What is YOU?

YOU is a book of tips to help you be more effective in your personality type. It contains the 16 personality types measured by the Myers-Briggs Type Indicator® (MBTI®) and the 20 facets that underlie these types.

What makes this book unique?

It contains the only research that relates MBTI types to effectiveness data at work. For the first time, we have related MBTI types to effectiveness patterns using data from a variety of data bases, including from the Center for Creative Leadership. For each type, we can say here are some likely strengths you have, here are some ways you may get into trouble, and here's what you can do about it.

We link how and why people differ to how those differences play out in behavior at work. *YOU* explains why some skills come more naturally and why others are tough to learn or even ignored.

We answer the *So what?* question. Being type wise can lead to better performance at work and better relationships while you're at it!

Who is YOU for?

- People who want to grow and enhance their skills.

- HR professionals who want to be able to relate personal characteristics to skills and effectiveness and who want practical but research-based development suggestions.

- Experienced MBTI users (e.g., executive coaches, OD consultants, training and development professionals) who want to directly relate type preference to increasing the competence at work.

Why should you read it?

- This book will help make you more type wise.

- This book will help you understand yourself better, understand others better, and understand what happens when two different people interact.

- This book offers tips on how to be more effective, given your particular type.

- This book surfaces typical interaction problems and shows how to solve them to be more effective.

YOU: BEING MORE EFFECTIVE IN YOUR MBTI® TYPE

ROGER R. PEARMAN, ED.D.
MICHAEL M. LOMBARDO, ED.D.
ROBERT W. EICHINGER, PH.D.

YOU: Being More Effective in Your MBTI® Type

Published by LOMINGER LIMITED, INC.
Minneapolis, Minnesota 55416
Tel. 952-345-3600 • Fax. 952-345-3601 • www.lominger.com

Printed in the United States of America
by TM Associates, Inc.
Cover Design: Punch-Design, Inc.

ISBN: 0-9745892-8-4
Lominger reorder part number: 11030

FIRST EDITION MAY 2005

ACKNOWLEDGMENTS

I want to acknowledge the patience and encouragement of my wife, Angela, daughter, Olivia, and son, Lukas during the execution of this project. In addition, I am grateful for the thoughtful support of the Qualifying.org staff: Ann Coleman, Dan Ahern, and Marg Dickson.

I am deeply appreciative of the collegial dialogue and profound insights of my co-authors during the development of this manuscript. In my professional life, I have rarely had the experience of working so closely with dedicated social scientists who are as deeply committed to the evidence as they are to the careful presentation of information for the enrichment of every reader. The Lominger organization is such a community of talents with whom I am proud to associate.

Roger R. Pearman

~~

First, we would like to give special thanks to the people of Lominger who have worked so hard on this book. Alex Stiber first thought of the idea of including cases, then worked extensively on all 16 types. Judy Chartrand managed the project of herding this book toward publication from draft to finished work. Lesley Kurke again demonstrated her diligence with a large, complex project and her electronic publishing wizardry to take us to print. Bonnie Parks, as always, carefully reviewed and edited our work to keep the structure clean, the syntax acceptable, and our sentences free of egregious errors.

Many people gave feedback on various chapters and sections of YOU. We would like to thank Lourine Clark, Larry Clark, Linda Rodman, Linda Hodge, Cara Capretta Raymond, Adrienne Johns, Kathy Sterner, Davis Klaila, and Michael Friedman for their comments and support.

Finally, without the superb research of Roger Pearman and his considerable insight into the interesting world of the MBTI, this book would not have been possible. To him we give a special thanks.

Mike Lombardo and Bob Eichinger

TABLE OF CONTENTS

Page

SECTION II 553

Extraverting–Introverting Facets 557

Sensing–Intuiting Facets 591

Thinking–Feeling Facets 633

Judging–Perceiving Facets 675

Page

SECTION III   719

TABLE OF CONTENTS

Introduction to *YOU* (and the MBTI)

It is, after all, all about YOU!

Each of us is unique. We all look different. We all have different experiences. We all act somewhat differently.

Being successful and effective in life and work has a lot to do with all of the differences noted above. We all behave somewhat differently based upon our experiences and our nature. Sometimes how we behave works well and other times it doesn't.

So, a lot of life's joys and disappointments are all about YOU and how you go about being that person.

Most of us have a relatively consistent and predictable YOU. A YOU we actually like to be. Most YOUs have a consistent and predictable pattern of things we generally do well and things we generally do less well. Our strengths have been, are, and for most of us will be about the same. Our weaknesses also have been, are, and will be approximately the same.

Other than YOU, there are THEM.

Each THEM is as unique as YOU, with the same pattern of preferences, strengths, and not-so-strongs.

Success in life and work has a fairly simple formula as far as working with people to get things done goes. We call it being type wise.

- ■ First, "Know thyself" (borrowing from Socrates). Know your YOU. The research findings are clear and simple. Successful and effective people know themselves better. The research also says that most people don't really know themselves very well. So, this is a big gap and an opportunity for most. The more you know about YOU, the better.

- ■ Second, know THEM. While you know thousands of people, it is somewhat simpler than that. There are 16 general types of YOUs, plus, at a deeper level, 20 pairs of facets or behavioral patterns beneath the 16 types. The more you know about others, the more successful you will be with others.

■ Third, understand how people of similar and different types (all the YOUs) match and mesh. If YOU have a relatively consistent package of strengths and weaknesses (you like going fast) and a person you are interacting with to get something done has a relatively consistent package of strengths and weaknesses (he or she prefers a deliberate and slower pace), what happens? There will generally be discomfort and possible dysfunction. You will both be frustrated. He/she is going slower than you like and YOU are going faster than he/she likes. The simple solution is for you to go a little slower and him/her to go a little faster—you meet in the middle. But this is not how it usually goes. If it's a boss and a report, it probably goes the way the boss prefers. If it's peers, usually the more vocal of the two wins. If it is spouses, who knows? While meeting in the middle is logical, practical, and a no-brainer, the frequency of that happening is relatively low. Most people like to stay in their YOU. Unless people really have the desire and motivation to work cooperatively together and to respect differences, conflict is more common than pleasant interactions.

■ Fourth, understand the demand characteristics of situations for YOU. Which YOU would work best in this situation? What needs to be done? What strengths and skills would work the best? What weaknesses would hamper getting things done? Who are the players? What are their goals and objectives? Does the situation call for speed or paced deliberation?

So, if you want to be successful and effective in life and work, become more type wise:

1. Know yourself (your YOU) as completely and totally as you can.

2. Understand THEM as completely and totally as you can.

3. Understand what happens when YOUs who are different have to work together to get something done.

4. Understand what the situations you find yourself in require from your YOU, and learn how to be agile in your type—contouring and shaping what and how you get things done.

This book will help you make progress on all four tasks—this book is about being type wise.

Our intention is not to change YOU. We don't think that is the path most people want to pursue. We suggest the path of being a more effective YOU. You can do that by first understanding YOU, particularly your consistent portfolio of strengths and weaknesses. Then, understanding the portfolio of the significant THEMs (people with whom you need to interact). Then, using the effectiveness tips in this book, modify some of your behavior to get something done with that person in that situation. If it feels good, continue to learn to behave that way more frequently. If it was very uncomfortable and didn't feel good or didn't work, return to the YOU you are and try something else.

The MBTI

Millions of people around the world have taken the MBTI, and many have taken the instrument multiple times. Many people, in casual conversation at work and in social life, will know their "type" and most share that information comfortably. MBTI popularity is due to ease of understanding some typical ways we behave every day:

■   Do we prefer to engage in conversation or reflect within ourselves?

■   Do we prefer concrete, pragmatic experience or the world of ideas and possibilities?

■   Do we seek closure through logic or prefer to consider values and feelings?

The answers to questions like these determine your type, and this forms much of the YOU people see as you go through your daily tasks. These commonsense and commonplace distinctions are what makes the MBTI so accessible and familiar. We all know people who love to plan their weekends and those for whom the thought depresses them. We all know people who go for solutions first and those who go for possibilities. We also know that a planner seldom becomes comfortably loose or a solutions-first person seldom becomes reflective. We cover the full power of the MBTI as a personal diagnostic in the introduction to SECTION I of this book.

As popular as the MBTI is, increasingly we hear the question, *So what?* While it's nice, even valuable to know what my type is, as millions do (We have seen license plates with the owner's MBTI type displayed!), what is the payoff for being type wise? What's the relationship to effectiveness?

How do I integrate the typical patterns of an ISTJ into what makes an ISTJ more effective? Now that I know my type, what do I do next?

The answer has always been a bit murky. Now we can say that each type has a fingerprint of typical strengths, typical problems it struggles with, and typical behaviors it can do too much of. While any type can be effective, what it takes to be effective is very different.

How do we know this? Because, for the first time, we have related MBTI types to effectiveness patterns using data from a variety of data bases, including from the Center for Creative Leadership, repeatedly voted the number one organization in the world for leadership development. For each type, we can say here are some likely strengths you have, here are some ways you may get into trouble, and here's what you can do about it.

This book brings together two streams of research: the fifty-plus years of research done on the Myers-Briggs Type Indicator, including the award-winning research of Roger Pearman on the MBTI, and the research by Lominger Limited, Inc. on the LEADERSHIP ARCHITECT® Competencies. By meshing the results, we can make statements or strong likelihoods such as:

- INTJs often synthesize ideas ahead of the crowd and get impatient for others to catch up.

- ESTJs can be too speedy.

- INTPs are uncomfortable with public speaking.

- And in all cases, here are tips if you have this problem.

Do we mean that all the patterns are true for you just because they were found in a research study? Of course not, but they should hit at least three times as often as they miss. To pretest this book, we sent it to many people familiar with their type. The feedback we received was that people found about a 75–80% hit between their preferred type and typical developmental needs we described. Some said the fit was 100%.

In SECTION I of this book, we combined the research on the 16 MBTI personality types with the competency research done by Lominger. Type information is contained in Forms M and Q of the MBTI. For each type, we cover:

- Typical strengths.

- Typical patterns of behavior.

- Typical challenges in becoming more effective in your type.

- What to do when you overdo an aspect of your type.

- A case (Application) to help you think through how your type plays out in typical work situations.

Each of the 16 chapters follows the above format. Our advice is to:

- Read through the typical strengths and patterns of behavior, noting which of those are most typical for you.

- Read through the typical Being More Effective challenges and see which tips speak to feedback you have received in performance discussions or in 360° feedback.

- Scan through the Overusing Tendencies tips for problems that arise when your pattern goes into overdrive. These problems arise when you are so INTJ or too much ENTP, for example.

- For your most typical issues, what developmental tips might help you be more effective?

SECTION II of this book covers the 20 facet pairs which underlie the familiar type designations of Extraverting–Introverting, Sensing–Intuiting, Thinking–Feeling, and Judging–Perceiving. Isabel Myers described multiple facets of each dimension of the MBTI tool. Later research confirmed these facets as aspects of each of her dimensions. For example, an individual could be scored for Extraversion but also be described by the facets as being Quiet or Contained, which are associated with Introversion. In other words, having a preference for one type in general does not mean that all aspects of that preference are accurate descriptors. In commonsense terms, this is why all ESTJs are not alike. There are some quiet extraverts. Another way to think about facets is that there are a minority of pure types. There are few pure INTJs or ESTJs, for example. There are more mixed types. This information is contained in Form Q of the MBTI.

Each of the 20 facet pair descriptions follows this format:

■ Description of the facet.

■ Tips on how to be more of this facet.

■ Tips on what to do if you overdo this facet.

Guiding Principles Behind the Developmental Tips

1. **Brief.** Most people want to get started right away. You want the low-hanging fruit. You want quick help. The tips were designed to help you get started quickly and see results as soon as you begin executing the tips.

2. **Things everyone could and would do.** There are many more complex and involved problem-solving methods, for example, that are not included here. If you have a need, we assume that you're not very good at whatever you're reading about, and would appreciate tips that don't assume you are practiced or proficient. You just want to get started and do something.

3. **Just the key tips.** Hard as it was to hold ourselves down, we tried to include those tips that will do you the most good. As these topics are quite complex, we recommend books as well.

4. **Quick results.** While some of our tips involve longer-term effort, most are things you can do tomorrow and hopefully see some quick improvement in effectiveness.

Where Did the Developmental Tips Come From?

Where they existed, we used research findings—on creativity or composure, for example. There is a fairly rich array of research on competencies—what experiences teach them, what they look like, what their elements are. You'll see references to the best books that we've seen on the various topics in the pages that follow.

Additionally, the authors have been in the development business for a combined 80 years, on both the research end and the practical end. During feedback sessions, we've heard thousands of executives and managers describe their difficulties, figured out with them what's getting in their way, and have tested our ideas for fixing things with them. We know from experience and research what tips are most likely to work.

Book Recommendations

Each of the 16 chapters in SECTION I has numerous sources for further reading. We used these selection criteria:

- **ROI**—Is there a significant and immediate payoff for reading this book? Are there suggestions busy people can implement?

- **Organization**—Is the book well laid out? Is it easy to find what you are looking for?

- **Ease**—Is it well written?

- **Solid**—Is the advice more than opinion?

- **Prolific**—Are there lots of tips and examples?

- **Available**—Can the book be found without a search?

To ensure that the books were solid, we relied heavily on the *Library Journal,* which reviews and recommends the best business books every year. So the books are substantive and mostly available through your local public library.

Second, we relied on Soundview so many of the books would be conveniently available in eight-page summaries. (Soundview Executive Book Summaries, 10 LaCrue Avenue, Concordville, PA 19331. www.summary.com 1-800-521-1227. International calls outside the US and Canada +1-610-558-9495.)

Third, we checked major booksellers (Barnes & Noble, B. Dalton, Borders) to see what they stock. In general, they are similar in coverage to Soundview.

Finally, we checked MBA syllabi to see what universities regard as substantive for business people.

SECTIONS I and II give you many themes to consider. Once you have selected some to consider, go to SECTION III on Effectiveness and Development Planning, where you will find strategies to:

1. Build the skill(s) for temporary or permanent use.

2. Substitute something else for the lack of skill.

3. Use workarounds to neutralize the lack of skill.

4. Compensate for overused skills (usually strengths).

5. Learn to live with it. Know your strongest competencies and leverage them more often.

About the Authors

Roger R. Pearman is an internationally known expert on the Myers-Briggs Type Indicator, winner of the Myers Research (1997) and McCaulley Contribution (1999) Awards, and past president of the International Association for Psychological Type. He has qualified over 5,000 professionals in the MBTI and trained 10,000 managers in its interpretation.

Roger is the senior author of *I'm Not Crazy, I'm Just Not You: The Real Meaning of the Sixteen Personality Types* (1997), author of *Hardwired Leadership: Unleashing Personality for the New Millennium Leader* (1998), a contributor to the *MBTI Manual* (1999), author of *Enhancing Leadership Effectiveness* (2000), *Leadership Advantage* (2001), and *Introduction to Type and Emotional Intelligence* (2002).

Roger is founder of Leadership Performance Systems, located in Winston-Salem, NC and Qualifying.org, a Web-based blended learning approach which offers certification on the Myers-Briggs Type Indicator and other well-established psychological tools. Roger has two decades of experience as a senior adjunct staff member with the Center for Creative Leadership.

Mike Lombardo has over 25 years experience in executive and management research and in executive coaching and training. He has worked with hundreds of corporations in the US and Europe. He is one of the founders of Lominger Limited, Inc., publishers of the LEADERSHIP ARCHITECT® Suite. With Bob Eichinger, Mike has authored 20 products for the suite, including *The Leadership Machine, FYI For Your Improvement™, 100 Things You Need to Know*, the CAREER ARCHITECT®, CHOICES ARCHITECT®, and VOICES®, the first electronic 360° instrument. The LEADERSHIP ARCHITECT® suite contains products that deal with employee development, interviewing for selection, succession planning, feedback, learning skills, performance management, culture assessment, and team building.

During his 15 years at the Center for Creative Leadership, Mike was a co-author of *The Lessons of Experience,* which detailed the experiences that can teach the competencies needed to be successful. He also co-authored the research on executive derailment revealing how personal flaws and overdone strengths caused otherwise effective executives to get into career trouble, BENCHMARKS®, one of the first 360° feedback instruments, and the LOOKING GLASS® simulation, a simulation of managerial work that is used internationally. With Bob Eichinger, he developed the popular program, "Tools for Developing Successful Executives," an international offering of the Center for Creative Leadership.

Mike has continued his research interests at Lominger. He has conducted numerous validation studies of Lominger instruments. He has won four national awards for research on managerial and executive development. He has co-authored or edited seven books and over 50 publications in popular and professional journals.

Bob Eichinger is CEO of Lominger Limited, Inc. and, along with Mike Lombardo, co-creator of The LEADERSHIP ARCHITECT® Suite of manager and executive development products and co-author of *The Leadership Machine,* a source book on developing people. Bob has over 40 years experience in management and executive development. He held executive development positions at PepsiCo and Pillsbury and has consulted with hundreds of organizations on succession planning and development. He has lectured extensively on the topic of executive and management development and has served on the Board of the Human Resource Planning Society, a professional association of people charged with the responsibility of management and executive development in their organizations. He has been a one-on-one feedback giver and coach from both inside and outside organizations. Bob has worked personally with over 1,000 managers and executives during his career. He has served on feedback teams within courses and off-sites in various organizations and public courses.

SECTION I

An Introduction to the MBTI Instrument and Theory

Millions of people have taken the MBTI tool and benefited from the self-knowledge they acquired. However, only a small percentage of users ever learn about the rich psychological theory on which the tool is based. In many cases, the MBTI instrument is presented as the theory itself, leaving out the overall framework. In this introduction we will provide you with a thorough understanding of both the tool and the underlying psychological model.

Basic Type Theory: The 16 Types

When you pick up the paper to read the headlines or when you begin a meeting that you are facilitating, you are using some basic mental resources to achieve this task. In fact, you have an automatic "default" in the kinds of things you pay attention to and act on. Obviously, if such patterns are pervasive for you, these are likely to show up in your leadership and management behavior and have reasonably predictable results.

Think of times when you:

- Sought out others to make personal connections and to show empathetic regard.
- Rehearsed your internal thoughts to gain clarity.
- Focused on specific, real-time information.
- Explored and shared various ideas, possibilities, hopes.
- Provided an expert analysis on a topic or issue.
- Settled on the "right" option, given the mission and purpose of those involved.
- Completed an analysis of pros/cons and comparisons.
- Imagined future outcomes of various options.

These behaviors reflect eight different mental processes that are critical for you to access and use. The way you use these processes and how often produces your interpersonal style. The whole system of psychological type proposes that all eight of these processes are at work within each of us;

however, we are usually more aware of and more facile with some than others. What we pay attention to first (and last) affects our performance.

The MBTI instrument is an assessment tool for understanding your preference for using the eight mental processes, which are organized into four pairs: Extraversion–Introversion, Sensing–Intuition, Thinking–Feeling, and Judging–Perceiving.

The four pairs, or dichotomies, describe preferences for:

Drawing Energy (Where you are initially energized.)

■ **Extraverting (E):** Seeking external experience by engaging the outer world of people, activities, and actions; or immediate focus, physical activity, brainstorming, critiquing, and engaging in conversation.

■ **Introverting (I):** Seeking awareness of ideas, emotions, and impressions; or reflecting on details, imagining future options, analyzing options, or evaluating the merit of a situation.

Perceiving Information (Where you tend to focus for information.)

■ **Sensing (S):** By focusing on the actual and observable; or through concrete, realistic experience with enjoyment of the pragmatic, or internally by rehearsal to clarify details, cataloging information.

■ **Intuiting (N):** By focusing on patterns and interrelationships; or through seeing ideas, innovations, possible linkages, or by engaging idea generation and sharing possibilities.

Making Decisions (How you sort and prioritize information for decisions.)

■ **Thinking (T):** Through consideration of logical outcomes; or externally critiquing, seeking closure and reasonable order using specific logic or criteria, or internally analyzing, finding the internal logic of a situation or circumstance.

■ **Feeling (F):** Through consideration of ideals and outcomes on others; or externally expressing empathetic regard, seeking harmony in relationships, or internally evaluating outcomes by the believed mission, ideal, or value bases in a situation or circumstance.

Dealing With the World (Which strategy you employ for managing life.)

■ **Judging (J):** Through planning, decisiveness, and organization; or a desire for closure through analysis or evaluative action, seeking structure and order as a way of making sense of experience.

■ **Perceiving (P):** Through spontaneity, flexibility, and keeping options open; or a desire for in-the-moment information or big-picture thinking about a situation, seeking "flow," open outcomes as a way of making sense of experience.

The assessment questions that make up these categories produce a sort such as ESTJ, ESFP, INTJ, INFP, etc., with 16 combinations. Each person is identified as having a preference for one of the 16 types shown below.

MBTI Type Percentages of Population and Managers*

ISTJ	ISFJ	INFJ	INTJ
11.6% of Population	13.8% of Population	1.5% of Population	2.1% of Population
17% of Managers	3.4% of Managers	1.9% of Managers	10.0% of Managers
ISTP	**ISFP**	**INFP**	**INTP**
5.4% of Population	8.8% of Population	4.4% of Population	3.3% of Population
3.4% of Managers	1.2% of Managers	2.7% of Managers	6.6% of Managers
ESTP	**ESFP**	**ENFP**	**ENTP**
4.3% of Population	8.5% of Population	8.1% of Population	3.2% of Population
3.2% of Managers	1.4% of Managers	5.1% of Managers	8.1% of Managers
ESTJ	**ESFJ**	**ENFJ**	**ENTJ**
8.7% of Population	12.3% of Population	2.5% of Population	1.8% of Population
15.8% of Managers	3.6% of Managers	3.4% of Managers	13.1% of Managers

*Type Distribution of the National Representative Sample (Base Population) and Multicultural Type Distribution Samples of Managers from: *MBTI Manual: A Guide to the Development and Use of the Myers-Briggs Type Indicator* (3rd ed.). Palo Alto, CA: Consulting Psychologists Press, 1998 (pp. 298, 383).

MBTI Step II Results

The author of the MBTI instrument, Isabel Briggs Myers, realized that people with the same type sometimes behave differently. She believed that each of the four dichotomies is made up of component parts, or facets. So, in the 1940s she began work on a tool that would identify individual differences within the 16 types. The outcome of her work is evident in the MBTI Step II instrument, which measures the 20 facet pairs shown below.

Extraverting ↔ Introverting			Thinking ↔ Feeling		
Initiating	↔	Receiving	Logical	↔	Empathetic
Expressive	↔	Contained	Reasonable	↔	Compassionate
Gregarious	↔	Intimate	Questioning	↔	Accommodating
Active	↔	Reflective	Critical	↔	Accepting
Enthusiastic	↔	Quiet	Tough	↔	Tender
Sensing ↔ Intuiting			**Judging ↔ Perceiving**		
Concrete	↔	Abstract	Systematic	↔	Casual
Realistic	↔	Imaginative	Planful	↔	Open-Ended
Practical	↔	Conceptual	Early Starting	↔	Pressure-Prompted
Experiential	↔	Theoretical	Scheduled	↔	Spontaneous
Traditional	↔	Original	Methodical	↔	Emergent

SECTION II of this book provides a thorough description of each facet and how it relates to performance behaviors. The facets give you a more detailed explanation of your type and explain possible inconsistencies (e.g., being an ISTP who prefers Early Starting to Pressure-Prompted). You will need to complete the MBTI Step II instrument to receive feedback on the 20 facets. Although the MBTI Step II is quickly becoming the assessment of choice in leadership programs, it is necessary to distinguish between the MBTI Step I (Form M), which yields only the 16 types and the MBTI Step II (Form Q), which yields both type and facet scores.

Type Dynamics

The basic theory featuring the 16 types is easily understood. But this is only the first part of the story. The four letters are intended to suggest an order in the use of the eight mental processes. Understanding the order of the mental processes results in a deeper and more meaningful use of the MBTI instrument. The processes and the order in which they are accessed by each type is outlined below.

Eight Mental Processes	Typical Behaviors/Reactions
SE (Sensing that is Extraverted)	**External Focus** • Immediate awareness of situation, individual facts. • Focus on present, concrete, practical elements. • Demonstrates a sense of urgency.
SI (Sensing that is Introverted)	**Internal Rehearsal** • Rehearses and reviews information for clarity. • Awareness of personal reactions, physical sensations. • Specific and realistic memory.
NE (Intuiting that is Extraverted)	**Expressive of Ideas, Associations** • Sees links, associations. • Generates possibilities, ideas, concepts. • Looks for context and "big picture."
NI (Intuiting that is Introverted)	**Imagining Future** • Imagines future outcomes. • Anticipates next steps. • Makes interconnections of ideas, feelings, concepts.
TE (Thinking that is Extraverted)	**Critiquing, Logical** • Critiques to make things better. • Responds to order, structure, logic of a situation. • Questions assumptions, outcomes, long-term action.
TI (Thinking that is Introverted)	**Precise Analysis** • Analyzes to find the best framework. • Precise about information. • Sees logical weaknesses quickly.
FE (Feeling that is Extraverted)	**Empathy, Connection** • Actively seeks connections with others. • Shows empathy quickly. • Demonstrates interest in alignment of action with values.
FI (Feeling that is Introverted)	**Evaluation of Merit** • Acts out of mission and value orientation. • Seeks interrelated meaning of ideas, actions, purposes. • Evaluates the "worth" and "merit" of a situation.

INTRODUCTION TO THE MBTI INSTRUMENT AND THEORY

Although all of us use these eight processes, they are often accessed in a preferred order. The first four tend to be used the most, and the last four are often less developed. According to type theory and practice, the more we use all eight processes, the more able and effective our behavior can become. For example, an INTJ is often bursting with ideas (Introverted Intuiting). Some of the lesser used processes, especially Introverted Thinking, can serve as a balance to sort through and give some priority order to those ideas. Otherwise, an INTJ can overdo idea generation and overwhelm those around him or her.

The following table indicates how each type accesses the eight mental processes. Note that use of the first four processes are generally accepted as central to type dynamics. The theory proposes the other four processes are actively, though unconsciously, at work within you.

Ordering of the Eight Mental Processes for Introverts								
Typical Process Order	ISTJ	ISFJ	INFJ	INTJ	ISTP	ISFP	INFP	INTP
Primary	S_I	S_I	N_I	N_I	T_I	F_I	F_I	T_I
Secondary	T_E	F_E	F_E	T_E	S_E	S_E	N_E	N_E
Third	F_E	T_E	T_E	F_E	N_E	N_E	S_E	S_E
Fourth	N_E	N_E	S_E	S_E	F_E	T_E	T_E	F_E
Fifth	S_E	S_E	N_E	N_E	T_E	F_E	F_E	T_E
Sixth	T_I	F_I	F_I	T_I	S_I	S_I	N_I	N_I
Seventh	F_I	T_I	T_I	F_I	N_I	N_I	S_I	S_I
Eighth	N_I	N_I	S_I	S_I	F_I	T_I	T_I	F_I
Ordering of the Eight Mental Processes for Extraverts								
Typical Process Order	ESTJ	ESFJ	ENFJ	ENTJ	ESTP	ESFP	ENFP	ENTP
Primary	T_E	F_E	F_E	T_E	S_E	S_E	N_E	N_E
Secondary	S_I	S_I	N_I	N_I	T_I	F_I	F_I	T_I
Third	N_I	N_I	S_I	S_I	F_I	T_I	T_I	F_I
Fourth	F_I	T_I	T_I	F_I	N_I	N_I	S_I	S_I
Fifth	T_I	F_I	F_I	T_I	S_I	S_I	N_I	N_I
Sixth	S_E	S_E	N_E	N_E	T_E	F_E	F_E	T_E
Seventh	N_E	N_E	S_E	S_E	F_E	T_E	T_E	F_E
Eighth	F_E	T_E	T_E	F_E	N_E	N_E	S_E	S_E

Type theory suggests that the eight mental processes organize in a variety of ways in each person, and it is this order that produces rich differences among the 16 types. For example, the code ESTJ means that people who are like this extravert Thinking and introvert Sensing. As such, they are likely to be analytical with a legion of facts and evidence supporting the critical perspective of the ESTJ. Further, the third and fourth processes of Introverted Intuiting and Introverted Feeling suggest they are likely to have a vision of how they want things to come out and that they are quite passionate about this ideal. Consequently, ESTJs often appear very driven, ambitious, critical, and unbending in their point of view.

To illustrate these principles further, we will compare the behavioral tendencies of an ESTJ with an ENTJ. According to type theory, both are Extraverted Thinking types with one having Introverted Sensing as the ordinary way of perceiving and the other having Introverted Intuiting. As a result, the ESTJ is more likely to argue a point of view from verifiable facts, while the ENTJ is likely to use concepts, ideas, and theoretical research to back up a discussion. It is the auxiliary, or second process, that blends with the lead process to produce profound differences in what the type pays attention to and the language they use. This does not mean that the ESTJ cannot rely on concepts or theories; it is just that the ESTJ will start with facts, data, and verifiable information before theory is brought into the picture. Likewise, the ENTJ is likely to rely on those facts that support the perceived underlying concepts in a situation.

For each of the 16 types, there is a "lead" or dominant process, a second, third, and so forth for the eight processes. It is this combination of using the processes that generates the "typical ness" we observe that leads to "type." All of us use all eight processes but in varying degrees. To focus on the four-letter code would be to miss the dynamic and judge a book by the cover and not by the story.

All eight mental processes feed our world view and style, and the more we become aware of these processes and their contributions to our behavior, the more we are likely to use them appropriately. If you begin to reflect on the richness of your own psychological system, you immediately see the common sense value of understanding these eight mental processes and how they affect your choices to lead and influence others. The model is not about understanding others per se; it is about understanding and gaining more control over yourself.

This "organization" of the eight processes within the 16 types adds considerable complexity to the model. Yet, it makes perfect sense that just because an individual may more frequently rely on an Extraverted Thinking process **does not mean** he or she cannot use Extraverted Feeling. In fact, the more developed individual knows that he/she is using a critical, analytical voice, realizes this may not always be effective, and learns to use cooperative, encouraging language in appropriate situations.

All behavior can be said to be an expression of one or a combination of the eight processes of type. The first four processes for each of the 16 types use the most energy and are most evident in our behavior. For this reason, in the 16 type chapters that follow, we will focus on how these top four processes combine to impact how we tend to display our various strengths and flat sides. Most of the tips are written around more effective use of the first four processes for each type, but all eight get some consideration. Simply stated, working on all eight processes helps us balance our behavior and become more effective in our type.

Roger Pearman's organization, Qualifying.org, offers certification in a blended learning format on the MBTI and other psychological instruments.

THE
SIXTEEN
TYPES

ISTJ	ISFJ	INFJ	INTJ
ISTP	ISFP	INFP	INTP
ESTP	ESFP	ENFP	ENTP
ESTJ	ESFJ	ENFJ	ENTJ

CHAPTER 1

ISTJ
Introverted Sensing
with
Extraverted Thinking

■■■■■■■■■■■■■■■■■

11.6% of Population
17% of Managers

■■■■■■■■■■■■■■■■■

Typical Strengths

Orderly
Persevering
Responsible
Task Oriented
Honest, Fair-Minded, and Loyal
Business Oriented, Interested in Trends

ISTJ	ISFJ	INFJ	INTJ
ISTP	ISFP	INFP	INTP
ESTP	ESFP	ENFP	ENTP
ESTJ	ESFJ	ENFJ	ENTJ

The focus on details and reliance on logical analysis has never led me wrong.
– An ISTJ Manager

Basic Habits of Mind

As an Introverted Sensing type, ISTJs seek precision and clarity in information—spoken or written. These two qualities promote a thorough and practical concentration on the task at hand. As Extraverted Thinkers, ISTJs are likely to appear as focused, orderly, critical, and decisive people who trust facts and structure.

Their Extraverted Feeling and Extraverted Intuiting often show in the sense of mission and intensity they display when tackling problems. Unfortunately, these qualities are sometimes misinterpreted as demanding, rigid, and stubborn.

Typical Communication Patterns

- Carefully share tested and verifiable data.

- Decisive, predictable, and realistic in expression of information.

- Logical, matter-of-fact, and detailed presentation.

- When overplayed, ISTJs may appear to be too mechanical and not take people's needs into account.

General Learning Strategy

- ISTJs usually learn best with clearly stated objectives and procedures; prefer to analyze, examine, and think it through before telling others.

- Their preferred learning strategies are likely to be analyzing, identifying the facts first, labeling, then categorizing information.

- Their learning is helped by clear directions, prework with "doing" activities included such as answering questions and engaging in some competitive challenge.

Interpersonal Qualities Related to Motivation

- They generally attempt to motivate others with precise, accurate, and timely information.

- ISTJs are concise and analytical, figuring that logic and order will engage others.

Blind Spots

- Others may see their deliberate analytical behavior as manipulating, demanding, and impatient.

- They can often be seen as pressuring and blunt.

- Their commitment to careful precision is interpreted by some as guarded dogmatism.

Stress Related Behavior

- As an initial response to stress, ISTJs usually increase their efforts at thorough methodical strategies. This can look exaggerated, that they insist on control and heavy conformance to expectations.

- Under enough stress, their natural attention to precision can lead to anticipation of failure and seeing the incompetence of people and processes around them, for which they may find abundant evidence!

Potential Barriers to Effectiveness

- Typical needs for ISTJs are to create a more developmental climate and express more compassion for those who work with them. Both of these can cause career stumbles.

- Having a low tolerance for ambiguity, they may find it difficult to advance in organizations where teamwork orientation and strategic agility are essential.

Being a More Effective ISTJ

A Dealing With Ambiguity
B Showing Compassion and Caring
C Developing Others
D Innovation and Strategy
E Team Building

ISTJ	ISFJ	INFJ	INTJ
ISTP	ISFP	INFP	INTP
ESTP	ESFP	ENFP	ENTP
ESTJ	ESFJ	ENFJ	ENTJ

A Dealing With Ambiguity

ISTJs often prefer straightforward, methodical processes that they don't care to change. Dealing with change is a challenge.

1. **Incrementalism.** The essence of dealing comfortably with uncertainty is the tolerance of errors and mistakes, and absorbing the possible heat and criticism that follow. Acting on an ill-defined problem with no precedents to follow means shooting in the dark with as informed a decision as you can make at the time. People who are good at this are incrementalists. They make a series of smaller decisions, get instant feedback, correct the course, get a little more data, move forward a little more, until the bigger problem is under control. They don't try to get it right the first time. Many problem-solving studies show that the second or third try is when we really understand the underlying dynamics of problems. They also know that the more uncertain the situation is, the more likely it is they will make mistakes in the beginning. So, you need to work on two practices: Start small so you can recover more quickly. Do little somethings as soon as you can and get used to heat.

2. **Perfectionist?** Need or prefer or want to be 100% sure? Lots might prefer that. Perfectionism is tough to let go of because most people see it as a positive trait for themselves. Recognize your perfectionism for what it might be—collecting more information than others to improve your confidence in making a fault-free decision and thereby avoiding risk and criticism. Try to decrease your need for data and your need to be right all the time slightly every week until you reach a more reasonable balance between thinking it through and taking action. Try making some small decisions on little or no data. Anyone with a brain and 100% of the data can make good decisions. The real test is who can act the soonest with a reasonable amount, but not all, of the data. Some studies suggest successful general managers are about 65% correct. Trust your intuition. Let your brain do the calculations.

3. **Locate the essence of the problem.** What are the key factors or elements in this problem? Experts usually solve problems by figuring out what the deep, underlying principles are and working forward from there; the less adept focus on desired outcomes/solutions and either work backward or concentrate on the surface facts. What are the deep principles of what you're working on? Once you've done this, search the past for parallels—your past, the business past, the historical past. One common mistake here is to search in parallel organizations because "only they would know." Backing up and asking a broader question will aid in the search for solutions. When Motorola wanted to find out how to process orders more quickly, they went not to other electronics firms, but to Domino's Pizza and Federal Express.

4. **Patterns.** Look for patterns in personal, organization, or the world, in general successes and failures. What was common to each success or what was present in each failure but never present in a success? Focus on the successes; failures are easier to analyze but don't in themselves tell you what would work. Comparing successes, while less exciting, yields more information about underlying principles. The bottom line is to reduce your insights to principles or rules of thumb you think might be repeatable. When faced with the next new problem, those general underlying principles will apply again.

5. **Finishing.** Do you prefer to finish what you have started? Do you have a high need to complete tasks? Wrap them up in nice clean packages? Working well with ambiguity and under uncertainty means moving from incomplete task to incomplete task. Some may be abandoned, some may never be finished. They'll probably only ever get 80% done, and you'll constantly have to edit your actions and decisions. Change your internal reward process toward feeling good about fixing mistakes and moving things forward incrementally, more than finishing any given project.

B Showing Compassion and Caring

ISTJs often care but have trouble expressing it and are uncomfortable with strong displays of emotion.

1. **Compassion is understanding.** A primary reason for problems with compassion is that you don't know how to deal with strong feelings and may appear distant or uninterested. You're uncomfortable with strong displays of emotion and calls for personal help. Simply

imagine how you would feel in this situation and respond with that. Tell the person how sorry you are this has happened or has to be dealt with. Offer whatever help is reasonable. A day off. A loan. A resource. If you can, offer hope of a better day. This is what the person can use most.

2. **Compassion is sometimes just listening.** Sometimes people just need to talk it out. Compassion is quiet listening. Nod and maintain eye contact to indicate listening. When he/she pauses, respond with how he/she must feel, and suggest something you could do to help (e.g., if he/she needs to be gone for awhile, you'll see that his/her work is covered).

3. **Compassion is not always advice.** Don't offer advice unless asked. Indicate support through listening and a helpful gesture. There will be time for advice when the situation isn't so emotionally charged. Many times managers are too quick with advice before they really understand the problem.

4. **Compassion is not therapy or counseling.** Another reason people have trouble with compassion is thinking that a counselor role isn't appropriate at work. You can be brief and compassionate by following three rules:

   ■ Let people say what's on their mind without saying anything other than you know they're upset. Don't judge. Don't advise.

   ■ Summarize when they start repeating. This signals that you heard them, but keeps them from consuming so much time that you begin to feel like a counselor.

   ■ If someone overdoes it, invite him/her to talk with you outside of work hours or refer him/her to another resource like employee assistance. This shows others that you cared, you listened and are willing to help if possible, while not putting you in the counselor role that is making you uncomfortable.

5. **Compassion isn't judgment or agreement.** Be candid with yourself. Is there a group or groups you don't like or are uncomfortable with? Do you judge individual members of that group without really knowing if your stereotype is true? Most of us do. Do you show compassion for one group's problems but not another's? To deal with this:

   ■ Put yourself in their case. Why would you act that way? What do you think they're trying to achieve? Assume that however they act is rational to them; it must have paid off or they wouldn't be doing it. Don't use your internal standards.

■ Avoid putting groups in buckets. Many of us bucket groups as friendly or unfriendly, good or bad, like me or not like me. Once we do, we generally don't show as much compassion toward them and may question their motives. Apply the logic of why people belong to the group in the first place. See if you can predict accurately what the group will say or do across situations to test your understanding of the group. Don't use your agreement program.

■ Listen. Even though this tip may seem obvious, many of us tune out when dealing with difficult or not-well-understood groups, or reject what they're saying before they say it. Just listen. Mentally summarize their views, and see if you can figure out what they want from what they say and mean. The true test is whether you can clearly figure it out, even though you don't think that way.

6. **Many people who need your compassion most aren't the most pleasant people.**

■ For the cynical—delegate responsibility to them for what they are most cynical about.

■ For the helpless and dependent—ask yourself what would make them feel the most powerful?

■ For the truly resentful or hostile—don't encourage them to air all of their gripes in detail. This merely reinforces their views. Instead, find out what is bothering them the most at work, and give them something new to do where they have the authority to make a difference.

C Developing Others

ISTJs are quite responsible and often overload themselves with work. Since they think it's easier to do it themselves, they tend not to delegate or develop others well.

1. **You have to invest some time.** For most managers, time is what they have the least of to give. For the purposes of developing others beyond today's job, you need to allocate about eight hours per year per direct report. If you have a normal span of seven direct reports, that's 7 of 220 working days or 3% of your annual time. Two of the

eight hours are for an annual in-depth appraisal of the person in terms of current strengths and weaknesses and of the competencies he/she needs to develop to move on to the next step. Two of the eight hours are for an in-depth career discussion with each person. What does he/she want? What will he/she sacrifice to get there? What is his/her own appraisal of his/her skills? Two of the eight hours are for creating a three- to five-year development plan and sharing it with the person. The last two hours are to present your findings and recommendations to the organization, usually in a succession planning process, and arranging for developmental events for each person. Start thinking of yourself as a coach or mentor. It's your job to help your people grow.

2. **Help people focus on the right things.** In their study of successful vs. average careers, Citrin and Smith found that the most successful people force themselves into experiences they need for growth. They do not play it safe. While they demonstrate early competence in a specific area, they also don't overdo working on basic job requirements. They do enough work on the basics while searching for mission-critical job elements and trying to overdeliver on them. They add unexpected value. They call this the 20/80 principle of performance—focusing on the 20% that makes 80% of the difference. In doing so, the successful rack up career freedom points by tackling these tough assignments.

3. **Do you help your people learn by looking for repeating patterns?** Help them look for patterns in the situations and problems they deal with. What succeeded and what failed? Ask them what they have learned to increase their skills and understanding, making them better managers or professionals. Ask them what they can do now that they couldn't do a year ago. Reinforce this and encourage more of it. Developing is learning in as many ways as possible.

4. **More what and why, less how.** The best delegators are crystal clear on what and when, and more open on how. People are more motivated when they can determine the how for themselves. Inexperienced delegators include the hows, which turn the people into task automatons instead of an empowered and energized staff. Tell them what and when and for how long, and let them figure out how on their own. Give them leeway. Encourage them to try things. Besides being more motivating, it's also more developmental for them. Add the larger context. Although it is not necessary to get the task done, people are more motivated when they know where this task fits in the bigger picture. Take three extra minutes and tell them why this task

needs to be done, where it fits in the grander scheme, and its importance to the goals and objectives of the unit.

5. **How to delegate?** Communicate, set time frames and goals, and get out of the way. People need to know what it is you expect. What does the outcome look like? When do you need it by? What's the budget? What resources do they get? What decisions can they make? Do you want checkpoints along the way? How will we both know and measure how well the task is done? One of the most common problems with delegation is incomplete or cryptic up-front communication leading to frustration, a job not well done the first time, rework, and a reluctance to delegate next time. Poor communicators always have to take more time managing because of rework. Analyze recent projects that went well and didn't go well. How did you delegate? Too much? Not enough? Unwanted pieces? Major chunks of responsibility? Workload distributed properly? Did you set measures? Overmanage or abdicate? Find out what your best practices are. Set up a series of delegation practices that can be used as if you're not there. What do you have to be informed of? What feedback loops can people use for midcourse correction? What questions should be answered as the work proceeds? What steps should be followed? What are the criteria to be followed? When will you be available to help?

6. **Feedback.** People need continuous feedback from you and others to grow. Some tips about feedback:

■ Arrange for them to get feedback from multiple people, including yourself, on what matters for success in their future jobs; arrange for your direct reports to get 360° feedback about every two years.

■ Give them progressively stretching tasks that are first-time and different for them so that they can give themselves feedback as they go.

■ If they have direct reports and peers, another technique to recommend is to ask their associates for comments on what they should stop doing, start doing, and keep doing to be more successful.

■ You have to be willing to be straight with your people and give them accurate but balanced feedback. Give as much real-time feedback as you have time for. Most people are motivated by process feedback against agreed-upon goals for three reasons.

First, it helps them adjust what they are doing along the way in time to better achieve the goal; they can make midcourse corrections. Second, it shows them what they are doing is important and that you're there to help. Third, it's not the "gotcha" game of negative and critical feedback after the fact. If there are negatives, they need to know as soon as possible.

■ Set up a buddy system so people can get continuing feedback.

■ If your organization has a mentoring program, find out how it works. Best practices begin with those to be mentored writing down goals, objectives, and development needs. They are then carefully matched with mentors and the relationship is outlined. How often will the people meet? On what topics is the mentor to be helpful? What are the responsibilities of the person to be mentored? If your organization doesn't have such a program, look at setting one up within your unit or function.

7. **Development planning.** You need to put together a development plan that, if followed, actually would work. At least 70% of reported skill development comes from having challenging, uncomfortable tasks/assignments. Development means that you do the new skill or fail at something important to you. Tasks that develop anything are those in which not doing it is not a viable option. Another 20% comes from studying and working with others to see useful behavior and get feedback. This can take the form of studying a role model, working with a developmental partner, keeping a written summary of what's working and not working, or preferably a formal assessment like a 360° process. Without this continuous feedback, even the best developmental plans fail. About 10% of development comes from thinking differently or having new ways to think about things. Typically these come from coursework, books, or mentors; the lion's share is learning from tough tasks and the learning from other people that comes from feedback. A good plan would have 70% job and task content; 20% people to study, listen to, and work with; and 10% courses and readings.

D Innovation and Strategy

ISTJs' commitment and loyalty to their organization often keeps their focus on the tried-and-true. They may think they are focusing on innovation and strategy, but tend to actually focus on little things and can get blindsided by emerging trends. They often focus on tweaks, not breakthroughs.

1. **Innovation involves three skills.** The first is a total understanding of the marketplace for your products and services. That's knowing what sells and why. What more do your customers want? What features would be most attractive to them? And what do your non-customers want that they don't find in your products? The second is being able to select from among many possible creative ideas for new products and services, those which would have the highest likelihood of success in the marketplace. The third skill is taking the raw idea and managing its transition into a successful product in the marketplace.

2. **Managing the creative process.** You need raw creative ideas to be able to manage innovation. While you may not be and don't need to be the source for the creative ideas, you need to understand the process. Creative thought processes do not follow the formal rules of logic where one uses cause and effect to prove or solve something. The rules of creative thought lie not in using existing concepts but in changing them—moving from one concept or way of looking at things to another. It involves challenging the status quo and generating ideas without judging them initially. Jumping from one idea to another without justifying the jump. Looking for the least likely and the odd. The creative process requires freedom and openness and a non-judgmental environment. The creative process can't be timed. Setting a goal and a time schedule to be creative will most likely chill creativity.

3. **Getting creativity out of a group.** Many times the creative idea comes from a group, not single individuals. When working on a new idea for a product or service, have them come up with as many questions about it as you can. Often we think too quickly of solutions. In studies of problem-solving sessions, solutions outweigh questions 8 to 1. Asking more questions helps people rethink the problem and come to more and different solutions. Have the group take a current product you are dissatisfied with and represent it visually—a flowchart or a series of pictures. Cut it up into its component pieces and shuffle them. Examine the pieces to see if a different order would help, or how you could combine three pieces into one. Try many experiments or trials to find something that will work. Have the group think beyond current boundaries. What are some of the most sacred rules or practices in your organization? Unit? Think about smashing them— what would your unit be doing if you broke the rules? Talk to the most irreverent person you know about this. Buffer the group. It's difficult to work on something new if they are besieged with all the

25

distractions you have to deal with, particularly if people are looking over your shoulder asking why isn't anything happening.

4. **Narrow perspective?** Some are sharply focused on what they do and do it very well. They have prepared themselves for a narrow but satisfying career. Then someone tells them their job has changed, and they now have to be strategic. Being strategic requires a broad perspective. In addition to knowing one thing well, it requires that you know about a lot of things somewhat. You need to understand business. You need to understand markets. You need to understand how the world operates. You need to put all that together and figure out what all that means to your organization.

5. **Too busy?** Strategy is always last on the list. Solving today's problems, of which there are many, is job one. You have to make time for strategy. A good strategy releases future time because it makes choices clear and leads to less wasted effort, but it takes time to do. Delegation is usually the main key. Give away as much tactical day-to-day stuff as you can. Ask your people what they think they could do to give you more time for strategic reflection. Another key is better time management. Put an hour a week on your calendar for strategic reading and reflection throughout the year. Don't wait until one week before the strategic plan is due. Keep a log of ideas you get from others, magazines, etc. Focus on how these impact your organization or function.

6. **Can't think strategically?** Strategy is linking several variables together to come up with the most likely scenario. Think of it as the search for and application of relevant parallels. It involves making projections of several variables at once to see how they come together. These projections are in the context of shifting markets, international affairs, monetary movements, and government interventions. It involves a lot of uncertainty, making risk assumptions, and understanding how things work together. How many reasons would account for sales going down? Up? How are advertising and sales linked? If the dollar is cheaper in Asia, what does that mean for our product in Japan? If the world population is aging and they have more money, how will that change buying patterns? Not everyone enjoys this kind of pie-in-the-sky thinking and not everyone is skilled at doing it.

7. **Don't know how to be strategic?** The simplest problem is someone who wants to be strategic and wants to learn. Strategy is a reasonably well-known field. Read the gurus (Michael Porter, Ram Charan, C.K.

Prahalad, Gary Hamel, Fred Wiersema, and Vijay Govindarajan). Scan the *Harvard Business Review* and *Sloan Review* regularly. Read the three to five strategic case studies in *BusinessWeek* every issue. Go to a three-day strategy course taught by one of the gurus. Get someone from the organization's strategic group to tutor you in strategy. Watch CEOs talk about their businesses on cable. Volunteer to serve on a task force on a strategic issue. Join the Strategic Leadership Forum for a year, read their publication, *Strategy and Leadership*, and attend one national convention. Attend The Conference Board's Annual Conference on Strategy, where CEOs talk about their companies. Read 10 annual reports a year outside your industry and study their strategies.

8. **Become a strategic activist.** Pick one distinctive competence or driving force. That's what the mediocre companies who became successful over time did in James Collins' latest research. Create a strategic plan for your unit around one distinctive competence— include breakthrough process and product improvements, justify your conclusions by pointing to hard data that points toward your conclusions. Have the plan reviewed by people you trust. Form a consortium with three other individuals or companies; each of you will present a strategic issue and a plan backed up with data and rationale. Agree to review your thinking every three months with this group and write down lessons learned. Analyze three business/ organizational success stories in your area and the same number of failures. What did each have in common? How would these principles apply in your situation? What was common to the failures that was never present in the successes?

E Team Building

ISTJs are usually individual achievers who are not attracted to the messiness of teams.

1. **Don't believe in teams.** If you don't believe in teams, you are probably a strong individual achiever who doesn't like the mess and sometimes the slowness of due-process relationships and team processes. You are very results oriented and truly believe the best way to do that is to manage one person at a time. To balance this thinking, observe and talk with three excellent team builders and ask them why they manage that way. What do they consider rewarding about building teams? What advantages do they get from using the team format? Read *The Wisdom of Teams* by Katzenbach and Smith. If you can't see the value in teams, none of the following tips will help much.

2. **Don't have the time; teaming takes longer.** That's true and not true. While building a team takes longer than managing one person at a time, having a well-functioning team increases results, builds in a sustaining capability to perform, maximizes collective strengths and covers individual weaknesses, and actually releases more time for the manager because the team members help each other. Many managers get caught in the trap of thinking it takes up too much time to build a team and end up taking more time managing one-on-one.

3. **Would like to build a team but don't know how.** High performance teams have four common characteristics: (1) They have a shared mind-set. They have a common vision. Everyone knows the goals and measures. (2) They trust one another. They know "you will cover me if I get in trouble." They know you will pitch in and help even though it may be difficult for you. They know you will be honest with them. They know you will bring problems to them directly and won't go behind their backs. (3) They have the talent collectively to do the job. While not any one member may have it all, collectively they have every task covered. (4) They know how to operate efficiently and effectively. They have good team skills. They run effective meetings. They have efficient ways to communicate. They have ways to deal with internal conflict.

4. **Cement relationships.** Even though some—maybe including you—will resist it, parties, roasts, gag awards, picnics, and outings help build group cohesion. Allow roles to evolve naturally rather than being specified by job descriptions. Some research indicates that people gravitate naturally to eight roles, and that successful teams are not those where everyone does the same thing. Successful teams specialize, cover for each other, and only sometimes demand that everyone participate in identical activities.

5. **Not good at motivating people beyond being results oriented?** Play the motivation odds. According to research by Rewick and Lawler, the top motivators at work are: (1) Job challenge; (2) Accomplishing something worthwhile; (3) Learning new things; (4) Personal development; and (5) Autonomy. Pay (12th), Friendliness (14th), Praise (15th), or Chance of Promotion (17th) are not insignificant but are superficial compared with the five top motivators. Provide challenges, paint pictures of why this is worthwhile, set up chances to learn and grow, and provide autonomy, and you'll hit the vast majority of people's hot buttons.

6. **Follow the basic rules of inspiring others** as outlined in classic books like *People Skills* by Robert Bolton or *Thriving on Chaos* by Tom Peters. Communicate to people that what they do is important. Say thanks. Offer help and ask for it. Provide autonomy in how people do their work. Provide a variety of tasks. "Surprise" people with enriching, challenging assignments. Show an interest in their careers. Adopt a learning attitude toward mistakes. Celebrate successes, have visible accepted measures of achievement, and so on. Too often people behave correctly but there are no consequences. Although it's easy to get too busy to acknowledge, celebrate, and occasionally criticize, don't forget to reinforce what you want. As a rule of thumb, 4 to 1 positive to negative is best.

7. **To better figure out what drives people, look to: What do they do first?** What do they emphasize in their speech? What do they display emotion around? What values play out for them?

   - First things. Does this person go to others first, hole up and study, complain, discuss feelings, or take action? These are the basic orientations of people that reveal what's important to them. Use these to motivate.

   - Speech content. People might focus on details, concepts, feelings, or other people in their speech. This can tell you again how to appeal to them by mirroring their speech emphasis. Although most of us naturally adjust—we talk details with detail-oriented people—chances are good that in problem relationships you're not finding the common ground. She talks "detail" and you talk "people," for example.

   - Emotion. You need to know what people's hot buttons are because one mistake can get you labeled as insensitive with some people. The only cure here is to see what turns up the volume for them—either literally or what they're concerned about.

   - Values. Apply the same thinking to the values of others. Do they talk about money, recognition, integrity, efficiency in their normal work conversation? Figuring out what their drivers are tells you another easy way to appeal to anyone.

8. **Establish a common cause and a shared mind-set.** A common thrust is what energizes dream teams. As in light lasers, alignment adds focus, power, and efficiency. It's best to get each team member involved in setting the common vision. Establish goals and measures.

Most people like to be measured. People like to have checkpoints along the way to chart their progress. Most people perform better with goals that are stretching. Again, letting the team participate in setting the goals is a plus.

9. **Learn to be a cultural anthropologist.** In assessing groups, ask yourself: What makes their blood boil? What do they believe? What are they trying to accomplish together? What do they smile at? What norms and customs do they have? What practices and behaviors do they share? Do they not like it if you stand too close? If you get right down to business? Do they like first names or are they more formal? If a Japanese manager presents his card, do you know what to do? Why do they have their cards printed in two languages and executives from the U.S. don't? Do you know what jokes are okay to tell? What do they believe about you and your group or groups? Positive? Neutral? Negative? What's been the history of their group and yours? Is this a first contact or a long history? Don't blunder in; nothing will kill you quicker with a group than showing utter disregard—read disrespect—for it and its norms, or having no idea of how they view your group. Ask people for insights who deal with this group often. If it's an important group to you and your business, read about it.

Overusing ISTJ Tendencies

If you sometimes overdo your preferred behaviors, you may need to work on:

A Becoming More Approachable

B Curbing Arrogance

C Better Listening and Patience

D Not Leaving a Trail of Bodies

ISTJ	ISFJ	INFJ	INTJ
ISTP	ISFP	INFP	INTP
ESTP	ESFP	ENFP	ENTP
ESTJ	ESFJ	ENFJ	ENTJ

A Becoming More Approachable

ISTJs can be quiet and reserved.

1. **Watch your non-verbals.** Approachable people appear and sound open and relaxed. They smile. They are calm. They keep eye contact. They nod while the other person is talking. They have an open body posture. They speak in a paced and pleasant tone. Eliminate any disruptive habits, such as speaking too rapidly or forcefully, using strongly worded or loaded language, or going into too much detail. Watch out for signaling disinterest with actions like glancing at your watch, fiddling with paperwork, or giving your impatient "I'm busy" look.

2. **The magic of questions.** Many people don't ask enough curiosity questions when in their work mode. There are too many informational statements, conclusions, suggestions, and solutions and not enough "what if," "what are you thinking," "how do you see that." In studies, statements outweighed questions 8 to 1. Ask more questions than others. Make fewer solution statements early in a discussion. Keep probing until you understand what they are trying to tell you.

3. **The first three minutes.** Managing the first three minutes is essential. The tone is set. First impressions are formed. Work on being open and approachable, and take in information during the beginning of a transaction. This means putting others at ease so that they feel okay about disclosing. It means initiating rapport, listening, sharing, understanding, and comforting. Approachable people get more information, know things earlier, and can get others to do more

31

things. The more you can get them to initiate and say early in the transaction, the more you'll know about where they are coming from, and the better you can tailor your approach.

4. **Have more fun.** Properly used and delivered, humor can be a constructive influence on those around you. It can increase a feeling of well-being and belonging, it can take the bite out of tension, and it can balance a negative situation for someone or the whole team. There are topics that can be near universally humorous. There are universal traits. Misers, bad drivers, absent-minded people, anything that is understood worldwide as the human condition. There are things that are funny about your life. Have funny kids, pets, hobbies? What's a ridiculous situation you've been caught in lately? There are funny things in the workplace. The jargon of it, memos, ironic rules. Stories from the picnic or the off-site. There is providing relief from our problems. The weather, taxes, any of life's little indignities and embarrassments. And there is always the news. Most programs have at least one humorous tale, and sometimes the news is funny enough as it is. There are cartoons that most find humorous in the work setting (*The Far Side* and *Dilbert* currently). There are funny jokes that most find funny. Humor that unites people rather than puts down people or groups is always safe. Begin to look for and remember the humor around you. Begin to pass on your observation to a few safe people to test your humor judgment.

5. **Self-humor.** Self-humor is usually safe, seen as positive by others, and most of the time leads to increased respect. Funny and embarrassing things that happened to you (when the airline lost your luggage and you had to wash your underwear in an airport restroom and dry it under the hand dryer). Your flaws and foibles (when you were so stressed over your taxes that you locked the keys in your car with the motor running). Mistakes you've made. Blunders you've committed. Besides adding humor to the situation, it humanizes you and endears people to you. Anything can of course be overdone, so balance it with seriousness.

6. **Informing.** Do you hold back information unless it's part of a task or directive? Do you parcel out information on your schedule? Do people around you know what you're doing and why? Are you aware of things others would benefit from, but you don't take the time to communicate? In most organizations, these things and things like it will get you in trouble. Organizations function on the flow of information. Being on your own and preferring peace and privacy are okay as long as you communicate things to bosses, peers, and

teammates that they need to know and would feel better if they knew. Don't be the source of surprises.

B Curbing Arrogance

Because ISTJs are orderly, factual, and dedicated, they can come across as know-it-alls.

1. **Arrogant?** Arrogant people are seen as distant and impersonal loners who prefer their own ideas to anyone else's. They purposefully, or not, devalue others and their contributions. This usually results in people feeling diminished, rejected, and angry. Why? Answers. Solutions. Conclusions. Statements. Dictates. That's the staple of arrogant people. Not listening. Instant output. Sharp reactions. Don't want to be that way? Read your audience. Do you know what people look like when they are uncomfortable with you? Do they back up? Stumble over words? Cringe? Stand at the door hoping not to get invited in? You should work doubly hard at observing others. Especially during the first three minutes of an important transaction, work to make the person or group comfortable with you before the real agenda starts. Ask a question unrelated to the topic. Offer them a drink. Share something personal.

2. **Does your style chill the transaction?** Arrogant? Insensitive? Distant? Too busy to pay attention? Too quick to get into the agenda? Always select your interpersonal approach from the other person in, not from you out. Your best choice of approach will always be determined by the other person or group, not you. Think about each transaction as if the other person were a customer you wanted. How would you craft an approach?

3. **Arrogance is a major blockage to building self-knowledge.** Research says that successful people know themselves better. Many people who have a towering strength or lots of success get less feedback and roll along thinking they are perfect until their careers get in trouble. If you are viewed as arrogant, your best chance of understanding it is to get facilitated 360° feedback where the respondents can remain anonymous. It is unlikely you could get useful data from people directly since they don't think you listen, and it has been painful in the past to try to influence you. Arrogant people typically overrate themselves. Their ratings from others may be lower than they should be because people believe they need to make it look worse than it is to

get through your defiance shield. If you are seen as devaluing others, they will return the favor.

4. **Watch your non-verbals.** Arrogant people look, talk, and act arrogantly. As you try to become less arrogant, you need to find out what your non-verbals are. All arrogant people do a series of things that can be viewed by a neutral party and judged to give off the signals of arrogance. Washboard brow. Facial expressions. Body shifting, especially turning away. Impatient finger or pencil tapping. False smile. Tight lips. Looking away. Find out from a trusted friend what you do, and try to eliminate those behaviors.

C Better Listening and Patience

ISTJs have high standards and a strongly developed sense of right and wrong. They can come across as harsh on those who don't work as diligently, run slow processes, lack follow-through, or just generally waste their time.

1. **Blame and vengeance?** Do you feel a need to punish the people and groups that set you off? Do you become hostile, angry, sarcastic, or vengeful? While all that may be temporarily satisfying to you, they will all backfire and you will lose in the long term. When someone attacks you, rephrase it as an attack on a problem. Reverse the argument—ask what they would do if they were in your shoes. When the other side takes a rigid position, don't reject it. Ask why: What are the principles behind the offer? How do we know it's fair? What's the theory of the case? Play out what would happen if their position was accepted. Let the other side vent frustration or blow off steam, but don't react.

2. **Listening.** Interpersonally skilled people are very good at listening. They listen to understand and take in information to select their response. They listen without interrupting. They ask clarifying questions. They don't instantly judge. Judgment might come later. They restate what the other person has said to signal understanding. They nod. They might jot down notes. Listeners get more data.

3. **Try to listen without judging initially.** Turn off your "I agree; I don't agree" filter. You don't have to agree with it; just listen to understand. Assume when people tell you something they are looking for understanding; indicate that by being able to summarize what they said. Don't offer advice or solutions unless it's obvious the person wants to know what you would do. While offering instant solutions is

a good thing to do in many circumstances, it's chilling where the goal is to get people to talk to you more freely.

4. **Impatience triggers.** Some people probably bring out your impatience more than others. Who are they? What is it about them that makes you more impatient? Pace? Language? Thought process? Accent? These people may include people you don't like, who ramble, who whine and complain, or who are repetitive advocates for things you have already rejected. Mentally rehearse some calming tactics before meeting with people who trigger your impatience. Work on understanding their positions without judging them—you can always judge later. In all cases, focus them on the issues or problems to be discussed, return them to the point, interrupt to summarize, and state your position. Try to gently train them to be more efficient with you next time without damaging them in the process.

5. **Rein in your horse.** Impatient people provide answers, conclusions, and solutions too early in the process. Others haven't even understood the problem yet. Providing solutions too quickly will make your people dependent and irritated. If you don't teach them how you think and how you can come up with solutions so fast, they will never learn. Take the time to really define the problem—not impatiently throw out a solution. Brainstorm what questions need to be answered in order to resolve it. Give your people the task to think about for a day and come back with some solutions. Be a teacher instead of a dictator of solutions. Study yourself. Keep a journal of what triggered your behavior and what the observed consequences were. Learn to detect and control your triggers before they get you in trouble.

6. **Let others be humorous.** Sometimes people who aren't very humorous (or are very serious) chill and suppress humor in others. Even if you're not going to work on being more humorous or funny, at least let others be. That will actually help you be seen as at least more tolerant of humor than you were in the past. Eventually, you may even be tempted to join in.

7. **Build a sense of fun for those around you.** Parties, roasts, gag awards, and outings build cohesion. Start celebrating wins, honor those who have gone the extra mile, but don't honor anyone twice before everyone has been honored once. Working with the whole person tends to build teams.

D Not Leaving a Trail of Bodies

ISTJs can appear quite judgmental and blaming with low performers and those they disagree with. They can be too quick to act, don't put enough effort into development, and expect miracle turnarounds.

1. **Cooperative relations.** The opposite of conflict is cooperation. Developing cooperative relationships involves demonstrating real and perceived equity, the other side feeling understood and respected, and taking a problem-oriented point of view. To do this more: Increase the realities and perceptions of fairness—don't try to win every battle and take all the spoils; focus on the common-ground issues and interests of both sides—find wins on both sides, give in on little points; avoid starting with entrenched positions—show respect for them and their positions; and reduce any remaining conflicts to the smallest size possible.

2. **Causing unnecessary conflict.** Language, words, and timing set the tone and can cause unnecessary conflict that has to be managed before you can get anything done. Do you use insensitive language? Do you raise your voice often? Do you use terms and phrases that challenge others? Do you use demeaning terms? Do you use negative humor? Do you offer conclusions, solutions, statements, dictates, or answers early in the transaction? Give reasons first, solutions last. When you give solutions first, people often directly challenge the solutions instead of defining the problem. Pick words that are other-person neutral. Pick words that don't challenge or sound one-sided. Pick tentative and probabilistic words that give others a chance to maneuver and save face. Pick words that are about the problem and not the person. Avoid direct blaming remarks; describe the problem and its impact.

3. **Delivering firm messages.** Be succinct. You have limited attention span in tough feedback situations. Don't waste time with a long preamble, particularly if the feedback is negative. If the feedback is negative and the recipient is likely to know it, go ahead and say it directly. They won't hear anything positive you have to say anyway. Don't overwhelm the person/group, even if you have a lot to say. Go from specific to general points. Keep it to the facts. Don't embellish to make your point. No passion or inflammatory language. Don't do it to harm or out of vengeance. Don't do it in anger. If feelings are involved for you, wait until you can describe them, not show them. Managerial courage comes in search of a better outcome, not

destroying others. Stay calm and cool. If others are not composed, don't respond. Just return to the message.

4. **Are your problem performers confused?** Do they know what's expected of them? You may not set clear enough performance standards, goals, and objectives. You may be a seat-of-the-pants manager, and some people are struggling because they don't know what is expected or it changes. You may be a cryptic communicator. You may be too busy to communicate. You may communicate to some and not to others. You may have given up on some and stopped communicating. Or you may think they would know what to do if they're any good, but that's not really true because you have not properly communicated what you want. The first task is to outline the 5 to 10 key results areas and what indicators of success would be. Involve your problem direct reports on both ends—the standards and the indicators. Provide them with a fair way to measure their own progress. Employees with goals and standards are usually harder on themselves than you'll ever be. Often they set higher standards than you would. Sometimes the problem is behavioral, as in someone who can't control outbursts, and only affects performance on the back end in lost cooperation or sabotage. Then the best approach is to note the gap between behavior and expectations, and point out what some of the observed consequences are. If the person agrees, then coaching may suffice. If the person balks, then a 360° feedback process with follow-up may be needed to illuminate the depth of the problem before any help can be given.

5. **Bring a solution if you can.** Nobody likes a critic. Everybody appreciates a problem solver. Give people ways to improve; don't just dump and leave. Tell others what you think would be better—paint a different outcome. Help others see the consequences—you can ask them what they think, and you can tell them what the consequences are from your side if you are personally involved ("I'd be reluctant to work with you on X again").

The results that are gained from my work tend to reinforce what I consider effective, but I tend to bruise people. I have rarely considered other approaches, which I need to do.

– An ISTJ Manager

APPLICATION

Your personal preferences play out in day-to-day problems and situations you face. Below is a case about your type dealing with such a situation. Use this to think through how you will integrate the tips you've considered and coach yourself to be more effective in your type.

ISTJ Application Situation (Part 1)

You're the Chairman of the Board of Directors of an organization in the transportation industry, and before retirement you were CEO of an innovative and successful start-up that developed air navigation systems. The organization you now chair is undergoing profound change, as is your industry, based on a number of interrelated factors, including environmental pressures, more demanding customers, and investor anxiety. This has resulted in a good deal of internal turmoil between upper and middle management, and between front-line management and line employees.

Your CEO, John, has been with the company for 20 years, having risen from his first job as a front-line supervisor, up through the ranks by virtue of being a careful, conscientious, serious-minded and detail-oriented achiever. He also has a steel-trap memory, and in some quarters he's referred to (not without some sarcasm) as "the history professor."

Those characteristics served John well in all his previous roles, but now he's facing new challenges and seems to be staggering. You've decided to work more closely with him on a one-to-one basis because you think he can continue to be an asset, but only if he makes some changes.

Thinking It Through: Strategy

■ In preparation for your meeting with John, what kind of data do you want to get, and where do you think you should get it?

■ What's your approach going to be in talking with him?

Planning It Out: Tactics

■ What barriers to John's effectiveness (i.e., actions, behaviors) do you anticipate you'd find if you were to interview his peers and direct reports?

■ What particular areas would present developmental challenges to John, and what competencies would you want to see him put into play in order to help him meet the new demands of the job?

■ Which of the tactics described in the Being More Effective section are applicable in this situation?

■ Which Overused Tendencies are most likely to come into play here?

ISTJ Application Situation (Part 2)

■ You interviewed other members of the executive team and you gathered the multi-rater assessment data. You also had John complete the MBTI, and his type was identified as ISTJ.

Here's some of what you learned:

■ John's self-assessed strength as a detail-oriented, thorough, and cautious decision maker is actually viewed by others as an overused strength that is inhibiting innovation and change.

■ What John considers to be thoughtfulness and judiciousness, other members of the Board and of the executive team consider to be lack of impact and excess reserve.

Reflection

■ Where are you going to begin in coaching John? What should he work on?

■ What in his profile can John continue to rely on, what must he minimize, and do you think he has a good chance of making it?

SUGGESTED READINGS

■■■■■■■■ Being a More Effective ISTJ ■■■■■■■■

Dealing With Ambiguity

Anderson, Dean and Linda S. Ackerman Anderson. *Beyond Change Management: Advanced Strategies for Today's Transformational Leaders.* San Francisco: Jossey-Bass, Inc., 2001.

Bellman, Geoffrey M. *Getting Things Done When You Are Not in Charge.* San Francisco: Berrett-Koehler Publishers, Inc., 2001.

Black, J. Stewart and Hal B. Gregersen. *Leading Strategic Change: Breaking Through the Brain Barrier.* Upper Saddle River, NJ: Financial Times/Prentice Hall, 2002.

Burke, W. Warner and William Trahant with Richard Koonce. *Business Climate Shifts: Profiles of Change Makers.* Boston: Butterworth-Heinemann, 2000.

Luecke, Richard. *Managing Change and Transition.* Boston: Harvard Business School Publishing, 2003.

Showing Compassion and Caring

Autry, James A. *The Art of Caring Leadership.* New York: William Morrow and Company, Inc., 1991.

Brantley, Jeffrey and Jon Kabat-Zinn. *Calming Your Anxious Mind: How Mindfulness and Compassion Can Free You From Anxiety, Fear, and Panic.* Oakland, CA: New Harbinger Publications, 2003.

Daniels, Aubrey C. *Bringing Out the Best in People.* New York: McGraw-Hill, Inc., 1994.

Kouzes, James M. and Barry Z. Posner. *Encouraging the Heart: A Leader's Guide to Rewarding and Recognizing Others.* San Francisco: Jossey-Bass, Inc., 2003.

Stone, Douglas. *Difficult Conversations: How to Discuss What Matters Most.* New York: Penguin Books, 2000.

Developing Others

Charan, Ram, James L. Noel and Steve Drotter. *The Leadership Pipeline: How to Build the Leadership Powered Company.* New York: John Wiley & Sons, Inc., 2000.

Daniels, Aubrey C. *Bringing Out the Best in People.* New York: McGraw-Hill, Inc., 1994.

Fulmer, Robert M. and Jay A. Conger. *Growing Your Company's Leaders.* New York: AMACOM, 2004.

Lombardo, Michael M. and Robert W. Eichinger. *The Leadership Machine.* Minneapolis, MN: Lominger Limited, Inc., 2004.

Innovation and Strategy

Bandrowski, James F. *Corporate Imagination Plus—Five Steps to Translating Innovative Strategies Into Action.* New York: The Free Press, 2000.

Birch, Paul and Brian Clegg. *Imagination Engineering—The Toolkit for Business Creativity.* London: Pitman Publishing, 1996.

Chakravorti, Bhaskar. *The Slow Pace of Fast Change: Bringing Innovations to Market in a Connected World.* Boston: Harvard Business School Press, 2003.

Charan, Ram. *What the CEO Wants You to Know: How Your Company Really Works.* New York: Crown Business Publishing, 2001.

Christensen, Clayton M. and Michael E. Raynor. *The Innovator's Solution.* Harvard Business School Press, 2003.

Collins, James C. *Good to Great: Why Some Companies Make the Leap...And Others Don't.* New York: HarperCollins, 2001.

DeGraff, Jeff and Katherine A. Lawrence. *Creativity at Work: Developing the Right Practices to Make Innovation Happen.* San Francisco: Jossey-Bass, Inc., 2002.

Dudik, Evan Matthew. *Strategic Renaissance: New Thinking and Innovative Tools to Create Great Corporate Strategies Using Insights From History and Science.* New York: AMACOM, 2000.

The Futurist Magazine. http://www.wfs.org

Gaynor, Gerard H. *Innovation by Design.* New York: AMACOM, 2002.

Hamel, Gary. *Leading the Revolution*. Boston: Harvard Business School Press, 2002.

Hargadon, Andrew and Kathleen M. Eisenhardt. *How Breakthroughs Happen: The Surprising Truth About How Companies Innovate*. Boston: Harvard Business School Press, 2003.

Harvard Business Review. Phone: 800-988-0886 (US and Canada). Fax: 617-496-1029. Mail: Harvard Business Review. Subscriber Services, P.O. Box 52623. Boulder, CO 80322-2623 USA. http://www.hbsp.harvard.edu/products/hbr

Kaplan, Robert S. and David P. Norton. *The Strategy-Focused Organization: How Balanced Scorecard Companies Thrive in the New Business Environment*. Boston: Harvard Business School Press, 2000.

Porter, Michael E. *Competitive Strategy: Techniques for Analyzing Industries and Competitors*. New York: The Free Press, 1998.

Prahalad, C.K. and Venkat Ramaswamy. *The Future of Competition: Co-Creating Unique Value With Customers*. Boston: Harvard Business School Press, 2004.

Team Building

Bolton, Robert. *People Skills*. New York: Simon & Schuster, 1979.

Fisher, Kimball and Mareen Duncan Fisher. *The Distance Manager: A Hands-On Guide to Managing Off-Site Employees and Virtual Teams*. New York: McGraw-Hill Trade, 2000.

Harvard Business School Press. *Harvard Business Review on Teams That Succeed*. Boston: Harvard Business School Press, 2004.

Katzenbach, Jon R. and Douglas K. Smith. *The Wisdom of Teams: Creating the High-Performance Organization*. New York: HarperBusiness, 2003.

Parker, Glenn M. *Cross-Functional Teams: Working With Allies, Enemies, and Other Strangers*. San Francisco: Jossey-Bass, Inc., 2002.

Peters, Tom. *Thriving on Chaos: Handbook for a Management Revolution*. New York: HarperCollins, 1987.

Raymond, Cara Capretta, Robert W. Eichinger and Michael M. Lombardo. *FYI for Teams*. Minneapolis, MN: Lominger Limited, Inc., 2001–2004.

Robbins, Harvey and Michael Finley. *The New Why Teams Don't Work— What Goes Wrong and How to Make It Right.* San Francisco: Berrett-Koehler Publishers, Inc., 2000.

■■■■■■■ **Overusing ISTJ Tendencies** ■■■■■■■

Becoming More Approachable

Benton, D.A. *Executive Charisma: Six Steps to Mastering the Art of Leadership.* New York: McGraw-Hill Trade, 2003.

Brooks, Michael. *Instant Rapport.* New York: Warner Books, 1989.

Maxwell, John C. *Relationships 101.* London: Thomas Nelson, 2004.

Silberman, Melvin L. and Freda Hansburg. *Peoplesmart: Developing Your Interpersonal Intelligence.* San Francisco: Berrett-Koehler Publishers, Inc., 2000.

Curbing Arrogance

Bolton, Robert and Dorothy Grover Bolton. *People Styles at Work—Making Bad Relationships Good and Good Relationships Better.* New York: AMACOM, 1996.

Carter, Les. *The Anger Trap: Free Yourself From the Frustrations That Sabotage Your Life.* New York: John Wiley & Sons, Inc., 2003.

Ellis, Albert, Ph.D. *How to Control Your Anxiety Before It Controls You.* New York: Citadel Press, 2000.

Waldroop, James, Ph.D. and Timothy Butler, Ph.D. *Maximum Success: Changing the 12 Behavior Patterns That Keep You From Getting Ahead.* New York: Doubleday, 2000.

Better Listening and Patience

Barker, Larry, Ph.D. and Kittie Watson, Ph.D. *Listen Up: At Home, at Work, in Relationships: How to Harness the Power of Effective Listening.* Irvine, CA: Griffin Trade Paperback, 2001.

Bolton, Robert and Dorothy Grover Bolton. *People Styles at Work—Making Bad Relationships Good and Good Relationships Better.* New York: AMACOM, 1996.

Burley-Allen, Madelyn. *Listening: The Forgotten Skill.* New York: John Wiley & Sons, Inc., 1995.

Gonthier, Giovinella and Kevin Morrissey. *Rude Awakenings: Overcoming the Civility Crisis in the Workplace.* Chicago: Dearborn Trade Publishing, 2002.

Ryan, Mary Jane. *The Power of Patience: How to Slow the Rush and Enjoy More Happiness, Success, and Peace of Mind Everyday.* New York: Broadway Press, 2003.

Not Leaving a Trail of Bodies

Cloke, Ken and Joan Goldsmith. *Resolving Conflicts at Work: A Complete Guide for Everyone on the Job.* San Francisco: Jossey-Bass, Inc., 2000.

Dana, Daniel. *Conflict Resolution.* New York: McGraw-Hill Trade, 2000.

Graham, Gini. *A Survival Guide for Working With Humans: Dealing With Whiners, Back-Stabbers, Know-It-Alls, and Other Difficult People.* New York: AMACOM, 2004.

Guttman, Howard M. *When Goliaths Clash: Managing Executive Conflict to Build a More Dynamic Organization.* New York: AMACOM, 2003.

Levin, Robert A. and Joseph G. Rosse. *Talent Flow: A Strategic Approach to Keeping Good Employees, Helping Them Grow, and Letting Them Go.* New York: John Wiley & Sons, Inc., 2001.

Masters, Marick Francis and Robert R. Albright. *The Complete Guide to Conflict Resolution in the Workplace.* New York: AMACOM, 2002.

Solomon, Muriel. *Working With Difficult People.* New York: Prentice Hall, 2002.

CHAPTER 2

ISFJ
Introverted Sensing
with
Extraverted Feeling

■■■■■■■■■■■■■■■■■

13.8% of Population
3.4% of Managers

■■■■■■■■■■■■■■■■■

Typical Strengths

To Serve and Protect
Helpful to Others
Sympathetic
Team Oriented
Loyal and Dependable

ISTJ	ISFJ	INFJ	INTJ
ISTP	ISFP	INFP	INTP
ESTP	ESFP	ENFP	ENTP
ESTJ	ESFJ	ENFJ	ENTJ

I figure if I do my job, keep people happy, everyone will stay out of my hair.
– An ISFJ Manager

Basic Habits of Mind

Introverted Sensing drives ISFJs to be realistic, calm, consistent, and to be careful with facts. Loyal and reliable, they trust in the truth of their experience as a guide. Extraverted Feeling leads them to develop cooperative and sympathetic behaviors. Seen as warm and thoughtful, they usually express interest in people rather than things.

The effects of Extraverted Thinking and Extraverted Intuiting are more subtle as they may stick doggedly to a plan and feel quite convinced of their frame of reference. These qualities can make them appear stubborn and slow to change.

Typical Communication Patterns

■ ISFJs seek to be helpful to others without asserting their own needs.

■ Unhurried and focused, others may see them as patient, thorough realists.

■ They are careful to achieve balance in their work and personal life and often assume others do so as well. They get the job done before the deadline to prevent disruptive last-minute effort.

General Learning Strategy

■ A visual learner, ISFJs will usually prefer "show and tell," seeing a video, and reading cases that illustrate the points being made.

■ Their preferred learning strategies are likely to be observing, graphing, organizing, and applying.

■ They learn best in small-group, cooperative-learning discussions that focus on personal experiences.

Interpersonal Qualities Related to Motivation

- ISFJs like organized and concise information and assume that others will as well.

- They put energy into confirming "the facts" before taking action, and feel that others know they are reliable.

- They usually follow the tactic of if you show and tell, you will get people to understand the job that needs to be done.

Blind Spots

- ISFJs can sometimes appear to be so conventional that they seem self-centered, uncompromising, and lacking in innovation.

- They might be surprised to learn that their behavior can be seen as stingy, overly conventional, and rigid.

Stress Related Behavior

- As an initial response to stress, ISFJs may become very reserved and obsessive about procedure or conventions. They tend to be very attentive to the use of resources.

- Under prolonged stress, they may see evidence in the smallest events that the future is gloomy and is unlikely to be enjoyable. In this situation they may actually seem impulsive and unrealistic in their expectations.

Potential Barriers to Effectiveness

- Being overdependent on structures and standard operating procedures with a high sense of control, they may have difficulty with staff relationships and innovation.

- Their lack of interest in the limelight means that they often do not get their views aired enough. They may behave in ways to diminish the social presence needed to influence others.

Being a More Effective ISFJ

A   Letting Go of Structure
B   Being More Personally Flexible
C   Taking Charge
D   Dealing With Conflict
E   Being More Innovative
F   Dealing With Problem Performers

ISTJ	ISFJ	INFJ	INTJ
ISTP	ISFP	INFP	INTP
ESTP	ESFP	ENFP	ENTP
ESTJ	ESFJ	ENFJ	ENTJ

A   Letting Go of Structure

ISFJs prefer structure and organization. They sometimes lack action orientation and don't take risks.

1. **Analysis paralysis?** Break out of your examine-it-to-death mode and just do it. Sometimes you hold back acting because you don't have all the information. Some like to be close to 100% sure before they act. Anyone with a brain and 100% of the data can make good decisions. The real test is who can act the soonest with a reasonable amount, but not all, of the data. Some studies suggest successful general managers are about 65% correct. If you learn to make smaller decisions more quickly, you can change course along the way to the correct decision. You may examine things to death because you are a chronic worrier who focuses on the downsides of action. Write down your worries, and for each one, write down the upside (a pro for each con). Once you consider both sides of the issue, you should be more willing to take action. Virtually any conceivable action has a downside, but it has an upside as well. Act, get feedback on the results, refine, and act again.

2. **Don't like risk?** Sometimes taking action involves pushing the envelope, taking chances, and trying bold new initiatives. Doing those things leads to more misfires and mistakes. Research says that successful executives have made more mistakes in their careers than those who didn't make it. Treat any mistakes or failures as chances to learn. Nothing ventured, nothing gained. Up your risk comfort. Start small so you can recover more quickly. Go for small wins. Don't blast into a major task to prove your boldness. Break it down into smaller tasks. Take the easiest one for you first. Then build up to the tougher ones. Review each one to see what you did well and not well, and set goals so you'll do something differently and better each time. End up accomplishing the big goal and taking the bold action. Challenge

yourself. See how creative you can be in taking action a number of different ways.

3. **Stuck with what you know?** Do you feel best when you know everything that's going on around you and you are in control? Most do. Few are motivated by uncertainty and chaos. But many are challenged by it. They enjoy solving problems no one has solved before. They enjoy cutting paths where no one has been before. You need to become more comfortable being a pioneer. Explore new ground. Learn new things. Practice in your life. Go to theme restaurants you know nothing about. Vacation at places without doing a lot of research. Go to ethnic festivals for groups you have little knowledge about.

4. **Problem definition.** Under uncertainty, it really helps to get as firm a handle as possible on the problem. Figure out what causes it. Keep asking why. See how many causes you can come up with and how many organizing buckets you can put them in. This increases the chance of a better solution because you can see more connections. The evidence from decision-making research makes it clear that thorough problem definition with appropriate questions to answer leads to better decisions. Focusing on solutions or information first often slows things down since we have no conceptual buckets in which to organize our thinking. Learn to ask more questions. In one study of problem solving, 7% of comments were questions and about half were solutions.

5. **Finishing.** Do you prefer to finish what you have started? Do you have a high need to complete tasks? Wrap them up in nice clean packages? Working well with ambiguity and under uncertainty means moving from incomplete task to incomplete task. Some may be abandoned, some may never be finished. They'll probably only ever get 80% done, and you'll constantly have to edit your actions and decisions. Change your internal reward process toward feeling good about fixing mistakes and moving things forward incrementally, more than finishing any given project.

B Being More Personally Flexible

ISFJs can be rather rigid about their beliefs, behavior, and values. Changing behavior doesn't come easily.

1. **You may be seen as rigid in your values stances and unwilling to accept, or even see, those of others.** Rigid stances often come from childhood and early adult experiences. You need to know why you hold these values and critically examine if they are appropriate here. Statements of belief are pronouncements—a true value holds up to action scrutiny; you can say why you hold it, how it plays out in different situations, and what happens when it conflicts with other values. You may have reduced your beliefs to rigid commandments.

2. **Are you rule oriented, more likely to follow a plan than create one?** You may follow procedures and schedules, but need more flexible options in planning. To plan better:

   ■ Lay out tasks and work. Most successful projects begin with a good plan. What do I need to accomplish? What are the goals? What's the time line? What resources will I need? How many of the resources do I control? Who controls the rest of the resources—people, funding, tools, materials, support—I need? Lay out the work from A to Z. Many people are seen as lacking a plan because they don't write down the sequence or parts of the work and leave something out. Ask others to comment on ordering and what's missing.

   ■ Vision the plan in process. What could go wrong? Run scenarios in your head. Think along several paths. Rank the potential problems from highest likelihood to lowest likelihood. Think about what you would do if the highest likelihood things were to occur. Create a contingency plan for each. Pay attention to the weakest links, which are usually groups or elements you have the least interface with or control over (perhaps someone in a remote location, a consultant, or supplier). Stay doubly in touch with the potential weak links.

3. **Pick people who are quite different from you and observe what they do and how they do it.** Then ask for their help on a problem. Just ask questions and understand their perspective. Don't make any judgments about the rightness or wrongness of their approach.

4. **Pick some tough critics to talk with.** Don't go to the few people you truly like, most likely because you share similar perspectives. Go to some you know will disagree with you and hear them out.

5. **Incrementalism.** The essence of dealing comfortably with uncertainty is the tolerance of errors and mistakes, and absorbing the possible heat and criticism that follow. Acting on an ill-defined problem with no precedents to follow means shooting in the dark with as informed a decision as you can make at the time. People who are good at this are incrementalists. They make a series of smaller decisions, get instant feedback, correct the course, get a little more data, move forward a little more, until the bigger problem is under control. They don't try to get it right the first time. Many problem-solving studies show that the second or third try is when we really understand the underlying dynamics of problems. They also know that the more uncertain the situation is, the more likely it is they will make mistakes in the beginning. So, you need to work on two practices: Start small so you can recover more quickly. Do little somethings as soon as you can and get used to heat.

6. **Transitions.** Which transitions are the toughest for you? Write down the five toughest for you. What do you have a hard time switching to and from? Use this knowledge to assist you in making a list of discontinuities (tough transitions) you face, such as confronting people vs. being approachable and accepting, leading vs. following, going from firing someone to a business-as-usual staff meeting. Write down how each of these discontinuities makes you feel and what you may do that gets you in trouble. For example, you may not shift gears well after a confrontation, or you may have trouble taking charge again after passively sitting in a meeting all day. Create a plan to attack each of the tough transitions.

7. **Control your instant responses to shifts.** Many of us respond to the fragmentation and discontinuities of work as if they were threats instead of the way life is. Sometimes our emotions and fears are triggered by switching from active to passive or soft to tough. This initial anxious response lasts 45–60 seconds, and we need to buy some time before we say or do something inappropriate. Research shows that generally somewhere between the second and third thing you think to say or do is the best option. Practice holding back your first response long enough to think of a second and a third. Manage your shifts, don't be a prisoner of them.

8. **Use mental rehearsal to think about different ways you could carry out a transaction.** Try to see yourself acting in opposing ways to get the same thing done—when to be tough, when to let them decide, when to deflect the issue because it's not ready to decide. What cues would you look for to select an approach that matches? Practice trying to get the same thing done with two different groups with two different approaches. Did they both work?

C Taking Charge

ISFJs don't usually take charge when trouble comes. They often don't get their views aired or know how to sell their ideas.

1. **Leading is riskier than following.** While there are a lot of personal rewards for leading, leading puts you in the limelight. Think about what happens to political leaders and the scrutiny they face. Leaders have to be internally secure. Do you feel good about yourself? They have to please themselves first that they are on the right track. Can you defend to a critical and impartial audience the wisdom of what you're doing? They have to accept lightning bolts from detractors. Can you take the heat? People will always say it should have been done differently. Listen to them, but be skeptical. Even great leaders are wrong sometimes. They accept personal responsibility for errors and move on to lead some more. Don't let criticism prevent you from taking the lead. Build up your heat shield. Conduct a postmortem immediately after finishing milestone efforts. This will indicate to all that you're open to continuous improvement whether the result was stellar or not.

2. **Against the grain tough stands.** Taking a tough stand demands confidence in what you're saying along with the humility that you might be wrong—one of life's paradoxes. To prepare to take the lead on a tough issue, work on your stand through mental interrogation until you can clearly state in a few sentences what your stand is and why you hold it. Build the business case. How do others win? People don't line up behind laundry lists or ambiguous objectives. Ask others for advice—scope the problem, consider options, pick one, develop a rationale, then go with it until proven wrong. Then redo the process. If this doesn't help, find out where the pain is for you. What have you been avoiding? Examine your past and see where taking-charge behavior has gotten you in trouble or you thought it would get you in trouble. Isolate the most troublesome elements, such as forgetting things under pressure, trouble with fierce debate, problems with

unpopular stands, and things moving too fast. Devise counter-strategies.

3. **Selling your leadership.** While some people may welcome what you say and want to do, others will go after you or even try to minimize the situation. Some will sabotage. To sell your leadership, keep your eyes on the prize but don't specify how to get there. Present the outcomes, targets, and goals without the how to's. Welcome their ideas—good and bad. Any negative response is a positive if you learn from it. Allow them to fill in the blanks, ask questions, and disagree without appearing impatient with them. Allow others to save face; concede small points, invite criticism of your own. Help them figure out how to win. Keep to the facts and the problem before the group; stay away from personal clashes.

D Dealing With Conflict

Due to the ISFJ's focus on relationships and worry about any harm coming to those relationships, they tend to be conflict averse. When they do deal with conflict, they tend to be rule bound (it's always been that way) and values driven (a question of ideals rather than facts). They need to detach from relationships and look at the problem alone.

1. **Clear problem-focused communication.** Follow the rule of equity: Explain your thinking and ask them to explain theirs. Be able to state their position as clearly as they do whether you agree or not—give it legitimacy. Separate facts from opinions and assumptions. Generate a variety of possibilities first rather than stake out positions. Keep your speaking to 30–60 second bursts. Try to get them to do the same. Don't give the other side the impression you're lecturing or criticizing them. Explain objectively why you hold a view; make the other side do the same. Ask lots of questions, make fewer statements. To identify interests behind positions, ask why they hold them or why they wouldn't want to do something. Always restate their position to their satisfaction before offering a response.

2. **Downsizing the conflict.** Almost all conflicts have common points that get lost in the heat of the battle. After a conflict has been presented and understood, start by saying that it might be helpful to see if we agree on anything. Write them on the flip chart. Then write down the areas left open. Focus on common goals, priorities, and problems. Keep the open conflicts as small as possible and concrete. The more abstract it gets, "We don't trust your unit," the more

unmanageable it gets. To this respond, "Tell me your specific concern—why exactly don't you trust us; can you give me an example?" Usually after calm discussion, they don't trust your unit on this specific issue under these specific conditions. That's easier to deal with. Allow others to save face by conceding small points that are not central to the issue—don't try to hit a home run every time. If you can't agree on a solution, agree on a procedure to move forward. Collect more data. Appeal to a higher power. Get a third-party arbitrator. Something. This creates some positive motion and breaks stalemates.

E Being More Innovative

ISFJs tend to be traditionalists, not very interested in change and innovation.

1. **Being creative involves:** (1) Immersing yourself in a problem; (2) Looking broadly for connections—in the past, what other organizations do, brainstorming with others; (3) Letting your ideas incubate; (4) The breakthrough which usually occurs when you are distracted or in a relaxed state; and (5) Picking one or more to pilot. Most of us are capable of being more creative than we demonstrate. Upbringing, schooling, and the narrowness of many jobs can have a chilling effect on creativity. Many of us are or have been taught to be restrained, narrow, focused, hesitant, cautious, conservative, afraid to err, and unwilling to make a fool of ourselves. All of that chills the creativity already inside us. One process is to lift those restraints. The other involves adding creative skills. There are research-based and experience-tested techniques that, if followed, will produce a more creative process from a person or a group. Creativity is a valued skill because most organizations need innovation in their products and services to succeed.

2. **Remove the restraints.** What's preventing you from being more creative? Perfectionist? Being creative operates at well below having everything right. Cautious and reluctant to speculate? Being creative is the opposite. Worried about what people may think? Afraid you won't be able to defend your idea? By its very nature, being creative means throwing uncertain things up for review and critique. Narrow perspective; most comfortable with your technology and profession? Being creative is looking everywhere. More comfortable with what is very practical? Being creative begins as being impractical. Too busy to reflect and ruminate? Being creative takes time. Get out of your comfort zone. Many busy people rely too much on solutions from

their own history. They rely on what has happened to them in the past. They see sameness in problems that isn't there. Beware of "I have always..." or "Usually, I...." Always pause and look under rocks and ask yourself is this really like the problems you have solved in the past? You don't have to change who you are and what you're comfortable with other than when you need to be more creative. Then think and act differently; try new things; break free of your restraints.

3. **Value-added approaches.** To be more personally creative, immerse yourself in the problem. Getting fresh ideas is not a speedboating process; it requires looking deeply.

- Carve out dedicated time—study the problem deeply, talk with others, look for parallels in other organizations and in remote areas totally outside your field. If your response to this is that you don't have the time, that also usually explains why you're not having any fresh ideas.

- Think out loud. Many people don't know what they know until they talk it out. Find a good sounding board and talk to him/her to increase your understanding of a problem or a technical area. Talk to an expert in an unrelated field. Talk to the most irreverent person you know. Your goal is not to get his/her input, but rather his/her help in figuring out what you know—what your principles and rules of thumb are.

- Practice picking out anomalies—unusual facts that don't quite fit, like sales going down when they should have gone up. What do these odd things imply for strategy? Naturally creative people are much more likely to think in opposite cases when confronted with a problem. Turn the problem upside down: Ask what is the least likely thing it could be, what the problem is not, what's missing from the problem, or what the mirror image of the problem is.

- Look for distant parallels. Don't fall into the mental trap of searching only in parallel organizations because "only they would know." Back up and ask a broader question to aid in the search for solutions. When Motorola wanted to find out how to process orders more quickly, they went not to other electronics firms, but to Domino's Pizza and Federal Express. For more ideas, an interesting—and fun—book on the topic is *Take the Road to Creativity and Get Off Your Dead End* by David Campbell.

F Dealing With Problem Performers

ISFJs can be quite impatient with those who don't appear to have the same degree of loyalty and work ethic that they do. At times, they can come across as blunt to these people.

1. **The message.** Be succinct. You have limited attention span in tough feedback situations. Don't waste time with a long preamble, particularly if the feedback is negative. If the feedback is negative and the recipient is likely to know it, go ahead and say it directly. They won't hear anything positive you have to say anyway. Don't overwhelm the person/group, even if you have a lot to say. Go from specific to general points. Keep it to the facts. Don't embellish to make your point. No passion or inflammatory language. Don't do it to harm or out of vengeance. Don't do it in anger. If feelings are involved for you, wait until you can describe them, not show them. Managerial courage comes in search of a better outcome, not destroying others. Stay calm and cool. If others are not composed, don't respond. Just return to the message.

2. **Creating and communicating standards.** Are your problem performers confused? Do they know what's expected of them? You may not set clear enough performance standards, goals, and objectives. You may be a seat-of-the-pants manager, and some people are struggling because they don't know what is expected or it changes. You may be a cryptic communicator. You may be too busy to communicate. You may communicate to some and not to others. You may have given up on some and stopped communicating. Or you may think they would know what to do if they're any good, but that's not really true because you have not properly communicated what you want. The first task is to outline the 5 to 10 key results areas and what indicators of success would be. Involve your problem direct reports on both ends—the standards and the indicators. Provide them with a fair way to measure their own progress. Employees with goals and standards are usually harder on themselves than you'll ever be. Often they set higher standards than you would. Sometimes the problem is behavioral, as in someone who can't control outbursts, and only affects performance on the back end in lost cooperation or sabotage. Then the best approach is to note the gap between behavior and expectations, and point out what some of the observed consequences are. If the person agrees, then coaching may suffice. If the person balks, then a 360° feedback process with follow-up may be

needed to illuminate the depth of the problem before any help can be given.

3. **Bring a solution if you can.** Nobody likes a critic. Everybody appreciates a problem solver. Give people ways to improve; don't just dump and leave. Tell others what you think would be better—paint a different outcome. Help others see the consequences—you can ask them what they think, and you can tell them what the consequences are from your side if you are personally involved ("I'd be reluctant to work with you on X again").

4. **Feedback.** People need continuous feedback from you and others to grow. Some tips about feedback:

   ■ Arrange for them to get feedback from multiple people, including yourself, on what matters for success in their future jobs; arrange for your direct reports to get 360° feedback about every two years.

   ■ Give them progressively stretching tasks that are first-time and different for them so that they can give themselves feedback as they go.

   ■ If they have direct reports and peers, another technique to recommend is to ask their associates for comments on what they should stop doing, start doing, and keep doing to be more successful.

   ■ You have to be willing to be straight with your people and give them accurate but balanced feedback. Give as much real-time feedback as you have time for. Most people are motivated by process feedback against agreed-upon goals for three reasons. First, it helps them adjust what they are doing along the way in time to better achieve the goal; they can make midcourse corrections. Second, it shows them what they are doing is important and that you're there to help. Third, it's not the "gotcha" game of negative and critical feedback after the fact. If there are negatives, they need to know as soon as possible.

   ■ Set up a buddy system so people can get continuing feedback.

   ■ If your organization has a mentoring program, find out how it works. Best practices begin with those to be mentored writing down goals, objectives, and development needs. They are then carefully matched with mentors and the relationship is outlined.

How often will the people meet? On what topics is the mentor to be helpful? What are the responsibilities of the person to be mentored? If your organization doesn't have such a program, look at setting one up within your unit or function.

Overusing ISFJ Tendencies

If you sometimes overdo your preferred behaviors, you may need to work on:

A Informing With Others in Mind

B Working Better With Peers

C Developing Direct Reports

D Having a Broader Perspective

E Sensitivity to Criticism

F Becoming More Visible

ISTJ	ISFJ	INFJ	INTJ
ISTP	ISFP	INFP	INTP
ESTP	ESFP	ENFP	ENTP
ESTJ	ESFJ	ENFJ	ENTJ

A Informing With Others in Mind

ISFJs tend to inform based on their own agenda, not that of others.

1. **Don't inform enough.** Are you a minimalist? Do you tell people only what they need to know to do their little piece of the puzzle? People are motivated by being aware of the bigger picture. They want to know what to do in order to do their jobs and more. How does what they are doing fit into the larger picture? What are the other people working on and why? Many people think that's unnecessary information and that it would take too much time to do. They're wrong. The sense of doing something worthwhile is the number two motivator at work! It results in a high return on motivation and productivity. (Try to increase the amount of more-than-your-job information you share.) Focus on the impact on others by figuring out who information affects. Put five minutes on your meeting agenda. Ask people what they want to know and, assuming it's not confidential information, tell them. Pick a topic each month to tell your people about.

2.   **A loner.** Do you keep to yourself? Work alone or try to? Do you hold back information? Do you parcel out information on your schedule? Do you share information to get an advantage or to win favor? Do people around you know what you're doing and why? Are you aware of things others would benefit from, but you don't take the time to communicate? In most organizations, these things and things like it will get you in trouble. Organizations function on the flow of information. Being on your own and preferring peace and privacy are okay as long as you communicate things to bosses, peers, and teammates that they need to know and would feel better if they knew. Don't be the source of surprises.

3.   **Cryptic informer.** Some people just aren't good at informing. Their communication styles are not effective. According to behavioral research studies, the most effective communicators: speak often, but briefly (15–30 seconds); ask more questions than others; make fewer solution statements early in a discussion; headline their points in a sentence or two; summarize frequently, and make more frequent "here's where we are" statements; invite everyone to share their views; and typically interject their views after others have had a chance to speak, unless they are passing on decisions. Compare these practices to yours. Work on those that are not up to standard.

4.   **Inconsistent informing.** Have an information checklist detailing what information should go to whom; pass on summaries or copies of important communications. Determine the information checklist by: keeping tabs on unpleasant surprises people report to you; ask direct reports what they'd like to know to do their jobs better; and check with boss, peers, and customers to see if you pass along too little, enough, or too much of the right kinds of information. It's important to know what to pass, to whom to pass, and when to pass, to become an effective informer.

5.   **Audience sensitivity.** Unfortunately, one method or style of informing does not play equally well across audiences. Many times you will have to adjust the tone, pace, style, and even the message and how you couch it for different audiences. If you are delivering the same message to multiple people or audiences, always ask yourself how are they different? Some differences among people or audiences include level of sophistication, friendly vs. unfriendly, time sensitivity, whether they prefer it in writing or not, and whether a logical or emotional argument will play better. Write or tell? Writing is usually best for the extremes—complex descriptions complete with background and five or six progressive arguments, or on the other

side, straightforward, unambiguous things people need to know. You should generally tell when it requires discussion or you are alerting them to a problem. Make a read on each person and each audience and adjust accordingly.

B Working Better With Peers

ISFJs can have trouble working with peers who are quite different.

1. **Influencing.** Peers generally do not have power over each other. That means that influence skills, understanding, and trading are the currencies to use. Don't just ask for things; find some common ground where you can provide help. What do the peers you're contacting need? Do you really know how they see the issue? Is it even important to them? How does what you're working on affect them? If it affects them negatively, can you trade something, appeal to the common good, figure out some way to minimize the work (volunteering staff help, for example)? Go into peer relationships with a trading mentality.

2. **Separate working smoothly with peers from personal relationships,** contests, competing for incentives, one-upsmanship, not-invented-here, pride, and ego. Working well with peers over the long term helps everyone, makes sense for the organization, and builds a capacity for the organization to do greater things. Usually the least-used resource in an organization is lateral exchanges of information and resources.

3. **Monitor yourself in tough situations to get a sense of how you are coming across.** What's the first thing you attend to? How often do you take a stand vs. make an accommodating gesture? What proportion of your comments deals with relationships vs. the issue to be addressed? Mentally rehearse for worst-case scenarios/hard-to-deal-with people. Anticipate what the person might say and have responses prepared so as not to be caught off guard.

C Developing Direct Reports

ISFJs tend to choose goals that are reinforcing of their skill set so they can control the pace and process. As a result, they typically don't develop people well and can be seen as overly protective.

1. **Help people focus on the right things.** In their study of successful vs. average careers, Citrin and Smith found that the most successful

people force themselves into experiences they need for growth. They do not play it safe. While they demonstrate early competence in a specific area, they also don't overdo working on basic job requirements. They do enough work on the basics while searching for mission-critical job elements and trying to overdeliver on them. They add unexpected value. They call this the 20/80 principle of performance—focusing on the 20% that makes 80% of the difference. In doing so, the successful rack up career freedom points by tackling these tough assignments.

2. **Development planning.** You need to put together a development plan that, if followed, actually would work. At least 70% of reported skill development comes from having challenging, uncomfortable tasks/assignments. Development means that you do the new skill or fail at something important to you. Tasks that develop anything are those in which not doing it is not a viable option. Another 20% comes from studying and working with others to see useful behavior and get feedback. This can take the form of studying a role model, working with a developmental partner, keeping a written summary of what's working and not working, or preferably a formal assessment like a 360° process. Without this continuous feedback, even the best developmental plans fail. About 10% of development comes from thinking differently or having new ways to think about things. Typically these come from coursework, books, or mentors; the lion's share is learning from tough tasks and the learning from other people that comes from feedback. A good plan would have 70% job and task content; 20% people to study, listen to, and work with; and 10% courses and readings.

3. **Delegate for development.** Brainstorm with your direct reports all the tasks that aren't being done but are important to do. Ask them for a list of tasks that are no longer challenging for them. (You can also use parts of your own job to develop others. Take three tasks that are no longer developmental for you, but would be for others, and delegate them.) Trade tasks and assignments between two direct reports; have them do each other's work. Assign each of your direct reports an out-of-comfort-zone task that meets the following criteria: The task needs to be done, the person hasn't done it or isn't good at it, and the task calls for a skill the person needs to develop. Remember to focus on varied assignments—more of the same isn't developmental.

4. **Remember, meaningful development is not the stress-reduction business.** It is not cozy or safe; it comes from varied, stressful, even

adverse tasks that require we learn to do something new or different, or fail. Real development involves real work the person largely hasn't done before. Real development is rewarding but scary. Be open with your people about this. Everyone won't want to be developed in new areas. Some are satisfied to do what they do, even if it limits their career options. While you should advise them of the consequences, all organizations need strong performers dedicated to skill building in their current area only. Don't imply that a pure tactician must become a strategist to be valued. Instead, create more ways for people to excel and get status recognition. For most of us this is a powerful need—some studies show that people in prestigious jobs are less likely to get seriously ill, regardless of their personal habits. If a person wants to be a customer service representative for life, recognize that as critical, and help the person develop in every way possible within that area—coaching, training, and networking with other experts.

5. **Do you help your people learn by looking for repeating patterns?** Help them look for patterns in the situations and problems they deal with. What succeeded and what failed? What was common to each success or what was present in each failure but never present in a success? Focus on the successes; failures are easier to analyze but don't in themselves tell you what would work. Comparing successes, while less exciting, yields more information. The bottom line is help them reduce insights to principles or rules of thumb that might be repeatable. Ask them what they have learned to increase their skills and understanding, making them better managers or professionals. Ask them what they can do now that they couldn't do a year ago. Reinforce this and encourage more of it. Developing is learning in as many ways as possible.

6. **More what and why, less how.** The best delegators are crystal clear on what and when, and more open on how. People are more motivated when they can determine the how for themselves. Inexperienced delegators include the hows, which turn the people into task automatons instead of an empowered and energized staff. Tell them what and when and for how long, and let them figure out how on their own. Give them leeway. Encourage them to try things. Besides being more motivating, it's also more developmental for them. Add the larger context. Although it is not necessary to get the task done, people are more motivated when they know where this task fits in the bigger picture. Take three extra minutes and tell them why this task needs to be done, where it fits in the grander scheme, and its importance to the goals and objectives of the unit.

7. **Set goals.** You should set goals before assigning projects, work, and tasks. Goals help focus people's time and efforts. It allows people to perform more effectively and efficiently. Most people don't want to waste time. Most people want to perform well. Learn about MBO—managing by objectives. Read a book about it. While you may not be interested in a full-blown application, all of the principles of setting goals will be in the book. Go to a course on goal setting.

8. **Engage your people in the goal-setting effort.** People are more motivated when they have a say in how goals are set and measured. Most won't sandbag the effort by lobbying for low goals. They are just as likely to set the goals higher than you might.

D Having a Broader Perspective

ISFJs often show little interest in the future and what may be different. They are usually task focused and appeal to the past as precedent.

1. **Don't know how to be strategic?** The simplest problem is someone who wants to be strategic and wants to learn. Strategy is a reasonably well-known field. Read the gurus (Michael Porter, Ram Charan, C.K. Prahalad, Gary Hamel, Fred Wiersema, and Vijay Govindarajan). Scan the *Harvard Business Review* and *Sloan Review* regularly. Read the three to five strategic case studies in *BusinessWeek* every issue. Go to a three-day strategy course taught by one of the gurus. Get someone from the organization's strategic group to tutor you in strategy. Watch CEOs talk about their businesses on cable. Volunteer to serve on a task force on a strategic issue. Join the Strategic Leadership Forum for a year, read their publication, *Strategy and Leadership*, and attend one national convention. Attend The Conference Board's Annual Conference on Strategy, where CEOs talk about their companies. Read 10 annual reports a year outside your industry and study their strategies.

2. **Figure out the rules of the game.** Reduce your understanding of how business operates to personal rules of thumb or insights. Write them down in your own words. An example would be, "What are the drivers in marketing anything?" One executive had 25 such drivers that he continually edited, scratched through, and replaced with more up-to-date thinking. Use these rules of thumb to analyze a business that you know something about, possibly one of your hobbies or a sport you are enthusiastic about. Pick what you know. Then pick two businesses that have pulled off clever strategies, one related to yours and one not. Study what they did, talk to people who know what

happened, and see what you can learn. Then study two businesses that were not successful and see what they didn't do.

3. **Don't know enough about your business?** Study your annual report and various other financial reports. If you don't know how, the major investment firms have basic documents explaining how to read financial documents. After you've done this, consult a pro and ask him/her what he/she looks at and why. Ask for lunch or just a meeting with the person who is in charge of the strategic planning process in your company. Have him/her explain the strategic plan for the organization. Particularly, have him/her point out the mission-critical functions and capabilities the organization needs to be on the leading edge to win.

E Sensitivity to Criticism

ISFJs like to follow the rules and put a premium on personal competence. They can be overly sensitive to any criticism indicating that they have not performed as expected.

1. **Develop a philosophical stance toward failure/criticism.** After all, most innovations fail, most new products fail, most change efforts fail, anything worth doing takes repeated effort, anything could always have been done better. To increase learning, build in immediate feedback loops. Look for something that is common to each failure and that is never present when there is a success. There will be many mistakes and failures in innovation; after all, no one knows what to do. The best tack is to ask what can we learn from this? What caused it? What do we need to do differently? Don't expect to get it right the first time. This leads to safe, less-than-innovative solutions. Many problem-solving studies show that the second or third try is when we come up with the best solution.

2. **Increasing impulse control.** People say and do inappropriate things when they lose their composure. The problem is that they say or do the first thing that occurs to them. Research shows that generally somewhere between the second and third thing you think of to say or do is the best option. Practice holding back your first response long enough to think of a second. When you can do that, wait long enough to think of a third before you choose. By that time, 50% of your composure problems should go away.

3. **Count to 10.** Our thinking and judgment are not at their best during the emotional response. Create and practice delaying tactics. Go get a

pencil out of your briefcase. Go get a cup of coffee. Ask a question and listen. Go up to the flip chart and write something. Take notes. See yourself in a setting you find calming. Go to the bathroom. You need about a minute to regain your composure after the emotional response is triggered. Don't do or say anything until the minute has passed.

4. **Your defensive response.** You will need to work on keeping yourself in a calm state when getting negative feedback. You need to change your thinking. When getting the feedback, your only task is to accurately understand what people are trying to tell you. It is not your task at that point to accept or reject. That comes later. Mentally rehearse how you will calmly react to tough feedback situations before they happen. Develop automatic tactics to shut down or delay your usual emotional response. Some useful tactics are to slow down, take notes, ask clarifying questions, ask them for concrete examples, and thank them for telling you since you know it's not easy for them.

5. **Once you have understood the feedback,** and after the event, write down all of the criticisms on 3" x 5" cards or Post-it® Notes. Create two piles: These criticisms are probably true of me and these are probably not. Ask someone you trust, who knows you well, to help you so you don't delude yourself. For those that are true, signal the people who gave you the feedback that you have understood, think it was accurate, and will try to do something about it. For those that are not true, resort the pile into criticisms that are important to you and those that are small and trivial or unimportant. Throw the unimportant pile away. With those that are probably not true but important, re-sort into a career-threatening pile—if people above me really thought this was true about me, my career would be damaged—and a not-career-stopping pile. Throw the not-career-stopping pile away. With the remaining pile, review them with your boss and/or mentor to see what the general opinion is about you. This leaves you with two piles: those that people do believe—even though they are not true—and those they don't. Throw the don't believe pile away. With the remaining pile, plot a strategy to convince people around you—by deeds, not words—that those criticisms are untrue of you.

6. **Show others you take your development seriously.** Share your developmental needs and ask for their help. One of the best ways to avoid criticism is to bring it up yourself first and let others just fill in the details. Research shows that people are much more likely to help and give the benefit of the doubt to those who admit their shortcomings and try to do something about them. They know it takes courage.

F Becoming More Visible

Many ISFJs stay off the radar and have low social presence. Becoming incrementally more visible is a need.

1. **How good are you?** How good could you be? Are you underselling yourself? You may be too critical of yourself. Get a good, confidential 360° assessment. Are your ratings lower than those of others? Sit down with an experienced facilitator. The process should be, "How good could I be with this foundation of strengths? What do others think are my strengths that I don't see? What should I work on next to progress?" Build up your confidence. Take a course or work with a tutor to bolster your confidence in an area. Behave as if you were confident and successful. Reward yourself if you're a doubter. Master a skill. Prepare for meetings better than anyone else does. And learn how to cope with your mistakes. Acknowledge them, inform everyone affected, learn from them, and then move on. Remember, you don't have to be good at everything or mistake-free to succeed.

2. **Not comfortable marketing yourself?** You don't know how to get promoted. You dislike people who blow their own horns. Here's how to do it. Build a performance track record of variety—start up things, fix things, innovate, make plans, come under budget. This is what will get you promoted. All organizations are looking for broad thinkers to give fresh opportunities to. Start by thinking more broadly.

3. **Stage fright?** Nervous? Anxious? Didn't sleep well? Stomach's not working well? All normal. There is not a person in your audience who has not passed through that stage to become a competent presenter. Aside from death, speaking in front of large audiences is the most feared activity for adults. All of the things you think might happen don't. You won't pass out. You won't freeze and not be able to continue. You won't speak in tongues. You won't have to go to the bathroom midway through. You may run out of breath. Stop and breathe. Your mouth may get dry. Drink something. You may forget what you wanted to say. Refer to your notes. You may stumble on a word. Pause and repeat it. A sweat drop may run down your nose. Wipe it off. You may shake. Hold on to the podium. Look at three different people in the audience who are smiling and receptive. Avoid looking at frowners and head shakers.

4. **Practice, practice, practice.** Rehearse what you are going to do several times so you can do it as naturally as possible; this gives you time to deal with questions and unexpected reactions more comfortably.

Record yourself on videotape. Did you speak no longer than 5 to 10 minutes per major point? Anything you went into with so much detail that you sounded like an almanac? Did you vary tone and volume or was it monotone? Will they remember your key points 15 minutes after the meeting ends?

I am reserved and casual, and this leads me to be less forceful than I need to be in certain situations. The higher I go in the organization, the more forceful, assertive, and initiating I need to become.

— An ISFJ Manager

APPLICATION

Your personal preferences play out in day-to-day problems and situations you face. Below is a case about your type dealing with such a situation. Use this to think through how you will integrate the tips you've considered and coach yourself to be more effective in your type.

ISFJ Application Situation (Part 1)

Interoffice Memorandum
To: Bruce L.
From: Mark P.
Re: Follow-up on Jackie W.—Career Coaching Op.

When Jackie came to me looking for career coaching, I was stumped. For one thing, I didn't understand how someone at the Director level, particularly in the HR function, would be complaining about her distaste for management meetings. And then there were contradictions in things she said. For example, she told me that on the one hand her boss doesn't give her enough direction, and then in the next breath she's telling me how he's always telling her to speak up more, be more strategic, "act like a 'player.'"

I asked Jackie what she enjoyed most about her job, and she told me that she preferred working with individual employees and managers, that she felt she was accomplishing something when she was helping someone understand policy and procedural details and complete paperwork. But after eight years of solid performance in the senior management group, where she felt she'd been a "good soldier," she was confused by these new demands that she "work as a strategic partner" in determining better ways of meeting more demanding business goals.

Frankly, she feared she was starting to fail in her job and wanted help. That's why I've come to you. There are issues here that fall outside the scope of my expertise, which, as you know, is in interpreting and summarizing assessment data. I can tell you that Jackie is an ISFJ and is of above-average intelligence. I really appreciate your willingness to see her. Thanks again, and let me know if there's any other information you want.

Thinking It Through: Strategy

- What would you want to accomplish by the end of this first meeting?

- Do you have ideas, based on what you know so far, about whether Jackie is going to be successful in adapting to the new expectations for her role?

Planning It Out: Tactics

- In preparing to meet with Jackie, is there anything else you'd like to know?

- Besides the assessment data, and information about what her boss thinks, who else would you confer with about Jackie?

- Which of the tactics described in the Being More Effective section are applicable in this situation?

- Which Overused Tendencies are most likely to come into play here?

ISFJ Application Situation (Part 2)

■ You meet with Jackie and she tells you that she thinks she may be ready for a new job, and perhaps outside of Human Resources. "The only problem," she says, "is that I don't really know much about anything else."

Reflection

■ Where do you go with this one?

SUGGESTED READINGS

■■■■■■■■ Being a More Effective ISFJ ■■■■■■■■

Letting Go of Structure

Anderson, Dean and Linda S. Ackerman Anderson. *Beyond Change Management: Advanced Strategies for Today's Transformational Leaders.* San Francisco: Jossey-Bass, Inc., 2001.

Black, J. Stewart and Hal B. Gregersen. *Leading Strategic Change: Breaking Through the Brain Barrier.* Upper Saddle River, NJ: Financial Times/Prentice Hall, 2002.

Block, Peter. *The Answer to How Is Yes: Acting on What Matters.* San Francisco: Berrett-Koehler Publishers, Inc., 2001.

Bossidy, Larry, Ram Charan and Charles Burck (Contributor). *Execution: The Discipline of Getting Things Done.* New York: Crown Business Publishing, 2002.

Burke, W. Warner and William Trahant with Richard Koonce. *Business Climate Shifts: Profiles of Change Makers.* Boston: Butterworth-Heinemann, 2000.

Luecke, Richard. *Managing Change and Transition.* Boston: Harvard Business School Publishing, 2003.

Pfeffer, Jeffrey and Robert I. Sutton. *The Knowing-Doing Gap: How Smart Companies Turn Knowledge Into Action.* Boston: Harvard Business School Press, 2000.

Being More Personally Flexible

Bellman, Geoffrey M. *Getting Things Done When You Are Not in Charge.* San Francisco: Berrett-Koehler Publishers, Inc., 2001.

Brim, Gilbert. *Ambition: How We Manage Success and Failure Throughout Our Lives.* New York: Backinprint.com, 2000.

Christian, Ken. *Your Own Worst Enemy: Breaking the Habit of Adult Underachievement.* New York: Regan Books, 2004.

Jackson, Paul Z. and Mark McKergow. *The Solutions Focus.* Yarmouth, ME: Nicholas Brealey Publishing, 2002.

Mitroff, Ian I. and Gus Anagnos. *Managing Crises Before They Happen.* New York: AMACOM, 2001.

Taking Charge

Badaracco, Joseph L., Jr. *Defining Moments — When Managers Must Choose Between Right and Right.* Boston: Harvard Business School Press, 1997.

Bennis, Warren G. and Burt Nanus. *Leaders: Strategies for Taking Charge.* New York: HarperBusiness, 2003.

Calvert, Gene. *Highwire Management.* San Francisco: Jossey-Bass, Inc., 1993.

Chaleff, Ira. *The Courageous Follower: Standing Up to and for Our Leaders.* San Francisco: Berrett-Koehler Publishers, Inc., 2003.

Coponigro, Jeffrey R. *The Crisis Counselor: A Step-by-Step Guide to Managing a Business Crisis.* New York: McGraw-Hill/Contemporary Books, 2000.

Cox, Danny and John Hoover. *Leadership When the Heat's On.* New York: McGraw-Hill Trade, 2002.

Linsky, Martin and Ronald A. Heifetz. *Leadership on the Line: Staying Alive Through the Dangers of Leading.* Boston: Harvard Business School Press, 2002.

Dealing With Conflict

Cloke, Ken and Joan Goldsmith. *Resolving Conflicts at Work: A Complete Guide for Everyone on the Job.* San Francisco: Jossey-Bass, Inc., 2000.

Dana, Daniel. *Conflict Resolution.* New York: McGraw-Hill Trade, 2000.

Guttman, Howard M. *When Goliaths Clash: Managing Executive Conflict to Build a More Dynamic Organization.* New York: AMACOM, 2003.

Masters, Marick Francis and Robert R. Albright. *The Complete Guide to Conflict Resolution in the Workplace.* New York: AMACOM, 2002.

Being More Innovative

Birch, Paul and Brian Clegg. *Imagination Engineering—The Toolkit for Business Creativity.* London: Pitman Publishing, 1996.

Campbell, David. *Take the Road to Creativity and Get Off Your Dead End.* Greensboro, NC: Center for Creative Leadership, 1985.

DeGraff, Jeff and Katherine A. Lawrence. *Creativity at Work: Developing the Right Practices to Make Innovation Happen.* San Francisco: Jossey-Bass, Inc., 2002.

Lucas, Robert W. *The Creative Training Idea Book: Inspired Tips and Techniques for Engaging and Effective Learning.* New York: AMACOM, 2003.

Von Oech, Roger. *Expect the Unexpected or You Won't Find It: A Creativity Tool Based on the Ancient Wisdom of Heraclitus.* San Francisco: Berrett-Koehler Publishers, Inc., 2002.

Dealing With Problem Performers

Graham, Gini. *A Survival Guide for Working With Humans: Dealing With Whiners, Back-Stabbers, Know-It-Alls, and Other Difficult People.* New York: AMACOM, 2004.

Levin, Robert A. and Joseph G. Rosse. *Talent Flow: A Strategic Approach to Keeping Good Employees, Helping Them Grow, and Letting Them Go.* New York: John Wiley & Sons, Inc., 2001.

Solomon, Muriel. *Working With Difficult People.* New York: Prentice Hall, 2002.

■■■■■■■ Overusing ISFJ Tendencies ■■■■■■■

Informing With Others in Mind

Arredondo, Lani. *Communicating Effectively.* New York: McGraw-Hill Trade, 2000.

Keyton, Joann. *Communicating in Groups: Building Relationships for Effective Decision Making.* New York: WCB/McGraw-Hill, 2002.

McCormack, Mark H. *On Communicating.* Los Angeles: Dove Books, 1998.

Zeuschner, Raymond F. *Communicating Today: The Essentials.* Boston: Allyn & Bacon, 2002.

Working Better With Peers

Baker, Wayne E. *Networking Smart.* New York: Backinprint.com, 2000.

Bolton, Robert and Dorothy Grover Bolton. *People Styles at Work—Making Bad Relationships Good and Good Relationships Better.* New York: AMACOM, 1996.

Cartwright, Tatula. *Managing Conflict With Peers.* Greensboro, NC: Center for Creative Leadership, 2003.

Patterson, Kerry, Joseph Grenny, Ron McMillan, Al Switzler and Stephen R. Covey. *Crucial Conversations: Tools for Talking When Stakes Are High.* New York: McGraw-Hill/Contemporary Books, 2002.

Developing Direct Reports

Charan, Ram, James L. Noel and Steve Drotter. *The Leadership Pipeline: How to Build the Leadership Powered Company.* New York: John Wiley & Sons, Inc., 2000.

Daniels, Aubrey C. *Bringing Out the Best in People.* New York: McGraw-Hill, Inc., 1994.

Fulmer, Robert M. and Jay A. Conger. *Growing Your Company's Leaders.* New York: AMACOM, 2004.

Lombardo, Michael M. and Robert W. Eichinger. *The Leadership Machine.* Minneapolis, MN: Lominger Limited, Inc., 2004.

Having a Broader Perspective

Chakravorti, Bhaskar. *The Slow Pace of Fast Change: Bringing Innovations to Market in a Connected World.* Boston: Harvard Business School Press, 2003.

Charan, Ram. *What the CEO Wants You to Know: How Your Company Really Works.* New York: Crown Business Publishing, 2001.

Collins, James C. *Good to Great: Why Some Companies Make the Leap...And Others Don't.* New York: HarperCollins, 2001.

Dudik, Evan Matthew. *Strategic Renaissance: New Thinking and Innovative Tools to Create Great Corporate Strategies Using Insights From History and Science.* New York: AMACOM, 2000.

The Futurist Magazine. http://www.wfs.org

Hamel, Gary. *Leading the Revolution.* Boston: Harvard Business School Press, 2002.

Hargadon, Andrew and Kathleen M. Eisenhardt. *How Breakthroughs Happen: The Surprising Truth About How Companies Innovate.* Boston: Harvard Business School Press, 2003.

Harvard Business Review. Phone: 800-988-0886 (US and Canada). Fax: 617-496-1029. Mail: Harvard Business Review. Subscriber Services, P.O. Box 52623. Boulder, CO 80322-2623 USA. http://www.hbsp.harvard.edu/products/hbr

Kaplan, Robert S. and David P. Norton. *The Strategy-Focused Organization: How Balanced Scorecard Companies Thrive in the New Business Environment.* Boston: Harvard Business School Press, 2000.

Porter, Michael E. *Competitive Strategy: Techniques for Analyzing Industries and Competitors.* New York: The Free Press, 1998.

Prahalad, C.K. and Venkat Ramaswamy. *The Future of Competition: Co-Creating Unique Value With Customers.* Boston: Harvard Business School Press, 2004.

Sensitivity to Criticism

Brim, Gilbert. *Ambition: How We Manage Success and Failure Throughout Our Lives.* New York: Backinprint.com, 2000.

Carter, Les. *The Anger Trap: Free Yourself From the Frustrations That Sabotage Your Life.* New York: John Wiley & Sons, Inc., 2003.

Ellis, Albert, Ph.D. *How to Control Your Anxiety Before It Controls You.* New York: Citadel Press, 2000.

Lerner, Harriet. *The Dance of Connection: How to Talk to Someone When You're Mad, Hurt, Scared, Frustrated, Insulted, Betrayed, or Desperate.* New York: Quill/HarperCollins, 2002.

Patterson, Kerry, Joseph Grenny, Ron McMillan, Al Switzler and Stephen R. Covey. *Crucial Conversations: Tools for Talking When Stakes Are High.* New York: McGraw-Hill/Contemporary Books, 2002.

Becoming More Visible

Bolles, Richard N. *What Color Is Your Parachute? 2004: A Practical Manual for Job-Hunters & Career-Changers.* Berkeley, CA: Ten Speed Press, 2004.

Christian, Ken. *Your Own Worst Enemy: Breaking the Habit of Adult Underachievement.* New York: Regan Books, 2004.

Citrin, James M. and Richard A. Smith. *The Five Patterns of Extraordinary Careers.* New York: Crown Business, 2003.

Dominguez, Linda R. *How to Shine at Work.* New York: McGraw-Hill Trade, 2003.

Morgan, Nick. *Working the Room: How to Move People to Action Through Audience-Centered Speaking.* Boston: Harvard Business School Press, 2003.

Niven, David. *The 100 Simple Secrets of Successful People: What Scientists Have Learned and How You Can Use It.* New York: HarperBusiness, 2002.

CHAPTER 3

INFJ
Introverted Intuiting
with
Extraverted Feeling

■■■■■■■■■■■■■■■■■

1.5% of Population
1.9% of Managers

■■■■■■■■■■■■■■■■■

Typical Strengths

Understand Others
Praising and Harmonious
Work for the Common Good
Quietly Forceful and Determined
Believe in Human Potential
Leading Small Groups
Constructively Confronting Others
Comfortable With Complexity

ISTJ	ISFJ	INFJ	INTJ
ISTP	ISFP	INFP	INTP
ESTP	ESFP	ENFP	ENTP
ESTJ	ESFJ	ENFJ	ENTJ

*I usually have a sense about how things are going to turn out,
and I work relentlessly toward that goal.*

– An INFJ Manager

Basic Habits of Mind

Introverted Intuiting helps INFJs see the complexity of interpersonal relationships and circumstances of situations. Understanding the various connections among people and situations is helped by Extraverted Feeling. This drives them to engage with other people and to evaluate the events around them with an awareness of the consequences on people and treasured ideals. Interested in harmony, they tend to quietly form strong networks of friends and colleagues.

Extraverted Thinking leads them to focus on selective "facts" and "principles." As a result, when they take a position on an issue, they can come across as insistent and stubborn. Extraverted Sensing contributes by swiftly directing their attention to only those external observations that "prove the point." As a result, INFJs may be quietly studious until an issue signals an abuse to their value system. Then they can intensely object, seem aloof, and put themselves above the issue.

Typical Communication Patterns

- INFJs are usually appreciative of others' efforts and attentive in ways that communicate empathy and regard.

- They value information (especially concepts and ideals) and put special emphasis on decisions that keep people in mind. They communicate more around values than facts.

- They are often seen as warm, cooperative, and sympathetic in their interactions with others.

- They spend a lot of time getting "buy in" from others.

General Learning Strategy

- INFJs like to reframe situations in unique ways before testing ideas and seek to clarify with open-ended questions.

- Their likely learning strategies are: write about it before talking about it, illustrate ideas, and use cooperative learning simulations.

- Their learning is generally enhanced by small group discussions, creating a supportive climate, and having opportunities to elaborate and change their point of view.

Interpersonal Qualities Related to Motivation

- INFJs are generally motivated by and seek to engage others through cooperation and by acting on those values which they see as promoting human well-being.

- Inclusive of others, they put energy into tasks and activities that help establish enduring relationships.

- Typically driven by their vision of human well-being, they often put other people and their causes before their personal needs.

Blind Spots

- While generally seen as resourceful, INFJs might be surprised to learn that others can see an overdependence in their relationships, undeveloped criteria for hiring staff, and too low in social presence to have the influence needed to address change situations in organizations.

- Their style can be seen as unsupportive of management initiatives. Being independent and cause-driven, they often go their own way.

- Once they form a strong relationship, they can be too trusting and others can take advantage of them.

Stress Related Behavior

- As an initial response to stress, INFJs often become more intense and reserved.

- They may appear to disregard others and communicate unrealistic expectations.

- If stress is extensive, they might exhibit a relentless concern about the events of the day.

- This obsession with current events and specific information can lead to indicating to others that everything is in a "sorry condition."

- When something goes wrong, it all goes wrong. Once they hit the tipping point—a breach of trust or something that offends their values—they can reject and withdraw.

Potential Barriers to Effectiveness

- Their interpersonal style, although warm and caring, can also be seen as dogmatic, guarded, and pressuring.

- Because they seek out autonomy, they can act as if this gives them a special perspective. However, this can undermine trust and promote a feeling of the absence of fair play when dealing with the boss.

- INFJs need to be careful that their empathy and demonstrated interest in fostering relationships is not translated as a loss of appropriate boundaries within their work roles.

- While loyal to both people and the organization, human needs usually come first.

Being a More Effective INFJ

A Fairness in Relationships
B Problems With Higher Management
C Taking Charge
D Staffing
E Getting Results

ISTJ	ISFJ	INFJ	INTJ
ISTP	ISFP	INFP	INTP
ESTP	ESFP	ENFP	ENTP
ESTJ	ESFJ	ENFJ	ENTJ

A Fairness in Relationships

INFJs see complexity and uniqueness in all relationships. Sometimes consistency and finding common ground is called for.

1. **Equity with information.** Follow the rule of equity of information with everyone. Explain your thinking and ask them to explain theirs. When discussing issues, give reasons first, solutions last. When you give solutions first, people often don't listen to your reasons. Some people get overly directive with some of their reports, and they, in turn, feel that you're not interested in what they think. Invite their thinking and their reasons before settling on solutions. Don't provide information selectively. Don't use information as a reward or a relationship builder with one or just a few and not others.

2. **If a fairness issue hits a core value of yours, pause to:**

   ■ Edit your actions before you act. Before you speak or act in problem situations, ask yourself if you would do the same thing in a parallel situation. Is your value really what should be operating here?

   ■ Pick your battles. Make sure you only pull rank and impose your values on others in really mission-critical situations.

3. **Influencing.** Peers generally do not have power over each other. That means that influence skills, understanding, and trading are the currencies to use. Don't just ask for things; find some common ground where you can provide help. What do the peers you're contacting need? Do you really know how they see the issue? Is it even important to them? How does what you're working on affect them? If it affects them negatively, can you trade something, appeal to the common good, figure out some way to minimize the work (volunteering staff help, for example)? Go into peer relationships with a trading mentality.

4. **Sometimes the problem is maneuvering through the complex maze called the organization.** How do you get things done sideways? Who are the movers and shakers in the organization? How do they get things done? Who do they rely on for expediting things through the maze? Who are the major gatekeepers who control the flow of resources, information, and decisions? Who are the guides and the helpers? Get to know them better. Who are the major resisters and stoppers? Try to avoid or go around them.

5. **Monitor yourself in tough situations to get a sense of how you are coming across.** What's the first thing you attend to? How often do you take a stand vs. make an accommodating gesture? What proportion of your comments deals with relationships vs. the issue to be addressed? Mentally rehearse for worst-case scenarios/hard-to-deal-with people. Anticipate what the person might say and have responses prepared so as not to be caught off guard.

6. **Avoid early rigid positions.** It's just physics. Action gets equal reaction. Strong statements. Strongly worded positions. Casting blame. Absolutes. Lines in the sand. Unnecessary passion. All of these will be responded to in kind, will waste time, cause ill will, and possibly prevent a win-win or a something-something. It only has a place in one-time, either/or negotiations, and even there it isn't recommended. Similarly, watch out for overcommitment to any need

or course of action. Look for information that goes against your preferences. Be able to adjust your position and your wants. If you can't, your ego is getting the best of you. If you can't walk away until you get X, you'll probably either overpay or blow the negotiation. Don't negotiate around a single issue if you can add another. This is another situation that leads to rigidity.

B Problems With Higher Management

INFJs can have a rebellious streak and go after those in power in unproductive ways, confronting the wrong people at the wrong time.

1. **Consider who bothers you.** If only certain higher-ups bother you and others don't, take a piece of paper and list the styles of the two groups/individuals. What are the similarities? Why does one style bother you and the other doesn't? With the groups/individuals that bother you, how could you respond more comfortably and effectively? Perhaps you could use some of the techniques you use with the more comfortable groups. Probably you should prime yourself to take nothing in personal terms and, no matter what happens, return to a discussion of the problem.

2. **Get to know more top managers.** Try to meet and interact with higher-ups in informal settings like receptions, social or athletic events, charity events, off-sites, etc. You will probably learn that higher-ups are just regular people who are older and therefore higher than you in the hierarchy. You may then feel more comfortable with them when back in the work setting.

3. **Focus on the three key problems you need to work on with your boss and do them.** Keep your head down. Keep your conversations with the boss directed at these core agenda. Focus on expectations, ask what results indicate success. Find out about your boss's job and what sorts of pressures he/she is under. Do you know what drives your boss? Do you talk detail and he's a big-picture person? Do you fight his/her style which is more action oriented than yours? Do you get in unproductive values debates? Do you use words that set the boss off?

4. **Find out how top managers think.** Read the biographies of five "great" people; see what is said about them and their views of people like you. Read five autobiographies and see what they said about themselves and how they viewed people in your position. Write down five things you can do differently or better.

5. **Be ready for Q&A.** Many people get in trouble during questions and answers. Don't fake answers; most high-level managers will tolerate a "Don't know but I'll get back to you on that." Think of all the questions ahead of time; ask someone else to look at what you are going to say and do and to think of questions they would ask. Rehearse the answers to the questions. Another place people get in trouble when challenged is by retreating to a safe recitation of facts; executives are usually asking for logic and problem analysis, not a repackaging of what you've already said. The worst case, of course, is when an executive rejects your argument. If this happens, draw the person out to see if you've been misunderstood and clarify. If that's not the case, let the disagreement be as it is. Few executives respect someone who drops an argument as soon as challenged. You should listen carefully and respond with logic in 30 seconds or less per point. Don't repeat the entire argument; long answers often backfire since people have already heard it and few may agree with the questioner. In haste to be thorough, you may just look defensive.

6. **Quit arguing.** Most of the time, you may be delivering someone else's view of the future. Top management and a consultant created the mission, vision, and strategy off somewhere in the woods all by themselves. You may or may not have been asked for any input. You may even have some doubts about it yourself. Your role is to manage this vision and mission, not your personal one. Do not offer conditional statements to your audience: "I've got some concerns myself." Don't let it be known to others that you are not fully on board. Your job is to deliver and manage the message. While it's okay to admit your problems in dealing with change, it's not okay to admit them in dealing with this change. If you have better ideas, try to get them to the people who form missions in your organization.

C Taking Charge

INFJs are forceful, but usually behind the scenes. They also worry about offending anyone and what the human costs will be, even if the costs will be worse if they don't take charge.

1. **Not comfortable being out front?** Leading is riskier than following. While there are a lot of personal rewards for taking tough stands, it puts you into the limelight. Look at what happens to political leaders and the scrutiny they face. People who choose to stand alone have to be internally secure. Do you feel good about yourself? Can you defend to a critical and impartial audience the wisdom of what you're

doing? They have to please themselves first that they are on the right track. They have to accept lightning bolts from detractors. Can you take the heat? People will always say it should have been done differently. Even great leaders are wrong sometimes. They accept personal responsibility for errors and move on to lead some more. Don't let criticism prevent you from taking a stand. Build up your heat shield. If you know you're right, standing alone is well worth the heat. If it turns out you're wrong, admit it and move on.

2. **Against the grain tough stands.** Taking a tough stand demands confidence in what you're saying along with the humility that you might be wrong—one of life's paradoxes. To prepare to take the lead on a tough issue, work on your stand through mental interrogation until you can clearly state in a few sentences what your stand is and why you hold it. Build the business case. How do others win? Ask others for advice. Scope the problem, consider options, pick one, develop a rationale, then go with it until proven wrong. Consider the opposing view. Develop a strong case against your stand. Prepare responses to it. Expect pushback.

3. **Selling your stand.** While some people may welcome what you say and what you do, others will go after you or even try to minimize you or the situation your stand relates to. Some will sabotage. To sell your views, keep your eyes on the prize but don't specify everything about how to get there. Give others room to maneuver. Present the outcomes, targets, and goals without the how to's. Welcome ideas— good and bad. Any negative response is a positive if you learn from it. Invite criticism of what you're doing. Even though you're going it alone, you need the advice and support of others to get there. Stay away from personal clashes.

4. **Afraid of nasty questions or ones you can't answer?** Think about the 10 most likely questions you could be asked. Rehearse what you would say. Some rules. Practice 10- to 30-second answers. Ask the questioner if that answered his/her question. Many spend too much time on the answers. Make sure you know what the question is. Many answer the wrong question. Ask one clarifying question if you're unsure: "Do you mean how would this product work in a foreign or domestic market?" If someone just won't let go, say, "We must really have different experiences. It's apparent we don't agree, so let's just agree to disagree for now, but thanks for the debate." If the question is hot, "Why are women so discriminated against in this organization?" extract the main issues and respond with, "Here are three things you can do about it." As a general rule, don't answer such

questions as given because they are negative, and stay away from classification (women, men, accountants) answers. Get it in your mind that questions are your friends because they reveal opportunities to solve problems and headline the difficulties you face. You just need five techniques to deal with them, including the dreaded "I don't know, but I'll find out and get back to you on that."

5. **Think more in political terms.** People who are politically savvy work from the outside (audience, person, group) in. They determine the demand characteristics or requirements of each situation and each person they face and select from among their various skills, tone, and styles to find the best approach to make things work. Practice not thinking inside/out when you are around others.

6. **Strong advocates for narrow views don't usually fare well politically in organizations.** Initially be tentative. Give others some room to maneuver. Make the business or organizational case first. Be prepared to counter arguments that your objective is less important than theirs. A lot of political noise is caused by making extreme statements right out of the box.

7. **Selective savvy?** Is there a group or groups you have more trouble with politically than others? Is it because you don't like or are uncomfortable with them? To work better with problem groups, put yourself in their case. Turn off your "I like—I don't like; I agree—I don't agree" switch. Ask yourself why would you act that way? What do you think they're trying to achieve? Establish reciprocity. Relationships don't last unless you provide something and so do they. Find out what they want and tell them what you want. Strike a bargain.

8. **Keep political conflicts small and concrete.** The more abstract it gets, the more unmanageable it becomes. Separate the people from the problem. Attack problems by looking at the nature of the problem, not the person presenting the problem. Avoid direct blaming remarks; describe the problem and its impact. If you can't agree on a solution, agree on procedure, or agree on a few things, and list all the issues remaining. This creates some motion and breaks political stalemates.

9. **Delivering firm messages.** Be succinct. You have limited attention span in tough feedback situations. Don't waste time with a long preamble, particularly if the feedback is negative. If the feedback is negative and the recipient is likely to know it, go ahead and say it directly. They won't hear anything positive you have to say anyway.

Don't overwhelm the person/group, even if you have a lot to say. Go from specific to general points. Keep it to the facts. Don't embellish to make your point. No passion or inflammatory language. Don't do it to harm or out of vengeance. Don't do it in anger. If feelings are involved for you, wait until you can describe them, not show them. Managerial courage comes in search of a better outcome, not destroying others. Stay calm and cool. If others are not composed, don't respond. Just return to the message.

10. **Everybody appreciates a problem solver.** Use your natural strength to "see" possible ideas and take the initiative and share them. Give people ways to improve. Tell others what you think would be better— paint a different outcome. Help others see the consequences—you can ask them what they think, and you can tell them what the consequences are from your side if you are personally involved ("I'd be reluctant to work with you on X again").

11. **Is it personal?** If you are personally involved and you are delivering a message to someone who didn't meet your expectations, stick to the facts and the consequences for you. Separate the event from the person. It's okay to be upset with the behavior, less so with the person, unless it's a repetitive transgression. Most of the time he/she won't accept it the first time you deliver the message. "I'm not happy with the way you presented my position in the staff meeting." Many people are defensive. Don't go for the close in every delivery situation. Just deliver the message enough so you are sure he/she understood it. Give him/her time to absorb it. Don't seek instant acceptance. Just deliver the message clearly and firmly. Don't threaten.

D Staffing

INFJs believe so strongly in human potential, that they often have undeveloped criteria for differentiating the skill sets of others.

1. **When you make a hiring decision** or are deciding whom to work with on a problem or project, do you think you have a tendency to clone yourself too much? Do you have a preference for people who think and act as you do? What characteristics do you value too much? What downsides do you ignore or excuse away? This is a common human tendency. The key is to seek balance, variety, and diversity. Shore up your weaknesses when hiring others. People good at this

competency can comfortably surround themselves with people not like them.

2. **Make sure you know what matters most.** Read sources that focus on key competencies at work, such as *The Extraordinary Leader* by Zenger and Folkman or *The Leadership Machine* by Lombardo and Eichinger. Look at the research-based lists of competencies that appear on standardized competency instruments such as VOICES®, PROFILOR®, or BENCHMARKS®.

3. **Become a student of the people around you.** First, try to outline their strengths and weaknesses, their preferences and beliefs. Watch out for traps—it is rarely general intelligence or pure personality that spells the difference in people. Most people are smart enough, and many personality characteristics don't matter that much for performance. Ask a second question. Look below surface descriptions of smart, approachable, technically skilled people to describe specifics. Then try to predict ahead of time what they would do in specific circumstances. What percent of the time are your predictions correct? Try to increase the percent over time.

4. **Can you interview for talent?** There are commonly agreed-upon methods to find talent in an interview. A couple of keys: Look for evidence of rapid learning, excitement about the kinds of tasks that are critical in the role, and a penchant for going into new situations. See *The INTERVIEW ARCHITECT®* or ask someone in the recruiting and staffing area in your organization for guidance on how to conduct a good interview. Research indicates that structured interviewing is the best selection method, vastly better than unstructured interviewing.

5. **What differences make a difference?** For each job, role, task, or assignment, try to create a success profile of what would be required for success. What skills, knowledge, and competencies would be mission-critical to getting the job done? This means that they differentiate superior from average performance. Don't include competencies that, while important, most people on a job would be expected to already have. (For example, integrity is a must, but if people already have it, it can't predict success. Similarly, time management and planning are important, but most people have demonstrated a reasonable proficiency in those in order to be employable. They wouldn't distinguish superior from average performers often.) Go for the critical few, not the important many. Which competencies don't make a difference?

6. **Volunteer to be part of an assessment center team,** or take a course on assessment. You will be trained to observe and assess people as they are going through a number of tasks and assignments. As part of the process, you will compare your notes and assessments with others on the team. That way, you will learn to calibrate your assessments.

E Getting Results

When results clash with people concerns, INFJs can get off task.

1. **Priorities?** You don't have a correct set of priorities. Some people get results, but on the wrong things. Effective managers typically spend about half their time on two or three key priorities. What should you spend half your time on? Can you name five things that are less critical? If you can't, you're not differentiating well. Or even if you know the priorities, your team doesn't. You communicate that everything is important and has a deadline of yesterday. They see their jobs as 97 things that need to be done right now. To deal with this, ask yourself what would happen if they only did four or five things today? What would they be? Ask what the three things they spend the most time on are, and what they would be if we were doing things better? Find out what the 10–20% most time-consuming activities are, and either eliminate them or structure them through processes and policies to take less time.

2. **Set goals for yourself and others.** Most people work better if they have a set of goals and objectives to achieve and a standard everyone agrees to measure accomplishments against. Most people like stretch goals. They like them even better if they have had a hand in setting them. Set checkpoints along the way to be able to measure progress. Give yourself and others as much feedback as you can.

3. **How to get things done.** Some don't know the best way to produce results. There is a well-established set of best practices for producing results—TQM, ISO and Six Sigma. If you are not disciplined in how to design work flows and processes for yourself and others, buy one book on each of these topics. Go to one workshop on efficient and effective work design. Ask those responsible for total work systems in your organization for help.

Overusing INFJ Tendencies

If you sometimes overdo your preferred behaviors, you may need to work on:

A   Becoming More Career Ambitious

B   Being Less Dependent on a Few Relationships

C   Being More Open-Minded

D   Better Delegation and Team Building

E   Not Jumping to Conclusions

F   Better Composure and Less Defensiveness

ISTJ	ISFJ	INFJ	INTJ
ISTP	ISFP	INFP	INTP
ESTP	ESFP	ENFP	ENTP
ESTJ	ESFJ	ENFJ	ENTJ

A   Becoming More Career Ambitious

INFJs don't often put career first. They don't market themselves well and usually avoid public speaking.

1. **Many people don't know how careers are built.** Most are put off by the popular myth of getting ahead. All of us have seen *How to Succeed in Business Without Really Trying* or something like it. It's easy to get cynical and believe that successful people are political or sell out, suck up, knife people in the back, it's who you know, and so on. The facts are dramatically different from this. Those behaviors get people in trouble eventually. What has staying power is performing and problem solving on the current job, having a few notable strengths, and seeking new tasks you don't know how to do. It's solving every problem with tenacity, while looking for what you haven't yet done and getting yourself in a position to do it. Read *The Lessons of Experience* by McCall, Lombardo and Morrison for the careers of men and *Breaking the Glass Ceiling* by Morrison, White and Van Velsor for the careers of women to see how successful careers really happen.

2. **Break out of your career comfort zone.** Maybe you haven't seen enough. Pick some activities you haven't done before but might find exciting. Take a course in a new area. Task trade—switch tasks with a peer. Volunteer for task forces and projects that are multi-functional or multi-business in nature. Read more broadly.

3. **Don't know what it takes?** Think of five successful people in your organization/field whom you know well and ask what drives them? What sorts of jobs have they held? What are their technical skills? Behavioral skills? Use common competency lists such as those in *FYI For Your Improvement* to determine what the 10 key skills of each person are; compare this list with your own self-assessment and feedback. Ask Human Resources if they have a success profile for some of the jobs you may be interested in. Make a list of what you need to work on next. If you want to be a star, figure out what is important about your job to higher management. If you're an accountant, help management pinpoint high costs; if a chemist, a cheaper way to do what you're now doing. Learn to love the details that affect your field. If your strengths are not technical, help out coworkers or look for a management or organizational problem around you to solve.

4. **Focus on the right things.** In their study of successful vs. average careers, Citrin and Smith found that the most successful people force themselves into experiences they need for growth. They do not play it safe. While they demonstrate early competence in a specific area, they also don't overdo working on basic job requirements. They do enough work on the basics while searching for mission-critical job elements and trying to overdeliver on them. They add unexpected value. They call this the 20/80 principle of performance—focusing on the 20% that makes 80% of the difference. In doing so, the successful rack up career freedom points by tackling these tough assignments.

5. **Getting noticed by top decision makers.** Top managers aren't as interested in glitz as many would have you believe. They're interested in people who take care of problems, spot opportunities, ward off disaster, and have a broad repertoire of skills. They are looking for bold performers. But a better mousetrap alone is not enough. Volunteer for projects that will require interacting/presenting with higher management. Focus on activities that are the core of what your organization does. Find a business opportunity and make a reasoned case for it. Pick a big problem and work maniacally to solve it. You need to be seen and heard—but on substance, not fluff.

6. **Take on public speaking like you would any complex task.** Make a checklist. What's your objective? What's your point? What are five things you want them to remember? What would the ideal audience member say if interviewed 15 minutes after you finish? Who's your audience? How much do they know? What are five techniques you will use to hold their attention? What presentation technology would

work best? What questions will the audience have? What's the setting? How much time do you have—always take a few minutes less, never more.

7. **Preparing a speech.** State your message or purpose in a single sentence. In other words, do the ending first. Then outline the three to five chunks of your argument to support your thesis. Any more and the audience won't follow it. Sometimes putting main concepts on index cards and shuffling them into order can accomplish this. A famous minister said, "No souls are saved after 20 minutes." Many speeches must be longer than this, but can still be divided into sections with clear conclusions, and a hard bridge to the next related topic. What introduction will grab the audience and rivet them on your message? A story, a fact, a comparison, a quote, a photo, a cartoon? For example, one speaker selected a comparison to introduce a series of research findings on career success by saying, "How can you take identical twins, hired for the same entry job in the same organization, and 20 years later, one of them succeeds and one of them doesn't?" She then returned to the twins periodically as she went through her argument on the different developmental experiences they had with the corporation. In organizing your talk, you should resist telling them all you know. What are your priority points, and how will you explain them? Some points are made better by example, some by the logic of the argument, some by facts or stories. You should vary how you drive home your point because you will reach more people. Use memory devices—state points in threes; repeat key words and phrases—"I have a dream"; use understatement and overstatement; use antithesis—"Ask not what your country can do for you; ask what you can do for your country." One nasty shock many learning presenters experience is that writing is different from speaking. A well-written speech is one that sounds right spoken, not read. Do not fall in love with what you have written until you record it on tape and listen to it. The cadence and pace is different in writing than in speaking. Writing doesn't take breathing into account. If your computer has a speech synthesizer, let the computer say your speech. Or have someone else read it to you. Never deliver a written speech until you have heard it spoken. Subscribe to *Presentations* magazine for tips, www.presentations.com.

8. **Rehearsing.** If you are just building your presentation skills, rehearsals are very helpful. The best is to rehearse in the actual setting of the presentation. To get ready, practice in front of a video camera, in front of someone who can give you feedback, by using an

audiotape or, worst case, in front of a mirror by yourself. Focus on time spent per major point—usually 5 to 10 minutes. For your longest point, did you go into too much detail? Vary your volume and tone—sameness lulls the audience. Use your hands and body. Vary facial expression—if the words and the music don't match, people don't buy the message. Use pauses—for effect, to drive in a point. Be careful of repeating the same words too often. If you're stumped for something to say, pause—uhs, ahs, and you knows distract and turn off some listeners. If you go blank, pause, then repeat your last statement in a paraphrasing of it. While you play for time, ask yourself what you can connect to that statement. Avoid speaking too forcefully or using loaded terms that will annoy some audience members. The best speech is the one that looks totally natural. It is usually the one that has been rehearsed a lot. If you can deliver the presentation on autopilot, you can scan the audience and adjust as you go.

B | Being Less Dependent on a Few Relationships

INFJs can depend on just a few relationships, limiting perspective and networking.

1. **Pick people who are quite different from you and observe what they do and how they do it.** Then ask for their help on a problem. Just ask questions and understand their perspective. Don't make any judgments about the rightness or wrongness of their approach.

2. **Pick some tough critics to talk with.** Don't go to the few people you truly like, most likely because you share similar perspectives. Go to some you know will disagree with you and hear them out.

3. **Spend most of your time with just a few people?** Developed a comfort and liking for the few? Expand your repertoire to get your relationship quota up. Be an early adopter of something. Find some new thing, technique, software, tool, system, process, or skill relevant to your activity. Privately become an expert in it. Read the books. Get certified. Visit a location where it's being done. Then surprise everyone and be the first to introduce it into your world. Sell it. Train others. Integrate it into your work.

4. **Pick three tasks you've never done before and go do them.** If you don't know much about customers, work in a store or handle customer complaints; if you don't know what engineering does, go find out; task trade with someone. Meet with your colleagues from

other areas and tell each other what and, more importantly, how you do what you do.

5. **Volunteer for task forces,** especially those working with people who are quite different from yourself. Task forces/projects are a great opportunity to learn new things in a low-risk environment. Task forces are one of the most common developmental events listed by successful executives. Such projects require learning other functions, businesses, or nationalities well enough that in a tight time frame you can appreciate how they think and why their area/position is important. In so doing, you get out of your own experience and start to see connections to a broader world—how international trade works; or more at home, how the pieces of your organization fit together.

6. **Pick a person in the organization who is different in some aspects from your advocate/mentor.** Observe what he/she does and how he/she does it. He/she is as successful as your advocate/mentor but does it in other ways. If possible, ask for a meeting/lunch to discuss his/her success and the things he/she has learned. See if he/she has any interest in teaching you something and being a temporary coach. Get to know other potential advocates on and off work. Go for maximum variety in the towering strengths they possess.

C Being More Open-Minded

INFJs may be so idealistic and principle-driven on certain issues that they can become intolerant of others whose values appear to be different.

1. **Being closed-minded.** You may either be stubborn or may be signaling being stubborn, rigid, and closed to new or different points of view. You must learn to turn off your instant evaluator/rejector filter and listen. Your first task is to understand; your second task is to let the other person know you understand by repeating or rephrasing; and your third task can be to reject, with a fuller explanation of why than you now do. Ask more questions: "How did you get there? Do you prefer this to that or to what we're now doing?" If you disagree, give your reasons first. Then invite criticism. Turn the disagreement back to the nature of the problem or strategy: "What are we trying to solve? What causes it? What questions should be answered? What objective standards could we use to measure success?"

2. **Control?** Are you somewhat of a perfectionist? Need to have everything just so? Create plans and expect them to be followed? Very

jealous of your time? Another source of loss of composure is when things do not go exactly as planned. Put slack in your plans. Expect the unexpected. Lengthen the time line. Plan for delays. List worst-case scenarios. Most of the time you will be pleasantly surprised, and the rest of the time you won't get so upset.

3. **If you're seen as intolerant or closed,** people will often stumble over words in their haste to talk with you or shortcut their argument since they assume you're not listening anyway. Ask a question, invite them to disagree with you, present their argument back to them softly, let them save face no matter what. Add a 15-second pause into your transactions before you say anything, and add two clarifying questions per transaction to signal you're listening and want to understand.

4. **You may be seen as rigid in your values stances and unwilling to accept, or even see, those of others.** Rigid stances often come from childhood and early adult experiences. You need to know why you hold these values and critically examine if they are appropriate here. Statements of belief are pronouncements—a true value holds up to action scrutiny; you can say why you hold it, how it plays out in different situations, and what happens when it conflicts with other values. You may have reduced your beliefs to rigid commandments.

5. **Read three texts on how people differ.** Go to a college bookstore and get an introductory textbook on the theory of personality. Find a copy of *Gifts Differing* by Isabel Myers, a book about the background of the Myers-Briggs Type Indicator. Find *Competence at Work* by Spencer and Spencer which outlines 40 years of study on the differing characteristics people need to be successful in different jobs. Watch out for your personal biases—do you think you have a tendency to favor clones of yourself? Do you have a preference for people who think and act like you do? What characteristics do you value too much? What downsides do you ignore or excuse away? People good at this competency can see, describe, and value the competencies of people not like them.

D Better Delegation and Team Building

Although INFJs are team oriented, they tend to overcommit or focus too much on the needs and problems of selected others. Often the Extraverted Feeling aspect of INFJs will lead to making too many commitments to others, since they see this as part of their relationship responsibility. This unfortunately leads to doing C tasks when they should focus on A tasks. Further, they often anticipate so well that they figure they might as well do the job, given they have a hunch about what needs to be done. They see this as efficient, but, in fact, it keeps others uninformed or prematurely satisfied. If INFJs detect that the relationships are essential to their mission, they may become unstoppable and drive themselves into a morass of personal issues with a sure conviction of what needs to be done. This can ruin teaming.

1. **How to delegate?** Communicate, set time frames and goals, and get out of the way. People need to know what it is you expect. What does the outcome look like? When do you need it by? What's the budget? What resources do they get? What decisions can they make? Do you want checkpoints along the way? How will we both know and measure how well the task is done? One of the most common problems with delegation is incomplete or cryptic up-front communication leading to frustration, a job not well done the first time, rework, and a reluctance to delegate next time. Poor communicators always have to take more time managing because of rework. Analyze recent projects that went well and didn't go well. How did you delegate? Too much? Not enough? Unwanted pieces? Major chunks of responsibility? Workload distributed properly? Did you set measures? Overmanage or abdicate? Find out what your best practices are. Set up a series of delegation practices that can be used as if you're not there. What do you have to be informed of? What feedback loops can people use for midcourse correction? What questions should be answered as the work proceeds? What steps should be followed? What are the criteria to be followed? When will you be available to help?

2. **More what and why, less how.** The best delegators are crystal clear on what and when, and more open on how. People are more motivated when they can determine the how for themselves. Inexperienced delegators include the hows, which turn the people into task automatons instead of an empowered and energized staff. Tell them what and when and for how long, and let them figure out how on their own. Give them leeway. Encourage them to try things. Besides

being more motivating, it's also more developmental for them. Add the larger context. Although it is not necessary to get the task done, people are more motivated when they know where this task fits in the bigger picture. Take three extra minutes and tell them why this task needs to be done, where it fits in the grander scheme, and its importance to the goals and objectives of the unit.

3. **Would like to build a team but don't know how.** High performance teams have four common characteristics: (1) They have a shared mind-set. They have a common vision. Everyone knows the goals and measures. (2) They trust one another. They know "you will cover me if I get in trouble." They know you will pitch in and help even though it may be difficult for you. They know you will be honest with them. They know you will bring problems to them directly and won't go behind their backs. (3) They have the talent collectively to do the job. While not any one member may have it all, collectively they have every task covered. (4) They know how to operate efficiently and effectively. They have good team skills. They run effective meetings. They have efficient ways to communicate. They have ways to deal with internal conflict.

4. **Can't seem to get people motivated to be a team.** Follow the basic rules of inspiring others as outlined in classic books like *People Skills* by Robert Bolton or *Thriving on Chaos* by Tom Peters. Communicate to people that what they do is important. Say thanks. Offer help and ask for it. Provide autonomy in how people do their work. Provide a variety of tasks. "Surprise" people with enriching, challenging assignments. Show an interest in their careers. Adopt a learning attitude toward mistakes. Celebrate successes, have visible accepted measures of achievement, and so on. Try to get everyone to participate in the building of the team so they have a stake in the outcome.

E Not Jumping to Conclusions

INFJs often push solutions based on their vision before the analysis is complete.

1. **Check yourself for these common errors in thinking:** Do you state as facts things that are really opinions or assumptions? Are you sure these assertions are facts? State opinions and assumptions as that and don't present them as facts. Do you attribute cause and effect to relationships when you don't know if one causes the other? If sales are down, and we increase advertising and sales go up, this doesn't prove causality. They are simply related. Say we know that the relationship

between sales/advertising is about the same as sales/number of employees. If sales go down, we probably wouldn't hire more people, so make sure one thing causes the other before acting on it. Do you generalize from a single example without knowing if that single example does generalize?

2. **Defining the problem.** Instant and early conclusions, solutions, statements, suggestions, and how we solved it in the past, are the enemies of good problem solving. Studies show that defining the problem and taking action occur almost simultaneously for most people, so the more effort you put on the front end, the easier it is to come up with a good solution. Stop and first define what the problem is and isn't. Since providing solutions is so easy for everyone, it would be nice if they were offering solutions to the right problem. Figure out what causes it. Keep asking why. See how many causes you can come up with and how many organizing buckets you can put them in. This increases the chance of a better solution because you can see more connections. Be a chess master. Chess masters recognize thousands of patterns of chess pieces. Look for patterns in data; don't just collect information. Put it in categories that make sense to you. Ask lots of questions. Allot at least 50% of the time to defining the problem.

F Better Composure and Less Defensiveness

When they feel pushed on their values, INFJs can shut down and appear to be very defensive. They reject and withdraw or come out firing once they have passed their tipping point.

1. **Decreasing triggers.** Write down the last 25 times you lost your composure. Most people who have composure problems have three to five repeating triggers. Criticism. Loss of control. A certain kind of person. An enemy. Being surprised. Spouse. Children. Money. Authority. Angry at yourself because you can't say no? Try to group 90% of the events into three to five categories. Once you have the groupings, ask yourself why these are a problem. Is it ego? Losing face? Being caught short? Being found out? Causing you more work? In each grouping, what would be a more mature response? Mentally and physically rehearse a better response. Try to decrease by 10% a month the number of times you lose your composure.

2. **Increasing impulse control.** People say and do inappropriate things when they lose their composure. The problem is that they say or do the first thing that occurs to them. Research shows that generally

95

somewhere between the second and third thing you think of to say or do is the best option. Practice holding back your first response long enough to think of a second. When you can do that, wait long enough to think of a third before you choose. By that time, 50% of your composure problems should go away.

3. **Count to 10.** Our thinking and judgment are not at their best during the emotional response. Create and practice delaying tactics. Go get a pencil out of your briefcase. Go get a cup of coffee. Ask a question and listen. Go up to the flip chart and write something. Take notes. See yourself in a setting you find calming. Go to the bathroom. You need about a minute to regain your composure after the emotional response is triggered. Don't do or say anything until the minute has passed.

4. **Maybe your fuse is too long.** You may wait and wait, let the pressure build, keep your concerns to yourself, then explode as a pressure release. Write down what you're concerned about, then talk about the issues with confidantes and coworkers before you blow up. If the pressure interferes with your thought processes at work (you're supposed to be listening, but you're fretting instead), pick a time to worry. Say to yourself, "I'll write this down, then think about it on the way home." Train yourself to stay in the present.

5. **Your defensive response.** You will need to work on keeping yourself in a calm state when getting negative feedback. You need to change your thinking. When getting the feedback, your only task is to accurately understand what people are trying to tell you. It is not your task at that point to accept or reject. That comes later. Mentally rehearse how you will calmly react to tough feedback situations before they happen. Develop automatic tactics to shut down or delay your usual emotional response. Some useful tactics are to slow down, take notes, ask clarifying questions, ask them for concrete examples, and thank them for telling you since you know it's not easy for them.

I enjoy ideas and possibilities so much that I often overlook the details of what needs to be practically done to make an idea real. While I am good with people, I often do not demonstrate enough analytical ability for others to take me seriously.

— An INFJ Manager

■ ■ ■ ■ ■ ■ ■ ■ ■ ■ ■ ■ ■ ■ ■ ■

APPLICATION

Your personal preferences play out in day-to-day problems and situations you face. Below is a case about your type dealing with such a situation. Use this to think through how you will integrate the tips you've considered and coach yourself to be more effective in your type.

INFJ Application Situation (Part 1)

"I remember one thing above all else that my client, Susan, said to me when I told her I was going to give up my consulting business and take a job as Director of IS for EFG Manufacturing: 'Watch your back. You don't have a political bone in your body, and I'd hate to see you get eaten alive.'

"At the time, I didn't really know what she was talking about. I guess you could say that was my blind spot. Anyway, I'm relieved to tell you that I haven't been eaten alive. On the other hand, I seem to be stalled in my role and don't see how I'm going to move up. And around here, sooner or later, it's up or out. They don't seem to understand or have much tolerance for people who are just looking to stay in place and strive for work/life balance."

Listening to Alex as he went on about himself, I noticed he sometimes tended to stare off into the distance, almost dreamily, as if he were actually reliving things in the past as he talked about them.

"How would you describe your relationships with your staff?" I asked him.

"Well, I've managed a staff of eleven people for the six years I've been here, and turnover has been reasonably low, unusually low, I'd say, for this field. Especially given the company's fast-track policies around advancement and succession." He looked off in the distance again, then turned back to me.

"I've worked hard at building good relationships with them. One guy left the company early on, but I'm pretty sure it had more to do with where he wanted to go with his career than with me."

"Would it surprise you to learn that in talking with your staff, I got a very strong consensus that you don't share sufficient information with them?"

Alex's brow furrowed and eyes narrowed. "I can't imagine where that's coming from. No one values cooperation more than I do."

Thinking It Through: Strategy

■ If you were in the role of Alex's coach, with knowledge that his Myers-Briggs type is INFJ, how would you proceed from this point in the conversation?

■ What would you want to accomplish by the end of this first meeting?

Planning It Out: Tactics

■ What other information about Alex would you like to have?

■ What would be the best sources for getting it?

■ Which of the tactics described in the Being More Effective section are applicable in this situation?

■ Which Overused Tendencies are most likely to come into play here?

INFJ Application Situation (Part 2)

■ In gathering more information, you learned that Alex is very much involved in community life and works on weekends in an academic program for economically disadvantaged inner-city kids. The director of the program reports that he feels fortunate to have someone like Alex, who is sociable and sympathetic, working with them, but confesses to occasionally being puzzled when Alex is unresponsive to requests for feedback on how things are going.

Reflection

■ What do you want to work on with Alex over the longer term?

SUGGESTED READINGS

■■■■■■■■ Being a More Effective INFJ ■■■■■■■■

Fairness in Relationships

Arredondo, Lani. *Communicating Effectively.* New York: McGraw-Hill Trade, 2000.

Bolton, Robert and Dorothy Grover Bolton. *People Styles at Work—Making Bad Relationships Good and Good Relationships Better.* New York: AMACOM, 1996.

Cartwright, Tatula. *Managing Conflict With Peers.* Greensboro, NC: Center for Creative Leadership, 2003.

Daniels, Aubrey C. *Bringing Out the Best in People.* New York: McGraw-Hill, Inc., 1994.

Goleman, Daniel, Annie McKee and Richard E. Boyatzis. *Primal Leadership: Realizing the Power of Emotional Intelligence.* Boston: Harvard Business School Press, 2002.

Problems With Higher Management

Charan, Ram. *What the CEO Wants You to Know: How Your Company Really Works.* New York: Crown Business Publishing, 2001.

Dobson, Michael Singer. *Managing Up! 59 Ways to Build a Career-Advancing Relationship With Your Boss.* New York: AMACOM, 2000.

Dominguez, Linda R. *How to Shine at Work.* New York: McGraw-Hill Trade, 2003.

Jay, Ros. *How to Manage Your Boss: Developing the Perfect Working Relationship.* London: Financial Times Management, 2002.

Taking Charge

Badaracco, Joseph L., Jr. *Defining Moments—When Managers Must Choose Between Right and Right.* Boston: Harvard Business School Press, 1997.

Bennis, Warren G. and Burt Nanus. *Leaders: Strategies for Taking Charge.* New York: HarperBusiness, 2003.

Calvert, Gene. *Highwire Management.* San Francisco: Jossey-Bass, Inc., 1993.

Chaleff, Ira. *The Courageous Follower: Standing Up to and for Our Leaders.* San Francisco: Berrett-Koehler Publishers, Inc., 2003.

Coponigro, Jeffrey R. *The Crisis Counselor: A Step-by-Step Guide to Managing a Business Crisis.* New York: McGraw-Hill/Contemporary Books, 2000.

Cox, Danny and John Hoover. *Leadership When the Heat's On.* New York: McGraw-Hill Trade, 2002.

Linsky, Martin and Ronald A. Heifetz. *Leadership on the Line: Staying Alive Through the Dangers of Leading.* Boston: Harvard Business School Press, 2002.

Staffing

Harvard Business School Press. *Hiring and Keeping the Best People.* Boston: Harvard Business School Press, 2003.

Levin, Robert A. and Joseph G. Rosse. *Talent Flow: A Strategic Approach to Keeping Good Employees, Helping Them Grow, and Letting Them Go.* New York: John Wiley & Sons, Inc., 2001.

Lombardo, Michael M. and Robert W. Eichinger. *The Leadership Machine.* Minneapolis, MN: Lominger Limited, Inc., 2004.

Michaels, Ed, Helen Handfield-Jones and Beth Axelrod. *The War for Talent.* Boston: Harvard Business School Press, 2001.

Myers, Isabel Briggs with Peter B. Myers. *Gifts Differing: Understanding Personality Type.* Palo Alto, CA: Davies-Black Publishing, 1995.

Poundstone, William. *How Would You Move Mount Fiji? Microsoft's Cult of the Puzzle—How the World's Smartest Company Selects the Most Creative Thinkers.* Boston: Little, Brown, 2003.

Smart, Bradford D., Ph.D. *Topgrading—How Leading Companies Win: Hiring, Coaching and Keeping the Best People.* New York: Prentice Hall, 1999.

Zenger, John H. and Joseph Folkman. *The Extraordinary Leader: Turning Good Managers Into Great Leaders.* New York: McGraw-Hill, Inc., 2002.

Getting Results

Block, Peter. *The Answer to How Is Yes: Acting On What Matters.* San Francisco: Berrett-Koehler Publishers, Inc., 2001.

Bossidy, Larry, Ram Charan and Charles Burck (Contributor). *Execution: The Discipline of Getting Things Done.* New York: Crown Business Publishing, 2002.

Collins, James C. *Good to Great: Why Some Companies Make the Leap...And Others Don't.* New York: HarperCollins, 2001.

Longenecker, Clinton O. and Jack L. Simonetti. *Getting Results: Five Absolutes for High Performance.* New York: John Wiley & Sons, Inc., 2001.

Zook, Chris and James Allen. *Profit From the Core.* Boston: Harvard Business School Press, 2001.

■■■■■■■ **Overusing INFJ Tendencies** ■■■■■■■

Becoming More Career Ambitious

Bolles, Richard N. *What Color Is Your Parachute? 2004: A Practical Manual for Job-Hunters & Career-Changers.* Berkeley, CA: Ten Speed Press, 2004.

Christian, Ken. *Your Own Worst Enemy: Breaking the Habit of Adult Underachievement.* New York: Regan Books, 2004.

Citrin, James M. and Richard A. Smith. *The Five Patterns of Extraordinary Careers.* New York: Crown Business, 2003.

Dominguez, Linda R. *How to Shine at Work.* New York: McGraw-Hill Trade, 2003.

Lombardo, Michael M. and Robert W. Eichinger. *FYI For Your Improvement* (4th ed.). Minneapolis, MN: Lominger Limited, Inc., 1996–2004.

McCall, Morgan W., Michael M. Lombardo and Ann M. Morrison. *The Lessons of Experience.* Lexington, MA: Lexington Books, 1988.

Morgan, Nick. *Working the Room: How to Move People to Action Through Audience-Centered Speaking.* Boston: Harvard Business School Press, 2003.

Morrison, Ann M., Randall P. White, Ellen Van Velsor and the Center for Creative Leadership. *Breaking the Glass Ceiling: Can Women Reach the Top of America's Largest Corporations?* Reading, MA: Addison-Wesley Publishing Company, 1992.

Niven, David. *The 100 Simple Secrets of Successful People: What Scientists Have Learned and How You Can Use It.* New York: HarperBusiness, 2002.

Being Less Dependent on a Few Relationships

Benton, D.A. *Executive Charisma: Six Steps to Mastering the Art of Leadership.* New York: McGraw-Hill Trade, 2003.

Bolton, Robert and Dorothy Grover Bolton. *People Styles at Work—Making Bad Relationships Good and Good Relationships Better.* New York: AMACOM, 1996.

Brooks, Michael. *Instant Rapport.* New York: Warner Books, 1989.

Maxwell, John C. *Relationships 101.* London: Thomas Nelson, 2004.

Niven, David. *The 100 Simple Secrets of Successful People: What Scientists Have Learned and How You Can Use It.* New York: HarperBusiness, 2002.

Silberman, Melvin L. and Freda Hansburg. *Peoplesmart: Developing Your Interpersonal Intelligence.* San Francisco: Berrett-Koehler Publishers, Inc., 2000.

Being More Open-Minded

Christian, Ken. *Your Own Worst Enemy: Breaking the Habit of Adult Underachievement.* New York: Regan Books, 2004.

Dotlich, David L. and Peter C. Cairo. *Why CEOs Fail.* San Francisco: Jossey-Bass, Inc., 2003.

Ellis, Albert, Ph.D. *How to Control Your Anxiety Before It Controls You.* New York: Citadel Press, 2000.

Glickman, Rosalene. *Optimal Thinking: How to Be Your Best Self.* New York: John Wiley & Sons, Inc., 2002.

Spencer, L. and S. Spencer. *Competence at Work: Models for Superior Performance.* New York: John Wiley & Sons, Inc., 1993.

Waldroop, James, Ph.D. and Timothy Butler, Ph.D. *Maximum Success: Changing the 12 Behavior Patterns That Keep You From Getting Ahead*. New York: Doubleday, 2000.

Better Delegation and Team Building

Bolton, Robert. *People Skills*. New York: Simon & Schuster, 1979.

Peters, Tom. *Thriving on Chaos: Handbook for a Management Revolution*. New York: HarperCollins, 1987.

Fisher, Kimball and Mareen Duncan Fisher. *The Distance Manager: A Hands-On Guide to Managing Off-Site Employees and Virtual Teams*. New York: McGraw-Hill Trade, 2000.

Genett, Donna M. *If You Want It Done Right, You Don't Have to Do It Yourself! The Power of Effective Delegation*. Sanger, CA: Quill Driver Books, 2004.

Harvard Business School Press. *Harvard Business Review on Teams That Succeed*. Boston: Harvard Business School Press, 2004.

Katzenbach, Jon R. and Douglas K. Smith. *The Wisdom of Teams: Creating the High-Performance Organization*. New York: HarperBusiness, 2003.

Parker, Glenn M. *Cross-Functional Teams: Working With Allies, Enemies, and Other Strangers*. San Francisco: Jossey-Bass, Inc., 2002.

Peters, Tom. *Thriving on Chaos: Handbook for a Management Revolution*. New York: HarperCollins, 1987.

Raymond, Cara Capretta, Robert W. Eichinger and Michael M. Lombardo. *FYI for Teams*. Minneapolis, MN: Lominger Limited, Inc., 2001–2004.

Robbins, Harvey and Michael Finley. *The New Why Teams Don't Work— What Goes Wrong and How to Make It Right*. San Francisco: Berrett-Koehler Publishers, Inc., 2000.

Not Jumping to Conclusions

Flynn, Daniel J. *Intellectual Morons: How Ideology Makes Smart People Fall for Stupid Ideas*. New York: Crown Business Publishing, 2004.

Hammond, John S., Ralph L. Keeney and Howard Raiffer. *Smart Choices*. Boston: Harvard University Press, 1999.

Nutt, Paul C. *Why Decisions Fail: Avoiding the Blunders and Traps That Lead to Decision Debacles.* San Francisco: Berrett-Koehler Publishers, Inc., 2002.

Sofo, Francesco. *Six Myths of Critical Thinking.* Business & Professional Publishing, 2003.

Sternberg, Robert J. *Thinking Styles.* Boston: Cambridge University Press, 1997.

Yates, J. Frank. *Decision Management: How to Assure Better Decisions in Your Company.* San Francisco: Jossey-Bass, Inc., 2003.

Better Composure and Less Defensiveness

Brim, Gilbert. *Ambition: How We Manage Success and Failure Throughout Our Lives.* New York: Backinprint.com, 2000.

Carter, Les. *The Anger Trap: Free Yourself From the Frustrations That Sabotage Your Life.* New York: John Wiley & Sons, Inc., 2003.

Ellis, Albert, Ph.D. *How to Control Your Anxiety Before It Controls You.* New York: Citadel Press, 2000.

Lerner, Harriet. *The Dance of Connection: How to Talk to Someone When You're Mad, Hurt, Scared, Frustrated, Insulted, Betrayed, or Desperate.* New York: Quill/HarperCollins, 2002.

Patterson, Kerry, Joseph Grenny, Ron McMillan, Al Switzler and Stephen R. Covey. *Crucial Conversations: Tools for Talking When Stakes Are High.* New York: McGraw-Hill/Contemporary Books, 2002.

CHAPTER 4

INTJ
Introverted Intuiting
with
Extraverted Thinking

■■■■■■■■■■■■■■■■■

2.1% of Population
10.0% of Managers

■■■■■■■■■■■■■■■■■

Typical Strengths

Original
High Standards
Autonomous
Practical
Strategic
Visionary
Decision Quality

ISTJ	ISFJ	INFJ	INTJ
ISTP	ISFP	INFP	INTP
ESTP	ESFP	ENFP	ENTP
ESTJ	ESFJ	ENFJ	ENTJ

I see the big picture easily; getting people to buy in to it is the hard part.

– An INTJ Manager

Basic Habits of Mind

Introverted Intuiting leads INTJs to see possibilities and have complex ideas. Often they see relationships among apparently unrelated events or facts, and have a tendency to look for a "strategic view" that can lead to an uncanny awareness of situations and capability to predict what will happen. They use Extraverted Thinking to examine their environment with analytical and critical precision.

Extraverted Feeling and Extraverted Sensing lead to the special ability to read others in a situation and be able to quickly adapt to emerging demands. This information does not necessarily alter their plan; it informs them on the next strategy to employ. This quality also sometimes leads to a perception of being unapproachable, arrogant, and overbearing.

Typical Communication Patterns

■ Because Extraverted Thinking is used as a primary mode of engaging people, INTJs can seem questioning and skeptical.

■ Due to the INTJ tendency to collect theories and ideas, they are likely to find a model to make sense of most any situation.

■ Being logical, orderly, and systematic is typical.

■ They can appear very intense and have difficulty expressing all of the complexity that their Introverted Intuiting has spotted.

General Learning Strategy

■ INTJs usually prefer to learn about global frameworks, to envision possibilities, to speculate, and to actively make connections between ideas.

■ Their typical learning strategies are independent analysis, debating, researching a problem, and connecting their experience to an abstraction or model.

■ Their learning is usually enhanced by pursuing open-ended questions, providing time for analysis before discussing, and having freedom to brainstorm and design.

Interpersonal Qualities Related to Motivation

■ INTJs appreciate mental versatility, systematic analysis, and high aspirations.

■ They are likely to try to motivate others by explaining overall frameworks for action. They often connect actions and motives to outcomes and provide a "formula" to explain their experiences.

Blind Spots

■ They may be unaware that their decisive analytical style can appear dogmatic, impatient, and manipulating. INTJs may need to know more about how their interpersonal style affects their effectiveness in relationships.

■ Their independent nature is often interpreted as not supporting management decisions or strategic directions.

Stress Related Behavior

■ INTJs can become more skeptical and questioning with stress. This may appear as being hardheaded or condescending.

■ When the pressure is great enough, they may become obsessed with a fact that they beat to death. In these cases, they may insist on hairsplitting precision.

Potential Barriers to Effectiveness

■ The need to strengthen relationships, to demonstrate more compassion and sensitivity, and to be careful about disagreements with management decisions are usually critical to addressing barriers to effectiveness for INTJs.

■ What feels like open, direct communication and clear, critical questions about decisions being made is often seen by others as being opinionated, detached, and manipulative.

Being a More Effective INTJ

A Handling Disagreements
B Informing
C Patience
D Interpersonal Savvy
E Boss Relationships
F Dislike of Standard Operating
   Procedures

ISTJ	ISFJ	INFJ	INTJ
ISTP	ISFP	INFP	INTP
ESTP	ESFP	ENFP	ENTP
ESTJ	ESFJ	ENFJ	ENTJ

A Handling Disagreements

INTJs often get in disputes with those who don't grasp their vision and can become pushy and dismissive.

1. **Cooperative relations.** The opposite of conflict is cooperation. Developing cooperative relationships involves demonstrating real and perceived equity, the other side feeling understood and respected, and taking a problem-oriented point of view. To do this more: Increase the realities and perceptions of fairness—don't try to win every battle and take all the spoils; focus on the common-ground issues and interests of both sides—find wins on both sides, give in on little points; avoid starting with entrenched positions—show respect for them and their positions; and reduce any remaining conflicts to the smallest size possible.

2. **Causing unnecessary conflict.** Language, words, and timing set the tone and can cause unnecessary conflict that has to be managed before you can get anything done. Do you use insensitive language? Do you raise your voice often? Do you use terms and phrases that challenge others? Do you use demeaning terms? Do you use negative humor? Do you offer conclusions, solutions, statements, dictates, or answers early in the transaction? Give reasons first, solutions last. When you give solutions first, people often directly challenge the solutions instead of defining the problem. Pick words that are other-person neutral. Pick words that don't challenge or sound one-sided. Pick tentative and probabilistic words that give others a chance to maneuver and save face. Pick words that are about the problem and not the person. Avoid direct blaming remarks; describe the problem and its impact.

3. **Practice Aikido,** the ancient art of absorbing the energy of your opponent and using it to manage him/her. Let the other side vent frustration or blow off steam, but don't react. Listen. Nod. Ask clarifying questions. Ask open-ended questions like, "What one change could you make so we could achieve our objectives better?" "What could I do that would help the most?" Restate their position periodically to signal you have understood. But don't react. Keep them talking until they run out of venom. When the other side takes a rigid position, don't reject it. Ask why: What are the principles behind the position? How do we know it's fair? What's the theory of the case? Play out what would happen if their position was accepted. Then explore the underlying concern. Separate the people from the problem. When someone attacks you, rephrase it as an attack on the problem. In response to threats, say you'll only negotiate on merit and fairness. If the other side won't play fair, surface their game—"It looks like you're playing good cop, bad cop. Why don't you settle your differences and tell me one thing?" In response to unreasonable proposals, attacks, or a non-answer to a question, you can always say nothing. People will usually respond by saying more, coming off their position a bit, or at least revealing their true interests. Many times, with unlimited venting and your understanding, the actual conflict shrinks.

4. **Downsizing the conflict.** Almost all conflicts have common points that get lost in the heat of the battle. After a conflict has been presented and understood, start by saying that it might be helpful to see if we agree on anything. Write them on the flip chart. Then write down the areas left open. Focus on common goals, priorities, and problems. Keep the open conflicts as small as possible and concrete. The more abstract it gets, "We don't trust your unit," the more unmanageable it gets. To this respond, "Tell me your specific concern—why exactly don't you trust us; can you give me an example?" Usually after calm discussion, they don't trust your unit on this specific issue under these specific conditions. That's easier to deal with. Allow others to save face by conceding small points that are not central to the issue—don't try to hit a home run every time. If you can't agree on a solution, agree on a procedure to move forward. Collect more data. Appeal to a higher power. Get a third-party arbitrator. Something. This creates some positive motion and breaks stalemates.

5. **Get a bit too tough?** Do your statements have an edge to them? In conflict situations, what reactions do you have (such as impatience or

non-verbals like flushing or drumming your pen or fingers)? Learn to recognize those as soon as they start and substitute something more neutral. Most emotional responses to conflict come from personalizing the issue. Separate people issues from the problem at hand, and deal with people issues separately and later if they persist. Always return to facts and the problem before the group; stay away from personal clashes. Attack the problem by looking at common interests and underlying concerns, not people and their positions. Try on their views for size—the emotion as well as the content. Ask yourself if you understand their feelings. Ask what they would do if they were in your shoes. See if you can restate each other's position and advocate it for a minute to get inside each other's place. If you get emotional, pause and collect yourself. You are not your best when you get emotional. Then return to the problem.

6. **Bargaining and trading.** Since you can't absolutely win all conflicts unless you keep pulling rank, you have to learn to horse-trade and bargain. What do they need that I have? What could I do for them outside this conflict that could allow them to give up something I need now in return? How can we turn this into a win for both of us?

7. **Clear problem-focused communication.** Follow the rule of equity: Explain your thinking and ask them to explain theirs. Be able to state their position as clearly as they do whether you agree or not—give it legitimacy. Separate facts from opinions and assumptions. Generate a variety of possibilities first rather than stake out positions. Keep your speaking to 30–60 second bursts. Try to get them to do the same. Don't give the other side the impression you're lecturing or criticizing them. Explain objectively why you hold a view; make the other side do the same. Ask lots of questions, make fewer statements. To identify interests behind positions, ask why they hold them or why they wouldn't want to do something. Always restate their position to their satisfaction before offering a response.

8. **Questions.** In win-win and something-something negotiations, the more information you have about the other side, the more you will have to work with. What can you learn about what they know before going in? What will they do if they don't reach an agreement with you? In the negotiation, ask more questions, make fewer statements. Ask clarifying questions: "What did you mean by that?" Probes: "Why do you say that?" Motives: "What led you to that position?" Get everything out that you can. Don't negotiate assumptions, negotiate facts.

9. **Avoid early rigid positions.** It's just physics. Action gets equal reaction. Strong statements. Strongly worded positions. Casting blame. Absolutes. Lines in the sand. Unnecessary passion. All of these will be responded to in kind, will waste time, cause ill will, and possibly prevent a win-win or a something-something. It only has a place in one-time, either/or negotiations, and even there it isn't recommended. Similarly, watch out for overcommitment to any need or course of action. Look for information that goes against your preferences. Be able to adjust your position and your wants. If you can't, your ego is getting the best of you. If you can't walk away until you get X, you'll probably either overpay or blow the negotiation. Don't negotiate around a single issue if you can add another. This is another situation that leads to rigidity.

10. **Selective resistance.** Do you adapt to some and not to others? You probably have good people buckets and bad people buckets and signal your disagreement with them to the bad bucket groups or individuals. You may have good group buckets and bad group buckets—gender, race, age, origin. Learn to understand without accepting or judging. Listen, take notes, ask questions, and be able to make their case as well as they can. Pick something in their argument you agree with. Present your argument in terms of the problem only—why you think this is the best manner to deal with a mutually agreed-upon problem. A careful observer should not be able to tell your assessment of people or their arguments at the time. Find someone who is a fair observer and get a critique. Was I fair? Did I treat everyone the same? Were my objections based on reasoning against standards and not directed at people?

B Informing

INTJs often don't inform people well. They think it's obvious or sometimes don't think at that level of detail.

1. **Share your thinking.** To help those around you grow and learn from what you know, you have to sometimes think out loud. You have to share your thinking from the initial presentation of the issue through to conclusion. Most of us are on thinking autopilot. We don't think about thinking. When someone else has to or wants to understand how you came up with a decision, it's sometimes difficult to unravel it in your mind. You have to go step-by-step and recreate your thinking. Sometimes it helps if other people ask the questions. They can probably guide you through how you came up with an answer or

a decision better than you can. Once in a while, you should document a decision or two. What was the issue? What were the pros and cons you considered? How did you weight things? Then you can use those examples to demonstrate to others how you make decisions.

2. **Don't inform enough.** Are you a minimalist? Do you tell people only what they need to know to do their little piece of the puzzle? People are motivated by being aware of the bigger picture. They want to know what to do in order to do their jobs and more. How does what they are doing fit into the larger picture? What are the other people working on and why? Many people think that's unnecessary information and that it would take too much time to do. They're wrong. The sense of doing something worthwhile is the number two motivator at work! It results in a high return on motivation and productivity. (Try to increase the amount of more-than-your-job information you share.) Focus on the impact on others by figuring out who information affects. Put five minutes on your meeting agenda. Ask people what they want to know and, assuming it's not confidential information, tell them. Pick a topic each month to tell your people about.

3. **A loner.** Do you keep to yourself? Work alone or try to? Do you hold back information? Do you parcel out information on your schedule? Do you share information to get an advantage or to win favor? Do people around you know what you're doing and why? Are you aware of things others would benefit from, but you don't take the time to communicate? In most organizations, these things and things like it will get you in trouble. Organizations function on the flow of information. Being on your own and preferring peace and privacy are okay as long as you communicate things to bosses, peers, and teammates that they need to know and would feel better if they knew. Don't be the source of surprises.

4. **Cryptic informer.** Some people just aren't good at informing. Their communication styles are not effective. According to behavioral research studies, the most effective communicators: speak often, but briefly (15–30 seconds); ask more questions than others; make fewer solution statements early in a discussion; headline their points in a sentence or two; summarize frequently, and make more frequent "here's where we are" statements; invite everyone to share their views; and typically interject their views after others have had a chance to speak, unless they are passing on decisions. Compare these practices to yours. Work on those that are not up to standard.

5. **Inconsistent informing.** Have an information checklist detailing what information should go to whom; pass on summaries or copies of important communications. Determine the information checklist by: keeping tabs on unpleasant surprises people report to you; ask direct reports what they'd like to know to do their jobs better; and check with boss, peers, and customers to see if you pass along too little, enough, or too much of the right kinds of information. It's important to know what to pass, to whom to pass, and when to pass, to become an effective informer.

6. **Audience sensitivity.** Unfortunately, one method or style of informing does not play equally well across audiences. Many times you will have to adjust the tone, pace, style, and even the message and how you couch it for different audiences. If you are delivering the same message to multiple people or audiences, always ask yourself how are they different? Some differences among people or audiences include level of sophistication, friendly vs. unfriendly, time sensitivity, whether they prefer it in writing or not, and whether a logical or emotional argument will play better. Write or tell? Writing is usually best for the extremes—complex descriptions complete with background and five or six progressive arguments, or on the other side, straightforward, unambiguous things people need to know. You should generally tell when it requires discussion or you are alerting them to a problem. Make a read on each person and each audience and adjust accordingly.

C Patience

If INTJs have a fatal flaw, lack of patience is likely to be it. They can show great disdain for people who are slow to grasp something or don't express themselves precisely or quickly.

1. **Listening chillers?** Don't interrupt before they have finished. Don't suggest words when they hesitate or pause. Don't finish their sentences for them. Don't wave off any further input by saying, "Yes, I know that." "Yes, I know where you're going." "Yes, I have heard that before." If time is really important, you can say, "Let me see if I know where this is going…," or "I wonder if we could summarize to save both of us some time?" Finally, early in a transaction, answers, solutions, conclusions, statements, and dictates shut many people down. You've told them your mind is already made up. Listen first, solve second.

2. **Questions.** Good listeners ask lots of questions to get to a good understanding. Probing questions. Clarifying questions. Confirming—is this what you are saying—questions. Ask one more question than you do now and add to that until people signal you that they think you are truly listening.

3. **Watch out for negative humor.** Some people use humor to deliver negative messages. They are sarcastic and barbed in their humor. In a tense confrontation with an employee, to say, "I hope your résumé is up to date," instead of saying, "Your performance is not what I expected. It has to improve or I will have to reconsider your continued employment," is not acceptable. There is a very simple rule. Do not use humor to deliver a critical point to a person or a group. Negative humor hurts more than a straightforward statement. Say directly what you mean.

4. **Listening to those who waste a lot of time.** With those you don't have time to listen to, switch to being a teacher. Try to help them craft their communications to you in a more acceptable way. Interrupt to summarize. Tell them to be shorter next time. Come with more/less data. Structure the conversation by helping them come up with categories and structures to stop their rambling. Good listeners don't signal to the "bad" people that they are not listening or are not interested. Don't signal to anyone what bucket they're in. Put your mind in neutral, nod, ask questions, be helpful.

5. **Listening to people you don't like.** What do people see in them who do like them or can at least get along with them? What are their strengths? Do you have any common interests? Talk less and ask more questions to give them a second chance. Don't judge their motives and intentions—do that later.

6. **Listening to people you like but...**

   ■ They are disorganized. Interrupt to summarize and keep the discussion focused. While interrupting is generally not a good tactic, it's necessary here.

   ■ They just want to chat. Ask questions to focus them; don't respond to chatty remarks.

   ■ They want to unload a problem. Assume when people tell you something they are looking for understanding; indicate that by being able to summarize what they said. Don't offer any advice.

- They are chronic complainers. Ask them to write down problems and solutions and then let's discuss it. This turns down the volume while, hopefully, moving them off complaining.

- They like to complain about others. Ask if they've talked to the person. Encourage them to do so. If that doesn't work, summarize what they have said without agreeing or disagreeing.

7. **Impatience triggers.** Some people probably bring out your impatience more than others. Who are they? What is it about them that makes you more impatient? Pace? Language? Thought process? Accent? These people may include people you don't like, who ramble, who whine and complain, or who are repetitive advocates for things you have already rejected. Mentally rehearse some calming tactics before meeting with people who trigger your impatience. Work on understanding their positions without judging them—you can always judge later. In all cases, focus them on the issues or problems to be discussed, return them to the point, summarize, and state your position. Try to gently train them to be more efficient with you next time without damaging them in the process.

8. **Work on your openness and approachability.** Impatient people don't get as much information as patient listeners do. They are more often surprised by events when others knew they were coming. People are hesitant to talk to impatient people. It's too painful. People don't pass on hunches, unbaked thoughts, maybes, and possibles to impatient people. You will be out of the information loop and miss important information you need to know to be effective. Suspend judgment on informal communications. Just take it in. Acknowledge that you understand. Ask a question or two. Follow up later.

9. **Rein in your horse.** Impatient people provide answers, conclusions, and solutions too early in the process. Others haven't even understood the problem yet. Providing solutions too quickly will make your people dependent and irritated. If you don't teach them how you think and how you can come up with solutions so fast, they will never learn. Take the time to really define the problem—not impatiently throw out a solution. Brainstorm what questions need to be answered in order to resolve it. Give your people the task to think about for a day and come back with some solutions. Be a teacher instead of a dictator of solutions. Study yourself. Keep a journal of what triggered your behavior and what the observed consequences

were. Learn to detect and control your triggers before they get you in trouble.

10. **Task impatience.** Impatient people check in a lot. How's it coming. Is it done yet? When will it be finished? Let me see what you've done so far. That is disruptive to due process and wastes time. When you give out a task or assign a project, establish agreed-upon time checkpoints. You can also assign percentage checkpoints. Check in with me when you are about 25% finished so we can make midcourse corrections and 75% finished so we can make final corrections. Let them figure out how to do the task. Hold back from checking in at other than the agreed-upon times and percentages.

D Interpersonal Savvy

People often come in a distant second to ideas for INTJs. Change and efficiency are usually much more important to them. As a result, their relationships can suffer, and they can have trouble expressing compassion.

1. **Personalizing.** Approachable people work to know and remember important things about the people they work around, for, and with. Know three things about everybody—their interests or their children or something you can chat about other than the business agenda. Treat life as a small world. If you ask a few questions, you'll find you have something in common with virtually anyone. Establish things you can talk about with each person you work with that go beyond strictly work transactions. These need not be social—they could be issues of strategy, global events, market shifts. The point is to forge common ground and connections.

2. **Ask the first question.** For low-risk practice, talk to strangers off-work. Set a goal of meeting 10 new people at a social gathering; find out what you have in common with them. Initiate contact at your place of worship, at PTA meetings, in the neighborhood, at the supermarket, on the plane, and on the bus.

3. **The first three minutes.** Managing the first three minutes is essential. The tone is set. First impressions are formed. Work on being open and approachable, and take in information during the beginning of a transaction. This means putting others at ease so that they feel okay about disclosing. It means initiating rapport, listening, sharing, understanding, and comforting. Approachable people get more information, know things earlier, and can get others to do more things. The more you can get them to initiate and say early in the

transaction, the more you'll know about where they are coming from, and the better you can tailor your approach.

4. **To understand the differences among people,** look to the obvious first. What do they do first? What do they emphasize in their speech? People focus on different things—taking action, details, concepts, feelings, other people. What's their interaction style? People come in different styles—pushy, tough, soft, matter-of-fact, and so on. To figure these out, listen for the values behind their words and note what they have passion and emotion around. One key to getting anything of value done in the work world is the ability to see differences in people and to manage against and use those differences for everyone's benefit. Interpersonal savvy is meeting each person where he/she is to get done what you need to get done. Basically, people respond favorably to ease of transaction. If you make it easy by accepting their normal mode of doing things, not fighting their style, and neither defending your own nor letting style get in the way of performance, things will generally run smoothly.

5. **Show more understanding.** A primary reason for problems with showing compassion is that you don't know how to deal with strong feelings and appear distant or uninterested. You're uncomfortable with strong displays of emotion and calls for personal help. Simply imagine how you would feel in this situation and respond with that. Tell the person how sorry you are this has happened or has to be dealt with. Offer whatever help is reasonable. A day off. A loan. A resource. If you can, offer hope of a better day. This is what the person can use most.

6. **You don't have to be a therapist or counselor.** Another reason people have trouble with compassion is thinking that a counselor role isn't appropriate at work. You can be brief and compassionate by following three rules:

   ■ Let people say what's on their mind without saying anything other than you know they're upset. Don't judge. Don't advise.

   ■ Summarize when they start repeating. This signals that you heard them, but keeps them from consuming so much time that you begin to feel like a counselor.

   ■ If someone overdoes it, invite him/her to talk with you outside of work hours or refer him/her to another resource like employee assistance.

This shows others that you cared, you listened and are willing to help if possible, while not putting you in the counselor role that is making you uncomfortable.

7. **Showing compassion isn't judgment or agreement.** It's showing empathy for others. Be candid with yourself. Is there a group or groups you don't like or are uncomfortable with? Do you judge individual members of that group without really knowing if your stereotype is true? Most of us do. Do you show compassion for one group's problems but not another's? To deal with this:

    ■ Put yourself in their case. Why would you act that way? What do you think they're trying to achieve? Assume that however they act is rational to them; it must have paid off or they wouldn't be doing it. Don't use your internal standards.

    ■ Avoid putting groups in buckets. Many of us bucket groups as friendly or unfriendly, good or bad, like me or not like me. Once we do, we generally don't show as much compassion toward them and may question their motives. Apply the logic of why people belong to the group in the first place. See if you can predict accurately what the group will say or do across situations to test your understanding of the group. Don't use your agreement program.

    ■ Listen. Even though this tip may seem obvious, many of us tune out when dealing with difficult or not-well-understood groups, or reject what they're saying before they say it. Just listen. Mentally summarize their views, and see if you can figure out what they want from what they say and mean. The true test is whether you can clearly figure it out, even though you don't think that way.

8. **Many people who need your compassion most aren't the most pleasant people.**

    ■ For the cynical—delegate responsibility to them for what they are most cynical about.

    ■ For the helpless and dependent—ask yourself what would make them feel the most powerful?

    ■ For the truly resentful or hostile—don't encourage them to air all of their gripes in detail. This merely reinforces their views. Instead, find out what is bothering them the most at work, and give them something new to do where they have the authority to make a difference.

E   Boss Relationships

INTJs are loyal to innovation and continuous improvement and tend to scoff at or reject authority. If they decide their boss is not very competent or is resisting change, sparks fly.

1. **Facing the boss.** Try to have a series of informal, relaxed discussions with your boss about what the problem might be, leading with your contributions—we are seldom completely in the right—to the problem first; then give him/her an opportunity to add to the discussion. Make it easy for him/her by indicating, "You are doing me a favor. I need your help." In return for your boss's help, offer some in return. What are your boss's weakest areas or what can you do to make the job easier? Figure out what those are and pitch in. This is good practice because relationships don't often prosper unless there is some equity built in. Give to get or your boss may soon be uncomfortable with the one-way nature of the help.

2. **Some rules to follow:** Describe. Say "I" not "you." Focus on how to accomplish work better. (If you think the boss is blocking you, instead of saying this, say, "I need help in getting this done. I've tried the following things, but....")

    ■   If your boss is reluctant to give criticism, help by making statements rather than asking questions. Saying "I think I focus too much on operations and miss some of the larger strategic connections" is easier for most people to reply to than a question which asks them to tell you this point.

    ■   If your manager is uninvolved, you will need to provide the structure and aim for a sign-off on your objectives.

    ■   If you work for a detail-driven micromanager, ask what results you must achieve to be successful (and left alone more).

    ■   If your manager is well-meaning, but a nuisance, ask if you can check in with him because you are trying to be more autonomous.

    ■   If you believe the boss is blocking you, access your network for performance help, think of five ways to accomplish anything, and try them all.

3. **Learn to depersonalize and be neutral.** Try to separate the person from the boss role he/she is in; try to objectify the situation. Someone made her/him boss for a reason, and you are never going to please everyone. Deal with him/her as your boss more than as a person. While you don't ever have to invite her/him to your home, you do have to deal with this person as a boss. Ask yourself why you dislike your boss so much or don't like to work with him/her. Write down everything you don't like on the left-hand side of a page. On the right-hand side write a strategy for dealing with it. Consider these strategies: Ask what strengths you can appeal to; ask what you can provide that the boss needs; ask what the boss would like for you to do to be more effective; design a project that you can do together so you can have a success experience; and consult with others for advice. What do people think who have a favorable impression of your boss? Do you share any common interests? Write down everything you've heard him/her say that was favorable. Play to the boss's good points. Whatever you do, don't signal what you think. Put your judgments on hold, nod, ask questions, summarize as you would with anyone else. A fly on the wall should not be able to tell whether you're talking to friend or foe. You can always talk less and ask more questions.

4. **Keep your cool.** Being nervous, anxious, and uncomfortable around one or more higher-ups is fairly normal; the key is not allowing that to prevent you from doing your best. Being uncomfortable can sometimes lead to physical reactions like sweating, hesitating or stuttering speech, mispronounced words, flushing of the face, grumbling in the stomach, running out of breath while talking, etc. When that happens, stop a second or two, take a deep breath, compose yourself, and continue what you were doing; they all have been there before. Remember, all you can do is the best you can do. You probably know more about this topic than they do. You're well prepared—being anxious can prevent you from demonstrating your expertise.

F Dislike of Standard Operating Procedures

INTJs are interested in models for the future, not the necessary techniques of the present. They tend to question routines and standard operating procedures because they are boring and because the past holds no special value to them.

1. **Focus more in the here and now.** Pick a plan or procedure and do a historical analysis of how it came to be and why it is necessary. Resist the urge to change it or question its usefulness. Understand it first.

2. **Turn off your answer program.** We all have a need to provide answers as soon as possible to questions and problems. We all have preconceived notions, favorite solutions, and prejudices that prevent our intellectual skills from dealing with the real facts of the problem. For one-half of the time you have to deal with an issue or a problem, shut off your solution machine and just take in the facts.

3. **Compensate for your dislikes.** Find a person you admire and respect to deal with all the procedures you find oppressive. Let this person tell you if anything needs changing. Otherwise, trust his or her judgment.

Overusing INTJ Tendencies

If you sometimes overdo your preferred behaviors, you may need to work on:

A   Not Jumping to Conclusions

B   Improving Team Building

C   Developing Others

D   Understanding Others

E   Curbing Arrogance

F   Better Relationships With Higher Management

ISTJ	ISFJ	INFJ	INTJ
ISTP	ISFP	INFP	INTP
ESTP	ESFP	ENFP	ENTP
ESTJ	ESFJ	ENFJ	ENTJ

A   Not Jumping to Conclusions

Since INTJs often see ahead clearly and are very able thinkers, they also jump ahead to conclusions without explaining their thinking or what alternatives were considered.

1. **Defining the problem.** Instant and early conclusions, solutions, statements, suggestions, and how we solved it in the past, are the enemies of good problem solving. Studies show that defining the problem and taking action occur almost simultaneously for most people, so the more effort you put on the front end, the easier it is to come up with a good solution. Stop and first define what the problem is and isn't. Since providing solutions is so easy for everyone, it would be nice if they were offering solutions to the right problem. Figure out what causes it. Keep asking why. See how many causes you can come up with and how many organizing buckets you can put them in. This

increases the chance of a better solution because you can see more connections. Be a chess master. Chess masters recognize thousands of patterns of chess pieces. Look for patterns in data; don't just collect information. Put it in categories that make sense to you. Ask lots of questions. Allot at least 50% of the time to defining the problem.

2. **Watch your biases.** Some people have solutions in search of problems. They have favorite solutions. They have biases. They have universal solutions to most situations. They pre-judge what the problem is without stopping to consider the nuances of this specific problem. Do honest and open analysis first. Did you state as facts things that are really assumptions or opinions? Are you sure these assertions are facts? Did you generalize from a single example? One of your solutions may in fact fit, but wait to see if you're right about the problem.

3. **Do you help your people learn by looking for repeating patterns?** Help them look for patterns in the situations and problems they deal with. What succeeded and what failed? What was common to each success or what was present in each failure but never present in a success? Focus on the successes; failures are easier to analyze but don't in themselves tell you what would work. Comparing successes, while less exciting, yields more information. The bottom line is help them reduce insights to principles or rules of thumb that might be repeatable. Ask them what they have learned to increase their skills and understanding, making them better managers or professionals. Ask them what they can do now that they couldn't do a year ago. Reinforce this and encourage more of it. Developing is learning in as many ways as possible.

4. **Asking others for input.** Many try to do too much themselves. They don't delegate, listen, or ask others for input. Even if you think you have the solution, ask some others for input just to make sure. Access your network. Find someone who makes a good sounding board and talk to her/him, not just for ideas, but to increase your understanding of the problem. Or do it more formally. Set up a competition between two teams, both acting as your advisors. Call a problem-solving meeting and give the group two hours to come up with something that will at least be tried. Find a buddy group in another function or organization that faces the same or a similar problem and both of you experiment.

5. **You probably have good people buckets and bad people buckets** and signal to the bad bucket groups or individuals your disagreement with them. Learn to understand without either accepting or judging. Listen, take notes, ask questions, and be able to make their case as well as they can even though you don't agree. Pick something in their argument you agree with. Present your argument in terms of the problem only—why you think this is the best manner to deal with a mutually agreed-upon problem.

6. **You may be highly intelligent and quite skilled in your area.** You may work around people who aren't as informed or educated as you are. You may be in a position of essentially dictating what should be done. But you don't have to make it demeaning or painful. You need to switch to a teacher/guru role—tell them how you think about an issue, don't just fire out solutions. Tell them what you think the problem is, what questions need to be asked and answered, how you would go about finding out, and what you think some likely solutions might be. Work to pass on your knowledge and skills.

B Improving Team Building

INTJs usually lack interest in the messiness and time-consuming nature of teams. They may ignore the need and value of teams. They often have a huge vision that they can't externalize fast enough and teams get in the way.

1. **Don't believe in teams.** If you don't believe in teams, you are probably a strong individual achiever who doesn't like the mess and sometimes the slowness of due-process relationships and team processes. You are very results oriented and truly believe the best way to do that is to manage one person at a time. To balance this thinking, observe and talk with three excellent team builders and ask them why they manage that way. What do they consider rewarding about building teams? What advantages do they get from using the team format? Read *The Wisdom of Teams* by Katzenbach and Smith. If you can't see the value in teams, none of the following tips will help much.

2. **Don't have the time; teaming takes longer.** That's true and not true. While building a team takes longer than managing one person at a time, having a well-functioning team increases results, builds in a sustaining capability to perform, maximizes collective strengths and covers individual weaknesses, and actually releases more time for the manager because the team members help each other. Many managers

get caught in the trap of thinking it takes up too much time to build a team and end up taking more time managing one-on-one.

3. **Not a people person?** Many managers are better with things, ideas, and projects than they are with people. They may be driven and very focused on producing results and have little time left to develop their people skills. It really doesn't take too much. There is communicating. People are more motivated and do better work when they know what's going on. They want to know more than just their little piece. There is listening. Nothing motivates more than a boss who will listen, not interrupt, not finish your sentences, and not complete your thoughts. Increase your listening time 30 seconds in each transaction. There is caring. Caring is questions. Caring is asking about me and what I think and what I feel. Ask one more question per transaction than you do now.

4. **Would like to build a team but don't know how.** High performance teams have four common characteristics: (1) They have a shared mind-set. They have a common vision. Everyone knows the goals and measures. (2) They trust one another. They know "you will cover me if I get in trouble." They know you will pitch in and help even though it may be difficult for you. They know you will be honest with them. They know you will bring problems to them directly and won't go behind their backs. (3) They have the talent collectively to do the job. While not any one member may have it all, collectively they have every task covered. (4) They know how to operate efficiently and effectively. They have good team skills. They run effective meetings. They have efficient ways to communicate. They have ways to deal with internal conflict.

5. **Can't seem to get people motivated to be a team.** Follow the basic rules of inspiring others as outlined in classic books like *People Skills* by Robert Bolton or *Thriving on Chaos* by Tom Peters. Communicate to people that what they do is important. Say thanks. Offer help and ask for it. Provide autonomy in how people do their work. Provide a variety of tasks. "Surprise" people with enriching, challenging assignments. Show an interest in their careers. Adopt a learning attitude toward mistakes. Celebrate successes, have visible accepted measures of achievement, and so on. Try to get everyone to participate in the building of the team so they have a stake in the outcome.

6. **Cement relationships.** Even though some—maybe including you—will resist it, parties, roasts, gag awards, picnics, and outings help build group cohesion. Allow roles to evolve naturally rather than

being specified by job descriptions. Some research indicates that people gravitate naturally to eight roles, and that successful teams are not those where everyone does the same thing. Successful teams specialize, cover for each other, and only sometimes demand that everyone participate in identical activities.

7. **Not good at motivating people beyond being results oriented?** Play the motivation odds. According to research by Rewick and Lawler, the top motivators at work are: (1) Job challenge; (2) Accomplishing something worthwhile; (3) Learning new things; (4) Personal development; and (5) Autonomy. Pay (12th), Friendliness (14th), Praise (15th), or Chance of Promotion (17th) are not insignificant but are superficial compared with the five top motivators. Provide challenges, paint pictures of why this is worthwhile, set up chances to learn and grow, and provide autonomy, and you'll hit the vast majority of people's hot buttons.

8. **Use goals to motivate.** Most people are turned on by reasonable goals. They like to measure themselves against a standard. They like to see who can run the fastest, score the most, and work the best. They like goals to be realistic but stretching. People try hardest when they have somewhere between one-half and two-thirds chance of success and some control over how they go about it. People are even more motivated when they participate in setting the goals. Set just-out-of-reach challenges and tasks that will be first time for people—their first negotiation, their first solo presentation, etc.

C Developing Others

INTJs would rather do it themselves, are typically in a hurry to do so, and can overmanage.

1. **How to delegate?** Communicate, set time frames and goals, and get out of the way. People need to know what it is you expect. What does the outcome look like? When do you need it by? What's the budget? What resources do they get? What decisions can they make? Do you want checkpoints along the way? How will we both know and measure how well the task is done? One of the most common problems with delegation is incomplete or cryptic up-front communication leading to frustration, a job not well done the first time, rework, and a reluctance to delegate next time. Poor communicators always have to take more time managing because of rework. Analyze recent projects that went well and didn't go well.

How did you delegate? Too much? Not enough? Unwanted pieces? Major chunks of responsibility? Workload distributed properly? Did you set measures? Overmanage or abdicate? Find out what your best practices are. Set up a series of delegation practices that can be used as if you're not there. What do you have to be informed of? What feedback loops can people use for midcourse correction? What questions should be answered as the work proceeds? What steps should be followed? What are the criteria to be followed? When will you be available to help?

2. **More what and why, less how.** The best delegators are crystal clear on what and when, and more open on how. People are more motivated when they can determine the how for themselves. Inexperienced delegators include the hows, which turn the people into task automatons instead of an empowered and energized staff. Tell them what and when and for how long, and let them figure out how on their own. Give them leeway. Encourage them to try things. Besides being more motivating, it's also more developmental for them. Add the larger context. Although it is not necessary to get the task done, people are more motivated when they know where this task fits in the bigger picture. Take three extra minutes and tell them why this task needs to be done, where it fits in the grander scheme, and its importance to the goals and objectives of the unit.

3. **Monitoring delegated tasks.** Do you micromanage? If you're constantly looking over shoulders, you're not delegating. A properly communicated and delegated task doesn't need to be monitored. If you must monitor, set time-definite checkpoints: by the calendar, every Monday, by percentage, after each 10% is complete, or by outcome—such as when you have the first draft. Be approachable for help, but not intrusive. Intervene only when agreed-upon criteria are not being followed or expectations are not being met. This focuses on the task, not the person. Let people finish their work.

4. **Delegate for development.** Brainstorm with your direct reports all the tasks that aren't being done but are important to do. Ask them for a list of tasks that are no longer challenging for them. (You can also use parts of your own job to develop others. Take three tasks that are no longer developmental for you, but would be for others, and delegate them.) Trade tasks and assignments between two direct reports; have them do each other's work. Assign each of your direct reports an out-of-comfort-zone task that meets the following criteria: The task needs to be done, the person hasn't done it or isn't good at it,

and the task calls for a skill the person needs to develop. Remember to focus on varied assignments—more of the same isn't developmental.

5. **Remember, meaningful development is not the stress-reduction business.** It is not cozy or safe; it comes from varied, stressful, even adverse tasks that require we learn to do something new or different, or fail. Real development involves real work the person largely hasn't done before. Real development is rewarding but scary. Be open with your people about this. Everyone won't want to be developed in new areas. Some are satisfied to do what they do, even if it limits their career options. While you should advise them of the consequences, all organizations need strong performers dedicated to skill building in their current area only. Don't imply that a pure tactician must become a strategist to be valued. Instead, create more ways for people to excel and get status recognition. For most of us this is a powerful need—some studies show that people in prestigious jobs are less likely to get seriously ill, regardless of their personal habits. If a person wants to be a customer service representative for life, recognize that as critical, and help the person develop in every way possible within that area—coaching, training, and networking with other experts.

D Understanding Others

INTJs often miss, or make note of but ignore, the passions of people—their affiliations and needs. They may consider them a drag in implementing their vision.

1. **Learn to be a cultural anthropologist.** In assessing groups, ask yourself: What makes their blood boil? What do they believe? What are they trying to accomplish together? What do they smile at? What norms and customs do they have? What practices and behaviors do they share? Do they not like it if you stand too close? If you get right down to business? Do they like first names or are they more formal? If a Japanese manager presents his card, do you know what to do? Why do they have their cards printed in two languages and executives from the U.S. don't? Do you know what jokes are okay to tell? What do they believe about you and your group or groups? Positive? Neutral? Negative? What's been the history of their group and yours? Is this a first contact or a long history? Don't blunder in; nothing will kill you quicker with a group than showing utter disregard—read disrespect—for it and its norms, or having no idea of how they view your group. Ask people for insights who deal with this group often. If it's an important group to you and your business, read about it.

2. **Working with groups.** To deal effectively with groups, establish reciprocity. Relationships don't last unless you provide something and so do they. Find out what they want and tell them what you want. Strike a bargain. If one group usually gets the benefit, the other group will eventually become uncooperative and balky. Learn their conceptual categories. People who went on to become successful executives often spoke of their first time dealing with another function. The most common tack for a marketing person dealing with finance for the first time was to show them something he/she was working on and ask them how they would analyze it. What questions would they ask? What were the key numbers and why? What were the four or five key factors they were looking at? Be able to speak their language. Speaking their language shows respect and makes it easier for them to talk with you. Tell them your conceptual categories. To deal with you, they also need to know how you think and why. Tell them your perspective—the questions you ask, the factors you're interested in. If you can't explain your thinking, they won't know how to deal with you effectively.

3. **Stereotypes?** You have to understand your own subtle stereotyping. Helen Astin's research showed that both men and women rated women managers at the extremes (very high or very low) while they rated men on a normal curve. Do you think redheads have tempers? Blondes have more fun? Overweight people are lazy? Women are more emotional at work? Men can't show emotion? Find out your own pattern. Attend a course which delves into perception of others. Most stereotyping is false. Even if there are surface differences, they don't make a difference in performance.

E Curbing Arrogance

INTJs can easily come across as know-it-alls. They often know themselves well, but neither seek nor get the feedback necessary for growth and improved relationships.

1. **Arrogance is a major blockage to building self-knowledge.** Research says that successful people know themselves better. Many people who have a towering strength or lots of success get less feedback and roll along thinking they are perfect until their careers get in trouble. If you are viewed as arrogant, your best chance of understanding it is to get facilitated 360° feedback where the respondents can remain anonymous. It is unlikely you could get useful data from people directly since they don't think you listen, and it has been painful in the past to try to influence you. Arrogant people typically overrate

themselves. Their ratings from others may be lower than they should be because people believe they need to make it look worse than it is to get through your defiance shield. If you are seen as devaluing others, they will return the favor.

2. **There are two possibilities.** You are really talented and near perfect and people just have had a hard time getting used to you mostly being right, or you're not perfect but you act as if you are. If you are in fact really, really bright and successful and knowledgeable and right most of the time, you have to stop making people feel bad and rejected because of your special gifts. If you're not almost perfect, there is no reason to act as if you are. In either case, you have to work on being more behaviorally open and approachable and help people deal with you comfortably.

3. **You may view feedback as information,** but this can come across that you just don't care and can increase perceptions of aloofness. Make sure to say thank you for the feedback. Because you may be seen as quite powerful and having high standards, if you don't say thank you or find something to praise or verify in the feedback, you can be seen as indifferent or dismissive.

4. **Although INTJs are rarely defensive,** they can be if the feedback comes when they are upset about performance or slowness. You will need to work on keeping yourself in a calm state when getting negative feedback. You need to change your thinking. When getting the feedback, your only task is to accurately understand what people are trying to tell you. It is not your task at that point to accept or reject. That comes later. Mentally rehearse how you will calmly react to tough feedback situations before they happen. Develop automatic tactics to shut down or delay your usual emotional response. Some useful tactics are to slow down, take notes, ask clarifying questions, ask them for concrete examples, and thank them for telling you since you know it's not easy for them.

5. **Do you value feedback only from those you feel have the experience and expertise to offer it?** If someone points out that you could be somewhat more accommodating, is your reaction to whom, for what purpose, and will that move us toward the goal? Go to the people you respect most and get their feedback on your pluses and minuses. Then think about what modifications in your behavior would help you push your vision through more effectively.

6. **Watch your non-verbals.** Arrogant people look, talk, and act arrogantly. As you try to become less arrogant, you need to find out what your non-verbals are. All arrogant people do a series of things that can be viewed by a neutral party and judged to give off the signals of arrogance. Washboard brow. Facial expressions. Body shifting, especially turning away. Impatient finger or pencil tapping. False smile. Tight lips. Looking away. Find out from a trusted friend what you do, and try to eliminate those behaviors.

7. **Answers. Solutions. Conclusions. Statements. Dictates.** That's the staple of arrogant people. Instant output. Sharp reactions. This may be getting you in trouble. You jump to conclusions, categorically dismiss what others say, use challenging words in an absolute tone. People then see you as closed to their input or combative. More negatively, they may believe you think they're stupid or ill-informed. Give people a chance to talk without interruption. If you're seen as intolerant or closed, people will often stumble over words in their haste to talk with you or shortcut their argument since they assume you're not listening anyway. Ask a question, invite them to disagree with you, present their argument back to them softly, let them save face no matter what. Add a 15-second pause into your transactions before you say anything, and add two clarifying questions per transaction to signal you're listening and want to understand.

8. **Read your audience.** Do you know what people look like when they are uncomfortable with your arrogance? Do they back up? Frown? Flush? Shut down? Cringe? Stand at the door hoping not to get invited in? You should work doubly hard at observing others. Especially during the first three minutes of an important transaction, work to make one person or group comfortable with you before the agenda starts. Ask a question unrelated to the topic. Offer them a drink. Tell them something you did last weekend that you found interesting.

9. **Arrogant people keep their distance** and don't share much personal data. You may believe you shouldn't mix personal with business. You may believe it's wise to keep distance between you and others you work around and with. Since it's hard for others to relate to an arrogant person in the first place, your reputation may be based on only short, unsatisfactory transactions. The kinds of disclosures people enjoy are: the reasons behind why you do and decide what you do; your self-appraisal; things you know behind what's happening in the business that they don't know—that you are at liberty to disclose; things both good and embarrassing that have

happened to you in the past; comments about what's going on around you—without being too negative about others; and things you are interested in and do outside of work. These are areas which you should learn to disclose more than you now do.

F Better Relationships With Higher Management

INTJs have a rebellious streak and can go after those in power in unproductive ways, confronting the wrong people at the wrong time.

1. **Consider who bothers you.** If only certain higher-ups bother you and others don't, take a piece of paper and list the styles of the two groups/individuals. What are the similarities? Why does one style bother you and the other doesn't? With the groups/individuals that bother you, how could you respond more comfortably and effectively? Perhaps you could use some of the techniques you use with the more comfortable groups. Probably you should prime yourself to take nothing in personal terms and, no matter what happens, return to a discussion of the problem.

2. **Get to know more top managers.** Try to meet and interact with higher-ups in informal settings like receptions, social or athletic events, charity events, off-sites, etc. You will probably learn that higher-ups are just regular people who are older and therefore higher than you in the hierarchy. You may then feel more comfortable with them when back in the work setting.

3. **Find out how top managers think.** Read the biographies of five "great" people; see what is said about them and their views of people like you. Read five autobiographies and see what they said about themselves and how they viewed people in your position. Write down five things you can do differently or better.

4. **Be ready for Q&A.** Many people get in trouble during questions and answers. Don't fake answers; most high-level managers will tolerate a "Don't know but I'll get back to you on that." Think of all the questions ahead of time; ask someone else to look at what you are going to say and do and to think of questions they would ask. Rehearse the answers to the questions. Another place people get in trouble when challenged is by retreating to a safe recitation of facts; executives are usually asking for logic and problem analysis, not a repackaging of what you've already said. The worst case, of course, is when an executive rejects your argument. If this happens, draw the person out to see if you've been misunderstood and clarify. If that's

not the case, let the disagreement be as it is. Few executives respect someone who drops an argument as soon as challenged. You should listen carefully and respond with logic in 30 seconds or less per point. Don't repeat the entire argument; long answers often backfire since people have already heard it and few may agree with the questioner. In haste to be thorough, you may just look defensive.

5. **Quit arguing.** Most of the time, you may be delivering someone else's view of the future. Top management and a consultant created the mission, vision, and strategy off somewhere in the woods all by themselves. You may or may not have been asked for any input. You may even have some doubts about it yourself. Your role is to manage this vision and mission, not your personal one. Do not offer conditional statements to your audience: "I've got some concerns myself." Don't let it be known to others that you are not fully on board. Your job is to deliver and manage the message. While it's okay to admit your problems in dealing with change, it's not okay to admit them in dealing with this change. If you have better ideas, try to get them to the people who form missions in your organization.

I overdo concepts and do not pay enough attention to data, leading to judgments that are too quick. I need to be more inclusive of others and show appreciation.

– An INTJ Manager

■ ■ ■ ■ ■ ■ ■ ■ ■ ■ ■ ■ ■ ■ ■

APPLICATION

Your personal preferences play out in day-to-day problems and situations you face. Below is a case about your type dealing with such a situation. Use this to think through how you will integrate the tips you've considered and coach yourself to be more effective in your type.

INTJ Application Situation (Part 1)

You're a product manager preparing for a meeting tomorrow with your organization's executive team (CEO, COO, CFO, CTO, EVP-Marketing) to review a proposal you've submitted for a new line of business. Your boss, the VP of your business unit, has just come into your office to "give you some coaching." In brief, he's told you that he expects you to be the meeting leader, not merely the content expert, and to not only facilitate a discussion but impose your will. He's also prepared you to understand that he is going to take an aggressive contrary position to what he anticipates will be the senior leaders' position on pricing for the new line, and he expects your support. As he leaves your office, he says, "Remember, be forceful, take control."

During the afternoon, while you're putting your thoughts together and preparing a few PowerPoint slides to frame the discussion, you get a phone call from a salesperson at a software development company who, coincidentally, wants to talk with you about selling your company a software system. The system is in almost all key respects very much like the one at the heart of your new line of business, which you have all along anticipated having to build in-house with resources that have, in the past, been less than fully reliable.

After you get off the phone with the salesperson, you do some initial cost-benefit comparisons to inform the make vs. buy decision you're now contemplating. Energized by this new possibility, you start revising the presentation you're going to use tomorrow to frame your discussion with the executive team. You can already anticipate how impressed they're going to be with your new approach.

Thinking It Through: Strategy

- What are you trying to accomplish?

- What do you need to be concerned about?

Planning It Out: Tactics

- What are your goals and objectives?

- What potential barriers to your effectiveness (i.e., actions, behaviors) are inherent in this situation based on your personality type (INTJ)?

- What particular areas would present developmental challenges to you, and what competencies would you want to put into play in order not only to accomplish your objectives but assure that relationships are preserved?

- Which of the tactics described in the Being More Effective section are applicable in this situation?

- Which Overused Tendencies are most likely to come into play here?

INTJ Application Situation (Part 2)

You arrive at the meeting on time, everyone is there, and the CTO is already at the head of the table, at the flip chart, explaining how he's going to deploy his team of programmers on your project.

- As an INTJ, what do you need to guard against, and what competencies do you need to put into play to adjust to this situation and get a win-win outcome?

- Whose interests do you need to consider, and how will you address those while still asserting your own goals and rationale?

Reflection

- Given the situation narrated above, what would you have done between Part 1 and Part 2 that wasn't included in the narration?

- What do you think are the advantages of being an INTJ in such a situation?

- What are the potential liabilities?

SUGGESTED READINGS

■■■■■■■■ Being a More Effective INTJ ■■■■■■■■

Handling Disagreements

Cloke, Ken and Joan Goldsmith. *Resolving Conflicts at Work: A Complete Guide for Everyone on the Job.* San Francisco: Jossey-Bass, Inc., 2000.

Dana, Daniel. *Conflict Resolution.* New York: McGraw-Hill Trade, 2000.

Graham, Gini. *A Survival Guide for Working With Humans: Dealing With Whiners, Back-Stabbers, Know-It-Alls, and Other Difficult People.* New York: AMACOM, 2004.

Guttman, Howard M. *When Goliaths Clash: Managing Executive Conflict to Build a More Dynamic Organization.* New York: AMACOM, 2003.

Levin, Robert A. and Joseph G. Rosse. *Talent Flow: A Strategic Approach to Keeping Good Employees, Helping Them Grow, and Letting Them Go.* New York: John Wiley & Sons, Inc., 2001.

Masters, Marick Francis and Robert R. Albright. *The Complete Guide to Conflict Resolution in the Workplace.* New York: AMACOM, 2002.

Solomon, Muriel. *Working With Difficult People.* New York: Prentice Hall, 2002.

Informing

Arredondo, Lani. *Communicating Effectively.* New York: McGraw-Hill Trade, 2000.

Keyton, Joann. *Communicating in Groups: Building Relationships for Effective Decision Making.* New York: WCB/McGraw-Hill, 2002.

McCormack, Mark H. *On Communicating.* Los Angeles: Dove Books, 1998.

Zeuschner, Raymond F. *Communicating Today: The Essentials.* Boston: Allyn & Bacon, 2002.

Patience

Barker, Larry, Ph.D. and Kittie Watson, Ph.D. *Listen Up: At Home, at Work, in Relationships: How to Harness the Power of Effective Listening.* Irvine, CA: Griffin Trade Paperback, 2001.

Bolton, Robert and Dorothy Grover Bolton. *People Styles at Work—Making Bad Relationships Good and Good Relationships Better.* New York: AMACOM, 1996.

Burley-Allen, Madelyn. *Listening: The Forgotten Skill.* New York: John Wiley & Sons, Inc., 1995.

Gonthier, Giovinella and Kevin Morrissey. *Rude Awakenings: Overcoming the Civility Crisis in the Workplace.* Chicago: Dearborn Trade Publishing, 2002.

Ryan, Mary Jane. *The Power of Patience: How to Slow the Rush and Enjoy More Happiness, Success, and Peace of Mind Everyday.* New York: Broadway Press, 2003.

Interpersonal Savvy

Autry, James A. *The Art of Caring Leadership.* New York: William Morrow and Company, Inc., 1991.

Benton, D.A. *Executive Charisma: Six Steps to Mastering the Art of Leadership.* New York: McGraw-Hill Trade, 2003.

Bolton, Robert and Dorothy Grover Bolton. *People Styles at Work—Making Bad Relationships Good and Good Relationships Better.* New York: AMACOM, 1996.

Brooks, Michael. *Instant Rapport.* New York: Warner Books, 1989.

Kouzes, James M. and Barry Z. Posner. *Encouraging the Heart: A Leader's Guide to Rewarding and Recognizing Others.* San Francisco: Jossey-Bass, Inc., 2003.

Maxwell, John C. *Relationships 101.* London: Thomas Nelson, 2004.

Silberman, Melvin L. and Freda Hansburg. *Peoplesmart: Developing Your Interpersonal Intelligence.* San Francisco: Berrett-Koehler Publishers, Inc., 2000.

Boss Relationships

Carson, Kerry, Ph.D. and Paula Phillips Carson, Ph.D. *Defective Bosses—Working for the Dysfunctional Dozen.* New York: The Haworth Press, 1998.

Charan, Ram. *What the CEO Wants You to Know: How Your Company Really Works.* New York: Crown Business Publishing, 2001.

Dobson, Michael Singer. *Managing Up! 59 Ways to Build a Career-Advancing Relationship With Your Boss.* New York: AMACOM, 2000.

Dominguez, Linda R. *How to Shine at Work.* New York: McGraw-Hill Trade, 2003.

Jay, Ros. *How to Manage Your Boss: Developing the Perfect Working Relationship.* London: Financial Times Management, 2002.

Dislike of Standard Operating Procedures

Bossidy, Larry, Ram Charan and Charles Burck (Contributor). *Execution: The Discipline of Getting Things Done.* New York: Crown Business Publishing, 2002.

Keen, Peter G.W. *The Process Edge—Creating Value Where It Counts.* Boston: Harvard Business School Press, 1998.

Lawler, Edward E., III, Susan Albers Mohrman and George Benson. *Organizing for High Performance: Employee Involvement, TQM, Reengineering, and Knowledge Management in the Fortune 1000: The CEO Report.* San Francisco: Jossey-Bass, Inc., 2001.

Niven, P.R. *Balanced Scorecard Step-by-Step: Maximizing Performance and Maintaining Results.* New York: John Wiley & Sons, Inc., 2002.

■■■■■■■ Overusing INTJ Tendencies ■■■■■■■

Not Jumping to Conclusions

Flynn, Daniel J. *Intellectual Morons: How Ideology Makes Smart People Fall for Stupid Ideas.* New York: Crown Business Publishing, 2004.

Hammond, John S., Ralph L. Keeney and Howard Raiffer. *Smart Choices.* Boston: Harvard University Press, 1999.

Nutt, Paul C. *Why Decisions Fail: Avoiding the Blunders and Traps That Lead to Decision Debacles.* San Francisco: Berrett-Koehler Publishers, Inc., 2002.

Sofo, Francesco. *Six Myths of Critical Thinking.* Business & Professional Publishing, 2003.

Sternberg, Robert J. *Thinking Styles.* Boston: Cambridge University Press, 1997.

Yates, J. Frank. *Decision Management: How to Assure Better Decisions in Your Company.* San Francisco: Jossey-Bass, Inc., 2003.

Improving Team Building

Bolton, Robert. *People Skills.* New York: Simon & Schuster, 1979.

Fisher, Kimball and Mareen Duncan Fisher. *The Distance Manager: A Hands-On Guide to Managing Off-Site Employees and Virtual Teams.* New York: McGraw-Hill Trade, 2000.

Genett, Donna M. *If You Want It Done Right, You Don't Have to Do It Yourself! The Power of Effective Delegation.* Sanger, CA: Quill Driver Books, 2004.

Harvard Business School Press. *Harvard Business Review on Teams That Succeed.* Boston: Harvard Business School Press, 2004.

Katzenbach, Jon R. and Douglas K. Smith. *The Wisdom of Teams: Creating the High-Performance Organization.* New York: HarperBusiness, 2003.

Parker, Glenn M. *Cross-Functional Teams: Working With Allies, Enemies, and Other Strangers.* San Francisco: Jossey-Bass, Inc., 2002.

Peters, Tom. *Thriving on Chaos: Handbook for a Management Revolution.* New York: HarperCollins, 1987.

Raymond, Cara Capretta, Robert W. Eichinger and Michael M. Lombardo. *FYI for Teams.* Minneapolis, MN: Lominger Limited, Inc., 2001–2004.

Robbins, Harvey and Michael Finley. *The New Why Teams Don't Work— What Goes Wrong and How to Make It Right.* San Francisco: Berrett-Koehler Publishers, Inc., 2000.

Developing Others

Charan, Ram, James L. Noel and Steve Drotter. *The Leadership Pipeline: How to Build the Leadership Powered Company.* New York: John Wiley & Sons, Inc., 2000.

Daniels, Aubrey C. *Bringing Out the Best in People.* New York: McGraw-Hill, Inc., 1994.

Fulmer, Robert M. and Jay A. Conger. *Growing Your Company's Leaders.* New York: AMACOM, 2004.

Lombardo, Michael M. and Robert W. Eichinger. *The Leadership Machine.* Minneapolis, MN: Lominger Limited, Inc., 2004.

Understanding Others

Ashkenas, Ronald N. (Ed.), Dave Ulrich, Todd Jick, Steve Kerr and Lawrence A. Bossidy. *The Boundaryless Organization: Breaking the Chains of Organization Structure, Revised and Updated.* New York: John Wiley & Sons, Inc., 2002.

Belbin, R. Meredith. *Management Teams.* Boston: Butterworth-Heinemann, 2004.

Bolton, Robert and Dorothy Grover Bolton. *People Styles at Work—Making Bad Relationships Good and Good Relationships Better.* New York: AMACOM, 1996.

Crainer, Stuart. *Motivating the New Generation—Modern Motivation Techniques.* New York: BrownHerron Publishing, 2001.

Deems, Richard S. and Terri A. Deems. *Leading in Tough Times: The Manager's Guide to Responsibility, Trust, and Motivation.* Amherst, MA: HRD Press, 2003.

Glanz, Barbara A. *Handle With CARE: Motivating and Retaining Employees.* New York: McGraw-Hill Trade, 2002.

Curbing Arrogance

Bolton, Robert and Dorothy Grover Bolton. *People Styles at Work—Making Bad Relationships Good and Good Relationships Better.* New York: AMACOM, 1996.

Carter, Les. *The Anger Trap: Free Yourself From the Frustrations That Sabotage Your Life.* New York: John Wiley & Sons, Inc., 2003.

Ellis, Albert, Ph.D. *How to Control Your Anxiety Before It Controls You.* New York: Citadel Press, 2000.

Waldroop, James, Ph.D. and Timothy Butler, Ph.D. *Maximum Success: Changing the 12 Behavior Patterns That Keep You From Getting Ahead.* New York: Doubleday, 2000.

Better Relationships With Higher Management

Bolton, Robert and Dorothy Grover Bolton. *People Styles at Work—Making Bad Relationships Good and Good Relationships Better.* New York: AMACOM, 1996.

Chaleff, Ira. *The Courageous Follower: Standing Up to and for Our Leaders.* San Francisco: Berrett-Koehler Publishers, Inc., 2003.

Charan, Ram. *What the CEO Wants You to Know: How Your Company Really Works.* New York: Crown Business Publishing, 2001.

Gittines, Roger and Rosanne Badowski. *Managing Up: How to Forge an Effective Relationship With Those Above You.* New York: Currency, 2003.

Guttman, Howard M. *When Goliaths Clash: Managing Executive Conflict to Build a More Dynamic Organization.* New York: AMACOM, 2003.

CHAPTER 5

ISTP
Introverted Thinking
with
Extraverted Sensing

■■■■■■■■■■■■■■■■■

5.4% of Population
3.4% of Managers

■■■■■■■■■■■■■■■■■

Typical Strengths

Independent
Effective Troubleshooters
Enjoy Challenge
Know How and Why Things Work
Using Tools and Instruments
Solving Concrete Problems
Very Action Oriented

ISTJ	ISFJ	INFJ	INTJ
ISTP	ISFP	INFP	INTP
ESTP	ESFP	ENFP	ENTP
ESTJ	ESFJ	ENFJ	ENTJ

I simply don't let emotions get in the way.

– An ISTP Manager

Basic Habits of Mind

Introverted Thinking leads ISTPs to be decisive, concerned with precision and exactness. It further pulls them toward being reflective, skeptical, and analytical. Aided by Extraverted Sensing, which provides an acute awareness of the present situation, their thinking is adaptable as long as logical order can be made out of the situation.

Extraverted Intuiting and Extraverted Feeling also aid ISTPs. External Intuiting leads to scanning the environment, and the external direction of Feeling means they communicate intensity. In fact, the "mission" for this type is for precision and analytical elegance in hands-on problem solving. This can also come off as condescending, aloof, and unforgiving.

Typical Communication Patterns

- ISTPs appear reflective, but when engaged they are quick on their feet, quite ingenious, and realistic in their remarks.

- Seen as good-natured.

- They know the who, what, where, and when of situations.

- They are often people of few words, except in their areas of interest.

General Learning Strategy

- ISTPs typically learn by actively "doing" and experimenting with ideas.

- Typical learning strategies employed are demonstrations of ideas, analyzing in the moment, creating structure and order, and adapting the current best model.

- Their learning is usually helped by structure, variety of tasks, and clearly stated competency goals.

Interpersonal Qualities Related to Motivation

■ Motivated by dealing with practical concerns.

■ ISTPs want to get things done that are within their experience and frameworks.

■ They enjoy analyzing their world and enjoy talking about how to get a specific outcome.

■ Tangible goals get their "juices moving."

Blind Spots

■ ISTPs might be surprised to know that they are sometimes seen as blunt, detached, guarded, impersonal, and low on demonstrated empathy.

■ While they think of themselves as able to competently maneuver social settings, their social behavior often fails to make the impression they imagined was true. For example, they selectively include others and engage animatedly on selected topics. They talk about these topics whether anyone else is interested or not. They can get distant if the conversation gets out of their area of expertise.

Stress Related Behavior

■ ISTPs typically become silent for long periods of time during stress. When they do speak up, their critical, analytical, logical expressions can become increasingly intense.

■ As stress increases, they often seem restless and nonconforming.

■ After an extended stressful period, they might become unusually sensitive to people's verbal and non-verbal behavior, seeing rejection and disregard in the simplest of events.

Potential Barriers to Effectiveness

■ Making strategic transitions during organizational change is seen as a potential barrier to effectiveness for ISTPs.

■ In addition, in environments where change is frequent, they may discover their logical, critical comments are seen as disagreeing with upper management. They come across as just critical and not trying to improve the situation when, in fact, they are.

- They like to change things, are natural-born troubleshooters, but usually don't care to implement others' changes.

- ISTPs usually spend little energy on the vagaries of people or interpersonal conflict.

- At times, they can be seen as rigid and unapproachable. They insist on precision and immediate attention to priorities. This sets them up to be seen as unable to see the big picture and hard to influence.

Being a More Effective ISTP

A Being More Flexible
B Being More Engaging
C Being More Reflective Problem Solvers
D Boss and Peer Relationships
E Seeing the Bigger Picture
F Dislike of Routine and Procedures

ISTJ	ISFJ	INFJ	INTJ
ISTP	ISFP	INFP	INTP
ESTP	ESFP	ENFP	ENTP
ESTJ	ESFJ	ENFJ	ENTJ

A Being More Flexible

ISTPs typically do not like ambiguous situations or those that call for changing behavior rapidly. They like to move in a straightforward, linear fashion through problems and dispose of them.

1. **Making transitions.** Which transitions are the toughest for you? Write down the five toughest for you. What do you have a hard time switching to and from? Use this knowledge to assist you in making a list of discontinuities (tough transitions) you face, such as confronting people vs. being approachable and accepting, leading vs. following, going from firing someone to a business-as-usual staff meeting. Write down how each of these discontinuities makes you feel and what you may do that gets you in trouble. For example, you may not shift gears well after a confrontation, or you may have trouble taking charge again after passively sitting in a meeting all day. Create a plan to attack each of the tough transitions.

2. **Go for more variety at work.** Take a risk, then play it safe. Set tasks for yourself that force you to shift gears, such as being a spokesperson for your organization when tough questions are expected, making peace with an enemy, or managing people who are novices at a task.

If you already have these tasks as part of your job, use them to observe yourself and try new behaviors.

3. **Use mental rehearsal to think about different ways you could carry out a transaction.** Try to see yourself acting in opposing ways to get the same thing done—when to be tough, when to let them decide, when to deflect the issue because it's not ready to decide. What cues would you look for to select an approach that matches? Practice trying to get the same thing done with two different groups with two different approaches. Did they both work?

4. **Incrementalism.** The essence of dealing comfortably with uncertainty is the tolerance of errors and mistakes, and absorbing the possible heat and criticism that follow. Acting on an ill-defined problem with no precedents to follow means shooting in the dark with as informed a decision as you can make at the time. People who are good at this are incrementalists. They make a series of smaller decisions, get instant feedback, correct the course, get a little more data, move forward a little more, until the bigger problem is under control. They don't try to get it right the first time. Many problem-solving studies show that the second or third try is when we really understand the underlying dynamics of problems. They also know that the more uncertain the situation is, the more likely it is they will make mistakes in the beginning. So, you need to work on two practices: Start small so you can recover more quickly. Do little somethings as soon as you can and get used to heat.

5. **Perfectionist?** Need or prefer or want to be 100% sure? Lots might prefer that. Perfectionism is tough to let go of because most people see it as a positive trait for themselves. Recognize your perfectionism for what it might be—collecting more information than others to improve your confidence in making a fault-free decision and thereby avoiding risk and criticism. Try to decrease your need for data and your need to be right all the time slightly every week until you reach a more reasonable balance between thinking it through and taking action. Try making some small decisions on little or no data. Anyone with a brain and 100% of the data can make good decisions. The real test is who can act the soonest with a reasonable amount, but not all, of the data. Some studies suggest successful general managers are about 65% correct. Trust your intuition. Let your brain do the calculations.

6. **Finishing.** Do you prefer to finish what you have started? Do you have a high need to complete tasks? Wrap them up in nice clean packages? Working well with ambiguity and under uncertainty

means moving from incomplete task to incomplete task. Some may be abandoned, some may never be finished. They'll probably only ever get 80% done, and you'll constantly have to edit your actions and decisions. Change your internal reward process toward feeling good about fixing mistakes and moving things forward incrementally, more than finishing any given project.

B Being More Engaging

ISTPs usually spend little time considering other people or what they want or need. They like activities and dislike talking about people or emotional states. They can particularly have problems with people who are more theoretical, like to talk about action more than doing, avoid risk, or just like to follow standard operating procedures.

1. **You start.** Being approachable means you have to initiate the transaction. You have to put out your hand first. Make first eye contact. Note the color of the person's eyes to ensure good eye contact. You have to ask the first question or share the first piece of information. You have to make the first three minutes comfortable for the other person or group so they can accomplish what they came to you to do.

2. **Listen.** Approachable people are very good at listening. They listen without interrupting. They ask clarifying questions. They don't instantly judge. They listen to understand. Judgment may come later. They restate what the other person has said to signal understanding. They nod. They may jot down notes. Listeners don't always offer advice or solutions unless it's obvious the person wants to know what they would do.

3. **Do people confuse you?** You may be a fact-based person. Since to you the facts dictate everything, you may be baffled as to why people would see it any differently than you do. The reason they see it differently is that there is a higher order of values at work. People compare across situations to check for common themes, equity, and parity. They ask questions like who wins and loses here, who is being favored, is this a play for advantage? Since you are a here-and-now person, you will look inconsistent to them across slightly different situations. You need to drop back and ask what will others hear, not what you want to say. Go below the surface. Tell them why you're saying something. Ask them what they think.

4. **Customer focus.** People who are good at this work from the outside (the customer, the audience, the person, the situation) in, not from the inside out. ("What do I want to do in this situation; what would make me happy and feel good?") Practice not thinking inside/out when you are around others. What are the demand characteristics of this situation? How does this person or audience best learn? Which of my approaches or styles would work best? How can I best accomplish my goals? How can I alter my approach and tactics to be the most effective? The one-trick pony can only perform once per show. If the audience doesn't like that particular trick, no oats for the pony.

5. **Personalizing.** Approachable people work to know and remember important things about the people they work around, for, and with. Know three things about everybody—their interests or their children or something you can chat about other than the business agenda. Treat life as a small world. If you ask a few questions, you'll find you have something in common with virtually anyone. Establish things you can talk about with each person you work with that go beyond strictly work transactions. These need not be social—they could be issues of strategy, global events, market shifts. The point is to forge common ground and connections.

6. **Watch your non-verbals.** Approachable people appear and sound open and relaxed. They smile. They are calm. They keep eye contact. They nod while the other person is talking. They have an open body posture. They speak in a paced and pleasant tone. Eliminate any disruptive habits, such as speaking too rapidly or forcefully, using strongly worded or loaded language, or going into too much detail. Watch out for signaling disinterest with actions like glancing at your watch, fiddling with paperwork, or giving your impatient "I'm busy" look.

7. **The magic of questions.** Many people don't ask enough curiosity questions when in their work mode. There are too many informational statements, conclusions, suggestions, and solutions and not enough "what if," "what are you thinking," "how do you see that." In studies, statements outweighed questions 8 to 1. Ask more questions than others. Make fewer solution statements early in a discussion. Keep probing until you understand what they are trying to tell you.

8. **One key to getting anything of value done in the work world** is the ability to see differences in people and to manage against and use those differences for everyone's benefit. Interpersonal savvy is

meeting each person where he/she is to get done what you need to get done. Basically, people respond favorably to ease of transaction and feeling included. If you make it easy by accepting their normal mode of doing things, not fighting their style, and neither defending your own nor letting style get in the way of performance, things will generally run smoothly.

9. **Set a goal of meeting new people at every social gathering;** find out what you have in common with them. Initiate contact at your place of worship, at PTA meetings, in the neighborhood, at the supermarket, on the plane, and on the bus.

C Being More Reflective Problem Solvers

ISTPs are likely to just do it and be convinced they have examined the problem. They love to troubleshoot and are driven by trial-and-error learning instead of a longer-term perspective.

1. **Solutions first, understanding second?** You might be seen as someone who jumps to conclusions and solutions before others have had a chance to finish their statement of the problem. Take the time to really define the problem. Let people finish. Try not to interrupt. Don't finish others' sentences. Ask clarifying questions. Restate the problem in your own words to everyone's satisfaction. Then decide.

2. **Share your thinking.** To help those around you grow and learn from what you know, you have to sometimes think out loud. You have to share your thinking from the initial presentation of the issue through to conclusion. Most of us are on thinking autopilot. We don't think about thinking. When someone else has to or wants to understand how you came up with a decision, it's sometimes difficult to unravel it in your mind. You have to go step-by-step and recreate your thinking. Sometimes it helps if other people ask the questions. They can probably guide you through how you came up with an answer or a decision better than you can. Once in a while, you should document a decision or two. What was the issue? What were the pros and cons you considered? How did you weight things? Then you can use those examples to demonstrate to others how you make decisions.

3. **Check yourself for these common errors in thinking:** Do you state as facts things that are really opinions or assumptions? Are you sure these assertions are facts? State opinions and assumptions as that and don't present them as facts. Do you attribute cause and effect to relationships when you don't know if one causes the other? If sales are

down, and we increase advertising and sales go up, this doesn't prove causality. They are simply related. Say we know that the relationship between sales/advertising is about the same as sales/number of employees. If sales go down, we probably wouldn't hire more people, so make sure one thing causes the other before acting on it. Do you generalize from a single example without knowing if that single example does generalize?

4. **Do you do enough analysis?** Thoroughly define the problem. Figure out what causes it. Keep asking why. See how many causes you can come up with and how many organizing buckets you can put them in. This increases the chance of a better solution because you can see more connections. Look for patterns in data, don't just collect information. Put it in categories that make sense to you. A good rule of thumb is to analyze patterns and causes to come up with alternatives. Many of us just collect data, which numerous studies show increases our confidence but doesn't increase decision accuracy. Think out loud with others; see how they view the problem. Studies show that defining the problem and taking action usually occur simultaneously, so to break out of analysis paralysis, figure out what the problem is first. Then when a good alternative appears, you're likely to recognize it immediately.

5. **Do a historical analysis.** Do an objective analysis of decisions you have made in the past and what the percentage correct was. Break the decisions into topics or areas of your life. For most of us, we make better decisions in some areas than others. Maybe your decision-making skills need help in one or two limited areas, like decisions about people, decisions about your career, political decisions, technical, etc.

6. **Holster your gun.** Life is a balance between waiting and doing. Many in management put a premium on doing over waiting. Most could make close to 100% good decisions given all of the data and unlimited time. Life affords us neither the data nor the time. You may need to try to discipline yourself to wait just a little longer than you usually do for more, but not all, the data to come in. Push yourself to always get one more piece of data than you did before until your correct decision percent becomes more acceptable. Instead of just doing it, ask what questions would need to be answered before we'd know which way to go. In one study of problem solving, answers outnumbered questions 8 to 1. We jump to solutions based on what has worked in the past. So collect data to answer these questions, then shoot.

7. **Value-added approaches.** To be more personally creative, immerse yourself in the problem. Getting fresh ideas is not a speedboating process; it requires looking deeply.

- Carve out dedicated time—study the problem deeply, talk with others, look for parallels in other organizations and in remote areas totally outside your field. If your response to this is that you don't have the time, that also usually explains why you're not having any fresh ideas.

- Think out loud. Many people don't know what they know until they talk it out. Find a good sounding board and talk to him/her to increase your understanding of a problem or a technical area. Talk to an expert in an unrelated field. Talk to the most irreverent person you know. Your goal is not to get his/her input, but rather his/her help in figuring out what you know—what your principles and rules of thumb are.

- Practice picking out anomalies—unusual facts that don't quite fit, like sales going down when they should have gone up. What do these odd things imply for strategy? Naturally creative people are much more likely to think in opposite cases when confronted with a problem. Turn the problem upside down: Ask what is the least likely thing it could be, what the problem is not, what's missing from the problem, or what the mirror image of the problem is.

- Look for distant parallels. Don't fall into the mental trap of searching only in parallel organizations because "only they would know." Back up and ask a broader question to aid in the search for solutions. When Motorola wanted to find out how to process orders more quickly, they went not to other electronics firms, but to Domino's Pizza and Federal Express. For more ideas, an interesting—and fun—book on the topic is *Take the Road to Creativity and Get Off Your Dead End* by David Campbell.

8. **Unearthing creative ideas.** Creative thought processes do not follow the formal rules of logic, where one uses cause and effect to prove or solve something. Some rules of creative thought are:

- Not using concepts but changing them; imagining this were something else.

- Move from one concept or way of looking at things to another, such as from economic to political.

- Generate ideas without judging them initially.

- Use information to restructure and come up with new patterns.

- Jump from one idea to another without justifying the jump.

- Look for the least likely and odd.

- Look for parallels far from the problem, such as how is an organization like a big oak tree?

- Ask what's missing or what's not here.

- Fascination with mistakes and failure as learning devices.

D Boss and Peer Relationships

Because ISTPs rely on past performance as their primary guide to effectiveness, they can be quite critical when they perceive that change will affect their tried-and-true practices. They then can lock horns with boss and peers.

1. **Focus on your boss more.** Focus on the three key problems you need to work on with him/her and do them. Keep your head down. Keep your conversations with the boss directed at these core agenda. Focus on expectations, ask what results indicate success. Find out about your boss's job and what sorts of pressures he/she is under.

2. **Deal with him/her as your boss more than as a person.** While you don't ever have to invite her/him to your home, you do have to deal with this person as a boss. Ask yourself why you dislike your boss so much or don't like to work with him/her. Write down everything you don't like on the left-hand side of a page. On the right-hand side write a strategy for dealing with it. Consider these strategies: Ask what strengths you can appeal to; ask what you can provide that the boss needs; ask what the boss would like for you to do to be more effective; design a project that you can do together so you can have a success experience; and consult with others for advice.

3. **Some rules to follow:** Describe. Say "I" not "you." Focus on how to accomplish work better. (If you think the boss is blocking you, instead of saying this, say, "I need help in getting this done. I've tried the following things, but....")

    - If your boss is reluctant to give criticism, help by making statements rather than asking questions. Saying "I think I focus too much on operations and miss some of the larger strategic connections" is easier for most people to reply to than a question which asks them to tell you this point.

- If your manager is uninvolved, you will need to provide the structure and aim for a sign-off on your objectives.

- If you work for a detail-driven micromanager, ask what results you must achieve to be successful (and left alone more).

- If your manager is well-meaning, but a nuisance, ask if you can check in with him because you are trying to be more autonomous.

- If you believe the boss is blocking you, access your network for performance help, think of five ways to accomplish anything, and try them all.

4. **Influencing peers.** Peers generally do not have power over each other. That means that influence skills, understanding, and trading are the currencies to use. Don't just ask for things; find some common ground where you can provide help. What do the peers you're contacting need? Do you really know how they see the issue? Is it even important to them? How does what you're working on affect them? If it affects them negatively, can you trade something, appeal to the common good, figure out some way to minimize the work (volunteering staff help, for example)? Go into peer relationships with a trading mentality.

5. **Sometimes the problem is maneuvering through the complex maze called the organization.** How do you get things done sideways? Who are the movers and shakers in the organization? How do they get things done? Who do they rely on for expediting things through the maze? Who are the major gatekeepers who control the flow of resources, information, and decisions? Who are the guides and the helpers? Get to know them better. Who are the major resisters and stoppers? Try to avoid or go around them.

E Seeing the Bigger Picture

ISTPs excel at hands-on endeavors. They do not tend to look ahead to the longer-term issues.

1. **Not curious?** Many managers are so wrapped up in today's problems that they aren't curious about tomorrow. They really don't care about the long-term future. They may not even be in the organization when the strategic plan is supposed to happen. They believe there won't be much of a future until we perform today. Being a visionary and a good strategist requires curiosity and imagination. It requires playing "what ifs." What are the implications of the growing gap between rich and poor? The collapse of retail pricing? The increasing influence of brand names? What if it turns out there is life on other planets, and we get the first message? What will that change? Will they need our products? What will happen when a larger percentage of the world's population is over the age of 65? The effects of terrorism? What if cancer is cured? Heart disease? AIDS? Obesity? What if the government outlaws or severely regulates some aspect of your business? True, nobody knows the answers, but good strategists know the questions. Work at developing broader interests outside your business. Subscribe to different magazines. Pick new shows to watch. Meet different people. Join a new organization. Look under some rocks. Think about tomorrow. Talk to others about what they think the future will bring.

2. **Narrow perspective?** Some are sharply focused on what they do and do it very well. They have prepared themselves for a narrow but satisfying career. Then someone tells them their job has changed, and they now have to be strategic. Being strategic requires a broad perspective. In addition to knowing one thing well, it requires that you know about a lot of things somewhat. You need to understand business. You need to understand markets. You need to understand how the world operates. You need to put all that together and figure out what all that means to your organization.

3. **Too busy?** Strategy is always last on the list. Solving today's problems, of which there are many, is job one. You have to make time for strategy. A good strategy releases future time because it makes choices clear and leads to less wasted effort, but it takes time to do. Delegation is usually the main key. Give away as much tactical day-to-day stuff as you can. Ask your people what they think they could do to give you more time for strategic reflection. Another key is better

time management. Put an hour a week on your calendar for strategic reading and reflection throughout the year. Don't wait until one week before the strategic plan is due. Keep a log of ideas you get from others, magazines, etc. Focus on how these impact your organization or function.

4. **The most likely scenario.** Think of it as the search for and application of relevant parallels. It involves making projections of several variables at once to see how they come together. These projections are in the context of shifting markets, international affairs, monetary movements, and government interventions. It involves a lot of uncertainty, making risk assumptions, and understanding how things work together. How many reasons would account for sales going down? Up? How are advertising and sales linked? If the dollar is cheaper in Asia, what does that mean for our product in Japan? If the world population is aging and they have more money, how will that change buying patterns? Not everyone enjoys this kind of pie-in-the-sky thinking and not everyone is skilled at doing it.

5. **You have to help your people envision what a long-term change will look like.** To do this, you need a clear, succinct mission statement. C.K. Prahalad, one of the leading strategic consultants, believes that in order to qualify as a mission statement, it should take less than three minutes to explain it clearly to an audience. Really effective mission statements are simple, compelling, and capable of capturing people's imagination. Mission statements should help everyone allot his/her time. They should signal what's mission-critical and explain what's rewarded in the organization and what's not. Create a simple obvious symbol, visual, or slogan to make the cause come alive. Ford's "Quality is Job One" seems clear enough. Nordstrom's "The Customer is Always Right" tells employees how they should do their jobs. Although the actual mission and vision document would be longer, the message needs to be finely crafted to capture the essence of what's important around here.

6. **A good mission statement leads to a common mind-set.** The power of a mission and vision communication is providing everyone in the organization with a road map on how they are going to be part of something grand and exciting. Establish common cause. Imagine what the change would look like if fully implemented, then describe the outcome often—how things will look in the future. Help people

see how their efforts fit in by creating simple, obvious measures of achievement like bar or thermometer charts. Be succinct. People don't line up behind laundry lists or ambiguous objectives. Missions and visions should be more about where we are going and less about how we are going to get there. Keep your eyes on the prize.

F Dislike of Routine and Procedures

ISTPs are interested in hands-on, on-line problem solving. They excel in a crisis, but can become bored and skeptical with the familiar. They tend to question the routines and standard operating procedures of others because they know they can improve on it and do it better.

1. **Try to see the value in routines.** Pick a plan or procedure and do a historical analysis of how it came to be and why it is necessary. Resist the urge to change it or question its usefulness. Understand it first.

2. **Turn off your answer program.** We all have a need to provide answers as soon as possible to questions and problems. We all have preconceived notions, favorite solutions, and prejudices that prevent our intellectual skills from dealing with the real facts of the problem. For one-half of the time you have to deal with an issue or a problem, shut off your solution machine and just take in the facts.

3. **Compensate for your dislikes.** Find a person you admire and respect to deal with all the procedures you find oppressive. Let this person tell you if anything needs changing. Otherwise, trust his or her judgment.

Overusing ISTP Tendencies

If you sometimes overdo your preferred behaviors, you may need to work on:

A Better Team Building

B Motivating Others

C Not Going It Alone

D Reading Others

E Broadening Career Perspective

F Not Trying to Win Every Battle

ISTJ	ISFJ	INFJ	INTJ
ISTP	ISFP	INFP	INTP
ESTP	ESFP	ENFP	ENTP
ESTJ	ESFJ	ENFJ	ENTJ

A Better Team Building

ISTPs enjoy working in a hands-on fashion in a team environment to solve problems. They often excel at judging the strengths and capabilities of those who work with them. But at heart they are individual achievers.

1. **Don't believe in teams.** If you don't believe in teams, you are probably a strong individual achiever who doesn't like the mess and sometimes the slowness of due-process relationships and team processes. You are very results oriented and truly believe the best way to do that is to manage one person at a time. To balance this thinking, observe and talk with three excellent team builders and ask them why they manage that way. What do they consider rewarding about building teams? What advantages do they get from using the team format? Read *The Wisdom of Teams* by Katzenbach and Smith. If you can't see the value in teams, none of the following tips will help much.

2. **Don't have the time; teaming takes longer.** That's true and not true. While building a team takes longer than managing one person at a time, having a well-functioning team increases results, builds in a sustaining capability to perform, maximizes collective strengths and covers individual weaknesses, and actually releases more time for the manager because the team members help each other. Many managers get caught in the trap of thinking it takes up too much time to build a team and end up taking more time managing one-on-one.

3. **Would like to build a team but don't know how.** High performance teams have four common characteristics: (1) They have a shared mind-set. They have a common vision. Everyone knows the goals and measures. (2) They trust one another. They know "you will cover me if I get in trouble." They know you will pitch in and help even though it may be difficult for you. They know you will be honest with them. They know you will bring problems to them directly and won't go behind their backs. (3) They have the talent collectively to do the job. While not any one member may have it all, collectively they have every task covered. (4) They know how to operate efficiently and effectively. They have good team skills. They run effective meetings. They have efficient ways to communicate. They have ways to deal with internal conflict.

4. **Cement relationships.** Even though some—maybe including you—will resist it, parties, roasts, gag awards, picnics, and outings help build group cohesion. Allow roles to evolve naturally rather than being specified by job descriptions. Some research indicates that people gravitate naturally to eight roles, and that successful teams are not those where everyone does the same thing. Successful teams specialize, cover for each other, and only sometimes demand that everyone participate in identical activities.

5. **Not good at motivating people beyond being results oriented?** Play the motivation odds. According to research by Rewick and Lawler, the top motivators at work are: (1) Job challenge; (2) Accomplishing something worthwhile; (3) Learning new things; (4) Personal development; and (5) Autonomy. Pay (12th), Friendliness (14th), Praise (15th), or Chance of Promotion (17th) are not insignificant but are superficial compared with the five top motivators. Provide challenges, paint pictures of why this is worthwhile, set up chances to learn and grow, and provide autonomy, and you'll hit the vast majority of people's hot buttons.

B Motivating Others

ISTPs are not usually attracted to murky issues like motivation or developing others. They tend to lead by example and focus on tasks, missing some of the nuances of people's behavior.

1. **Follow the basic rules of inspiring others** as outlined in classic books like *People Skills* by Robert Bolton or *Thriving on Chaos* by Tom Peters. Communicate to people that what they do is important. Say thanks.

Offer help and ask for it. Provide autonomy in how people do their work. Provide a variety of tasks. "Surprise" people with enriching, challenging assignments. Show an interest in their careers. Adopt a learning attitude toward mistakes. Celebrate successes, have visible accepted measures of achievement, and so on. Too often people behave correctly but there are no consequences. Although it's easy to get too busy to acknowledge, celebrate, and occasionally criticize, don't forget to reinforce what you want. As a rule of thumb, 4 to 1 positive to negative is best.

2. **Use goals to motivate.** Most people are turned on by reasonable goals. They like to measure themselves against a standard. They like to see who can run the fastest, score the most, and work the best. They like goals to be realistic but stretching. People try hardest when they have somewhere between one-half and two-thirds chance of success and some control over how they go about it. People are even more motivated when they participate in setting the goals. Set just-out-of-reach challenges and tasks that will be first time for people—their first negotiation, their first solo presentation, etc.

3. **More what and why, less how.** The best delegators are crystal clear on what and when, and more open on how. People are more motivated when they can determine the how for themselves. Inexperienced delegators include the hows, which turn the people into task automatons instead of an empowered and energized staff. Tell them what and when and for how long, and let them figure out how on their own. Give them leeway. Encourage them to try things. Besides being more motivating, it's also more developmental for them. Add the larger context. Although it is not necessary to get the task done, people are more motivated when they know where this task fits in the bigger picture. Take three extra minutes and tell them why this task needs to be done, where it fits in the grander scheme, and its importance to the goals and objectives of the unit.

4. **Monitoring delegated tasks.** Do you micromanage? If you're constantly looking over shoulders, you're not delegating. A properly communicated and delegated task doesn't need to be monitored. If you must monitor, set time-definite checkpoints: by the calendar, every Monday, by percentage, after each 10% is complete, or by outcome—such as when you have the first draft. Be approachable for help, but not intrusive. Intervene only when agreed-upon criteria are not being followed or expectations are not being met. This focuses on the task, not the person. Let people finish their work.

5. **Delegate for development.** Brainstorm with your direct reports all the tasks that aren't being done but are important to do. Ask them for a list of tasks that are no longer challenging for them. (You can also use parts of your own job to develop others. Take three tasks that are no longer developmental for you, but would be for others, and delegate them.) Trade tasks and assignments between two direct reports; have them do each other's work. Assign each of your direct reports an out-of-comfort-zone task that meets the following criteria: The task needs to be done, the person hasn't done it or isn't good at it, and the task calls for a skill the person needs to develop. Remember to focus on varied assignments—more of the same isn't developmental.

C Not Going It Alone

ISTPs can be loners.

1. **Not a people person?** Many managers are better with things, ideas, and projects than they are with people. They may be driven and very focused on producing results and have little time left to develop their people skills. It really doesn't take too much. There is communicating. People are more motivated and do better work when they know what's going on. They want to know more than just their little piece. There is listening. Nothing motivates more than a boss who will listen, not interrupt, not finish your sentences, and not complete your thoughts. Increase your listening time 30 seconds in each transaction. There is caring. Caring is questions. Caring is asking about me and what I think and what I feel. Ask one more question per transaction than you do now.

2. **A loner.** Do you keep to yourself? Work alone or try to? Do you hold back information? Do you parcel out information on your schedule? Do you share information to get an advantage or to win favor? Do people around you know what you're doing and why? Are you aware of things others would benefit from, but you don't take the time to communicate? In most organizations, these things and things like it will get you in trouble. Organizations function on the flow of information. Being on your own and preferring peace and privacy are okay as long as you communicate things to bosses, peers, and teammates that they need to know and would feel better if they knew. Don't be the source of surprises.

D Reading Others

ISTPs read others' skills well. They do not typically read below the surface.

1. **Maybe you run a bad tape in your head.** Under enough stress, you start to question others' motives, judge them negatively, and feel slighted. Check it out. Ask people what is going on. Don't assume you know or that whatever they are doing has anything to do with you. Ask them what you should keep doing, start doing, and stop doing. If this is left unchecked, you might appear judgmental and unforgiving to others due to slights, real or not real.

2. **To better figure out what drives people, look to**: What do they do first? What do they emphasize in their speech? What do they display emotion around? What values play out for them?

   ■ First things. Does this person go to others first, hole up and study, complain, discuss feelings, or take action? These are the basic orientations of people that reveal what's important to them. Use these to motivate.

   ■ Speech content. People might focus on details, concepts, feelings, or other people in their speech. This can tell you again how to appeal to them by mirroring their speech emphasis. Although most of us naturally adjust—we talk details with detail-oriented people—chances are good that in problem relationships you're not finding the common ground. She talks "detail" and you talk "people," for example.

   ■ Emotion. You need to know what people's hot buttons are because one mistake can get you labeled as insensitive with some people. The only cure here is to see what turns up the volume for them—either literally or what they're concerned about.

   ■ Values. Apply the same thinking to the values of others. Do they talk about money, recognition, integrity, efficiency in their normal work conversation? Figuring out what their drivers are tells you another easy way to appeal to anyone.

3. **You must observe and listen to be good at reading others.** You must watch the reactions of people to what you are doing while you are doing it to gauge their response. Are they bored? Change the pace. Are they confused? State it in a different way. Are they angry? Stop and ask what the problem is. Are they too quiet? Stop and get them

involved in what you are doing. Are they fidgeting, scribbling on their pads, or staring out the window? They may not be interested in what you are doing. Move to the end of your presentation or task, end it, and exit. Check in with your audience frequently and select a different tactic if necessary. As Warren Bennis notes, "Being a first-class noticer allows leaders to recognize talent, identify opportunities, and avoid pitfalls. Leaders who succeed...are geniuses at grasping context."

4. **Pay particular attention to non-verbal cues.** Common signals of trouble are changes in body posture (especially turning away), crossed arms, staring, or the telltale glancing at one's watch, tapping fingers or the pencil, frowns, and washboard foreheads. When this occurs, pause. Ask a question. Ask how we're doing. Do a live process check. Some people use the same body language to signal that they are done or not interested in what's going on. Get to know their signals. Construct an alternative plan for the five people you work with closely: When Bill begins to stare, I will.... When Sally interrupts for the third time, I will....

E Broadening Career Perspective

Troubleshooting is a valuable skill. But ISTPs run the risk of knowing how to do one thing, albeit superbly. This can lead to career dead-ends.

1. **Many people don't know how careers are built.** Most are put off by the popular myth of getting ahead. All of us have seen *How to Succeed in Business Without Really Trying* or something like it. It's easy to get cynical and believe that successful people are political or sell out, suck up, knife people in the back, it's who you know, and so on. The facts are dramatically different from this. Those behaviors get people in trouble eventually. What has staying power is performing and problem solving on the current job, having a few notable strengths, and seeking new tasks you don't know how to do. It's solving every problem with tenacity, while looking for what you haven't yet done and getting yourself in a position to do it. Read *The Lessons of Experience* by McCall, Lombardo and Morrison for the careers of men and *Breaking the Glass Ceiling* by Morrison, White and Van Velsor for the careers of women to see how successful careers really happen.

2. **Break out of your career comfort zone.** Maybe you haven't seen enough. Pick some activities you haven't done before but might find exciting. Take a course in a new area. Task trade—switch tasks with a

peer. Volunteer for task forces and projects that are multi-functional or multi-business in nature. Read more broadly.

3. **Focus on the right things.** In their study of successful vs. average careers, Citrin and Smith found that the most successful people force themselves into experiences they need for growth. They do not play it safe. While they demonstrate early competence in a specific area, they also don't overdo working on basic job requirements. They do enough work on the basics while searching for mission-critical job elements and trying to overdeliver on them. They add unexpected value. They call this the 20/80 principle of performance—focusing on the 20% that makes 80% of the difference. In doing so, the successful rack up career freedom points by tackling these tough assignments.

4. **Teach others.** Form a study group and take turns presenting on new, different, or unknown aspects of the technology. Having to teach it will force you to conceptualize and understand it more deeply. The relationships you form in such groups pay off in other ways as well. One company found its technicians learned more from coffee break conversations than from manuals.

5. **Think carefully about your next natural point for an assignment change.** This time, press your boss, business unit, or organization for something different. Could be different geography, same job but different business unit, same job but different assignments, or a completely different job. Sometimes if you have been in something too long, you may have to take a lateral or even a short-term downgrading to get on a different track.

6. **Volunteer for task forces and study teams outside your area.**

7. **Attend off-sites and meetings of functions and units other than yours.**

8. **In addition to the literature you now read in your specialty, expand to a broader selection of journals and magazines.**

9. **Take a seminar or workshop outside your area just for the fun of it.**

10. **Vacation more broadly than you now do.** Get out of your comfort zone and explore new places. If you can arrange it, vacation outside of your home country.

11. **Find someone who is as specialized as you are who also is seeking expansion** and teach your specialties to each other. Get together a small group; have each person agree to present a new technology or

business topic each month to the group. Teaching something new for you is one of the best ways to learn it yourself.

12. **Look to some people in your area who are in higher level jobs than you are.** Are they as specialized as you are? Are they struggling in their new roles because they are as specialized as you are? Read *Career Mastery* by Harry Levinson.

13. **Find some experts in what you need to learn.** Interview them; find out how they think about their area. Take something to them in their area and ask them how they figure it out. What are the five key things they look for?

14. **Pick three people who are broadly skilled.** Ask them how they got to be that way. What job experiences have they had? What do they read? Watch on TV? Who do they like to learn from?

F Not Trying to Win Every Battle

Intensely competitive, ISTPs really want to win. They enjoy being one up on the competition. This can cause lots of problems with peers and in conflict situations.

1. **Cooperative relations.** The opposite of conflict is cooperation. Developing cooperative relationships involves demonstrating real and perceived equity, the other side feeling understood and respected, and taking a problem-oriented point of view. To do this more: Increase the realities and perceptions of fairness—don't try to win every battle and take all the spoils; focus on the common-ground issues and interests of both sides—find wins on both sides, give in on little points; avoid starting with entrenched positions—show respect for them and their positions; and reduce any remaining conflicts to the smallest size possible.

2. **Causing unnecessary conflict.** Language, words, and timing set the tone and can cause unnecessary conflict that has to be managed before you can get anything done. Do you use insensitive language? Do you raise your voice often? Do you use terms and phrases that challenge others? Do you use demeaning terms? Do you use negative humor? Do you offer conclusions, solutions, statements, dictates, or answers early in the transaction? Give reasons first, solutions last. When you give solutions first, people often directly challenge the solutions instead of defining the problem. Pick words that are other-person neutral. Pick words that don't challenge or sound one-sided. Pick tentative and probabilistic words that give others a chance to

maneuver and save face. Pick words that are about the problem and not the person. Avoid direct blaming remarks; describe the problem and its impact.

3. **Practice Aikido,** the ancient art of absorbing the energy of your opponent and using it to manage him/her. Let the other side vent frustration or blow off steam, but don't react. Listen. Nod. Ask clarifying questions. Ask open-ended questions like, "What one change could you make so we could achieve our objectives better?" "What could I do that would help the most?" Restate their position periodically to signal you have understood. But don't react. Keep them talking until they run out of venom. When the other side takes a rigid position, don't reject it. Ask why: What are the principles behind the position? How do we know it's fair? What's the theory of the case? Play out what would happen if their position was accepted. Then explore the concern underlying the answer. Separate the people from the problem. When someone attacks you, rephrase it as an attack on the problem. In response to threats, say you'll only negotiate on merit and fairness. If the other side won't play fair, surface their game—"It looks like you're playing good cop, bad cop. Why don't you settle your differences and tell me one thing?" In response to unreasonable proposals, attacks, or a non-answer to a question, you can always say nothing. People will usually respond by saying more, coming off their position a bit, or at least revealing their true interests. Many times, with unlimited venting and your understanding, the actual conflict shrinks.

4. **Downsizing the conflict.** Almost all conflicts have common points that get lost in the heat of the battle. After a conflict has been presented and understood, start by saying that it might be helpful to see if we agree on anything. Write them on the flip chart. Then write down the areas left open. Focus on common ground. Keep the open conflicts as small as possible and concrete. The more abstract it gets, "We don't trust your unit," the more unmanageable it gets. To this respond, "Tell me your specific concern—why exactly don't you trust us; can you give me an example?" Usually after calm discussion, they don't trust your unit on this specific issue under these specific conditions. That's easier to deal with. Allow others to save face by conceding small points that are not central to the issue—don't try to hit a home run every time. If you can't agree on a solution, agree on a procedure to move forward. Collect more data. Appeal to a higher power. Get a third-party arbitrator. Something. This creates some positive motion and breaks stalemates.

5. **If peers see you as excessively competitive,** they will cut you out of the loop and may sabotage your cross-border attempts. To be seen as more cooperative, always explain your thinking and invite them to explain theirs. Generate a variety of possibilities first rather than stake out positions. Be tentative, allowing them room to customize the situation. Focus on common goals, priorities, and problems. Invite criticism of your ideas.

6. **Monitor yourself in tough situations** to get a sense of how you are coming across. What's the first thing you attend to? How often do you take a stand vs. make an accommodating gesture? What proportion of your comments deals with relationships vs. the issue to be addressed? Mentally rehearse for worst-case scenarios/hard-to-deal-with people. Anticipate what the person might say and have responses prepared so as not to be caught off guard.

7. **Clear problem-focused communication.** Follow the rule of equity: Explain your thinking and ask them to explain theirs. Be able to state their position as clearly as they do whether you agree or not—give it legitimacy. Separate facts from opinions and assumptions. Generate a variety of possibilities first rather than stake out positions. Keep your speaking to 30–60 second bursts. Try to get them to do the same. Don't give the other side the impression you're lecturing or criticizing them. Explain objectively why you hold a view; make the other side do the same. Ask lots of questions, make fewer statements. To identify interests behind positions, ask why they hold them or why they wouldn't want to do something. Always restate their position to their satisfaction before offering a response.

8. **Questions.** In win-win and something-something negotiations, the more information you have about the other side, the more you will have to work with. What can you learn about what they know before going in? What will they do if they don't reach an agreement with you? In the negotiation, ask more questions, make fewer statements. Ask clarifying questions: "What did you mean by that?" Probes: "Why do you say that?" Motives: "What led you to that position?" Get everything out that you can. Don't negotiate assumptions, negotiate facts.

9. **Avoid early rigid positions.** It's just physics. Action gets equal reaction. Strong statements. Strongly worded positions. Casting blame. Absolutes. Lines in the sand. Unnecessary passion. All of these will be responded to in kind, will waste time, cause ill will, and possibly prevent a win-win or a something-something. It only has a

place in one-time, either/or negotiations, and even there it isn't recommended. Similarly, watch out for overcommitment to any need or course of action. Look for information that goes against your preferences. Be able to adjust your position and your wants. If you can't, your ego is getting the best of you. If you can't walk away until you get X, you'll probably either overpay or blow the negotiation. Don't negotiate around a single issue if you can add another. This is another situation that leads to rigidity.

I prefer to take action. I superficially listen to things I deem irrelevant. This, along with my determination, gets misread as not being a team player.

— An ISTP Manager

APPLICATION

Your personal preferences play out in day-to-day problems and situations you face. Below is a case about your type dealing with such a situation. Use this to think through how you will integrate the tips you've considered and coach yourself to be more effective in your type.

ISTP Application Situation (Part 1)

"I'm not interested in moving up. I like the job I have. What's wrong with being a General Manager?"

This isn't the first time Barry's wife, Arlene, has heard this exclamation. And it frustrates her, because she knows Barry has what it takes to run the global company, not just manage the National Fire Safety group. But, coupling the personal stake she has in Barry's success with the insight and knowledge she has as a practicing counseling psychologist, it is hard for her to distance herself from the situation.

"Let me ask you this, Barry," she said. "You know how I've sometimes gotten upset with you because you leave me out of the loop on things that are important to both of us, and how you think you're doing me a big favor by solving family issues and problems without involving me or the kids?"

Barry had heard it before and said, "Well, I actually do think I'm doing you guys a favor when I solve things without taking up your time."

Arlene didn't like where this was going. She wanted to help him focus on work and his career at the company, but, as it often did when Barry sensed he was being attacked, the conversation was taking an unproductive personal turn. She tried to redirect it. "Okay, I appreciate your concern for my time, honey. But what you're doing at home is probably very much like what you're doing at work."

"Well, I know what I know. If I'm the expert, why do I need other people's involvement?"

Thinking It Through: Strategy

- If you were going to coach Barry on what you gleaned from this conversation, and if, as someone intimate with Myers-Briggs types, you knew what the implications were for his being an ISTP, how would you proceed in your first meeting with Barry?

- What would you want to accomplish?

Planning It Out: Tactics

- What other information about Barry would you like to have?

- What would be the best sources for getting it?

- Which of the tactics described in the Being More Effective section are applicable in this situation?

- Which Overused Tendencies are most likely to come into play here?

ISTP Application Situation (Part 2)

Good thing you spent some time thinking about the answers to those questions because you've been engaged by Barry's company to provide him with coaching. In preparation for it, here's what else you've learned so far:

■ His 360° report reveals him to be perceived as dedicated, detail oriented, and focused, but often independent, inadequately concerned with sharing information, and insensitive to others' needs. His boss commented that Barry needs to learn how to coach others.

Reflection

■ What's your direction with Barry?

SUGGESTED READINGS

■■■■■■■■ Being a More Effective ISTP ■■■■■■■■

Being More Flexible

Anderson, Dean and Linda S. Ackerman Anderson. *Beyond Change Management: Advanced Strategies for Today's Transformational Leaders.* San Francisco: Jossey-Bass, Inc., 2001.

Bellman, Geoffrey M. *Getting Things Done When You Are Not in Charge.* San Francisco: Berrett-Koehler Publishers, Inc., 2001.

Black, J. Stewart and Hal B. Gregersen. *Leading Strategic Change: Breaking Through the Brain Barrier.* Upper Saddle River, NJ: Financial Times/Prentice Hall, 2002.

Burke, W. Warner and William Trahant with Richard Koonce. *Business Climate Shifts: Profiles of Change Makers.* Boston: Butterworth-Heinemann, 2000.

Fullan, Michael. *Leading in a Culture of Change.* New York: John Wiley & Sons, Inc., 2001.

Gilley, Jerry W. *The Manager As Change Agent.* Cambridge, MA: Perseus Publishing, 2001.

Luecke, Richard. *Managing Change and Transition.* Boston: Harvard Business School Publishing, 2003.

Being More Engaging

Benton, D.A. *Executive Charisma: Six Steps to Mastering the Art of Leadership.* New York: McGraw-Hill Trade, 2003.

Brooks, Michael. *Instant Rapport.* New York: Warner Books, 1989.

Maxwell, John C. *Relationships 101.* London: Thomas Nelson, 2004.

Silberman, Melvin L. and Freda Hansburg. *Peoplesmart: Developing Your Interpersonal Intelligence.* San Francisco: Berrett-Koehler Publishers, Inc., 2000.

Being More Reflective Problem Solvers

Campbell, David. *Take the Road to Creativity and Get Off Your Dead End.* Greensboro, NC: Center for Creative Leadership, 1985.

DeGraff, Jeff and Katherine A. Lawrence. *Creativity at Work: Developing the Right Practices to Make Innovation Happen.* San Francisco: Jossey-Bass, Inc., 2002.

Flynn, Daniel J. *Intellectual Morons: How Ideology Makes Smart People Fall for Stupid Ideas.* New York: Crown Business Publishing, 2004.

Hammond, John S., Ralph L. Keeney and Howard Raiffer. *Smart Choices.* Boston: Harvard University Press, 1999.

Lucas, Robert W. *The Creative Training Idea Book: Inspired Tips and Techniques for Engaging and Effective Learning.* New York: AMACOM, 2003.

Nutt, Paul C. *Why Decisions Fail: Avoiding the Blunders and Traps That Lead to Decision Debacles.* San Francisco: Berrett-Koehler Publishers, Inc., 2002.

Sofo, Francesco. *Six Myths of Critical Thinking.* Business & Professional Publishing, 2003.

Sternberg, Robert J. *Thinking Styles.* Boston: Cambridge University Press, 1997.

Yates, J. Frank. *Decision Management: How to Assure Better Decisions in Your Company.* San Francisco: Jossey-Bass, Inc., 2003.

Boss and Peer Relationships

Baker, Wayne E. *Networking Smart.* New York: Backinprint.com, 2000.

Bolton, Robert and Dorothy Grover Bolton. *People Styles at Work—Making Bad Relationships Good and Good Relationships Better.* New York: AMACOM, 1996.

Carson, Kerry, Ph.D. and Paula Phillips Carson, Ph.D. *Defective Bosses— Working for the Dysfunctional Dozen.* New York: The Haworth Press, 1998.

Cartwright, Tatula. *Managing Conflict With Peers.* Greensboro, NC: Center for Creative Leadership, 2003.

Dobson, Michael Singer. *Managing Up! 59 Ways to Build a Career-Advancing Relationship With Your Boss.* New York: AMACOM, 2000.

Dominguez, Linda R. *How to Shine at Work.* New York: McGraw-Hill Trade, 2003.

Jay, Ros. *How to Manage Your Boss: Developing the Perfect Working Relationship.* London: Financial Times Management, 2002.

Seeing the Bigger Picture

Chakravorti, Bhaskar. *The Slow Pace of Fast Change: Bringing Innovations to Market in a Connected World.* Boston: Harvard Business School Press, 2003.

Charan, Ram. *What the CEO Wants You to Know: How Your Company Really Works.* New York: Crown Business Publishing, 2001.

Collins, James C. *Good to Great: Why Some Companies Make the Leap...And Others Don't.* New York: HarperCollins, 2001.

Dudik, Evan Matthew. *Strategic Renaissance: New Thinking and Innovative Tools to Create Great Corporate Strategies Using Insights From History and Science.* New York: AMACOM, 2000.

The Futurist Magazine. http://www.wfs.org

Hamel, Gary. *Leading the Revolution.* Boston: Harvard Business School Press, 2002.

Hargadon, Andrew and Kathleen M. Eisenhardt. *How Breakthroughs Happen: The Surprising Truth About How Companies Innovate.* Boston: Harvard Business School Press, 2003.

Harvard Business Review. Phone: 800-988-0886 (US and Canada). Fax: 617-496-1029. Mail: Harvard Business Review. Subscriber Services, P.O. Box 52623. Boulder, CO 80322-2623 USA. http://www.hbsp.harvard.edu/products/hbr

Kaplan, Robert S. and David P. Norton. *The Strategy-Focused Organization: How Balanced Scorecard Companies Thrive in the New Business Environment.* Boston: Harvard Business School Press, 2000.

Porter, Michael E. *Competitive Strategy: Techniques for Analyzing Industries and Competitors.* New York: The Free Press, 1998.

Prahalad, C.K. and Venkat Ramaswamy. *The Future of Competition: Co-Creating Unique Value With Customers.* Boston: Harvard Business School Press, 2004.

Dislike of Routine and Procedures

Bossidy, Larry, Ram Charan and Charles Burck (Contributor). *Execution: The Discipline of Getting Things Done.* New York: Crown Business Publishing, 2002.

Keen, Peter G.W. *The Process Edge—Creating Value Where It Counts.* Boston: Harvard Business School Press, 1998.

Lawler, Edward E., III, Susan Albers Mohrman and George Benson. *Organizing for High Performance: Employee Involvement, TQM, Reengineering, and Knowledge Management in the Fortune 1000: The CEO Report.* San Francisco: Jossey-Bass, Inc., 2001.

Niven, P.R. *Balanced Scorecard Step-by-Step: Maximizing Performance and Maintaining Results.* New York: John Wiley & Sons, Inc., 2002.

■■■■■■■ Overusing ISTP Tendencies ■■■■■■■

Better Team Building

Bolton, Robert. *People Skills.* New York: Simon & Schuster, 1979.

Fisher, Kimball and Mareen Duncan Fisher. *The Distance Manager: A Hands-On Guide to Managing Off-Site Employees and Virtual Teams.* New York: McGraw-Hill Trade, 2000.

Genett, Donna M. *If You Want It Done Right, You Don't Have to Do It Yourself! The Power of Effective Delegation.* Sanger, CA: Quill Driver Books, 2004.

Harvard Business School Press. *Harvard Business Review on Teams That Succeed.* Boston: Harvard Business School Press, 2004.

Katzenbach, Jon R. and Douglas K. Smith. *The Wisdom of Teams: Creating the High-Performance Organization.* New York: HarperBusiness, 2003.

Parker, Glenn M. *Cross-Functional Teams: Working With Allies, Enemies, and Other Strangers.* San Francisco: Jossey-Bass, Inc., 2002.

Peters, Tom. *Thriving on Chaos: Handbook for a Management Revolution.* New York: HarperCollins, 1987.

Raymond, Cara Capretta, Robert W. Eichinger and Michael M. Lombardo. *FYI for Teams.* Minneapolis, MN: Lominger Limited, Inc., 2001–2004.

Robbins, Harvey and Michael Finley. *The New Why Teams Don't Work— What Goes Wrong and How to Make It Right.* San Francisco: Berrett-Koehler Publishers, Inc., 2000.

Motivating Others

Crainer, Stuart. *Motivating the New Generation—Modern Motivation Techniques.* New York: BrownHerron Publishing, 2001.

Daniels, Aubrey C. *Bringing Out the Best in People.* New York: McGraw-Hill, Inc., 1994.

Fulmer, Robert M. and Jay A. Conger. *Growing Your Company's Leaders.* New York: AMACOM, 2004.

Glanz, Barbara A. *Handle With CARE: Motivating and Retaining Employees.* New York: McGraw-Hill Trade, 2002.

Hiam, Alexander. *Motivational Management: Inspiring Your People for Maximum Performance.* New York: AMACOM, 2003.

Lombardo, Michael M. and Robert W. Eichinger. *The Leadership Machine.* Minneapolis, MN: Lominger Limited, Inc., 2004.

Not Going It Alone

Bossidy, Larry, Ram Charan and Charles Burck (Contributor). *Execution: The Discipline of Getting Things Done.* New York: Crown Business Publishing, 2002.

Dess, Gregory G. and Joseph C. Picken. *Beyond Productivity: How Leading Companies Achieve Superior Performance by Leveraging Their Human Capital.* New York: AMACOM, 1999.

Drucker, Peter F. *The Effective Executive.* New York: HarperBusiness, 2002.

Goleman, Daniel. *Leadership That Gets Results.* Boston: Harvard Business School Press, 2002.

Lawler, Edward E., III, Susan Albers Mohrman and George Benson. *Organizing for High Performance: Employee Involvement, TQM, Reengineering, and Knowledge Management in the Fortune 1000: The CEO Report.* San Francisco: Jossey-Bass, Inc., 2001.

Stone, Florence M. and Randi T. Sachs. *The High-Value Manager—Developing the Core Competencies Your Organization Needs.* New York: AMACOM, 1995.

Ulrich, David, Jack Zenger and Norman Smallwood. *Results-Based Leadership.* Boston: Harvard Business School Press, 1999.

Reading Others

Bolton, Robert and Dorothy Grover Bolton. *People Styles at Work—Making Bad Relationships Good and Good Relationships Better.* New York: AMACOM, 1996.

Brinkman, Rick, Ph.D. and Dr. Rick Kirschner. *Dealing With People You Can't Stand.* New York: McGraw-Hill, Inc., 1994.

Caro, Mike. *Caro's Book of Poker Tells.* New York: Simon & Schuster, 2003.

Mazzarella, Mark C. and Jo-Ellan Dimitrius. *Reading People: How to Understand People and Predict Their Behavior—Anytime, Anyplace.* New York: Ballantine Books, 1999.

Myers, Isabel Briggs with Peter B. Myers. *Gifts Differing: Understanding Personality Type.* Palo Alto, CA: Davies-Black Publishing, 1995.

Wainright, Gordon R. *Teach Yourself Body Language.* New York: McGraw-Hill/Contemporary Books, 2003.

Broadening Career Perspective

Bennis, Warren G. and Robert J. Thomas. *Geeks and Geezers.* Boston: Harvard Business School Press, 2002.

Bolles, Richard N. *What Color Is Your Parachute? 2004: A Practical Manual for Job-Hunters & Career-Changers.* Berkeley, CA: Ten Speed Press, 2004.

Christian, Ken. *Your Own Worst Enemy: Breaking the Habit of Adult Underachievement.* New York: Regan Books, 2004.

Citrin, James M. and Richard A. Smith. *The Five Patterns of Extraordinary Careers.* New York: Crown Business, 2003.

Dominguez, Linda R. *How to Shine at Work.* New York: McGraw-Hill Trade, 2003.

Levinson, Harry. *Career Mastery.* San Francisco, CA: Berrett-Koehler Publishers, Inc., 1992.

McCall, Morgan W., Michael M. Lombardo and Ann M. Morrison. *The Lessons of Experience*. Lexington, MA: Lexington Books, 1988.

Morrison, Ann M., Randall P. White, Ellen Van Velsor and the Center for Creative Leadership. *Breaking the Glass Ceiling: Can Women Reach the Top of America's Largest Corporations?* Reading, MA: Addison-Wesley Publishing Company, 1992.

Niven, David. *The 100 Simple Secrets of Successful People: What Scientists Have Learned and How You Can Use It*. New York: HarperBusiness, 2002.

Not Trying to Win Every Battle

Cloke, Ken and Joan Goldsmith. *Resolving Conflicts at Work: A Complete Guide for Everyone on the Job*. San Francisco: Jossey-Bass, Inc., 2000.

Dana, Daniel. *Conflict Resolution*. New York: McGraw-Hill Trade, 2000.

Dawson, Roger. *Secrets of Power Negotiating: Inside Secrets From a Master Negotiator*. Franklin Lakes, NJ: Career Press, 2001.

Graham, Gini. *A Survival Guide for Working With Humans: Dealing With Whiners, Back-Stabbers, Know-It-Alls, and Other Difficult People*. New York: AMACOM, 2004.

Guttman, Howard M. *When Goliaths Clash: Managing Executive Conflict to Build a More Dynamic Organization*. New York: AMACOM, 2003.

Masters, Marick Francis and Robert R. Albright. *The Complete Guide to Conflict Resolution in the Workplace*. New York: AMACOM, 2002.

Oliver, David. *How to Negotiate Effectively*. London: Kogan Page, 2003.

Solomon, Muriel. *Working With Difficult People*. New York: Prentice Hall, 2002.

CHAPTER 6

ISFP
Introverted Feeling
with
Extraverted Sensing

■■■■■■■■■■■■■■■■■

8.8% of Population
1.2% of Managers

■■■■■■■■■■■■■■■■■

Typical Strengths

Quiet but Warm
Loyal; Team Oriented
Building Relationships
Values Driven
Free Spirit
Artistic
Live in the Action of the Moment
Like to Have an Impact

ISTJ	ISFJ	INFJ	INTJ
ISTP	**ISFP**	INFP	INTP
ESTP	ESFP	ENFP	ENTP
ESTJ	ESFJ	ENFJ	ENTJ

I work best behind the scenes. . .but I'm told the best jobs are for those who know how to socialize in a big way.

– An ISFP Manager

Basic Habits of Mind

Introverted Feeling leads ISFPs to make decisions based on their matrix of relationships. Introverted Feeling leads to finding supportive environments and to developing strong—though few—interpersonal relationships. Aided by Extraverted Sensing, they are aware of the immediate situation in which they find themselves and the practical considerations of any decisions. ISFPs tend to be very gentle and often respectfully defer to others. Focusing on one issue, they tend to be out of sync with larger issues.

Extraverted Intuiting and Extraverted Thinking also aid ISFPs. In practical terms, Extraverted Intuiting contributes to astutely scanning the environment and Extraverted Thinking leads to succinctly reporting on what is experienced.

This combination is sometimes seen as curt and cool. Due to their selectivity and limited sharing of information, ISFPs can be misinterpreted as holding back something for advantage. This can lead to being seen as opportunistic and "slow."

Typical Communication Patterns

- ISFPs' typical comments are factual, good-natured, and concise.

- They show their intentions and real commitments more by actions than by words.

- But in their conversation, they know the who, what, where, and when of people and situations, which they believe is evidence of truly caring about others and situations.

General Learning Strategy

- ISFPs generally prefer to work cooperatively with small groups, will concretely test ideas, and prefer to do things that have personal meaning.

178

- They like to find personal meaning in experiences and relate this to their values.

- Their learning is usually enhanced by tasks that have personal meaning and opportunities to identify, rather than create, models or categories of information.

- They usually attend to tasks with personal meaning, not intellectual tasks.

Interpersonal Qualities Related to Motivation

- ISFPs are energized by taking practical action to help people.

- They gently encourage others to act and quietly act to address an issue or situation.

- Personal, matter-of-fact, hands-on assistance excites ISFPs.

Blind Spots

- ISFPs are often seen as overdependent on a select few, not concerned enough with making a good impression, and lacking in social presence.

- Relative to others, this type is unaware of how yielding or deferring to others may be seen as having merely "gone along," which is sometimes misattributed as having difficulties with upper management.

- The absence of critical questions can lead to the perception of being mediocre contributors.

Stress Related Behavior

- When stressed, ISFPs can become undependable in follow-through and suspicious of others' intentions.

- Under extended stress, they can become hypercritical of others and find an endless list of reasons for the unacceptability of some action or fact. A skeptical, touchy interpersonal style may emerge.

Potential Barriers to Effectiveness

- Often seen as guarded and at times impatient, these behaviors get in the way of their effectiveness.

- Observers would like to see a more strategic-minded demonstration from ISFPs.

- While often good with their direct reports and bosses, they can have unusual difficulty in getting their peers to appreciate their gifts.

Being a More Effective ISFP

A Taking Charge
B Communicating More Forcefully
C Expanding Ways to Learn
D Seeing the Bigger Picture
E Problems With Peers
F Dislike of Routine and Repetition
G Delegation

A Taking Charge

Although ISFPs enjoy taking action and may respond well in a crisis, they usually don't step up and take the lead and can be seen as passive.

1. **Build up your confidence.** Maybe you're slow to act because you don't think you're up to the task. If you boldly act, others will shoot you down and find you out. Take a course or work with a tutor to bolster your confidence in one skill or area at a time. Focus on the strengths you do have; think of ways you can use these strengths when making nerve-wracking actions. If you are interpersonally skilled, for example, see yourself smoothly dealing with questions and objections to your actions. The only way you will ever know what you can do is to act and find out.

2. **Don't like risk?** Sometimes taking action involves pushing the envelope, taking chances, and trying bold new initiatives. Doing those things leads to more misfires and mistakes. Research says that successful executives have made more mistakes in their careers than those who didn't make it. Treat any mistakes or failures as chances to learn. Nothing ventured, nothing gained. Up your risk comfort. Start small so you can recover more quickly. Go for small wins. Don't blast into a major task to prove your boldness. Break it down into smaller tasks. Take the easiest one for you first. Then build up to the tougher ones. Review each one to see what you did well and not well, and set goals so you'll do something differently and better each time. End up

accomplishing the big goal and taking the bold action. Challenge yourself. See how creative you can be in taking action a number of different ways.

3. **Lost your passion?** Run out of gas? Heart's not in it anymore? Not 100% committed? Doing the same sort of work a long time and you're bored with it? Seen it all; done the same tasks, made the same decisions, worked with the same people? To make the best of this, make a list of what you like and don't like to do. Concentrate on doing at least a couple of liked activities each day. Work to delegate or task trade the things that are no longer motivating to you. Do your least preferred activities first; focus not on the activity, but your sense of accomplishment. Change your work activity to mirror your interests as much as you can. Volunteer for task forces and projects that would be motivating for you.

4. **Leading is riskier than following.** While there are a lot of personal rewards for leading, leading puts you in the limelight. Think about what happens to political leaders and the scrutiny they face. Leaders have to be internally secure. Do you feel good about yourself? They have to please themselves first that they are on the right track. Can you defend to a critical and impartial audience the wisdom of what you're doing? They have to accept lightning bolts from detractors. Can you take the heat? People will always say it should have been done differently. Listen to them, but be skeptical. Even great leaders are wrong sometimes. They accept personal responsibility for errors and move on to lead some more. Don't let criticism prevent you from taking the lead. Build up your heat shield. Conduct a postmortem immediately after finishing milestone efforts. This will indicate to all that you're open to continuous improvement whether the result was stellar or not.

5. **Against the grain tough stands.** Taking a tough stand demands confidence in what you're saying along with the humility that you might be wrong—one of life's paradoxes. To prepare to take the lead on a tough issue, work on your stand through mental interrogation until you can clearly state in a few sentences what your stand is and why you hold it. Build the business case. How do others win? People don't line up behind laundry lists or ambiguous objectives. Ask others for advice—scope the problem, consider options, pick one, develop a rationale, then go with it until proven wrong. Then redo the process. If this doesn't help, find out where the pain is for you. What have you been avoiding? Examine your past and see where taking-charge behavior has gotten you in trouble or you thought it would get you in

trouble. Isolate the most troublesome elements, such as forgetting things under pressure, trouble with fierce debate, problems with unpopular stands, and things moving too fast. Devise counter-strategies.

B Communicating More Forcefully

Many ISFPs are artistic, more interested in the visual and performing arts. They often are not that interested in expressing themselves verbally and can be seen as quiet and yielding to others.

1. **You may clam up around talkative people** because you are busy processing what they said, and you have just finished point one when they are already on point four. This can make you appear inscrutable or perhaps disinterested in what they have to say. If you are around a true talker, this may be the one time you need to interrupt. Wave a hand. Smile. Make a comment or ask a question. The goal is not to disagree or cause turmoil, but simply to slow them down.

2. **Leadership presence.** Leading takes presence. You have to look and sound like a leader. Voice is strong. Eye contact. Intensity. Confidence. A lot of leadership presence has to do with forceful presentation skills. Giving good presentations is a known technology. There are several books and workshops you can take. Look to workshops that use videotaping. Join your local Toastmasters Club for some low-risk training and practice. Look to small things such as do you look like a leader? What colors do you wear? Do you dress the part? Are your glasses right? Is your office configured right? Do you sound confident? Do you whine and complain or do you solve problems? If I met you for the first time in a group of 10, would I pick you as the leader?

3. **Clear problem-focused communication.** Follow the rule of equity: Explain your thinking and ask them to explain theirs. Be able to state their position as clearly as they do whether you agree or not—give it legitimacy. Separate facts from opinions and assumptions. Generate a variety of possibilities first rather than stake out positions. Keep your speaking to 30–60 second bursts. Try to get them to do the same. Don't give the other side the impression you're lecturing or criticizing them. Explain objectively why you hold a view; make the other side do the same. Ask lots of questions, make fewer statements. To identify interests behind positions, ask why they hold them or why they

wouldn't want to do something. Always restate their position to their satisfaction before offering a response.

4. **Share your thinking.** To help those around you grow and learn from what you know, you have to sometimes think out loud. You have to share your thinking from the initial presentation of the issue through to conclusion. Most of us are on thinking autopilot. We don't think about thinking. When someone else has to or wants to understand how you came up with a decision, it's sometimes difficult to unravel it in your mind. You have to go step-by-step and recreate your thinking. Sometimes it helps if other people ask the questions. They can probably guide you through how you came up with an answer or a decision better than you can. Once in a while, you should document a decision or two. What was the issue? What were the pros and cons you considered? How did you weight things? Then you can use those examples to demonstrate to others how you make decisions.

5. **Don't inform enough.** Are you a minimalist? Do you tell people only what they need to know to do their little piece of the puzzle? People are motivated by being aware of the bigger picture. They want to know what to do in order to do their jobs and more. How does what they are doing fit into the larger picture? What are the other people working on and why? Many people think that's unnecessary information and that it would take too much time to do. They're wrong. The sense of doing something worthwhile is the number two motivator at work! It results in a high return on motivation and productivity. (Try to increase the amount of more-than-your-job information you share.) Focus on the impact on others by figuring out who information affects. Put five minutes on your meeting agenda. Ask people what they want to know and, assuming it's not confidential information, tell them. Pick a topic each month to tell your people about.

6. **Cryptic informer.** Some people just aren't good at informing. Their communication styles are not effective. According to behavioral research studies, the most effective communicators: speak often, but briefly (15–30 seconds); ask more questions than others; make fewer solution statements early in a discussion; headline their points in a sentence or two; summarize frequently, and make more frequent "here's where we are" statements; invite everyone to share their views; and typically interject their views after others have had a chance to speak, unless they are passing on decisions. Compare these practices to yours. Work on those that are not up to standard.

7. **Preparing.** Make a checklist. What's your objective? What's your point? What are five things you want them to remember? What would the ideal audience member say if interviewed 15 minutes after you finish? Who's your audience? How much do they know? What are five techniques you will use to hold their attention? What presentation technology would work best? What questions will the audience have? What's the setting? How much time do you have—always take a few minutes less, never more.

8. **Preparing a speech.** State your message or purpose in a single sentence. In other words, do the ending first. Then outline the three to five chunks of your argument to support your thesis. Any more and the audience won't follow it. Sometimes putting main concepts on index cards and shuffling them into order can accomplish this. A famous minister said, "No souls are saved after 20 minutes." Many speeches must be longer than this, but can still be divided into sections with clear conclusions, and a hard bridge to the next related topic. What introduction will grab the audience and rivet them on your message? A story, a fact, a comparison, a quote, a photo, a cartoon? For example, one speaker selected a comparison to introduce a series of research findings on career success by saying, "How can you take identical twins, hired for the same entry job in the same organization, and 20 years later, one of them succeeds and one of them doesn't?" She then returned to the twins periodically as she went through her argument on the different developmental experiences they had with the corporation. In organizing your talk, you should resist telling them all you know. What are your priority points, and how will you explain them? Some points are made better by example, some by the logic of the argument, some by facts or stories. You should vary how you drive home your point because you will reach more people. Use memory devices—state points in threes; repeat key words and phrases—"I have a dream"; use understatement and overstatement; use antithesis—"Ask not what your country can do for you; ask what you can do for your country." One nasty shock many learning presenters experience is that writing is different from speaking. A well-written speech is one that sounds right spoken, not read. Do not fall in love with what you have written until you record it on tape and listen to it. The cadence and pace is different in writing than in speaking. Writing doesn't take breathing into account. If your computer has a speech synthesizer, let the computer say your speech. Or have someone else read it to you. Never deliver a written speech until you have heard it spoken. Subscribe to *Presentations* magazine for tips, www.presentations.com.

C Expanding Ways to Learn

ISFPs tend to learn from direct experience and often aren't that interested in analysis, reading, or more abstract ways of knowing.

1. **Personal experience is a very limited way to learn.** Even accessing others' experiences still leaves major gaps. For adults, most learning either comes from taking action and learning from the consequences or searching for parallel experiences in the past.

2. **When faced with a new issue, challenge, or problem, figure out what causes it.** Keep asking why. See how many causes you can come up with and how many organizing buckets you can put them in. This increases the chance of a better solution because you can see more connections. Chess masters recognize thousands of possible patterns of chess pieces. Look for patterns in data; don't just collect information. Put it in categories that make sense to you. To better understand new and difficult learning, read *The Future of Leadership* by White, Hodgson and Crainer.

3. **Locate the essence of the problem.** What are the key factors or elements in this problem? Experts usually solve problems by figuring out what the deep, underlying principles are and working forward from there; the less adept focus on desired outcomes/solutions and either work backward or concentrate on the surface facts. What are the deep principles of what you're working on? Once you've done this, search the past for parallels—your past, the business past, the historical past. One common mistake here is to search in parallel organizations because "only they would know." Backing up and asking a broader question will aid in the search for solutions. When Motorola wanted to find out how to process orders more quickly, they went not to other electronics firms, but to Domino's Pizza and Federal Express.

4. **Patterns.** Look for patterns in personal, organization, or the world, in general successes and failures. What was common to each success or what was present in each failure but never present in a success? Focus on the successes; failures are easier to analyze but don't in themselves tell you what would work. Comparing successes, while less exciting, yields more information about underlying principles. The bottom line is to reduce your insights to principles or rules of thumb you think might be repeatable. When faced with the next new problem, those general underlying principles will apply again.

5. **Use oddball tactics.** What is a direct analogy between something you are working on and a natural occurrence? Ask what in nature parallels your problem. When the terrible surfs and motion of the tide threatened to defeat their massive dam project, the Delta Works, the Dutch used the violence of the North Sea to drive in the pilings, ending the danger of the south of the Netherlands flooding. Practice picking out anomalies—unusual facts that don't quite fit, like sales going down when they should have gone up. What do these odd things imply for strategy?

6. **Encourage yourself to do quick experiments and trials.** Studies show that 80% of innovations occur in the wrong place, are created by the wrong people (dye makers developed detergent; Post-it® Notes was an error in a glue formula), and 30–50% of technical innovations fail in tests within the company. Even among those that make it to the marketplace, 70–90% fail. The bottom line on change is a 95% failure rate, and the most successful innovators try lots of quick, inexpensive experiments to increase the chances of success.

7. **Access great minds.** Study a few great thinkers and philosophers like John Stuart Mill who outlined the basic logic of problem solving. Read their biographies or autobiographies for clues into how they used their intellectual skills.

8. **Do you do enough analysis?** Thoroughly define the problem. Look for patterns in data, don't just collect information. Put it in categories that make sense to you. A good rule of thumb is to analyze patterns and causes to come up with alternatives. Many of us just collect data, which numerous studies show increases our confidence but doesn't increase decision accuracy. Think out loud with others; see how they view the problem. Studies show that defining the problem and taking action usually occur simultaneously, so to break out of analysis paralysis, figure out what the problem is first. Then when a good alternative appears, you're likely to recognize it immediately.

D   Seeing the Bigger Picture

ISFPs don't often speculate since they generally prefer the action of the moment and seeking impact now. This can hurt their effectiveness because they fail to connect immediate problems to longer-term ones.

1. **Not curious?** Many managers are so wrapped up in today's problems that they aren't curious about tomorrow. They really don't care about the long-term future. They may not even be in the organization when the strategic plan is supposed to happen. They believe there won't be much of a future until we perform today. Being a visionary and a good strategist requires curiosity and imagination. It requires playing "what ifs." What are the implications of the growing gap between rich and poor? The collapse of retail pricing? The increasing influence of brand names? What if it turns out there is life on other planets, and we get the first message? What will that change? Will they need our products? What will happen when a larger percentage of the world's population is over the age of 65? The effects of terrorism? What if cancer is cured? Heart disease? AIDS? Obesity? What if the government outlaws or severely regulates some aspect of your business? True, nobody knows the answers, but good strategists know the questions. Work at developing broader interests outside your business. Subscribe to different magazines. Pick new shows to watch. Meet different people. Join a new organization. Look under some rocks. Think about tomorrow. Talk to others about what they think the future will bring.

2. **Narrow perspective?** Some are sharply focused on what they do and do it very well. They have prepared themselves for a narrow but satisfying career. Then someone tells them their job has changed, and they now have to be strategic. Being strategic requires a broad perspective. In addition to knowing one thing well, it requires that you know about a lot of things somewhat. You need to understand business. You need to understand markets. You need to understand how the world operates. You need to put all that together and figure out what all that means to your organization.

3. **Too busy?** Strategy is always last on the list. Solving today's problems, of which there are many, is job one. You have to make time for strategy. A good strategy releases future time because it makes choices clear and leads to less wasted effort, but it takes time to do. Delegation is usually the main key. Give away as much tactical day-to-day stuff as you can. Ask your people what they think they could

do to give you more time for strategic reflection. Another key is better time management. Put an hour a week on your calendar for strategic reading and reflection throughout the year. Don't wait until one week before the strategic plan is due. Keep a log of ideas you get from others, magazines, etc. Focus on how these impact your organization or function.

4. **Can't think strategically?** Strategy is linking several variables together to come up with the most likely scenario. Think of it as the search for and application of relevant parallels. It involves making projections of several variables at once to see how they come together. These projections are in the context of shifting markets, international affairs, monetary movements, and government interventions. It involves a lot of uncertainty, making risk assumptions, and understanding how things work together. How many reasons would account for sales going down? Up? How are advertising and sales linked? If the dollar is cheaper in Asia, what does that mean for our product in Japan? If the world population is aging and they have more money, how will that change buying patterns? Not everyone enjoys this kind of pie-in-the-sky thinking and not everyone is skilled at doing it.

5. **Managing remotely** is the true test of seeing the larger picture. It's impossible for you to do it all. Successful managers report high involvement in setting parameters, exceptions they want to be notified of, and expected outcomes. They detail what requires their involvement and what doesn't. When people call them for a decision, they always ask, "What do you think? What impact will it have on you—customers, etc.—if we do this?" rather than just render a judgment. If you don't, people will begin to delegate upward, and you'll be a close-in manager from a remote location. Help people think things through, and trust them to follow the plan. Delegation requires this clear communication about expectations and releasing the authority to decide and act.

E Problems With Peers

Due to their gentle natures, ISFPs often lack the presence to influence peers.

1. **Influencing.** Peers generally do not have power over each other. That means that influence skills, understanding, and trading are the currencies to use. Don't just ask for things; find some common ground where you can provide help. What do the peers you're contacting

need? Do you really know how they see the issue? Is it even important to them? How does what you're working on affect them? If it affects them negatively, can you trade something, appeal to the common good, figure out some way to minimize the work (volunteering staff help, for example)? Go into peer relationships with a trading mentality.

2. **Tentativeness can be viewed as a lack of confidence** and/or withholding information and viewpoints. You may not be expressive enough and don't build rapport in an active way. Say more often, "I'm glad to see you." "I'm looking forward to working with you." "I'm looking forward to your contribution." "Here's the contribution I'm hoping to make." Any of these statements can help you connect with others.

3. **Sometimes the problem is maneuvering through the complex maze called the organization.** How do you get things done sideways? Who are the movers and shakers in the organization? How do they get things done? Who do they rely on for expediting things through the maze? Who are the major gatekeepers who control the flow of resources, information, and decisions? Who are the guides and the helpers? Get to know them better. Who are the major resisters and stoppers? Try to avoid or go around them.

4. **If you see your peers as excessively competitive,** you may cut them out of the loop. Instead, give them a chance to be as cooperative as you think they should be. Ask them to explain their thinking and generate possibilities rather than stake out positions. Give them a second chance.

5. **Without agreeing or disagreeing, try on their views for size.** Can you understand their viewpoint? When peers blow off steam, don't react; return to facts and the problem, staying away from personal clashes. When a peer takes a rigid position, don't reject it. Ask why: What are the principles behind the position? How do we know it's fair? What's the theory of the case? Play out what would happen if his/her position was accepted.

6. **If a peer doesn't play fair, avoid telling others all about it.** This often boomerangs. What goes around comes around. Confront the peer directly, politely, and privately. Describe the unfair situation; explain the impact on you. Don't blame. Give the peer the chance to explain, ask questions, let him/her save some face, and see if you can resolve

the matter. Even if you don't totally accept what is said, it's better to solve the problem than win the argument.

7. **Monitor yourself in tough situations to get a sense of how you are coming across.** What's the first thing you attend to? How often do you take a stand vs. make an accommodating gesture? What proportion of your comments deals with relationships vs. the issue to be addressed? Mentally rehearse for worst-case scenarios/hard-to-deal-with people. Anticipate what the person might say and have responses prepared so as not to be caught off guard.

F Dislike of Routine and Repetition

ISFPs are very autonomous and like to live in the moment. As a consequence, they are generally bored with routine or repetition.

1. **Try to see the value in routine.** Pick a plan or procedure and do a historical analysis of how it came to be and why it is necessary. Resist the urge to change it or question its usefulness. Understand it first.

2. **Turn off your answer program.** We all have a need to provide answers as soon as possible to questions and problems. We all have preconceived notions, favorite solutions, and prejudices that prevent our intellectual skills from dealing with the real facts of the problem. For one-half of the time you have to deal with an issue or a problem, shut off your solution machine and just take in the facts.

3. **Compensate for your dislikes.** Find a person you admire and respect to deal with all the procedures you find oppressive. Let this person tell you if anything needs changing. Otherwise, trust his or her judgment.

G Delegation

Why bother teaching others when ISFPs like to do it themselves?

1. **How to delegate?** Communicate, set time frames and goals, and get out of the way. People need to know what it is you expect. What does the outcome look like? When do you need it by? What's the budget? What resources do they get? What decisions can they make? Do you want checkpoints along the way? How will we both know and measure how well the task is done? One of the most common problems with delegation is incomplete or cryptic up-front communication leading to frustration, a job not well done the first time,

rework, and a reluctance to delegate next time. Poor communicators always have to take more time managing because of rework. Analyze recent projects that went well and didn't go well. How did you delegate? Too much? Not enough? Unwanted pieces? Major chunks of responsibility? Workload distributed properly? Did you set measures? Overmanage or abdicate? Find out what your best practices are. Set up a series of delegation practices that can be used as if you're not there. What do you have to be informed of? What feedback loops can people use for midcourse correction? What questions should be answered as the work proceeds? What steps should be followed? What are the criteria to be followed? When will you be available to help?

2. **More what and why, less how.** The best delegators are crystal clear on what and when, and more open on how. People are more motivated when they can determine the how for themselves. Inexperienced delegators include the hows, which turn the people into task automatons instead of an empowered and energized staff. Tell them what and when and for how long, and let them figure out how on their own. Give them leeway. Encourage them to try things. Besides being more motivating, it's also more developmental for them. Add the larger context. Although it is not necessary to get the task done, people are more motivated when they know where this task fits in the bigger picture. Take three extra minutes and tell them why this task needs to be done, where it fits in the grander scheme, and its importance to the goals and objectives of the unit.

3. **Do you help your people learn by looking for repeating patterns?** Help them look for patterns in the situations and problems they deal with. What succeeded and what failed? What was common to each success or what was present in each failure but never present in a success? Focus on the successes; failures are easier to analyze but don't in themselves tell you what would work. Comparing successes, while less exciting, yields more information. The bottom line is help them reduce insights to principles or rules of thumb that might be repeatable. Ask them what they have learned to increase their skills and understanding, making them better managers or professionals. Ask them what they can do now that they couldn't do a year ago. Reinforce this and encourage more of it. Developing is learning in as many ways as possible.

Overusing ISFP Tendencies

If you sometimes overdo your preferred behaviors, you may need to work on:

A   Being Less Hypercritical

B   Working Faster

C   Being Less Dependent on a Few Relationships

D   Being More Active With Higher Management

E   Facing Conflict

ISTJ	ISFJ	INFJ	INTJ
ISTP	ISFP	INFP	INTP
ESTP	ESFP	ENFP	ENTP
ESTJ	ESFJ	ENFJ	ENTJ

A   Being Less Hypercritical

Under enough stress, ISFPs can appear suspicious and skeptical with others.

1. **Under extended stress,** you can become hypercritical of others and find an endless list of reasons for the unacceptability of some action or fact. You appear skeptical and touchy. Accept this for what it is—you. Think of it as your personal preferences speaking rather than reality. Seek feedback to find out what is really going on.

2. **You should work doubly hard at observing others.** Always select your interpersonal approach from the other person in, not from you out. Your best choice of approach will always be determined by the other person or group, not you. Think about each transaction as if the other person were a customer you wanted. How would you craft an approach?

3. **Listening.** Interpersonally skilled people are very good at listening. They listen to understand and take in information to select their response. They listen without interrupting. They ask clarifying questions. They don't instantly judge. Judgment might come later. They restate what the other person has said to signal understanding. They nod. They might jot down notes. Listeners get more data.

B Working Faster

ISFPs enjoy doing things and doing them well. Sometimes they work too long on one thing and don't pay enough attention to priorities or follow through once a task is done to their satisfaction. They may over commit and under deliver.

1. **Perfectionist?** Need or prefer or want to be 100% sure? Want to make sure that all or at least most of your decisions are right? A lot of people prefer that. Perfectionism is tough to let go of because most people see it as a positive trait for them. They pride themselves on never being wrong. Recognize perfectionism for what it might be—collecting more information than others do to improve confidence in making a fault-free decision and thereby avoiding the risk and criticism that would come from making decisions faster. Anyone with a brain, unlimited time, and 100% of the data can make good decisions. The real test is who can act the soonest, being right the most, with less than all the data. Some studies suggest even successful general managers are about 65% correct. If you need to be more timely, you need to reduce your own internal need for data and the need to be perfect. Try to decrease your need for data and your need to be right all the time slightly every week until you reach a more reasonable balance between thinking it through and taking action. Try making some small decisions on little or no data. Trust your intuition more. Your experience won't let you stray too far. Let your brain do the calculations.

2. **Procrastinator?** Are you a procrastinator? Get caught short on deadlines? Do it all at the last minute? Not only will you not be timely, your decision quality and accuracy will be poor. Procrastinators miss deadlines and performance targets. If you procrastinate, you might not produce consistent decisions. Start earlier. Always do 10% of thinking about the decision immediately after it is assigned so you can better gauge what it is going to take to finish the rest. Divide decisions into thirds or fourths, and schedule time to work on them spaced over the delivery period. Remember one of Murphy's Laws: It takes 90% of the time to do 90% of the project, and another 90% of the time to finish the remaining 10%. Always leave more time than you think it's going to take. Set up checkpoints for yourself along the way. Schedule early data collection and analysis. Don't wait until the last moment. Set an internal deadline one week before the real one.

3. **Set better priorities.** You may not have the correct set of priorities. Some people take action but on the wrong things. Effective managers typically spend about half their time on two or three key priorities. What should you spend half your time on? Can you name five things that you have to do that are less critical? If you can't, you're not differentiating well. People without priorities see their jobs as 97 things that need to be done right now—that will actually slow you down. Pick a few mission-critical things and get them done. Don't get diverted by trivia.

4. **Overcommitting.** A lot of trouble follows overcommitting. Overcommitting usually comes from wanting to please everyone or not wanting to face the conflict if you say no. You can only do so much. Only commit to that which you can actually do. Commit to a specific time for delivery. Write it down. Learn to say "no" pleasantly. Learn to pass it off to someone else who has the time—"Gee no, but I'm sure Susan could help you with that." Learn to say, "Yes, but it will take longer than you might want to wait," and give them the option of withdrawing the request. Learn to say, "Yes, but what else that I have already committed to do for you would you like to delay to get this done?"

5. **Do an upstream and downstream check with the people you work for,** work around, and those who work for you, to create a list of the administrative slip-ups you do that give them the most trouble. Be sure to ask them for help creating the list. That way, you have a focused list of the things you need to fix first. If you fix the top 10, maybe that will do and the rest of your habits can stay the same.

6. **Lay out the process.** Most well-running processes start out with a plan. What do I need to accomplish? What's the time line? What resources will I need? Who controls the resources—people, funding, tools, materials, support—I need? What's my currency? How can I pay for or repay the resources I need? Who wins if I win? Who might lose? Buy a flowcharting software program that does PERT and GANTT charts. Become an expert in its use. Use the output of the software to communicate your plans to others. Use the flowcharts in your presentations. Nothing helps move a process along better than a good plan. It helps the people who have to work under the plan. It leads to better use of resources. It gets things done faster. It helps anticipate problems before they occur. Lay out the work from A to Z. Many people are seen as lacking because they don't write down the sequence or parts of the work and leave something out. Ask others to comment on your ordering and note what's missing.

C Being Less Dependent on a Few Relationships

Generally, ISFPs gravitate to a few close relationships. This limits their perspective and their network in an organization.

1. **Pick people who are quite different from you and observe what they do and how they do it.** Then ask for their help on a problem. Just ask questions and understand their perspective. Don't make any judgments about the rightness or wrongness of their approach.

2. **Pick some tough critics to talk with.** Don't go to the few people you truly like, most likely because you share similar perspectives. Go to some you know will disagree with you and hear them out.

3. **Spend most of your time with just a few people?** Developed a comfort and liking for the few? Expand your repertoire to get your relationship quota up. Be an early adopter of something. Find some new thing, technique, software, tool, system, process, or skill relevant to your activity. Privately become an expert in it. Read the books. Get certified. Visit a location where it's being done. Then surprise everyone and be the first to introduce it into your world. Sell it. Train others. Integrate it into your work.

4. **Pick three tasks you've never done before and go do them.** If you don't know much about customers, work in a store or handle customer complaints; if you don't know what engineering does, go find out; task trade with someone. Meet with your colleagues from other areas and tell each other what and, more importantly, how you do what you do.

5. **Volunteer for task forces.** Task forces/projects are a great opportunity to learn new things in a low-risk environment. Task forces are one of the most common developmental events listed by successful executives. Such projects require learning other functions, businesses, or nationalities well enough that in a tight time frame you can appreciate how they think and why their area/position is important. In so doing, you get out of your own experience and start to see connections to a broader world—how international trade works; or more at home, how the pieces of your organization fit together.

6. **Pick a person in the organization who is different in some aspects from your advocate/mentor.** Observe what he/she does and how he/she does it. He/she is as successful as your advocate/mentor but does it in other ways. If possible, ask for a meeting/lunch to discuss his/her success and the things he/she has learned. See if he/she has

any interest in teaching you something and being a temporary coach. Get to know other potential advocates on and off work. Go for maximum variety in the towering strengths they possess.

7. **Are you the same in your personal life?** Do you eat at the same restaurants? Vacation at the same places? Holidays are always done the same as in the past? Buy the same make or type car over and over again? Have the same insurance agent your father had? Expand yourself. Go on adventures with the family. Travel to places you have not been before. Never vacation at the same place again. Eat at different theme restaurants. Go to events and meetings of groups you have never really met. Go to ethnic festivals and sample the cultures. Go to athletic events you've never attended before. Each week, you and your family should go on a personal learning adventure. See how many different perspectives you can add to your knowledge.

D Being More Active With Higher Management

ISFPs are not natural marketers of self. Because they are present focused, they are often seen as lacking career ambition and not being comfortable around higher management.

1. **Don't know what it takes?** Think of five successful people in your organization/field whom you know well and ask what drives them? What sorts of jobs have they held? What are their technical skills? Behavioral skills? Use standard competency lists such as those in *FYI For Your Improvement* to determine what the 10 key skills of each person are; compare this list with your own self-assessment and feedback. Ask Human Resources if they have a success profile for some of the jobs you may be interested in. Make a list of what you need to work on next. If you want to be a star, figure out what is important about your job to higher management. If you're an accountant, help management pinpoint high costs; if a chemist, a cheaper way to do what you're now doing. Learn to love the details that affect your field. If your strengths are not technical, help out coworkers or look for a management or organizational problem around you to solve.

2. **Not comfortable marketing yourself?** You don't know how to get promoted. You dislike people who blow their own horns. Here's how to do it. Build a performance track record of variety—start up things, fix things, innovate, make plans, come under budget. This is what will

get you promoted. All organizations are looking for broad thinkers to give fresh opportunities to. Start by thinking more broadly.

3. **Getting noticed by top decision makers.** Top managers aren't as interested in glitz as many would have you believe. They're interested in people who take care of problems, spot opportunities, ward off disaster, and have a broad repertoire of skills. They are looking for bold performers. But a better mousetrap alone is not enough. Volunteer for projects that will require interacting/presenting with higher management. Focus on activities that are the core of what your organization does. Find a business opportunity and make a reasoned case for it. Pick a big problem and work maniacally to solve it. You need to be seen and heard—but on substance, not fluff.

4. **Many people don't know how careers are built.** Most are put off by the popular myth of getting ahead. It's easy to get cynical and believe that successful people are political or sell out, suck up, knife people in the back, it's who you know, and so on. The facts are dramatically different from this. Those behaviors get people in trouble eventually. What has staying power is performing and problem solving on the current job, having a few notable strengths, and seeking new tasks you don't know how to do. It's solving every problem with tenacity, while looking for what you haven't yet done and getting yourself in a position to do it. Read *The Lessons of Experience* by McCall, Lombardo and Morrison for the careers of men and *Breaking the Glass Ceiling* by Morrison, White and Van Velsor for the careers of women to see how successful careers really happen.

5. **Be ready for Q&A from higher management.** Many people get in trouble during questions and answers. Don't fake answers; most high-level managers will tolerate a "Don't know but I'll get back to you on that." Think of all the questions ahead of time; ask someone else to look at what you are going to say and do and to think of questions they would ask. Rehearse the answers to the questions. Another place people get in trouble when challenged is by retreating to a safe recitation of facts; executives are usually asking for logic and problem analysis, not a repackaging of what you've already said. The worst case, of course, is when an executive rejects your argument. If this happens, draw the person out to see if you've been misunderstood and clarify. If that's not the case, let the disagreement be as it is. Few executives respect someone who drops an argument as soon as challenged. You should listen carefully and respond with logic in 30 seconds or less per point. Don't repeat the entire argument; long answers often backfire since people have already heard it and few

may agree with the questioner. In haste to be thorough, you may just look defensive.

6. **Find a confidant.** Ask a member of top management you know well and trust for advice on how you could feel better and perform more effectively when you transact with him/her and the rest of the team. Share your anxieties with a trusted colleague and ask for suggestions and observations. Find someone who appears comfortable in the settings you find difficult and ask how to do it.

7. **Don't know enough about your business?** Study your annual report and various other financial reports. If you don't know how, the major investment firms have basic documents explaining how to read financial documents. After you've done this, consult a pro and ask him/her what he/she looks at and why. Ask for lunch or just a meeting with the person who is in charge of the strategic planning process in your company. Have him/her explain the strategic plan for the organization. Particularly, have him/her point out the mission-critical functions and capabilities the organization needs to be on the leading edge to win.

E Facing Conflict

Preferring pleasantness, many ISFPs avoid conflict and don't freely express their opinions. It would be helpful if they would separate the personal aspects from the problem and focus there.

1. **Clear problem-focused communication.** Follow the rule of equity: Explain your thinking and ask them to explain theirs. Be able to state their position as clearly as they do whether you agree or not—give it legitimacy. Separate facts from opinions and assumptions. Generate a variety of possibilities first rather than stake out positions. Keep your speaking to 30–60 second bursts. Try to get them to do the same. Don't give the other side the impression you're lecturing or criticizing them. Explain objectively why you hold a view; make the other side do the same. Ask lots of questions, make fewer statements. To identify interests behind positions, ask why they hold them or why they wouldn't want to do something. Always restate their position to their satisfaction before offering a response.

2. **Tend to shy away from managerial courage situations?** Why? What's getting in your way? Are you prone to give up in tough situations, fear exposing yourself, don't like conflict, what? Ask yourself—what's the downside of delivering a message you think is right and will

eventually help the organization but may cause someone short-term pain. What if it turns out you were wrong? Treat any misinterpretations as chances to learn. What if you were the target person or group? Even though it might hurt, would you appreciate it if someone brought the data to your attention in time for you to fix it with minimal damage? What would you think of a person whom you later found out knew about it and didn't come forward, and you had to spend inordinate amounts of time and political currency to fix it? Follow your convictions. Follow due process. Step up to the plate and be responsible, win or lose. People will think better of you in the long term.

3. **Tough messages.** Be succinct. You have limited attention span in tough feedback situations. Don't waste time with a long preamble, particularly if the feedback is negative. If the feedback is negative and the recipient is likely to know it, go ahead and say it directly. They won't hear anything positive you have to say anyway. Don't overwhelm the person/group, even if you have a lot to say. Go from specific to general points. Keep it to the facts. Don't embellish to make your point. No passion or inflammatory language. Don't do it to harm or out of vengeance. Don't do it in anger. If feelings are involved for you, wait until you can describe them, not show them. Managerial courage comes in search of a better outcome, not destroying others. Stay calm and cool. If others are not composed, don't respond. Just return to the message.

4. **Listening under duress.** What if you're being criticized or attacked personally? What if people are wrong in what they are saying? The rules remain the same. You need to work on keeping yourself in a calm state when getting negative feedback. You need to shift your thinking. When getting the feedback, your only task is to accurately understand what the person is trying to tell you. It is not, at that point, to accept or refute. That comes later. Practice verbal Aikido, the ancient art of absorbing the energy of your opponent, and using it to manage him/her. Let the other side vent but don't react directly. Listen. Nod. Ask clarifying questions. But don't vent yourself. Don't judge. Keep him/her talking until he/she runs out of venom. Separate the person from the feedback.

I am easygoing and patient because I do not like to be distracted by emotions. I like to operate in crisis situations because my demeanor is a strength there.

— An ISFP Manager

■ ■ ■ ■ ■ ■ ■ ■ ■ ■ ■ ■ ■ ■ ■ ■ ■

APPLICATION

Your personal preferences play out in day-to-day problems and situations you face. Below is a case about your type dealing with such a situation. Use this to think through how you will integrate the tips you've considered and coach yourself to be more effective in your type.

ISFP Application Situation (Part 1)

When Jerry was given his severance, he had reached Vice President of Operations at the furniture company where he had worked since high school. During that time, he had completed an undergraduate degree in business administration while learning all facets of the business—from manufacturing through sales and distribution.

"I'm disillusioned and hurt at being fired," he tells you. "Nobody worked harder and longer hours than I did, and no one cared more about their direct reports. I just don't get it."

To this you respond, "Well, I'm a recruiter, not a counselor, and sometimes in situations like this it's useful for you to be talking with both. There are some things you and I can do to move forward. The first part of that, I think, is to do some assessment, and if you have access to performance reviews and 360° feedback, that would be helpful for me to see."

Jerry rummages through his briefcase and finds some reports in a couple of folders. He passes them to you, smiling deferentially and saying, "The outplacement material said you'd want to see these things." He reaches into his briefcase and pulls out another report, offering it to you. "It's my Myers-Briggs results."

Among the things you note in reviewing the various reports: Jerry's type is ISFP; his last two performance reviews (since being promoted to VP) both contained ratings that were generally at "meeting expectations," with a few exceptions where he was below expectations; there were comments from his boss about the need to delegate more effectively; and Jerry's 360° data showed his direct reports found him to be very accessible but didn't feel as though they were getting adequate development opportunities.

Thinking It Through: Strategy

■ Based on what you know from the summary above and what you know about the ISFP type, what do you think you're going to want to focus on with Jerry?

■ What do you want the outcome of this initial meeting to be?

Planning It Out: Tactics

■ What tendencies and preferences in Jerry's type (ISFP) indicate the kind of role you think he should explore in his job search?

■ What one thing would you urge Jerry to work on to improve his skills in the higher leadership functions, such as long-term planning?

■ Which of the tactics described in the Being More Effective section are applicable in this situation?

■ Which Overused Tendencies are most likely to come into play here?

ISFP Application Situation (Part 2)

■ The next time you meet with Jerry, it takes awhile to get down to work because when you ask him how he is, he starts out by telling you that he is upset about things going poorly at home. Seems the family was planning a vacation but Jerry felt as though he was burdened with having to do everything, and also his wife told him that he is too rigid and touchy and that he sometimes says unkind things to her.

Reflection

■ What do you suggest to Jerry at this point?

SUGGESTED READINGS

■■■■■■■■ Being a More Effective ISFP ■■■■■■■■

Taking Charge

Badaracco, Joseph L., Jr. *Defining Moments—When Managers Must Choose Between Right and Right.* Boston: Harvard Business School Press, 1997.

Bennis, Warren G. and Burt Nanus. *Leaders: Strategies for Taking Charge.* New York: HarperBusiness, 2003.

Calvert, Gene. *Highwire Management.* San Francisco: Jossey-Bass, Inc., 1993.

Chaleff, Ira. *The Courageous Follower: Standing Up to and for Our Leaders.* San Francisco: Berrett-Koehler Publishers, Inc., 2003.

Coponigro, Jeffrey R. *The Crisis Counselor: A Step-by-Step Guide to Managing a Business Crisis.* New York: McGraw-Hill/Contemporary Books, 2000.

Cox, Danny and John Hoover. *Leadership When the Heat's On.* New York: McGraw-Hill Trade, 2002.

Linsky, Martin and Ronald A. Heifetz. *Leadership on the Line: Staying Alive Through the Dangers of Leading.* Boston: Harvard Business School Press, 2002.

Communicating More Forcefully

Baldoni, John. *Great Communication Secrets of Great Leaders.* New York: McGraw-Hill, Inc., 2003.

Booher, Dianna. *Speak With Confidence: Powerful Presentations That Inform, Inspire, and Persuade.* New York: McGraw-Hill, Inc., 2002.

Collins, Patrick J. *Say It With Confidence.* New York: Prentice Hall, 1998.

Giuliani, Rudolph W. and Ken Kurson. *Leadership.* New York: Miramax, 2002.

Expanding Ways to Learn

DeGraff, Jeff and Katherine A. Lawrence. *Creativity at Work: Developing the Right Practices to Make Innovation Happen.* San Francisco: Jossey-Bass, Inc., 2002.

Flynn, Daniel J. *Intellectual Morons: How Ideology Makes Smart People Fall for Stupid Ideas.* New York: Crown Business Publishing, 2004.

Hammond, John S., Ralph L. Keeney and Howard Raiffer. *Smart Choices.* Boston: Harvard University Press, 1999.

Lucas, Robert W. *The Creative Training Idea Book: Inspired Tips and Techniques for Engaging and Effective Learning.* New York: AMACOM, 2003.

Von Oech, Roger. *Expect the Unexpected or You Won't Find It: A Creativity Tool Based on the Ancient Wisdom of Heraclitus.* San Francisco: Berrett-Koehler Publishers, Inc., 2002.

White, R.P., P. Hodgson and S. Crainer. *The Future of Leadership.* London: Pitman, 1996.

Yates, J. Frank. *Decision Management: How to Assure Better Decisions in Your Company.* San Francisco: Jossey-Bass, Inc., 2003.

Seeing the Bigger Picture

Chakravorti, Bhaskar. *The Slow Pace of Fast Change: Bringing Innovations to Market in a Connected World.* Boston: Harvard Business School Press, 2003.

Charan, Ram. *What the CEO Wants You to Know: How Your Company Really Works.* New York: Crown Business Publishing, 2001.

Collins, James C. *Good to Great: Why Some Companies Make the Leap...And Others Don't.* New York: HarperCollins, 2001.

Dudik, Evan Matthew. *Strategic Renaissance: New Thinking and Innovative Tools to Create Great Corporate Strategies Using Insights From History and Science.* New York: AMACOM, 2000.

The Futurist Magazine. http://www.wfs.org

Hamel, Gary. *Leading the Revolution.* Boston: Harvard Business School Press, 2002.

Hargadon, Andrew and Kathleen M. Eisenhardt. *How Breakthroughs Happen: The Surprising Truth About How Companies Innovate.* Boston: Harvard Business School Press, 2003.

Harvard Business Review. Phone: 800-988-0886 (US and Canada). Fax: 617-496-1029. Mail: Harvard Business Review. Subscriber Services, P.O. Box 52623. Boulder, CO 80322-2623 USA. http://www.hbsp.harvard.edu/products/hbr

Kaplan, Robert S. and David P. Norton. *The Strategy-Focused Organization: How Balanced Scorecard Companies Thrive in the New Business Environment.* Boston: Harvard Business School Press, 2000.

Porter, Michael E. *Competitive Strategy: Techniques for Analyzing Industries and Competitors.* New York: The Free Press, 1998.

Prahalad, C.K. and Venkat Ramaswamy. *The Future of Competition: Co-Creating Unique Value With Customers.* Boston: Harvard Business School Press, 2004.

Problems With Peers

Baker, Wayne E. *Networking Smart.* New York: Backinprint.com, 2000.

Bolton, Robert and Dorothy Grover Bolton. *People Styles at Work—Making Bad Relationships Good and Good Relationships Better.* New York: AMACOM, 1996.

Cartwright, Tatula. *Managing Conflict With Peers.* Greensboro, NC: Center for Creative Leadership, 2003.

Patterson, Kerry, Joseph Grenny, Ron McMillan, Al Switzler and Stephen R. Covey. *Crucial Conversations: Tools for Talking When Stakes Are High.* New York: McGraw-Hill/Contemporary Books, 2002.

Dislike of Routine and Repetition

Bossidy, Larry, Ram Charan and Charles Burck (Contributor). *Execution: The Discipline of Getting Things Done.* New York: Crown Business Publishing, 2002.

Keen, Peter G.W. *The Process Edge—Creating Value Where It Counts.* Boston: Harvard Business School Press, 1998.

Lawler, Edward E., III, Susan Albers Mohrman and George Benson. *Organizing for High Performance: Employee Involvement, TQM, Reengineering, and Knowledge Management in the Fortune 1000: The CEO Report.* San Francisco: Jossey-Bass, Inc., 2001.

Niven, P.R. *Balanced Scorecard Step-by-Step: Maximizing Performance and Maintaining Results.* New York: John Wiley & Sons, Inc., 2002.

Delegation

Allen, David. *Getting Things Done: The Art of Stress-Free Productivity.* New York: Penguin Books, 2003.

Bossidy, Larry, Ram Charan and Charles Burck (Contributor). *Execution: The Discipline of Getting Things Done.* New York: Crown Business Publishing, 2002.

Daniels, Aubrey C. *Bringing Out the Best in People.* New York: McGraw-Hill, Inc., 1994.

Genett, Donna M. *If You Want It Done Right, You Don't Have to Do It Yourself! The Power of Effective Delegation.* Sanger, CA: Quill Driver Books, 2004.

■■■■■■■■ Overusing ISFP Tendencies ■■■■■■■■

Being Less Hypercritical

Carter, Les. *The Anger Trap: Free Yourself From the Frustrations That Sabotage Your Life.* New York: John Wiley & Sons, Inc., 2003.

Ellis, Albert, Ph.D. *How to Control Your Anxiety Before It Controls You.* New York: Citadel Press, 2000.

Lerner, Harriet. *The Dance of Connection: How to Talk to Someone When You're Mad, Hurt, Scared, Frustrated, Insulted, Betrayed, or Desperate.* New York: Quill/HarperCollins, 2002.

Patterson, Kerry, Joseph Grenny, Ron McMillan, Al Switzler and Stephen R. Covey. *Crucial Conversations: Tools for Talking When Stakes Are High.* New York: McGraw-Hill/Contemporary Books, 2002.

Working Faster

Block, Peter. *The Answer to How Is Yes: Acting On What Matters.* San Francisco: Berrett-Koehler Publishers, Inc., 2001.

Byfield, Marilyn. *It's Hard to Make a Difference When You Can't Find Your Keys: The Seven-Step Path to Becoming Truly Organized.* New York: Viking Press, 2003.

Carrison, Dan. *Deadline! How Premier Organizations Win the Race Against Time.* New York: AMACOM, 2003.

Emmett, Rita. *The Procrastinator's Handbook: Mastering the Art of Doing It Now.* New York: Walker & Company, 2000.

Jennings, Jason and Laurence Haughton. *It's Not the Big That Eat the Small...It's the Fast That Eat the Slow.* New York: HarperCollins, 2001.

Murnighan, John Keith and John C. Mowen. *The Art of High-Stakes Decision-Making: Tough Calls in a Speed-Driven World.* New York: John Wiley & Sons, Inc., 2002.

Being Less Dependent on a Few Relationships

Benton, D.A. *Executive Charisma: Six Steps to Mastering the Art of Leadership.* New York: McGraw-Hill Trade, 2003.

Bolton, Robert and Dorothy Grover Bolton. *People Styles at Work—Making Bad Relationships Good and Good Relationships Better.* New York: AMACOM, 1996.

Brooks, Michael. *Instant Rapport.* New York: Warner Books, 1989.

Maxwell, John C. *Relationships 101.* London: Thomas Nelson, 2004.

Niven, David. *The 100 Simple Secrets of Successful People: What Scientists Have Learned and How You Can Use It.* New York: HarperBusiness, 2002.

Silberman, Melvin L. and Freda Hansburg. *Peoplesmart: Developing Your Interpersonal Intelligence.* San Francisco: Berrett-Koehler Publishers, Inc., 2000.

Being More Active With Higher Management

Bing, Stanley. *Throwing the Elephant: Zen and the Art of Managing Up.* New York: HarperBusiness, 2002.

Bolles, Richard N. *What Color Is Your Parachute? 2004: A Practical Manual for Job-Hunters & Career-Changers.* Berkeley, CA: Ten Speed Press, 2004.

Christian, Ken. *Your Own Worst Enemy: Breaking the Habit of Adult Underachievement.* New York: Regan Books, 2004.

Citrin, James M. and Richard A. Smith. *The Five Patterns of Extraordinary Careers.* New York: Crown Business, 2003.

Dominguez, Linda R. *How to Shine at Work.* New York: McGraw-Hill Trade, 2003.

Lombardo, Michael M. and Robert W. Eichinger. *FYI For Your Improvement* (4th ed.). Minneapolis, MN: Lominger Limited, Inc., 1996–2004.

McCall, Morgan W., Michael M. Lombardo and Ann M. Morrison. *The Lessons of Experience.* Lexington, MA: Lexington Books, 1988.

Morrison, Ann M., Randall P. White, Ellen Van Velsor and the Center for Creative Leadership. *Breaking the Glass Ceiling: Can Women Reach the Top of America's Largest Corporations?* Reading, MA: Addison-Wesley Publishing Company, 1992.

Facing Conflict

Cloke, Ken and Joan Goldsmith. *Resolving Conflicts at Work: A Complete Guide for Everyone on the Job.* San Francisco: Jossey-Bass, Inc., 2000.

Dana, Daniel. *Conflict Resolution.* New York: McGraw-Hill Trade, 2000.

Guttman, Howard M. *When Goliaths Clash: Managing Executive Conflict to Build a More Dynamic Organization.* New York: AMACOM, 2003.

Masters, Marick Francis and Robert R. Albright. *The Complete Guide to Conflict Resolution in the Workplace.* New York: AMACOM, 2002.

CHAPTER 7

INFP
Introverted Feeling
with
Extraverted Intuiting

■■■■■■■■■■■■■■■■

4.4% of Population
2.7% of Managers

■■■■■■■■■■■■■■■■

Typical Strengths

A Peacekeeper
Caring
Idealistic
Good at Projects
Participative
Understanding Individual Differences

ISTJ	ISFJ	INFJ	INTJ
ISTP	ISFP	INFP	INTP
ESTP	ESFP	ENFP	ENTP
ESTJ	ESFJ	ENFJ	ENTJ

I focus on what is really important and leave everything else to others.

– An INFP Manager

Basic Habits of Mind

Introverted Feeling drives INFPs to match outcomes with their values and sense of purpose. Aided by Extraverted Intuiting, which seeks out possibilities and patterns, they use this to evaluate how acceptable people, ideas, and events are.

Extraverted Sensing is used to pick up subtle shifts in body language and acute awareness of their environment. INFPs usually read places well, and feel comfortable or uncomfortable intuitively. Extraverted Thinking acts as an evaluator, making INFPs appear critical and unnecessarily skeptical at times.

Typical Communication Patterns

- INFPs like to discuss future actions that might be taken.

- They ask questions to "get along" with the people with whom they are talking.

- Curious about others and their lives, they are usually well liked.

- Their curiosity about people often leads to some unconventional speculation about situations.

- Their passion is to cause no harm, so they have to consider all options.

- They often give complex, reflective summaries of their thoughts and ideas.

General Learning Strategy

- INFPs usually prefer holistic models and frameworks when learning. They need to see how the learning will be valuable to life mission and goals.

- Typical learning strategies are journal writing, attending seminars, and using creative expression to illustrate learning.

- Their learning is generally enhanced by providing minimal structure with a few open-ended questions. Role plays or other simulations and non-competitive situations are also appealing.

Interpersonal Qualities Related to Motivation

- INFPs are generally motivated by autonomy and enjoy the complexity of dealing with people and situations.

- Introspective and gentle, they like to keep their options open.

- When they feel there is less room to find alternate solutions to problems, their motivation decreases.

- They will usually put a great deal of energy into actualizing personal values.

Blind Spots

- INFPs are usually not aware that they appear to be overdependent on a select group, unconcerned with making a good impression, and too reserved to be effective.

- A general lack of follow-through in a timely manner is considered an issue by observers of this type.

Stress Related Behavior

- Even INFPs can get surprised with how touchy and unrealistic they become when they are under stress.

- They can become noticeably distracted and impulsive as the stress increases.

- When stress is extended, they can become very critical and petty, seeming harsh and very negative toward others.

Potential Barriers to Effectiveness

- Being guarded, detached, impatient, and at times dogmatic and opinionated are considered unattractive qualities for this type.

- Although likable, their reserved nature leads to a lack of sociability that can give people discomfort.

Being a More Effective INFP

A   Approachability
B   Taking Charge
C   Dealing With Conflict
D   Technical Focus
E   Drive for Results
F   Informing

ISTJ	ISFJ	INFJ	INTJ
ISTP	ISFP	INFP	INTP
ESTP	ESFP	ENFP	ENTP
ESTJ	ESFJ	ENFJ	ENTJ

A   Approachability

As much as INFPs care deeply about others, they can appear quite reserved, although they are rarely shy. They desire to have meaningful contact with others and don't put out effort if they don't think it will be reciprocated.

1. **You may clam up around talkative people** because you are busy processing what they said, and you have just finished point one when they are already on point four. This can make you appear inscrutable or perhaps disinterested in what they have to say. If you are around a true talker, this may be the one time you need to interrupt. Wave a hand. Smile. Make a comment or ask a question. The goal is not to disagree or cause turmoil, but simply to slow them down.

2. **Lower your expectations.** INFPs care more than most people and it's a bit unrealistic to expect others to care as much as you do. In your case, the golden rule doesn't usually work. Instead, look for small wins and take pleasure that some other types of people are giving as much as they can.

3. **Personalizing.** Approachable people work to know and remember important things about the people they work around, for, and with. Know three things about everybody—their interests or their children or something you can chat about other than the business agenda. Treat life as a small world. If you ask a few questions, you'll find you have something in common with virtually anyone. Establish things you can talk about with each person you work with that go beyond strictly work transactions. These need not be social—they could be issues of strategy, global events, market shifts. The point is to forge common ground and connections.

4. **Practice.** For low-risk practice, talk to strangers off-work. Set a goal of meeting 10 new people at a social gathering; find out what you have in common with them. Initiate contact at your place of worship, at

PTA meetings, in the neighborhood, at the supermarket, on the plane, and on the bus.

5. **The first three minutes.** Managing the first three minutes is essential. The tone is set. First impressions are formed. Work on being open and approachable, and take in information during the beginning of a transaction. This means putting others at ease so that they feel okay about disclosing. It means initiating rapport, listening, sharing, understanding, and comforting. Approachable people get more information, know things earlier, and can get others to do more things. The more you can get them to initiate and say early in the transaction, the more you'll know about where they are coming from, and the better you can tailor your approach.

6. **To understand the differences among people,** look to the obvious first. What do they do first? What do they emphasize in their speech? People focus on different things—taking action, details, concepts, feelings, other people. What's their interaction style? People come in different styles—pushy, tough, soft, matter-of-fact, and so on. To figure these out, listen for the values behind their words and note what they have passion and emotion around. One key to getting anything of value done in the work world is the ability to see differences in people and to manage against and use those differences for everyone's benefit. Interpersonal savvy is meeting each person where he/she is to get done what you need to get done. Basically, people respond favorably to ease of transaction. If you make it easy by accepting their normal mode of doing things, not fighting their style, and neither defending your own nor letting style get in the way of performance, things will generally run smoothly.

B Taking Charge

INFPs don't seek the limelight and can be seen as too interested in harmony, even when more decisive action is called for.

1. **Leading is riskier than following.** While there are a lot of personal rewards for leading, leading puts you in the limelight. Think about what happens to political leaders and the scrutiny they face. Leaders have to be internally secure. Do you feel good about yourself? They have to please themselves first that they are on the right track. Can you defend to a critical and impartial audience the wisdom of what you're doing? They have to accept lightning bolts from detractors. Can you take the heat? People will always say it should have been

done differently. Listen to them, but be skeptical. Even great leaders are wrong sometimes. They accept personal responsibility for errors and move on to lead some more. Don't let criticism prevent you from taking the lead. Build up your heat shield. Conduct a postmortem immediately after finishing milestone efforts. This will indicate to all that you're open to continuous improvement whether the result was stellar or not.

2. **Against the grain tough stands.** Taking a tough stand demands confidence in what you're saying along with the humility that you might be wrong—one of life's paradoxes. To prepare to take the lead on a tough issue, work on your stand through mental interrogation until you can clearly state in a few sentences what your stand is and why you hold it. Build the business case. How do others win? People don't line up behind laundry lists or ambiguous objectives. Ask others for advice—scope the problem, consider options, pick one, develop a rationale, then go with it until proven wrong. Then redo the process. If this doesn't help, find out where the pain is for you. What have you been avoiding? Examine your past and see where taking-charge behavior has gotten you in trouble or you thought it would get you in trouble. Isolate the most troublesome elements, such as forgetting things under pressure, trouble with fierce debate, problems with unpopular stands, and things moving too fast. Devise counter-strategies.

3. **Selling your leadership.** While some people may welcome what you say and want to do, others will go after you or even try to minimize the situation. Some will sabotage. To sell your leadership, keep your eyes on the prize but don't specify how to get there. Present the outcomes, targets, and goals without the how to's. Welcome their ideas—good and bad. Any negative response is a positive if you learn from it. Allow them to fill in the blanks, ask questions, and disagree without appearing impatient with them. Allow others to save face; concede small points, invite criticism of your own. Help them figure out how to win. Keep to the facts and the problem before the group; stay away from personal clashes.

C Dealing With Conflict

The primary issue for INFPs is keeping perspective. Conflict becomes very visceral to them. They need to step back and realize it's not about them. INFPs often tend to take on the problems of others as if they were their own. While admirable, they can't fix everything and can get frustrated and become volatile.

1. **Clear problem-focused communication.** Follow the rule of equity: Explain your thinking and ask them to explain theirs. Be able to state their position as clearly as they do whether you agree or not—give it legitimacy. Separate facts from opinions and assumptions. Generate a variety of possibilities first rather than stake out positions. Keep your speaking to 30–60 second bursts. Try to get them to do the same. Don't give the other side the impression you're lecturing or criticizing them. Explain objectively why you hold a view; make the other side do the same. Ask lots of questions, make fewer statements. To identify interests behind positions, ask why they hold them or why they wouldn't want to do something. Always restate their position to their satisfaction before offering a response.

2. **Downsizing the conflict.** Almost all conflicts have common points that get lost in the heat of the battle. After a conflict has been presented and understood, start by saying that it might be helpful to see if we agree on anything. Write them on the flip chart. Then write down the areas left open. Focus on common goals, priorities, and problems. Keep the open conflicts as small as possible and concrete. The more abstract it gets, "We don't trust your unit," the more unmanageable it gets. To this respond, "Tell me your specific concern—why exactly don't you trust us; can you give me an example?" Usually after calm discussion, they don't trust your unit on this specific issue under these specific conditions. That's easier to deal with. Allow others to save face by conceding small points that are not central to the issue—don't try to hit a home run every time. If you can't agree on a solution, agree on a procedure to move forward. Collect more data. Appeal to a higher power. Get a third-party arbitrator. Something. This creates some positive motion and breaks stalemates.

3. **Cooperative relations.** The opposite of conflict is cooperation. Developing cooperative relationships involves demonstrating real and perceived equity, the other side feeling understood and respected, and taking a problem-oriented point of view. To do this more: Increase the realities and perceptions of fairness—don't try to win every battle

and take all the spoils; focus on the common-ground issues and interests of both sides—find wins on both sides, give in on little points; avoid starting with entrenched positions—show respect for them and their positions; and reduce any remaining conflicts to the smallest size possible.

4. **Practice Aikido,** the ancient art of absorbing the energy of your opponent and using it to manage him/her. Let the other side vent frustration or blow off steam, but don't react. Listen. Nod. Ask clarifying questions. Ask open-ended questions like, "What one change could you make so we could achieve our objectives better?" "What could I do that would help the most?" Restate their position periodically to signal you have understood. But don't react. Keep them talking until they run out of venom. When the other side takes a rigid position, don't reject it. Ask why: What are the principles behind the position? How do we know it's fair? What's the theory of the case? Play out what would happen if their position was accepted. Then explore the concern underlying the answer. Separate the people from the problem. When someone attacks you, rephrase it as an attack on the problem. In response to threats, say you'll only negotiate on merit and fairness. If the other side won't play fair, surface their game—"It looks like you're playing good cop, bad cop. Why don't you settle your differences and tell me one thing?" In response to unreasonable proposals, attacks, or a non-answer to a question, you can always say nothing. People will usually respond by saying more, coming off their position a bit, or at least revealing their true interests. Many times, with unlimited venting and your understanding, the actual conflict shrinks.

5. **Get a bit too touchy under stress?** Do your statements have an edge to them? In conflict situations, what reactions do you have (such as impatience or non-verbals like flushing or drumming your pen or fingers)? Learn to recognize those as soon as they start and substitute something more neutral. Most emotional responses to conflict come from personalizing the issue. Separate people issues from the problem at hand, and deal with people issues separately and later if they persist. Always return to facts and the problem before the group; stay away from personal clashes. Attack the problem by looking at common interests and underlying concerns, not people and their positions. Try on their views for size—the emotion as well as the content. Ask yourself if you understand their feelings. Ask what they would do if they were in your shoes. See if you can restate each other's position and advocate it for a minute to get inside each other's

place. If you get emotional, pause and collect yourself. You are not your best when you get emotional. Then return to the problem.

6. **Bargaining and trading.** Since you can't absolutely win all conflicts unless you keep pulling rank, you have to learn to horse-trade and bargain. What do they need that I have? What could I do for them outside this conflict that could allow them to give up something I need now in return? How can we turn this into a win for both of us?

7. **Questions.** In win-win and something-something negotiations, the more information you have about the other side, the more you will have to work with. What can you learn about what they know before going in? What will they do if they don't reach an agreement with you? In the negotiation, ask more questions, make fewer statements. Ask clarifying questions: "What did you mean by that?" Probes: "Why do you say that?" Motives: "What led you to that position?" Get everything out that you can. Don't negotiate assumptions, negotiate facts.

D Technical Focus

INFPs often are global thinkers who don't get into detail much.

1. **Check yourself for these common errors in thinking:** Do you state as facts things that are really opinions or assumptions? Are you sure these assertions are facts? State opinions and assumptions as that and don't present them as facts. Do you attribute cause and effect to relationships when you don't know if one causes the other? If sales are down, and we increase advertising and sales go up, this doesn't prove causality. They are simply related. Say we know that the relationship between sales/advertising is about the same as sales/number of employees. If sales go down, we probably wouldn't hire more people, so make sure one thing causes the other before acting on it. Do you generalize from a single example without knowing if that single example does generalize?

2. **Do you do enough analysis?** Thoroughly define the problem. Figure out what causes it. Keep asking why. See how many causes you can come up with and how many organizing buckets you can put them in. This increases the chance of a better solution because you can see more connections. Look for patterns in data, don't just collect information. Put it in categories that make sense to you. A good rule of thumb is to analyze patterns and causes to come up with alternatives. Many of us just collect data, which numerous studies

show increases our confidence but doesn't increase decision accuracy. Think out loud with others; see how they view the problem. Studies show that defining the problem and taking action usually occur simultaneously, so to break out of analysis paralysis, figure out what the problem is first. Then when a good alternative appears, you're likely to recognize it immediately.

3. **Locate a pro.** Find the seasoned master professional in the technology or function, and ask whether he/she would mind showing you the ropes and tutoring you. Most don't mind having a few "apprentices" around. Help him or her teach you. Ask, "How do you know what's important? What do you look at first? Second? What are the five keys you always look at or for? What do you read? Who do you go to for advice?"

4. **Sign up.** Almost all functions have national and sometimes regional professional associations made up of hundreds of people who do well what you need to learn every day. Sign up as a member. Buy some of the introductory literature. Go to some of their workshops. Go to the annual conference.

5. **Learn to think as an expert in the technology thinks.** Take problems to him/her and ask what are the keys he/she looks for; observe what he/she considers significant and not significant. Chunk up data into categories so you can remember it. Devise five key areas or questions you can consider each time a technical issue comes up. Don't waste your time learning facts; they won't be useful unless you have conceptual buckets to put them in.

6. **Teach others.** Form a study group and take turns presenting on new, different, or unknown aspects of the technology. Having to teach it will force you to conceptualize and understand it more deeply. The relationships you form in such groups pay off in other ways as well. One company found its technicians learned more from coffee break conversations than from manuals.

E Drive for Results

While INFPs love to work on projects and get results on them, many times the larger issue of results gets neglected in favor of their latest cause. At other times, they may become perfectionistic, because anything less would let down the people they care about.

1. **Priorities?** You don't have a correct set of priorities. Some people get results, but on the wrong things. Effective managers typically spend about half their time on two or three key priorities. What should you spend half your time on? Can you name five things that are less critical? If you can't, you're not differentiating well. Or even if you know the priorities, your team doesn't. You communicate that everything is important and has a deadline of yesterday. They see their jobs as 97 things that need to be done right now. To deal with this, ask yourself what would happen if they only did four or five things today? What would they be? Ask what the three things they spend the most time on are, and what they would be if we were doing things better? Find out what the 10–20% most time-consuming activities are, and either eliminate them or structure them through processes and policies to take less time.

2. **Set goals for yourself and others.** Most people work better if they have a set of goals and objectives to achieve and a standard everyone agrees to measure accomplishments against. Most people like stretch goals. They like them even better if they have had a hand in setting them. Set checkpoints along the way to be able to measure progress. Give yourself and others as much feedback as you can.

3. **How to get things done.** Some don't know the best way to produce results. There is a well-established set of best practices for producing results—TQM, ISO and Six Sigma. If you are not disciplined in how to design work flows and processes for yourself and others, buy one book on each of these topics. Go to one workshop on efficient and effective work design. Ask those responsible for total work systems in your organization for help.

4. **When you are stuck, write down the pros and cons for each option.** Check what effect each would have both on the short and long term. Are there cost differences? Is one resource more efficient than the other? Is one apt to be more successful than the other? Think about the interaction of both short- and long-term goals. Sometimes what you decide to do today will hurt you or the organization downstream.

When making either a short-term or long-term choice, stop for a second and ask what effect this might have on the other. Adjust as necessary.

5. **Perfectionist?** Need or prefer or want to be 100% sure? Lots might prefer that. Perfectionism is tough to let go of because most people see it as a positive trait for themselves. Recognize your perfectionism for what it might be—collecting more information than others to improve your confidence in making a fault-free decision and thereby avoiding risk and criticism. Try to decrease your need for data and your need to be right all the time slightly every week until you reach a more reasonable balance between thinking it through and taking action. Try making some small decisions on little or no data. Anyone with a brain and 100% of the data can make good decisions. The real test is who can act the soonest with a reasonable amount, but not all, of the data. Some studies suggest successful general managers are about 65% correct. Trust your intuition. Let your brain do the calculations.

6. **Give up after one or two tries?** If you have trouble going back the second or third time to get something done, then switch approaches. Sometimes people get stuck in a repeating groove that's not working. Do something different next time. If you visited the office of someone you have difficulties with, invite him/her to your office next time. Think about multiple ways to get the same outcome. For example, to push a decision through, you could meet with stakeholders first, go to a single key stakeholder, study and present the problem to a group, call a problem-solving session, or call in an outside expert. Be prepared to do them all when obstacles arise.

7. **Focus on measures.** How would you tell if the goal was accomplished? If the things I asked others to do were done right, what outcomes could we all agree on as measures of success? Most groups can easily come up with success measures that are different from, and more important to them, than formal measures. Ask them to do so.

8. **Start earlier.** Always do 10% of thinking about the decision immediately after it is assigned so you can better gauge what it is going to take to finish the rest. Divide decisions into thirds or fourths, and schedule time to work on them spaced over the delivery period. Remember one of Murphy's Laws: It takes 90% of the time to do 90% of the project, and another 90% of the time to finish the remaining 10%. Always leave more time than you think it's going to take. Set up checkpoints for yourself along the way. Schedule early data collection

and analysis. Don't wait until the last moment. Set an internal deadline one week before the real one.

F Informing

While informative when related to their mission, many INFPs don't get into enough detail to keep others well informed on more ordinary matters. They are more likely to work through it themselves and not be explicit enough.

1. **Don't inform enough.** Are you a minimalist? Do you tell people only what they need to know to do their little piece of the puzzle? People are motivated by being aware of the bigger picture. They want to know what to do in order to do their jobs and more. How does what they are doing fit into the larger picture? What are the other people working on and why? Many people think that's unnecessary information and that it would take too much time to do. They're wrong. The sense of doing something worthwhile is the number two motivator at work! It results in a high return on motivation and productivity. (Try to increase the amount of more-than-your-job information you share.) Focus on the impact on others by figuring out who information affects. Put five minutes on your meeting agenda. Ask people what they want to know and, assuming it's not confidential information, tell them. Pick a topic each month to tell your people about.

2. **A loner.** Do you keep to yourself? Work alone or try to? Do you hold back information? Do you parcel out information on your schedule? Do you share information to get an advantage or to win favor? Do people around you know what you're doing and why? Are you aware of things others would benefit from, but you don't take the time to communicate? In most organizations, these things and things like it will get you in trouble. Organizations function on the flow of information. Being on your own and preferring peace and privacy are okay as long as you communicate things to bosses, peers, and teammates that they need to know and would feel better if they knew. Don't be the source of surprises.

Overusing INFP Tendencies

If you sometimes overdo your preferred behaviors, you may need to work on:

A Being More Personally Flexible

B Being More Patient

C Developing Better Presence

D Better Follow-Through

E Being Less Dependent on a Few Relationships

F Better Relationships With Higher Management

ISTJ	ISFJ	INFJ	INTJ
ISTP	ISFP	INFP	INTP
ESTP	ESFP	ENFP	ENTP
ESTJ	ESFJ	ENFJ	ENTJ

A Being More Personally Flexible

INFPs are generally very flexible and adaptable until they bump into something related to their sense of mission and purpose, and then people find they have run into a 100-million-mile-thick iron wall.

1. **You may be seen as rigid in your values stances and unwilling to accept, or even see, those of others.** Rigid stances often come from childhood and early adult experiences. You may have reduced your beliefs to rigid commandments. You need to know why you hold these values and critically examine whether they are appropriate here. Statements of belief are pronouncements—a true value holds up to action scrutiny; you can say why you hold it, how it plays out in different situations, and what happens when it conflicts with other values.

2. **Incrementalism.** The essence of dealing comfortably with uncertainty is the tolerance of errors and mistakes, and absorbing the possible heat and criticism that follow. Acting on an ill-defined problem with no precedents to follow means shooting in the dark with as informed a decision as you can make at the time. People who are good at this are incrementalists. They make a series of smaller decisions, get instant feedback, correct the course, get a little more data, move forward a little more, until the bigger problem is under control. They

don't try to get it right the first time. Many problem-solving studies show that the second or third try is when we really understand the underlying dynamics of problems. They also know that the more uncertain the situation is, the more likely it is they will make mistakes in the beginning. So, you need to work on two practices: Start small so you can recover more quickly. Do little somethings as soon as you can and get used to heat.

3. **Transitions.** Which transitions are the toughest for you? Write down the five toughest for you. What do you have a hard time switching to and from? Use this knowledge to assist you in making a list of discontinuities (tough transitions) you face, such as confronting people vs. being approachable and accepting, leading vs. following, going from firing someone to a business-as-usual staff meeting. Write down how each of these discontinuities makes you feel and what you may do that gets you in trouble. For example, you may not shift gears well after a confrontation, or you may have trouble taking charge again after passively sitting in a meeting all day. Create a plan to attack each of the tough transitions.

4. **Control your instant responses to shifts.** Many of us respond to the fragmentation and discontinuities of work as if they were threats instead of the way life is. Sometimes our emotions and fears are triggered by switching from active to passive or soft to tough. This initial anxious response lasts 45–60 seconds, and we need to buy some time before we say or do something inappropriate. Research shows that generally somewhere between the second and third thing you think to say or do is the best option. Practice holding back your first response long enough to think of a second and a third. Manage your shifts, don't be a prisoner of them.

5. **Use mental rehearsal to think about different ways you could carry out a transaction.** Try to see yourself acting in opposing ways to get the same thing done—when to be tough, when to let them decide, when to deflect the issue because it's not ready to decide. What cues would you look for to select an approach that matches? Practice trying to get the same thing done with two different groups with two different approaches. Did they both work?

6. **Avoid early rigid positions.** It's just physics. Action gets equal reaction. Strong statements. Strongly worded positions. Casting blame. Absolutes. Lines in the sand. Unnecessary passion. All of these will be responded to in kind, will waste time, cause ill will, and possibly prevent a win-win or a something-something. It only has a

place in one-time, either/or negotiations, and even there it isn't recommended. Similarly, watch out for overcommitment to any need or course of action. Look for information that goes against your preferences. Be able to adjust your position and your wants. If you can't, your ego is getting the best of you. If you can't walk away until you get X, you'll probably either overpay or blow the negotiation. Don't negotiate around a single issue if you can add another. This is another situation that leads to rigidity.

7. **Selective resistance.** Do you adapt to some and not to others? You probably have good people buckets and bad people buckets and signal your disagreement with them to the bad bucket groups or individuals. You may have good group buckets and bad group buckets—gender, race, age, origin. Learn to understand without accepting or judging. Listen, take notes, ask questions, and be able to make their case as well as they can. Pick something in their argument you agree with. Present your argument in terms of the problem only—why you think this is the best manner to deal with a mutually agreed-upon problem. A careful observer should not be able to tell your assessment of people or their arguments at the time. Find someone who is a fair observer and get a critique. Was I fair? Did I treat everyone the same? Were my objections based on reasoning against standards and not directed at people?

B Being More Patient

INFPs lack patience with themselves under stress. They feel they have let others down. Regardless, they can express criticism toward others as well or shut down and appear somewhat indifferent.

1. **Under extended stress,** you can become hypercritical of others and find an endless list of reasons for the unacceptability of some action or fact. You appear skeptical and touchy. Accept this for what it is—you. Think of it as your personal preferences speaking rather than reality. Seek feedback to find out what is really going on.

2. **Blame and vengeance?** Do you feel a need to punish the people and groups that set you off? Do you become hostile, angry, sarcastic, or vengeful? While all that may be temporarily satisfying to you, they will all backfire and you will lose in the long term. When someone attacks you, rephrase it as an attack on a problem. Reverse the argument—ask what they would do if they were in your shoes. When the other side takes a rigid position, don't reject it. Ask why: What are

the principles behind the offer? How do we know it's fair? What's the theory of the case? Play out what would happen if their position was accepted. Let the other side vent frustration or blow off steam, but don't react. When you do reply to an attack, keep it to the facts and their impact on you. It's fine for you to draw conclusions about the impact on yourself—"I felt blindsided." It's not fine for you to tell others their motives—"You blindsided me" means you did it, probably meant to, and I know the meaning of your behavior. So state the meaning for yourself; ask others what their actions meant.

3. **Questions.** Good listeners ask lots of questions to get to a good understanding. Probing questions. Clarifying questions. Confirming— is this what you are saying—questions. Ask one more question than you do now and add to that until people signal you that they think you are truly listening.

4. **Listening to those who waste a lot of time.** With those you don't have time to listen to, switch to being a teacher. Try to help them craft their communications to you in a more acceptable way. Tell them to be shorter next time. Come with more/less data. Structure the conversation by helping them come up with categories and structures to stop their rambling. Good listeners don't signal to the "bad" people that they are not listening or are not interested. Don't signal to anyone what bucket they're in. Put your mind in neutral, nod, ask questions, be helpful.

5. **Listening to people you don't like.** What do people see in them who do like them or can at least get along with them? What are their strengths? Do you have any common interests? Talk less and ask more questions to give them a second chance. Don't judge their motives and intentions—do that later.

6. **Listening to people you like but...**

   ■ They are disorganized. Interrupt to summarize and keep the discussion focused. While interrupting is generally not a good tactic, it's necessary here.

   ■ They just want to chat. Ask questions to focus them; don't respond to chatty remarks.

   ■ They want to unload a problem. Assume when people tell you something they are looking for understanding; indicate that by being able to summarize what they said. Don't offer any advice.

- They are chronic complainers. Ask them to write down problems and solutions and then let's discuss it. This turns down the volume while, hopefully, moving them off complaining.

- They like to complain about others. Ask if they've talked to the person. Encourage them to do so. If that doesn't work, summarize what they have said without agreeing or disagreeing.

7. **Impatience triggers.** Some people probably bring out your impatience more than others. Who are they? What is it about them that makes you more impatient? Pace? Language? Thought process? Accent? These people may include people you don't like, who ramble, who whine and complain, or who are repetitive advocates for things you have already rejected. Mentally rehearse some calming tactics before meeting with people who trigger your impatience. Work on understanding their positions without judging them—you can always judge later. In all cases, focus them on the issues or problems to be discussed, return them to the point, interrupt to summarize, and state your position. Try to gently train them to be more efficient with you next time without damaging them in the process.

8. **Work on your openness and approachability.** Impatient people don't get as much information as patient listeners do. They are more often surprised by events when others knew they were coming. People are hesitant to talk to impatient people. It's too painful. People don't pass on hunches, unbaked thoughts, maybes, and possibles to impatient people. You will be out of the information loop and miss important information you need to know to be effective. Suspend judgment on informal communications. Just take it in. Acknowledge that you understand. Ask a question or two. Follow up later.

9. **Rein in your horse.** Impatient people provide answers, conclusions, and solutions too early in the process. Others haven't even understood the problem yet. Providing solutions too quickly will make your people dependent and irritated. If you don't teach them how you think and how you can come up with solutions so fast, they will never learn. Take the time to really define the problem—not impatiently throw out a solution. Brainstorm what questions need to be answered in order to resolve it. Give your people the task to think about for a day and come back with some solutions. Be a teacher instead of a dictator of solutions. Study yourself. Keep a journal of what triggered your behavior and what the observed consequences

were. Learn to detect and control your triggers before they get you in trouble.

10. **Task impatience.** Impatient people check in a lot. How's it coming. Is it done yet? When will it be finished? Let me see what you've done so far. That is disruptive to due process and wastes time. When you give out a task or assign a project, establish agreed-upon time checkpoints. You can also assign percentage checkpoints. Check in with me when you are about 25% finished so we can make midcourse corrections and 75% finished so we can make final corrections. Let them figure out how to do the task. Hold back from checking in at other than the agreed-upon times and percentages.

C   Developing Better Presence

INFPs can act in a very tentative fashion because they fear their decisions can be wrong and affect many people. They typically have not developed their presence, speaking skills, or assertiveness.

1. **Leadership presence.** Leading takes presence. You have to look and sound like a leader. Voice is strong. Eye contact. Intensity. Confidence. A lot of leadership presence has to do with forceful presentation skills. Giving good presentations is a known technology. There are several books and workshops you can take. Look to workshops that use videotaping. Join your local Toastmasters Club for some low-risk training and practice. Look to small things such as do you look like a leader? What colors do you wear? Do you dress the part? Are your glasses right? Is your office configured right? Do you sound confident? Do you whine and complain or do you solve problems? If I met you for the first time in a group of 10, would I pick you as the leader?

2. **Tentativeness can be viewed as a lack of confidence** and/or withholding information and viewpoints. You may not be expressive enough and don't build rapport in an active way. Say more often, "I'm glad to see you." "I'm looking forward to working with you." "I'm looking forward to your contribution." "Here's the contribution I'm hoping to make." Any of these statements can help you connect with others.

3. **Share your thinking.** To help those around you grow and learn from what you know, you have to sometimes think out loud. You have to share your thinking from the initial presentation of the issue through to conclusion. Most of us are on thinking autopilot. We don't think

about thinking. When someone else has to or wants to understand how you came up with a decision, it's sometimes difficult to unravel it in your mind. You have to go step-by-step and recreate your thinking. Sometimes it helps if other people ask the questions. They can probably guide you through how you came up with an answer or a decision better than you can. Once in a while, you should document a decision or two. What was the issue? What were the pros and cons you considered? How did you weight things? Then you can use those examples to demonstrate to others how you make decisions.

4. **The first rule of public speaking is to make a checklist.** What's your objective? What's your point? What are five things you want them to remember? What would the ideal audience member say if interviewed 15 minutes after you finish? Who's your audience? How much do they know? What are five techniques you will use to hold their attention? What presentation technology would work best? What questions will the audience have? What's the setting? How much time do you have—always take a few minutes less, never more.

5. **Preparing a speech.** State your message or purpose in a single sentence. In other words, do the ending first. Then outline the three to five chunks of your argument to support your thesis. Any more and the audience won't follow it. Sometimes putting main concepts on index cards and shuffling them into order can accomplish this. A famous minister said, "No souls are saved after 20 minutes." Many speeches must be longer than this, but can still be divided into sections with clear conclusions, and a hard bridge to the next related topic. What introduction will grab the audience and rivet them on your message? A story, a fact, a comparison, a quote, a photo, a cartoon? For example, one speaker selected a comparison to introduce a series of research findings on career success by saying, "How can you take identical twins, hired for the same entry job in the same organization, and 20 years later, one of them succeeds and one of them doesn't?" She then returned to the twins periodically as she went through her argument on the different developmental experiences they had with the corporation. In organizing your talk, you should resist telling them all you know. What are your priority points, and how will you explain them? Some points are made better by example, some by the logic of the argument, some by facts or stories. You should vary how you drive home your point because you will reach more people. Use memory devices—state points in threes; repeat key words and phrases—"I have a dream"; use understatement and overstatement; use antithesis—"Ask not what your country can do for

you; ask what you can do for your country." One nasty shock many learning presenters experience is that writing is different from speaking. A well-written speech is one that sounds right spoken, not read. Do not fall in love with what you have written until you record it on tape and listen to it. The cadence and pace is different in writing than in speaking. Writing doesn't take breathing into account. If your computer has a speech synthesizer, let the computer say your speech. Or have someone else read it to you. Never deliver a written speech until you have heard it spoken. Subscribe to *Presentations* magazine for tips, www.presentations.com.

D Better Follow-Through

INFPs get caught up in trying to get everything just right in the service of others. They often don't follow through and aren't very timely.

1. **Simple commitments.** Do you return phone calls in a timely manner? Do you forward material you promised? Did you pass on information you promised to get? Did you carry through on a task you promised someone you would take care of? Failing to do things like this damages relationships. If you tend to forget things, write them down. If you run out of time, set up a specific time each day to follow through on commitments. If you are going to miss a deadline, let them know and give them a second date you will be sure to make.

2. **Overcommitting.** A lot of trouble follows overcommitting. Overcommitting usually comes from wanting to please everyone or not wanting to face the conflict if you say no. You can only do so much. Only commit to that which you can actually do. Commit to a specific time for delivery. Write it down. Learn to say "no" pleasantly. Learn to pass it off to someone else who has the time—"Gee no, but I'm sure Susan could help you with that." Learn to say, "Yes, but it will take longer than you might want to wait," and give them the option of withdrawing the request. Learn to say, "Yes, but what else that I have already committed to do for you would you like to delay to get this done?"

3. **Manage your time efficiently.** Plan your time and manage against it. Be time sensitive. Value time. Figure out what you are worth per hour and minute by taking your gross salary plus overhead and benefits. Attach a monetary value on your time. Then ask, is this worth $56 of my time? Review your calendar over the past 90 days to figure out what your three largest time wasters are, and reduce them 50% by

batching activities and using efficient communications like e-mail and voice mail for routine matters. Make a list of points to be covered in phone calls; set deadlines for yourself; use your best time of day for the toughest projects—if you're best in the morning, don't waste it on B and C level tasks.

4. **Another common time waster is inadequate disengagement skills.** Some poor time managers can't shut down transactions. Either they continue to talk beyond what would be necessary or, more commonly, they can't get the other party to quit talking. When it's time to move on, just say, "I have to get on to the next thing I have to do; we can pick this up some other time."

5. **Do an upstream and downstream check with the people you work for,** work around, and those who work for you, to create a list of the administrative slip-ups you do that give them the most trouble. Be sure to ask them for help creating the list. That way, you have a focused list of the things you need to fix first. If you fix the top 10, maybe that will do and the rest of your habits can stay the same.

6. **Always out of time?** Do you intend to get to things but never have the time? Do you always estimate shorter times to get things done that then take longer? There is a well-established science and a set of best practices in time management. There are a number of books you can buy in any business bookstore, and there are a number of good courses you can attend. Delegating also helps you use your time more effectively.

7. **Visualize.** Set up a process to monitor progress against the goals. People like running measures. They like to gauge their pace. It's like the United Way Thermometer in the lobby.

8. **Feedback.** Give as much in-process feedback as you have time for. Most people are motivated by process feedback against agreed-upon goals for three reasons:

   ■ First, it helps them adjust what they are doing along the way in time to achieve the goal; they can make midcourse corrections.

   ■ Second, it shows them what they are doing is important and that you're eager to help.

   ■ Third, it's not the "gotcha" game of negative and critical feedback after the fact.

E Being Less Dependent on a Few Relationships

Generally, INFPs gravitate to a few close relationships. This limits their perspective and their network in an organization.

1. **Pick people who are quite different from you and observe what they do and how they do it.** Then ask for their help on a problem. Just ask questions and understand their perspective. Don't make any judgments about the rightness or wrongness of their approach.

2. **Pick some tough critics to talk with.** Don't go to the few people you truly like, most likely because you share similar perspectives. Go to some you know will disagree with you and hear them out.

3. **Spend most of your time with just a few people?** Developed a comfort and liking for the few? Expand your repertoire to get your relationship quota up. Be an early adopter of something. Find some new thing, technique, software, tool, system, process, or skill relevant to your activity. Privately become an expert in it. Read the books. Get certified. Visit a location where it's being done. Then surprise everyone and be the first to introduce it into your world. Sell it. Train others. Integrate it into your work.

4. **Pick three tasks you've never done before and go do them.** If you don't know much about customers, work in a store or handle customer complaints; if you don't know what engineering does, go find out; task trade with someone. Meet with your colleagues from other areas and tell each other what and, more importantly, how you do what you do.

5. **Volunteer for task forces.** Task forces/projects are a great opportunity to learn new things in a low-risk environment. Task forces are one of the most common developmental events listed by successful executives. Such projects require learning other functions, businesses, or nationalities well enough that in a tight time frame you can appreciate how they think and why their area/position is important. In so doing, you get out of your own experience and start to see connections to a broader world—how international trade works; or more at home, how the pieces of your organization fit together.

6. **Pick a person in the organization who is different in some aspects from your advocate/mentor.** Observe what he/she does and how he/she does it. He/she is as successful as your advocate/mentor but does it in other ways. If possible, ask for a meeting/lunch to discuss

his/her success and the things he/she has learned. See if he/she has any interest in teaching you something and being a temporary coach. Get to know other potential advocates on and off work. Go for maximum variety in the towering strengths they possess.

7. **Are you the same in your personal life?** Do you eat at the same restaurants? Vacation at the same places? Holidays are always done the same as in the past? Buy the same make or type car over and over again? Have the same insurance agent your father had? Expand yourself. Go on adventures with the family. Travel to places you have not been before. Never vacation at the same place again. Eat at different theme restaurants. Go to events and meetings of groups you have never really met. Go to ethnic festivals and sample the cultures. Go to athletic events you've never attended before. Each week, you and your family should go on a personal learning adventure. See how many different perspectives you can add to your knowledge.

F Better Relationships With Higher Management

INFPs have a rebellious streak and can go after those in power in unproductive ways, confronting the wrong people at the wrong time.

1. **Consider who bothers you.** If only certain higher-ups bother you and others don't, take a piece of paper and list the styles of the two groups/individuals. What are the similarities? Why does one style bother you and the other doesn't? With the groups/individuals that bother you, how could you respond more comfortably and effectively? Perhaps you could use some of the techniques you use with the more comfortable groups. Probably you should prime yourself to take nothing in personal terms and, no matter what happens, return to a discussion of the problem.

2. **Get to know more top managers.** Try to meet and interact with higher-ups in informal settings like receptions, social or athletic events, charity events, off-sites, etc. You will probably learn that higher-ups are just regular people who are older and therefore higher than you in the hierarchy. You may then feel more comfortable with them when back in the work setting.

3. **Focus on the three key problems you need to work on with your boss and do them.** Keep your head down. Keep your conversations with the boss directed at these core agenda. Focus on expectations, ask what results indicate success. Find out about your boss's job and what sorts of pressures he/she is under. Do you know what drives your

boss? Do you talk detail and he's a big-picture person? Do you fight his/her style which is more action oriented than yours? Do you get in unproductive values debates? Do you use words that set the boss off?

4. **Find out how top managers think.** Read the biographies of five "great" people; see what is said about them and their views of people like you. Read five autobiographies and see what they said about themselves and how they viewed people in your position. Write down five things you can do differently or better.

5. **Be ready for Q&A.** Many people get in trouble during questions and answers. Don't fake answers; most high-level managers will tolerate a "Don't know but I'll get back to you on that." Think of all the questions ahead of time; ask someone else to look at what you are going to say and do and to think of questions they would ask. Rehearse the answers to the questions. Another place people get in trouble when challenged is by retreating to a safe recitation of facts; executives are usually asking for logic and problem analysis, not a repackaging of what you've already said. The worst case, of course, is when an executive rejects your argument. If this happens, draw the person out to see if you've been misunderstood and clarify. If that's not the case, let the disagreement be as it is. Few executives respect someone who drops an argument as soon as challenged. You should listen carefully and respond with logic in 30 seconds or less per point. Don't repeat the entire argument; long answers often backfire since people have already heard it and few may agree with the questioner. In haste to be thorough, you may just look defensive.

6. **Quit arguing.** Most of the time, you may be delivering someone else's view of the future. Top management and a consultant created the mission, vision, and strategy off somewhere in the woods all by themselves. You may or may not have been asked for any input. You may even have some doubts about it yourself. Your role is to manage this vision and mission, not your personal one. Do not offer conditional statements to your audience: "I've got some concerns myself." Don't let it be known to others that you are not fully on board. Your job is to deliver and manage the message. While it's okay to admit your problems in dealing with change, it's not okay to admit them in dealing with this change. If you have better ideas, try to get them to the people who form missions in your organization.

*I am so determined to get my unit to work toward my ideal
that I am sometimes too demanding.*

– An INFP Manager

■　■　■　■　■　■　■　■　■　■　■　■　■　■　■

APPLICATION

Your personal preferences play out in day-to-day problems and situations
you face. Below is a case about your type dealing with such a situation. Use
this to think through how you will integrate the tips you've considered and
coach yourself to be more effective in your type.

INFP Application Situation (Part 1)

"Angela, you've got a problem," her boss was saying. "You've got great
ideas, but something is getting lost in translation, and it's disrupting your
effectiveness."

"What are you suggesting?" Angela asked, grimacing somewhat self-
effacingly. Her boss wondered if he had offended her.

Angela had recently been named Managing Director of the Advertising
Department. As a team-building exercise, the team had completed various
forms of assessment and one of the pieces was the MBTI. Angela's boss had
experience with the instrument in a previous organization and was
prepared to coach her, using information from a 360° assessment along with
her MBTI, which categorized Angela as an INFP.

"Only that I'd like to help you," Angela's boss said. Sensing a little
guardedness in Angela's body language as she crossed her arms over her
chest, he added, "Let's not forget, people respect your creativity and quality
orientation. And it's widely recognized that your high touch with people
and your readiness to help out and recognize others is valued here."

Angela relaxed a little. "OK, shoot," she said, and smirked.

"Well, first I'd like to try something out, if you don't mind."

Angela nodded.

"I've written up a list of things I've summarized from your 360° assessment, and I'd like you to use what you've learned about yourself from your MBTI profile to see if there are some parallels you can draw. Oh, and by the way, you'll probably notice what appear to be some contradictions in the list. See what you can make of those."

"I'll give it a try," she agreed.

Thinking It Through: Strategy

- What is Angela's boss trying to accomplish here?

- How might this approach be useful?

Planning It Out: Tactics

- As an INFP, what are some of the behaviors in Angela's profile that raters (peers and direct reports) have identified as problematic for her?

- What particular areas would present developmental challenges to Angela, and what competencies would she want to put into play?

- Which of the tactics described in the Being More Effective section are applicable in this situation?

- Which Overused Tendencies are most likely to come into play here?

INFP Application Situation (Part 2)

Here is the list of observations from feedback that Angela's boss presented to her (and space for her to fill in relevant information from her MBTI):

■ Seems withholding in sharing ideas.

■ Has good, complex, and useful ideas.

■ Is idealistic and has a strong sense of values.

■ Seems easily offended, abrupt.

■ Is hard to get to know.

■ Presents ideas with passion, but somehow lacks impact.

Reflection

■ What factors in her personality type should Angela continue to rely on?

■ What is Angela going to have to do more of, and what will she need to do less of, in order to succeed in her role?

SUGGESTED READINGS

■■■■■■■■ Being a More Effective INFP ■■■■■■■■

Approachability

Benton, D.A. *Executive Charisma: Six Steps to Mastering the Art of Leadership.* New York: McGraw-Hill Trade, 2003.

Brooks, Michael. *Instant Rapport.* New York: Warner Books, 1989.

Maxwell, John C. *Relationships 101.* London: Thomas Nelson, 2004.

Silberman, Melvin L. and Freda Hansburg. *Peoplesmart: Developing Your Interpersonal Intelligence.* San Francisco: Berrett-Koehler Publishers, Inc., 2000.

Taking Charge

Badaracco, Joseph L., Jr. *Defining Moments — When Managers Must Choose Between Right and Right.* Boston: Harvard Business School Press, 1997.

Bennis, Warren G. and Burt Nanus. *Leaders: Strategies for Taking Charge.* New York: HarperBusiness, 2003.

Calvert, Gene. *Highwire Management.* San Francisco: Jossey-Bass, Inc., 1993.

Chaleff, Ira. *The Courageous Follower: Standing Up to and for Our Leaders.* San Francisco: Berrett-Koehler Publishers, Inc., 2003.

Coponigro, Jeffrey R. *The Crisis Counselor: A Step-by-Step Guide to Managing a Business Crisis.* New York: McGraw-Hill/Contemporary Books, 2000.

Cox, Danny and John Hoover. *Leadership When the Heat's On.* New York: McGraw-Hill Trade, 2002.

Linsky, Martin and Ronald A. Heifetz. *Leadership on the Line: Staying Alive Through the Dangers of Leading.* Boston: Harvard Business School Press, 2002.

Dealing With Conflict

Cloke, Ken and Joan Goldsmith. *Resolving Conflicts at Work: A Complete Guide for Everyone on the Job.* San Francisco: Jossey-Bass, Inc., 2000.

Dana, Daniel. *Conflict Resolution.* New York: McGraw-Hill Trade, 2000.

Guttman, Howard M. *When Goliaths Clash: Managing Executive Conflict to Build a More Dynamic Organization.* New York: AMACOM, 2003.

Masters, Marick Francis and Robert R. Albright. *The Complete Guide to Conflict Resolution in the Workplace.* New York: AMACOM, 2002.

Technical Focus

DeGraff, Jeff and Katherine A. Lawrence. *Creativity at Work: Developing the Right Practices to Make Innovation Happen.* San Francisco: Jossey-Bass, Inc., 2002.

Drummond, Helga. *The Art of Decision Making.* New York: John Wiley & Sons, Inc., 2001.

Flynn, Daniel J. *Intellectual Morons: How Ideology Makes Smart People Fall for Stupid Ideas.* New York: Crown Business Publishing, 2004.

Hammond, John S., Ralph L. Keeney and Howard Raiffer. *Smart Choices.* Boston: Harvard University Press, 1999.

Lucas, Robert W. *The Creative Training Idea Book: Inspired Tips and Techniques for Engaging and Effective Learning.* New York: AMACOM, 2003.

Yates, J. Frank. *Decision Management: How to Assure Better Decisions in Your Company.* San Francisco: Jossey-Bass, Inc., 2003.

Drive for Results

Block, Peter. *The Answer to How Is Yes: Acting On What Matters.* San Francisco: Berrett-Koehler Publishers, Inc., 2001.

Bossidy, Larry, Ram Charan and Charles Burck (Contributor). *Execution: The Discipline of Getting Things Done.* New York: Crown Business Publishing, 2002.

Collins, James C. *Good to Great: Why Some Companies Make the Leap...And Others Don't.* New York: HarperCollins, 2001.

Loehr, Jim and Tony Schwartz. *The Power of Full Engagement: Managing Energy, Not Time, Is the Key to High Performance and Personal Renewal.* New York: The Free Press, 2003.

Longenecker, Clinton O. and Jack L. Simonetti. *Getting Results: Five Absolutes for High Performance.* New York: John Wiley & Sons, Inc., 2001.

Informing

Arredondo, Lani. *Communicating Effectively.* New York: McGraw-Hill Trade, 2000.

Keyton, Joann. *Communicating in Groups: Building Relationships for Effective Decision Making.* New York: WCB/McGraw-Hill, 2002.

McCormack, Mark H. *On Communicating.* Los Angeles: Dove Books, 1998.

Zeuschner, Raymond F. *Communicating Today: The Essentials.* Boston: Allyn & Bacon, 2002.

■■■■■■■■ Overusing INFP Tendencies ■■■■■■■■

Being More Personally Flexible

Bellman, Geoffrey M. *Getting Things Done When You Are Not in Charge.* San Francisco: Berrett-Koehler Publishers, Inc., 2001.

Brim, Gilbert. *Ambition: How We Manage Success and Failure Throughout Our Lives.* New York: Backinprint.com, 2000.

Christian, Ken. *Your Own Worst Enemy: Breaking the Habit of Adult Underachievement.* New York: Regan Books, 2004.

Glickman, Rosalene. *Optimal Thinking: How to Be Your Best Self.* New York: John Wiley & Sons, Inc., 2002.

Jackson, Paul Z. and Mark McKergow. *The Solutions Focus.* Yarmouth, ME: Nicholas Brealey Publishing, 2002.

Being More Patient

Barker, Larry, Ph.D. and Kittie Watson, Ph.D. *Listen Up: At Home, at Work, in Relationships: How to Harness the Power of Effective Listening.* Irvine, CA: Griffin Trade Paperback, 2001.

Bolton, Robert and Dorothy Grover Bolton. *People Styles at Work—Making Bad Relationships Good and Good Relationships Better.* New York: AMACOM, 1996.

Burley-Allen, Madelyn. *Listening: The Forgotten Skill.* New York: John Wiley & Sons, Inc., 1995.

Gonthier, Giovinella and Kevin Morrissey. *Rude Awakenings: Overcoming the Civility Crisis in the Workplace.* Chicago: Dearborn Trade Publishing, 2002.

Ryan, Mary Jane. *The Power of Patience: How to Slow the Rush and Enjoy More Happiness, Success, and Peace of Mind Everyday.* New York: Broadway Press, 2003.

Developing Better Presence

Baldoni, John. *Great Communication Secrets of Great Leaders.* New York: McGraw-Hill, Inc., 2003.

Booher, Dianna. *Speak With Confidence: Powerful Presentations That Inform, Inspire, and Persuade.* New York: McGraw-Hill, Inc., 2002.

Collins, Patrick J. *Say It With Confidence.* New York: Prentice Hall, 1998.

Giuliani, Rudolph W. and Ken Kurson. *Leadership.* New York: Miramax, 2002.

Better Follow-Through

Byfield, Marilyn. *It's Hard to Make a Difference When You Can't Find Your Keys: The Seven-Step Path to Becoming Truly Organized.* New York: Viking Press, 2003.

Emmett, Rita. *The Procrastinator's Handbook: Mastering the Art of Doing It Now.* New York: Walker & Company, 2000.

Gleeson, Kerry. *The Personal Efficiency Program: How to Get Organized to Do More Work in Less Time.* New York: John Wiley & Sons, Inc., 2000.

MacKenzie, Alec. *The Time Trap: The Classic Book on Time Management.* Fine Communications, 2002.

Being Less Dependent on a Few Relationships

Benton, D.A. *Executive Charisma: Six Steps to Mastering the Art of Leadership.* New York: McGraw-Hill Trade, 2003.

Bolton, Robert and Dorothy Grover Bolton. *People Styles at Work—Making Bad Relationships Good and Good Relationships Better.* New York: AMACOM, 1996.

Brooks, Michael. *Instant Rapport.* New York: Warner Books, 1989.

Maxwell, John C. *Relationships 101.* London: Thomas Nelson, 2004.

Niven, David. *The 100 Simple Secrets of Successful People: What Scientists Have Learned and How You Can Use It.* New York: HarperBusiness, 2002.

Silberman, Melvin L. and Freda Hansburg. *Peoplesmart: Developing Your Interpersonal Intelligence.* San Francisco: Berrett-Koehler Publishers, Inc., 2000.

Better Relationships With Higher Management

Bolton, Robert and Dorothy Grover Bolton. *People Styles at Work—Making Bad Relationships Good and Good Relationships Better.* New York: AMACOM, 1996.

Chaleff, Ira. *The Courageous Follower: Standing Up to and for Our Leaders.* San Francisco: Berrett-Koehler Publishers, Inc., 2003.

Charan, Ram. *What the CEO Wants You to Know: How Your Company Really Works.* New York: Crown Business Publishing, 2001.

Gittines, Roger and Rosanne Badowski. *Managing Up: How to Forge an Effective Relationship With Those Above You.* New York: Currency, 2003.

Guttman, Howard M. *When Goliaths Clash: Managing Executive Conflict to Build a More Dynamic Organization.* New York: AMACOM, 2003.

CHAPTER 8

INTP
Introverted Thinking
with
Extraverted Intuiting

■■■■■■■■■■■■■■■■

3.3% of Population
6.6% of Managers

■■■■■■■■■■■■■■■■

Typical Strengths
The World of Ideas
Willpower
Conceptual and Analytical
Writing Skills
Strategic
Enjoy Creating Something From Nothing
Non-Defensive

ISTJ	ISFJ	INFJ	INTJ
ISTP	ISFP	INFP	**INTP**
ESTP	ESFP	ENFP	ENTP
ESTJ	ESFJ	ENFJ	ENTJ

I like it best when I can solve the problem by myself.

– An INTP Manager

Basic Habits of Mind

Introverted Thinking drives INTPs to relentlessly question causes and outcomes in a situation. This focus is with such passion that interpersonal relationships can be ignored. Extraverted Intuiting aids their logical nature by spotting complexity in the environment. This leads to their seeing situations as fluid, complex, and paradoxical.

Extraverted Sensing and Extraverted Feeling also aid INTPs. These serve to both focus and communicate a passion for thoroughness in their style. This can be misunderstood as cool and intellectually arrogant. Highly selective about sharing observations, this can magnify views of their interpersonal style.

This combination sometimes is misperceived as uncaring, skeptical, arrogant, and condescending.

Typical Communication Patterns

- INTPs usually have a working theory for the way things are or an outright skepticism about how to make sense of things.

- They see paradox and irony in almost everything they do, which leads to unconventional and imaginative remarks.

- They are autonomous problem solvers but are willing to validate their analysis of events through conversation when invited to do so.

General Learning Strategy

- INTPs generally prefer the freedom to explore. They insist on a variety of tasks and creative opportunities for learning and testing theories.

- They generally learn by analyzing "it" first before actually testing it. They will then compare and contrast with other experiences.

■ Their learning is enhanced by intellectual challenges and opportunities to write or illustrate abstractions. They like to clarify through elaborate analysis.

Interpersonal Qualities Related to Motivation

■ INTPs are motivated by intellectual and complex challenge.

■ The tougher the problem, the greater their interest.

■ They gain a great deal of energy from talking about theoretical models and find debate invigorating.

Blind Spots

■ INTPs might be surprised to learn that they do not put people at ease as quickly as they imagine.

■ They may appear pressuring, blunt, impatient, and having difficulty with follow-through.

■ As a result of these occasional behaviors, they can have more relationship issues than they initially think.

Stress Related Behavior

■ As stress increases, INTPs can become restless and defensive.

■ They view the big picture through a critical lens. This only feeds an urgency to solve the problem. This can lead to a rebellious action because "no one else can grasp the scope of the problem."

■ If high-level stress continues over time, they can become hypersensitive and show disappointment in the lack of diligence others show.

Potential Barriers to Effectiveness

■ According to observers, learning to build and mend peer and report relationships is critical to their future success.

■ If INTPs do not learn the lessons of interpersonal relatedness, then others will see them as having a poor work team commitment and a poor confrontation record.

Being a More Effective INTP

A **Problems With Peers**
B **Problems With Direct Reports**
C **Organizing**
D **Patience**
E **Interpersonal Relationships**

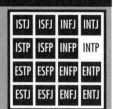

ISTJ	ISFJ	INFJ	INTJ
ISTP	ISFP	INFP	INTP
ESTP	ESFP	ENFP	ENTP
ESTJ	ESFJ	ENFJ	ENTJ

A Problems With Peers

INTPs can be quite solitary and not eager to communicate. Their influence skills often need work, especially in situations calling for interpersonal or political savvy.

1. **Influencing.** Peers generally do not have power over each other. That means that influence skills, understanding, and trading are the currencies to use. Don't just ask for things; find some common ground where you can provide help. What do the peers you're contacting need? Do you really know how they see the issue? Is it even important to them? How does what you're working on affect them? If it affects them negatively, can you trade something, appeal to the common good, figure out some way to minimize the work (volunteering staff help, for example)? Go into peer relationships with a trading mentality.

2. **Sometimes the problem is maneuvering through the complex maze called the organization.** How do you get things done sideways? Who are the movers and shakers in the organization? How do they get things done? Who do they rely on for expediting things through the maze? Who are the major gatekeepers who control the flow of resources, information, and decisions? Who are the guides and the helpers? Get to know them better. Who are the major resisters and stoppers? Try to avoid or go around them.

3. **If peers see you as excessively competitive,** they will cut you out of the loop and may sabotage your cross-border attempts. To be seen as more cooperative, always explain your thinking and invite them to explain theirs. Generate a variety of possibilities first rather than stake out positions. Be tentative, allowing them room to customize the situation. Focus on common goals, priorities, and problems. Invite criticism of your ideas.

4. **If peers think you lack respect for them or what they do, try to keep conflicts as small and concrete as possible.** Separate the people from the problem. Don't get personal. Don't give peers the impression you're trying to dominate or push something on them. Without agreeing or disagreeing, try on their views for size. Can you understand their viewpoint? When peers blow off steam, don't react; return to facts and the problem, staying away from personal clashes. Allow others to save face; concede small points; don't try to hit a home run every time. When a peer takes a rigid position, don't reject it. Ask why: What are the principles behind the position? How do we know it's fair? What's the theory of the case? Play out what would happen if his/her position was accepted.

5. **Separate working smoothly with peers from personal relationships,** contests, competing for incentives, one-upsmanship, not-invented-here, pride, and ego. Working well with peers over the long term helps everyone, makes sense for the organization, and builds a capacity for the organization to do greater things. Usually the least-used resource in an organization is lateral exchanges of information and resources.

6. **If a peer doesn't play fair, avoid telling others all about it.** This often boomerangs. What goes around comes around. Confront the peer directly, politely, and privately. Describe the unfair situation; explain the impact on you. Don't blame. Give the peer the chance to explain, ask questions, let him/her save some face, and see if you can resolve the matter. Even if you don't totally accept what is said, it's better to solve the problem than win the argument.

7. **Monitor yourself in tough situations to get a sense of how you are coming across.** What's the first thing you attend to? How often do you take a stand vs. make an accommodating gesture? What proportion of your comments deals with relationships vs. the issue to be addressed? Mentally rehearse for worst-case scenarios/hard-to-deal-with people. Anticipate what the person might say and have responses prepared so as not to be caught off guard.

B Problems With Direct Reports

Many INTPs are poor delegators, preferring to work alone. If a task isn't being done to their satisfaction, they would rather take it on themselves. They often project an air of near indifference and do not praise others easily. They can be rough on problem performers who don't live up to INTP standards.

1. **Caring is listening.** Many bosses are marginal listeners. They are action oriented and more apt to cut off people mid-sentence than listen. They also are impatient and finish people's sentences for them when they hesitate. All of these impatient behaviors come across to others as a lack of caring. It's being insensitive to the needs and feelings of others. So, step one in caring is listening longer.

2. **Caring is sharing and disclosing.** Share your thinking on a business issue and invite the advice of direct reports. Pass on tidbits of information you think will help people do their jobs better or broaden their perspectives. Reveal things people don't need to know to do their jobs, but which will be interesting to them—and help them feel valued. Disclose some things about yourself as well. It's hard for people to relate to a stone. Tell them how you arrive at decisions. Explain your intentions, your reasons, and your thinking when announcing decisions. If you offer solutions first, you invite resistance and feelings of not being cared about—"He/she just dumps things on us."

3. **Caring is knowing.** Know three non-work things about everybody— their interests and hobbies or their children or something you can chat about. Life is a small world. If you ask your people a few personal questions, you'll find you have something in common with virtually anyone. Having something in common will help bond the relationship.

4. **Caring is accepting.** Try to listen without judging initially. Turn off your "I agree; I don't agree" filter. You don't have to agree with it; just listen to understand. Assume when people tell you something they are looking for understanding; indicate that by being able to summarize what they said. Don't offer advice or solutions unless it's obvious the person wants to know what you would do. While offering instant solutions is a good thing to do in many circumstances, it's chilling where the goal is to get people to talk to you more freely.

5. **Caring is understanding.** Study the people you work with. Without judging them, collect evidence on how they think and what they do. What drives them to do what they do? Try to predict what they will do in given situations. Use this to understand how to relate to them. What are their hot buttons? What would they like for you to care about?

6. **Feedback.** People need continuous feedback from you and others to grow. Some tips about feedback:

■ Arrange for them to get feedback from multiple people, including yourself, on what matters for success in their future jobs; arrange for your direct reports to get 360° feedback about every two years.

■ Give them progressively stretching tasks that are first-time and different for them so that they can give themselves feedback as they go.

■ If they have direct reports and peers, another technique to recommend is to ask their associates for comments on what they should stop doing, start doing, and keep doing to be more successful.

■ You have to be willing to be straight with your people and give them accurate but balanced feedback. Give as much real-time feedback as you have time for. Most people are motivated by process feedback against agreed-upon goals for three reasons. First, it helps them adjust what they are doing along the way in time to better achieve the goal; they can make midcourse corrections. Second, it shows them what they are doing is important and that you're there to help. Third, it's not the "gotcha" game of negative and critical feedback after the fact. If there are negatives, they need to know as soon as possible.

■ Set up a buddy system so people can get continuing feedback.

■ If your organization has a mentoring program, find out how it works. Best practices begin with those to be mentored writing down goals, objectives, and development needs. They are then carefully matched with mentors and the relationship is outlined. How often will the people meet? On what topics is the mentor to be helpful? What are the responsibilities of the person to be mentored? If your organization doesn't have such a program, look at setting one up within your unit or function.

7. **Do you help your people learn by looking for repeating patterns?** Help them look for patterns in the situations and problems they deal with. What succeeded and what failed? What was common to each success or what was present in each failure but never present in a success? Focus on the successes; failures are easier to analyze but don't in themselves tell you what would work. Comparing successes, while less exciting, yields more information. The bottom line is help them reduce insights to principles or rules of thumb that might be repeatable. Ask them what they have learned to increase their skills and understanding, making them better managers or professionals. Ask them what they can do now that they couldn't do a year ago. Reinforce this and encourage more of it. Developing is learning in as many ways as possible.

8. **How to delegate?** Communicate, set time frames and goals, and get out of the way. People need to know what it is you expect. What does the outcome look like? When do you need it by? What's the budget? What resources do they get? What decisions can they make? Do you want checkpoints along the way? How will we both know and measure how well the task is done? One of the most common problems with delegation is incomplete or cryptic up-front communication leading to frustration, a job not well done the first time, rework, and a reluctance to delegate next time. Poor communicators always have to take more time managing because of rework. Analyze recent projects that went well and didn't go well. How did you delegate? Too much? Not enough? Unwanted pieces? Major chunks of responsibility? Workload distributed properly? Did you set measures? Overmanage or abdicate? Find out what your best practices are. Set up a series of delegation practices that can be used as if you're not there. What do you have to be informed of? What feedback loops can people use for midcourse correction? What questions should be answered as the work proceeds? What steps should be followed? What are the criteria to be followed? When will you be available to help?

9. **More what and why, less how.** The best delegators are crystal clear on what and when, and more open on how. People are more motivated when they can determine the how for themselves. Inexperienced delegators include the hows, which turn the people into task automatons instead of an empowered and energized staff. Tell them what and when and for how long, and let them figure out how on their own. Give them leeway. Encourage them to try things. Besides being more motivating, it's also more developmental for them. Add

the larger context. Although it is not necessary to get the task done, people are more motivated when they know where this task fits in the bigger picture. Take three extra minutes and tell them why this task needs to be done, where it fits in the grander scheme, and its importance to the goals and objectives of the unit.

10. **Are your problem performers confused?** Do they know what's expected of them? You may not set clear enough performance standards, goals, and objectives. You may be a seat-of-the-pants manager, and some people are struggling because they don't know what is expected or it changes. You may be a cryptic communicator. You may be too busy to communicate. You may communicate to some and not to others. You may have given up on some and stopped communicating. Or you may think they would know what to do if they're any good, but that's not really true because you have not properly communicated what you want. The first task is to outline the 5 to 10 key results areas and what indicators of success would be. Involve your problem direct reports on both ends—the standards and the indicators. Provide them with a fair way to measure their own progress. Employees with goals and standards are usually harder on themselves than you'll ever be. Often they set higher standards than you would. Sometimes the problem is behavioral, as in someone who can't control outbursts, and only affects performance on the back end in lost cooperation or sabotage. Then the best approach is to note the gap between behavior and expectations, and point out what some of the observed consequences are. If the person agrees, then coaching may suffice. If the person balks, then a 360° feedback process with follow-up may be needed to illuminate the depth of the problem before any help can be given.

11. **Realism.** They are not performing up to standard? It's common to see 90-day improve-or-else plans that no one can accomplish: be more strategic, improve your interpersonal skills, learn about the business, be less arrogant. Ask yourself how long did it take you to become proficient at what you are criticizing this person for? Because managers hesitate delivering negative messages, we get to people late. Sometimes the last five managers this person reported to saw the same difficulty, but none of them confronted the person. Get to people as soon as they do not meet agreed-upon standards of performance. Don't wait. Early is the easiest time to do it with the highest return on investment for you, them, and the organization. Most people who have reached the problem performer status will take one to two years to turn around under the best of circumstances. It's cruel and unusual

punishment to require a fixed-time turnaround or improvement plan. If your organization demands a 90-day wonder, fight it. Tell them that while a bit of improvement can be seen in that period, substantive change is not like producing a quarterly earnings statement.

C Organizing

INTPs are usually not detail people. Procedures and day-to-day management are often ignored or glossed over.

1. **Set goals.** You should set goals before assigning projects, work, and tasks. Goals help focus people's time and efforts. It allows people to perform more effectively and efficiently. Most people don't want to waste time. Most people want to perform well. Learn about MBO— managing by objectives. Read a book about it. While you may not be interested in a full-blown application, all of the principles of setting goals will be in the book. Go to a course on goal setting.

2. **Focus on measures.** How would you tell if the goal was accomplished? If the things I asked others to do were done right, what outcomes could we all agree on as measures of success? Most groups can easily come up with success measures that are different from, and more important to them, than formal measures. Ask them to do so.

3. **Visualize.** Set up a process to monitor progress against the goals. People like running measures. They like to gauge their pace. It's like the United Way Thermometer in the lobby.

4. **Feedback.** Give as much in-process feedback as you have time for. Most people are motivated by process feedback against agreed-upon goals for three reasons:

   ■ First, it helps them adjust what they are doing along the way in time to achieve the goal; they can make midcourse corrections.

   ■ Second, it shows them what they are doing is important and that you're eager to help.

   ■ Third, it's not the "gotcha" game of negative and critical feedback after the fact.

5. **Laying out the work.** Most resourcefulness starts out with a plan. What do I need to accomplish? What's the time line? What resources will I need? Who controls the resources—people, funding, tools, materials, support—I need? What's my currency? How can I pay for

or repay the resources I need? Who wins if I win? Who might lose? Lay out the work from A to Z. Many people are seen as disorganized because they don't write down the sequence or parts of the work and leave something out. Ask others to comment on ordering and what's missing.

6. **Bargaining for resources.** What do I have to trade? What can I buy? What can I borrow? What do I need to trade for? What do I need that I can't pay or trade for?

7. **Rallying support.** Share your mission and goals with the people you need to support you. Try to get their input. People who are asked tend to cooperate more than people who are not asked. Figure out how the people who support your effort can win along with you.

D Patience

It is not in the nature of INTPs to be especially patient. They are inclined toward the next discovery, and waiting is in itself stressful to them. They often see normal process as slow and inefficient and can react sharply.

1. **Blame and vengeance?** Do you feel a need to punish the people and groups that set you off? Do you become hostile, angry, sarcastic, or vengeful? While all that may be temporarily satisfying to you, they will all backfire and you will lose in the long term. When someone attacks you, rephrase it as an attack on a problem. Reverse the argument—ask what they would do if they were in your shoes. Let the other side vent frustration or blow off steam, but don't react. When you do reply to an attack, keep it to the facts and their impact on you. It's fine for you to draw conclusions about the impact on yourself—"I felt blindsided." It's not fine for you to tell others their motives—"You blindsided me" means you did it, probably meant to, and I know the meaning of your behavior. So state the meaning for yourself; ask others what their actions meant.

2. **Listening chillers?** Don't interrupt before they have finished. Don't suggest words when they hesitate or pause. Don't finish their sentences for them. Don't wave off any further input by saying, "Yes, I know that." "Yes, I know where you're going." "Yes, I have heard that before." If time is really important, you can say, "Let me see if I know where this is going...," or "I wonder if we could summarize to save both of us some time?" Finally, early in a transaction, answers, solutions, conclusions, statements, and dictates shut many people

down. You've told them your mind is already made up. Listen first, solve second.

3. **Questions.** Good listeners ask lots of questions to get to a good understanding. Probing questions. Clarifying questions. Confirming—is this what you are saying—questions. Ask one more question than you do now and add to that until people signal you that they think you are truly listening.

4. **Watch out for negative humor.** Some people use humor to deliver negative messages. They are sarcastic and barbed in their humor. In a tense confrontation with an employee, to say, "I hope your résumé is up to date," instead of saying, "Your performance is not what I expected. It has to improve or I will have to reconsider your continued employment," is not acceptable. There is a very simple rule. Do not use humor to deliver a critical point to a person or a group. Negative humor hurts more than a straightforward statement. Say directly what you mean.

5. **Listening to those who waste a lot of time.** With those you don't have time to listen to, switch to being a teacher. Try to help them craft their communications to you in a more acceptable way. Tell them to be shorter next time. Come with more/less data. Structure the conversation by helping them come up with categories and structures to stop their rambling. Good listeners don't signal to the "bad" people that they are not listening or are not interested. Don't signal to anyone what bucket they're in. Put your mind in neutral, nod, ask questions, be helpful.

6. **Listening to people you don't like.** What do people see in them who do like them or can at least get along with them? What are their strengths? Do you have any common interests? Talk less and ask more questions to give them a second chance. Don't judge their motives and intentions—do that later.

7. **Listening to people you like but...**

   ■ They are disorganized. Interrupt to summarize and keep the discussion focused. While interrupting is generally not a good tactic, it's necessary here.

   ■ They just want to chat. Ask questions to focus them; don't respond to chatty remarks.

- They want to unload a problem. Assume when people tell you something they are looking for understanding; indicate that by being able to summarize what they said. Don't offer any advice.

- They are chronic complainers. Ask them to write down problems and solutions and then let's discuss it. This turns down the volume while, hopefully, moving them off complaining.

- They like to complain about others. Ask if they've talked to the person. Encourage them to do so. If that doesn't work, summarize what they have said without agreeing or disagreeing.

8. **Impatience triggers.** Some people probably bring out your impatience more than others. Who are they? What is it about them that makes you more impatient? Pace? Language? Thought process? Accent? These people may include people you don't like, who ramble, who whine and complain, or who are repetitive advocates for things you have already rejected. Mentally rehearse some calming tactics before meeting with people who trigger your impatience. Work on understanding their positions without judging them—you can always judge later. In all cases, focus them on the issues or problems to be discussed, return them to the point, summarize, and state your position. Try to gently train them to be more efficient with you next time without damaging them in the process.

9. **Work on your openness and approachability.** Impatient people don't get as much information as patient listeners do. They are more often surprised by events when others knew they were coming. People are hesitant to talk to impatient people. It's too painful. People don't pass on hunches, unbaked thoughts, maybes, and possibles to impatient people. You will be out of the information loop and miss important information you need to know to be effective. Suspend judgment on informal communications. Just take it in. Acknowledge that you understand. Ask a question or two. Follow up later.

10. **Rein in your horse.** Impatient people provide answers, conclusions, and solutions too early in the process. Others haven't even understood the problem yet. Providing solutions too quickly will make your people dependent and irritated. If you don't teach them how you think and how you can come up with solutions so fast, they will never learn. Take the time to really define the problem—not impatiently throw out a solution. Brainstorm what questions need to be answered in order to resolve it. Give your people the task to think

about for a day and come back with some solutions. Be a teacher instead of a dictator of solutions. Study yourself. Keep a journal of what triggered your behavior and what the observed consequences were. Learn to detect and control your triggers before they get you in trouble.

11. **Task impatience.** Impatient people check in a lot. How's it coming. Is it done yet? When will it be finished? Let me see what you've done so far. That is disruptive to due process and wastes time. When you give out a task or assign a project, establish agreed-upon time checkpoints. You can also assign percentage checkpoints. Check in with me when you are about 25% finished so we can make midcourse corrections and 75% finished so we can make final corrections. Let them figure out how to do the task. Hold back from checking in at other than the agreed-upon times and percentages.

E Interpersonal Relationships

Reserved by nature, INTPs can appear detached and their questioning nature can come across as skeptical. Although usually soft-hearted, they don't approach and deal with people as easily as many other types.

1. **Personalizing.** Approachable people work to know and remember important things about the people they work around, for, and with. Know three things about everybody—their interests or their children or something you can chat about other than the business agenda. Treat life as a small world. If you ask a few questions, you'll find you have something in common with virtually anyone. Establish things you can talk about with each person you work with that go beyond strictly work transactions. These need not be social—they could be issues of strategy, global events, market shifts. The point is to forge common ground and connections.

2. **You may clam up around talkative people** because you are busy processing what they said, and you have just finished point one when they are already on point four. This can make you appear inscrutable or perhaps disinterested in what they have to say. If you are around a true talker, this may be the one time you need to interrupt. Wave a hand. Smile. Make a comment or ask a question. The goal is not to disagree or cause turmoil, but simply to slow them down.

3. **Shy?** Trouble with appearing vulnerable? Afraid of how people will react? Not sure of your social skills? Want to appear—while shaking inside—not shy? Hand first. Consistent eye contact. Ask the first question. For low-risk practice, talk to strangers off-work. Set a goal of meeting 10 new people at a social gathering; find out what you have in common with them. Initiate contact at your place of worship, at PTA meetings, in the neighborhood, at the supermarket, on the plane, and on the bus. See if any of the bad and scary things you think might happen to you if you initiate people contact actually happen.

4. **The first three minutes.** Managing the first three minutes is essential. The tone is set. First impressions are formed. Work on being open and approachable, and take in information during the beginning of a transaction. This means putting others at ease so that they feel okay about disclosing. It means initiating rapport, listening, sharing, understanding, and comforting. Approachable people get more information, know things earlier, and can get others to do more things. The more you can get them to initiate and say early in the transaction, the more you'll know about where they are coming from, and the better you can tailor your approach.

5. **To understand the differences among people,** look to the obvious first. What do they do first? What do they emphasize in their speech? People focus on different things—taking action, details, concepts, feelings, other people. What's their interaction style? People come in different styles—pushy, tough, soft, matter-of-fact, and so on. To figure these out, listen for the values behind their words and note what they have passion and emotion around. One key to getting anything of value done in the work world is the ability to see differences in people and to manage against and use those differences for everyone's benefit. Interpersonal savvy is meeting each person where he/she is to get done what you need to get done. Basically, people respond favorably to ease of transaction. If you make it easy by accepting their normal mode of doing things, not fighting their style, and neither defending your own nor letting style get in the way of performance, things will generally run smoothly.

Overusing INTP Tendencies

If you sometimes overdo your preferred behaviors, you may need to work on:

A Overcoming Arrogance

B Communicating More Clearly

C Dealing With Conflict

D Giving More Praise

E Better Follow-Through

F Better Team Building

ISTJ	ISFJ	INFJ	INTJ
ISTP	ISFP	INFP	INTP
ESTP	ESFP	ENFP	ENTP
ESTJ	ESFJ	ENFJ	ENTJ

A Overcoming Arrogance

INTPs can become very restless under enough stress. They then tend to nitpick or attack what they see as low standards of performance or poor thinking. On the other hand, they are usually non-defensive when confronted about their behavior, viewing it as information.

1. **Under extended stress,** you can become hypercritical of others and find an endless list of reasons for the unacceptability of some action or fact. You appear skeptical and touchy. Accept this for what it is—you. Think of it as your personal preferences speaking rather than reality. Seek feedback to find out what is really going on.

2. **Watch your non-verbals.** Arrogant people look, talk, and act arrogantly. As you try to become less arrogant, you need to find out what your non-verbals are. All arrogant people do a series of things that can be viewed by a neutral party and judged to give off the signals of arrogance. Washboard brow. Facial expressions. Body shifting, especially turning away. Impatient finger or pencil tapping. False smile. Tight lips. Looking away. Find out from a trusted friend what you do, and try to eliminate those behaviors.

3. **Answers. Solutions. Conclusions. Statements. Dictates.** That's the staple of arrogant people. Instant output. Sharp reactions. This may be getting you in trouble. You jump to conclusions, categorically dismiss what others say, use challenging words in an absolute tone. People then see you as closed to their input or combative. More negatively,

they may believe you think they're stupid or ill-informed. Give people a chance to talk without interruption. If you're seen as intolerant or closed, people will often stumble over words in their haste to talk with you or shortcut their argument since they assume you're not listening anyway. Ask a question, invite them to disagree with you, present their argument back to them softly, let them save face no matter what. Add a 15-second pause into your transactions before you say anything, and add two clarifying questions per transaction to signal you're listening and want to understand.

4. **You may be highly intelligent and quite skilled in your area.** You may work around people who aren't as informed or educated as you are. You may be in a position of essentially dictating what should be done. But you don't have to make it demeaning or painful. You need to switch to a teacher/guru role—tell them how you think about an issue, don't just fire out solutions. Tell them what you think the problem is, what questions need to be asked and answered, how you would go about finding out, and what you think some likely solutions might be. Work to pass on your knowledge and skills.

5. **You should work doubly hard at observing others.** Always select your interpersonal approach from the other person in, not from you out. Your best choice of approach will always be determined by the other person or group, not you. Think about each transaction as if the other person were a customer you wanted. How would you craft an approach?

6. **You may view feedback as information,** but this can come across that you just don't care and can increase perceptions of aloofness. Make sure to say thank you for the feedback. Because you may be seen as quite powerful and having high standards, if you don't say thank you or find something to praise or verify in the feedback, you can be seen as indifferent or dismissive.

7. **Although INTPs are rarely defensive,** they can be if the feedback comes when they are upset about performance or slowness. You will need to work on keeping yourself in a calm state when getting negative feedback. You need to change your thinking. When getting the feedback, your only task is to accurately understand what people are trying to tell you. It is not your task at that point to accept or reject. That comes later. Mentally rehearse how you will calmly react to tough feedback situations before they happen. Develop automatic tactics to shut down or delay your usual emotional response. Some useful tactics are to slow down, take notes, ask clarifying questions,

ask them for concrete examples, and thank them for telling you since you know it's not easy for them.

8. **Do you value feedback only from those you feel have the experience and expertise to offer it?** If someone points out that you could be somewhat more accommodating, is your reaction to whom, for what purpose, and will that move us toward the goal? Go to the people you respect most and get their feedback on your pluses and minuses. Then think about what modifications in your behavior would help you push your vision through more effectively.

B Communicating More Clearly

INTPs are often terse in verbal communications, preferring to elaborate only in writing. They can avoid informing sessions and speech making. Sometimes when they do inform, they tell people too much rather than hitting the highlights.

1. **Don't inform enough.** Are you a minimalist? Do you tell people only what they need to know to do their little piece of the puzzle? People are motivated by being aware of the bigger picture. They want to know what to do in order to do their jobs and more. How does what they are doing fit into the larger picture? What are the other people working on and why? Many people think that's unnecessary information and that it would take too much time to do. They're wrong. The sense of doing something worthwhile is the number two motivator at work! It results in a high return on motivation and productivity. (Try to increase the amount of more-than-your-job information you share.) Focus on the impact on others by figuring out who information affects. Put five minutes on your meeting agenda. Ask people what they want to know and, assuming it's not confidential information, tell them. Pick a topic each month to tell your people about.

2. **A loner.** Do you keep to yourself? Work alone or try to? Do you hold back information? Do you parcel out information on your schedule? Do you share information to get an advantage or to win favor? Do people around you know what you're doing and why? Are you aware of things others would benefit from, but you don't take the time to communicate? In most organizations, these things and things like it will get you in trouble. Organizations function on the flow of information. Being on your own and preferring peace and privacy are okay as long as you communicate things to bosses, peers, and

teammates that they need to know and would feel better if they knew. Don't be the source of surprises.

3. **Share your thinking.** To help those around you grow and learn from what you know, you have to sometimes think out loud. You have to share your thinking from the initial presentation of the issue through to conclusion. Most of us are on thinking autopilot. We don't think about thinking. When someone else has to or wants to understand how you came up with a decision, it's sometimes difficult to unravel it in your mind. You have to go step-by-step and recreate your thinking. Sometimes it helps if other people ask the questions. They can probably guide you through how you came up with an answer or a decision better than you can. Once in a while, you should document a decision or two. What was the issue? What were the pros and cons you considered? How did you weight things? Then you can use those examples to demonstrate to others how you make decisions.

4. **Preparing a speech.** State your message or purpose in a single sentence. In other words, do the ending first. Then outline the three to five chunks of your argument to support your thesis. Any more and the audience won't follow it. Sometimes putting main concepts on index cards and shuffling them into order can accomplish this. A famous minister said, "No souls are saved after 20 minutes." Many speeches must be longer than this, but can still be divided into sections with clear conclusions, and a hard bridge to the next related topic. What introduction will grab the audience and rivet them on your message? A story, a fact, a comparison, a quote, a photo, a cartoon? For example, one speaker selected a comparison to introduce a series of research findings on career success by saying, "How can you take identical twins, hired for the same entry job in the same organization, and 20 years later, one of them succeeds and one of them doesn't?" She then returned to the twins periodically as she went through her argument on the different developmental experiences they had with the corporation. In organizing your talk, you should resist telling them all you know. What are your priority points, and how will you explain them? Some points are made better by example, some by the logic of the argument, some by facts or stories. You should vary how you drive home your point because you will reach more people. Use memory devices—state points in threes; repeat key words and phrases—"I have a dream"; use understatement and overstatement; use antithesis—"Ask not what your country can do for you; ask what you can do for your country." One nasty shock many learning presenters experience is that writing is different from

speaking. A well-written speech is one that sounds right spoken, not read. Do not fall in love with what you have written until you record it on tape and listen to it. The cadence and pace is different in writing than in speaking. Writing doesn't take breathing into account. If your computer has a speech synthesizer, let the computer say your speech. Or have someone else read it to you. Never deliver a written speech until you have heard it spoken. Subscribe to *Presentations* magazine for tips, www.presentations.com.

5. **The first rule of presentations is to make a checklist.** What's your objective? What's your point? What are five things you want them to remember? What would the ideal audience member say if interviewed 15 minutes after you finish? Who's your audience? How much do they know? What are five techniques you will use to hold their attention? What presentation technology would work best? What questions will the audience have? What's the setting? How much time do you have—always take a few minutes less, never more.

C   Dealing With Conflict

INTPs are often conflict avoiders, as they are extremely uncomfortable with tense, emotional situations. When forced to deal with conflict, they expect everything to be resolved logically, have problems with emotional outbursts, and tend to stick tenaciously to what they see as the "right answer."

1. **Clear problem-focused communication.** Follow the rule of equity: Explain your thinking and ask them to explain theirs. Be able to state their position as clearly as they do whether you agree or not—give it legitimacy. Separate facts from opinions and assumptions. Generate a variety of possibilities first rather than stake out positions. Keep your speaking to 30–60 second bursts. Try to get them to do the same. Don't give the other side the impression you're lecturing or criticizing them. Explain objectively why you hold a view; make the other side do the same. Ask lots of questions, make fewer statements. To identify interests behind positions, ask why they hold them or why they wouldn't want to do something. Always restate their position to their satisfaction before offering a response.

2. **Downsizing the conflict.** Almost all conflicts have common points that get lost in the heat of the battle. After a conflict has been presented and understood, start by saying that it might be helpful to see if we agree on anything. Write them on the flip chart. Then write down the areas left open. Focus on common goals, priorities, and

problems. Keep the open conflicts as small as possible and concrete. The more abstract it gets, "We don't trust your unit," the more unmanageable it gets. To this respond, "Tell me your specific concern—why exactly don't you trust us; can you give me an example?" Usually after calm discussion, they don't trust your unit on this specific issue under these specific conditions. That's easier to deal with. Allow others to save face by conceding small points that are not central to the issue—don't try to hit a home run every time. If you can't agree on a solution, agree on a procedure to move forward. Collect more data. Appeal to a higher power. Get a third-party arbitrator. Something. This creates some positive motion and breaks stalemates.

3. **Cooperative relations.** The opposite of conflict is cooperation. Developing cooperative relationships involves demonstrating real and perceived equity, the other side feeling understood and respected, and taking a problem-oriented point of view. To do this more: Increase the realities and perceptions of fairness—don't try to win every battle and take all the spoils; focus on the common-ground issues and interests of both sides—find wins on both sides, give in on little points; avoid starting with entrenched positions—show respect for them and their positions; and reduce any remaining conflicts to the smallest size possible.

4. **Causing unnecessary conflict.** Language, words, and timing set the tone and can cause unnecessary conflict that has to be managed before you can get anything done. Do you use insensitive language? Do you raise your voice often? Do you use terms and phrases that challenge others? Do you use demeaning terms? Do you use negative humor? Do you offer conclusions, solutions, statements, dictates, or answers early in the transaction? Give reasons first, solutions last. When you give solutions first, people often directly challenge the solutions instead of defining the problem. Pick words that are other-person neutral. Pick words that don't challenge or sound one-sided. Pick tentative and probabilistic words that give others a chance to maneuver and save face. Pick words that are about the problem and not the person. Avoid direct blaming remarks; describe the problem and its impact.

5. **Practice Aikido,** the ancient art of absorbing the energy of your opponent and using it to manage him/her. Let the other side vent frustration or blow off steam, but don't react. Listen. Nod. Ask clarifying questions. Ask open-ended questions like, "What one change could you make so we could achieve our objectives better?"

"What could I do that would help the most?" Restate their position periodically to signal you have understood. But don't react. Keep them talking until they run out of venom. When the other side takes a rigid position, don't reject it. Ask why: What are the principles behind the position? How do we know it's fair? What's the theory of the case? Play out what would happen if their position was accepted. Then explore the concern underlying the answer. Separate the people from the problem. When someone attacks you, rephrase it as an attack on the problem. In response to threats, say you'll only negotiate on merit and fairness. If the other side won't play fair, surface their game—"It looks like you're playing good cop, bad cop. Why don't you settle your differences and tell me one thing?" In response to unreasonable proposals, attacks, or a non-answer to a question, you can always say nothing. People will usually respond by saying more, coming off their position a bit, or at least revealing their true interests. Many times, with unlimited venting and your understanding, the actual conflict shrinks.

6. **Get a bit too tough?** Do your statements have an edge to them? In conflict situations, what reactions do you have (such as impatience or non-verbals like flushing or drumming your pen or fingers)? Learn to recognize those as soon as they start and substitute something more neutral. Most emotional responses to conflict come from personalizing the issue. Separate people issues from the problem at hand, and deal with people issues separately and later if they persist. Always return to facts and the problem before the group; stay away from personal clashes. Attack the problem by looking at common interests and underlying concerns, not people and their positions. Try on their views for size—the emotion as well as the content. Ask yourself if you understand their feelings. Ask what they would do if they were in your shoes. See if you can restate each other's position and advocate it for a minute to get inside each other's place. If you get emotional, pause and collect yourself. You are not your best when you get emotional. Then return to the problem.

7. **Bargaining and trading.** Since you can't absolutely win all conflicts unless you keep pulling rank, you have to learn to horse-trade and bargain. What do they need that I have? What could I do for them outside this conflict that could allow them to give up something I need now in return? How can we turn this into a win for both of us?

8. **Questions.** In win-win and something-something negotiations, the more information you have about the other side, the more you will have to work with. What can you learn about what they know before

going in? What will they do if they don't reach an agreement with you? In the negotiation, ask more questions, make fewer statements. Ask clarifying questions: "What did you mean by that?" Probes: "Why do you say that?" Motives: "What led you to that position?" Get everything out that you can. Don't negotiate assumptions, negotiate facts.

D Giving More Praise

INTPs often don't think to praise others, seeing a job well done as the reward.

1. **Follow through with positive and negative rewards and consequences.** Celebrate the exceeders, compliment the just-made-its, and sit down and discuss what happened with the missers. Actually deliver the reward or consequence you communicated. If you don't do what you said you were going to do, no one will pay attention to the next goal and consequence you set.

2. **Follow the basic rules of inspiring others** as outlined in classic books like *People Skills* by Robert Bolton or *Thriving on Chaos* by Tom Peters. Communicate to people that what they do is important. Say thanks. Offer help and ask for it. Provide autonomy in how people do their work. Provide a variety of tasks. "Surprise" people with enriching, challenging assignments. Show an interest in their careers. Adopt a learning attitude toward mistakes. Celebrate successes, have visible accepted measures of achievement, and so on. Too often people behave correctly but there are no consequences. Although it's easy to get too busy to acknowledge, celebrate, and occasionally criticize, don't forget to reinforce what you want. As a rule of thumb, 4 to 1 positive to negative is best.

3. **Know and play the motivation odds.** According to research by Rewick and Lawler, the top motivators at work are: (1) Job challenge; (2) Accomplishing something worthwhile; (3) Learning new things; (4) Personal development; and (5) Autonomy. Pay (12th), Friendliness (14th), Praise (15th), or Chance of Promotion (17th) are not insignificant but are superficial compared with the more powerful motivators. Provide challenges, paint pictures of why this is worthwhile, create a common mind-set, set up chances to learn and grow, and provide autonomy, and you'll hit the vast majority of people's hot buttons.

4. **Use goals to motivate.** Most people are turned on by reasonable goals. They like to measure themselves against a standard. They like to see

who can run the fastest, score the most, and work the best. They like goals to be realistic but stretching. People try hardest when they have somewhere between one-half and two-thirds chance of success and some control over how they go about it. People are even more motivated when they participate in setting the goals. Set just-out-of-reach challenges and tasks that will be first time for people—their first negotiation, their first solo presentation, etc.

5. **Be able to speak their language at their level.** It shows respect for their way of thinking. Speaking their language makes it easier for them to talk with you and give you the information you need to motivate.

E Better Follow-Through

INTPs tend to be passionate about problems they find interesting. Due to this, other things can fall off their plate or get left dangling.

1. **Simple commitments.** Do you return phone calls in a timely manner? Do you forward material you promised? Did you pass on information you promised to get? Did you carry through on a task you promised someone you would take care of? Failing to do things like this damages relationships. If you tend to forget things, write them down. If you run out of time, set up a specific time each day to follow through on commitments. If you are going to miss a deadline, let them know and give them a second date you will be sure to make.

2. **Overcommitting.** A lot of trouble follows overcommitting. Overcommitting usually comes from wanting to please everyone or not wanting to face the conflict if you say no. You can only do so much. Only commit to that which you can actually do. Commit to a specific time for delivery. Write it down. Learn to say "no" pleasantly. Learn to pass it off to someone else who has the time—"Gee no, but I'm sure Susan could help you with that." Learn to say, "Yes, but it will take longer than you might want to wait," and give them the option of withdrawing the request. Learn to say, "Yes, but what else that I have already committed to do for you would you like to delay to get this done?"

3. **Do an upstream and downstream check with the people you work for,** work around, and those who work for you, to create a list of the administrative slip-ups you do that give them the most trouble. Be sure to ask them for help creating the list. That way, you have a

focused list of the things you need to fix first. If you fix the top 10, maybe that will do and the rest of your habits can stay the same.

4. **Always out of time?** Do you intend to get to things but never have the time? Do you always estimate shorter times to get things done that then take longer? There is a well-established science and a set of best practices in time management. There are a number of books you can buy in any business bookstore, and there are a number of good courses you can attend. Delegating also helps you use your time more effectively.

5. **Visualize.** Set up a process to monitor progress against the goals. People like running measures. They like to gauge their pace. It's like the United Way Thermometer in the lobby.

6. **Feedback.** Give as much in-process feedback as you have time for. Most people are motivated by process feedback against agreed-upon goals for three reasons:

    ■   First, it helps them adjust what they are doing along the way in time to achieve the goal; they can make midcourse corrections.

    ■   Second, it shows them what they are doing is important and that you're eager to help.

    ■   Third, it's not the "gotcha" game of negative and critical feedback after the fact.

F Better Team Building

Many INTPs are the ultimate individual achievers. They would rather solve it themselves and have to be convinced of the value in teams.

1. **Don't believe in teams.** If you don't believe in teams, you are probably a strong individual achiever who doesn't like the mess and sometimes the slowness of due-process relationships and team processes. You are very results oriented and truly believe the best way to do that is to manage one person at a time. To balance this thinking, observe and talk with three excellent team builders and ask them why they manage that way. What do they consider rewarding about building teams? What advantages do they get from using the team format? Read *The Wisdom of Teams* by Katzenbach and Smith. If you can't see the value in teams, none of the following tips will help much.

2. **Don't have the time; teaming takes longer.** That's true and not true. While building a team takes longer than managing one person at a time, having a well-functioning team increases results, builds in a sustaining capability to perform, maximizes collective strengths and covers individual weaknesses, and actually releases more time for the manager because the team members help each other. Many managers get caught in the trap of thinking it takes up too much time to build a team and end up taking more time managing one-on-one.

3. **Not a people person?** Many managers are better with things, ideas, and projects than they are with people. They may be driven and very focused on producing results and have little time left to develop their people skills. It really doesn't take too much. There is communicating. People are more motivated and do better work when they know what's going on. They want to know more than just their little piece. There is listening. Nothing motivates more than a boss who will listen, not interrupt, not finish your sentences, and not complete your thoughts. Increase your listening time 30 seconds in each transaction. There is caring. Caring is questions. Caring is asking about me and what I think and what I feel. Ask one more question per transaction than you do now.

4. **Would like to build a team but don't know how.** High performance teams have four common characteristics: (1) They have a shared mind-set. They have a common vision. Everyone knows the goals and measures. (2) They trust one another. They know "you will cover me if I get in trouble." They know you will pitch in and help even though it may be difficult for you. They know you will be honest with them. They know you will bring problems to them directly and won't go behind their backs. (3) They have the talent collectively to do the job. While not any one member may have it all, collectively they have every task covered. (4) They know how to operate efficiently and effectively. They have good team skills. They run effective meetings. They have efficient ways to communicate. They have ways to deal with internal conflict.

5. **Cement relationships.** Even though some—maybe including you— will resist it, parties, roasts, gag awards, picnics, and outings help build group cohesion. Allow roles to evolve naturally rather than being specified by job descriptions. Some research indicates that people gravitate naturally to eight roles, and that successful teams are not those where everyone does the same thing. Successful teams specialize, cover for each other, and only sometimes demand that everyone participate in identical activities.

I am too methodical and too unwilling to open up to suggestions and thoughts of others. People have a hard time figuring me out.

– An INTP Manager

■ ■ ■ ■ ■ ■ ■ ■ ■ ■ ■ ■ ■ ■ ■ ■

APPLICATION

Your personal preferences play out in day-to-day problems and situations you face. Below is a case about your type dealing with such a situation. Use this to think through how you will integrate the tips you've considered and coach yourself to be more effective in your type.

INTP Application Situation (Part 1)

You're the Manager of a team of research scientists in a pharmaceutical lab and are hoping for a promotion to Director of the center's labs based on a solid track record of successes. You are gratified that your theories about how research should be conducted have resulted in a steady stream of innovative products. You are also pleased that you have managed to keep a group of highly competent researchers and developers intact despite the lure of competing companies and jobs in a tight labor market. These are significant indicators of success, you think, and should position you well for the promotion.

The VP for Research Operations, who is ultimately going to decide whether to promote you or bring someone else in from outside, however, has some concerns. He has told you that he has heard there is often conflict in your team, especially between you and some of the members. He has asked you to do some self-reflection and to try to understand why some of your team has issues with you.

To complement your self-assessment, which you recognize is likely to be flawed, you decide to have a 360° assessment conducted, and you also complete the MBTI, which tells you that your type is INTP.

Thinking It Through: Strategy

■ What are your goals and objectives in your assessment?

■ What potential barriers to your effectiveness might prevent you from becoming an effective Director of Lab Operations?

Planning It Out: Tactics

■ As an INTP, what are the behaviors in your profile that have led some team members to have issues with your leadership style?

■ What kinds of things in your interaction with your team members do you think you'll need to be more concerned about?

■ What particular areas would present developmental challenges to you, and what competencies would you want to put into play in order not only to accomplish your objectives but to assure that relationships are preserved?

■ Which of the tactics described in the Being More Effective section are applicable in this situation?

■ Which Overused Tendencies are most likely to come into play here?

INTP Application Situation (Part 2)

■ You have a meeting scheduled with your VP to discuss the feedback from the 360° assessment. Your VP has brought in a coach from HR to help you understand the feedback. In summary, he tells you that there's a consensus among your direct reports that while your relentless focus on methodology, thoroughness, and your own ideas has accounted for a good deal of success, your apparent indifference to the needs of others and your attention to nit-picking has led to unnecessary conflict and inhibited team development and innovation.

Reflection

■ What factors in your personality type can you rely on while you work on reducing the "noise" that your direct reports are perceiving?

■ What are you going to have to do more of, and what are you going to have to do less of, in order to succeed at higher levels of leadership?

SUGGESTED READINGS

■■■■■■■ Being a More Effective INTP ■■■■■■■

Problems With Peers

Ashkenas, Ronald N. (Ed.), Dave Ulrich, Todd Jick, Steve Kerr and Lawrence A. Bossidy. *The Boundaryless Organization: Breaking the Chains of Organization Structure, Revised and Updated.* New York: John Wiley & Sons, Inc., 2002.

Aubuchon, Norbert. *The Anatomy of Persuasion.* New York: AMACOM, 1997.

Baker, Wayne E. *Networking Smart.* New York: Backinprint.com, 2000.

Bolton, Robert and Dorothy Grover Bolton. *People Styles at Work—Making Bad Relationships Good and Good Relationships Better.* New York: AMACOM, 1996.

Brache, Alan P. *How Organizations Work.* New York: John Wiley & Sons, Inc., 2002.

Cartwright, Tatula. *Managing Conflict With Peers.* Greensboro, NC: Center for Creative Leadership, 2003.

Dobson, Michael S. and Deborah S. Dobson. *Enlightened Office Politics: Understanding, Coping With and Winning the Game—Without Losing Your Soul.* New York: AMACOM, 2001.

Problems With Direct Reports

Autry, James A. *The Art of Caring Leadership.* New York: William Morrow and Company, Inc., 1991.

Genett, Donna M. *If You Want It Done Right, You Don't Have to Do It Yourself! The Power of Effective Delegation.* Sanger, CA: Quill Driver Books, 2004.

Kouzes, James M. and Barry Z. Posner. *Encouraging the Heart: A Leader's Guide to Rewarding and Recognizing Others.* San Francisco: Jossey-Bass, Inc., 2003.

Levin, Robert A. and Joseph G. Rosse. *Talent Flow: A Strategic Approach to Keeping Good Employees, Helping Them Grow, and Letting Them Go.* New York: John Wiley & Sons, Inc., 2001.

Solomon, Muriel. *Working With Difficult People.* New York: Prentice Hall, 2002.

Stone, Douglas. *Difficult Conversations: How to Discuss What Matters Most.* New York: Penguin Books, 2000.

Organizing

Allen, David. *Getting Things Done: The Art of Stress-Free Productivity.* New York: Penguin Books, 2003.

Bossidy, Larry, Ram Charan and Charles Burck (Contributor). *Execution: The Discipline of Getting Things Done.* New York: Crown Business Publishing, 2002.

Drucker, Peter F. *The Effective Executive.* New York: HarperBusiness, 2002.

Stone, Florence M. and Randi T. Sachs. *The High-Value Manager— Developing the Core Competencies Your Organization Needs.* New York: AMACOM, 1995.

Ulrich, David, Jack Zenger and Norman Smallwood. *Results-Based Leadership.* Boston: Harvard Business School Press, 1999.

Patience

Barker, Larry, Ph.D. and Kittie Watson, Ph.D. *Listen Up: At Home, at Work, in Relationships: How to Harness the Power of Effective Listening.* Irvine, CA: Griffin Trade Paperback, 2001.

Bolton, Robert and Dorothy Grover Bolton. *People Styles at Work—Making Bad Relationships Good and Good Relationships Better.* New York: AMACOM, 1996.

Burley-Allen, Madelyn. *Listening: The Forgotten Skill.* New York: John Wiley & Sons, Inc., 1995.

Gonthier, Giovinella and Kevin Morrissey. *Rude Awakenings: Overcoming the Civility Crisis in the Workplace.* Chicago: Dearborn Trade Publishing, 2002.

Ryan, Mary Jane. *The Power of Patience: How to Slow the Rush and Enjoy More Happiness, Success, and Peace of Mind Everyday.* New York: Broadway Press, 2003.

Interpersonal Relationships

Benton, D.A. *Executive Charisma: Six Steps to Mastering the Art of Leadership.* New York: McGraw-Hill Trade, 2003.

Bolton, Robert and Dorothy Grover Bolton. *People Styles at Work—Making Bad Relationships Good and Good Relationships Better.* New York: AMACOM, 1996.

Brooks, Michael. *Instant Rapport.* New York: Warner Books, 1989.

Maxwell, John C. *Relationships 101.* London: Thomas Nelson, 2004.

Silberman, Melvin L. and Freda Hansburg. *Peoplesmart: Developing Your Interpersonal Intelligence.* San Francisco: Berrett-Koehler Publishers, Inc., 2000.

■■■■■■■ Overusing INTP Tendencies ■■■■■■■

Overcoming Arrogance

Bolton, Robert and Dorothy Grover Bolton. *People Styles at Work—Making Bad Relationships Good and Good Relationships Better.* New York: AMACOM, 1996.

Carter, Les. *The Anger Trap: Free Yourself From the Frustrations That Sabotage Your Life.* New York: John Wiley & Sons, Inc., 2003.

Ellis, Albert, Ph.D. *How to Control Your Anxiety Before It Controls You.* New York: Citadel Press, 2000.

Waldroop, James, Ph.D. and Timothy Butler, Ph.D. *Maximum Success: Changing the 12 Behavior Patterns That Keep You From Getting Ahead.* New York: Doubleday, 2000.

Communicating More Clearly

Arredondo, Lani. *Communicating Effectively.* New York: McGraw-Hill Trade, 2000.

Booher, Dianna. *Speak With Confidence: Powerful Presentations That Inform, Inspire, and Persuade.* New York: McGraw-Hill, Inc., 2002.

Harvard Business School Press (Ed.). *Presentations That Persuade and Motivate (The Results-Driven Manager Series).* Boston: Harvard Business School Press, 2004.

McCormack, Mark H. *On Communicating*. Los Angeles: Dove Books, 1998.

Zeuschner, Raymond F. *Communicating Today: The Essentials*. Boston: Allyn & Bacon, 2002.

Dealing With Conflict

Cloke, Ken and Joan Goldsmith. *Resolving Conflicts at Work: A Complete Guide for Everyone on the Job*. San Francisco: Jossey-Bass, Inc., 2000.

Dana, Daniel. *Conflict Resolution*. New York: McGraw-Hill Trade, 2000.

Graham, Gini. *A Survival Guide for Working With Humans: Dealing With Whiners, Back-Stabbers, Know-It-Alls, and Other Difficult People*. New York: AMACOM, 2004.

Guttman, Howard M. *When Goliaths Clash: Managing Executive Conflict to Build a More Dynamic Organization*. New York: AMACOM, 2003.

Masters, Marick Francis and Robert R. Albright. *The Complete Guide to Conflict Resolution in the Workplace*. New York: AMACOM, 2002.

Giving More Praise

Bolton, Robert. *People Skills*. New York: Simon & Schuster, 1979.

Crainer, Stuart. *Motivating the New Generation—Modern Motivation Techniques*. New York: BrownHerron Publishing, 2001.

Glanz, Barbara A. *Handle With CARE: Motivating and Retaining Employees*. New York: McGraw-Hill Trade, 2002.

Hiam, Alexander. *Motivational Management: Inspiring Your People for Maximum Performance*. New York: AMACOM, 2003.

Peters, Tom. *Thriving on Chaos: Handbook for a Management Revolution*. New York: HarperCollins, 1987.

Better Follow-Through

Byfield, Marilyn. *It's Hard to Make a Difference When You Can't Find Your Keys: The Seven-Step Path to Becoming Truly Organized*. New York: Viking Press, 2003.

Gleeson, Kerry. *The Personal Efficiency Program: How to Get Organized to Do More Work in Less Time*. New York: John Wiley & Sons, Inc., 2000.

MacKenzie, Alec. *The Time Trap: The Classic Book on Time Management.* Fine Communications, 2002.

Winston, Stephanie. *The Organized Executive: The Classic Program for Productivity: New Ways to Manage Time, People, and the Digital Office.* New York: Warner Business, 2001.

Better Team Building

Fisher, Kimball and Mareen Duncan Fisher. *The Distance Manager: A Hands-On Guide to Managing Off-Site Employees and Virtual Teams.* New York: McGraw-Hill Trade, 2000.

Genett, Donna M. *If You Want It Done Right, You Don't Have to Do It Yourself! The Power of Effective Delegation.* Sanger, CA: Quill Driver Books, 2004.

Harvard Business School Press. *Harvard Business Review on Teams That Succeed.* Boston: Harvard Business School Press, 2004.

Katzenbach, Jon R. and Douglas K. Smith. *The Wisdom of Teams: Creating the High-Performance Organization.* New York: HarperBusiness, 2003.

Parker, Glenn M. *Cross-Functional Teams: Working With Allies, Enemies, and Other Strangers.* San Francisco: Jossey-Bass, Inc., 2002.

Raymond, Cara Capretta, Robert W. Eichinger and Michael M. Lombardo. *FYI for Teams.* Minneapolis, MN: Lominger Limited, Inc., 2001–2004.

Robbins, Harvey and Michael Finley. *The New Why Teams Don't Work— What Goes Wrong and How to Make It Right.* San Francisco: Berrett-Koehler Publishers, Inc., 2000.

CHAPTER 9

ESTP
Extraverted Sensing
with
Introverted Thinking

■■■■■■■■■■■■■■■■

4.3% of Population
3.2% of Managers

■■■■■■■■■■■■■■■■

Typical Strengths

Fast Paced
Good-Natured
Fact Based
Crisis Management
Decisive
Social Presence
Pick Up on Non-Verbal Cues
Good Negotiator
Charismatic

ISTJ	ISFJ	INFJ	INTJ
ISTP	ISFP	INFP	INTP
ESTP	ESFP	ENFP	ENTP
ESTJ	ESFJ	ENFJ	ENTJ

Make the numbers and forget the rest.

– An ESTP Manager

Basic Habits of Mind

Extraverted Sensing is the dominant mental process. ESTPs are in a state of relentless awareness of the environment and people. As a result of this awareness, they tend to quickly respond and to move at a fast pace. Aided by Introverted Thinking, they are busy constructing logical paths to follow.

Introverted Feeling and Introverted Intuiting also help ESTPs. Introverted Feeling promotes a sense of purpose and direction, again as applied to practical ends. Introverted Intuiting plays out as moving forward with confidence.

This combination sometimes is misunderstood as impatient, opportunistic, and self-centered. ESTPs can be seen as trying to win at others' expense.

Typical Communication Patterns

- ESTPs are energetic, fast-paced communicators who enjoy whatever they are doing at the moment.

- They are good-natured and realistic in their interactions.

- Often good at easing tensions due to their sense of humor, ESTPs are also very critical and analytical when exploring situations.

- They actively seek facts followed by concise questioning of others.

General Learning Strategy

- ESTPs usually prefer quick-paced, "hands-on," and challenging opportunities to learn.

- Their typical learning strategies are active testing of ideas, trial-and-error rather than reflective learning, and physically active learning.

- Their learning is generally enhanced by competitive opportunities, clear instructions, and a chance to socialize.

Interpersonal Qualities Related to Motivation

■ ESTPs are energized by being on the move, focusing on the present, and quickly acting to efficiently solve problems.

■ Put them on the "emergency team" or the "disaster recovery team" and you may see them at their highest level of motivation.

■ Although fast movers, ESTPs can appear inactive when they are, in fact, looking for the quickest, shortest route between two points.

Blind Spots

■ According to observers, ESTPs do not demonstrate the same degree of resourcefulness and responsibility they imagine others see.

■ They are sometimes seen as noncommittal, detached, and abrasive.

Stress Related Behavior

■ When stressed, ESTPs often become more aggressive in seeking information and forceful in expecting people to conform.

■ If the stress persists and is constant enough, they may seem to obsess about dire possibilities. They can convince themselves that they know how terrible a situation is before checking it out with someone.

Potential Barriers to Effectiveness

■ ESTPs can stumble in their work if they do not build a developmental climate in the workplace, demonstrate as much empathy as criticism, and take the time to show their interest in the long-range strategic future of the organization.

Being a More Effective ESTP

A Showing Caring
B Developing Others
C Team Building
D Analyzing Problems
E Seeing the Bigger Picture
F Attention to Process and Plans

ISTJ	ISFJ	INFJ	INTJ
ISTP	ISFP	INFP	INTP
ESTP	ESFP	ENFP	ENTP
ESTJ	ESFJ	ENFJ	ENTJ

A | Showing Caring

While good-natured and good with others, many ESTPs move too fast to show much caring or to listen to others.

1. **Caring is listening.** Many bosses are marginal listeners. They are action oriented and more apt to cut off people mid-sentence than listen. They also are impatient and finish people's sentences for them when they hesitate. All of these impatient behaviors come across to others as a lack of caring. It's being insensitive to the needs and feelings of others. So, step one in caring is listening longer.

2. **Caring is sharing and disclosing.** Share your thinking on a business issue and invite the advice of direct reports. Pass on tidbits of information you think will help people do their jobs better or broaden their perspectives. Reveal things people don't need to know to do their jobs, but which will be interesting to them—and help them feel valued. Disclose some things about yourself as well. It's hard for people to relate to a stone. Tell them how you arrive at decisions. Explain your intentions, your reasons, and your thinking when announcing decisions. If you offer solutions first, you invite resistance and feelings of not being cared about—"He/she just dumps things on us."

3. **Caring is knowing.** Know three non-work things about everybody— their interests and hobbies or their children or something you can chat about. Life is a small world. If you ask your people a few personal questions, you'll find you have something in common with virtually anyone. Having something in common will help bond the relationship.

4. **Caring is accepting.** Try to listen without judging initially. Turn off your "I agree; I don't agree" filter. You don't have to agree with it; just

listen to understand. Assume when people tell you something they are looking for understanding; indicate that by being able to summarize what they said. Don't offer advice or solutions unless it's obvious the person wants to know what you would do. While offering instant solutions is a good thing to do in many circumstances, it's chilling where the goal is to get people to talk to you more freely.

5. **Caring is understanding.** Study the people you work with. Without judging them, collect evidence on how they think and what they do. What drives them to do what they do? Try to predict what they will do in given situations. Use this to understand how to relate to them. What are their hot buttons? What would they like for you to care about?

6. **Feedback.** People need continuous feedback from you and others to grow. Some tips about feedback:

- Arrange for them to get feedback from multiple people, including yourself, on what matters for success in their future jobs; arrange for your direct reports to get 360° feedback about every two years.

- Give them progressively stretching tasks that are first-time and different for them so that they can give themselves feedback as they go.

- If they have direct reports and peers, another technique to recommend is to ask their associates for comments on what they should stop doing, start doing, and keep doing to be more successful.

- You have to be willing to be straight with your people and give them accurate but balanced feedback. Give as much real-time feedback as you have time for. Most people are motivated by process feedback against agreed-upon goals for three reasons. First, it helps them adjust what they are doing along the way in time to better achieve the goal; they can make midcourse corrections. Second, it shows them what they are doing is important and that you're there to help. Third, it's not the "gotcha" game of negative and critical feedback after the fact. If there are negatives, they need to know as soon as possible.

- Set up a buddy system so people can get continuing feedback.

■ If your organization has a mentoring program, find out how it works. Best practices begin with those to be mentored writing down goals, objectives, and development needs. They are then carefully matched with mentors and the relationship is outlined. How often will the people meet? On what topics is the mentor to be helpful? What are the responsibilities of the person to be mentored? If your organization doesn't have such a program, look at setting one up within your unit or function.

B Developing Others

Development is a long-term process, and present focused ESTPs are not usually very interested in the development of others. They are on to the next project.

1. **You have to invest some time.** For most managers, time is what they have the least of to give. For the purposes of developing others beyond today's job, you need to allocate about eight hours per year per direct report. If you have a normal span of seven direct reports, that's 7 of 220 working days or 3% of your annual time. Two of the eight hours are for an annual in-depth appraisal of the person in terms of current strengths and weaknesses and of the competencies he/she needs to develop to move on to the next step. Two of the eight hours are for an in-depth career discussion with each person. What does he/she want? What will he/she sacrifice to get there? What is his/her own appraisal of his/her skills? Two of the eight hours are for creating a three- to five-year development plan and sharing it with the person. The last two hours are to present your findings and recommendations to the organization, usually in a succession planning process, and arranging for developmental events for each person. Start thinking of yourself as a coach or mentor. It's your job to help your people grow.

2. **Help people focus on the right things.** In their study of successful vs. average careers, Citrin and Smith found that the most successful people force themselves into experiences they need for growth. They do not play it safe. While they demonstrate early competence in a specific area, they also don't overdo working on basic job requirements. They do enough work on the basics while searching for mission-critical job elements and trying to overdeliver on them. They add unexpected value. They call this the 20/80 principle of performance—focusing on the 20% that makes 80% of the difference. In doing so, the successful rack up career freedom points by tackling these tough assignments.

3. **Do you help your people learn by looking for repeating patterns?** Help them look for patterns in the situations and problems they deal with. What succeeded and what failed? What was common to each success or what was present in each failure but never present in a success? Focus on the successes; failures are easier to analyze but don't in themselves tell you what would work. Comparing successes, while less exciting, yields more information. The bottom line is help them reduce insights to principles or rules of thumb that might be repeatable. Ask them what they have learned to increase their skills and understanding, making them better managers or professionals. Ask them what they can do now that they couldn't do a year ago. Reinforce this and encourage more of it. Developing is learning in as many ways as possible.

4. **How to delegate?** Communicate, set time frames and goals, and get out of the way. People need to know what it is you expect. What does the outcome look like? When do you need it by? What's the budget? What resources do they get? What decisions can they make? Do you want checkpoints along the way? How will we both know and measure how well the task is done? One of the most common problems with delegation is incomplete or cryptic up-front communication leading to frustration, a job not well done the first time, rework, and a reluctance to delegate next time. Poor communicators always have to take more time managing because of rework. Analyze recent projects that went well and didn't go well. How did you delegate? Too much? Not enough? Unwanted pieces? Major chunks of responsibility? Workload distributed properly? Did you set measures? Overmanage or abdicate? Find out what your best practices are. Set up a series of delegation practices that can be used as if you're not there. What do you have to be informed of? What feedback loops can people use for midcourse correction? What questions should be answered as the work proceeds? What steps should be followed? What are the criteria to be followed? When will you be available to help?

5. **More what and why, less how.** The best delegators are crystal clear on what and when, and more open on how. People are more motivated when they can determine the how for themselves. Inexperienced delegators include the hows, which turn the people into task automatons instead of an empowered and energized staff. Tell them what and when and for how long, and let them figure out how on their own. Give them leeway. Encourage them to try things. Besides being more motivating, it's also more developmental for them. Add

the larger context. Although it is not necessary to get the task done, people are more motivated when they know where this task fits in the bigger picture. Take three extra minutes and tell them why this task needs to be done, where it fits in the grander scheme, and its importance to the goals and objectives of the unit.

C Team Building

ESTPs usually lack the patience for process that teams demand. They like to work on many projects at once. Teams can slow them down.

1. **Don't believe in teams.** If you don't believe in teams, you are probably a strong individual achiever who doesn't like the mess and sometimes the slowness of due-process relationships and team processes. You are very results oriented and truly believe the best way to do that is to manage one person at a time. To balance this thinking, observe and talk with three excellent team builders and ask them why they manage that way. What do they consider rewarding about building teams? What advantages do they get from using the team format? Read *The Wisdom of Teams* by Katzenbach and Smith. If you can't see the value in teams, none of the following tips will help much.

2. **Don't have the time; teaming takes longer.** That's true and not true. While building a team takes longer than managing one person at a time, having a well-functioning team increases results, builds in a sustaining capability to perform, maximizes collective strengths and covers individual weaknesses, and actually releases more time for the manager because the team members help each other. Many managers get caught in the trap of thinking it takes up too much time to build a team and end up taking more time managing one-on-one.

3. **Would like to build a team but don't know how.** High performance teams have four common characteristics: (1) They have a shared mind-set. They have a common vision. Everyone knows the goals and measures. (2) They trust one another. They know "you will cover me if I get in trouble." They know you will pitch in and help even though it may be difficult for you. They know you will be honest with them. They know you will bring problems to them directly and won't go behind their backs. (3) They have the talent collectively to do the job. While not any one member may have it all, collectively they have every task covered. (4) They know how to operate efficiently and effectively. They have good team skills. They run effective meetings.

They have efficient ways to communicate. They have ways to deal with internal conflict.

4. **Can't seem to get people motivated to be a team.** Follow the basic rules of inspiring others as outlined in classic books like *People Skills* by Robert Bolton or *Thriving on Chaos* by Tom Peters. Communicate to people that what they do is important. Say thanks. Offer help and ask for it. Provide autonomy in how people do their work. Provide a variety of tasks. "Surprise" people with enriching, challenging assignments. Show an interest in their careers. Adopt a learning attitude toward mistakes. Celebrate successes, have visible accepted measures of achievement, and so on. Try to get everyone to participate in the building of the team so they have a stake in the outcome.

5. **Cement relationships.** Even though some—maybe including you—will resist it, parties, roasts, gag awards, picnics, and outings help build group cohesion. Allow roles to evolve naturally rather than being specified by job descriptions. Some research indicates that people gravitate naturally to eight roles, and that successful teams are not those where everyone does the same thing. Successful teams specialize, cover for each other, and only sometimes demand that everyone participate in identical activities.

6. **Not good at motivating people beyond being results oriented?** Play the motivation odds. According to research by Rewick and Lawler, the top motivators at work are: (1) Job challenge; (2) Accomplishing something worthwhile; (3) Learning new things; (4) Personal development; and (5) Autonomy. Pay (12th), Friendliness (14th), Praise (15th), or Chance of Promotion (17th) are not insignificant but are superficial compared with the five top motivators. Provide challenges, paint pictures of why this is worthwhile, set up chances to learn and grow, and provide autonomy, and you'll hit the vast majority of people's hot buttons.

D   Analyzing Problems

Present focused and crisis oriented, ESTPs are usually seen as not interested in detailed analysis. They are much more likely to pull something from their bag of tricks.

1. **Holster your gun.** Life is a balance between waiting and doing. Many in management put a premium on doing over waiting. Most could make close to 100% good decisions given all of the data and unlimited time. Life affords us neither the data nor the time. You may need to try

to discipline yourself to wait just a little longer than you usually do for more, but not all, the data to come in. Push yourself to always get one more piece of data than you did before until your correct decision percent becomes more acceptable. Instead of just doing it, ask what questions would need to be answered before we'd know which way to go. In one study of problem solving, answers outnumbered questions 8 to 1. We jump to solutions based on what has worked in the past. So collect data to answer these questions, then shoot.

2. **Do you do enough analysis?** Thoroughly define the problem. Look for patterns in data, don't just collect information. Put it in categories that make sense to you. A good rule of thumb is to analyze patterns and causes to come up with alternatives. Many of us just collect data, which numerous studies show increases our confidence but doesn't increase decision accuracy. Think out loud with others; see how they view the problem. To break out of analysis paralysis, figure out what the problem is first. Then when a good alternative appears, you're likely to recognize it immediately.

3. **Defining the problem.** Instant and early conclusions, solutions, statements, suggestions, and how we solved it in the past, are the enemies of good problem solving. Studies show that defining the problem and taking action occur almost simultaneously for most people, so the more effort you put on the front end, the easier it is to come up with a good solution. Stop and first define what the problem is and isn't. Since providing solutions is so easy for everyone, it would be nice if they were offering solutions to the right problem. Figure out what causes it. Keep asking why. See how many causes you can come up with and how many organizing buckets you can put them in. This increases the chance of a better solution because you can see more connections. Be a chess master. Chess masters recognize thousands of patterns of chess pieces. Look for patterns in data; don't just collect information. Put it in categories that make sense to you. Ask lots of questions. Allot at least 50% of the time to defining the problem.

4. **Watch your biases.** Some people have solutions in search of problems. They have favorite solutions. They have biases. They have universal solutions to most situations. They pre-judge what the problem is without stopping to consider the nuances of this specific problem. Do honest and open analysis first. One of your solutions may in fact fit, but wait to see if you're right about the problem.

5. **Check yourself for these common errors in thinking:** Do you state as facts things that are really opinions or assumptions? Are you sure

these assertions are facts? State opinions and assumptions as that and don't present them as facts. Do you attribute cause and effect to relationships when you don't know if one causes the other? If sales are down, and we increase advertising and sales go up, this doesn't prove causality. They are simply related. Say we know that the relationship between sales/advertising is about the same as sales/number of employees. If sales go down, we probably wouldn't hire more people, so make sure one thing causes the other before acting on it. Do you generalize from a single example without knowing if that single example does generalize?

E Seeing the Bigger Picture

ESTPs are present focused. Strategy usually holds no special interest.

1. **Not curious?** Many managers are so wrapped up in today's problems that they aren't curious about tomorrow. They really don't care about the long-term future. They may not even be in the organization when the strategic plan is supposed to happen. They believe there won't be much of a future until we perform today. Being a visionary and a good strategist requires curiosity and imagination. It requires playing "what ifs." What are the implications of the growing gap between rich and poor? The collapse of retail pricing? The increasing influence of brand names? What if it turns out there is life on other planets, and we get the first message? What will that change? Will they need our products? What will happen when a larger percentage of the world's population is over the age of 65? The effects of terrorism? What if cancer is cured? Heart disease? AIDS? Obesity? What if the government outlaws or severely regulates some aspect of your business? True, nobody knows the answers, but good strategists know the questions. Work at developing broader interests outside your business. Subscribe to different magazines. Pick new shows to watch. Meet different people. Join a new organization. Look under some rocks. Think about tomorrow. Talk to others about what they think the future will bring.

2. **Narrow perspective?** Some are sharply focused on what they do and do it very well. They have prepared themselves for a narrow but satisfying career. Then someone tells them their job has changed, and they now have to be strategic. Being strategic requires a broad perspective. In addition to knowing one thing well, it requires that you know about a lot of things somewhat. You need to understand business. You need to understand markets. You need to understand

how the world operates. You need to put all that together and figure out what all that means to your organization.

3. **Too busy?** Strategy is always last on the list. Solving today's problems, of which there are many, is job one. You have to make time for strategy. A good strategy releases future time because it makes choices clear and leads to less wasted effort, but it takes time to do. Delegation is usually the main key. Give away as much tactical day-to-day stuff as you can. Ask your people what they think they could do to give you more time for strategic reflection. Another key is better time management. Put an hour a week on your calendar for strategic reading and reflection throughout the year. Don't wait until one week before the strategic plan is due. Keep a log of ideas you get from others, magazines, etc. Focus on how these impact your organization or function.

4. **Can't think strategically?** Strategy is linking several variables together to come up with the most likely scenario. Think of it as the search for and application of relevant parallels. It involves making projections of several variables at once to see how they come together. These projections are in the context of shifting markets, international affairs, monetary movements, and government interventions. It involves a lot of uncertainty, making risk assumptions, and understanding how things work together. How many reasons would account for sales going down? Up? How are advertising and sales linked? If the dollar is cheaper in Asia, what does that mean for our product in Japan? If the world population is aging and they have more money, how will that change buying patterns? Not everyone enjoys this kind of pie-in-the-sky thinking and not everyone is skilled at doing it.

5. **Managing remotely requires a broader view.** It's impossible for you to do it all. Successful managers report high involvement in setting parameters, exceptions they want to be notified of, and expected outcomes. They detail what requires their involvement and what doesn't. When people call them for a decision, they always ask, "What do you think? What impact will it have on you—customers, etc.—if we do this?" rather than just render a judgment. If you don't, people will begin to delegate upward, and you'll be a close-in manager from a remote location. Help people think things through, and trust them to follow the plan. Delegation requires this clear communication about expectations and releasing the authority to decide and act.

F Attention to Process and Plans

ESTPs are rarely planful. They are fixers, hard-driving problem solvers who lack the patience to lay things out carefully.

1. **Lay out tasks and work.** Most successful projects begin with a good plan. What do I need to accomplish? What are the goals? What's the time line? What resources will I need? How many of the resources do I control? Who controls the rest of the resources—people, funding, tools, materials, support—I need? Lay out the work from A to Z. Many people are seen as lacking a plan because they don't write down the sequence or parts of the work and leave something out. Ask others to comment on ordering and what's missing.

2. **Set goals.** You should set goals before assigning projects, work, and tasks. Goals help focus people's time and efforts. It allows people to perform more effectively and efficiently. Most people don't want to waste time. Most people want to perform well. Learn about MBO—managing by objectives. Read a book about it. While you may not be interested in a full-blown application, all of the principles of setting goals will be in the book. Go to a course on goal setting.

3. **Focus on measures.** How would you tell if the goal was accomplished? If the things I asked others to do were done right, what outcomes could we all agree on as measures of success? Most groups can easily come up with success measures that are different from, and more important to them, than formal measures. Ask them to do so.

4. **Vision the plan in process.** What could go wrong? Run scenarios in your head. Think along several paths. Rank the potential problems from highest likelihood to lowest likelihood. Think about what you would do if the highest likelihood things were to occur. Create a contingency plan for each. Pay attention to the weakest links, which are usually groups or elements you have the least interface with or control over (perhaps someone in a remote location, a consultant, or supplier). Stay doubly in touch with the potential weak links.

5. **Visualize.** Set up a process to monitor progress against the goals. People like running measures. They like to gauge their pace. It's like the United Way Thermometer in the lobby.

6. **Bargaining for resources.** What do I have to trade? What can I buy? What can I borrow? What do I need to trade for? What do I need that I can't pay or trade for?

7. **Rallying support.** Share your mission and goals with the people you need to support you. Try to get their input. People who are asked tend to cooperate more than people who are not asked. Figure out how the people who support your effort can win along with you.

Overusing ESTP Tendencies

If you sometimes overdo your preferred behaviors, you may need to work on:

A Being Appropriately Ambitious

B Being Less Pressuring

C Dealing With Ambiguity Better

D Better Follow-Through

E Dealing With Routine and Procedures

F Not Trying to Win Every Battle

ISTJ	ISFJ	INFJ	INTJ
ISTP	ISFP	INFP	INTP
ESTP	ESFP	ENFP	ENTP
ESTJ	ESFJ	ENFJ	ENTJ

A Being Appropriately Ambitious

ESTPs like to win, and will win at the expense of others at times.

1. **Self-marketing needs to be done with great political care.** Don't wear out your welcome. While people are usually positive about moderate self-promotion, they turn off quickly to what they consider too much or self-promotion that's too loud. Who really matters? Approach them once or twice carefully and with moderation. Don't share your ambitions with people who don't play a part in your future. And never, never bad-mouth competitors for a promotion. This will say far more about you than it says about them.

2. **How much time do you spend helping others solve problems vs. pushing your own agenda?** Are you viewed as a loner? Do you help peers, help direct reports develop, visibly work to build a team? You may be trying to blame others for things you should take responsibility for. You may be making up excuses that are not real to cover for yourself. You may be trying to make your rivals look bad so that you look better. You may hedge when asked a tough question. You may slap things together to look good when what's underneath wouldn't pass the test. You may be disorganized and your actions

cause problems for others. You may indicate little or no concern for others. If you do any of these things or things like it, you will eventually be found out, and you will lose the future you have been marketing yourself for. Stop them all.

3. **Values or facts?** You may be a fact-based person. Since to you the facts dictate everything, you may be baffled as to why people would see it any differently than you do. The reason they see it differently is that there is a higher order of values at work. People compare across situations to check for common themes, equity, and parity. They ask questions like who wins and loses here, who is being favored, is this a play for advantage? Since you are a here-and-now person, you will look inconsistent to them across slightly different situations. You need to drop back and ask what will others hear, not what you want to say. Go below the surface. Tell them why you're saying something. Ask them what they think.

4. **Do you promote the careers of others as well as your own?** Do you help other people solve their problems or do they only help you solve yours? People will tolerate more ambition from you if you have a demonstrated track record of helping others get ahead as well.

5. **Do you do all the presenting for your group to top management?** Sometimes that's a sign of being overly ambitious. Let others present sometimes. Try to gain stature with top management through the success of your people. Usually that's just as fast a track to a career as is doing everything yourself. Executives quickly notice people builders, those who surround themselves with high performers.

6. **Answers. Solutions. Conclusions. Statements. Dictates.** That's the staple of arrogant people. Instant output. Sharp reactions. This may be getting you in trouble. You jump to conclusions, categorically dismiss what others say, use challenging words in an absolute tone. People then see you as closed to their input or combative. More negatively, they may believe you think they're stupid or ill-informed. Give people a chance to talk without interruption. If you're seen as intolerant or closed, people will often stumble over words in their haste to talk with you or shortcut their argument since they assume you're not listening anyway. Ask a question, invite them to disagree with you, present their argument back to them softly, let them save face no matter what. Add a 15-second pause into your transactions before you say anything, and add two clarifying questions per transaction to signal you're listening and want to understand.

7. **Too independent?** You set your own rules, smash through obstacles, see yourself as tough, action oriented, and results oriented. You get it done. The problem is, you wreak havoc for others; they don't know which of your actions will create headaches for them in their own unit or with customers. You don't often worry about whether others think like you do. You operate from the inside out. What's important to you is what you think and what you judge to be right and just. In a sense, admirable. In a sense, not smart. You live in an organization that has both formal and informal commonly held standards, beliefs, ethics, and values. You can't survive long without knowing what they are and bending yours to fit. To find out, focus on the impact on others and how they see the issue. This will be hard at first since you spend your energy justifying your own actions.

B Being Less Pressuring

ESTPs can write off people, not listen, ignore, or go around anyone or anything that blocks their path.

1. **Under extended stress, you can become hypercritical of others** and find an endless list of reasons for the unacceptability of some action or fact. You appear skeptical and touchy. Accept this for what it is—you. Think of it as your personal preferences speaking rather than reality. Seek feedback to find out what is really going on.

2. **Do you meddle in the work of others when they are blocking your efforts?** Let your team help you. Periodically, send out a memo asking each person whether there is anything he or she thinks he/she could do that you are now doing or monitoring too closely. Pick one or two things per person and empower them to do it on their own. Make sure the up-front communication is adequate for them to perform well. Explain your standards—what the outcome should be, the key things that need to be taken care of—then ask them to figure out how to do it themselves.

3. **If you are impatient and find yourself checking in too frequently,** set up a timetable with your people with agreed-upon checkpoints and in-progress checks. Let them initiate this on a schedule you are comfortable with. Ask yourself who your most motivating bosses were. Chances are they gave you a lot of leeway, encouraged you to try things, were good sounding boards, and cheered your successes. Do what they did with you.

4. **Blame and vengeance?** Do you feel a need to punish the people and groups that set you off? Do you become hostile, angry, sarcastic, or vengeful? While all that may be temporarily satisfying to you, they will all backfire and you will lose in the long term. When someone attacks you, rephrase it as an attack on a problem. Reverse the argument—ask what they would do if they were in your shoes. When the other side takes a rigid position, don't reject it. Ask why: What are the principles behind the offer? How do we know it's fair? What's the theory of the case? Play out what would happen if their position was accepted. Let the other side vent frustration or blow off steam, but don't react. When you do reply to an attack, keep it to the facts and their impact on you. It's fine for you to draw conclusions about the impact on yourself—"I felt blindsided." It's not fine for you to tell others their motives—"You blindsided me" means you did it, probably meant to, and I know the meaning of your behavior. So state the meaning for yourself; ask others what their actions meant.

5. **Listening chillers?** Don't interrupt before they have finished. Don't suggest words when they hesitate or pause. Don't finish their sentences for them. Don't wave off any further input by saying, "Yes, I know that." "Yes, I know where you're going." "Yes, I have heard that before." If time is really important, you can say, "Let me see if I know where this is going...," or "I wonder if we could summarize to save both of us some time?" Finally, early in a transaction, answers, solutions, conclusions, statements, and dictates shut many people down. You've told them your mind is already made up. Listen first, solve second.

6. **Listening to those who waste a lot of time.** With those you don't have time to listen to, switch to being a teacher. Try to help them craft their communications to you in a more acceptable way. Tell them to be shorter next time. Come with more/less data. Structure the conversation by helping them come up with categories and structures to stop their rambling. Good listeners don't signal to the "bad" people that they are not listening or are not interested. Don't signal to anyone what bucket they're in. Put your mind in neutral, nod, ask questions, be helpful.

7. **Listening to people you don't like.** What do people see in them who do like them or can at least get along with them? What are their strengths? Do you have any common interests? Talk less and ask more questions to give them a second chance. Don't judge their motives and intentions—do that later.

8. **Listening to people you like but...**

- They are disorganized. Interrupt to summarize and keep the discussion focused. While interrupting is generally not a good tactic, it's necessary here.

- They just want to chat. Ask questions to focus them; don't respond to chatty remarks.

- They want to unload a problem. Assume when people tell you something they are looking for understanding; indicate that by being able to summarize what they said. Don't offer any advice.

- They are chronic complainers. Ask them to write down problems and solutions and then let's discuss it. This turns down the volume while, hopefully, moving them off complaining.

- They like to complain about others. Ask if they've talked to the person. Encourage them to do so. If that doesn't work, summarize what they have said without agreeing or disagreeing.

9. **Impatience triggers.** Some people probably bring out your impatience more than others. Who are they? What is it about them that makes you more impatient? Pace? Language? Thought process? Accent? These people may include people you don't like, who ramble, who whine and complain, or who are repetitive advocates for things you have already rejected. Mentally rehearse some calming tactics before meeting with people who trigger your impatience. Work on understanding their positions without judging them—you can always judge later. In all cases, focus them on the issues or problems to be discussed, return them to the point, summarize, and state your position. Try to gently train them to be more efficient with you next time without damaging them in the process.

10. **Work on your openness and approachability.** Impatient people don't get as much information as patient listeners do. They are more often surprised by events when others knew they were coming. People are hesitant to talk to impatient people. It's too painful. People don't pass on hunches, unbaked thoughts, maybes, and possibles to impatient people. You will be out of the information loop and miss important information you need to know to be effective. Suspend judgment on informal communications. Just take it in. Acknowledge that you understand. Ask a question or two. Follow up later.

11. **Rein in your horse.** Impatient people provide answers, conclusions, and solutions too early in the process. Others haven't even understood the problem yet. Providing solutions too quickly will make your people dependent and irritated. If you don't teach them how you think and how you can come up with solutions so fast, they will never learn. Take the time to really define the problem—not impatiently throw out a solution. Brainstorm what questions need to be answered in order to resolve it. Give your people the task to think about for a day and come back with some solutions. Be a teacher instead of a dictator of solutions. Study yourself. Keep a journal of what triggered your behavior and what the observed consequences were. Learn to detect and control your triggers before they get you in trouble.

12. **Task impatience.** Impatient people check in a lot. How's it coming. Is it done yet? When will it be finished? Let me see what you've done so far. That is disruptive to due process and wastes time. When you give out a task or assign a project, establish agreed-upon time checkpoints. You can also assign percentage checkpoints. Check in with me when you are about 25% finished so we can make midcourse corrections and 75% finished so we can make final corrections. Let them figure out how to do the task. Hold back from checking in at other than the agreed-upon times and percentages.

C Dealing With Ambiguity Better

ESTPs usually prefer the concrete and reject the ambiguous. They tend to try solutions from their past and hip shoot.

1. **Incrementalism.** The essence of dealing comfortably with uncertainty is the tolerance of errors and mistakes, and absorbing the possible heat and criticism that follow. Acting on an ill-defined problem with no precedents to follow means shooting in the dark with as informed a decision as you can make at the time. People who are good at this are incrementalists. They make a series of smaller decisions, get instant feedback, correct the course, get a little more data, move forward a little more, until the bigger problem is under control. They don't try to get it right the first time. Many problem-solving studies show that the second or third try is when we really understand the underlying dynamics of problems. They also know that the more uncertain the situation is, the more likely it is they will make mistakes in the beginning. So, you need to work on two practices: Start small so

you can recover more quickly. Do little somethings as soon as you can and get used to heat.

2. **Transitions.** Which transitions are the toughest for you? Write down the five toughest for you. What do you have a hard time switching to and from? Use this knowledge to assist you in making a list of discontinuities (tough transitions) you face, such as confronting people vs. being approachable and accepting, leading vs. following, going from firing someone to a business-as-usual staff meeting. Write down how each of these discontinuities makes you feel and what you may do that gets you in trouble. For example, you may not shift gears well after a confrontation, or you may have trouble taking charge again after passively sitting in a meeting all day. Create a plan to attack each of the tough transitions.

3. **Control your instant responses to shifts.** Many of us respond to the fragmentation and discontinuities of work as if they were threats instead of the way life is. Sometimes our emotions and fears are triggered by switching from active to passive or soft to tough. This initial anxious response lasts 45–60 seconds, and we need to buy some time before we say or do something inappropriate. Research shows that generally somewhere between the second and third thing you think to say or do is the best option. Practice holding back your first response long enough to think of a second and a third. Manage your shifts, don't be a prisoner of them.

4. **Use mental rehearsal** to think about different ways you could carry out a transaction. Try to see yourself acting in opposing ways to get the same thing done—when to be tough, when to let them decide, when to deflect the issue because it's not ready to decide. What cues would you look for to select an approach that matches? Practice trying to get the same thing done with two different groups with two different approaches. Did they both work?

5. **Avoid early rigid positions.** It's just physics. Action gets equal reaction. Strong statements. Strongly worded positions. Casting blame. Absolutes. Lines in the sand. Unnecessary passion. All of these will be responded to in kind, will waste time, cause ill will, and possibly prevent a win-win or a something-something. It only has a place in one-time, either/or negotiations, and even there it isn't recommended. Similarly, watch out for overcommitment to any need or course of action. Look for information that goes against your preferences. Be able to adjust your position and your wants. If you can't, your ego is getting the best of you. If you can't walk away until

you get X, you'll probably either overpay or blow the negotiation. Don't negotiate around a single issue if you can add another. This is another situation that leads to rigidity.

6. **Selective resistance.** Do you adapt to some and not to others? You probably have good people buckets and bad people buckets and signal your disagreement with them to the bad bucket groups or individuals. You may have good group buckets and bad group buckets—gender, race, age, origin. Learn to understand without accepting or judging. Listen, take notes, ask questions, and be able to make their case as well as they can. Pick something in their argument you agree with. Present your argument in terms of the problem only— why you think this is the best manner to deal with a mutually agreed-upon problem. A careful observer should not be able to tell your assessment of people or their arguments at the time. Find someone who is a fair observer and get a critique. Was I fair? Did I treat everyone the same? Were my objections based on reasoning against standards and not directed at people?

D Better Follow-Through

ESTPs tend to choose projects they can finish. Others they don't tackle, especially those that are more complex and long term. As such, they can be seen as getting bored easily, not following through, having trouble with deadlines, and failure to take on complex/strategic challenges.

1. **Pick someone you respect and get back on track.** Talk to this person with the goal of being told when enough is enough, what's a good use of your time, and to get validation of your priorities.

2. **Are you pressure-prompted?** Can you not get really excited about a project unless the deadline is drawing near? Set fake deadlines. One of the reasons you delay is that you like pressure and dislike the ordinary. So, fool yourself. Always start 10% of each attempt immediately after it is apparent it will be needed and tell yourself it's due on Friday, that you can't leave for the weekend until you've made some progress. This has the added benefit of helping you better gauge what it is going to take to finish it. Always assume it will take more time than you think it's going to take.

3. **Finishing.** While it's true that sometimes you get 80% of what you are pushing for with the first 20% of the effort, it unfortunately then takes another 80% of the time to finish the last 20%. In a fast-paced world, it's sometimes tough to pull the cart all the way to the finish line when

the race is over. Not all tasks have to be completely finished. For some, 80% would be acceptable. For those who need all the i's dotted and the t's crossed, it will take perseverance. The devil is in the details. When you get caught in this situation, create a checklist with the 20% that remains to be done. Plan to do a little on it each day. Cross things off and celebrate each time you get to take something off the list. Remember, it's going to challenge your motivation and attention. Try to delegate finishing to someone who would see the 20% as a fresh challenge. Get a consultant to finish it. Task trade with someone else's 20% so you both would have something fresh to do.

4. **Simple commitments.** Do you return phone calls in a timely manner? Do you forward material you promised? Did you pass on information you promised to get? Did you carry through on a task you promised someone you would take care of? Failing to do things like this damages relationships. If you tend to forget things, write them down. If you run out of time, set up a specific time each day to follow through on commitments. If you are going to miss a deadline, let them know and give them a second date you will be sure to make.

5. **Do an upstream and downstream check with the people you work for,** work around, and those who work for you, to create a list of the administrative slip-ups you do that give them the most trouble. Be sure to ask them for help creating the list. That way, you have a focused list of the things you need to fix first. If you fix the top 10, maybe that will do and the rest of your habits can stay the same.

6. **Visualize.** Set up a process to monitor progress against the goals. People like running measures. They like to gauge their pace. It's like the United Way Thermometer in the lobby.

7. **Feedback.** Give as much in-process feedback as you have time for. Most people are motivated by process feedback against agreed-upon goals for three reasons:

   ■ First, it helps them adjust what they are doing along the way in time to achieve the goal; they can make midcourse corrections.

   ■ Second, it shows them what they are doing is important and that you're eager to help.

   ■ Third, it's not the "gotcha" game of negative and critical feedback after the fact.

8. **Disorganized?** Lose interest in anything not directly in your area of expertise? Move from task to task until you find one you want to do?

Short attention span? You can't operate helter-skelter and persevere. Perseverance takes focus and continuity of effort. Get better organized and disciplined. Keep a task progress log. Keep a "top 10 things I have to do" list. Stick with tasks longer than you now do.

E Dealing With Routine and Procedures

ESTPs are interested in hands-on, on-line problem solving. They excel in a crisis, but can become bored and skeptical with the familiar. They tend to question the routines and standard operating procedures of others because they know they can improve on it and do it better.

1. **Try to see the value in routines.** Pick a plan or procedure and do a historical analysis of how it came to be and why it is necessary. Resist the urge to change it or question its usefulness. Understand it first.

2. **Turn off your answer program.** We all have a need to provide answers as soon as possible to questions and problems. We all have preconceived notions, favorite solutions, and prejudices that prevent our intellectual skills from dealing with the real facts of the problem. For one-half of the time you have to deal with an issue or a problem, shut off your solution machine and just take in the facts.

3. **Compensate for your dislikes.** Find a person you admire and respect to deal with all the procedures you find oppressive. Let this person tell you if anything needs changing. Otherwise, trust his or her judgment.

F Not Trying to Win Every Battle

Intensely competitive, ESTPs really want to win. They enjoy being one up on the competition. This causes them lots of problems with peers and in conflict situations.

1. **Cooperative relations.** The opposite of conflict is cooperation. Developing cooperative relationships involves demonstrating real and perceived equity, the other side feeling understood and respected, and taking a problem-oriented point of view. To do this more: Increase the realities and perceptions of fairness—don't try to win every battle and take all the spoils; focus on the common-ground issues and interests of both sides—find wins on both sides, give in on little points; avoid starting with entrenched positions—show respect for them and their positions; and reduce any remaining conflicts to the smallest size possible.

2. **Causing unnecessary conflict.** Language, words, and timing set the tone and can cause unnecessary conflict that has to be managed before you can get anything done. Do you use insensitive language? Do you raise your voice often? Do you use terms and phrases that challenge others? Do you use demeaning terms? Do you use negative humor? Do you offer conclusions, solutions, statements, dictates, or answers early in the transaction? Give reasons first, solutions last. When you give solutions first, people often directly challenge the solutions instead of defining the problem. Pick words that are other-person neutral. Pick words that don't challenge or sound one-sided. Pick tentative and probabilistic words that give others a chance to maneuver and save face. Pick words that are about the problem and not the person. Avoid direct blaming remarks; describe the problem and its impact.

3. **Practice Aikido,** the ancient art of absorbing the energy of your opponent and using it to manage him/her. Let the other side vent frustration or blow off steam, but don't react. Listen. Nod. Ask clarifying questions. Ask open-ended questions like, "What one change could you make so we could achieve our objectives better?" "What could I do that would help the most?" Restate their position periodically to signal you have understood. But don't react. Keep them talking until they run out of venom. Then explore the concern. Separate the people from the problem. When someone attacks you, rephrase it as an attack on the problem. In response to threats, say you'll only negotiate on merit and fairness. If the other side won't play fair, surface their game—"It looks like you're playing good cop, bad cop. Why don't you settle your differences and tell me one thing?" In response to unreasonable proposals, attacks, or a non-answer to a question, you can always say nothing. People will usually respond by saying more, coming off their position a bit, or at least revealing their true interests. Many times, with unlimited venting and your understanding, the actual conflict shrinks.

4. **Downsizing the conflict.** Almost all conflicts have common points that get lost in the heat of the battle. After a conflict has been presented and understood, start by saying that it might be helpful to see if we agree on anything. Write them on the flip chart. Then write down the areas left open. Focus on common goals, priorities, and problems. Keep the open conflicts as small as possible and concrete. The more abstract it gets, "We don't trust your unit," the more unmanageable it gets. To this respond, "Tell me your specific concern—why exactly don't you trust us; can you give me an

example?" Usually after calm discussion, they don't trust your unit on this specific issue under these specific conditions. That's easier to deal with. Allow others to save face by conceding small points that are not central to the issue—don't try to hit a home run every time. If you can't agree on a solution, agree on a procedure to move forward. Collect more data. Appeal to a higher power. Get a third-party arbitrator. Something. This creates some positive motion and breaks stalemates.

5. **If peers see you as excessively competitive,** they will cut you out of the loop and may sabotage your cross-border attempts. To be seen as more cooperative, always explain your thinking and invite them to explain theirs. Generate a variety of possibilities first rather than stake out positions. Be tentative, allowing them room to customize the situation. Focus on common ground. Invite criticism of your ideas.

6. **Monitor yourself in tough situations** to get a sense of how you are coming across. What's the first thing you attend to? How often do you take a stand vs. make an accommodating gesture? What proportion of your comments deals with relationships vs. the issue to be addressed? Mentally rehearse for worst-case scenarios/hard-to-deal-with people. Anticipate what the person might say and have responses prepared so as not to be caught off guard.

7. **Follow the rule of equity:** Explain your thinking and ask them to explain theirs. Be able to state their position as clearly as they do whether you agree or not—give it legitimacy. Separate facts from opinions and assumptions. Generate a variety of possibilities first rather than stake out positions. Keep your speaking to 30–60 second bursts. Try to get them to do the same. Don't give the other side the impression you're lecturing or criticizing them. Explain objectively why you hold a view; make the other side do the same. Ask lots of questions, make fewer statements. To identify interests behind positions, ask why they hold them or why they wouldn't want to do something. Always restate their position to their satisfaction before offering a response.

8. **Questions.** In win-win and something-something negotiations, the more information you have about the other side, the more you will have to work with. What can you learn about what they know before going in? What will they do if they don't reach an agreement with you? In the negotiation, ask more questions, make fewer statements. Ask clarifying questions: "What did you mean by that?" Probes: "Why do you say that?" Motives: "What led you to that position?" Get

everything out that you can. Don't negotiate assumptions, negotiate facts.

I am competitive to a fault.

– An ESTP Manager

■ ■ ■ ■ ■ ■ ■ ■ ■ ■ ■ ■ ■ ■ ■ ■

APPLICATION

Your personal preferences play out in day-to-day problems and situations you face. Below is a case about your type dealing with such a situation. Use this to think through how you will integrate the tips you've considered and coach yourself to be more effective in your type.

ESTP Application Situation (Part 1)

As President of your computer software company, you've kept your eye on one of the sales managers, Alexandra, who you think has particular potential to move up. You've noted with a great deal of satisfaction that she has consistently lived up to your expectations and her goals. Her bonuses, usually the biggest in the sales group over a fifteen-year stretch, attest to her action orientation and have earned her the nickname, "The Killer."

During your annual succession planning meetings, though, you and others have expressed concern that Alexandra seems reluctant to pursue or accept promotions because she's protective of the fast-paced work that she considers to be fun.

In reviewing her portfolio, you note that her boss reports that she's action oriented, clever, an improviser. Members of her sales team have characterized her as a straight-talking, observant go-getter.

But in spite of Alexandra's conspicuous success and straight-ahead, goal-oriented approach to her job, there's something that's not quite right. You've heard, for example, that in her zeal to meet her goals, she can be impulsive, near-sighted, and single-pointed in her focus. While she is admired for her accomplishments, people on her team rarely turn to her for advice or input on challenges they're facing. You'd like Alexandra's boss to provide coaching to her, but he doesn't seem to understand what is underlying the issues that are affecting her performance. And as an "if it ain't broke don't fix it" guy, he's often said, "Why bother arguing with success?"

But you're determined to work with Alexandra, not only for her own benefit but for the greater benefit of her team and the organization. And so, whether or not she wants to move up, you've decided to take her on as a developmental project for the greater good. And you think a good place to start understanding her is in finding out what her Myers-Briggs type is, which you learn to be ESTP.

Thinking It Through: Strategy

- What facets in Alexandra's type might account for why her team members don't see her as a source for advice?

- How does her behavior likely affect her relationships with those around her?

Planning It Out: Tactics

- How can you present your insights to Alexandra without her getting caught up in the details at the expense of the bigger picture?

- What kinds of developmental challenges can you give to her that will require looking beyond the moment?

- What particular areas would present developmental challenges to her, and what competencies would you want to put into play in order to accomplish your objectives for Alexandra without discouraging her?

- Which of the tactics described in the Being More Effective section are applicable for Alexandra in this situation?

- Which Overused Tendencies are most likely to come into play here?

ESTP Application Situation (Part 2)

■ You meet with Alexandra, and after telling her what a terrific job she's been doing and how greatly the company values her, you tell her you'd like to see her take on a new sales associate as a mentee. You tell her, though, that if she's going to be successful, there are some things she'll need to focus on and do differently. Ask her to list some areas she could work on.

Reflection

■ What do you hope she'll list?

■ What do you need to help Alexandra focus on so that her development plan is longer-term and balanced?

■ What do you have to be concerned about so that you don't discourage a top performer?

SUGGESTED READINGS

■■■■■■■■ Being a More Effective ESTP ■■■■■■■■

Showing Caring

Autry, James A. *The Art of Caring Leadership*. New York: William Morrow and Company, Inc., 1991.

Brantley, Jeffrey and Jon Kabat-Zinn. *Calming Your Anxious Mind: How Mindfulness and Compassion Can Free You From Anxiety, Fear, and Panic*. Oakland, CA: New Harbinger Publications, 2003.

Daniels, Aubrey C. *Bringing Out the Best in People*. New York: McGraw-Hill, Inc., 1994.

Kouzes, James M. and Barry Z. Posner. *Encouraging the Heart: A Leader's Guide to Rewarding and Recognizing Others*. San Francisco: Jossey-Bass, Inc., 2003.

Stone, Douglas. *Difficult Conversations: How to Discuss What Matters Most*. New York: Penguin Books, 2000.

Developing Others

Charan, Ram, James L. Noel and Steve Drotter. *The Leadership Pipeline: How to Build the Leadership Powered Company*. New York: John Wiley & Sons, Inc., 2000.

Daniels, Aubrey C. *Bringing Out the Best in People*. New York: McGraw-Hill, Inc., 1994.

Fulmer, Robert M. and Jay A. Conger. *Growing Your Company's Leaders*. New York: AMACOM, 2004.

Lombardo, Michael M. and Robert W. Eichinger. *The Leadership Machine*. Minneapolis, MN: Lominger Limited, Inc., 2004.

Team Building

Bolton, Robert. *People Skills*. New York: Simon & Schuster, 1979.

Fisher, Kimball and Mareen Duncan Fisher. *The Distance Manager: A Hands-On Guide to Managing Off-Site Employees and Virtual Teams*. New York: McGraw-Hill Trade, 2000.

Harvard Business School Press. *Harvard Business Review on Teams That Succeed.* Boston: Harvard Business School Press, 2004.

Katzenbach, Jon R. and Douglas K. Smith. *The Wisdom of Teams: Creating the High-Performance Organization.* New York: HarperBusiness, 2003.

Parker, Glenn M. *Cross-Functional Teams: Working With Allies, Enemies, and Other Strangers.* San Francisco: Jossey-Bass, Inc., 2002.

Peters, Tom. *Thriving on Chaos: Handbook for a Management Revolution.* New York: HarperCollins, 1987.

Raymond, Cara Capretta, Robert W. Eichinger and Michael M. Lombardo. *FYI for Teams.* Minneapolis, MN: Lominger Limited, Inc., 2001–2004.

Robbins, Harvey and Michael Finley. *The New Why Teams Don't Work— What Goes Wrong and How to Make It Right.* San Francisco: Berrett-Koehler Publishers, Inc., 2000.

Analyzing Problems

Flynn, Daniel J. *Intellectual Morons: How Ideology Makes Smart People Fall for Stupid Ideas.* New York: Crown Business Publishing, 2004.

Hammond, John S., Ralph L. Keeney and Howard Raiffer. *Smart Choices.* Boston: Harvard University Press, 1999.

Nutt, Paul C. *Why Decisions Fail: Avoiding the Blunders and Traps That Lead to Decision Debacles.* San Francisco: Berrett-Koehler Publishers, Inc., 2002.

Sofo, Francesco. *Six Myths of Critical Thinking.* Business & Professional Publishing, 2003.

Sternberg, Robert J. *Thinking Styles.* Boston: Cambridge University Press, 1997.

Yates, J. Frank. *Decision Management: How to Assure Better Decisions in Your Company.* San Francisco: Jossey-Bass, Inc., 2003.

Seeing the Bigger Picture

Bandrowski, James F. *Corporate Imagination Plus—Five Steps to Translating Innovative Strategies Into Action.* New York: The Free Press, 2000.

Birch, Paul and Brian Clegg. *Imagination Engineering—The Toolkit for Business Creativity.* London: Pitman Publishing, 1996.

Chakravorti, Bhaskar. *The Slow Pace of Fast Change: Bringing Innovations to Market in a Connected World.* Boston: Harvard Business School Press, 2003.

Charan, Ram. *What the CEO Wants You to Know: How Your Company Really Works.* New York: Crown Business Publishing, 2001.

Christensen, Clayton M. and Michael E. Raynor. *The Innovator's Solution.* Harvard Business School Press, 2003.

Collins, James C. *Good to Great: Why Some Companies Make the Leap...And Others Don't.* New York: HarperCollins, 2001.

DeGraff, Jeff and Katherine A. Lawrence. *Creativity at Work: Developing the Right Practices to Make Innovation Happen.* San Francisco: Jossey-Bass, Inc., 2002.

Dudik, Evan Matthew. *Strategic Renaissance: New Thinking and Innovative Tools to Create Great Corporate Strategies Using Insights From History and Science.* New York: AMACOM, 2000.

The Futurist Magazine. http://www.wfs.org

Gaynor, Gerard H. *Innovation by Design.* New York: AMACOM, 2002.

Hamel, Gary. *Leading the Revolution.* Boston: Harvard Business School Press, 2002.

Hargadon, Andrew and Kathleen M. Eisenhardt. *How Breakthroughs Happen: The Surprising Truth About How Companies Innovate.* Boston: Harvard Business School Press, 2003.

Harvard Business Review. Phone: 800-988-0886 (US and Canada). Fax: 617-496-1029. Mail: Harvard Business Review. Subscriber Services, P.O. Box 52623. Boulder, CO 80322-2623 USA. http://www.hbsp.harvard.edu/products/hbr

Kaplan, Robert S. and David P. Norton. *The Strategy-Focused Organization: How Balanced Scorecard Companies Thrive in the New Business Environment.* Boston: Harvard Business School Press, 2000.

Porter, Michael E. *Competitive Strategy: Techniques for Analyzing Industries and Competitors.* New York: The Free Press, 1998.

Prahalad, C.K. and Venkat Ramaswamy. *The Future of Competition: Co-Creating Unique Value With Customers.* Boston: Harvard Business School Press, 2004.

Attention to Process and Plans

Allen, David. *Getting Things Done: The Art of Stress-Free Productivity.* New York: Penguin Books, 2003.

Bossidy, Larry, Ram Charan and Charles Burck (Contributor). *Execution: The Discipline of Getting Things Done.* New York: Crown Business Publishing, 2002.

Drucker, Peter F. *The Effective Executive.* New York: HarperBusiness, 2002.

Stone, Florence M. and Randi T. Sachs. *The High-Value Manager — Developing the Core Competencies Your Organization Needs.* New York: AMACOM, 1995.

Ulrich, David, Jack Zenger and Norman Smallwood. *Results-Based Leadership.* Boston: Harvard Business School Press, 1999.

■■■■■■■ Overusing ESTP Tendencies ■■■■■■■

Being Appropriately Ambitious

Champy, James and Nitin Nohria. *The Arc of Ambition.* Cambridge, MA: Perseus Publishing, 2000.

Dotlich, David L. and Peter C. Cairo. *Why CEOs Fail.* San Francisco: Jossey-Bass, Inc., 2003.

Schweich, Thomas A. *Staying Power: 30 Secrets Invincible Executives Use for Getting to the Top — And Staying There.* New York: McGraw-Hill, Inc., 2003.

Waldroop, James, Ph.D. and Timothy Butler, Ph.D. *Maximum Success: Changing the 12 Behavior Patterns That Keep You From Getting Ahead.* New York: Doubleday, 2000.

Being Less Pressuring

Barker, Larry, Ph.D. and Kittie Watson, Ph.D. *Listen Up: At Home, at Work, in Relationships: How to Harness the Power of Effective Listening.* Irvine, CA: Griffin Trade Paperback, 2001.

Bolton, Robert and Dorothy Grover Bolton. *People Styles at Work—Making Bad Relationships Good and Good Relationships Better.* New York: AMACOM, 1996.

Carter, Les. *The Anger Trap: Free Yourself From the Frustrations That Sabotage Your Life.* New York: John Wiley & Sons, Inc., 2003.

Ellis, Albert, Ph.D. *How to Control Your Anxiety Before It Controls You.* New York: Citadel Press, 2000.

Lerner, Harriet. *The Dance of Connection: How to Talk to Someone When You're Mad, Hurt, Scared, Frustrated, Insulted, Betrayed, or Desperate.* New York: Quill/HarperCollins, 2002.

Patterson, Kerry, Joseph Grenny, Ron McMillan, Al Switzler and Stephen R. Covey. *Crucial Conversations: Tools for Talking When Stakes Are High.* New York: McGraw-Hill/Contemporary Books, 2002.

Dealing With Ambiguity Better

Anderson, Dean and Linda S. Ackerman Anderson. *Beyond Change Management: Advanced Strategies for Today's Transformational Leaders.* San Francisco: Jossey-Bass, Inc., 2001.

Bellman, Geoffrey M. *Getting Things Done When You Are Not in Charge.* San Francisco: Berrett-Koehler Publishers, Inc., 2001.

Black, J. Stewart and Hal B. Gregersen. *Leading Strategic Change: Breaking Through the Brain Barrier.* Upper Saddle River, NJ: Financial Times/Prentice Hall, 2002.

Burke, W. Warner and William Trahant with Richard Koonce. *Business Climate Shifts: Profiles of Change Makers.* Boston: Butterworth-Heinemann, 2000.

Luecke, Richard. *Managing Change and Transition.* Boston: Harvard Business School Publishing, 2003.

Better Follow-Through

Byfield, Marilyn. *It's Hard to Make a Difference When You Can't Find Your Keys: The Seven-Step Path to Becoming Truly Organized.* New York: Viking Press, 2003.

Gleeson, Kerry. *The Personal Efficiency Program: How to Get Organized to Do More Work in Less Time.* New York: John Wiley & Sons, Inc., 2000.

MacKenzie, Alec. *The Time Trap: The Classic Book on Time Management.* Fine Communications, 2002.

Winston, Stephanie. *The Organized Executive: The Classic Program for Productivity: New Ways to Manage Time, People, and the Digital Office.* New York: Warner Business, 2001.

Dealing With Routine and Procedures

Bossidy, Larry, Ram Charan and Charles Burck (Contributor). *Execution: The Discipline of Getting Things Done.* New York: Crown Business Publishing, 2002.

Keen, Peter G.W. *The Process Edge—Creating Value Where It Counts.* Boston: Harvard Business School Press, 1998.

Lawler, Edward E., III, Susan Albers Mohrman and George Benson. *Organizing for High Performance: Employee Involvement, TQM, Reengineering, and Knowledge Management in the Fortune 1000: The CEO Report.* San Francisco: Jossey-Bass, Inc., 2001.

Niven, P.R. *Balanced Scorecard Step-by-Step: Maximizing Performance and Maintaining Results.* New York: John Wiley & Sons, Inc., 2002.

Not Trying to Win Every Battle

Cloke, Ken and Joan Goldsmith. *Resolving Conflicts at Work: A Complete Guide for Everyone on the Job.* San Francisco: Jossey-Bass, Inc., 2000.

Dana, Daniel. *Conflict Resolution.* New York: McGraw-Hill Trade, 2000.

Dawson, Roger. *Secrets of Power Negotiating: Inside Secrets From a Master Negotiator.* Franklin Lakes, NJ: Career Press, 2001.

Graham, Gini. *A Survival Guide for Working With Humans: Dealing With Whiners, Back-Stabbers, Know-It-Alls, and Other Difficult People.* New York: AMACOM, 2004.

Guttman, Howard M. *When Goliaths Clash: Managing Executive Conflict to Build a More Dynamic Organization.* New York: AMACOM, 2003.

Masters, Marick Francis and Robert R. Albright. *The Complete Guide to Conflict Resolution in the Workplace.* New York: AMACOM, 2002.

Oliver, David. *How to Negotiate Effectively.* London: Kogan Page, 2003.

Solomon, Muriel. *Working With Difficult People.* New York: Prentice Hall, 2002.

CHAPTER 10

ESFP

Extraverted Sensing
with
Introverted Feeling

■■■■■■■■■■■■■■■■■

8.5% of Population
1.4% of Managers

■■■■■■■■■■■■■■■■■

Typical Strengths

Entertaining
Team Oriented
Accepting and Compassionate
Hands-On
Action Oriented
Warm
Praising

ISTJ	ISFJ	INFJ	INTJ
ISTP	ISFP	INFP	INTP
ESTP	ESFP	ENFP	ENTP
ESTJ	ESFJ	ENFJ	ENTJ

Are we having fun yet?

– An ESFP Manager

Basic Habits of Mind

Extraverted Sensing makes ESFPs aware of the concrete details and realistic circumstances of a situation. Due to the influence of Introverted Feeling, they seek out connections to people and people-related things in their environment. Eager to enjoy the moment, Extraverted Sensing types seek out direct experiences. Introverted Feeling is used to decide the acceptability of circumstances and the way to approach people. They usually move easily among many different types of people and situations.

Introverted Thinking and Introverted Intuiting also help ESFPs. Introverted Thinking contributes a talent for finding the most direct, concrete solutions to problems. Introverted Intuiting gives insight as to the probable outcomes of choices.

This combination sometimes is misunderstood as non-strategic and too soft to make "tough decisions."

Typical Communication Patterns

- ESFPs are naturals at expressing concern for and enjoyment of others. Their comments are generally focused on the here and now.

- They enjoy conversation and are easily engaged on most any topic of current interest.

- They are very active and put a great deal of energy into being inclusive and being included by others.

General Learning Strategy

- ESFPs usually prefer to learn by using concrete activities or objects to illustrate ideas and being involved in cooperative learning opportunities.

- Their typical learning strategies are creating small groups to explore information, acting things out to see others' reactions, and sharing the personal meaning of experiences.

- Their learning is generally enhanced by telling stories, visual aids, and concrete information.

Interpersonal Qualities Related to Motivation

- ESFPs focus on the outside world. They enjoy physical activity and focusing on problems of a practical nature.

- They like working in teams and find immediate action more satisfying than long-term goal setting, though they see the need for it.

- They engage others at a personal level, which usually means dealing with the immediate situation in front of them.

Blind Spots

- ESFPs might be surprised to learn that others see them as overdependent on a select group and slightly less self-controlled than other people.

- Their quick responsiveness and easygoing manner is interpreted by some as non-committal (having simply reacted).

Stress Related Behavior

- When they feel stressed, ESFPs can seem undependable, touchy, and rigid.

- They may appear opportunistic and unkind as stress increases.

- With enough stress, they can become reserved and guarded and imagine the worst possible outcomes to situations.

Potential Barriers to Effectiveness

- When they appear impatient, non-committal, and blunt, ESFPs are viewed as ineffective.

- They need to show that they will do what is needed to get the job done and that they can be a quick study.

Being a More Effective ESFP

A   Productive Work Habits
B   Increasing Ways to Learn
C   Analyzing Problems
D   Drive for Results
E   Taking Charge
F   Dealing With Ambiguity

ISTJ	ISFJ	INFJ	INTJ
ISTP	ISFP	INFP	INTP
ESTP	ESFP	ENFP	ENTP
ESTJ	ESFJ	ENFJ	ENTJ

A   Productive Work Habits

Born doers, ESFPs often substitute action for productive use of time. They can be impulsive and not stop to pay attention to detail.

1. **Manage your time efficiently.** Plan your time and manage against it. Be time sensitive. Value time. Figure out what you are worth per hour and minute by taking your gross salary plus overhead and benefits. Attach a monetary value on your time. Then ask, is this worth $56 of my time? Figure out what your three largest time wasters are, and reduce them 50% by batching activities and using efficient communications like e-mail and voice mail for routine matters.

2. **Lay out tasks and work.** Most successful projects begin with a good plan. What do I need to accomplish? What are the goals? What's the time line? What resources will I need? How many of the resources do I control? Who controls the rest of the resources—people, funding, tools, materials, support—I need? Lay out the work from A to Z. Many people are seen as lacking a plan because they don't write down the sequence or parts of the work and leave something out. Ask others to comment on ordering and what's missing.

3. **Watch out for the activity trap.** John Kotter, in *The General Managers*, found that effective managers spent about half their time working on one or two key priorities—priorities they described in their own terms, not in terms of what the business/organizational plan said. Further, they made no attempt to work as much on small but related issues that tend to add up to lots of activity. So, rather than consuming themselves and others on 97 seemingly urgent and related smaller activities, they always returned to the few issues that would gain the most mileage long term.

4. **Set goals and measures.** Nothing keeps projects on time and on budget like a goal, a plan, and a measure. Set goals for the whole project and the subtasks. Plan for all. Set measures so you and others can track progress against the goals.

5. **Manage efficiently.** Plan the budget and manage against it. Spend carefully. Have a reserve if the unanticipated comes up. Set up a funding time line so you can track ongoing expenditures against plan.

6. **Set up a process to monitor progress against the plan.** How would you know if the plan is on time? Could you estimate time to completion or percent finished at any time? Give progress feedback as you go to people involved in implementing the plan.

B Increasing Ways to Learn

ESFPs learn through taking action and through association with many other people. They are less likely to search for patterns or consider deep causes.

1. **Personal experience is a very limited way to learn.** Even accessing others' experiences still leaves major gaps. For adults, most learning either comes from taking action and learning from the consequences or searching for parallel experiences in the past.

2. **When faced with a new issue, challenge, or problem, figure out what causes it.** Keep asking why. See how many causes you can come up with and how many organizing buckets you can put them in. This increases the chance of a better solution because you can see more connections. Chess masters recognize thousands of possible patterns of chess pieces. Look for patterns in data; don't just collect information. Put it in categories that make sense to you. To better understand new and difficult learning, read *The Future of Leadership* by White, Hodgson and Crainer.

3. **Locate the essence of the problem.** What are the key factors or elements in this problem? Experts usually solve problems by figuring out what the deep, underlying principles are and working forward from there; the less adept focus on desired outcomes/solutions and either work backward or concentrate on the surface facts. What are the deep principles of what you're working on? Once you've done this, search the past for parallels—your past, the business past, the historical past. One common mistake here is to search in parallel organizations because "only they would know." Backing up and asking a broader question will aid in the search for solutions. When

Motorola wanted to find out how to process orders more quickly, they went not to other electronics firms, but to Domino's Pizza and Federal Express.

4. **Patterns.** Look for patterns in personal, organization, or the world, in general successes and failures. What was common to each success or what was present in each failure but never present in a success? Focus on the successes; failures are easier to analyze but don't in themselves tell you what would work. Comparing successes, while less exciting, yields more information about underlying principles. The bottom line is to reduce your insights to principles or rules of thumb you think might be repeatable. When faced with the next new problem, those general underlying principles will apply again.

5. **Use oddball tactics.** What is a direct analogy between something you are working on and a natural occurrence? Ask what in nature parallels your problem. When the terrible surfs and motion of the tide threatened to defeat their massive dam project, the Delta Works, the Dutch used the violence of the North Sea to drive in the pilings, ending the danger of the south of the Netherlands flooding. Practice picking out anomalies—unusual facts that don't quite fit, like sales going down when they should have gone up. What do these odd things imply for strategy?

6. **Encourage yourself to do quick experiments and trials.** Studies show that 80% of innovations occur in the wrong place, are created by the wrong people (dye makers developed detergent; Post-it® Notes was an error in a glue formula), and 30–50% of technical innovations fail in tests within the company. Even among those that make it to the marketplace, 70–90% fail. The bottom line on change is a 95% failure rate, and the most successful innovators try lots of quick, inexpensive experiments to increase the chances of success.

C Analyzing Problems

Present focused and crisis oriented, ESFPs are usually seen as not interested in detailed analysis. They are much more likely to pull something from their bag of tricks.

1. **Defining the problem.** Instant and early conclusions, solutions, statements, suggestions, and how we solved it in the past, are the enemies of good problem solving. Studies show that defining the problem and taking action occur almost simultaneously for most people, so the more effort you put on the front end, the easier it is to

come up with a good solution. Stop and first define what the problem is and isn't. Since providing solutions is so easy for everyone, it would be nice if they were offering solutions to the right problem. Ask lots of questions. Allot at least 50% of the time to defining the problem.

2. **Do you do enough analysis?** A good rule of thumb is to analyze patterns and causes to come up with alternatives. Many of us just collect data, which numerous studies show increases our confidence but doesn't increase decision accuracy. Think out loud with others; see how they view the problem. To break out of analysis paralysis, figure out what the problem is first. Then when a good alternative appears, you're likely to recognize it immediately.

3. **Watch your biases.** Some people have solutions in search of problems. They have favorite solutions. They have biases. They have universal solutions to most situations. They pre-judge what the problem is without stopping to consider the nuances of this specific problem. Do honest and open analysis first. One of your solutions may in fact fit, but wait to see if you're right about the problem.

4. **Check yourself for these common errors in thinking:** Do you state as facts things that are really opinions or assumptions? Are you sure these assertions are facts? State opinions and assumptions as that and don't present them as facts. Do you attribute cause and effect to relationships when you don't know if one causes the other? If sales are down, and we increase advertising and sales go up, this doesn't prove causality. They are simply related. Say we know that the relationship between sales/advertising is about the same as sales/number of employees. If sales go down, we probably wouldn't hire more people, so make sure one thing causes the other before acting on it. Do you generalize from a single example without knowing if that single example does generalize?

5. **Holster your gun.** Life is a balance between waiting and doing. Many in management put a premium on doing over waiting. Most could make close to 100% good decisions given all of the data and unlimited time. Life affords us neither the data nor the time. You may need to try to discipline yourself to wait just a little longer than you usually do for more, but not all, the data to come in. Push yourself to always get one more piece of data than you did before until your correct decision percent becomes more acceptable. Instead of just doing it, ask what questions would need to be answered before we'd know which way to go. In one study of problem solving, answers outnumbered

questions 8 to 1. We jump to solutions based on what has worked in the past. So collect data to answer these questions, then shoot.

D Drive for Results

ESFPs sometimes don't finish the task before they are off to another more exciting one. Results can suffer.

1. **Priorities?** You don't have a correct set of priorities. Some people get results, but on the wrong things. Effective managers typically spend about half their time on two or three key priorities. What should you spend half your time on? Can you name five things that are less critical? If you can't, you're not differentiating well. Or even if you know the priorities, your team doesn't. You communicate that everything is important and has a deadline of yesterday. They see their jobs as 97 things that need to be done right now. To deal with this, ask yourself what would happen if they only did four or five things today? What would they be? Ask what the three things they spend the most time on are, and what they would be if we were doing things better? Find out what the 10–20% most time-consuming activities are, and either eliminate them or structure them through processes and policies to take less time.

2. **Set goals for yourself and others.** Most people work better if they have a set of goals and objectives to achieve and a standard everyone agrees to measure accomplishments against. Most people like stretch goals. They like them even better if they have had a hand in setting them. Set checkpoints along the way to be able to measure progress. Give yourself and others as much feedback as you can.

3. **How to get things done.** Some don't know the best way to produce results. There is a well-established set of best practices for producing results—TQM, ISO and Six Sigma. If you are not disciplined in how to design work flows and processes for yourself and others, buy one book on each of these topics. Go to one workshop on efficient and effective work design. Ask those responsible for total work systems in your organization for help.

4. **When you are stuck, write down the pros and cons for each option.** Check what effect each would have both on the short and long term. Are there cost differences? Is one resource more efficient than the other? Is one apt to be more successful than the other? Think about the interaction of both short- and long-term goals. Sometimes what you decide to do today will hurt you or the organization downstream.

When making either a short-term or long-term choice, stop for a second and ask what effect this might have on the other. Adjust as necessary.

5. **Give up after one or two tries?** If you have trouble going back the second or third time to get something done, then switch approaches. Sometimes people get stuck in a repeating groove that's not working. Do something different next time. If you visited the office of someone you have difficulties with, invite him/her to your office next time. Think about multiple ways to get the same outcome. For example, to push a decision through, you could meet with stakeholders first, go to a single key stakeholder, study and present the problem to a group, call a problem-solving session, or call in an outside expert. Be prepared to do them all when obstacles arise.

6. **Focus on measures.** How would you tell if the goal was accomplished? If the things I asked others to do were done right, what outcomes could we all agree on as measures of success? Most groups can easily come up with success measures that are different from, and more important to them, than formal measures. Ask them to do so.

7. **Start earlier.** Always do 10% of thinking about the decision immediately after it is assigned so you can better gauge what it is going to take to finish the rest. Divide decisions into thirds or fourths, and schedule time to work on them spaced over the delivery period. Remember one of Murphy's Laws: It takes 90% of the time to do 90% of the project, and another 90% of the time to finish the remaining 10%. Always leave more time than you think it's going to take. Set up checkpoints for yourself along the way. Schedule early data collection and analysis. Don't wait until the last moment. Set an internal deadline one week before the real one.

E Taking Charge

While willing to move fast, ESFPs often use their personal presence to entertain and motivate others rather than to lead in tough situations.

1. **Leading is riskier than following.** While there are a lot of personal rewards for leading, leading puts you in the limelight. Think about what happens to political leaders and the scrutiny they face. Leaders have to be internally secure. Do you feel good about yourself? They have to please themselves first that they are on the right track. Can you defend to a critical and impartial audience the wisdom of what you're doing? They have to accept lightning bolts from detractors.

Can you take the heat? People will always say it should have been done differently. Listen to them, but be skeptical. Even great leaders are wrong sometimes. They accept personal responsibility for errors and move on to lead some more. Don't let criticism prevent you from taking the lead. Build up your heat shield. Conduct a postmortem immediately after finishing milestone efforts. This will indicate to all that you're open to continuous improvement whether the result was stellar or not.

2. **Against the grain tough stands.** Taking a tough stand demands confidence in what you're saying along with the humility that you might be wrong—one of life's paradoxes. To prepare to take the lead on a tough issue, work on your stand through mental interrogation until you can clearly state in a few sentences what your stand is and why you hold it. Build the business case. How do others win? People don't line up behind laundry lists or ambiguous objectives. Ask others for advice—scope the problem, consider options, pick one, develop a rationale, then go with it until proven wrong. Then redo the process. If this doesn't help, find out where the pain is for you. What have you been avoiding? Examine your past and see where taking-charge behavior has gotten you in trouble or you thought it would get you in trouble. Isolate the most troublesome elements, such as forgetting things under pressure, trouble with fierce debate, problems with unpopular stands, and things moving too fast. Devise counter-strategies.

3. **Selling your leadership.** While some people may welcome what you say and want to do, others will go after you or even try to minimize the situation. Some will sabotage. To sell your leadership, keep your eyes on the prize but don't specify how to get there. Present the outcomes, targets, and goals without the how to's. Welcome their ideas—good and bad. Any negative response is a positive if you learn from it. Allow them to fill in the blanks, ask questions, and disagree without appearing impatient with them. Allow others to save face; concede small points, invite criticism of your own. Help them figure out how to win. Keep to the facts and the problem before the group; stay away from personal clashes.

4. **Clear problem-focused communication.** Follow the rule of equity: Explain your thinking and ask them to explain theirs. Be able to state their position as clearly as they do whether you agree or not—give it legitimacy. Separate facts from opinions and assumptions. Generate a variety of possibilities first rather than stake out positions. Keep your speaking to 30–60 second bursts. Try to get them to do the same. Don't

give the other side the impression you're lecturing or criticizing them. Explain objectively why you hold a view; make the other side do the same. Ask lots of questions, make fewer statements. To identify interests behind positions, ask why they hold them or why they wouldn't want to do something. Always restate their position to their satisfaction before offering a response.

F Dealing With Ambiguity

ESFPs usually prefer the concrete and reject the ambiguous. They tend to try solutions from their past and hip shoot.

1. **Incrementalism.** The essence of dealing comfortably with uncertainty is the tolerance of errors and mistakes, and absorbing the possible heat and criticism that follow. Acting on an ill-defined problem with no precedents to follow means shooting in the dark with as informed a decision as you can make at the time. People who are good at this are incrementalists. They make a series of smaller decisions, get instant feedback, correct the course, get a little more data, move forward a little more, until the bigger problem is under control. They don't try to get it right the first time. Many problem-solving studies show that the second or third try is when we really understand the underlying dynamics of problems. They also know that the more uncertain the situation is, the more likely it is they will make mistakes in the beginning. So, you need to work on two practices: Start small so you can recover more quickly. Do little somethings as soon as you can and get used to heat.

2. **Transitions.** Which transitions are the toughest for you? Write down the five toughest for you. What do you have a hard time switching to and from? Use this knowledge to assist you in making a list of discontinuities (tough transitions) you face, such as confronting people vs. being approachable and accepting, leading vs. following, going from firing someone to a business-as-usual staff meeting. Write down how each of these discontinuities makes you feel and what you may do that gets you in trouble. For example, you may not shift gears well after a confrontation, or you may have trouble taking charge again after passively sitting in a meeting all day. Create a plan to attack each of the tough transitions.

3. **Control your instant responses to shifts.** Many of us respond to the fragmentation and discontinuities of work as if they were threats instead of the way life is. Sometimes our emotions and fears are

triggered by switching from active to passive or soft to tough. This initial anxious response lasts 45–60 seconds, and we need to buy some time before we say or do something inappropriate. Research shows that generally somewhere between the second and third thing you think to say or do is the best option. Practice holding back your first response long enough to think of a second and a third. Manage your shifts, don't be a prisoner of them.

4. **Use mental rehearsal to think about different ways you could carry out a transaction.** Try to see yourself acting in opposing ways to get the same thing done—when to be tough, when to let them decide, when to deflect the issue because it's not ready to decide. What cues would you look for to select an approach that matches? Practice trying to get the same thing done with two different groups with two different approaches. Did they both work?

Overusing ESFP Tendencies

If you sometimes overdo your preferred behaviors, you may need to work on:

A Toughness

B Sizing Up People

C New Thinking Strategies

D Seeing the Bigger Picture

E Better Follow-Through

ISTJ	ISFJ	INFJ	INTJ
ISTP	ISFP	INFP	INTP
ESTP	ESFP	ENFP	ENTP
ESTJ	ESFJ	ENFJ	ENTJ

A Toughness

ESFPs are often conflict avoiders. Getting along quite well with others, they don't step up in tough situations and have problems dealing with troubled performers.

1. **Laid back?** None of your business? Tend to shy away from managerial courage situations? Why? What's getting in your way? Are you prone to give up in tough situations, fear exposing yourself, don't like conflict, what? Ask yourself—what's the downside of delivering a message you think is right and will eventually help the organization but may cause someone short-term pain. What if it turns out you were wrong? Treat any misinterpretations as chances to learn.

What if you were the target person or group? Even though it might hurt, would you appreciate it if someone brought the data to your attention in time for you to fix it with minimal damage? What would you think of a person whom you later found out knew about it and didn't come forward, and you had to spend inordinate amounts of time and political currency to fix it? Follow your convictions. Follow due process. Step up to the plate and be responsible, win or lose. People will think better of you in the long term.

2. **Are your problem performers confused?** Do they know what's expected of them? You may not set clear enough performance standards, goals, and objectives. You may be a seat-of-the-pants manager, and some people are struggling because they don't know what is expected or it changes. You may be a cryptic communicator. You may be too busy to communicate. You may communicate to some and not to others. You may have given up on some and stopped communicating. Or you may think they would know what to do if they're any good, but that's not really true because you have not properly communicated what you want. The first task is to outline the 5 to 10 key results areas and what indicators of success would be. Involve your problem direct reports on both ends—the standards and the indicators. Provide them with a fair way to measure their own progress. Employees with goals and standards are usually harder on themselves than you'll ever be. Often they set higher standards than you would. Sometimes the problem is behavioral, as in someone who can't control outbursts, and only affects performance on the back end in lost cooperation or sabotage. Then the best approach is to note the gap between behavior and expectations, and point out what some of the observed consequences are. If the person agrees, then coaching may suffice. If the person balks, then a 360° feedback process with follow-up may be needed to illuminate the depth of the problem before any help can be given.

3. **The message.** Be succinct. You have limited attention span in tough feedback situations. Don't waste time with a long preamble, particularly if the feedback is negative. If the feedback is negative and the recipient is likely to know it, go ahead and say it directly. They won't hear anything positive you have to say anyway. Don't overwhelm the person/group, even if you have a lot to say. Go from specific to general points. Keep it to the facts. Don't embellish to make your point. No passion or inflammatory language. Don't do it to harm or out of vengeance. Don't do it in anger. If feelings are involved for you, wait until you can describe them, not show them. Managerial

courage comes in search of a better outcome, not destroying others. Stay calm and cool. If others are not composed, don't respond. Just return to the message.

4. **Bring a solution if you can.** Everybody appreciates a problem solver. Give people ways to improve; don't just dump and leave. Tell others what you think would be better—paint a different outcome. Help others see the consequences—you can ask them what they think, and you can tell them what the consequences are from your side if you are personally involved ("I'd be reluctant to work with you on X again").

5. **Tough concern.** Don't forget the pathos of the situation—even if you're totally right, feelings may run high. If you have to be critical, you can still empathize with how he/she feels, and you can help with encouragement when the discussion turns more positive. Mentally rehearse for worst-case scenarios. Anticipate what the person might say and have responses prepared so as not to be caught off guard.

6. **Managing the pushback.** Keep control of the discussion. Don't do fake listening—the obligatory "Now let's hear your side"—if you don't think there is another side. Discussions like this will trigger most people's natural defense routines. Expect that. That's not necessarily a sign of true disagreement or denial; it's just a natural thing to do. Say something like, "I understand you have a different view, but the performance just isn't there in this area. We've got to deal with this." The person may have 10 reasons why your appraisal isn't fair or accurate. Listen. Acknowledge that you understand what he/she has said. If the person persists, say "Let's talk about your view tomorrow after we've both had a chance to reflect on this discussion." Then, return to your agenda. Say, "I'm going to help you perform in this area." The best tack is to immediately schedule new work, trusting that the person will come through this time. You should discuss this as you would any other work assignment and not bring up the past. She/he has already heard what you said. (With a person who, in your opinion, lacks motivation not skill, raise the stakes. Sometimes a person who performs poorly at a C difficulty task performs well at an A difficulty task in exactly the same area.)

7. **Saying good-bye.** Just because the person can't do this job doesn't mean he/she is incompetent as a person or that he/she can't do 50 other things better than you can do them. Do nothing to generalize one performance failure to other situations, and point to the person's strengths in any way you can. Suggest what would be a better job match. Indicate what you can do to help; if you're willing to be a

reference for certain types of work, say so. Make the meeting short. Go back to see the person later and talk about his/her feelings if he/she is willing. You don't have to respond, just listen. Come up with some sort of parting gesture that indicates to the person that you are not rejecting him or her; it was simply a matter of one job that wasn't a fit. A party, a note, a phone call—whatever you can do that's genuine. Even if he/she rejects you, if you meant it, that's all you can do.

B Sizing Up People

Because they tend to shoot from the hip, ESFPs can have trouble with staffing because they often don't analyze or size up people well.

1. **Become a student of the people around you.** First, try to outline their strengths and weakness, their preferences and beliefs. Watch out for traps—it is rarely general intelligence or pure personality that spells the difference in people. Most people are smart enough, and many personality characteristics don't matter that much for performance. Ask a second question. Look below surface descriptions of smart, approachable, technically skilled people to describe specifics. Then try to predict ahead of time what they would do in specific circumstances. What percent of the time are your predictions correct? Try to increase the percent over time.

2. **When you make a hiring decision or are deciding whom to work with on a problem or project,** do you think you have a tendency to clone yourself too much? Do you have a preference for people who think and act as you do? What characteristics do you value too much? What downsides do you ignore or excuse away? This is a common human tendency. The key is to seek balance, variety, and diversity. Shore up your weaknesses when hiring others. People good at this competency can comfortably surround themselves with people not like them.

3. **Are your standards too high or too low?** Do you hire the first close candidate that comes along, or do you wait for the perfect candidate and leave the position open too long? Either tendency will probably get you and the organization in trouble. Always try to wait long enough to have choices but not long enough to lose a very good candidate while you wait for the perfect one to come along. Learn how to set reasonable standards by looking at a competency model and selecting key skills.

4. **Do you have a long-term view of the talent it's going to take to produce both current and long-term results?** Do you have a replacement plan for yourself? Do you use a success profile with the competencies you know you are going to need? Have you hired someone who now has, or will have in a short period of time, the ability to take your job? Have you selected someone you would sponsor for promotion to another job at your level, possibly passing you up in time? The best managers surround themselves with talent, and eventually some of the talent turns out to be better than the person who hired and trained them. That's a good thing and reason for a celebration.

C New Thinking Strategies

Taking action is only one way to learn. ESFPs like to talk about what is done, but tend to tell the same stories again and again. Some fresh thinking strategies are called for.

1. **Value-added approaches.** To be more personally creative, immerse yourself in the problem. Getting fresh ideas is not a speedboating process; it requires looking deeply.

   ■ Carve out dedicated time—study the problem deeply, talk with others, look for parallels in other organizations and in remote areas totally outside your field. If your response to this is that you don't have the time, that also usually explains why you're not having any fresh ideas.

   ■ Think out loud. Many people don't know what they know until they talk it out. Find a good sounding board and talk to him/her to increase your understanding of a problem or a technical area. Talk to an expert in an unrelated field. Talk to the most irreverent person you know. Your goal is not to get his/her input, but rather his/her help in figuring out what you know—what your principles and rules of thumb are.

   ■ Practice picking out anomalies—unusual facts that don't quite fit, like sales going down when they should have gone up. What do these odd things imply for strategy? Naturally creative people are much more likely to think in opposite cases when confronted with a problem. Turn the problem upside down: Ask what is the least likely thing it could be, what the problem is not, what's missing from the problem, or what the mirror image of the problem is.

- Look for distant parallels. Don't fall into the mental trap of searching only in parallel organizations because "only they would know." Back up and ask a broader question to aid in the search for solutions. When Motorola wanted to find out how to process orders more quickly, they went not to other electronics firms, but to Domino's Pizza and Federal Express. For more ideas, an interesting—and fun—book on the topic is *Take the Road to Creativity and Get Off Your Dead End* by David Campbell.

2. **Unearthing creative ideas.** Creative thought processes do not follow the formal rules of logic, where one uses cause and effect to prove or solve something. Some rules of creative thought are:

   - Not using concepts but changing them; imagining this were something else.

   - Move from one concept or way of looking at things to another, such as from economic to political.

   - Generate ideas without judging them initially.

   - Use information to restructure and come up with new patterns.

   - Jump from one idea to another without justifying the jump.

   - Look for the least likely and odd.

   - Look for parallels far from the problem, such as how is an organization like a big oak tree?

   - Ask what's missing or what's not here.

   - Fascination with mistakes and failure as learning devices.

3. **Apply some standard problem-solving skills.** There are many different ways to think through and solve a problem more creatively:

   - Ask more questions. In one study of problem solving, 7% of comments were questions and about half were answers. We jump to solutions based on what has worked in the past.

   - Complex problems are hard to visualize. They tend to be either oversimplified or too complex to solve unless they are put in a visual format. Cut it up into its component pieces. Examine the pieces to see if a different order would help, or how you could combine three pieces into one.

- Another technique is a pictorial chart called a storyboard, where a problem is illustrated by its components being depicted as pictures.

- A variation of this is to tell stories that illustrate the +'s and –'s of a problem, then flowchart those according to what's working and not working. Another is a fishbone diagram used in Total Quality Management.

- Sometimes going to extremes helps. Adding every condition, every worst case you can think of sometimes will suggest a different solution. Taking the present state of affairs and projecting into the future may indicate how and where the system will break down.

- Sleep on it. Take periodic breaks, whether stuck or not. This allows the brain to continue to work on the issue. Most breakthroughs come when we're "not thinking about it." Put it away; give it to someone else; sleep on it. Once you've come up with every idea you can think of, throw them all out and wait for more to occur to you. Force yourself to forget about the issue.

4. **Increasing group creativity:** Selecting a group. During World War II, it was discovered that teams of people with the widest diversity of backgrounds produced the most creative solutions to problems. The teams included people who knew absolutely nothing about the area (i.e., an English major working on a costing problem). When attacking a tough problem which has eluded attempts to solve it, get the broadest group you can. Involve different functions, levels, and disciplines. Pull in customers and colleagues from other organizations. Remember that you're looking for fresh approaches; you're not convening a work task force expected to implement or judge the practicality of the notions. Believe it or not, it doesn't matter if they know anything about the problem or the technology required to deal with it. That's your job.

5. **Increasing group creativity:** Define the problem first. A straightforward technique to enable creativity is brainstorming. Anything goes for an agreed-upon time. Throw out ideas, record them all, no evaluation allowed. Many people have had bad experiences with brainstorming. Silly ideas. Nothing practical. A waste of time. This usually happens because the problem gets defined in the same old way. First, define the problem well. Allot hours to this, not two minutes to sketch the problem. Challenge your thinking—are you

generalizing from one or two cases? How do you know the causes are really causes? They may simply be related. What is fact and what is assumption?

6. **Increasing group creativity:** Facilitating the process. Here are three methods commonly used:

- Brainstorming. Outline the problem for the group; tell them what you've tried and learned from the tries. Include things that may have happened only once. Invite the group to free-form respond. Any idea is okay—no criticism allowed. Record all ideas on a flip chart. When the group has exhausted the possibilities, take the most interesting ones and ask the group to first name positive features of the ideas, then negative features, and finally what's interesting about the ideas. Follow this process until you've covered all the ideas that interest you. Then ask the group what else they would select as interesting ideas to do a plus, minus, interesting analysis. This process can usually be done in an hour or two.

- The nominal group. After the problem definition above, have the group write down as many ideas as occur to them. Record them all on a flip chart for freewheeling discussion. People can add, combine or clarify—"What were you thinking when you said...," but no criticism allowed. After this, follow the plus, minus, interesting process above.

- Analogies. Lots of creative solutions come from analogies to nature or other fields. Come up with a list (electrical engineering, cats, trees, the sea, biology, shipbuilding), any list will do, and insert it after you describe the problem to the group in the first or second option. Many times this will trigger novel ideas that no other process will.

D Seeing the Bigger Picture

ESFPs are essentially interested in today. Tomorrow isn't often on the agenda.

1. **Not curious?** Many managers are so wrapped up in today's problems that they aren't curious about tomorrow. They really don't care about the long-term future. They may not even be in the organization when the strategic plan is supposed to happen. They believe there won't be much of a future until we perform today. Being a visionary and a good strategist requires curiosity and imagination. It requires playing

"what ifs." What are the implications of the growing gap between rich and poor? The collapse of retail pricing? The increasing influence of brand names? What if it turns out there is life on other planets, and we get the first message? What will that change? Will they need our products? What will happen when a larger percentage of the world's population is over the age of 65? The effects of terrorism? What if cancer is cured? Heart disease? AIDS? Obesity? What if the government outlaws or severely regulates some aspect of your business? True, nobody knows the answers, but good strategists know the questions. Work at developing broader interests outside your business. Subscribe to different magazines. Pick new shows to watch. Meet different people. Join a new organization. Look under some rocks. Think about tomorrow. Talk to others about what they think the future will bring.

2. **Narrow perspective?** Some are sharply focused on what they do and do it very well. They have prepared themselves for a narrow but satisfying career. Then someone tells them their job has changed, and they now have to be strategic. Being strategic requires a broad perspective. In addition to knowing one thing well, it requires that you know about a lot of things somewhat. You need to understand business. You need to understand markets. You need to understand how the world operates. You need to put all that together and figure out what all that means to your organization.

3. **Too busy?** Strategy is always last on the list. Solving today's problems, of which there are many, is job one. You have to make time for strategy. A good strategy releases future time because it makes choices clear and leads to less wasted effort, but it takes time to do. Delegation is usually the main key. Give away as much tactical day-to-day stuff as you can. Ask your people what they think they could do to give you more time for strategic reflection. Another key is better time management. Put an hour a week on your calendar for strategic reading and reflection throughout the year. Don't wait until one week before the strategic plan is due. Keep a log of ideas you get from others, magazines, etc. Focus on how these impact your organization or function.

4. **Can't think strategically?** Strategy is linking several variables together to come up with the most likely scenario. Think of it as the search for and application of relevant parallels. It involves making projections of several variables at once to see how they come together. These projections are in the context of shifting markets, international affairs, monetary movements, and government interventions. It

involves a lot of uncertainty, making risk assumptions, and understanding how things work together. How many reasons would account for sales going down? Up? How are advertising and sales linked? If the dollar is cheaper in Asia, what does that mean for our product in Japan? If the world population is aging and they have more money, how will that change buying patterns? Not everyone enjoys this kind of pie-in-the-sky thinking and not everyone is skilled at doing it.

5. **Managing remotely is another way to think more long term.** It's impossible for you to do it all. Successful managers report high involvement in setting parameters, exceptions they want to be notified of, and expected outcomes. They detail what requires their involvement and what doesn't. When people call them for a decision, they always ask, "What do you think? What impact will it have on you—customers, etc.—if we do this?" rather than just render a judgment. If you don't, people will begin to delegate upward, and you'll be a close-in manager from a remote location. Help people think things through, and trust them to follow the plan. Delegation requires this clear communication about expectations and releasing the authority to decide and act.

6. **Don't know enough about your business?** Study your annual report and various other financial reports. If you don't know how, the major investment firms have basic documents explaining how to read financial documents. After you've done this, consult a pro and ask him/her what he/she looks at and why. Ask for lunch or just a meeting with the person who is in charge of the strategic planning process in your company. Have him/her explain the strategic plan for the organization. Particularly, have him/her point out the mission-critical functions and capabilities the organization needs to be on the leading edge to win.

7. **Try some broader tasks.** Volunteer for task forces that include people outside your area of expertise. Work on some TQM, ISO or Six Sigma projects that cross functional or business unit boundaries to learn more about the business. Go talk with customers, work actually delivering the product or service, and write down five things you've learned about how the business works. Start up a mock business in something you know intimately. Write a business plan, complete the necessary forms, price equipment, and talk with people in this business about their problems.

8. **Get close to customers.** Customer service is the best place to learn about the business. Arrange a meeting with a counterpart in customer service. Have him or her explain the function to you. If you can, listen in on customer service calls or, even better, handle a couple yourself.

9. **Do you only think about your part of the business?** In order to be a well-running business, all of the pieces and parts need to work together. A business is a closed system. That means doing something in one area affects all of the other areas. Sunbeam decided to have an off-season discount in order to show more booked business in the fourth quarter. That was easy. Customers stocked up on the cheaper goods. Then plant production faltered in the next two quarters as orders decreased. Inventory prices went up for Sunbeam and its customers, which led to dissatisfaction. Margins decreased as Sunbeam tried to fix the problem. What happens in one area always affects everything else. When you make decisions in your area, do you think about possible negative consequences for the other functions? Document your understanding of the drivers that run your business to a few key drivers organized around things like marketing, sales, operations, etc. Share your conclusions with others from other functions or units to see how your key drivers affect them.

E Better Follow-Through

ESFPs get bored easily, don't follow through, and often have trouble with deadlines and finishing projects.

1. **Pick someone you respect and get back on track.** Talk to this person with the goal of being told when enough is enough, what's a good use of your time, and to get validation of your priorities.

2. **Are you pressure-prompted?** Can you not get really excited about a project unless the deadline is drawing near? Set fake deadlines. One of the reasons you delay is that you like pressure and dislike the ordinary. So, fool yourself. Always start 10% of each attempt immediately after it is apparent it will be needed and tell yourself it's due on Friday, that you can't leave for the weekend until you've made some progress. This has the added benefit of helping you better gauge what it is going to take to finish it. Always assume it will take more time than you think it's going to take.

3. **Disorganized?** Don't always get to everything on time? Forget deadlines? Lose requests for decisions? Forget to follow up on a request for more information? Lose interest in anything not right in

front of you? Move from task to task until you find one that's working? Short attention span? You can't operate helter-skelter and persevere. Perseverance takes focus and continuity of effort. Get better organized and disciplined. Keep a task progress log. Keep a "top 10 things I have to do" list. Stick with tasks longer than you now do.

4. **Simple commitments.** Do you return phone calls in a timely manner? Do you forward material you promised? Did you pass on information you promised to get? Did you carry through on a task you promised someone you would take care of? Failing to do things like this damages relationships. If you tend to forget things, write them down. If you run out of time, set up a specific time each day to follow through on commitments. If you are going to miss a deadline, let them know and give them a second date you will be sure to make.

5. **Overcommitting.** A lot of trouble follows overcommitting. Overcommitting usually comes from wanting to please everyone or not wanting to face the conflict if you say no. You can only do so much. Only commit to that which you can actually do. Commit to a specific time for delivery. Write it down. Learn to say "no" pleasantly. Learn to pass it off to someone else who has the time—"Gee no, but I'm sure Susan could help you with that." Learn to say, "Yes, but it will take longer than you might want to wait," and give them the option of withdrawing the request. Learn to say, "Yes, but what else that I have already committed to do for you would you like to delay to get this done?"

6. **Always out of time?** Do you intend to get to things but never have the time? Do you always estimate shorter times to get things done that then take longer? There is a well-established science and a set of best practices in time management. There are a number of books you can buy in any business bookstore, and there are a number of good courses you can attend. Delegating also helps you use your time more effectively.

7. **Another common time waster is inadequate disengagement skills.** Some poor time managers can't shut down transactions. Either they continue to talk beyond what would be necessary or, more commonly, they can't get the other party to quit talking. When it's time to move on, just say, "I have to get on to the next thing I have to do; we can pick this up some other time."

8. **Manage your time efficiently.** Plan your time and manage against it. Be time sensitive. Value time. Figure out what you are worth per hour and minute by taking your gross salary plus overhead and benefits. Attach a monetary value on your time. Then ask, is this worth $56 of my time? Review your calendar over the past 90 days to figure out what your three largest time wasters are, and reduce them 50% by batching activities and using efficient communications like e-mail and voice mail for routine matters. Make a list of points to be covered in phone calls; set deadlines for yourself; use your best time of day for the toughest projects—if you're best in the morning, don't waste it on B and C level tasks.

9. **Visualize.** Set up a process to monitor progress against the goals. People like running measures. They like to gauge their pace. It's like the United Way Thermometer in the lobby.

10. **Do an upstream and downstream check with the people you work for,** work around, and those who work for you, to create a list of the administrative slip-ups you do that give them the most trouble. Be sure to ask them for help creating the list. That way, you have a focused list of the things you need to fix first. If you fix the top 10, maybe that will do and the rest of your habits can stay the same.

11. **Feedback.** Give as much in-process feedback as you have time for. Most people are motivated by process feedback against agreed-upon goals for three reasons:

    ■ First, it helps them adjust what they are doing along the way in time to achieve the goal; they can make midcourse corrections.

    ■ Second, it shows them what they are doing is important and that you're eager to help.

    ■ Third, it's not the "gotcha" game of negative and critical feedback after the fact.

12. **Finishing.** While it's true that sometimes you get 80% of what you are pushing for with the first 20% of the effort, it unfortunately then takes another 80% of the time to finish the last 20%. In a fast-paced world, it's sometimes tough to pull the cart all the way to the finish line when the race is over. Not all tasks have to be completely finished. For some, 80% would be acceptable. For those who need all the i's dotted and the t's crossed, it will take perseverance. The devil is in the details. When you get caught in this situation, create a checklist with the 20% that remains to be done. Plan to do a little on it each day. Cross things

off and celebrate each time you get to take something off the list. Remember, it's going to challenge your motivation and attention. Try to delegate finishing to someone who would see the 20% as a fresh challenge. Get a consultant to finish it. Task trade with someone else's 20% so you both would have something fresh to do.

I overdo acting and underdo thinking. As a result, I am impulsive and impatient.

– An ESFP Manager

■ ■ ■ ■ ■ ■ ■ ■ ■ ■ ■ ■ ■ ■ ■ ■

APPLICATION

Your personal preferences play out in day-to-day problems and situations you face. Below is a case about your type dealing with such a situation. Use this to think through how you will integrate the tips you've considered and coach yourself to be more effective in your type.

ESFP Application Situation (Part 1)

As he uses his laser pointer to underscore key points in the data on yet another PowerPoint chart detailing the marketing segmentation study he and his staff have completed, Steve is explaining how the demographics correlate with seasonal variations in buying patterns, and how his talented staff collected and analyzed the information. Suddenly the VP of Sales clears her throat as a signal that she'd like to break in, then says, "This is all very thorough information, Steve, but can you take us up a level, give me the bigger picture, tell me what it means for our sales strategy?"

The Manager of Planning, impatient as always, jumps onboard, taking the opportunity to criticize Steve's presentation: "I agree with Helen. I'm less interested in all these numbers than in your view of what they suggest we need to do with our distribution strategy."

"I'm getting to that," Steve says, feeling slightly irritable with the interruptions, "but I think you need to understand the foundation for it first. I'm trying to be sensitive to your needs here, but I don't think you'll have enough to go on to make a good decision unless we all have a shared understanding of what this data that my team put together is telling us."

Turning back to his chart and pointing, he says excitedly, "For example, just look at this spike here…."

There is some uneasy shifting of people in the room as they realize they're in for a tedious meeting and worry that when the elaborate presentation is over, they may be no closer to a decision on the distribution strategy than they were before the meeting.

You're a consultant, brought in by the CEO to observe his senior team's meetings and to make some process suggestions about what can be done to improve them. One of the things you make note of is that it would be useful to have the members of the team complete the MBTI. The CEO agrees, and a few weeks later you come back to share the results with him and the members of his team, starting with Steve.

Thinking It Through: Strategy

- Steve is an ESFP. How does that reconcile with what you observed about him in the meeting?

- What do you want the outcome of this initial meeting to be?

Planning It Out: Tactics

- What tendencies and preferences in Steve's type (ESFP) would you focus on to help him appreciate what he might need to do less of and more of to better meet the needs of other members of the senior team?

- What one thing would you urge Steve to work on to improve his skills at persuasion?

- Which of the tactics described in the Being More Effective section are applicable in this situation?

- Which Overused Tendencies are most likely to come into play here?

ESFP Application Situation (Part 2)

■ When you meet with Steve, he starts out, reflectively, by telling you that he really never sought the job of Marketing Director, but rather was really enjoying being an analyst. When his boss suddenly left the company, he was recruited into the position. Steve knows that he is often perceived as indecisive and that he needs to be more politically savvy as well as more assertive. But, he says, "I really don't think it's in my nature."

Reflection

■ What do you suggest to Steve at this point?

SUGGESTED READINGS

■■■■■■■■ Being a More Effective ESFP ■■■■■■■■

Productive Work Habits

Allen, David. *Getting Things Done: The Art of Stress-Free Productivity.* New York: Penguin Books, 2003.

Bossidy, Larry, Ram Charan and Charles Burck (Contributor). *Execution: The Discipline of Getting Things Done.* New York: Crown Business Publishing, 2002.

Byfield, Marilyn. *It's Hard to Make a Difference When You Can't Find Your Keys: The Seven-Step Path to Becoming Truly Organized.* New York: Viking Press, 2003.

Drucker, Peter F. *The Effective Executive.* New York: HarperBusiness, 2002.

Gleeson, Kerry. *The Personal Efficiency Program: How to Get Organized to Do More Work in Less Time.* New York: John Wiley & Sons, Inc., 2000.

Kotter, John P. *The General Managers.* New York: The Free Press, 1982.

Stone, Florence M. and Randi T. Sachs. *The High-Value Manager—Developing the Core Competencies Your Organization Needs.* New York: AMACOM, 1995.

Increasing Ways to Learn

Nutt, Paul C. *Why Decisions Fail: Avoiding the Blunders and Traps That Lead to Decision Debacles.* San Francisco: Berrett-Koehler Publishers, Inc., 2002.

Sofo, Francesco. *Six Myths of Critical Thinking.* Business & Professional Publishing, 2003.

Sternberg, Robert J. *Thinking Styles.* Boston: Cambridge University Press, 1997.

White, R.P., P. Hodgson and S. Crainer. *The Future of Leadership.* London: Pitman, 1996.

Analyzing Problems

Flynn, Daniel J. *Intellectual Morons: How Ideology Makes Smart People Fall for Stupid Ideas.* New York: Crown Business Publishing, 2004.

Hammond, John S., Ralph L. Keeney and Howard Raiffer. *Smart Choices.* Boston: Harvard University Press, 1999.

Yates, J. Frank. *Decision Management: How to Assure Better Decisions in Your Company.* San Francisco: Jossey-Bass, Inc., 2003.

Drive for Results

Block, Peter. *The Answer to How Is Yes: Acting On What Matters.* San Francisco: Berrett-Koehler Publishers, Inc., 2001.

Bossidy, Larry, Ram Charan and Charles Burck (Contributor). *Execution: The Discipline of Getting Things Done.* New York: Crown Business Publishing, 2002.

Collins, James C. *Good to Great: Why Some Companies Make the Leap...And Others Don't.* New York: HarperCollins, 2001.

Loehr, Jim and Tony Schwartz. *The Power of Full Engagement: Managing Energy, Not Time, Is the Key to High Performance and Personal Renewal.* New York: The Free Press, 2003.

Longenecker, Clinton O. and Jack L. Simonetti. *Getting Results: Five Absolutes for High Performance.* New York: John Wiley & Sons, Inc., 2001.

Taking Charge

Badaracco, Joseph L., Jr. *Defining Moments—When Managers Must Choose Between Right and Right.* Boston: Harvard Business School Press, 1997.

Bennis, Warren G. and Burt Nanus. *Leaders: Strategies for Taking Charge.* New York: HarperBusiness, 2003.

Calvert, Gene. *Highwire Management.* San Francisco: Jossey-Bass, Inc., 1993.

Chaleff, Ira. *The Courageous Follower: Standing Up to and for Our Leaders.* San Francisco: Berrett-Koehler Publishers, Inc., 2003.

Coponigro, Jeffrey R. *The Crisis Counselor: A Step-by-Step Guide to Managing a Business Crisis.* New York: McGraw-Hill/Contemporary Books, 2000.

Cox, Danny and John Hoover. *Leadership When the Heat's On.* New York: McGraw-Hill Trade, 2002.

Linsky, Martin and Ronald A. Heifetz. *Leadership on the Line: Staying Alive Through the Dangers of Leading.* Boston: Harvard Business School Press, 2002.

Dealing With Ambiguity

Anderson, Dean and Linda S. Ackerman Anderson. *Beyond Change Management: Advanced Strategies for Today's Transformational Leaders.* San Francisco: Jossey-Bass, Inc., 2001.

Bellman, Geoffrey M. *Getting Things Done When You Are Not in Charge.* San Francisco: Berrett-Koehler Publishers, Inc., 2001.

Black, J. Stewart and Hal B. Gregersen. *Leading Strategic Change: Breaking Through the Brain Barrier.* Upper Saddle River, NJ: Financial Times/Prentice Hall, 2002.

Burke, W. Warner and William Trahant with Richard Koonce. *Business Climate Shifts: Profiles of Change Makers.* Boston: Butterworth-Heinemann, 2000.

Luecke, Richard. *Managing Change and Transition.* Boston: Harvard Business School Publishing, 2003.

■■■■■■■ Overusing ESFP Tendencies ■■■■■■■

Toughness

Chaleff, Ira. *The Courageous Follower: Standing Up to and for Our Leaders.* San Francisco: Berrett-Koehler Publishers, Inc., 2003.

Cloke, Ken and Joan Goldsmith. *Resolving Conflicts at Work: A Complete Guide for Everyone on the Job.* San Francisco: Jossey-Bass, Inc., 2000.

Downs, Alan. *The Fearless Executive: Finding the Courage to Trust Your Talents and Be the Leader You Are Meant to Be.* New York: AMACOM, 2000.

Graham, Gini. *A Survival Guide for Working With Humans: Dealing With Whiners, Back-Stabbers, Know-It-Alls, and Other Difficult People.* New York: AMACOM, 2004.

Guttman, Howard M. *When Goliaths Clash: Managing Executive Conflict to Build a More Dynamic Organization.* New York: AMACOM, 2003.

Levin, Robert A. and Joseph G. Rosse. *Talent Flow: A Strategic Approach to Keeping Good Employees, Helping Them Grow, and Letting Them Go.* New York: John Wiley & Sons, Inc., 2001.

Masters, Marick Francis and Robert R. Albright. *The Complete Guide to Conflict Resolution in the Workplace.* New York: AMACOM, 2002.

Patterson, Kerry, Joseph Grenny, Ron McMillan, Al Switzler and Stephen R. Covey. *Crucial Conversations: Tools for Talking When Stakes Are High.* New York: McGraw-Hill/Contemporary Books, 2002.

Solomon, Muriel. *Working With Difficult People.* New York: Prentice Hall, 2002.

Sizing Up People

Bolton, Robert and Dorothy Grover Bolton. *People Styles at Work—Making Bad Relationships Good and Good Relationships Better.* New York: AMACOM, 1996.

Harvard Business School Press. *Hiring and Keeping the Best People.* Boston: Harvard Business School Press, 2003.

Mazzarella, Mark C. and Jo-Ellan Dimitrius. *Reading People: How to Understand People and Predict Their Behavior—Anytime, Anyplace.* New York: Ballantine Books, 1999.

Myers, Isabel Briggs with Peter B. Myers. *Gifts Differing: Understanding Personality Type.* Palo Alto, CA: Davies-Black Publishing, 1995.

New Thinking Strategies
Campbell, David. *Take the Road to Creativity and Get Off Your Dead End.* Greensboro, NC: Center for Creative Leadership, 1985.

DeGraff, Jeff and Katherine A. Lawrence. *Creativity at Work: Developing the Right Practices to Make Innovation Happen.* San Francisco: Jossey-Bass, Inc., 2002.

Lucas, Robert W. *The Creative Training Idea Book: Inspired Tips and Techniques for Engaging and Effective Learning.* New York: AMACOM, 2003.

Von Oech, Roger. *Expect the Unexpected or You Won't Find It: A Creativity Tool Based on the Ancient Wisdom of Heraclitus.* San Francisco: Berrett-Koehler Publishers, Inc., 2002.

Seeing the Bigger Picture
Bandrowski, James F. *Corporate Imagination Plus—Five Steps to Translating Innovative Strategies Into Action.* New York: The Free Press, 2000.

Birch, Paul and Brian Clegg. *Imagination Engineering—The Toolkit for Business Creativity.* London: Pitman Publishing, 1996.

Chakravorti, Bhaskar. *The Slow Pace of Fast Change: Bringing Innovations to Market in a Connected World.* Boston: Harvard Business School Press, 2003.

Charan, Ram. *What the CEO Wants You to Know: How Your Company Really Works.* New York: Crown Business Publishing, 2001.

Christensen, Clayton M. and Michael E. Raynor. *The Innovator's Solution.* Harvard Business School Press, 2003.

Collins, James C. *Good to Great: Why Some Companies Make the Leap...And Others Don't.* New York: HarperCollins, 2001.

DeGraff, Jeff and Katherine A. Lawrence. *Creativity at Work: Developing the Right Practices to Make Innovation Happen.* San Francisco: Jossey-Bass, Inc., 2002.

Dudik, Evan Matthew. *Strategic Renaissance: New Thinking and Innovative Tools to Create Great Corporate Strategies Using Insights From History and Science.* New York: AMACOM, 2000.

The Futurist Magazine. http://www.wfs.org

Gaynor, Gerard H. *Innovation by Design.* New York: AMACOM, 2002.

Hamel, Gary. *Leading the Revolution.* Boston: Harvard Business School Press, 2002.

Hargadon, Andrew and Kathleen M. Eisenhardt. *How Breakthroughs Happen: The Surprising Truth About How Companies Innovate.* Boston: Harvard Business School Press, 2003.

Harvard Business Review. Phone: 800-988-0886 (US and Canada). Fax: 617-496-1029. Mail: Harvard Business Review. Subscriber Services, P.O. Box 52623. Boulder, CO 80322-2623 USA. http://www.hbsp.harvard.edu/products/hbr

Kaplan, Robert S. and David P. Norton. *The Strategy-Focused Organization: How Balanced Scorecard Companies Thrive in the New Business Environment.* Boston: Harvard Business School Press, 2000.

Porter, Michael E. *Competitive Strategy: Techniques for Analyzing Industries and Competitors.* New York: The Free Press, 1998.

Prahalad, C.K. and Venkat Ramaswamy. *The Future of Competition: Co-Creating Unique Value With Customers.* Boston: Harvard Business School Press, 2004.

Better Follow-Through

Byfield, Marilyn. *It's Hard to Make a Difference When You Can't Find Your Keys: The Seven-Step Path to Becoming Truly Organized.* New York: Viking Press, 2003.

Gleeson, Kerry. *The Personal Efficiency Program: How to Get Organized to Do More Work in Less Time.* New York: John Wiley & Sons, Inc., 2000.

MacKenzie, Alec. *The Time Trap: The Classic Book on Time Management.* Fine Communications, 2002.

Winston, Stephanie. *The Organized Executive: The Classic Program for Productivity: New Ways to Manage Time, People, and the Digital Office.* New York: Warner Business, 2001.

CHAPTER 11

ENFP
Extraverted Intuiting
with
Introverted Feeling

■■■■■■■■■■■■■■■■■

8.1% of Population
5.1% of Managers

■■■■■■■■■■■■■■■■■

Typical Strengths

Warm
Enthusiastic
Imaginative
Future Oriented
Relationship Builder
Developing Others
Appreciative
Leading Groups

ISTJ	ISFJ	INFJ	INTJ
ISTP	ISFP	INFP	INTP
ESTP	ESFP	**ENFP**	ENTP
ESTJ	ESFJ	ENFJ	ENTJ

The more I have to do that I care about, the more productive I am,
even if some things don't get attended to right away.

– An ENFP Manager

Basic Habits of Mind

Driven toward new ideas and possibilities by Extraverted Intuiting, ENFPs like "going with the flow." They connect current experience to possible future circumstances. Introverted Feeling aids their imagination through decisive judgments about whether situations and solutions are acceptable or not. Drawn toward people and people-related concerns, they try to understand relationships in context.

Introverted Thinking and Introverted Sensing also aid ENFPs. Introverted Thinking often provides incisive analysis that leads to questioning the current state. Introverted Sensing anchors or internally "grounds" experience and provides a sense of confidence about a course of action.

While on the inside ENFPs are indeed quite decisive once options have been explored, the face they show to others often appears as too open to possibilities, or lacking in direction, overly process oriented, and not planning thoroughly. They can fail to make their internal judgments known.

Typical Communication Patterns

■ ENFPs usually express enthusiasm about ideas and about being with people.

■ They openly reveal their observations and reactions to situations.

■ Eager to discuss the big picture, their language is expansive and filled with remarks about future possibilities.

■ Warmth and concern for others often come through as they enjoy engaging others in almost any task.

General Learning Strategy

■ ENFPs usually learn best when the whole context is clear and when they are brainstorming links and ideas. They like to explore questions.

■ Their typical learning strategies are active problem-solving discussions, exploring linkages among ideas or observations, and using graphics and visual representations. ENFPs are often the first to go to the flip chart or use mind mapping to explore linkages.

■ Their learning is generally enhanced by making linkages among ideas and personal values, and imagining the future use of information or ideas.

Interpersonal Qualities Related to Motivation

■ ENFPs are motivated by sharing ideas, brainstorming, and engaging with others to solve personal problems.

■ Flexible environments that encourage innovation and looking for new connections among experiences and ideas are great motivators for them.

Blind Spots

■ ENFPs might be surprised to learn that observers see them as somewhat overdependent on a small group of insiders, somewhat low in self-control, needing to be more straightforward, and to follow through more completely.

Stress Related Behavior

■ Stress often results in ENFPs increasing tempo, becoming more active, and being very talkative.

■ They can become more impulsive, hasty, noisy, and distracted as stress increases.

■ With long-term and persistent stress, they may become very quiet while they focus on a fact or two and obsess about its meaning (usually in very negative ways).

Potential Barriers to Effectiveness

■ ENFPs need to learn a greater range of confrontation skills, to be more supportive of upper management strategy, and to be more deliberate in their management of tasks.

■ When their values are pinched, they seem guarded, dogmatic, and hypersensitive, which interferes with their effectiveness.

Being a More Effective ENFP

A Day-to-Day Management
B Drive for Results
C Timely Decision Making
D Conflict Management
E Relationships With Higher Management

ISTJ	ISFJ	INFJ	INTJ
ISTP	ISFP	INFP	INTP
ESTP	ESFP	ENFP	ENTP
ESTJ	ESFJ	ENFJ	ENTJ

A Day-to-Day Management

ENFPs are excited by the sheer joy of new ideas, and having others applaud these ideas keeps them enthused. This enthusiasm often doesn't extend to details or disciplined work processes.

1. **Do an upstream and downstream check with the people you work for,** work around, and those who work for you, to create a list of the administrative slip-ups you do that give them the most trouble. Be sure to ask them for help creating the list. That way, you have a focused list of the things you need to fix first. If you fix the top 10, maybe that will do and the rest of your habits can stay the same.

2. **Put the things you have to do in two piles**—things I have to do that are for me, and things I have to do that are for others or that will affect others. Do the second pile first. Further divide the other pile into the mission-critical, important, and things that can wait. Do them in that order.

3. **Manage your time efficiently.** Plan your time and manage against it. Be time sensitive. Value time. Figure out what you are worth per hour and minute by taking your gross salary plus overhead and benefits. Attach a monetary value on your time. Then ask, is this worth $56 of my time? Figure out what your three largest time wasters are, and reduce them 50% by batching activities and using efficient communications like e-mail and voice mail for routine matters.

4. **Lay out tasks and work.** Most successful projects begin with a good plan. What do I need to accomplish? What are the goals? What's the time line? What resources will I need? How many of the resources do I control? Who controls the rest of the resources—people, funding, tools, materials, support—I need? Lay out the work from A to Z. Many people are seen as lacking a plan because they don't write

ENFP

down the sequence or parts of the work and leave something out. Ask others to comment on ordering and what's missing.

5. **Watch out for the activity trap.** John Kotter, in *The General Managers,* found that effective managers spent about half their time working on one or two key priorities—priorities they described in their own terms, not in terms of what the business/organizational plan said. Further, they made no attempt to work as much on small but related issues that tend to add up to lots of activity. So, rather than consuming themselves and others on 97 seemingly urgent and related smaller activities, they always returned to the few issues that would gain the most mileage long term.

6. **Set goals and measures.** Nothing keeps projects on time and on budget like a goal, a plan, and a measure. Set goals for the whole project and the subtasks. Plan for all. Set measures so you and others can track progress against the goals.

7. **Manage efficiently.** Plan the budget and manage against it. Spend carefully. Have a reserve if the unanticipated comes up. Set up a funding time line so you can track ongoing expenditures against plan.

8. **Set up a process to monitor progress against the plan.** How would you know if the plan is on time? Could you estimate time to completion or percent finished at any time? Give progress feedback as you go to people involved in implementing the plan.

B Drive for Results

For an ENFP, relationships and ideas are often more important than getting results.

1. **Priorities?** You don't have a correct set of priorities. Some people get results, but on the wrong things. Effective managers typically spend about half their time on two or three key priorities. What should you spend half your time on? Can you name five things that are less critical? If you can't, you're not differentiating well. Or even if you know the priorities, your team doesn't. You communicate that everything is important and has a deadline of yesterday. They see their jobs as 97 things that need to be done right now. To deal with this, ask yourself what would happen if they only did four or five things today? What would they be? Ask what the three things they spend the most time on are, and what they would be if we were doing things better? Find out what the 10–20% most time-consuming

351

activities are, and either eliminate them or structure them through processes and policies to take less time.

2. **Set goals for yourself and others.** Most people work better if they have a set of goals and objectives to achieve and a standard everyone agrees to measure accomplishments against. Most people like stretch goals. They like them even better if they have had a hand in setting them. Set checkpoints along the way to be able to measure progress. Give yourself and others as much feedback as you can.

3. **How to get things done.** Some don't know the best way to produce results. There is a well-established set of best practices for producing results—TQM, ISO and Six Sigma. If you are not disciplined in how to design work flows and processes for yourself and others, buy one book on each of these topics. Go to one workshop on efficient and effective work design. Ask those responsible for total work systems in your organization for help.

4. **When you are stuck, write down the pros and cons for each option.** Check what effect each would have both on the short and long term. Are there cost differences? Is one resource more efficient than the other? Is one apt to be more successful than the other? Think about the interaction of both short- and long-term goals. Sometimes what you decide to do today will hurt you or the organization downstream. When making either a short-term or long-term choice, stop for a second and ask what effect this might have on the other. Adjust as necessary.

5. **Give up after one or two tries?** If you have trouble going back the second or third time to get something done, then switch approaches. Sometimes people get stuck in a repeating groove that's not working. Do something different next time. If you visited the office of someone you have difficulties with, invite him/her to your office next time. Think about multiple ways to get the same outcome. For example, to push a decision through, you could meet with stakeholders first, go to a single key stakeholder, study and present the problem to a group, call a problem-solving session, or call in an outside expert. Be prepared to do them all when obstacles arise.

6. **Focus on measures.** How would you tell if the goal was accomplished? If the things I asked others to do were done right, what outcomes could we all agree on as measures of success? Most groups can easily come up with success measures that are different from, and more important to them, than formal measures. Ask them to do so.

C   Timely Decision Making

Working in bursts of energy and getting caught up in other people's issues can leave ENFPs scrambling at the last minute to get things done.

1. **Procrastinator?** Are you a procrastinator? Get caught short on deadlines? Do it all at the last minute? Not only will you not be timely, your decision quality and accuracy will be poor. Procrastinators miss deadlines and performance targets. If you procrastinate, you might not produce consistent decisions. Start earlier. Always do 10% of thinking about the decision immediately after it is assigned so you can better gauge what it is going to take to finish the rest. Divide decisions into thirds or fourths, and schedule time to work on them spaced over the delivery period. Remember one of Murphy's Laws: It takes 90% of the time to do 90% of the project, and another 90% of the time to finish the remaining 10%. Always leave more time than you think it's going to take. Set up checkpoints for yourself along the way. Schedule early data collection and analysis. Don't wait until the last moment. Set an internal deadline one week before the real one.

2. **Disorganized?** Don't always get to everything on time? Forget deadlines? Lose requests for decisions? Under time pressure and increased uncertainty, you have to put the keel in the water yourself. You can't operate helter-skelter and make quality timely decisions. You need to set tighter priorities. Focus more on the mission-critical few decisions. Don't get diverted by trivial work and other decisions. Get better organized and disciplined. Keep a decision log. When a decision opportunity surfaces, immediately log it along with the ideal date it needs to be made. Plan backwards to the work necessary to make the decision on time.

3. **Selective timeliness.** It's very common for people to be timely in some areas (budget decisions) and untimely in others (give an employee negative feedback). Sometimes we avoid certain areas. Create two columns. Left side are the areas where you seem to make timely and speedy decisions. What's common about those areas? Right side are the areas where you hold back, hesitate, and wait too long to decide. What's common to that list? Money involved? People? Risk? Higher management's involved? Are you avoiding detail or strategy or a technical area you dislike or know little about? Since you already make timely decisions in at least one area, transfer your decision behaviors and practices to the other areas. You already have the skills. You just need to get over the barriers (most likely attitude

barriers) in the more difficult areas. If you lack expertise, access your network. Go to the two wisest people you know on the decision, hire a consultant, convene a one-time problem-solving group. You don't have to be an expert in the area, but you do need to know how to access expertise to make timely decisions.

4. **Stress and conflict under time pressure.** Some are energized by time pressure. Some are stressed with time pressure. It actually slows us down. We lose our anchor. We are not at our best when we are pushed. We get more anxious, frustrated, upset. What brings out your emotional response? Write down why you get anxious under time pressure. What fears does it surface? Don't want to make a mistake? Afraid of the unknown consequences? Don't have the confidence to decide? When you get stressed, drop the problem for a moment. Go do something else. Come back to it when you are under better control. Let your brain work on it while you do something safer.

D Conflict Management

ENFPs handle other people's conflicts quite well; however, they often avoid their own. When situations aren't working for them, they can also imagine the worst and become quite suspicious.

1. **Check it out.** Lack of feedback or mixed signals doesn't mean there are necessarily any hidden agendas or ill will. Before you conclude that people are conspiring, go to the source and ask what is going on. Go to your most trusted person and ask him or her what is happening. Don't intuit a bad situation.

2. **Cooperative relations.** Don't reveal your suspicions. Treat other parties as if they share the same goals as you do. Developing cooperative relationships involves demonstrating real and perceived equity, the other side feeling understood and respected, and taking a problem-oriented point of view. To do this more, focus on the common-ground issues and interests of both sides. Find wins on both sides, give in on little points; show respect for them and their positions; and reduce any remaining conflicts to the smallest size possible.

3. **When others cause unnecessary conflict.** When you find yourself getting put off by the behavior of others (they use loaded words or don't share the same goals or fire out solutions instead of examining possibilities), take a deep breath. Return to defining the problem. Pick words that are other-person neutral. Pick words that don't challenge

or sound one-sided. Pick tentative and probabilistic words. Present a calm face. Don't allow yourself to get hooked by their behavior. Keep it from becoming personal.

4. **Practice Aikido,** the ancient art of absorbing the energy of your opponent and using it to manage him/her. Let the other side vent frustration or blow off steam, but don't react. Listen. Nod. Ask clarifying questions. Ask open-ended questions like, "What one change could you make so we could achieve our objectives better?" "What could I do that would help the most?" Restate their position periodically to signal you have understood. But don't react. Keep them talking until they run out of venom. Then explore the concern. Separate the people from the problem. When someone attacks you, rephrase it as an attack on the problem. In response to threats, say you'll only negotiate on merit and fairness. If the other side won't play fair, surface their game—"It looks like you're playing good cop, bad cop. Why don't you settle your differences and tell me one thing?" In response to unreasonable proposals, attacks, or a non-answer to a question, you can always say nothing. People will usually respond by saying more, coming off their position a bit, or at least revealing their true interests. Many times, with unlimited venting and your understanding, the actual conflict shrinks.

5. **Downsizing the conflict.** Almost all conflicts have common points that get lost in the heat of the battle. After a conflict has been presented and understood, start by saying that it might be helpful to see if we agree on anything. Write them on the flip chart. Then write down the areas left open. Focus on common goals, priorities, and problems. Keep the open conflicts as small as possible and concrete. The more abstract it gets, "We don't trust your unit," the more unmanageable it gets. To this respond, "Tell me your specific concern—why exactly don't you trust us; can you give me an example?" Usually after calm discussion, they don't trust your unit on this specific issue under these specific conditions. That's easier to deal with. Allow others to save face by conceding small points that are not central to the issue—don't try to hit a home run every time. If you can't agree on a solution, agree on a procedure to move forward. Collect more data. Appeal to a higher power. Get a third-party arbitrator. Something. This creates some positive motion and breaks stalemates.

6. **In conflict situations, what reactions do you have** (such as impatience or non-verbals like flushing or drumming your pen or fingers)? Learn to recognize those as soon as they start and substitute

something more neutral. Most emotional responses to conflict come from personalizing the issue. Separate people issues from the problem at hand, and deal with people issues separately and later if they persist. Always return to facts and the problem before the group; stay away from personal clashes. Attack the problem by looking at common interests and underlying concerns, not people and their positions. Try on their views for size—the emotion as well as the content. Ask yourself if you understand their feelings. Ask what they would do if they were in your shoes. See if you can restate each other's position and advocate it for a minute to get inside each other's place. If you get emotional, pause and collect yourself. You are not your best when you get emotional. Then return to the problem.

7. **Bargaining and trading.** Learn to horse-trade and bargain. What do they need that I have? What could I do for them outside this conflict that could allow them to give up something I need now in return? How can we turn this into a win for both of us?

8. **Clear problem-focused communication.** Follow the rule of equity: Explain your thinking and ask them to explain theirs. Be able to state their position as clearly as they do whether you agree or not—give it legitimacy. Separate facts from opinions and assumptions. Generate a variety of possibilities first rather than stake out positions. Keep your speaking to 30–60 second bursts. Try to get them to do the same. Don't give the other side the impression you're lecturing or criticizing them. Explain objectively why you hold a view; make the other side do the same. Ask lots of questions, make fewer statements. To identify interests behind positions, ask why they hold them or why they wouldn't want to do something. Always restate their position to their satisfaction before offering a response.

9. **Questions.** In win-win and something-something negotiations, the more information you have about the other side, the more you will have to work with. What can you learn about what they know before going in? What will they do if they don't reach an agreement with you? In the negotiation, ask more questions, make fewer statements. Ask clarifying questions: "What did you mean by that?" Probes: "Why do you say that?" Motives: "What led you to that position?" Get everything out that you can. Don't negotiate assumptions, negotiate facts.

10. **Watch out for overcommitment to any need or course of action.** Look for information that goes against your preferences. Be able to adjust your position and your wants. If you can't, your sense of mission is

getting the best of you. If you can't walk away until you get X, you'll probably either overpay or blow the negotiation. Don't negotiate around a single issue if you can add another. This is another situation that leads to rigidity.

11. **Selective resistance.** Do you do a lot of sorting? Do you adapt to some and not to others? You probably have good people buckets and bad people buckets and signal your disagreement with them to the bad bucket groups or individuals. Learn to understand without accepting or judging. Listen, take notes, ask questions, and be able to make their case as well as they can. Pick something in their argument you agree with. Present your argument in terms of the problem only—why you think this is the best manner to deal with a mutually agreed-upon problem. A careful observer should not be able to tell your assessment of people or their arguments at the time. Find someone who is a fair observer and get a critique. Was I fair? Did I treat everyone the same? Were my objections based on reasoning against standards and not directed at people?

E Relationships With Higher Management

Since values often come first, ENFPs can be seen as not that supportive of upper management strategy. If anything in the strategy crosses swords with a value of ENFPs, they can dig in their heels. Instead, they need to take the initiative in order to understand the points of view of bosses.

1. **Facing the boss.** Try to have a series of informal, relaxed discussions with your boss about what the problem might be, leading with your contributions—we are seldom completely in the right—to the problem first; then give him/her an opportunity to add to the discussion. Make it easy for him/her by indicating, "You are doing me a favor. I need your help." In return for your boss's help, offer some in return. What are your boss's weakest areas or what can you do to make the job easier? Figure out what those are and pitch in. This is good practice because relationships don't often prosper unless there is some equity built in. Give to get or your boss may soon be uncomfortable with the one-way nature of the help.

2. **Some rules to follow:** Describe. Say "I" not "you." Focus on how to accomplish work better. (If you think the boss is blocking you, instead of saying this, say, "I need help in getting this done. I've tried the following things, but....")

- If your boss is reluctant to give criticism, help by making statements rather than asking questions. Saying "I think I focus too much on operations and miss some of the larger strategic connections" is easier for most people to reply to than a question which asks them to tell you this point.

- If your manager is uninvolved, you will need to provide the structure and aim for a sign-off on your objectives.

- If you work for a detail-driven micromanager, ask what results you must achieve to be successful (and left alone more).

- If your manager is well-meaning, but a nuisance, ask if you can check in with him because you are trying to be more autonomous.

- If you believe the boss is blocking you, access your network for performance help, think of five ways to accomplish anything, and try them all.

3. **Learn to depersonalize and be neutral.** Try to separate the person from the boss role he/she is in; try to objectify the situation. Someone made her/him boss for a reason, and you are never going to please everyone. Deal with him/her as your boss more than as a person. While you don't ever have to invite her/him to your home, you do have to deal with this person as a boss. Ask yourself why you dislike your boss so much or don't like to work with him/her. Write down everything you don't like on the left-hand side of a page. On the right-hand side write a strategy for dealing with it. Consider these strategies: Ask what strengths you can appeal to; ask what you can provide that the boss needs; ask what the boss would like for you to do to be more effective; design a project that you can do together so you can have a success experience; and consult with others for advice. What do people think who have a favorable impression of your boss? Do you share any common interests? Write down everything you've heard him/her say that was favorable. Play to the boss's good points. Whatever you do, don't signal what you think. Put your judgments on hold, nod, ask questions, summarize as you would with anyone else. A fly on the wall should not be able to tell whether you're talking to friend or foe. You can always talk less and ask more questions.

4. **Keep your cool.** Being nervous, anxious, and uncomfortable around one or more higher-ups is fairly normal; the key is not allowing that to prevent you from doing your best. Being uncomfortable can sometimes lead to physical reactions like sweating, hesitating or

stuttering speech, mispronounced words, flushing of the face, grumbling in the stomach, running out of breath while talking, etc. When that happens, stop a second or two, take a deep breath, compose yourself, and continue what you were doing; they all have been there before. Remember, all you can do is the best you can do. You probably know more about this topic than they do. You're well prepared—being anxious can prevent you from demonstrating your expertise.

5. **You may be seen as rigid in your values stances and unwilling to accept, or even see, those of others.** Rigid stances often come from childhood and early adult experiences. You need to know why you hold these values and critically examine if they are appropriate here. Statements of belief are pronouncements—a true value holds up to action scrutiny; you can say why you hold it, how it plays out in different situations, and what happens when it conflicts with other values. You may have reduced your beliefs to rigid commandments.

Overusing ENFP Tendencies

If you sometimes overdo your preferred behaviors, you may need to work on:

A Composure

B Better Follow-Through

C Being Too Process Oriented

D Analyzing Problems More Fully

E Dealing With Routine and Procedures

F Being Less Dependent on a Few Relationships

ISTJ	ISFJ	INFJ	INTJ
ISTP	ISFP	INFP	INTP
ESTP	ESFP	ENFP	ENTP
ESTJ	ESFJ	ENFJ	ENTJ

A Composure

ENFPs are passionate people, and when the real world disappoints, they can become quite vocal and defensive or simply disappear.

1. **First, about emotions.** Emotions are electricity and chemistry. Emotions are designed to help you cope with emergencies and threats. Emotions trigger predictable body changes. Heart pumps faster and with greater pressure. Blood flows faster. Glucose is

released into the bloodstream for increased energy and strength. Eyes dilate to take in more light. Breathing rate increases to get more oxygen. Why is that? To either fight or flee from saber-toothed tigers, of course. Emotions are designed to help us with the so-called fight or flight response. It makes the body faster and stronger temporarily. The price? In order to increase energy to the muscles, the emotional response decreases resources for the stomach (that's why we get upset stomachs under stress) and the thinking brain (that's why we say and do dumb things under stress). Even though we might be able to lift a heavy object off a trapped person, we can't think of the right thing to say in a tense meeting. Once the emotional response is triggered, it has to run its course. If no threat follows the initial trigger, it lasts from 45–60 seconds in most people. That's why your grandmother told you to count to 10. Trouble is, people have saber-toothed tigers in their heads. In modern times, thoughts can trigger this emotional response. Events which are certainly not physically threatening, like being criticized, can trigger the response. Even worse, today people have added a third "f" to the fight or flight response—freeze. Emotions can shut you down and leave you speechless, neither choosing to fight (argue, respond) or flee (calmly shut down the transaction and exit). You'll have to fight these reactions to learn to be cool under pressure. Once you calm down, do a reality check. How do you know this is true? Don't jump to conclusions. Be a detective.

2. **Rein in your horse.** You may be in love with ideas, but providing them too quickly and often will make your people dependent, overwhelmed and irritated. Respect others' need to close out the discussion by moving on to a conclusion. Monitor how much time you spend spinning out possibilities and lessen it. Restrict yourself to three ideas per session. Go into a meeting expecting to come to some concrete outcome.

3. **Decreasing triggers.** Write down the last 25 times you lost your composure. Most people who have composure problems have three to five repeating triggers. Criticism. Loss of control. A certain kind of person. An enemy. Being surprised. Spouse. Children. Money. Authority. Angry at yourself because you can't say no? Try to group 90% of the events into three to five categories. Once you have the groupings, ask yourself why these are a problem. Is it ego? Losing face? Being caught short? Being found out? Causing you more work? In each grouping, what would be a more mature response? Mentally and physically rehearse a better response. Try to decrease by 10% a month the number of times you lose your composure.

4. **Increasing impulse control.** People say and do inappropriate things when they lose their composure. The problem is that they say or do the first thing that occurs to them. Research shows that generally somewhere between the second and third thing you think of to say or do is the best option. Practice holding back your first response long enough to think of a second. When you can do that, wait long enough to think of a third before you choose. By that time, 50% of your composure problems should go away.

5. **Count to 10.** Our thinking and judgment are not at their best during the emotional response. Create and practice delaying tactics. Go get a pencil out of your briefcase. Go get a cup of coffee. Ask a question and listen. Go up to the flip chart and write something. Take notes. See yourself in a setting you find calming. Go to the bathroom. You need about a minute to regain your composure after the emotional response is triggered. Don't do or say anything until the minute has passed.

6. **Delay of gratification.** Are you impatient? Do you get upset when the plane is delayed? The food is late? The car isn't ready? Your spouse is behind schedule? For most of us, life is one big delay. We always seem to be waiting for someone else to do something so we can do our something. People with composure problems often can't accept delay of what they want and what they think they deserve and have coming. When what they want is delayed, they get belligerent and demanding. Write down the last 25 delays that set you off. Group them into three to five categories. Create and rehearse a more mature response. Relax. Reward yourself with something enjoyable. Adopt a philosophical stance since there's little or nothing you can do about it. Think great thoughts while you're waiting. Force a smile or find something to laugh about.

7. **Blame and vengeance?** Do you feel a need to punish the people and groups that set you off? Do you become hostile, angry, sarcastic, or vengeful? While all that may be temporarily satisfying to you, they will all backfire and you will lose in the long term. When someone attacks you, rephrase it as an attack on a problem. Reverse the argument—ask what they would do if they were in your shoes. When the other side takes a rigid position, don't reject it. Ask why: What are the principles behind the offer? How do we know it's fair? What's the theory of the case? Play out what would happen if their position was accepted. Let the other side vent frustration or blow off steam, but don't react.

8. **The message.** Be succinct. You have limited attention span in tough feedback situations. Don't waste time with a long preamble, particularly if the feedback is negative. If the feedback is negative and the recipient is likely to know it, go ahead and say it directly. They won't hear anything positive you have to say anyway. Don't overwhelm the person/group, even if you have a lot to say. Go from specific to general points. Keep it to the facts. Don't embellish to make your point. No passion or inflammatory language. Don't do it to harm or out of vengeance. Don't do it in anger. If feelings are involved for you, wait until you can describe them, not show them. Managerial courage comes in search of a better outcome, not destroying others. Stay calm and cool. If others are not composed, don't respond. Just return to the message.

9. **Bring a solution if you can.** Nobody likes a critic. Everybody appreciates a problem solver. Give people ways to improve; don't just dump and leave. Tell others what you think would be better—paint a different outcome. Help others see the consequences—you can ask them what they think, and you can tell them what the consequences are from your side if you are personally involved ("I'd be reluctant to work with you on X again").

10. **Your defensive response.** You will need to work on keeping yourself in a calm state when getting negative feedback. You need to change your thinking. When getting the feedback, your only task is to accurately understand what people are trying to tell you. It is not your task at that point to accept or reject. That comes later. Mentally rehearse how you will calmly react to tough feedback situations before they happen. Develop automatic tactics to shut down or delay your usual emotional response. Some useful tactics are to slow down, take notes, ask clarifying questions, ask them for concrete examples, and thank them for telling you since you know it's not easy for them.

B Better Follow-Through

Not detail oriented by nature, and not terribly interested in procedures, ENFPs can fail to follow through. Attracted to ideas, they can also leave issues open too long as they look for more and fresher information.

1. **Pick someone you respect and get back on track.** Talk to this person with the goal of being told when enough is enough, what's a good use of your time, and to get validation of your priorities.

2. **Are you pressure-prompted?** Can you not get really excited about a project unless the deadline is drawing near? Set fake deadlines. One of the reasons you delay is that you like pressure and dislike the ordinary. So, fool yourself. Always start 10% of each attempt immediately after it is apparent it will be needed and tell yourself it's due on Friday, that you can't leave for the weekend until you've made some progress. This has the added benefit of helping you better gauge what it is going to take to finish it. Always assume it will take more time than you think it's going to take.

3. **Trying to avoid conflict?** Do you say what you need to say to get through the meeting or transaction but have little intention of doing what you said? Do you say things just to go along and not cause trouble? Do you say what you need to say to avoid disagreement or an argument? All these behaviors will eventually backfire when people find out you said something different in another setting or to another person, or they notice you didn't actually follow through and do what you said.

4. **Trying too hard to make the sale?** Does your enthusiasm to make the sale or get your point across cause you to commit to too many things in the heat of the transaction? The customers you get by unrealistic commitments are the customers you will lose forever when they find out you can't deliver.

5. **Simple commitments.** Do you return phone calls in a timely manner? Do you forward material you promised? Did you pass on information you promised to get? Did you carry through on a task you promised someone you would take care of? Failing to do things like this damages relationships. If you tend to forget things, write them down. If you run out of time, set up a specific time each day to follow through on commitments. If you are going to miss a deadline, let them know and give them a second date you will be sure to make.

6. **Overcommitting.** A lot of trouble follows overcommitting. Overcommitting usually comes from wanting to please everyone or not wanting to face the conflict if you say no. You can only do so much. Only commit to that which you can actually do. Commit to a specific time for delivery. Write it down. Learn to say "no" pleasantly. Learn to pass it off to someone else who has the time—"Gee no, but I'm sure Susan could help you with that." Learn to say, "Yes, but it will take longer than you might want to wait," and give them the option of withdrawing the request. Learn to say, "Yes, but what else that I

have already committed to do for you would you like to delay to get this done?"

7. **Always out of time?** Do you intend to get to things but never have the time? Do you always estimate shorter times to get things done that then take longer? There is a well-established science and a set of best practices in time management. There are a number of books you can buy in any business bookstore, and there are a number of good courses you can attend. Delegating also helps you use your time more effectively.

8. **Visualize.** Set up a process to monitor progress against the goals. People like running measures. They like to gauge their pace. It's like the United Way Thermometer in the lobby.

9. **Feedback.** Give as much in-process feedback as you have time for. Most people are motivated by process feedback against agreed-upon goals for three reasons:

   ■ First, it helps them adjust what they are doing along the way in time to achieve the goal; they can make midcourse corrections.

   ■ Second, it shows them what they are doing is important and that you're eager to help.

   ■ Third, it's not the "gotcha" game of negative and critical feedback after the fact.

10. **Follow through with positive and negative rewards and consequences.** Celebrate the exceeders, compliment the just-made-its, and sit down and discuss what happened with the missers. Actually deliver the reward or consequence you communicated. If you don't do what you said you were going to do, no one will pay attention to the next goal and consequence you set.

11. **Leave things undone?** Very action oriented? Impatient? Fingers in many pies? Interest wanes if it takes too long? On to new ideas? All of these result in unmet commitments. Try to discipline yourself to finish what you've started. Don't move on until it's done. Delegate finishing it to someone you trust. Check back to see that it was done. If you are not going to finish it, inform those concerned that you do not intend to complete the task with the reasons for your decision.

12. **Finishing.** While it's true that sometimes you get 80% of what you are pushing for with the first 20% of the effort, it unfortunately then takes another 80% of the time to finish the last 20%. In a fast-paced world,

it's sometimes tough to pull the cart all the way to the finish line when the race is over. Not all tasks have to be completely finished. For some, 80% would be acceptable. For those who need all the i's dotted and the t's crossed, it will take perseverance. The devil is in the details. When you get caught in this situation, create a checklist with the 20% that remains to be done. Plan to do a little on it each day. Cross things off and celebrate each time you get to take something off the list. Remember, it's going to challenge your motivation and attention. Try to delegate finishing to someone who would see the 20% as a fresh challenge. Get a consultant to finish it. Task trade with someone else's 20% so you both would have something fresh to do.

C Being Too Process Oriented

For ENFPs, enjoyment comes from their causes and the people around them. They can spend long amounts of time with others, get caught up in the process, and be seen as slow, intrusive, and even nosy. In these instances, they lose sight of the goal and don't take charge.

1. **You take too long to get things done because you focus on people and interpersonal process.** You need to determine a message and sell it. The power of a mission and vision communication is providing everyone in the organization with a road map on how they are going to be part of something grand and exciting. Establish common cause. Imagine what the change would look like if fully implemented, then describe the outcome often—how things will look in the future. Help people see how their efforts fit in by creating simple, obvious measures of achievement like bar or thermometer charts. Be succinct. People don't line up behind laundry lists or ambiguous objectives. Missions and visions should be more about where we are going and less about how we are going to get there. Keep your eyes on the prize.

2. **Leading is riskier than following.** While there are a lot of personal rewards for taking tough stands, it puts you into the limelight. Look at what happens to political leaders and the scrutiny they face. People who choose to stand alone have to be internally secure. Do you feel good about yourself? Can you defend to a critical and impartial audience the wisdom of what you're doing? They have to please themselves first that they are on the right track. They have to accept lightning bolts from detractors. Can you take the heat? People will always say it should have been done differently. Even great leaders are wrong sometimes. They accept personal responsibility for errors and move on to lead some more. Don't let criticism prevent you from

taking a stand. Build up your heat shield. If you know you're right, standing alone is well worth the heat. If it turns out you're wrong, admit it and move on.

3. **Against the grain tough stands.** Taking a tough stand demands confidence in what you're saying along with the humility that you might be wrong—one of life's paradoxes. To prepare to take the lead on a tough issue, work on your stand through mental interrogation until you can clearly state in a few sentences what your stand is and why you hold it. Build the business case. How do others win? Ask others for advice. Scope the problem, consider options, pick one, develop a rationale, then go with it until proven wrong. Consider the opposing view. Develop a strong case against your stand. Prepare responses to it. Expect pushback.

4. **Develop a philosophical stance toward failure/criticism.** After all, most innovations fail, most proposals fail, most efforts to lead change fail. Anything worth doing takes repeated effort. Anything could always have been done better. Research says that successful general managers have made more mistakes in their careers than the people they were promoted over. They got promoted because they had the courage to lead, not because they were always right. Other studies suggest really good general managers are right about 65% of the time. Put errors, mistakes, and failures on your menu. Everyone has to have some spinach for a balanced diet.

5. **Cutting line.** When all else fails, you may have to pull someone aside and say, "I have listened to all of your objections and have tried to understand them, but the train is moving on. Are you on or off?" Always follow the rules of dealing with conflict: depersonalize; keep it on the problem, not the person; try one last time to make your case; note the person's objections but don't concede anything; be clear; now is not the time for negotiation; give the person a day to think it over. Worst case, if the person is a direct report, you may have to ask him/her to leave the unit. If the person is a peer or colleague, inform your boss of the impasse and your intention to proceed without his/her support.

D Analyzing Problems More Fully

ENFPs are excellent idea generators but often don't do enough in close analysis.

1. **Personal experience is a very limited way to learn.** Even accessing others' experiences still leaves major gaps. For adults, most learning either comes from taking action and learning from the consequences or searching for parallel experiences in the past.

2. **Do you do enough analysis?** Thoroughly define the problem. Figure out what causes it. Keep asking why. See how many causes you can come up with and how many organizing buckets you can put them in. This increases the chance of a better solution because you can see more connections. Look for patterns in data, don't just collect information. Put it in categories that make sense to you. A good rule of thumb is to analyze patterns and causes to come up with alternatives. Many of us just collect data, which numerous studies show increases our confidence but doesn't increase decision accuracy. Think out loud with others; see how they view the problem. Studies show that defining the problem and taking action usually occur simultaneously, so to break out of analysis paralysis, figure out what the problem is first. Then when a good alternative appears, you're likely to recognize it immediately.

3. **Locate the essence of the problem.** What are the key factors or elements in this problem? Experts usually solve problems by figuring out what the deep, underlying principles are and working forward from there; the less adept focus on desired outcomes/solutions and either work backward or concentrate on the surface facts. What are the deep principles of what you're working on? Once you've done this, search the past for parallels—your past, the business past, the historical past. One common mistake here is to search in parallel organizations because "only they would know." Backing up and asking a broader question will aid in the search for solutions. When Motorola wanted to find out how to process orders more quickly, they went not to other electronics firms, but to Domino's Pizza and Federal Express.

4. **Check yourself for these common errors in thinking:** Do you state as facts things that are really opinions or assumptions? Are you sure these assertions are facts? State opinions and assumptions as that and don't present them as facts. Do you attribute cause and effect to relationships when you don't know if one causes the other? If sales are down, and we increase advertising and sales go up, this doesn't prove

causality. They are simply related. Say we know that the relationship between sales/advertising is about the same as sales/number of employees. If sales go down, we probably wouldn't hire more people, so make sure one thing causes the other before acting on it. Do you generalize from a single example without knowing if that single example does generalize?

E Dealing With Routine and Procedures

ENFPs are interested in causes and people, and they can become bored and skeptical with the familiar and the mundane.

1. **Try to see the value in routines.** Pick a plan or procedure and do a historical analysis of how it came to be and why it is necessary. Resist the urge to change it or question its usefulness. Understand it first.

2. **Turn off your idea-generation program.** Sometimes you need to just do it as designed. Four ideas to make a procedure better won't help the work get done today. Pick a few causes to change. For the others, just execute them.

3. **Compensate for your dislikes.** Find a person you admire and respect to deal with all the procedures you find oppressive. Let this person tell you if anything needs changing. Otherwise, trust his or her judgment.

F Being Less Dependent on a Few Relationships

Although very adept with people, ENFPs gravitate to a few close relationships and can be seen as dependent on a small group of insiders. This limits their perspective and their network in an organization. They often don't seek out contrasting views. Many are looking for yes-men to validate their perceptions of the world.

1. **Spend most of your time with just a few people?** Developed a comfort and liking for the few? Expand your repertoire to get your relationship quota up. Be an early adopter of something. Find some new thing, technique, software, tool, system, process, or skill relevant to your activity. Privately become an expert in it. Read the books. Get certified. Visit a location where it's being done. Then surprise everyone and be the first to introduce it into your world. Sell it. Train others. Integrate it into your work.

2. **Pick people who are quite different from you** and observe what they do and how they do it. Then ask for their help on a problem. Just ask

questions and understand their perspective. Don't make any judgments about the rightness or wrongness of their approach.

3. **Pick some tough critics to talk with.** Don't go to the few people you truly like, most likely because you share similar perspectives. Go to some you know will disagree with you and hear them out.

I generate many ideas—often too many, because others get overwhelmed.

— An ENFP Manager

APPLICATION

Your personal preferences play out in day-to-day problems and situations you face. Below is a case about your type dealing with such a situation. Use this to think through how you will integrate the tips you've considered and coach yourself to be more effective in your type.

ENFP Application Situation (Part 1)

"You'd think that after four years and four decent performance reviews in which she's generally been meeting expectations around her business goals and getting the same feedback on areas for development, Elaine would be more confident and need less reassurance about how she's doing, but she's still pretty time consuming and process oriented," her boss was saying to me over lunch. I finished chewing a bite of seared ahi tuna.

My name is Bob. I'm the owner of a leadership development and coaching business. Jay, who is Elaine's boss and VP of Operations, and I were having our monthly meeting in preparation for my company's work with his managers over the coming weeks.

At my prompting, Jay provided me with some examples of what constituted "time consuming," and I made some notes. While he was pretty certain that Elaine had not participated in a 360° assessment, he was aware that she had completed the MBTI and that her type is ENFP. Before coming here, Elaine was a faculty member at a small liberal arts college. Now, as Regional Business Director in this company, she has six direct reports. She is known for being great at generating ideas.

When I got back to my office, I debriefed Elaine's case with an associate who would be establishing the coaching relationship with her.

Thinking It Through: Strategy

- Based on your awareness of the ENFP type, what, other than the information noted above, do you think that Bob is likely to have heard about Elaine—both positive and negative—knowing that she's considered time consuming and concerned about process?

- What would you do to plan your initial meeting with Elaine and what would you want the outcome(s) of that meeting to be?

Planning It Out: Tactics

- What are some developmental steps you might suggest to Elaine in the very near term?

- What do you think stresses her?

- Which of the tactics described in the Being More Effective section are applicable in this situation?

- Which Overused Tendencies are most likely to come into play here?

ENFP Application Situation (Part 2)

- In the initial report you later received from the coaching associate, you read that when he met with Elaine, she seemed "irritable as well as suspicious of the motives behind the coaching." She also seemed to be "naive," according to his notes, and conveyed expectations for her role and for her relationship with her direct reports that seemed "unrealistic."

Reflection

- What do you think should be the next steps with Elaine? How would you suggest your associate proceed in helping her to use her understanding of characteristics of her type to develop?

SUGGESTED READINGS

■■■■■■■ Being a More Effective ENFP ■■■■■■■

Day-to-Day Management

Allen, David. *Getting Things Done: The Art of Stress-Free Productivity.* New York: Penguin Books, 2003.

Bossidy, Larry, Ram Charan and Charles Burck (Contributor). *Execution: The Discipline of Getting Things Done.* New York: Crown Business Publishing, 2002.

Byfield, Marilyn. *It's Hard to Make a Difference When You Can't Find Your Keys: The Seven-Step Path to Becoming Truly Organized.* New York: Viking Press, 2003.

Drucker, Peter F. *The Effective Executive.* New York: HarperBusiness, 2002.

Gleeson, Kerry. *The Personal Efficiency Program: How to Get Organized to Do More Work in Less Time.* New York: John Wiley & Sons, Inc., 2000.

Kotter, John P. *The General Managers.* New York: The Free Press, 1982.

Stone, Florence M. and Randi T. Sachs. *The High-Value Manager— Developing the Core Competencies Your Organization Needs.* New York: AMACOM, 1995.

Drive for Results

Block, Peter. *The Answer to How Is Yes: Acting On What Matters.* San Francisco: Berrett-Koehler Publishers, Inc., 2001.

Bossidy, Larry, Ram Charan and Charles Burck (Contributor). *Execution: The Discipline of Getting Things Done.* New York: Crown Business Publishing, 2002.

Collins, James C. *Good to Great: Why Some Companies Make the Leap...And Others Don't.* New York: HarperCollins, 2001.

Loehr, Jim and Tony Schwartz. *The Power of Full Engagement: Managing Energy, Not Time, Is the Key to High Performance and Personal Renewal.* New York: The Free Press, 2003.

Longenecker, Clinton O. and Jack L. Simonetti. *Getting Results: Five Absolutes for High Performance.* New York: John Wiley & Sons, Inc., 2001.

Timely Decision Making

Block, Peter. *The Answer to How Is Yes: Acting On What Matters.* San Francisco: Berrett-Koehler Publishers, Inc., 2001.

Byfield, Marilyn. *It's Hard to Make a Difference When You Can't Find Your Keys: The Seven-Step Path to Becoming Truly Organized.* New York: Viking Press, 2003.

Carrison, Dan. *Deadline! How Premier Organizations Win the Race Against Time.* New York: AMACOM, 2003.

Emmett, Rita. *The Procrastinator's Handbook: Mastering the Art of Doing It Now.* New York: Walker & Company, 2000.

Jennings, Jason and Laurence Haughton. *It's Not the Big That Eat the Small...It's the Fast That Eat the Slow.* New York: HarperCollins, 2001.

Murnighan, John Keith and John C. Mowen. *The Art of High-Stakes Decision-Making: Tough Calls in a Speed-Driven World.* New York: John Wiley & Sons, Inc., 2002.

Conflict Management

Cloke, Ken and Joan Goldsmith. *Resolving Conflicts at Work: A Complete Guide for Everyone on the Job.* San Francisco: Jossey-Bass, Inc., 2000.

Dana, Daniel. *Conflict Resolution.* New York: McGraw-Hill Trade, 2000.

Guttman, Howard M. *When Goliaths Clash: Managing Executive Conflict to Build a More Dynamic Organization.* New York: AMACOM, 2003.

Masters, Marick Francis and Robert R. Albright. *The Complete Guide to Conflict Resolution in the Workplace.* New York: AMACOM, 2002.

Relationships With Higher Management

Bolton, Robert and Dorothy Grover Bolton. *People Styles at Work—Making Bad Relationships Good and Good Relationships Better.* New York: AMACOM, 1996.

Chaleff, Ira. *The Courageous Follower: Standing Up to and for Our Leaders.* San Francisco: Berrett-Koehler Publishers, Inc., 2003.

Charan, Ram. *What the CEO Wants You to Know: How Your Company Really Works.* New York: Crown Business Publishing, 2001.

Gittines, Roger and Rosanne Badowski. *Managing Up: How to Forge an Effective Relationship With Those Above You.* New York: Currency, 2003.

Guttman, Howard M. *When Goliaths Clash: Managing Executive Conflict to Build a More Dynamic Organization.* New York: AMACOM, 2003.

■■■■■■■ Overusing ENFP Tendencies ■■■■■■■

Composure

Barker, Larry, Ph.D. and Kittie Watson, Ph.D. *Listen Up: At Home, at Work, in Relationships: How to Harness the Power of Effective Listening.* Irvine, CA: Griffin Trade Paperback, 2001.

Bolton, Robert and Dorothy Grover Bolton. *People Styles at Work—Making Bad Relationships Good and Good Relationships Better.* New York: AMACOM, 1996.

Carter, Les. *The Anger Trap: Free Yourself From the Frustrations That Sabotage Your Life.* New York: John Wiley & Sons, Inc., 2003.

Ellis, Albert, Ph.D. *How to Control Your Anxiety Before It Controls You.* New York: Citadel Press, 2000.

Lerner, Harriet. *The Dance of Connection: How to Talk to Someone When You're Mad, Hurt, Scared, Frustrated, Insulted, Betrayed, or Desperate.* New York: Quill/HarperCollins, 2002.

Patterson, Kerry, Joseph Grenny, Ron McMillan, Al Switzler and Stephen R. Covey. *Crucial Conversations: Tools for Talking When Stakes Are High.* New York: McGraw-Hill/Contemporary Books, 2002.

Better Follow-Through

Byfield, Marilyn. *It's Hard to Make a Difference When You Can't Find Your Keys: The Seven-Step Path to Becoming Truly Organized.* New York: Viking Press, 2003.

Gleeson, Kerry. *The Personal Efficiency Program: How to Get Organized to Do More Work in Less Time.* New York: John Wiley & Sons, Inc., 2000.

MacKenzie, Alec. *The Time Trap: The Classic Book on Time Management.* Fine Communications, 2002.

Winston, Stephanie. *The Organized Executive: The Classic Program for Productivity: New Ways to Manage Time, People, and the Digital Office.* New York: Warner Business, 2001.

Being Too Process Oriented

Bennis, Warren G. and Burt Nanus. *Leaders: Strategies for Taking Charge.* New York: HarperBusiness, 2003.

Cox, Danny and John Hoover. *Leadership When the Heat's On.* New York: McGraw-Hill Trade, 2002.

Dana, Daniel. *Conflict Resolution.* New York: McGraw-Hill Trade, 2000.

Dawson, Roger. *Secrets of Power Negotiating: Inside Secrets From a Master Negotiator.* Franklin Lakes, NJ: Career Press, 2001.

Oliver, David. *How to Negotiate Effectively.* London: Kogan Page, 2003.

Analyzing Problems More Fully

Flynn, Daniel J. *Intellectual Morons: How Ideology Makes Smart People Fall for Stupid Ideas.* New York: Crown Business Publishing, 2004.

Hammond, John S., Ralph L. Keeney and Howard Raiffer. *Smart Choices.* Boston: Harvard University Press, 1999.

Nutt, Paul C. *Why Decisions Fail: Avoiding the Blunders and Traps That Lead to Decision Debacles.* San Francisco: Berrett-Koehler Publishers, Inc., 2002.

Sofo, Francesco. *Six Myths of Critical Thinking.* Business & Professional Publishing, 2003.

Sternberg, Robert J. *Thinking Styles.* Boston: Cambridge University Press, 1997.

Yates, J. Frank. *Decision Management: How to Assure Better Decisions in Your Company.* San Francisco: Jossey-Bass, Inc., 2003.

Dealing With Routine and Procedures

Bossidy, Larry, Ram Charan and Charles Burck (Contributor). *Execution: The Discipline of Getting Things Done*. New York: Crown Business Publishing, 2002.

Keen, Peter G.W. *The Process Edge—Creating Value Where It Counts*. Boston: Harvard Business School Press, 1998.

Lawler, Edward E., III, Susan Albers Mohrman and George Benson. *Organizing for High Performance: Employee Involvement, TQM, Reengineering, and Knowledge Management in the Fortune 1000: The CEO Report*. San Francisco: Jossey-Bass, Inc., 2001.

Niven, P.R. *Balanced Scorecard Step-by-Step: Maximizing Performance and Maintaining Results*. New York: John Wiley & Sons, Inc., 2002.

Being Less Dependent on a Few Relationships

Benton, D.A. *Executive Charisma: Six Steps to Mastering the Art of Leadership*. New York: McGraw-Hill Trade, 2003.

Bolton, Robert and Dorothy Grover Bolton. *People Styles at Work—Making Bad Relationships Good and Good Relationships Better*. New York: AMACOM, 1996.

Brooks, Michael. *Instant Rapport*. New York: Warner Books, 1989.

Maxwell, John C. *Relationships 101*. London: Thomas Nelson, 2004.

Niven, David. *The 100 Simple Secrets of Successful People: What Scientists Have Learned and How You Can Use It*. New York: HarperBusiness, 2002.

Silberman, Melvin L. and Freda Hansburg. *Peoplesmart: Developing Your Interpersonal Intelligence*. San Francisco: Berrett-Koehler Publishers, Inc., 2000.

CHAPTER 12

ENTP
Extraverted Intuiting
with
Introverted Thinking

■■■■■■■■■■■■■■■■

3.2% of Population
8.1% of Managers

■■■■■■■■■■■■■■■■

Typical Strengths

Inventive
Can Argue Both Sides of an Issue
Stimulating
Can Work on Many Things at Once
Outspoken
Confident and Independent
Quick
Continuous Improver

ISTJ	ISFJ	INFJ	INTJ
ISTP	ISFP	INFP	INTP
ESTP	ESFP	ENFP	**ENTP**
ESTJ	ESFJ	ENFJ	ENTJ

I can do it, whatever it is. Just give me a chance.

– An ENTP Manager

Basic Habits of Mind

ENTPs seek to connect current experience to possible future circumstances. Driven toward new ideas and possibilities by their Extraverted Intuiting, these ideas go through their Introverted Thinking filter, resulting in a decisive judgment about the most attractive alternative. Drawn toward complex problems, ENTPs critique and question in an effort to find a complete and elegant solution. ENTPs often get caught up in wanting to be competent and cutting-edge at the same time, given the engagement of Extraverted Intuiting and the decisiveness of Introverted Thinking.

Introverted Feeling and Introverted Sensing also aid ENTPs. Introverted Feeling provides the passion for an ideal solution while Introverted Sensing polishes the analysis with a desire for precision. Introverted Feeling often shows up when ENTPs discover that the critical questioning of another person may have gone too far. Suddenly, they begin to soften their analysis. This can lead to perceptions of indecisiveness and an inability to stay the course and be consistently productive.

Typical Communication Patterns

- Enthusiastic about ideas and concepts.
- Openly reveal their observations and reactions to situations.
- Eager to discuss the big picture, ENTPs are often expansive and filled with remarks about future possibilities.
- They are eager to pursue questions and to enjoy the intellectual banter of analyzing ideas.

General Learning Strategy

- ENTPs usually prefer to understand the context and frame of reference when attacking problem solving.
- Typical learning strategies are active problem-solving discussions and rigorous debate.

- Their learning is generally helped by making linkages among ideas and important theories or concepts. In doing so, they visualize the future use of information or ideas.

Interpersonal Qualities Related to Motivation

- ENTPs are typically motivated by opportunities to share ideas, brainstorm, and engage in analytical give-and-take.

- Autonomy is important for them, so they prefer to be delegated to or to delegate to others. They assume this leads to environments that encourage innovation.

Blind Spots

- ENTPs might be surprised to learn that observers see them as somewhat overdependent on a small group of insiders, low in impulse control, and needing to follow through more completely.

Stress Related Behavior

- Stressors often result in ENTPs increasing their tempo, becoming more active and talkative.

- They can become more impulsive, hasty, noisy, and distracted as stress increases. With enough stress, they may become very quiet while they focus on a fact or two and obsess about its meaning (usually in very negative ways).

Potential Barriers to Effectiveness

- ENTPs are often blunt and abrupt. They often need to learn more constructive confrontation, to be more demonstratively a team player, and more deliberate in their management of tasks.

- Because of their analytical nature and their preference to push the boundaries, they may not be fully aware that others can see them as arrogant and insensitive.

Being a More Effective ENTP

A   Handling Disagreements
B   Team Building
C   Caring and Compassion
D   Planning and Organizing
E   Political Savvy
F   Quantity of Work Produced
G   Working With the Less Competent
H   Communicating More Fully

ISTJ	ISFJ	INFJ	INTJ
ISTP	ISFP	INFP	INTP
ESTP	ESFP	ENFP	ENTP
ESTJ	ESFJ	ENFJ	ENTJ

A Handling Disagreements

ENTPs often run over anything in their path. They can cause a lot of noise, especially if they think they are dealing with less-devoted or less-competent people.

1. **Turn down your intensity volume.** Although usually calm, once you have locked in to a position, you can get very hot in your comments. Impatience takes over and you deliver points with stinging honesty, then are surprised by the equally stinging reactions of others. After all, what you said was true, and you've heard others say exactly the same things with no terrible consequences. The problem here is that you are questioning, critical, and intense by nature. Your statements come across as you are putting the criticism into action immediately and burning down their house as well. Learn to be direct but diplomatic, candid but understated by practicing the tips below.

2. **Do you meddle in the work of others when they are blocking your efforts?** Let your team help you. Periodically, send out a memo asking each person whether there is anything he or she thinks he/she could do that you are now doing or monitoring too closely. Pick one or two things per person and empower them to do it on their own. Make sure the up-front communication is adequate for them to perform well. Explain your standards—what the outcome should be, the key things that need to be taken care of—then ask them to figure out how to do it themselves.

3. **Cooperative relations.** The opposite of conflict is cooperation. Developing cooperative relationships involves demonstrating real and perceived equity, the other side feeling understood and respected, and taking a problem-oriented point of view. To do this more: Increase the realities and perceptions of fairness—don't try to win every battle

and take all the spoils; focus on the common-ground issues and interests of both sides—find wins on both sides, give in on little points; avoid starting with entrenched positions—show respect for them and their positions; and reduce any remaining conflicts to the smallest size possible.

4. **Causing unnecessary conflict.** Language, words, and timing set the tone and can cause unnecessary conflict that has to be managed before you can get anything done. Do you use insensitive language? Do you raise your voice often? Do you use terms and phrases that challenge others? Do you use demeaning terms? Do you use negative humor? Do you offer conclusions, solutions, statements, dictates, or answers early in the transaction? Give reasons first, solutions last. When you give solutions first, people often directly challenge the solutions instead of defining the problem. Pick words that are other-person neutral. Pick words that don't challenge or sound one-sided. Pick tentative and probabilistic words that give others a chance to maneuver and save face. Pick words that are about the problem and not the person. Avoid direct blaming remarks; describe the problem and its impact.

5. **Practice Aikido,** the ancient art of absorbing the energy of your opponent and using it to manage him/her. Let the other side vent frustration or blow off steam, but don't react. Listen. Nod. Ask clarifying questions. Ask open-ended questions like, "What one change could you make so we could achieve our objectives better?" "What could I do that would help the most?" Restate their position periodically to signal you have understood. But don't react. Keep them talking until they run out of venom. Then explore the underlying concern. Separate the people from the problem. When someone attacks you, rephrase it as an attack on the problem. In response to threats, say you'll only negotiate on merit and fairness. If the other side won't play fair, surface their game—"It looks like you're playing good cop, bad cop. Why don't you settle your differences and tell me one thing?" In response to unreasonable proposals, attacks, or a non-answer to a question, you can always say nothing. People will usually respond by saying more, coming off their position a bit, or at least revealing their true interests. Many times, with unlimited venting and your understanding, the actual conflict shrinks.

6. **Downsizing the conflict.** Almost all conflicts have common points that get lost in the heat of the battle. After a conflict has been presented and understood, start by saying that it might be helpful to see if we agree on anything. Write them on the flip chart. Then write

down the areas left open. Focus on common goals, priorities, and problems. Keep the open conflicts as small as possible and concrete. The more abstract it gets, "We don't trust your unit," the more unmanageable it gets. To this respond, "Tell me your specific concern—why exactly don't you trust us; can you give me an example?" Usually after calm discussion, they don't trust your unit on this specific issue under these specific conditions. That's easier to deal with. Allow others to save face by conceding small points that are not central to the issue—don't try to hit a home run every time. If you can't agree on a solution, agree on a procedure to move forward. Collect more data. Appeal to a higher power. Get a third-party arbitrator. Something. This creates some positive motion and breaks stalemates.

7. **Bargaining and trading.** Since you can't absolutely win all conflicts unless you keep pulling rank, you have to learn to horse-trade and bargain. What do they need that I have? What could I do for them outside this conflict that could allow them to give up something I need now in return? How can we turn this into a win for both of us?

8. **Clear problem-focused communication.** Follow the rule of equity: Explain your thinking and ask them to explain theirs. Be able to state their position as clearly as they do whether you agree or not—give it legitimacy. Separate facts from opinions and assumptions. Generate a variety of possibilities first rather than stake out positions. Keep your speaking to 30–60 second bursts. Try to get them to do the same. Don't give the other side the impression you're lecturing or criticizing them. Ask lots of questions, make fewer statements. To identify interests behind positions, ask why they hold them or why they wouldn't want to do something. Always restate their position to their satisfaction before offering a response.

9. **Questions.** In win-win and something-something negotiations, the more information you have about the other side, the more you will have to work with. What can you learn about what they know before going in? What will they do if they don't reach an agreement with you? In the negotiation, ask more questions, make fewer statements. Ask clarifying questions: "What did you mean by that?" Probes: "Why do you say that?" Motives: "What led you to that position?" Explain objectively why you hold a view; make the other side do the same. When the other side takes a rigid position, don't reject it. Ask why: What are the principles behind the offer? How do we know it's fair? What's the theory of the case? Play out what would happen if

their position was accepted. Get everything out that you can. Don't negotiate assumptions, negotiate facts.

10. **Avoid early rigid positions.** It's just physics. Action gets equal reaction. Strong statements. Strongly worded positions. Casting blame. Absolutes. Lines in the sand. Unnecessary passion. All of these will be responded to in kind, will waste time, cause ill will, and possibly prevent a win-win or a something-something. It only has a place in one-time, either/or negotiations, and even there it isn't recommended. Similarly, watch out for overcommitment to any need or course of action. Look for information that goes against your preferences. Be able to adjust your position and your wants. If you can't, your ego is getting the best of you. If you can't walk away until you get X, you'll probably either overpay or blow the negotiation. Don't negotiate around a single issue if you can add another. This is another situation that leads to rigidity.

11. **Selective resistance.** Do you adapt to some and not to others? You probably have good people buckets and bad people buckets and signal your disagreement with them to the bad bucket groups or individuals. You may have good group buckets and bad group buckets—gender, race, age, origin. Learn to understand without accepting or judging. Listen, take notes, ask questions, and be able to make their case as well as they can. Pick something in their argument you agree with. Present your argument in terms of the problem only— why you think this is the best manner to deal with a mutually agreed- upon problem. A careful observer should not be able to tell your assessment of people or their arguments at the time. Find someone who is a fair observer and get a critique. Was I fair? Did I treat everyone the same? Were my objections based on reasoning against standards and not directed at people?

B Team Building

Although ENTPs can work on teams well when they think the other team members are competent, they often lack the patience and are too independent for the procedures, structures, intricate relationships, and emotional messiness of teams. They can have problems creating the kind of climate that produces group synergy.

1. **Don't believe in teams.** If you don't believe in teams, you are probably a strong individual achiever who doesn't like the mess and sometimes the slowness of due-process relationships and team processes. You are very results oriented and truly believe the best way

to do that is to manage one person at a time. To balance this thinking, observe and talk with three excellent team builders and ask them why they manage that way. What do they consider rewarding about building teams? What advantages do they get from using the team format? Read *The Wisdom of Teams* by Katzenbach and Smith. If you can't see the value in teams, none of the following tips will help much.

2. **Don't have the time; teaming takes longer.** That's true and not true. While building a team takes longer than managing one person at a time, having a well-functioning team increases results, builds in a sustaining capability to perform, maximizes collective strengths and covers individual weaknesses, and actually releases more time for the manager because the team members help each other. Many managers get caught in the trap of thinking it takes up too much time to build a team and end up taking more time managing one-on-one.

3. **Not a people person?** Many managers are better with things, ideas, and projects than they are with people. They may be driven and very focused on producing results and have little time left to develop their people skills. It really doesn't take too much. There is communicating. People are more motivated and do better work when they know what's going on. They want to know more than just their little piece. There is listening. Nothing motivates more than a boss who will listen, not interrupt, not finish your sentences, and not complete your thoughts. Increase your listening time 30 seconds in each transaction. There is caring. Caring is questions. Caring is asking about me and what I think and what I feel. Ask one more question per transaction than you do now.

4. **Would like to build a team but don't know how.** High performance teams have four common characteristics: (1) They have a shared mind-set. They have a common vision. Everyone knows the goals and measures. (2) They trust one another. They know "you will cover me if I get in trouble." They know you will pitch in and help even though it may be difficult for you. They know you will be honest with them. They know you will bring problems to them directly and won't go behind their backs. (3) They have the talent collectively to do the job. While not any one member may have it all, collectively they have every task covered. (4) They know how to operate efficiently and effectively. They have good team skills. They run effective meetings. They have efficient ways to communicate. They have ways to deal with internal conflict.

5. **Can't seem to get people motivated to be a team.** Follow the basic rules of inspiring others as outlined in classic books like *People Skills* by Robert Bolton or *Thriving on Chaos* by Tom Peters. Communicate to people that what they do is important. Say thanks. Offer help and ask for it. Provide autonomy in how people do their work. Provide a variety of tasks. "Surprise" people with enriching, challenging assignments. Show an interest in their careers. Adopt a learning attitude toward mistakes. Celebrate successes, have visible accepted measures of achievement, and so on. Try to get everyone to participate in the building of the team so they have a stake in the outcome.

6. **Cement relationships.** Even though some—maybe including you—will resist it, parties, roasts, gag awards, picnics, and outings help build group cohesion. Allow roles to evolve naturally rather than being specified by job descriptions. Some research indicates that people gravitate naturally to eight roles, and that successful teams are not those where everyone does the same thing. Successful teams specialize, cover for each other, and only sometimes demand that everyone participate in identical activities.

7. **Not good at motivating people beyond being results oriented?** Play the motivation odds. According to research by Rewick and Lawler, the top motivators at work are: (1) Job challenge; (2) Accomplishing something worthwhile; (3) Learning new things; (4) Personal development; and (5) Autonomy. Pay (12th), Friendliness (14th), Praise (15th), or Chance of Promotion (17th) are not insignificant but are superficial compared with the five top motivators. Provide challenges, paint pictures of why this is worthwhile, set up chances to learn and grow, and provide autonomy, and you'll hit the vast majority of people's hot buttons.

8. **Use goals to motivate.** Most people are turned on by reasonable goals. They like to measure themselves against a standard. They like to see who can run the fastest, score the most, and work the best. They like goals to be realistic but stretching. People try hardest when they have somewhere between one-half and two-thirds chance of success and some control over how they go about it. People are even more motivated when they participate in setting the goals. Set just-out-of-reach challenges and tasks that will be first time for people—their first negotiation, their first solo presentation, etc.

C Caring and Compassion

ENTPs often are put off by emotional outbursts and conflicts. They can appear quite disinterested, but it is more a matter of not knowing what to do in these situations.

1. **Caring is listening.** Many bosses are marginal listeners. They are action oriented and more apt to cut off people mid-sentence than listen. They also are impatient and finish people's sentences for them when they hesitate. All of these impatient behaviors come across to others as a lack of caring. It's being insensitive to the needs and feelings of others. So, step one in caring is listening longer.

2. **Caring is sharing and disclosing.** Share your thinking on a business issue and invite the advice of direct reports. Pass on tidbits of information you think will help people do their jobs better or broaden their perspectives. Reveal things people don't need to know to do their jobs, but which will be interesting to them—and help them feel valued. Disclose some things about yourself as well. It's hard for people to relate to a stone. Tell them how you arrive at decisions. Explain your intentions, your reasons, and your thinking when announcing decisions. If you offer solutions first, you invite resistance and feelings of not being cared about—"He/she just dumps things on us."

3. **Caring is knowing.** Know three non-work things about everybody—their interests and hobbies or their children or something you can chat about. Life is a small world. If you ask your people a few personal questions, you'll find you have something in common with virtually anyone. Having something in common will help bond the relationship.

4. **Caring is accepting.** Try to listen without judging initially. Turn off your "I agree; I don't agree" filter. You don't have to agree with it; just listen to understand. Assume when people tell you something they are looking for understanding; indicate that by being able to summarize what they said. Don't offer advice or solutions unless it's obvious the person wants to know what you would do. While offering instant solutions is a good thing to do in many circumstances, it's chilling where the goal is to get people to talk to you more freely.

5. **Caring is understanding.** Study the people you work with. Without judging them, collect evidence on how they think and what they do. What drives them to do what they do? Try to predict what they will

do in given situations. Use this to understand how to relate to them. What are their hot buttons? What would they like for you to care about?

6. **Feedback.** People need continuous feedback from you and others to grow. Some tips about feedback:

■ Arrange for them to get feedback from multiple people, including yourself, on what matters for success in their future jobs; arrange for your direct reports to get 360° feedback about every two years.

■ Give them progressively stretching tasks that are first-time and different for them so that they can give themselves feedback as they go.

■ If they have direct reports and peers, another technique to recommend is to ask their associates for comments on what they should stop doing, start doing, and keep doing to be more successful.

■ You have to be willing to be straight with your people and give them accurate but balanced feedback. Give as much real-time feedback as you have time for. Most people are motivated by process feedback against agreed-upon goals for three reasons. First, it helps them adjust what they are doing along the way in time to better achieve the goal; they can make midcourse corrections. Second, it shows them what they are doing is important and that you're there to help. Third, it's not the "gotcha" game of negative and critical feedback after the fact. If there are negatives, they need to know as soon as possible.

■ Set up a buddy system so people can get continuing feedback.

■ If your organization has a mentoring program, find out how it works. Best practices begin with those to be mentored writing down goals, objectives, and development needs. They are then carefully matched with mentors and the relationship is outlined. How often will the people meet? On what topics is the mentor to be helpful? What are the responsibilities of the person to be mentored? If your organization doesn't have such a program, look at setting one up within your unit or function.

D Planning and Organizing

ENTPs work on many projects at once. Planning and organizing are not very interesting to them compared with problem solving. They often ignore these skills.

1. **Watch out for the activity trap.** John Kotter, in *The General Managers*, found that effective managers spent about half their time working on one or two key priorities—priorities they described in their own terms, not in terms of what the business/organizational plan said. Further, they made no attempt to work as much on small but related issues that tend to add up to lots of activity. So, rather than consuming themselves and others on 97 seemingly urgent and related smaller activities, they always returned to the few issues that would gain the most mileage long term.

2. **Set goals and measures.** Nothing keeps projects on time and on budget like a goal, a plan, and a measure. Set goals for the whole project and the subtasks. Plan for all. Set measures so you and others can track progress against the goals.

3. **Manage efficiently.** Plan the budget and manage against it. Spend carefully. Have a reserve if the unanticipated comes up. Set up a funding time line so you can track ongoing expenditures against plan.

4. **Set up a process to monitor progress against the plan.** How would you know if the plan is on time? Could you estimate time to completion or percent finished at any time? Give progress feedback as you go to people involved in implementing the plan.

5. **Lay out the process.** Most well-running processes start out with a plan. What do I need to accomplish? What's the time line? What resources will I need? Who controls the resources—people, funding, tools, materials, support—I need? What's my currency? How can I pay for or repay the resources I need? Who wins if I win? Who might lose? Buy a flowcharting software program that does PERT and GANTT charts. Become an expert in its use. Use the output of the software to communicate your plans to others. Use the flowcharts in your presentations. Nothing helps move a process along better than a good plan. It helps the people who have to work under the plan. It leads to better use of resources. It gets things done faster. It helps anticipate problems before they occur. Lay out the work from A to Z. Many people are seen as lacking because they don't write down the sequence or parts of the work and leave something out. Ask others to comment on your ordering and note what's missing.

E Political Savvy

Being very outspoken, ENTPs can get into hot water often. Anything that violates or interferes with their sense of mission can get them started up.

1. **People who are politically savvy** work from the outside (audience, person, group) in. They determine the demand characteristics or requirements of each situation and each person they face and select from among their various skills, tone, and styles to find the best approach to make things work. Practice not thinking inside/out when you are around others.

2. **Strong advocates for narrow views** don't usually fare well politically in organizations. Initially be tentative. Give others some room to maneuver. Make the business or organizational case first. Be prepared to counter arguments that your objective is less important than theirs. A lot of political noise is caused by making extreme statements right out of the box.

3. **Selective savvy?** Is there a group or groups you have more trouble with politically than others? Is it because you don't like or are uncomfortable with them? To work better with problem groups, put yourself in their case. Turn off your "I like—I don't like; I agree—I don't agree" switch. Ask yourself why would you act that way? What do you think they're trying to achieve? Establish reciprocity. Relationships don't last unless you provide something and so do they. Find out what they want and tell them what you want. Strike a bargain.

4. **Keep political conflicts small and concrete.** The more abstract it gets, the more unmanageable it becomes. Separate the people from the problem. Attack problems by looking at the nature of the problem, not the person presenting the problem. Avoid direct blaming remarks; describe the problem and its impact. If you can't agree on a solution, agree on procedure, or agree on a few things, and list all the issues remaining. This creates some motion and breaks political stalemates.

F Quantity of Work Produced

ENTPs usually want to be both cutting-edge and fully competent and can get in a spiral of making whatever they are working on more and more perfect. They shine the piece to perfection and lose sight of other priorities. They get stuck on a specific task related to a goal, then pound on that issue, become distracted, and miss the deadline.

1. **Pick someone you respect and get back on track.** Talk to this person with the goal of being told when enough is enough, what's a good use of your time, and to get validation of your priorities.

2. **Are you pressure-prompted?** Can you not get really excited about a project unless the deadline is drawing near? Set fake deadlines. One of the reasons you delay is that you like pressure and dislike the ordinary. So, fool yourself. Always start 10% of each attempt immediately after it is apparent it will be needed and tell yourself it's due on Friday, that you can't leave for the weekend until you've made some progress. This has the added benefit of helping you better gauge what it is going to take to finish it. Always assume it will take more time than you think it's going to take.

3. **Finishing.** While you undoubtedly finish what you feel is reflective of your competence, other tasks get relegated to B status. ENTPs can be funny this way. You'll stick with something about which you feel strongly, but have trouble finishing as a general rule.

4. **Sometimes you get 80% of what you are pushing for with the first 20% of the effort;** it unfortunately then takes another 80% of the time to finish the last 20%. In a fast-paced world, it's sometimes tough to pull the cart all the way to the finish line when the race is over. Not all tasks have to be completely finished. For some, 80% would be acceptable. For those who need all the i's dotted and the t's crossed, it will take perseverance. The devil is in the details. When you get caught in this situation, create a checklist with the 20% that remains to be done. Plan to do a little on it each day. Cross things off and celebrate each time you get to take something off the list. Remember, it's going to challenge your motivation and attention. Try to delegate finishing to someone who would see the 20% as a fresh challenge. Get a consultant to finish it. Task trade with someone else's 20% so you both would have something fresh to do.

5. **Set better priorities.** You may not have the correct set of priorities. Some people take action but on the wrong things. Effective managers typically spend about half their time on two or three key priorities. What should you spend half your time on? Can you name five things that you have to do that are less critical? If you can't, you're not differentiating well. People without priorities see their jobs as 97 things that need to be done right now—that will actually slow you down. Pick a few mission-critical things and get them done. Don't get diverted by trivia.

6. **Working across borders and boundaries?** Do you have trouble when you have to go outside your unit to reach your goals and objectives? This means that influence skills, understanding, and trading are the currencies to use. Don't just ask for things; find some common ground where you can provide help. What do the peers you're contacting need? Are your results important to them? How does what you're working on affect their results? If it affects them negatively, can you trade something, appeal to the common good, figure out some way to minimize the work—volunteering staff help, for example? Go into peer relationships with a trading mentality. To be seen as more cooperative, always explain your thinking and invite them to explain theirs. Generate a variety of possibilities first rather than stake out positions. Be tentative, allowing them room to customize the situation. Focus on common goals, priorities, and problems. Invite criticism of your ideas.

7. **Manage your time efficiently.** Plan your time and manage against it. Be time sensitive. Value time. Figure out what you are worth per hour and minute by taking your gross salary plus overhead and benefits. Attach a monetary value on your time. Then ask, is this worth $56 of my time? Review your calendar over the past 90 days to figure out what your three largest time wasters are, and reduce them 50% by batching activities and using efficient communications like e-mail and voice mail for routine matters. Make a list of points to be covered in phone calls; set deadlines for yourself; use your best time of day for the toughest projects—if you're best in the morning, don't waste it on B and C level tasks.

G   Working With the Less Competent

ENTPs often write off problem performers without giving them a chance. Their combination of high standards and low tolerance for any delay gets in the way. As a result, they are often seen as playing favorites to high performers and giving short shrift to whomever they see as low performers.

1. **Are your problem performers confused?** Do they know what's expected of them? You may not set clear enough performance standards, goals, and objectives. You may be a seat-of-the-pants manager, and some people are struggling because they don't know what is expected or it changes. You may be a cryptic communicator. You may be too busy to communicate. You may communicate to some and not to others. You may have given up on some and stopped communicating. Or you may think they would know what to do if they're any good, but that's not really true because you have not properly communicated what you want. The first task is to outline the 5 to 10 key results areas and what indicators of success would be. Involve your problem direct reports on both ends—the standards and the indicators. Provide them with a fair way to measure their own progress. Employees with goals and standards are usually harder on themselves than you'll ever be. Often they set higher standards than you would. Sometimes the problem is behavioral, as in someone who can't control outbursts, and only affects performance on the back end in lost cooperation or sabotage. Then the best approach is to note the gap between behavior and expectations, and point out what some of the observed consequences are. If the person agrees, then coaching may suffice. If the person balks, then a 360° feedback process with follow-up may be needed to illuminate the depth of the problem before any help can be given.

2. **Realism.** They are not performing up to standard? It's common to see 90-day improve-or-else plans that no one can accomplish: be more strategic, improve your interpersonal skills, learn about the business, be less arrogant. Ask yourself how long did it take you to become proficient at what you are criticizing this person for? Because managers hesitate delivering negative messages, we get to people late. Sometimes the last five managers this person reported to saw the same difficulty, but none of them confronted the person. Get to people as soon as they do not meet agreed-upon standards of performance. Don't wait. Early is the easiest time to do it with the highest return on investment for you, them, and the organization. Most people who have reached the problem performer status will take one to two years

to turn around under the best of circumstances. It's cruel and unusual punishment to require a fixed-time turnaround or improvement plan. If your organization demands a 90-day wonder, fight it. Tell them that while a bit of improvement can be seen in that period, substantive change is not like producing a quarterly earnings statement.

3. **Starting the "improve or you're gone" process.** The first meeting. After you have made the assessment that a direct report just isn't making it, document your observations against the standards and arrange the first tough meeting. Experience directs that these first tough meetings should always be in the beginning of the week and in the mornings. They should not occur on Fridays or the day before holidays when most managers deliver them. They should not be at a time when the unit is on a bomb run getting ready for a big presentation. Start the meeting by saying "we" have a performance issue to talk about and fix. Be succinct. You have limited attention span in tough feedback situations. Don't waste time with a long preamble, just get to it. The recipient is likely to know the feedback is negative, so go ahead and say it first. They won't hear or remember anything positive you have to say anyway. Don't overwhelm the person, even if you have a lot to say. Pick the key areas and stick to them. Keep it to the facts and their impact on you, them, and your unit. Talk about specific events and situations. Plan for enough time. This is not a process to rush.

4. **Go in with an improvement plan.** Don't criticize without a solution and a plan. Tell the person what you want—paint a different outcome. Don't expect him/her to guess, and don't spend a lot of time rehashing the past. Suggest steps both of you can take to remedy the problem. Be positive but firm. Be constructive. Be optimistic in the beginning. Help him/her see the negative consequences and the potential timing—you can ask what he/she thinks and you can tell him/her what the consequences are from your side. Change starts with seeing an unacceptable consequence and a way out. "Improve or else" threats don't work.

H Communicating More Fully

ENTPs are often terse in their communications, assuming others understand the message.

1. **Don't inform enough.** Do you think that the big picture is obvious and should be transparent to them? No need to explain the links or

how they fit in? Being aware of the bigger picture motivates people. They want to know what to do in order to do their jobs and more. How does what they are doing fit into the larger picture? What are the other people working on and why? Many people think that's unnecessary information and that it would take too much time to do. They're wrong. The sense of doing something worthwhile is the number two motivator at work! It results in a high return on motivation and productivity. (Try to increase the amount of more-than-your-job information you share.) Focus on the impact on others by figuring out who information affects. Put five minutes on your meeting agenda. Ask people what they want to know and, assuming it's not confidential information, tell them. Pick a topic each month to tell your people about.

2. **Share your thinking.** To help those around you grow and learn from what you know, you have to sometimes think out loud. You have to share your thinking from the initial presentation of the issue through to conclusion. Most of us are on thinking autopilot. We don't think about thinking. When someone else has to or wants to understand how you came up with a decision, it's sometimes difficult to unravel it in your mind. You have to go step-by-step and recreate your thinking. Sometimes it helps if other people ask the questions. They can probably guide you through how you came up with an answer or a decision better than you can. Once in a while, you should document a decision or two. What was the issue? What were the pros and cons you considered? How did you weight things? Then you can use those examples to demonstrate to others how you make decisions.

Overusing ENTP Tendencies

If you sometimes overdo your preferred behaviors, you may need to work on:

A   Being Less Hypercritical

B   Arrogance

C   Composure/Impulsiveness

D   Being Appropriately Ambitious

E   Better Peer Relationships

F   Dealing With Routine and Procedures

G   More Work/Life Balance

ISTJ	ISFJ	INFJ	INTJ
ISTP	ISFP	INFP	INTP
ESTP	ESFP	ENFP	ENTP
ESTJ	ESFJ	ENFJ	ENTJ

A   Being Less Hypercritical

ENTPs are outspoken, which is both a virtue and a problem. "When," "why," and "why not" are typical questions for ENTPs. Sometimes these are seen as helpful and sometimes these are seen as disdainful and skeptical.

1.   **Under extended stress, you can become hypercritical of others** and find an endless list of reasons for the unacceptability of some action or fact. You appear skeptical and touchy. Accept this for what it is—you. Think of it as your personal preferences speaking rather than reality. Seek feedback to find out what is really going on.

2.   **Go to someone you trust and respect and ask this person to assess the people in question.** Ask them to tell you the assets of these people. When you get into hypercritical mode, you often don't see them.

3.   **Sometimes you ask too many questions,** not to be critical, but because your idea-generation program has been triggered. Although this may appear critical to others, the real issue is you need to turn your program off and just do it as designed. Four ideas to make a procedure better won't help the work get done today. Pick a few causes to change. For the others, just execute them.

4.   **In meetings, make sure you include everyone,** and don't direct substantially more remarks toward one person or subgroup to the

exclusion of others. Make sure you signal nothing negative to others; a neutral observer should not be able to tell from your demeanor whom you like and don't like. Help the quiet, shy, and reserved have their say. Quiet the loud, assertive, and passionate. Give everyone a fair chance to be heard.

5. **You should work doubly hard at observing others.** Always select your interpersonal approach from the other person in, not from you out. Your best choice of approach will always be determined by the other person or group, not you. Think about each transaction as if the other person were a customer you wanted. How would you craft an approach?

6. **Listening.** Interpersonally skilled people are very good at listening. They listen to understand and take in information to select their response. They listen without interrupting. They ask clarifying questions. They don't instantly judge. Judgment might come later. They restate what the other person has said to signal understanding. They nod. They might jot down notes. Listeners get more data.

7. **You must constantly observe others' reactions to you** to be good at adjusting to others. You must watch the reactions of people to what you are saying and doing while you are doing it in order to gauge their response. Are they bored? Change the pace. Are they confused? State it in a different way. Are they angry? Stop and ask what the problem is. Are they too quiet? Stop and get them involved in what you are doing. Are they fidgeting, scribbling on their pads, or staring out the window? They may not be interested in what you are doing. Move to the end of your presentation or task, end it, and exit. Check in with your audience frequently and select a different tactic if necessary. As Warren Bennis notes, "Being a first-class noticer allows leaders to recognize talent, identify opportunities, and avoid pitfalls. Leaders who succeed...are geniuses at grasping context."

8. **Equity with information.** Follow the rule of equity of information with everyone. Explain your thinking and ask them to explain theirs. When discussing issues, give reasons first, solutions last. When you give solutions first, people often don't listen to your reasons. Some people get overly directive with some of their reports, and they, in turn, feel that you're not interested in what they think. Invite their thinking and their reasons before settling on solutions. Don't provide information selectively. Don't use information as a reward or a relationship builder with one or just a few and not others.

9. **Pause to:**

    ■   Edit your actions before you act. Before you speak or act in problem situations, ask yourself if you would do the same thing in a parallel situation. Is your value really what should be operating here?

    ■   Pick your battles. Make sure you only pull rank and impose your values on others in really mission-critical situations.

B Arrogance

ENTPs are usually very accomplished at what they do and can transparently show their displeasure with slowness or lack of top performance.

1. **Watch your non-verbals.** Arrogant people look, talk, and act arrogantly. As you try to become less arrogant, you need to find out what your non-verbals are. All arrogant people do a series of things that can be viewed by a neutral party and judged to give off the signals of arrogance. Washboard brow. Facial expressions. Body shifting, especially turning away. Impatient finger or pencil tapping. False smile. Tight lips. Looking away. Find out from a trusted friend what you do, and try to eliminate those behaviors.

2. **You may view feedback as information,** but this can come across that you just don't care and can increase perceptions of aloofness. Make sure to say thank you for the feedback. Because you may be seen as quite powerful and having high standards, if you don't say thank you or find something to praise or verify in the feedback, you can be seen as indifferent or dismissive.

3. **Although ENTPs are rarely defensive,** they can be if the feedback comes when they are upset about performance or slowness. You will need to work on keeping yourself in a calm state when getting negative feedback. You need to change your thinking. When getting the feedback, your only task is to accurately understand what people are trying to tell you. It is not your task at that point to accept or reject. That comes later. Mentally rehearse how you will calmly react to tough feedback situations before they happen. Develop automatic tactics to shut down or delay your usual emotional response. Some useful tactics are to slow down, take notes, ask clarifying questions, ask them for concrete examples, and thank them for telling you since you know it's not easy for them.

4. **Do you value feedback only from those you feel have the experience and expertise to offer it?** If someone points out that you could be somewhat more accommodating, is your reaction to whom, for what purpose, and will that move us toward the goal? Go to the people you respect most and get their feedback on your pluses and minuses. Then think about what modifications in your behavior would help you push your vision through more effectively.

5. **Answers. Solutions. Conclusions. Statements. Dictates.** That's the staple of arrogant people. Instant output. Sharp reactions. This may be getting you in trouble. You jump to conclusions, categorically dismiss what others say, use challenging words in an absolute tone. People then see you as closed to their input or combative. More negatively, they may believe you think they're stupid or ill-informed. Give people a chance to talk without interruption. If you're seen as intolerant or closed, people will often stumble over words in their haste to talk with you or shortcut their argument since they assume you're not listening anyway. Ask a question, invite them to disagree with you, present their argument back to them softly, let them save face no matter what. Add a 15-second pause into your transactions before you say anything, and add two clarifying questions per transaction to signal you're listening and want to understand.

6. **You may be highly intelligent and quite skilled in your area.** You may work around people who aren't as informed or educated as you are. You may be in a position of essentially dictating what should be done. But you don't have to make it demeaning or painful. You need to switch to a teacher/guru role—tell them how you think about an issue, don't just fire out solutions. Tell them what you think the problem is, what questions need to be asked and answered, how you would go about finding out, and what you think some likely solutions might be. Work to pass on your knowledge and skills.

C Composure/Impulsiveness

ENTPs often lose their composure when disappointed.

1. **If you lose your composure with certain people but not others,** a good practice to follow is when your emotions rise to a challenge of your fairness, count to five in your head, then respond with a clarifying question. This serves the triple purpose of giving the person a second chance, allows you to compose yourself, and may prevent

you from jumping to an incorrect conclusion and taking precipitous action.

2. **Blame and vengeance?** Do you feel a need to punish the people and groups that set you off? Do you become hostile, angry, sarcastic, or vengeful? While all that may be temporarily satisfying to you, they will all backfire and you will lose in the long term. When someone attacks you, rephrase it as an attack on a problem. Reverse the argument—ask what they would do if they were in your shoes. When the other side takes a rigid position, don't reject it. Ask why: What are the principles behind the offer? How do we know it's fair? What's the theory of the case? Play out what would happen if their position was accepted. Let the other side vent frustration or blow off steam, but don't react. When you do reply to an attack, keep it to the facts and their impact on you. It's fine for you to draw conclusions about the impact on yourself—"I felt blindsided." It's not fine for you to tell others their motives—"You blindsided me" means you did it, probably meant to, and I know the meaning of your behavior. So state the meaning for yourself; ask others what their actions meant.

3. **Listening chillers?** Don't interrupt before they have finished. Don't suggest words when they hesitate or pause. Don't finish their sentences for them. Don't wave off any further input by saying, "Yes, I know that." "Yes, I know where you're going." "Yes, I have heard that before." If time is really important, you can say, "Let me see if I know where this is going...," or "I wonder if we could summarize to save both of us some time?" Finally, early in a transaction, answers, solutions, conclusions, statements, and dictates shut many people down. You've told them your mind is already made up. Listen first, solve second.

4. **Questions.** Good listeners ask lots of questions to get to a good understanding. Probing questions. Clarifying questions. Confirming— is this what you are saying—questions. Ask one more question than you do now and add to that until people signal you that they think you are truly listening.

5. **Listening to those who waste a lot of time.** With those you don't have time to listen to, switch to being a teacher. Try to help them craft their communications to you in a more acceptable way. Tell them to be shorter next time. Come with more/less data. Structure the conversation by helping them come up with categories and structures to stop their rambling. Good listeners don't signal to the "bad" people that they are not listening or are not interested. Don't signal to anyone

what bucket they're in. Put your mind in neutral, nod, ask questions, be helpful.

6. **Listening to people you don't like.** What do people see in them who do like them or can at least get along with them? What are their strengths? Do you have any common interests? Talk less and ask more questions to give them a second chance. Don't judge their motives and intentions—do that later.

7. **Listening to people you like but...**

   ■ They are disorganized. Interrupt to summarize and keep the discussion focused. While interrupting is generally not a good tactic, it's necessary here.

   ■ They just want to chat. Ask questions to focus them; don't respond to chatty remarks.

   ■ They want to unload a problem. Assume when people tell you something they are looking for understanding; indicate that by being able to summarize what they said. Don't offer any advice.

   ■ They are chronic complainers. Ask them to write down problems and solutions and then let's discuss it. This turns down the volume while, hopefully, moving them off complaining.

   ■ They like to complain about others. Ask if they've talked to the person. Encourage them to do so. If that doesn't work, summarize what they have said without agreeing or disagreeing.

8. **Impatience triggers.** Some people probably bring out your impatience more than others. Who are they? What is it about them that makes you more impatient? Pace? Language? Thought process? Accent? These people may include people you don't like, who ramble, who whine and complain, or who are repetitive advocates for things you have already rejected. Mentally rehearse some calming tactics before meeting with people who trigger your impatience. Work on understanding their positions without evaluating them. In all cases, focus them on the issues or problems to be discussed, return them to the point, summarize, and state your position. Try to gently train them to be more efficient with you next time without damaging them in the process.

9. **Work on your openness and approachability.** Impatient people don't get as much information as patient listeners do. They are more often

surprised by events when others knew they were coming. People are hesitant to talk to impatient people. It's too painful. People don't pass on hunches, unbaked thoughts, maybes, and possibles to impatient people. You will be out of the information loop and miss important information you need to know to be effective. Suspend judgment on informal communications. Just take it in. Acknowledge that you understand. Ask a question or two. Follow up later.

10. **Rein in your horse.** Impatient people provide answers, conclusions, and solutions too early in the process. Others haven't even understood the problem yet. Providing solutions too quickly will make your people dependent and irritated. If you don't teach them how you think and how you can come up with solutions so fast, they will never learn. Take the time to really define the problem—not impatiently throw out a solution. Brainstorm what questions need to be answered in order to resolve it. Give your people the task to think about for a day and come back with some solutions. Be a teacher instead of a dictator of solutions. Study yourself. Keep a journal of what triggered your behavior and what the observed consequences were. Learn to detect and control your triggers before they get you in trouble.

11. **Task impatience.** Impatient people check in a lot. How's it coming. Is it done yet? When will it be finished? Let me see what you've done so far. That is disruptive to due process and wastes time. When you give out a task or assign a project, establish agreed-upon time checkpoints. You can also assign percentage checkpoints. Check in with me when you are about 25% finished so we can make midcourse corrections and 75% finished so we can make final corrections. Let them figure out how to do the task. Hold back from checking in at other than the agreed-upon times and percentages.

12. **Defining the problem.** Instant and early conclusions, solutions, statements, suggestions, and how we solved it in the past, are the enemies of good problem solving. Studies show that defining the problem and taking action occur almost simultaneously for most people, so the more effort you put on the front end, the easier it is to come up with a good solution. Stop and first define what the problem is and isn't. Since providing solutions is so easy for everyone, it would be nice if they were offering solutions to the right problem. Figure out what causes it. Keep asking why. See how many causes you can come up with and how many organizing buckets you can put them in. This increases the chance of a better solution because you can see more connections. Be a chess master. Chess masters recognize thousands of

patterns of chess pieces. Look for patterns in data; don't just collect information. Put it in categories that make sense to you. Ask lots of questions. Allot at least 50% of the time to defining the problem.

13. **Watch your biases.** Some people have solutions in search of problems. They have favorite solutions. They have biases. They have universal solutions to most situations. They pre-judge what the problem is without stopping to consider the nuances of this specific problem. Do honest and open analysis first. Did you state as facts things that are really assumptions or opinions? Are you sure these assertions are facts? Did you generalize from a single example? One of your solutions may in fact fit, but wait to see if you're right about the problem.

14. **Asking others for input.** Many try to do too much themselves. They don't delegate, listen, or ask others for input. Even if you think you have the solution, ask some others for input just to make sure. Access your network. Find someone who makes a good sounding board and talk to her/him, not just for ideas, but to increase your understanding of the problem. Or do it more formally. Set up a competition between two teams, both acting as your advisors. Call a problem-solving meeting and give the group two hours to come up with something that will at least be tried. Find a buddy group in another function or organization that faces the same or a similar problem and both of you experiment.

D Being Appropriately Ambitious

ENTPs are always looking for the next challenge and can be seen as mainly out for themselves.

1. **Self-marketing needs to be done with great political care.** Don't wear out your welcome. While people are usually positive about moderate self-promotion, they turn off quickly to what they consider too much or self-promotion that's too loud. Who really matters? Approach them once or twice carefully and with moderation. Don't share your ambitions with people who don't play a part in your future. And never, never bad-mouth competitors for a promotion. This will say far more about you than it says about them.

2. **How much time do you spend helping others solve problems vs. pushing your own agenda?** Are you viewed as a loner? Do you help peers, help direct reports develop, visibly work to build a team? You may be trying to blame others for things you should take

responsibility for. You may be making up excuses that are not real to cover for yourself. You may be trying to make your rivals look bad so that you look better. You may hedge when asked a tough question. You may slap things together to look good when what's underneath wouldn't pass the test. You may be disorganized and your actions cause problems for others. You may indicate little or no concern for others. If you do any of these things or things like it, you will eventually be found out, and you will lose the future you have been marketing yourself for. Stop them all.

3. **Values or facts?** You may be a fact-based person. Since to you the facts dictate everything, you may be baffled as to why people would see it any differently than you do. The reason they see it differently is that there is a higher order of values at work. People compare across situations to check for common themes, equity, and parity. They ask questions like who wins and loses here, who is being favored, is this a play for advantage? Since you are a here-and-now person, you will look inconsistent to them across slightly different situations. You need to drop back and ask what will others hear, not what you want to say. Go below the surface. Tell them why you're saying something. Ask them what they think.

4. **Do you promote the careers of others as well as your own?** Do you help other people solve their problems or do they only help you solve yours? People will tolerate more ambition from you if you have a demonstrated track record of helping others get ahead as well.

5. **Do you do all the presenting for your group to top management?** Sometimes that's a sign of being overly ambitious. Let others present sometimes. Try to gain stature with top management through the success of your people. Usually that's just as fast a track to a career as is doing everything yourself. Executives quickly notice people builders, those who surround themselves with high performers.

6. **Too independent?** You set your own rules, smash through obstacles, see yourself as tough, action oriented, and results oriented. You get it done. The problem is, you wreak havoc for others; they don't know which of your actions will create headaches for them in their own unit or with customers. You don't often worry about whether others think like you do. You operate from the inside out. What's important to you is what you think and what you judge to be right and just. In a sense, admirable. In a sense, not smart. You live in an organization that has both formal and informal commonly held standards, beliefs, ethics, and values. You can't survive long without knowing what they are

and bending yours to fit. To find out, focus on the impact on others and how they see the issue. This will be hard at first since you spend your energy justifying your own actions.

E Better Peer Relationships

ENTPs' impatience often comes out with peers whom they perceive as blocking them or slowing them down.

1. **Influencing.** Peers generally do not have power over each other. That means that influence skills, understanding, and trading are the currencies to use. Don't just ask for things; find some common ground where you can provide help. What do the peers you're contacting need? Do you really know how they see the issue? Is it even important to them? How does what you're working on affect them? If it affects them negatively, can you trade something, appeal to the common good, figure out some way to minimize the work (volunteering staff help, for example)? Go into peer relationships with a trading mentality.

2. **Sometimes the problem is maneuvering through the complex maze called the organization.** How do you get things done sideways? Who are the movers and shakers in the organization? How do they get things done? Who do they rely on for expediting things through the maze? Who are the major gatekeepers who control the flow of resources, information, and decisions? Who are the guides and the helpers? Get to know them better. Who are the major resisters and stoppers? Try to avoid or go around them.

3. **If peers see you as excessively competitive,** they will cut you out of the loop and may sabotage your cross-border attempts. To be seen as more cooperative, always explain your thinking and invite them to explain theirs. Generate a variety of possibilities first rather than stake out positions. Be tentative, allowing them room to customize the situation. Focus on common goals, priorities, and problems. Invite criticism of your ideas.

4. **If peers think you lack respect for them or what they do,** try to keep conflicts as small and concrete as possible. Separate the people from the problem. Don't get personal. Don't give peers the impression you're trying to dominate or push something on them. Without agreeing or disagreeing, try on their views for size. Can you understand their viewpoint? When peers blow off steam, don't react; return to facts and the problem, staying away from personal clashes.

Allow others to save face; concede small points; don't try to hit a home run every time. When a peer takes a rigid position, don't reject it. Ask why: What are the principles behind the position? How do we know it's fair? What's the theory of the case? Play out what would happen if his/her position was accepted.

5. **Separate working smoothly with peers from personal relationships,** contests, competing for incentives, one-upsmanship, not-invented-here, pride, and ego. Working well with peers over the long term helps everyone, makes sense for the organization, and builds a capacity for the organization to do greater things. Usually the least-used resource in an organization is lateral exchanges of information and resources.

6. **If a peer doesn't play fair, avoid telling others all about it.** This often boomerangs. What goes around comes around. Confront the peer directly, politely, and privately. Describe the unfair situation; explain the impact on you. Don't blame. Give the peer the chance to explain, ask questions, let him/her save some face, and see if you can resolve the matter. Even if you don't totally accept what is said, it's better to solve the problem than win the argument.

7. **Monitor yourself in tough situations to get a sense of how you are coming across.** What's the first thing you attend to? How often do you take a stand vs. make an accommodating gesture? What proportion of your comments deals with relationships vs. the issue to be addressed? Mentally rehearse for worst-case scenarios/hard-to-deal-with people. Anticipate what the person might say and have responses prepared so as not to be caught off guard.

F Dealing With Routine and Procedures

ENTPs are interested in the hunt for solutions to many problems. Anything smacking of bureaucracy or restrictions irritates, and they will often ignore procedures.

1. **Try to see the value in routines.** Pick a plan or procedure and do a historical analysis of how it came to be and why it is necessary. Resist the urge to change it or question its usefulness. Understand it first.

2. **Turn off your answer program.** We all have a need to provide answers as soon as possible to questions and problems. We all have preconceived notions, favorite solutions, and prejudices that prevent our intellectual skills from dealing with the real facts of the problem.

For one-half of the time you have to deal with an issue or a problem, shut off your solution machine and just take in the facts.

3. **Compensate for your dislikes.** Find a person you admire and respect to deal with all the procedures you find oppressive. Let this person tell you if anything needs changing. Otherwise, trust his or her judgment.

G More Work/Life Balance

ENTPs can verge on being workaholics so likely are they to involve themselves in 50 things at once. They are always out of time.

1. **All your eggs in one basket?** Add things to your off-work life. This was a major finding of a stress study at AT&T of busy, high-potential women and men. It may seem counterintuitive, but the best-adjusted people forced themselves to structure off-work activities just as much as on-work activities. Otherwise work drives everything else out. Those with dual responsibilities (primary care giver and home manager and a full-time jobholder) need to use their management strengths and skills more at home. What makes your work life successful? Batch tasks, bundle similar activities together, delegate to children, or set up pools with coworkers or neighbors to share tasks, such as car pooling, soccer games, Scouts, etc. Pay to have some things done that are not mission-critical to your home needs. Organize and manage efficiently. Have a schedule. Set up goals and plans. Use some of your work skills more off-work.

2. **Balance has nothing to do with 50/50 or clock time.** It has to do with how we use the time we have. It doesn't mean for every hour of work, you must have an hour off-work. It means finding what is a reasonable balance for you. Is it a few hours a week unencumbered by work worries? Is it four breaks a day? Is it some solitude before bedtime? Is it playing with your kids more? Is it having an actual (rather than "Did you remember the dry cleaning?") conversation with your spouse (partner) each day? Is it a community, religious, or sports activity that you're passionate about? Schedule them; structure them into your life. Negotiate with your partner; don't just accept your life as a given. Define what balance is for you, and include your spouse or friends or family in the definition.

3. **What are your NOs?** If you don't have any, chances are you'll be frustrated on both sides of your life. Part of maturity is letting go of nice, even fun and probably valuable, activities. What are you

hanging on to? What can't you say no to at the office that really isn't a priority? Where do you make yourself a patsy? If your saying no irritates people initially, this may be the price. You can usually soften it, however, by explaining what you are trying to do. Most people won't take it personally if you say you're going to pick up your child or maybe coach his/her soccer team or you can't help with this project because of an explicit priority which is critical to your unit. Give reasons that don't downgrade the activity you're giving up. It's not that it's insignificant; it just didn't quite make the cut.

*Perfectionism has become an obsession with me.
I am critical and demanding of others, often leading me to reject solutions just because I don't think they are correct.*

– An ENTP Manager

APPLICATION

Your personal preferences play out in day-to-day problems and situations you face. Below is a case about your type dealing with such a situation. Use this to think through how you will integrate the tips you've considered and coach yourself to be more effective in your type.

ENTP Application Situation (Part 1)

You get a call from the CEO of a financial services firm, asking if you're available to provide some coaching to his new Vice President of Product Development. When Rebecca was hired, the executive team was impressed with her enthusiasm, innovative ideas, and her ability to move fluidly from one topic to another. They also felt that her quick wit would help her ease into the environment, and that her apparent agility in getting along with a variety of people would ensure a smooth integration. While they haven't changed their minds about her, the CEO admits that there is, at the highest levels, disappointment with results. You agree to meet with her.

In your initial meeting, you learn that Rebecca came into the organization with a mandate to be the "idea leader," the person who could look at the complex environment in which the organization competed, and leveraging her talent at improvising, point the way for the company to differentiate itself and gain market share. She is enthusiastic in telling you how inspired she is to do that. But she's frustrated by what she says seems to be a "plodding, overly cautious, detail-obsessed" group of peers.

"What kind of feedback have you gotten from your boss or your peers on your performance?" you ask her.

"Nothing direct," she says. "Just a feeling that they often seem to be impatient with me. Frankly, I've heard that there are a couple of them who seem to think I'm arrogant, and I'm really not. I'm not sure where that's coming from. As a matter of fact, as someone in product development, I'm always open to other people's ideas. At my previous place of employment, I was known as the 'Queen of Brainstorming,'" she laughs.

"Would you want to use a multi-rater process to get some data we could look at next time we meet?"

"Sure," she says, smiling enthusiastically. "Let's go for it. I'm sure there'll be plenty in there to chew on. Can I offer you some gum?" She takes a piece herself and holds out the packet to you.

"No thanks." You agree to help her with the multi-rater process and set up a meeting for four weeks out. "Oh, by the way," you turn at the door to ask, "do you happen to know your Myers-Briggs type?"

"Solidly ENTP," she says. "My previous employer had everyone to complete the inventory, but they didn't follow up very much on the results. Curious, since they spent so much money on the testing. But then again, that company spent money on a lot of things and then never followed up."

"I'll call you on Monday about the multi-rater," you say, as a way to close the deal, but also to bring the conversation back into focus as you leave.

Thinking It Through: Strategy

- What kinds of things do you want to look for in getting data to help Rebecca?

- Given your knowledge that she's an ENTP—which didn't surprise you—what particular areas will you focus on?

- What questions about her job performance (present and past) do you think you'd want to ask Rebecca in preparation for your next meeting with her?

Planning It Out: Tactics

- What barriers to Rebecca's effectiveness (i.e., actions, behaviors) do you anticipate you would find if you were to interview her peers and direct reports?

- What particular areas would present developmental challenges to Rebecca, and what competencies would you want to see her put into play in order to help her meet the expectations of the executive team?

- Which of the tactics described in the Being More Effective section are applicable in this situation?

- Which Overused Tendencies are most likely to come into play here?

ENTP Application Situation (Part 2)

You've gathered the multi-rater assessment data and conducted some interviews. Here's some of what you learned:

- There is strong rater agreement that Rebecca is weak at decision making.

- Her peers see her as easily distracted; her direct reports often feel left behind; her boss sees her as indifferent to details and follow-through.

Reflection

- Where are you going to begin in coaching Rebecca. What can she work on? What can she do to compensate for some of these improvement needs?

- What in her strengths can she rely on to improve her performance while she's working to minimize the liabilities?

SUGGESTED READINGS

■■■■■■■■ Being a More Effective ENTP ■■■■■■■■

Handling Disagreements

Carter, Les. *The Anger Trap: Free Yourself From the Frustrations That Sabotage Your Life*. New York: John Wiley & Sons, Inc., 2003.

Cloke, Ken and Joan Goldsmith. *Resolving Conflicts at Work: A Complete Guide for Everyone on the Job*. San Francisco: Jossey-Bass, Inc., 2000.

Dana, Daniel. *Conflict Resolution*. New York: McGraw-Hill Trade, 2000.

Guttman, Howard M. *When Goliaths Clash: Managing Executive Conflict to Build a More Dynamic Organization*. New York: AMACOM, 2003.

Masters, Marick Francis and Robert R. Albright. *The Complete Guide to Conflict Resolution in the Workplace*. New York: AMACOM, 2002.

Team Building

Bolton, Robert. *People Skills*. New York: Simon & Schuster, 1979.

Fisher, Kimball and Mareen Duncan Fisher. *The Distance Manager: A Hands-On Guide to Managing Off-Site Employees and Virtual Teams*. New York: McGraw-Hill Trade, 2000.

Harvard Business School Press. *Harvard Business Review on Teams That Succeed*. Boston: Harvard Business School Press, 2004.

Katzenbach, Jon R. and Douglas K. Smith. *The Wisdom of Teams: Creating the High-Performance Organization*. New York: HarperBusiness, 2003.

Parker, Glenn M. *Cross-Functional Teams: Working With Allies, Enemies, and Other Strangers*. San Francisco: Jossey-Bass, Inc., 2002.

Peters, Tom. *Thriving on Chaos: Handbook for a Management Revolution.* New York: HarperCollins, 1987.

Raymond, Cara Capretta, Robert W. Eichinger and Michael M. Lombardo. *FYI for Teams.* Minneapolis, MN: Lominger Limited, Inc., 2001–2004.

Robbins, Harvey and Michael Finley. *The New Why Teams Don't Work— What Goes Wrong and How to Make It Right.* San Francisco: Berrett-Koehler Publishers, Inc., 2000.

Caring and Compassion

Autry, James A. *The Art of Caring Leadership.* New York: William Morrow and Company, Inc., 1991.

Brantley, Jeffrey and Jon Kabat-Zinn. *Calming Your Anxious Mind: How Mindfulness and Compassion Can Free You From Anxiety, Fear, and Panic.* Oakland, CA: New Harbinger Publications, 2003.

Daniels, Aubrey C. *Bringing Out the Best in People.* New York: McGraw-Hill, Inc., 1994.

Kouzes, James M. and Barry Z. Posner. *Encouraging the Heart: A Leader's Guide to Rewarding and Recognizing Others.* San Francisco: Jossey-Bass, Inc., 2003.

Stone, Douglas. *Difficult Conversations: How to Discuss What Matters Most.* New York: Penguin Books, 2000.

Planning and Organizing

Allen, David. *Getting Things Done: The Art of Stress-Free Productivity.* New York: Penguin Books, 2003.

Bossidy, Larry, Ram Charan and Charles Burck (Contributor). *Execution: The Discipline of Getting Things Done.* New York: Crown Business Publishing, 2002.

Byfield, Marilyn. *It's Hard to Make a Difference When You Can't Find Your Keys: The Seven-Step Path to Becoming Truly Organized.* New York: Viking Press, 2003.

Drucker, Peter F. *The Effective Executive.* New York: HarperBusiness, 2002.

Gleeson, Kerry. *The Personal Efficiency Program: How to Get Organized to Do More Work in Less Time.* New York: John Wiley & Sons, Inc., 2000.

Kotter, John P. *The General Managers.* New York: The Free Press, 1982.

Stone, Florence M. and Randi T. Sachs. *The High-Value Manager — Developing the Core Competencies Your Organization Needs.* New York: AMACOM, 1995.

Political Savvy

Ashkenas, Ronald N. (Ed.), Dave Ulrich, Todd Jick, Steve Kerr and Lawrence A. Bossidy. *The Boundaryless Organization: Breaking the Chains of Organization Structure, Revised and Updated.* New York: John Wiley & Sons, Inc., 2002.

Aubuchon, Norbert. *The Anatomy of Persuasion.* New York: AMACOM, 1997.

Baker, Wayne E. *Networking Smart.* New York: Backinprint.com, 2000.

Bolton, Robert and Dorothy Grover Bolton. *People Styles at Work — Making Bad Relationships Good and Good Relationships Better.* New York: AMACOM, 1996.

Brache, Alan P. *How Organizations Work.* New York: John Wiley & Sons, Inc., 2002.

Dobson, Michael S. and Deborah S. Dobson. *Enlightened Office Politics: Understanding, Coping With and Winning the Game — Without Losing Your Soul.* New York: AMACOM, 2001.

Quantity of Work Produced

Block, Peter. *The Answer to How Is Yes: Acting On What Matters.* San Francisco: Berrett-Koehler Publishers, Inc., 2001.

Bossidy, Larry, Ram Charan and Charles Burck (Contributor). *Execution: The Discipline of Getting Things Done.* New York: Crown Business Publishing, 2002.

Holland, Winford E. Dutch. *Change Is the Rule: Practical Actions for Change: On Target, on Time, on Budget.* Chicago: Dearborn Trade Publishing, 2000.

Panella, Vince. *The 26 Hour Day: How to Gain at Least Two Hours a Day With Time Control.* Franklin Lakes, NJ: Career Press, 2002.

Working With the Less Competent

Graham, Gini. *A Survival Guide for Working With Humans: Dealing With Whiners, Back-Stabbers, Know-It-Alls, and Other Difficult People.* New York: AMACOM, 2004.

Levin, Robert A. and Joseph G. Rosse. *Talent Flow: A Strategic Approach to Keeping Good Employees, Helping Them Grow, and Letting Them Go.* New York: John Wiley & Sons, Inc., 2001.

Solomon, Muriel. *Working With Difficult People.* New York: Prentice Hall, 2002.

Communicating More Fully

Arredondo, Lani. *Communicating Effectively.* New York: McGraw-Hill Trade, 2000.

Keyton, Joann. *Communicating in Groups: Building Relationships for Effective Decision Making.* New York: WCB/McGraw-Hill, 2002.

McCormack, Mark H. *On Communicating.* Los Angeles: Dove Books, 1998.

Zeuschner, Raymond F. *Communicating Today: The Essentials.* Boston: Allyn & Bacon, 2002.

■■■■■■■■ Overusing ENTP Tendencies ■■■■■■■■

Being Less Hypercritical

Carter, Les. *The Anger Trap: Free Yourself From the Frustrations That Sabotage Your Life.* New York: John Wiley & Sons, Inc., 2003.

Ellis, Albert, Ph.D. *How to Control Your Anxiety Before It Controls You.* New York: Citadel Press, 2000.

Lerner, Harriet. *The Dance of Connection: How to Talk to Someone When You're Mad, Hurt, Scared, Frustrated, Insulted, Betrayed, or Desperate.* New York: Quill/HarperCollins, 2002.

Patterson, Kerry, Joseph Grenny, Ron McMillan, Al Switzler and Stephen R. Covey. *Crucial Conversations: Tools for Talking When Stakes Are High.* New York: McGraw-Hill/Contemporary Books, 2002.

Arrogance

Bolton, Robert and Dorothy Grover Bolton. *People Styles at Work—Making Bad Relationships Good and Good Relationships Better.* New York: AMACOM, 1996.

Carter, Les. *The Anger Trap: Free Yourself From the Frustrations That Sabotage Your Life.* New York: John Wiley & Sons, Inc., 2003.

Ellis, Albert, Ph.D. *How to Control Your Anxiety Before It Controls You.* New York: Citadel Press, 2000.

Waldroop, James, Ph.D. and Timothy Butler, Ph.D. *Maximum Success: Changing the 12 Behavior Patterns That Keep You From Getting Ahead.* New York: Doubleday, 2000.

Composure/Impulsiveness

Barker, Larry, Ph.D. and Kittie Watson, Ph.D. *Listen Up: At Home, at Work, in Relationships: How to Harness the Power of Effective Listening.* Irvine, CA: Griffin Trade Paperback, 2001.

Bolton, Robert and Dorothy Grover Bolton. *People Styles at Work—Making Bad Relationships Good and Good Relationships Better.* New York: AMACOM, 1996.

Carter, Les. *The Anger Trap: Free Yourself From the Frustrations That Sabotage Your Life.* New York: John Wiley & Sons, Inc., 2003.

Ellis, Albert, Ph.D. *How to Control Your Anxiety Before It Controls You.* New York: Citadel Press, 2000.

Lerner, Harriet. *The Dance of Connection: How to Talk to Someone When You're Mad, Hurt, Scared, Frustrated, Insulted, Betrayed, or Desperate.* New York: Quill/HarperCollins, 2002.

Patterson, Kerry, Joseph Grenny, Ron McMillan, Al Switzler and Stephen R. Covey. *Crucial Conversations: Tools for Talking When Stakes Are High.* New York: McGraw-Hill/Contemporary Books, 2002.

Being Appropriately Ambitious

Champy, James and Nitin Nohria. *The Arc of Ambition.* Cambridge, MA: Perseus Publishing, 2000.

Dotlich, David L. and Peter C. Cairo. *Why CEOs Fail.* San Francisco: Jossey-Bass, Inc., 2003.

Schweich, Thomas A. *Staying Power: 30 Secrets Invincible Executives Use for Getting to the Top—And Staying There.* New York: McGraw-Hill, Inc., 2003.

Waldroop, James, Ph.D. and Timothy Butler, Ph.D. *Maximum Success: Changing the 12 Behavior Patterns That Keep You From Getting Ahead.* New York: Doubleday, 2000.

Better Peer Relationships

Baker, Wayne E. *Networking Smart.* New York: Backinprint.com, 2000.

Bolton, Robert and Dorothy Grover Bolton. *People Styles at Work—Making Bad Relationships Good and Good Relationships Better.* New York: AMACOM, 1996.

Cartwright, Tatula. *Managing Conflict With Peers.* Greensboro, NC: Center for Creative Leadership, 2003.

Patterson, Kerry, Joseph Grenny, Ron McMillan, Al Switzler and Stephen R. Covey. *Crucial Conversations: Tools for Talking When Stakes Are High.* New York: McGraw-Hill/Contemporary Books, 2002.

Dealing With Routine and Procedures

Bossidy, Larry, Ram Charan and Charles Burck (Contributor). *Execution: The Discipline of Getting Things Done.* New York: Crown Business Publishing, 2002.

Keen, Peter G.W. *The Process Edge—Creating Value Where It Counts.* Boston: Harvard Business School Press, 1998.

Lawler, Edward E., III, Susan Albers Mohrman and George Benson. *Organizing for High Performance: Employee Involvement, TQM, Reengineering, and Knowledge Management in the Fortune 1000: The CEO Report.* San Francisco: Jossey-Bass, Inc., 2001.

Niven, P.R. *Balanced Scorecard Step-by-Step: Maximizing Performance and Maintaining Results.* New York: John Wiley & Sons, Inc., 2002.

More Work/Life Balance

Glanz, Barbara. *Balancing Acts.* Chicago, IL: Dearborn Trade Publishing, 2003.

Gordon, Gil E. *Turn It Off: How to Unplug From the Anytime-Anywhere Office Without Disconnecting Your Career.* New York: Three Rivers Press, 2001.

Merrill, A. Roger and Rebecca R. Merrill. *Life Matters: Creating a Dynamic Balance of Work, Family, Time & Money.* New York: McGraw-Hill, Inc., 2003.

St. James, Elaine. *Simplify Your Work Life: Ways to Change the Way You Work So You Have More Time to Live.* New York: Hyperion, 2001.

CHAPTER 13

ESTJ
Extraverted Thinking
with
Introverted Sensing

■■■■■■■■■■■■■■■■

8.7% of Population
15.8% of Managers

■■■■■■■■■■■■■■■■

Typical Strengths

Practical
Like to Run Things
Results Driven
Time Efficient
Organized
Decisive
Planful and Orderly
Team Approach

ISTJ	ISFJ	INFJ	INTJ
ISTP	ISFP	INFP	INTP
ESTP	ESFP	ENFP	ENTP
ESTJ	ESFJ	ENFJ	ENTJ

I haven't found a situation yet I couldn't tackle.
If you want to make things happen, put me in charge.

– An ESTJ Manager

Basic Habits of Mind

Extraverted Thinking casts a critical, analytical eye on experience. ESTJs usually place value on order and reasonableness via the "rules" and standard practices. Their decision process is aided by Introverted Sensing, which drives them to collect concrete information about experiences, people, and circumstances.

Introverted Intuiting and Introverted Feeling also help ESTJs. These are evident when ESTJs discuss long-term outcomes with passion and commitment. Introverted Intuiting provides this strong sense of future outcomes. Introverted Feeling promotes their passion for realistic and planful answers.

This combination is sometimes misinterpreted as demanding, rigid, impatient, and overly tactical.

Typical Communication Patterns

- Energetic and direct, ESTJs communicate practical and realistic information about situations before them.
- They like facts and are drawn to ask questions for clarity and precision.
- Their remarks are logical, orderly, and quite decisive.

General Learning Strategy

- ESTJs usually prefer sequential, active, competitive, problem-solving opportunities when learning new ideas or frameworks.
- Typical learning strategies are doing something with information— making lists, charts, and spreadsheets.
- Their learning is generally helped by demonstrations and hands-on, practical activities.

Interpersonal Qualities Related to Motivation

■ Give them the logical framework, the specific facts, and a method-ological way to address a situation, and ESTJs are highly motivated.

■ Thorough and orderly critiques move them to take action.

Blind Spots

■ ESTJs might be surprised to learn that others feel that they may develop problems with interpersonal relationships.

■ Others expect ESTJs will have difficulty in making strategic transitions.

Stress Related Behavior

■ They may become more demanding and instructive as stressors are pressing on them.

■ As stress increases, ESTJs can be seen as aggressive, arrogant, and stingy with resources.

■ With enough stress, they can become hypersensitive to rejection and focus on the incompetence of those around them.

Potential Barriers to Effectiveness

■ ESTJs need to learn more effective ways to build and mend relationships.

■ Of special attention, they usually need to focus on creating a devel-opmental climate with direct reports.

■ Often technically competent, they can mistake conformance to their instructions as respect for their ability.

Being a More Effective ESTJ

A **Interpersonal Savvy**
B **Developing Direct Reports**
C **Personal Creativity**
D **Dealing With Ambiguity**
E **Communicating More Completely**

ISTJ	ISFJ	INFJ	INTJ
ISTP	ISFP	INFP	INTP
ESTP	ESFP	ENFP	ENTP
ESTJ	ESFJ	ENFJ	ENTJ

A Interpersonal Savvy

ESTJs are speedy and task oriented. Sometimes this comes across to others as not being terribly interested in others. They often do not pick up or acknowledge the emotional side of life.

1. **One key to getting anything of value done in the work world** is the ability to see differences in people and to manage against and use those differences for everyone's benefit. Interpersonal savvy is meeting each person where he/she is to get done what you need to get done. Basically, people respond favorably to ease of transaction and inclusion. If you make it easy by accepting their normal mode of doing things, not fighting their style, and neither defending your own nor letting style get in the way of performance, things will generally run smoothly.

2. **If you're uncomfortable with strong displays of emotion and calls for personal help,** simply imagine how you would feel in this situation and respond with that. Tell the person how sorry you are this has happened or has to be dealt with. Offer whatever help is reasonable. A day off. A loan. A resource. If you can, offer hope of a better day. This is what the person can use most.

3. **You start.** Being approachable means you have to initiate the transaction. You have to put out your hand first. Make first eye contact. Note the color of the person's eyes to ensure good eye contact. You have to ask the first question or share the first piece of information. You have to make the first three minutes comfortable for the other person or group so they can accomplish what they came to you to do.

4. **How to start.** Start with three things you can talk about with almost anyone without risking uncomfortable personal disclosure. Vacations, hobbies, business interests, your thinking on business issues, children,

etc. Decide what they are and make a conscious effort to sprinkle them into some of your interactions with others you have generally had only a business relationship with before. Notice the reaction. Did they also share for the first time? Usually yes. And that's the point. Within limits, the more you know about each other, the better the working relationship will be.

5. **Listen.** Approachable people are very good at listening. They listen without interrupting. They ask clarifying questions. They don't instantly judge. They listen to understand. Judgment may come later. They restate what the other person has said to signal understanding. They nod. They may jot down notes. Listeners don't always offer advice or solutions unless it's obvious the person wants to know what they would do.

6. **Sharing.** Approachable people share more information and get more in return. Confide your thinking on a business issue and invite the response of others. Pass on tidbits of information you think will help people do their jobs better or broaden their perspectives. Disclose some things about yourself. It's hard for people to relate to an enigma. Reveal things that people don't need to know to do their jobs, but which will be interesting to them—and help them feel valued.

7. **Personalizing.** Approachable people work to know and remember important things about the people they work around, for, and with. Know three things about everybody—their interests or their children or something you can chat about other than the business agenda. Treat life as a small world. If you ask a few questions, you'll find you have something in common with virtually anyone. Establish things you can talk about with each person you work with that go beyond strictly work transactions. These need not be social—they could be issues of strategy, global events, market shifts. The point is to forge common ground and connections.

8. **Watch your non-verbals.** Approachable people appear and sound open and relaxed. They smile. They are calm. They keep eye contact. They nod while the other person is talking. They have an open body posture. They speak in a paced and pleasant tone. Eliminate any disruptive habits, such as speaking too rapidly or forcefully, using strongly worded or loaded language, or going into too much detail. Watch out for signaling disinterest with actions like glancing at your watch, fiddling with paperwork, or giving your impatient "I'm busy" look.

9. **The magic of questions.** Many people don't ask enough curiosity questions when in their work mode. There are too many informational statements, conclusions, suggestions, and solutions and not enough "what if," "what are you thinking," "how do you see that." In studies, statements outweighed questions 8 to 1. Ask more questions than others. Make fewer solution statements early in a discussion. Keep probing until you understand what they are trying to tell you.

B Developing Direct Reports

ESTJs tend to focus more on task completion and the good of the overall organization. They may not spend as much effort on individual development as they do on directing individuals to do work.

1. **Use goals to motivate.** Most people are turned on by reasonable goals. They like to measure themselves against a standard. They like to see who can run the fastest, score the most, and work the best. They like goals to be realistic but stretching. People try hardest when they have somewhere between one-half and two-thirds chance of success and some control over how they go about it. People are even more motivated when they participate in setting the goals. Set just-out-of-reach challenges and tasks that will be first time for people—their first negotiation, their first solo presentation, etc.

2. **More what and why, less how.** The best delegators are crystal clear on what and when, and more open on how. People are more motivated when they can determine the how for themselves. Inexperienced delegators include the hows, which turn the people into task automatons instead of an empowered and energized staff. Tell them what and when and for how long, and let them figure out how on their own. Give them leeway. Encourage them to try things. Besides being more motivating, it's also more developmental for them. Add the larger context. Although it is not necessary to get the task done, people are more motivated when they know where this task fits in the bigger picture. Take three extra minutes and tell them why this task needs to be done, where it fits in the grander scheme, and its importance to the goals and objectives of the unit.

3. **Monitoring delegated tasks.** Do you micromanage? If you're constantly looking over shoulders, you're not delegating. A properly communicated and delegated task doesn't need to be monitored. If you must monitor, set time-definite checkpoints: by the calendar,

every Monday, by percentage, after each 10% is complete, or by outcome—such as when you have the first draft. Be approachable for help, but not intrusive. Intervene only when agreed-upon criteria are not being followed or expectations are not being met. This focuses on the task, not the person. Let people finish their work.

4. **Delegate for development.** Brainstorm with your direct reports all the tasks that aren't being done but are important to do. Ask them for a list of tasks that are no longer challenging for them. (You can also use parts of your own job to develop others. Take three tasks that are no longer developmental for you, but would be for others, and delegate them.) Trade tasks and assignments between two direct reports; have them do each other's work. Assign each of your direct reports an out-of-comfort-zone task that meets the following criteria: The task needs to be done, the person hasn't done it or isn't good at it, and the task calls for a skill the person needs to develop. Remember to focus on varied assignments—more of the same isn't developmental.

5. **Do you help your people learn by looking for repeating patterns?** Help them look for patterns in the situations and problems they deal with. What succeeded and what failed? What was common to each success or what was present in each failure but never present in a success? Focus on the successes; failures are easier to analyze but don't in themselves tell you what would work. Comparing successes, while less exciting, yields more information. The bottom line is help them reduce insights to principles or rules of thumb that might be repeatable. Ask them what they have learned to increase their skills and understanding, making them better managers or professionals. Ask them what they can do now that they couldn't do a year ago. Reinforce this and encourage more of it. Developing is learning in as many ways as possible.

6. **Feedback.** People need continuous feedback from you and others to grow. Some tips about feedback:

   ■ Arrange for them to get feedback from multiple people, including yourself, on what matters for success in their future jobs; arrange for your direct reports to get 360° feedback about every two years.

   ■ Give them progressively stretching tasks that are first-time and different for them so that they can give themselves feedback as they go.

- If they have direct reports and peers, another technique to recommend is to ask their associates for comments on what they should stop doing, start doing, and keep doing to be more successful.

- You have to be willing to be straight with your people and give them accurate but balanced feedback. Give as much real-time feedback as you have time for. Most people are motivated by process feedback against agreed-upon goals for three reasons. First, it helps them adjust what they are doing along the way in time to better achieve the goal; they can make midcourse corrections. Second, it shows them what they are doing is important and that you're there to help. Third, it's not the "gotcha" game of negative and critical feedback after the fact. If there are negatives, they need to know as soon as possible.

- Set up a buddy system so people can get continuing feedback.

- If your organization has a mentoring program, find out how it works. Best practices begin with those to be mentored writing down goals, objectives, and development needs. They are then carefully matched with mentors and the relationship is outlined. How often will the people meet? On what topics is the mentor to be helpful? What are the responsibilities of the person to be mentored? If your organization doesn't have such a program, look at setting one up within your unit or function.

C Personal Creativity

ESTJs tend to be straight-ahead analytical thinkers. Many could benefit from taking risks outside of areas where they already know they'll be successful. They need to do more brainstorming and getting creativity out of a group.

1. **Unearthing creative ideas.** Creative thought processes do not follow the formal rules of logic, where one uses cause and effect to prove or solve something. Some rules of creative thought are:

   - Not using concepts but changing them; imagining this were something else.

   - Move from one concept or way of looking at things to another, such as from economic to political.

   - Generate ideas without judging them initially.

- Use information to restructure and come up with new patterns.

- Jump from one idea to another without justifying the jump.

- Look for the least likely and odd.

- Look for parallels far from the problem, such as how is an organization like a big oak tree?

- Ask what's missing or what's not here.

- Fascination with mistakes and failure as learning devices.

2. **Increasing group creativity:** Selecting a group. During World War II, it was discovered that teams of people with the widest diversity of backgrounds produced the most creative solutions to problems. The teams included people who knew absolutely nothing about the area (i.e., an English major working on a costing problem). When attacking a tough problem which has eluded attempts to solve it, get the broadest group you can. Involve different functions, levels, and disciplines. Pull in customers and colleagues from other organizations. Remember that you're looking for fresh approaches; you're not convening a work task force expected to implement or judge the practicality of the notions. Believe it or not, it doesn't matter if they know anything about the problem or the technology required to deal with it. That's your job.

3. **Increasing group creativity:** Define the problem first. A straightforward technique to enable creativity is brainstorming. Anything goes for an agreed-upon time. Throw out ideas, record them all, no evaluation allowed. Many people have had bad experiences with brainstorming. Silly ideas. Nothing practical. A waste of time. This usually happens because the problem gets defined in the same old way. First, define the problem well. Allot hours to this, not two minutes to sketch the problem. Challenge your thinking—are you generalizing from one or two cases? How do you know the causes are really causes? They may simply be related. What is fact and what is assumption?

4. **Increasing group creativity:** Facilitating the process. Here are three methods commonly used:

- Brainstorming. Outline the problem for the group; tell them what you've tried and learned from the tries. Include things that may have happened only once. Invite the group to free-form respond. Any idea is okay—no criticism allowed. Record all

425

ideas on a flip chart. When the group has exhausted the possibilities, take the most interesting ones and ask the group to first name positive features of the ideas, then negative features, and finally what's interesting about the ideas. Follow this process until you've covered all the ideas that interest you. Then ask the group what else they would select as interesting ideas to do a plus, minus, interesting analysis. This process can usually be done in an hour or two.

- The nominal group. After the problem definition above, have the group write down as many ideas as occur to them. Record them all on a flip chart for freewheeling discussion. People can add, combine or clarify—"What were you thinking when you said...," but no criticism allowed. After this, follow the plus, minus, interesting process above.

- Analogies. Lots of creative solutions come from analogies to nature or other fields. Come up with a list (electrical engineering, cats, trees, the sea, biology, shipbuilding), any list will do, and insert it after you describe the problem to the group in the first or second option. Many times this will trigger novel ideas that no other process will.

5. **Value-added approaches.** To be more personally creative, immerse yourself in the problem. Getting fresh ideas is not a speedboating process; it requires looking deeply.

- Carve out dedicated time—study the problem deeply, talk with others, look for parallels in other organizations and in remote areas totally outside your field. If your response to this is that you don't have the time, that also usually explains why you're not having any fresh ideas.

- Think out loud. Many people don't know what they know until they talk it out. Find a good sounding board and talk to him/her to increase your understanding of a problem or a technical area. Talk to an expert in an unrelated field. Talk to the most irreverent person you know. Your goal is not to get his/her input, but rather his/her help in figuring out what you know—what your principles and rules of thumb are.

- Practice picking out anomalies—unusual facts that don't quite fit, like sales going down when they should have gone up. What do these odd things imply for strategy? Naturally creative people are much more likely to think in opposite cases when confronted with a problem. Turn the problem upside down: Ask what is the least likely thing it could be, what the problem is not, what's missing from the problem, or what the mirror image of the problem is.

■ Look for distant parallels. Don't fall into the mental trap of searching only in parallel organizations because "only they would know." Back up and ask a broader question to aid in the search for solutions. When Motorola wanted to find out how to process orders more quickly, they went not to other electronics firms, but to Domino's Pizza and Federal Express. For more ideas, an interesting—and fun—book on the topic is *Take the Road to Creativity and Get Off Your Dead End* by David Campbell.

6. **Don't like risk?** Sometimes taking action involves pushing the envelope, taking chances, and trying bold new initiatives. Doing those things leads to more misfires and mistakes. Research says that successful executives have made more mistakes in their careers than those who didn't make it. Treat any mistakes or failures as chances to learn. Nothing ventured, nothing gained. Up your risk comfort. Start small so you can recover more quickly. Go for small wins. Don't blast into a major task to prove your boldness. Break it down into smaller tasks. Take the easiest one for you first. Then build up to the tougher ones. Review each one to see what you did well and not well, and set goals so you'll do something differently and better each time. End up accomplishing the big goal and taking the bold action. Challenge yourself. See how creative you can be in taking action a number of different ways.

7. **Experiment and learn.** Whether the ideas come from you or a brainstorming session, encourage yourself to do quick experiments and trials. Studies show that 80% of innovations occur in the wrong place, are created by the wrong people (dye makers developed detergent, Post-it® Notes was a failed glue experiment), and 30–50% of technical innovations fail in tests within the company. Even among those that make it to the marketplace, 70–90% fail. The bottom line on change is a 95% failure rate, and the most successful innovators try lots of quick, inexpensive experiments to increase the chances of success. Watch several episodes of *Modern Marvels*, a cable television program on the History Channel, which answers the question "How did they do that?" You can buy the series.

D Dealing With Ambiguity

ESTJs excel as doers and are concrete and specific in orientation. Ambiguous situations calling for intuition and redefinitions of issues are not easy for them.

1. **Incrementalism.** The essence of dealing comfortably with uncertainty is the tolerance of errors and mistakes, and absorbing the possible heat and criticism that follow. Acting on an ill-defined problem with no precedents to follow means shooting in the dark with as informed a decision as you can make at the time. People who are good at this are incrementalists. They make a series of smaller decisions, get instant feedback, correct the course, get a little more data, move forward a little more, until the bigger problem is under control. They don't try to get it right the first time. Many problem-solving studies show that the second or third try is when we really understand the underlying dynamics of problems. They also know that the more uncertain the situation is, the more likely it is they will make mistakes in the beginning. So, you need to work on two practices: Start small so you can recover more quickly. Do little somethings as soon as you can and get used to heat.

2. **Perfectionist?** Need or prefer or want to be 100% sure? Lots might prefer that. Perfectionism is tough to let go of because most people see it as a positive trait for themselves. Recognize your perfectionism for what it might be—collecting more information than others to improve your confidence in making a fault-free decision and thereby avoiding risk and criticism. Try to decrease your need for data and your need to be right all the time slightly every week until you reach a more reasonable balance between thinking it through and taking action. Try making some small decisions on little or no data. Anyone with a brain and 100% of the data can make good decisions. The real test is who can act the soonest with a reasonable amount, but not all, of the data. Some studies suggest successful general managers are about 65% correct. Trust your intuition. Let your brain do the calculations.

3. **Locate the essence of the problem.** What are the key factors or elements in this problem? Experts usually solve problems by figuring out what the deep, underlying principles are and working forward from there; the less adept focus on desired outcomes/solutions and either work backward or concentrate on the surface facts. What are the deep principles of what you're working on? Once you've done this, search the past for parallels—your past, the business past, the historical past.

4. **Finishing.** Do you prefer to finish what you have started? Do you have a high need to complete tasks? Wrap them up in nice clean packages? Working well with ambiguity and under uncertainty means moving from incomplete task to incomplete task. Some may be abandoned, some may never be finished. They'll probably only ever get 80% done, and you'll constantly have to edit your actions and decisions. Change your internal reward process toward feeling good about fixing mistakes and moving things forward incrementally, more than finishing any given project.

E Communicating More Completely

ESTJs excel as in-close communicators, but often are less comfortable with big-picture or mission statement communications. They tend to focus on facts and details and not think through how to influence their audience.

1. **Crafting the message.** C.K. Prahalad, one of the leading strategic consultants, believes that in order to qualify as a mission statement, it should take less than three minutes to explain it clearly to an audience. Really effective mission statements are simple, compelling, and capable of capturing people's imagination. Mission statements should help everyone allot his/her time. They should signal what's mission-critical and explain what's rewarded in the organization and what's not. Create a simple obvious symbol, visual, or slogan to make the cause come alive. Ford's "Quality is Job One" seems clear enough. Nordstrom's "The Customer is Always Right" tells employees how they should do their jobs. Although the actual mission and vision document would be longer, the message needs to be finely crafted to capture the essence of what's important around here.

2. **Common mind-set.** The power of a mission and vision communication is providing everyone in the organization with a road map on how they are going to be part of something grand and exciting. Establish common cause. Imagine what the change would look like if fully implemented, then describe the outcome often—how things will look in the future. Help people see how their efforts fit in by creating simple, obvious measures of achievement like bar or thermometer charts. Be succinct. People don't line up behind laundry lists or ambiguous objectives. Missions and visions should be more about where we are going and less about how we are going to get there. Keep your eyes on the prize.

3. **When public speaking, use your strengths.** Treat it as a technical task. Make a checklist. What's your objective? What's your point? What are five things you want them to remember? What would the ideal audience member say if interviewed 15 minutes after you finish? Who's your audience? How much do they know? What are five techniques you will use to hold their attention? What presentation technology would work best? What questions will the audience have? What's the setting? How much time do you have—always take a few minutes less, never more.

4. **Preparing a speech.** State your message or purpose in a single sentence. In other words, do the ending first. Then outline the three to five chunks of your argument to support your thesis. Any more and the audience won't follow it. Sometimes putting main concepts on index cards and shuffling them into order can accomplish this. A famous minister said, "No souls are saved after 20 minutes." Many speeches must be longer than this, but can still be divided into sections with clear conclusions, and a hard bridge to the next related topic.

5. **Walking someone else's talk.** A common paradox is having to support someone else's program or idea when you don't really think that way or agree with it. You have to be a member of the loyal opposition. Most of the time, you may be delivering someone else's view of the future. Top management and a consultant created the mission, vision, and strategy off somewhere in the woods. You may or may not have been asked for any input. You may even have some doubts about it yourself. Do not offer conditional statements to your audience. Don't let it be known to others that you are not fully on board. Your role is to manage this vision and mission, not your personal one. If you have strong contrary views, be sure to demand a voice next time around.

6. **Don't inform enough.** Are you a minimalist? Do you tell people only what they need to know to do their little piece of the puzzle? People are motivated by being aware of the bigger picture. They want to know what to do in order to do their jobs and more. How does what they are doing fit into the larger picture? What are the other people working on and why? Many people think that's unnecessary information and that it would take too much time to do. They're wrong. The sense of doing something worthwhile is the number two motivator at work! It results in a high return on motivation and productivity. (Try to increase the amount of more-than-your-job information you share.) Focus on the impact on others by figuring out

who information affects. Put five minutes on your meeting agenda. Ask people what they want to know and, assuming it's not confidential information, tell them. Pick a topic each month to tell your people about.

7. **A loner.** Do you keep to yourself? Work alone or try to? Do you hold back information? Do you parcel out information on your schedule? Do you share information to get an advantage or to win favor? Do people around you know what you're doing and why? Are you aware of things others would benefit from, but you don't take the time to communicate? In most organizations, these things and things like it will get you in trouble. Organizations function on the flow of information. Being on your own and preferring peace and privacy are okay as long as you communicate things to bosses, peers, and teammates that they need to know and would feel better if they knew. Don't be the source of surprises.

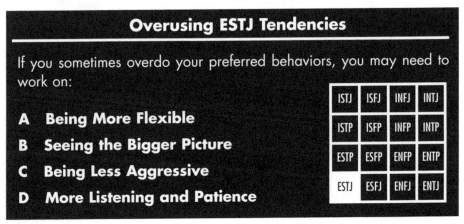

Overusing ESTJ Tendencies

If you sometimes overdo your preferred behaviors, you may need to work on:

A Being More Flexible

B Seeing the Bigger Picture

C Being Less Aggressive

D More Listening and Patience

ISTJ	ISFJ	INFJ	INTJ
ISTP	ISFP	INFP	INTP
ESTP	ESFP	ENFP	ENTP
ESTJ	ESFJ	ENFJ	ENTJ

A Being More Flexible

ESTJs can be impatient, not show much warmth, and confront people quite directly who act in less than a totally responsible way.

1. **You may be seen as rigid in your values stances and unwilling to accept, or even see, those of others.** Rigid stances often come from childhood and early adult experiences. You may have reduced your beliefs to rigid commandments. You need to know why you hold these values and critically examine whether they are appropriate here. Statements of belief are pronouncements—a true value holds up to action scrutiny; you can say why you hold it, how it plays out in

different situations, and what happens when it conflicts with other values.

2. **You may view feedback as information,** but this can come across that you just don't care and can increase perceptions of aloofness. Make sure to say thank you for the feedback. Because you may be seen as quite powerful and having high standards, if you don't say thank you or find something to praise or verify in the feedback, you can be seen as indifferent or dismissive.

3. **Although ESTJs are rarely defensive,** they can be if the feedback comes when they are upset about performance or slowness. You will need to work on keeping yourself in a calm state when getting negative feedback. You need to change your thinking. When getting the feedback, your only task is to accurately understand what people are trying to tell you. It is not your task at that point to accept or reject. That comes later. Mentally rehearse how you will calmly react to tough feedback situations before they happen. Develop automatic tactics to shut down or delay your usual emotional response. Some useful tactics are to slow down, take notes, ask clarifying questions, ask them for concrete examples, and thank them for telling you since you know it's not easy for them.

4. **Transitions.** Which transitions are the toughest for you? Write down the five toughest for you. What do you have a hard time switching to and from? Use this knowledge to assist you in making a list of discontinuities (tough transitions) you face, such as confronting people vs. being approachable and accepting, leading vs. following, going from firing someone to a business-as-usual staff meeting. Write down how each of these discontinuities makes you feel and what you may do that gets you in trouble. For example, you may not shift gears well after a confrontation, or you may have trouble taking charge again after passively sitting in a meeting all day. Create a plan to attack each of the tough transitions.

5. **Control your instant responses to shifts.** Many of us respond to the fragmentation and discontinuities of work as if they were threats instead of the way life is. Sometimes our emotions and fears are triggered by switching from active to passive or soft to tough. This initial anxious response lasts 45–60 seconds, and we need to buy some time before we say or do something inappropriate. Research shows that generally somewhere between the second and third thing you think to say or do is the best option. Practice holding back your first

response long enough to think of a second and a third. Manage your shifts, don't be a prisoner of them.

6. **Use mental rehearsal to think about different ways you could carry out a transaction.** Try to see yourself acting in opposing ways to get the same thing done—when to be tough, when to let them decide, when to deflect the issue because it's not ready to decide. What cues would you look for to select an approach that matches? Practice trying to get the same thing done with two different groups with two different approaches. Did they both work?

7. **Avoid early rigid positions.** It's just physics. Action gets equal reaction. Strong statements. Strongly worded positions. Casting blame. Absolutes. Lines in the sand. Unnecessary passion. All of these will be responded to in kind, will waste time, cause ill will, and possibly prevent a win-win or a something-something. It only has a place in one-time, either/or negotiations, and even there it isn't recommended. Similarly, watch out for overcommitment to any need or course of action. Look for information that goes against your preferences. Be able to adjust your position and your wants. If you can't, your ego is getting the best of you. If you can't walk away until you get X, you'll probably either overpay or blow the negotiation. Don't negotiate around a single issue if you can add another. This is another situation that leads to rigidity.

8. **Selective resistance.** Do you adapt to some and not to others? You probably have good people buckets and bad people buckets and signal your disagreement with them to the bad bucket groups or individuals. You may have good group buckets and bad group buckets—gender, race, age, origin. Learn to understand without accepting or judging. Listen, take notes, ask questions, and be able to make their case as well as they can. Pick something in their argument you agree with. Present your argument in terms of the problem only—why you think this is the best manner to deal with a mutually agreed-upon problem. A careful observer should not be able to tell your assessment of people or their arguments at the time. Find someone who is a fair observer and get a critique. Was I fair? Did I treat everyone the same? Were my objections based on reasoning against standards and not directed at people?

9. **Go for more variety at work.** Take a risk, then play it safe. Set tasks for yourself that force you to shift gears, such as being a spokesperson for your organization when tough questions are expected, making peace with an enemy, or managing people who are novices at a task.

If you already have these tasks as part of your job, use them to observe yourself and try new behaviors.

B Seeing the Bigger Picture

ESTJs often show little interest in broader issues which go beyond today's problems. At times they can appear disinterested in intangible issues.

1. **Not curious?** Many managers are so wrapped up in today's problems that they aren't curious about tomorrow. They really don't care about the long-term future. They may not even be in the organization when the strategic plan is supposed to happen. They believe there won't be much of a future until we perform today. Being a visionary and a good strategist requires curiosity and imagination. It requires playing "what ifs." What are the implications of the growing gap between rich and poor? The collapse of retail pricing? The increasing influence of brand names? What if it turns out there is life on other planets, and we get the first message? What will that change? Will they need our products? What will happen when a larger percentage of the world's population is over the age of 65? The effects of terrorism? What if cancer is cured? Heart disease? AIDS? Obesity? What if the government outlaws or severely regulates some aspect of your business? True, nobody knows the answers, but good strategists know the questions. Work at developing broader interests outside your business. Subscribe to different magazines. Pick new shows to watch. Meet different people. Join a new organization. Look under some rocks. Think about tomorrow. Talk to others about what they think the future will bring.

2. **Narrow perspective?** Some are sharply focused on what they do and do it very well. They have prepared themselves for a narrow but satisfying career. Then someone tells them their job has changed, and they now have to be strategic. Being strategic requires a broad perspective. In addition to knowing one thing well, it requires that you know about a lot of things somewhat. You need to understand business. You need to understand markets. You need to understand how the world operates. You need to put all that together and figure out what all that means to your organization.

3. **Too busy?** Strategy is always last on the list. Solving today's problems, of which there are many, is job one. You have to make time for strategy. A good strategy releases future time because it makes choices clear and leads to less wasted effort, but it takes time to do.

Delegation is usually the main key. Give away as much tactical day-to-day stuff as you can. Ask your people what they think they could do to give you more time for strategic reflection. Another key is better time management. Put an hour a week on your calendar for strategic reading and reflection throughout the year. Don't wait until one week before the strategic plan is due. Keep a log of ideas you get from others, magazines, etc. Focus on how these impact your organization or function.

4. **Can't think strategically?** Strategy is linking several variables together to come up with the most likely scenario. Think of it as the search for and application of relevant parallels. It involves making projections of several variables at once to see how they come together. These projections are in the context of shifting markets, international affairs, monetary movements, and government interventions. It involves a lot of uncertainty, making risk assumptions, and understanding how things work together. How many reasons would account for sales going down? Up? How are advertising and sales linked? If the dollar is cheaper in Asia, what does that mean for our product in Japan? If the world population is aging and they have more money, how will that change buying patterns? Not everyone enjoys this kind of pie-in-the-sky thinking and not everyone is skilled at doing it.

C Being Less Aggressive

ESTJs can get very aggressive when people don't perform up to their high expectations. They can be especially tough on problem performers. The issue, though, is that they often don't involve people enough and don't volunteer much feedback.

1. **Maybe you run a bad tape in your head.** Under enough stress, you start to question others' motives, judge them negatively, and feel slighted. Check it out. Ask people what is going on. Don't assume you know or that whatever they are doing has anything to do with you. Ask them what you should keep doing, start doing, and stop doing. If this is left unchecked, you might appear judgmental and unforgiving to others due to slights, real or not real.

2. **Go to someone you trust and respect and ask this person to assess the people in question.** Ask them to tell you the assets of these people. When you get into hypercritical mode, you often don't see them.

3. **Let your team help you.** Periodically, send out a memo asking each person whether there is anything he or she thinks he/she could do that you are now doing or monitoring too closely. Pick one or two things per person and empower them to do it on their own. Make sure the up-front communication is adequate for them to perform well. Explain your standards—what the outcome should be, the key things that need to be taken care of—then ask them to figure out how to do it themselves.

4. **If you are impatient and find yourself checking in too frequently,** set up a timetable with your people with agreed-upon checkpoints and in-progress checks. Let them initiate this on a schedule you are comfortable with. Ask yourself who your most motivating bosses were. Chances are they gave you a lot of leeway, encouraged you to try things, were good sounding boards, and cheered your successes. Do what they did with you.

5. **Are you hanging on to too much?** Are you a perfectionist, wanting everything to be just so? Do you have unrealistic expectations of others? Someone made you leader because you are probably better at doing what the team does than some or most of the members. Be careful to set the goals and objectives in a realistic and motivating manner.

6. **Do you delegate but withhold the power and authority to get the job done?** Delegating the work without the authority to make process or how-to decisions is demotivating. People grow if they have a chance to decide and succeed or fail on their own.

7. **What skill do you have that you could pass on to others?** Ask yourself why this is a strength for you. What are the first items you would teach as the keys to help others form umbrellas for understanding? Watch others carefully for their reactions when teaching and coaching. What works and doesn't work for you as a coach? Reveal things that people don't need to know to do their jobs, but which will be interesting to them—and help them feel valued.

8. **To better figure out what drives people, look to:** What do they do first? What do they emphasize in their speech? What do they display emotion around? What values play out for them?

   ■ First things. Does this person go to others first, hole up and study, complain, discuss feelings, or take action? These are the basic orientations of people that reveal what's important to them. Use these to motivate.

- Speech content. People might focus on details, concepts, feelings, or other people in their speech. This can tell you again how to appeal to them by mirroring their speech emphasis. Although most of us naturally adjust—we talk details with detail-oriented people—chances are good that in problem relationships you're not finding the common ground. She talks "detail" and you talk "people," for example.

- Emotion. You need to know what people's hot buttons are because one mistake can get you labeled as insensitive with some people. The only cure here is to see what turns up the volume for them—either literally or what they're concerned about.

- Values. Apply the same thinking to the values of others. Do they talk about money, recognition, integrity, efficiency in their normal work conversation? Figuring out what their drivers are tells you another easy way to appeal to anyone.

9. **Pay particular attention to non-verbal cues.** Common signals of trouble are changes in body posture (especially turning away), crossed arms, staring, or the telltale glancing at one's watch, scribbling on the pad, tapping fingers or the pencil, looking out the window, frowns, and washboard foreheads. When this occurs, pause. Ask a question. Ask how we're doing. Do a live process check. Some people use the same body language to signal that they are done or not interested in what's going on. Get to know their signals. Construct an alternative plan for the five people you work with closely: When Bill begins to stare, I will.... When Sally interrupts for the third time, I will....

10. **Are your problem performers confused?** Do they know what's expected of them? You may not set clear enough performance standards, goals, and objectives. You may be a seat-of-the-pants manager, and some people are struggling because they don't know what is expected or it changes. You may be a cryptic communicator. You may be too busy to communicate. You may communicate to some and not to others. You may have given up on some and stopped communicating. Or you may think they would know what to do if they're any good, but that's not really true because you have not properly communicated what you want. The first task is to outline the 5 to 10 key results areas and what indicators of success would be. Involve your problem direct reports on both ends—the standards and the indicators. Provide them with a fair way to measure their own

progress. Employees with goals and standards are usually harder on themselves than you'll ever be. Often they set higher standards than you would. Sometimes the problem is behavioral, as in someone who can't control outbursts, and only affects performance on the back end in lost cooperation or sabotage. Then the best approach is to note the gap between behavior and expectations, and point out what some of the observed consequences are. If the person agrees, then coaching may suffice. If the person balks, then a 360° feedback process with follow-up may be needed to illuminate the depth of the problem before any help can be given.

11. **Realism.** They are not performing up to standard? It's common to see 90-day improve-or-else plans that no one can accomplish: be more strategic, improve your interpersonal skills, learn about the business, be less arrogant. Ask yourself how long did it take you to become proficient at what you are criticizing this person for? Because managers hesitate delivering negative messages, we get to people late. Sometimes the last five managers this person reported to saw the same difficulty, but none of them confronted the person. Get to people as soon as they do not meet agreed-upon standards of performance. Don't wait. Early is the easiest time to do it with the highest return on investment for you, them, and the organization. Most people who have reached the problem performer status will take one to two years to turn around under the best of circumstances. It's cruel and unusual punishment to require a fixed-time turnaround or improvement plan. If your organization demands a 90-day wonder, fight it. Tell them that while a bit of improvement can be seen in that period, substantive change is not like producing a quarterly earnings statement.

12. **Starting the "improve or you're gone" process.** The first meeting. After you have made the assessment that a direct report just isn't making it, document your observations against the standards and arrange the first tough meeting. Experience directs that these first tough meetings should always be in the beginning of the week and in the mornings. They should not occur on Fridays or the day before holidays when most managers deliver them. They should not be at a time when the unit is on a bomb run getting ready for a big presentation. Start the meeting by saying "we" have a performance issue to talk about and fix. Be succinct. You have limited attention span in tough feedback situations. Don't waste time with a long preamble, just get to it. The recipient is likely to know the feedback is negative, so go ahead and say it first. They won't hear or remember anything positive you have to say anyway. Don't overwhelm the

person, even if you have a lot to say. Pick the key areas and stick to them. Keep it to the facts and their impact on you, them, and your unit. Talk about specific events and situations. Plan for enough time. This is not a process to rush.

13. **Go in with an improvement plan.** Don't criticize without a solution and a plan. Tell the person what you want—paint a different outcome. Don't expect him/her to guess, and don't spend a lot of time rehashing the past. Suggest steps both of you can take to remedy the problem. Be positive but firm. Be constructive. Be optimistic in the beginning. Help him/her see the negative consequences and the potential timing—you can ask what he/she thinks and you can tell him/her what the consequences are from your side. Change starts with seeing an unacceptable consequence and a way out. "Improve or else" threats don't work.

14. **Don't forget the pathos of the situation**—even if you're totally right, feelings will run high. If you have to be critical, you can still empathize with how he/she feels, and you can help with encouragement when the discussion turns more positive. Allow him/her to save face; concede some small points; don't rush the human process of grieving.

D More Listening and Patience

When they think standards are not being met, ESTJs can be very pressuring.

1. **Listening chillers?** Don't interrupt before they have finished. Don't suggest words when they hesitate or pause. Don't finish their sentences for them. Don't wave off any further input by saying, "Yes, I know that." "Yes, I know where you're going." "Yes, I have heard that before." If time is really important, you can say, "Let me see if I know where this is going...," or "I wonder if we could summarize to save both of us some time?" Finally, early in a transaction, answers, solutions, conclusions, statements, and dictates shut many people down. You've told them your mind is already made up. Listen first, solve second.

2. **Questions.** Good listeners ask lots of questions to get to a good understanding. Probing questions. Clarifying questions. Confirming—is this what you are saying—questions. Ask one more question than you do now and add to that until people signal you that they think you are truly listening.

3. **Selective listening.** Whom do you listen to? Whom don't you listen to? What factors account for the difference? Level? Age? Skills? Smarts? Like you/not like you? Gender? Direction (listen up but not down)? Setting? Situation? Your needs? Time available? Race? People I need/don't need? People who have something to offer/those who don't? Challenge yourself to practice listening to those you don't usually listen to. Listen for content. Separate the content from the person. Try to ferret out some value from everyone.

4. **Listening to those who waste a lot of time.** With those you don't have time to listen to, switch to being a teacher. Try to help them craft their communications to you in a more acceptable way. Tell them to be shorter next time. Come with more/less data. Structure the conversation by helping them come up with categories and structures to stop their rambling. Good listeners don't signal to the "bad" people that they are not listening or are not interested. Don't signal to anyone what bucket they're in. Put your mind in neutral, nod, ask questions, be helpful.

5. **Listening under duress.** What if you're being criticized or attacked personally? What if people are wrong in what they are saying? The rules remain the same. You need to work on keeping yourself in a calm state when getting negative feedback. You need to shift your thinking. When getting the feedback, your only task is to accurately understand what the person is trying to tell you. It is not, at that point, to accept or refute. That comes later. Practice verbal Aikido, the ancient art of absorbing the energy of your opponent, and using it to manage him/her. Let the other side vent but don't react directly. Listen. Nod. Ask clarifying questions. But don't vent yourself. Don't judge. Keep him/her talking until he/she runs out of venom. Separate the person from the feedback.

6. **Listening to people you don't like.** What do people see in them who do like them or can at least get along with them? What are their strengths? Do you have any common interests? Talk less and ask more questions to give them a second chance. Don't judge their motives and intentions—do that later.

7. **Listening to people you like but...**

- They are disorganized. Interrupt to summarize and keep the discussion focused. While interrupting is generally not a good tactic, it's necessary here.

- They just want to chat. Ask questions to focus them; don't respond to chatty remarks.

- They want to unload a problem. Assume when people tell you something they are looking for understanding; indicate that by being able to summarize what they said. Don't offer any advice.

- They are chronic complainers. Ask them to write down problems and solutions and then let's discuss it. This turns down the volume while, hopefully, moving them off complaining.

- They like to complain about others. Ask if they've talked to the person. Encourage them to do so. If that doesn't work, summarize what they have said without agreeing or disagreeing.

8. **Impatience triggers.** Some people probably bring out your impatience more than others. Who are they? What is it about them that makes you more impatient? Pace? Language? Thought process? Accent? These people may include people you don't like, who ramble, who whine and complain, or who are repetitive advocates for things you have already rejected. Mentally rehearse some calming tactics before meeting with people who trigger your impatience. Work on understanding their positions without judging them—you can always judge later. In all cases, focus them on the issues or problems to be discussed, return them to the point, summarize, and state your position. Try to gently train them to be more efficient with you next time without damaging them in the process.

9. **Rein in your horse.** Impatient people provide answers, conclusions, and solutions too early in the process. Others haven't even understood the problem yet. Providing solutions too quickly will make your people dependent and irritated. If you don't teach them how you think and how you can come up with solutions so fast, they will never learn. Take the time to really define the problem—not impatiently throw out a solution. Brainstorm what questions need to be answered in order to resolve it. Give your people the task to think about for a day and come back with some solutions. Be a teacher instead of a dictator of solutions. Study yourself. Keep a journal of

what triggered your behavior and what the observed consequences were. Learn to detect and control your triggers before they get you in trouble.

I have overdone the hard-driving, high-expectations, performance-at-any-cost trait until it has hurt relationships and caused others to stop challenging me.

– An ESTJ Manager

■ ■ ■ ■ ■ ■ ■ ■ ■ ■ ■ ■ ■ ■ ■ ■ ■

APPLICATION

Your personal preferences play out in day-to-day problems and situations you face. Below is a case about your type dealing with such a situation. Use this to think through how you will integrate the tips you've considered and coach yourself to be more effective in your type.

ESTJ Application Situation (Part 1)

You're Vice President of Manufacturing for XYZ Corp., a global company that designs, develops, and manufactures innovative sub-assemblies for the home appliance business. You've always been careful and thoughtful in planning your career, pursuing jobs and companies that would give you the wide range of experiences that would prepare you for higher-level challenges. And now, you find yourself with eight direct reports, four of whom are working in offices in countries outside of North America.

Not long after you started working at XYZ, you were assigned an executive coach with whom the company had a retainer agreement. In your first meeting with him, when he asked you to describe how you saw yourself, you offered, "thorough, analytical, logical, determined, task oriented, and results oriented." In your next meeting, your coach said that people from whom he had gotten feedback—among them, some of your peers and direct reports—noted that you were logical, determined, well organized, and very thorough about task-related issues. "That's the good news," he said. "But there are some things you need to work on, like teaming, and I'd like to talk to you about those in our next meeting. Do you have an hour on Wednesday, maybe over lunch?"

"How about now?"

Looking a bit surprised your coach says, "Before I tell you what those things are, I think it would be helpful to hear your general impressions of the people who report to you."

"Okay," you answer. "They're good people with plenty of potential, and they're cooperative, I think. But by and large they seem a little passive, and more often than not, I get the feeling that they're telling me what they think I want to hear instead of what they really think. I believe in having a strong team where everyone supports a common goal, and I'm sometimes not sure I really have their full commitment."

"Hmm, that's interesting," your coach remarks. "Can you think of any particular reason why they might act that way?"

"I'm not sure what you're getting at," you say, feeling a little defensive. "Are you suggesting it's something I do?"

"Well, I wasn't suggesting anything," your coach answers, and smiles at you. "But since you mention it, do you think that perhaps there is something in the way you interact with them that would get that sort of behavior from them?"

"I guess I'll need to think about that," you tell your coach.

Thinking It Through: Strategy

■ What is it in your "makeup" (i.e., type) that might lead others to respond to you in the way you have described?

■ What kinds of things do you think might lead other people to tell you what you want to hear rather than what they really think?

Planning It Out: Tactics

■ When you are interacting with your direct reports, what might you start doing more of if you really want to "build a team" of strong individuals?

■ What potential barriers to your effectiveness (i.e., actions, behaviors) are inherent in this situation based on your personality type (ESTJ)?

■ What particular areas would present developmental challenges to you, and what competencies would you want to put into play in order not only to accomplish your objectives but assure that relationships are preserved?

■ Which of the tactics described in the Being More Effective section are applicable in this situation?

■ Which Overused Tendencies are most likely to come into play here?

ESTJ Application Situation (Part 2)

You meet with your coach a few weeks later. Here's what he wants to know:

■ As an ESTJ, what do you need to guard against, and what competencies do you need to put into play so that your people feel more fully involved and comfortable in speaking their minds?

■ What should you do more of? Less of?

Reflection

■ What do you think are the advantages of ESTJs as team leaders?

■ What are the potential liabilities?

SUGGESTED READINGS

■■■■■■■■ Being a More Effective ESTJ ■■■■■■■■

Interpersonal Savvy

Benton, D.A. *Executive Charisma: Six Steps to Mastering the Art of Leadership.* New York: McGraw-Hill Trade, 2003.

Bolton, Robert and Dorothy Grover Bolton. *People Styles at Work—Making Bad Relationships Good and Good Relationships Better.* New York: AMACOM, 1996.

Brooks, Michael. *Instant Rapport.* New York: Warner Books, 1989.

Maxwell, John C. *Relationships 101.* London: Thomas Nelson, 2004.

Silberman, Melvin L. and Freda Hansburg. *Peoplesmart: Developing Your Interpersonal Intelligence.* San Francisco: Berrett-Koehler Publishers, Inc., 2000.

Developing Direct Reports

Charan, Ram, James L. Noel and Steve Drotter. *The Leadership Pipeline: How to Build the Leadership Powered Company.* New York: John Wiley & Sons, Inc., 2000.

Daniels, Aubrey C. *Bringing Out the Best in People.* New York: McGraw-Hill, Inc., 1994.

Fulmer, Robert M. and Jay A. Conger. *Growing Your Company's Leaders.* New York: AMACOM, 2004.

Lombardo, Michael M. and Robert W. Eichinger. *The Leadership Machine.* Minneapolis, MN: Lominger Limited, Inc., 2004.

Personal Creativity

Campbell, David. *Take the Road to Creativity and Get Off Your Dead End.* Greensboro, NC: Center for Creative Leadership, 1985.

Ceserani, Jonne. *Big Ideas: Putting the Zest Into Creativity & Innovation at Work.* London: Kogan Page, 2003.

DeGraff, Jeff and Katherine A. Lawrence. *Creativity at Work: Developing the Right Practices to Make Innovation Happen.* San Francisco: Jossey-Bass, Inc., 2002.

Foster, Jack. *Ideaship: How to Get Ideas Flowing in Your Workplace.* San Francisco: Berrett-Koehler Publishers, Inc., 2001.

Lucas, Robert W. *The Creative Training Idea Book: Inspired Tips and Techniques for Engaging and Effective Learning.* New York: AMACOM, 2003.

Von Oech, Roger. *Expect the Unexpected or You Won't Find It: A Creativity Tool Based on the Ancient Wisdom of Heraclitus.* San Francisco: Berrett-Koehler Publishers, Inc., 2002.

Dealing With Ambiguity

Anderson, Dean and Linda S. Ackerman Anderson. *Beyond Change Management: Advanced Strategies for Today's Transformational Leaders.* San Francisco: Jossey-Bass, Inc., 2001.

Bellman, Geoffrey M. *Getting Things Done When You Are Not in Charge.* San Francisco: Berrett-Koehler Publishers, Inc., 2001.

Hammond, John S., Ralph L. Keeney and Howard Raiffer. *Smart Choices.* Boston: Harvard University Press, 1999.

Nutt, Paul C. *Why Decisions Fail: Avoiding the Blunders and Traps That Lead to Decision Debacles.* San Francisco: Berrett-Koehler Publishers, Inc., 2002.

Sofo, Francesco. *Six Myths of Critical Thinking.* Business & Professional Publishing, 2003.

Sternberg, Robert J. *Thinking Styles.* Boston: Cambridge University Press, 1997.

Yates, J. Frank. *Decision Management: How to Assure Better Decisions in Your Company.* San Francisco: Jossey-Bass, Inc., 2003.

Communicating More Completely

Arredondo, Lani. *Communicating Effectively.* New York: McGraw-Hill Trade, 2000.

Booher, Dianna. *Speak With Confidence: Powerful Presentations That Inform, Inspire, and Persuade.* New York: McGraw-Hill, Inc., 2002.

Harvard Business School Press (Ed.). *Presentations That Persuade and Motivate (The Results-Driven Manager Series).* Boston: Harvard Business School Press, 2004.

McCormack, Mark H. *On Communicating*. Los Angeles: Dove Books, 1998.

Zeuschner, Raymond F. *Communicating Today: The Essentials*. Boston: Allyn & Bacon, 2002.

■■■■■■■ **Overusing ESTJ Tendencies** ■■■■■■■

Being More Flexible
Bellman, Geoffrey M. *Getting Things Done When You Are Not in Charge*. San Francisco: Berrett-Koehler Publishers, Inc., 2001.

Brooks, Michael. *Instant Rapport*. New York: Warner Books, 1989.

Butler, Gillian, Ph.D. and Tony Hope, M.D. *Managing Your Mind*. New York: Oxford University Press, 1995.

Carter, Les. *The Anger Trap: Free Yourself From the Frustrations That Sabotage Your Life*. New York: John Wiley & Sons, Inc., 2003.

Fullan, Michael. *Leading in a Culture of Change*. New York: John Wiley & Sons, Inc., 2001.

Glickman, Rosalene. *Optimal Thinking: How to Be Your Best Self*. New York: John Wiley & Sons, Inc., 2002.

Seeing the Bigger Picture
Bandrowski, James F. *Corporate Imagination Plus—Five Steps to Translating Innovative Strategies Into Action*. New York: The Free Press, 2000.

Birch, Paul and Brian Clegg. *Imagination Engineering—The Toolkit for Business Creativity*. London: Pitman Publishing, 1996.

Chakravorti, Bhaskar. *The Slow Pace of Fast Change: Bringing Innovations to Market in a Connected World*. Boston: Harvard Business School Press, 2003.

Charan, Ram. *What the CEO Wants You to Know: How Your Company Really Works*. New York: Crown Business Publishing, 2001.

Christensen, Clayton M. and Michael E. Raynor. *The Innovator's Solution*. Harvard Business School Press, 2003.

Collins, James C. *Good to Great: Why Some Companies Make the Leap...And Others Don't*. New York: HarperCollins, 2001.

DeGraff, Jeff and Katherine A. Lawrence. *Creativity at Work: Developing the Right Practices to Make Innovation Happen.* San Francisco: Jossey-Bass, Inc., 2002.

Dudik, Evan Matthew. *Strategic Renaissance: New Thinking and Innovative Tools to Create Great Corporate Strategies Using Insights From History and Science.* New York: AMACOM, 2000.

The Futurist Magazine. http://www.wfs.org

Gaynor, Gerard H. *Innovation by Design.* New York: AMACOM, 2002.

Hamel, Gary. *Leading the Revolution.* Boston: Harvard Business School Press, 2002.

Hargadon, Andrew and Kathleen M. Eisenhardt. *How Breakthroughs Happen: The Surprising Truth About How Companies Innovate.* Boston: Harvard Business School Press, 2003.

Harvard Business Review. Phone: 800-988-0886 (US and Canada). Fax: 617-496-1029. Mail: Harvard Business Review. Subscriber Services, P.O. Box 52623. Boulder, CO 80322-2623 USA. http://www.hbsp.harvard.edu/products/hbr

Kaplan, Robert S. and David P. Norton. *The Strategy-Focused Organization: How Balanced Scorecard Companies Thrive in the New Business Environment.* Boston: Harvard Business School Press, 2000.

Porter, Michael E. *Competitive Strategy: Techniques for Analyzing Industries and Competitors.* New York: The Free Press, 1998.

Prahalad, C.K. and Venkat Ramaswamy. *The Future of Competition: Co-Creating Unique Value With Customers.* Boston: Harvard Business School Press, 2004.

Being Less Aggressive

Allen, David. *Getting Things Done: The Art of Stress-Free Productivity.* New York: Penguin Books, 2003.

Badaracco, Joseph L., Jr. *Leading Quietly.* Boston: Harvard Business School Press, 2002.

Bolton, Robert and Dorothy Grover Bolton. *People Styles at Work — Making Bad Relationships Good and Good Relationships Better.* New York: AMACOM, 1996.

Bossidy, Larry, Ram Charan and Charles Burck (Contributor). *Execution: The Discipline of Getting Things Done.* New York: Crown Business Publishing, 2002.

Branham, L. *Keeping the People Who Keep You in Business.* New York: AMACOM, 2001.

Genett, Donna M. *If You Want It Done Right, You Don't Have to Do It Yourself! The Power of Effective Delegation.* Sanger, CA: Quill Driver Books, 2004.

Glanz, Barbara A. *Handle With CARE: Motivating and Retaining Employees.* New York: McGraw-Hill Trade, 2002.

More Listening and Patience

Barker, Larry, Ph.D. and Kittie Watson, Ph.D. *Listen Up: At Home, at Work, in Relationships: How to Harness the Power of Effective Listening.* Irvine, CA: Griffin Trade Paperback, 2001.

Bolton, Robert and Dorothy Grover Bolton. *People Styles at Work—Making Bad Relationships Good and Good Relationships Better.* New York: AMACOM, 1996.

Burley-Allen, Madelyn. *Listening: The Forgotten Skill.* New York: John Wiley & Sons, Inc., 1995.

Gonthier, Giovinella and Kevin Morrissey. *Rude Awakenings: Overcoming the Civility Crisis in the Workplace.* Chicago: Dearborn Trade Publishing, 2002.

Ryan, Mary Jane. *The Power of Patience: How to Slow the Rush and Enjoy More Happiness, Success, and Peace of Mind Everyday.* New York: Broadway Press, 2003.

CHAPTER 14

ESFJ
Extraverted Feeling
with
Introverted Sensing

■■■■■■■■■■■■■■■■■

12.3% of Population
3.6% of Managers

■■■■■■■■■■■■■■■■■

Typical Strengths

Warm-Hearted
Sociable
Caring
Strong Values
Involved
Loyal
Decisive
Results Oriented

ISTJ	ISFJ	INFJ	INTJ
ISTP	ISFP	INFP	INTP
ESTP	ESFP	ENFP	ENTP
ESTJ	ESFJ	ENFJ	ENTJ

If people would just do what I ask, we'll all get along.

– An ESFJ Manager

Basic Habits of Mind

Extraverted Feeling results in attention to people and how others react to situations. Immediately aware of relationships, ESFJs seek to understand others' experiences in order to understand their own. Introverted Sensing offers them immediate impressions of the environment. Their focus on others tends to be factual and detailed.

Introverted Intuiting and Introverted Thinking assist ESFJs. Introverted Intuiting provides a sense of place and belonging. Introverted Thinking focuses their attention on precise information.

This combination is sometimes seen as being too focused on a few pieces of information and not attuned to long-term business challenges.

Typical Communication Patterns

- ESFJs are warm and outgoing.

- While they like to make decisions, get clarity, and make sure instructions are clear, they are also eager to communicate inclusion by being empathetic.

- They make unassuming observations and like conversation that is focused on practical and people-related topics.

General Learning Strategy

- ESFJs prefer to learn in a cooperative environment with active personal sharing.

- Typical learning strategies are actively networking with others to share ideas, creating some order to their experiences, and looking for the practical lessons in situations.

- Their learning is generally helped by having specific ways to make the information or experience directly useful.

Interpersonal Qualities Related to Motivation

■ ESFJs are typically motivated by practical, realistic, hands-on action that drives completion of a project or task.

■ They enjoy the moment and are energized by their activities as long as these are guided by definitive guidelines, schedules, and timelines.

Blind Spots

■ Others believe that ESFJs may develop problems with interpersonal relationships if they fail to learn how to be more changeable and delegating.

■ ESFJs might be surprised to learn that others believe that they may develop problems when organizations are making strategic transitions and changes.

Stress Related Behavior

■ Under stress, ESFJs can become more energetic and insist on cooperation from others, which can lead to hasty observations and unrealistic expectations.

■ Under prolonged stress, they tend to overorganize to the point of distraction.

■ When stress is persistent and long term, they can seem unusually unemotional, overly conventional, and obsessive about the situation they are in.

Potential Barriers to Effectiveness

■ At times, their need for closure and focus comes across as blunt, abrasive, and manipulating.

■ When they appear pressuring, ESFJs are less effective.

■ Unless they demonstrate more self-awareness and support for innovation, they may not identify key opportunities for growth and development.

Being a More Effective ESFJ

A Enhancing Ways to Learn
B Dealing With Ambiguity
C Being More Innovative
D Dealing With Conflict
E Taking Charge
F Delegation and Staffing

ISTJ	ISFJ	INFJ	INTJ
ISTP	ISFP	INFP	INTP
ESTP	ESFP	ENFP	ENTP
ESTJ	ESFJ	ENFJ	ENTJ

A Enhancing Ways to Learn

ESFJs direct their energy toward people and somewhat limit the array of learning methods available to them.

1. **Personal experience is a very limited way to learn.** Even accessing others' experiences still leaves major gaps. For adults, most learning either comes from taking action and learning from the consequences or searching for parallel experiences in the past.

2. **Locate the essence of the problem.** What are the key factors or elements in this problem? Experts usually solve problems by figuring out what the deep, underlying principles are and working forward from there; the less adept focus on desired outcomes/solutions and either work backward or concentrate on the surface facts. What are the deep principles of what you're working on? Once you've done this, search the past for parallels—your past, the business past, the historical past. One common mistake here is to search in parallel organizations because "only they would know." Backing up and asking a broader question will aid in the search for solutions. When Motorola wanted to find out how to process orders more quickly, they went not to other electronics firms, but to Domino's Pizza and Federal Express.

3. **Patterns.** Look for patterns in personal, organization, or the world, in general successes and failures. What was common to each success or what was present in each failure but never present in a success? Focus on the successes; failures are easier to analyze but don't in themselves tell you what would work. Comparing successes, while less exciting, yields more information about underlying principles. The bottom line is to reduce your insights to principles or rules of thumb you think might be repeatable. When faced with the next new problem, those general underlying principles will apply again.

4. **Use oddball tactics.** What is a direct analogy between something you are working on and a natural occurrence? Ask what in nature parallels your problem. When the terrible surfs and motion of the tide threatened to defeat their massive dam project, the Delta Works, the Dutch used the violence of the North Sea to drive in the pilings, ending the danger of the south of the Netherlands flooding. Practice picking out anomalies—unusual facts that don't quite fit, like sales going down when they should have gone up. What do these odd things imply for strategy?

5. **Encourage yourself to do quick experiments and trials.** Studies show that 80% of innovations occur in the wrong place, are created by the wrong people (dye makers developed detergent; Post-it® Notes was an error in a glue formula), and 30–50% of technical innovations fail in tests within the company. Even among those that make it to the marketplace, 70–90% fail. The bottom line on change is a 95% failure rate, and the most successful innovators try lots of quick, inexpensive experiments to increase the chances of success.

B Dealing With Ambiguity

When things are ambiguous, ESFJs are often unsure of what is expected of them. Being quite organized by nature, they're not sure what to do when things are up in the air. They can become overwhelmed when a good many demands come toward them that do not seem to fit within a structure or set of ground rules. Although generally good at priority setting, in this instance they can lose sight of what is important on the list.

1. **Watch out for the activity trap.** John Kotter, in *The General Managers*, found that effective managers spent about half their time working on one or two key priorities—priorities they described in their own terms, not in terms of what the business/organizational plan said. Further, they made no attempt to work as much on small but related issues that tend to add up to lots of activity. So, rather than consuming themselves and others on 97 seemingly urgent and related smaller activities, they always returned to the few issues that would gain the most mileage long term.

2. **Incrementalism.** The essence of dealing comfortably with uncertainty is the tolerance of errors and mistakes, and absorbing the possible heat and criticism that follow. Acting on an ill-defined problem with no precedents to follow means shooting in the dark with as informed a decision as you can make at the time. People who are good at this

are incrementalists. They make a series of smaller decisions, get instant feedback, correct the course, get a little more data, move forward a little more, until the bigger problem is under control. They don't try to get it right the first time. Many problem-solving studies show that the second or third try is when we really understand the underlying dynamics of problems. They also know that the more uncertain the situation is, the more likely it is they will make mistakes in the beginning. So, you need to work on two practices: Start small so you can recover more quickly. Do little somethings as soon as you can and get used to heat.

3. **Problem definition.** Under uncertainty, it really helps to get as firm a handle as possible on the problem. Figure out what causes it. Keep asking why. See how many causes you can come up with and how many organizing buckets you can put them in. This increases the chance of a better solution because you can see more connections. The evidence from decision-making research makes it clear that thorough problem definition with appropriate questions to answer leads to better decisions. Focusing on solutions or information first often slows things down since we have no conceptual buckets in which to organize our thinking. Learn to ask more questions.

4. **Avoid early rigid positions.** It's just physics. Action gets equal reaction. Strong statements. Strongly worded positions. Casting blame. Absolutes. Lines in the sand. Unnecessary passion. All of these will be responded to in kind, will waste time, cause ill will, and possibly prevent a win-win or a something-something. It only has a place in one-time, either/or negotiations, and even there it isn't recommended. Similarly, watch out for overcommitment to any need or course of action. Look for information that goes against your preferences. Be able to adjust your position and your wants. If you can't, your ego is getting the best of you. If you can't walk away until you get X, you'll probably either overpay or blow the negotiation. Don't negotiate around a single issue if you can add another. This is another situation that leads to rigidity.

5. **Stress.** Some get stressed with increased ambiguity and uncertainty. We lose our anchor. We are not at our best when we are anxious, frustrated, upset, or when we lose our cool. What brings out your emotional response? Write down why you get anxious: when you don't know what to do; don't want to make a mistake; afraid of the unknown consequences; don't have the confidence to act. When you get emotional, drop the problem for awhile. Go do something else.

Come back to it when you are under better control. Let your brain work on it while you do something safer.

6. **Change is letting go of one trapeze in the air to catch the next one.** For a small amount of time, you have hold of nothing but thin air. The second gets you to a new platform and a new place. If you hang on to the first one, afraid you will fall, you will always return to the same old platform—safe but not new or different. Change is letting go. Stay informed about business/technological change and ask what it means for your work. Visualize a different and better outcome. Talk about it. Invite ideas. Interview those who have successfully pulled off changes. Experiment. The more you do this, the more comfortable you'll feel. To better understand dealing with change, read *The Future of Leadership* by White, Hodgson and Crainer.

7. **Finishing.** Do you prefer to finish what you have started? Do you have a high need to complete tasks? Wrap them up in nice clean packages? Working well with ambiguity and under uncertainty means moving from incomplete task to incomplete task. Some may be abandoned, some may never be finished. They'll probably only ever get 80% done, and you'll constantly have to edit your actions and decisions. Change your internal reward process toward feeling good about fixing mistakes and moving things forward incrementally, more than finishing any given project.

8. **Selective resistance.** Do you adapt to some and not to others? You probably have good people buckets and bad people buckets and signal your disagreement with them to the bad bucket groups or individuals. You may have good group buckets and bad group buckets—gender, race, age, origin. Learn to understand without accepting or judging. Listen, take notes, ask questions, and be able to make their case as well as they can. Pick something in their argument you agree with. Present your argument in terms of the problem only—why you think this is the best manner to deal with a mutually agreed-upon problem. A careful observer should not be able to tell your assessment of people or their arguments at the time. Find someone who is a fair observer and get a critique. Was I fair? Did I treat everyone the same? Were my objections based on reasoning against standards and not directed at people?

C Being More Innovative

ESFJs sometimes resist change in favor of maintaining traditional approaches.

1. **Try some different thinking strategies.** To be more personally creative, immerse yourself in the problem. Getting fresh ideas is not a speedboating process; it requires looking deeply.

2. **Carve out dedicated time**—study the problem deeply, talk with others, look for parallels in other organizations and in remote areas totally outside your field. If your response to this is that you don't have the time, that also usually explains why you're not having any fresh ideas.

3. **Think out loud.** Many people don't know what they know until they talk it out. Find a good sounding board and talk to him/her to increase your understanding of a problem or a technical area. Talk to an expert in an unrelated field. Talk to the most irreverent person you know. Your goal is not to get his/her input, but rather his/her help in figuring out what you know—what your principles and rules of thumb are.

4. **Practice picking out anomalies**—unusual facts that don't quite fit, like sales going down when they should have gone up. What do these odd things imply for strategy? Naturally creative people are much more likely to think in opposite cases when confronted with a problem. Turn the problem upside down: Ask what is the least likely thing it could be, what the problem is not, what's missing from the problem, or what the mirror image of the problem is.

5. **Look for distant parallels.** Don't fall into the mental trap of searching only in parallel organizations because "only they would know." Back up and ask a broader question to aid in the search for solutions. When Motorola wanted to find out how to process orders more quickly, they went not to other electronics firms, but to Domino's Pizza and Federal Express. For more ideas, an interesting—and fun—book on the topic is *Take the Road to Creativity and Get Off Your Dead End* by David Campbell.

6. **Unearthing creative ideas.** Creative thought processes do not follow the formal rules of logic, where one uses cause and effect to prove or solve something. Some rules of creative thought are:

   ■ Not using concepts but changing them; imagining this were something else.

- Move from one concept or way of looking at things to another, such as from economic to political.

- Generate ideas without judging them initially.

- Use information to restructure and come up with new patterns.

- Jump from one idea to another without justifying the jump.

- Look for the least likely and odd.

- Look for parallels far from the problem, such as how is an organization like a big oak tree?

- Ask what's missing or what's not here.

- Fascination with mistakes and failure as learning devices.

7. **Apply some standard problem-solving skills.** There are many different ways to think through and solve a problem more creatively:

- Ask more questions. In one study of problem solving, 7% of comments were questions and about half were answers. We jump to solutions based on what has worked in the past.

- Complex problems are hard to visualize. They tend to be either oversimplified or too complex to solve unless they are put in a visual format. Cut it up into its component pieces. Examine the pieces to see if a different order would help, or how you could combine three pieces into one.

- Another technique is a pictorial chart called a storyboard, where a problem is illustrated by its components being depicted as pictures.

- A variation of this is to tell stories that illustrate the +'s and -'s of a problem, then flowchart those according to what's working and not working. Another is a fishbone diagram used in Total Quality Management.

- Sometimes going to extremes helps. Adding every condition, every worst case you can think of sometimes will suggest a different solution. Taking the present state of affairs and projecting into the future may indicate how and where the system will break down.

- Sleep on it. Take periodic breaks, whether stuck or not. This allows the brain to continue to work on the issue. Most breakthroughs come when we're "not thinking about it." Put it away; give it to someone else; sleep on it. Once you've come up with every idea you can think of, throw them all out and wait for more to occur to you. Force yourself to forget about the issue.

8. **Increasing group creativity:** Selecting a group. During World War II, it was discovered that teams of people with the widest diversity of backgrounds produced the most creative solutions to problems. The teams included people who knew absolutely nothing about the area (i.e., an English major working on a costing problem). When attacking a tough problem which has eluded attempts to solve it, get the broadest group you can. Involve different functions, levels, and disciplines. Pull in customers and colleagues from other organizations. Remember that you're looking for fresh approaches; you're not convening a work task force expected to implement or judge the practicality of the notions. Believe it or not, it doesn't matter if they know anything about the problem or the technology required to deal with it. That's your job.

9. **Increasing group creativity:** Define the problem first. A straightforward technique to enable creativity is brainstorming. Anything goes for an agreed-upon time. Throw out ideas, record them all, no evaluation allowed. Many people have had bad experiences with brainstorming. Silly ideas. Nothing practical. A waste of time. This usually happens because the problem gets defined in the same old way. First, define the problem well. Allot hours to this, not two minutes to sketch the problem. Challenge your thinking—are you generalizing from one or two cases? How do you know the causes are really causes? They may simply be related. What is fact and what is assumption?

10. **Increasing group creativity:** Facilitating the process. Here are three methods commonly used:

■ Brainstorming. Outline the problem for the group; tell them what you've tried and learned from the tries. Include things that may have happened only once. Invite the group to free-form respond. Any idea is okay—no criticism allowed. Record all ideas on a flip chart. When the group has exhausted the possibilities, take the most interesting ones and ask the group to first name positive features of the ideas, then negative features, and finally what's interesting about the ideas. Follow this process until you've covered all the ideas that interest you. Then ask the group what else they would select as interesting ideas to do a plus, minus, interesting analysis. This process can usually be done in an hour or two.

- The nominal group. After the problem definition above, have the group write down as many ideas as occur to them. Record them all on a flip chart for freewheeling discussion. People can add, combine or clarify—"What were you thinking when you said...," but no criticism allowed. After this, follow the plus, minus, interesting process above.

- Analogies. Lots of creative solutions come from analogies to nature or other fields. Come up with a list (electrical engineering, cats, trees, the sea, biology, shipbuilding), any list will do, and insert it after you describe the problem to the group in the first or second option. Many times this will trigger novel ideas that no other process will.

D Dealing With Conflict

ESFJs believe in harmony and typically avoid dealing with conflict situations. When forced to, they can be too blunt, probably because they are so uncomfortable.

1. **Clear problem-focused communication.** Follow the rule of equity: Explain your thinking and ask them to explain theirs. Be able to state their position as clearly as they do whether you agree or not—give it legitimacy. Separate facts from opinions and assumptions. Generate a variety of possibilities first rather than stake out positions. Keep your speaking to 30–60 second bursts. Try to get them to do the same. Don't give the other side the impression you're lecturing or criticizing them. Explain objectively why you hold a view; make the other side do the same. Ask lots of questions, make fewer statements. To identify interests behind positions, ask why they hold them or why they wouldn't want to do something. Always restate their position to their satisfaction before offering a response.

2. **Downsizing the conflict.** Almost all conflicts have common points that get lost in the heat of the battle. After a conflict has been presented and understood, start by saying that it might be helpful to see if we agree on anything. Write them on the flip chart. Then write down the areas left open. Focus on common goals, priorities, and problems. Keep the open conflicts as small as possible and concrete. The more abstract it gets, "We don't trust your unit," the more unmanageable it gets. To this respond, "Tell me your specific concern—why exactly don't you trust us; can you give me an

example?" Usually after calm discussion, they don't trust your unit on this specific issue under these specific conditions. That's easier to deal with. Allow others to save face by conceding small points that are not central to the issue—don't try to hit a home run every time. If you can't agree on a solution, agree on a procedure to move forward. Collect more data. Appeal to a higher power. Get a third-party arbitrator. Something. This creates some positive motion and breaks stalemates.

3. **Practice Aikido,** the ancient art of absorbing the energy of your opponent and using it to manage him/her. Let the other side vent frustration or blow off steam, but don't react. Listen. Nod. Ask clarifying questions. Ask open-ended questions like, "What one change could you make so we could achieve our objectives better?" "What could I do that would help the most?" Restate their position periodically to signal you have understood. But don't react. Keep them talking until they run out of venom. Then explore the underlying concern. Separate the people from the problem. When someone attacks you, rephrase it as an attack on the problem. In response to threats, say you'll only negotiate on merit and fairness. If the other side won't play fair, surface their game—"It looks like you're playing good cop, bad cop. Why don't you settle your differences and tell me one thing?" In response to unreasonable proposals, attacks, or a non-answer to a question, you can always say nothing. People will usually respond by saying more, coming off their position a bit, or at least revealing their true interests. Many times, with unlimited venting and your understanding, the actual conflict shrinks.

4. **In conflict situations, what reactions do you have** (such as impatience or non-verbals like flushing or drumming your pen or fingers)? Learn to recognize those as soon as they start and substitute something more neutral. Most emotional responses to conflict come from personalizing the issue. Separate people issues from the problem at hand, and deal with people issues separately and later if they persist. Always return to facts and the problem before the group; stay away from personal clashes. Attack the problem by looking at common interests and underlying concerns, not people and their positions. Try on their views for size—the emotion as well as the content. Ask yourself if you understand their feelings. Ask what they would do if they were in your shoes. See if you can restate each other's position and advocate it for a minute to get inside each other's place. If you get emotional, pause and collect yourself. You are not your best when you get emotional. Then return to the problem.

5. **Questions.** In win-win and something-something negotiations, the more information you have about the other side, the more you will have to work with. What can you learn about what they know before going in? What will they do if they don't reach an agreement with you? In the negotiation, ask more questions, make fewer statements. Ask clarifying questions: "What did you mean by that?" Probes: "Why do you say that?" Motives: "What led you to that position?" When the other side takes a rigid position, don't reject it. Ask why: What are the principles behind the offer? How do we know it's fair? What's the theory of the case? Play out what would happen if their position was accepted. Get everything out that you can. Don't negotiate assumptions, negotiate facts.

E Taking Charge

ESFJs also dislike the conflict that comes with taking a hard stand. Whether dealing with a problem performer or a tough issue, they can benefit from keeping to the issue and not taking the situation too personally.

1. **Against the grain tough stands.** Taking a tough stand demands confidence in what you're saying along with the humility that you might be wrong—one of life's paradoxes. To prepare to take the lead on a tough issue, work on your stand through mental interrogation until you can clearly state in a few sentences what your stand is and why you hold it. Build the business case. How do others win? People don't line up behind laundry lists or ambiguous objectives. Ask others for advice—scope the problem, consider options, pick one, develop a rationale, then go with it until proven wrong. Then redo the process. If this doesn't help, find out where the pain is for you. What have you been avoiding? Examine your past and see where taking-charge behavior has gotten you in trouble or you thought it would get you in trouble. Isolate the most troublesome elements, such as forgetting things under pressure, trouble with fierce debate, problems with unpopular stands, and things moving too fast. Devise counterstrategies.

2. **Selling your leadership.** While some people may welcome what you say and want to do, others will go after you or even try to minimize the situation. Some will sabotage. To sell your leadership, keep your eyes on the prize but don't specify how to get there. Present the outcomes, targets, and goals without the how to's. Welcome their ideas—good and bad. Any negative response is a positive if you learn from it. Allow them to fill in the blanks, ask questions, and disagree

without appearing impatient with them. Allow others to save face; concede small points, invite criticism of your own. Help them figure out how to win. Keep to the facts and the problem before the group; stay away from personal clashes.

3. **Laid back?** None of your business? Tend to shy away from managerial courage situations? Why? What's getting in your way? Are you prone to give up in tough situations, fear exposing yourself, don't like conflict, what? Ask yourself—what's the downside of delivering a message you think is right and will eventually help the organization but may cause someone short-term pain. What if it turns out you were wrong? Treat any misinterpretations as chances to learn. What if you were the target person or group? Even though it might hurt, would you appreciate it if someone brought the data to your attention in time for you to fix it with minimal damage? What would you think of a person whom you later found out knew about it and didn't come forward, and you had to spend inordinate amounts of time and political currency to fix it? Follow your convictions. Follow due process. Step up to the plate and be responsible, win or lose. People will think better of you in the long term.

4. **Are your problem performers confused?** Do they know what's expected of them? You may not set clear enough performance standards, goals, and objectives. You may be a seat-of-the-pants manager, and some people are struggling because they don't know what is expected or it changes. You may be a cryptic communicator. You may be too busy to communicate. You may communicate to some and not to others. You may have given up on some and stopped communicating. Or you may think they would know what to do if they're any good, but that's not really true because you have not properly communicated what you want. The first task is to outline the 5 to 10 key results areas and what indicators of success would be. Involve your problem direct reports on both ends—the standards and the indicators. Provide them with a fair way to measure their own progress. Employees with goals and standards are usually harder on themselves than you'll ever be. Often they set higher standards than you would. Sometimes the problem is behavioral, as in someone who can't control outbursts, and only affects performance on the back end in lost cooperation or sabotage. Then the best approach is to note the gap between behavior and expectations, and point out what some of the observed consequences are. If the person agrees, then coaching may suffice. If the person balks, then a 360° feedback process with

follow-up may be needed to illuminate the depth of the problem before any help can be given.

5. **The message.** Be succinct. You have limited attention span in tough feedback situations. Don't waste time with a long preamble, particularly if the feedback is negative. If the feedback is negative and the recipient is likely to know it, go ahead and say it directly. They won't hear anything positive you have to say anyway. Don't overwhelm the person/group, even if you have a lot to say. Go from specific to general points. Keep it to the facts. Don't embellish to make your point. No passion or inflammatory language. Don't do it to harm or out of vengeance. Don't do it in anger. If feelings are involved for you, wait until you can describe them, not show them. Managerial courage comes in search of a better outcome, not destroying others. Stay calm and cool. If others are not composed, don't respond. Just return to the message.

6. **Bring a solution if you can.** Nobody likes a critic. Everybody appreciates a problem solver. Give people ways to improve; don't just dump and leave. Tell others what you think would be better—paint a different outcome. Help others see the consequences—you can ask them what they think, and you can tell them what the consequences are from your side if you are personally involved ("I'd be reluctant to work with you on X again").

F Delegation and Staffing

ESFJs may assume they know what people want and are more likely to decide what should be done without asking others. ESFJs are more directing than developing in their orientation.

1. **How to delegate?** Communicate, set time frames and goals, and get out of the way. People need to know what it is you expect. What does the outcome look like? When do you need it by? What's the budget? What resources do they get? What decisions can they make? Do you want checkpoints along the way? How will we both know and measure how well the task is done? One of the most common problems with delegation is incomplete or cryptic up-front communication leading to frustration, a job not well done the first time, rework, and a reluctance to delegate next time. Poor communicators always have to take more time managing because of rework. Analyze recent projects that went well and didn't go well. How did you delegate? Too much? Not enough? Unwanted pieces?

Major chunks of responsibility? Workload distributed properly? Did you set measures? Overmanage or abdicate? Find out what your best practices are. Set up a series of delegation practices that can be used as if you're not there. What do you have to be informed of? What feedback loops can people use for midcourse correction? What questions should be answered as the work proceeds? What steps should be followed? What are the criteria to be followed? When will you be available to help?

2. **More what and why, less how.** The best delegators are crystal clear on what and when, and more open on how. People are more motivated when they can determine the how for themselves. Inexperienced delegators include the hows, which turn the people into task automatons instead of an empowered and energized staff. Tell them what and when and for how long, and let them figure out how on their own. Give them leeway. Encourage them to try things. Besides being more motivating, it's also more developmental for them. Add the larger context. Although it is not necessary to get the task done, people are more motivated when they know where this task fits in the bigger picture. Take three extra minutes and tell them why this task needs to be done, where it fits in the grander scheme, and its importance to the goals and objectives of the unit.

3. **Do you help your people learn by looking for repeating patterns?** Help them look for patterns in the situations and problems they deal with. What succeeded and what failed? What was common to each success or what was present in each failure but never present in a success? Focus on the successes; failures are easier to analyze but don't in themselves tell you what would work. Comparing successes, while less exciting, yields more information. The bottom line is help them reduce insights to principles or rules of thumb that might be repeatable. Ask them what they have learned to increase their skills and understanding, making them better managers or professionals. Ask them what they can do now that they couldn't do a year ago. Reinforce this and encourage more of it. Developing is learning in as many ways as possible.

4. **Become a student of the people around you.** First, try to outline their strengths and weaknesses, their preferences and beliefs. Use a standard competency list such as that in *FYI For Your Improvement* to get more specific about people. Watch out for traps—it is rarely general intelligence or pure personality that spells the difference in people. Most people are smart enough, and many personality characteristics don't matter that much for performance. Ask a second

question. Look below surface descriptions of smart, approachable, technically skilled people to describe specifics. Then try to predict ahead of time what they would do in specific circumstances. What percent of the time are your predictions correct? Try to increase the percent over time.

5. **When you make a hiring decision or are deciding whom to work with on a problem or project,** do you think you have a tendency to clone yourself too much? Do you have a preference for people who think and act as you do? What characteristics do you value too much? What downsides do you ignore or excuse away? This is a common human tendency. The key is to seek balance, variety, and diversity. Shore up your weaknesses when hiring others. People good at this competency can comfortably surround themselves with people not like them.

6. **Are your standards too high or too low?** Do you hire the first close candidate that comes along, or do you wait for the perfect candidate and leave the position open too long? Either tendency will probably get you and the organization in trouble. Always try to wait long enough to have choices but not long enough to lose a very good candidate while you wait for the perfect one to come along. Learn how to set reasonable standards by looking at a competency model and selecting key skills.

7. **Do you have a long-term view of the talent it's going to take to produce both current and long-term results?** Do you have a replacement plan for yourself? Do you use a success profile with the competencies you know you are going to need? Have you hired someone who now has, or will have in a short period of time, the ability to take your job? Have you selected someone you would sponsor for promotion to another job at your level, possibly passing you up in time? The best managers surround themselves with talent, and eventually some of the talent turns out to be better than the person who hired and trained them. That's a good thing and reason for a celebration.

8. **Listening to people you don't like.** What do people see in them who do like them or can at least get along with them? What are their strengths? Do you have any common interests? Talk less and ask more questions to give them a second chance. Don't judge their motives and intentions—do that later.

9. Listening to people you like but...

- They are disorganized. Interrupt to summarize and keep the discussion focused. While interrupting is generally not a good tactic, it's necessary here.

- They just want to chat. Ask questions to focus them; don't respond to chatty remarks.

- They want to unload a problem. Assume when people tell you something they are looking for understanding; indicate that by being able to summarize what they said. Don't offer any advice.

- They are chronic complainers. Ask them to write down problems and solutions and then let's discuss it. This turns down the volume while, hopefully, moving them off complaining.

- They like to complain about others. Ask if they've talked to the person. Encourage them to do so. If that doesn't work, summarize what they have said without agreeing or disagreeing.

Overusing ESFJ Tendencies

If you sometimes overdo your preferred behaviors, you may need to work on:

A Self-Awareness

B Personal Growth

C Being More Flexible/Less Pressuring

D Being More Strategic

E Paying More Attention to Process

ISTJ	ISFJ	INFJ	INTJ
ISTP	ISFP	INFP	INTP
ESTP	ESFP	ENFP	ENTP
ESTJ	ESFJ	ENFJ	ENTJ

A Self-Awareness

Nice people often don't get much feedback, and ESFJs are hard to criticize. Well liked, it is easy for them to develop blind spots.

1. **Get feedback.** People are reluctant to give you feedback, especially negative or corrective information. Generally, to get it, you must ask for it. Seeking negative feedback increases both the accuracy of our

understanding and people's evaluation of our overall effectiveness. A person who wants to know the bad must be pretty good. People will increase their estimation of you as you seek out and accept more feedback. If people are reluctant to give criticism, help by making self-appraisal statements rather than asking questions. Saying, "I think I focus too much on operations and miss some of the larger strategic connections; what do you think?" is easier for most people to reply to than a question which asks them to volunteer this point.

2. **Confidential feedback**—a private discussion, a private 360°—tends to be more negative and more accurate than public—annual performance appraisal—feedback. Don't be lulled to sleep by your public feedback. For most of us, it's an excessively positive view. When the feedback giver knows results will be public, scores go up, accuracy goes down.

3. **Seek feedback from more than one source.** Different types of raters are likely to know more about and be more accurate about different competencies. Fruitful areas for bosses usually include: strategic grasp, selling-up skills, comfort around higher management, presentation of problems, solutions, clarity of thinking, team building, confronting and sizing up people skills. Customers generally know about responsiveness, listening, quality orientation, problem-solving skills, understanding of their business needs, persuasiveness. Peers know persuasion, selling, negotiation, listening to find common cause, keeping the interests of the organization in mind, follow-through on promises, and how well you maintain give-and-take in 50-50 relationships. Direct reports are best at the day-to-day behavior of leadership, management, team building, delegation, confronting, approachability, time use. When you get a piece of feedback, ask yourself if the person is in a position to know that about you. You may be the only one who doesn't know the truth about yourself. Other sources agree much more with one another about you than you will likely agree with any one of the sources. Even though your own view is important, don't accept it as fact until verified by more than one other person who should know.

4. **In choosing people to give you feedback,** 360° or otherwise, focus on those who know you best to get the most accurate feedback. Try not to stack the deck, picking either those you do best with or worst with. Both friend and foe tend to pick similar competencies as strengths and weaknesses. Friends will use higher scores than foes, but their highest and lowest competencies will usually be the same.

5. **When getting feedback,** focus on the highest and lowest items or competency results from each group. Spend less time worrying about whether your scores are high or low in an absolute sense. In development, you should worry about you relative to you, not you relative to anyone else. Your goal is simply to know yourself better. To do this, answer the following questions: Why am I this way? How did my strengths get to be strengths? What experiences shaped my pattern? Do I have strengths tipping over into weaknesses—"I'm intelligent but make others feel less so"; "I'm creative but disorganized." If you are clearly poor at something, what's getting in your way? Many times you'll find you don't like it and have a poor understanding of why and how it's done well. Think of tough situations for you where your strengths and weaknesses play out.

6. **Work to get continuous feedback;** don't wait for annual feedback events. There are three ways to get better, continued, high-quality feedback:

   ■ Prepare specific areas you are concerned about, and ask people to respond anonymously in writing. List the areas where you need feedback, and ask them what they would like for you to keep doing, start doing, and stop doing to improve.

   ■ Work with a development partner who knows what you're working on and gives up on-line feedback as you try new things.

   ■ In areas you are working on, ask others who have watched you to debrief events with you shortly after they happen.

7. **There will be three kinds of feedback:**

   ■ Things others see that you also see that are true about you.

   ■ Things others see that you don't see that are true about you— these will be strengths you have that you sell yourself short on and weaknesses you have that you deny or are unaware of (blind spots).

   ■ Things others think they see, but you don't agree and are not really true about you. The perceptions of others are facts to them, even though they may not be true about you. On just those incorrect observations that really matter, try to demonstrate by actions, not words, that their perceptions are wrong.

8. **Don't go it alone.** Regardless of how you get the feedback, get help in interpretation. Most 360° instruments can only be presented by a certified facilitator, but even if you get homegrown feedback, pick numerous people to talk with. Select people from each major constituency at work and people who know you best off-work. Don't ask them for general reactions. Select a few things from your feedback, state what you think the issue is, see if they agree, and ask them what they would like to see you do differently in this area.

9. **Your defensive response.** You will need to work on keeping yourself in a calm state when getting negative feedback. You need to change your thinking. When getting the feedback, your only task is to accurately understand what people are trying to tell you. It is not your task at that point to accept or reject. That comes later. Mentally rehearse how you will calmly react to tough feedback situations before they happen. Develop automatic tactics to shut down or delay your usual emotional response. Some useful tactics are to slow down, take notes, ask clarifying questions, ask them for concrete examples, and thank them for telling you since you know it's not easy for them.

B Personal Growth

ESFJs value stability and don't often seek personal change. This can severely limit their career prospects.

1. **Focus on the right things.** In their study of successful vs. average careers, Citrin and Smith found that the most successful people force themselves into experiences they need for growth. They do not play it safe. While they demonstrate early competence in a specific area, they also don't overdo working on basic job requirements. They do enough work on the basics while searching for mission-critical job elements and trying to overdeliver on them. They add unexpected value. They call this the 20/80 principle of performance—focusing on the 20% that makes 80% of the difference. In doing so, the successful rack up career freedom points by tackling these tough assignments.

2. **Strengths.** Leverage your strengths. A recent worldwide Gallup survey found that only 20% of employees thought their strengths were used every day. This is your greatest chance of success. What have you mastered? What do you learn quickly? What gives you the most satisfaction at work? If you are creative, what are three things you can start doing today? Where can you use your strengths to help others (so they will help you in return)? Can't use your strengths on

your current job? How about a project, special assignment, or a task trade? So, maintain the clear strengths you will need in the future by testing them in new task assignments. (You're good at conflict resolution—use this strength on a cross-functional problem-solving group while you learn about other functions.) Coach others in your strengths and ask for some help from them in their strengths.

3. **Balance your overdone strengths in important areas.** If you're creative, telling yourself to do less of this won't work—it's the primary reason for your success to date. The key is to leave it alone and focus on the unintended consequences. (You're seen as lacking in detail orientation or disorganized.) Get the downside of your strength up to neutral; the goal is not to be good at it, but rather to see that it doesn't hurt you.

4. **Weaknesses.** Weaknesses are best handled with a development plan which involves four keystones: stretching tasks in which you develop the skill or fail at the task (usually 70% of real development); continued feedback to help you understand how you're doing (usually 20% of learnings); building frameworks to understand through courses (about 10%); and ways to cement all your learnings so you can repeat them next time.

5. **You can also compensate for your weaknesses rather than build the skill.** We are all poor at something and beating on it is counterproductive. If you have failed repeatedly at sales, detail work, or public speaking, find others who do this well, change jobs, or restructure your current job. Sometimes you can find indirect ways to compensate. Lincoln managed his temper by writing nasty letters, extracting the key points from the letters, tearing the letters up, then dealing with the key points contained in the letter when he regained composure.

6. **Focus on untested areas.** Minimize weaknesses, but go after untested areas as well. In our research, we find that the profile of an individual contributor looks much like that of a manager which, in turn, looks much like that of an executive. Nobody's developing much across time. Few managers are good at developing others, few executives at managing vision and purpose. But did they ever have a real chance to develop in these areas? The key is to find out the core demands of performance in a role, then work on these a level before they are necessary. Get involved in small versions of your untested areas— write a strategic plan for your unit, then show it to people; negotiate the purchase of office furniture. Write down what you did well and

what you didn't. Then try a second, bigger task and again write down the +'s and −'s of your performance. At this point, you may want to read a book or attend a course in this area. Keep upping the size and stakes until you have the skill at the level you need it to be.

7. **Blind spots.** Be very careful of blind spots, since you think you're much better at this than do others. Resist trying challenging tasks involving this skill until you clearly understand your behavior, have a target model of excellent behavior, and a plan so you don't get yourself into trouble. Collect more data. Ask someone you trust to monitor you and give you feedback each time. Study three people who are good at this and compare what you do with what they do. Don't rest until you have cleared up the blind spot.

8. **Many people don't know how careers are built.** Most are put off by the popular myth of getting ahead. All of us have seen *How to Succeed in Business Without Really Trying* or something like it. It's easy to get cynical and believe that successful people are political or sell out, suck up, knife people in the back, it's who you know, and so on. The facts are dramatically different from this. Those behaviors get people in trouble eventually. What has staying power is performing and problem solving on the current job, having a few notable strengths, and seeking new tasks you don't know how to do. It's solving every problem with tenacity, while looking for what you haven't yet done and getting yourself in a position to do it. Read *The Lessons of Experience* by McCall, Lombardo and Morrison for the careers of men and *Breaking the Glass Ceiling* by Morrison, White and Van Velsor for the careers of women to see how successful careers really happen.

9. **Getting noticed by top decision makers.** Top managers aren't as interested in glitz as many would have you believe. They're interested in people who take care of problems, spot opportunities, ward off disaster, and have a broad repertoire of skills. They are looking for bold performers. But a better mousetrap alone is not enough. Volunteer for projects that will require interacting/presenting with higher management. Focus on activities that are the core of what your organization does. Find a business opportunity and make a reasoned case for it. Pick a big problem and work maniacally to solve it. You need to be seen and heard—but on substance, not fluff.

C Being More Flexible/Less Pressuring

When something threatens the sense of harmony and stability that ESFJs treasure, they can become pressuring and demanding.

1. **Rein in your horse.** Impatient people provide answers, conclusions, and solutions too early in the process. Others haven't even understood the problem yet. Providing solutions too quickly will make your people dependent and irritated. If you don't teach them how you think and how you can come up with solutions so fast, they will never learn. Take the time to really define the problem—not impatiently throw out a solution. Brainstorm what questions need to be answered in order to resolve it. Give your people the task to think about for a day and come back with some solutions. Be a teacher instead of a dictator of solutions. Study yourself. Keep a journal of what triggered your behavior and what the observed consequences were. Learn to detect and control your triggers before they get you in trouble.

2. **Task impatience.** Impatient people check in a lot. How's it coming. Is it done yet? When will it be finished? Let me see what you've done so far. That is disruptive to due process and wastes time. When you give out a task or assign a project, establish agreed-upon time checkpoints. You can also assign percentage checkpoints. Check in with me when you are about 25% finished so we can make midcourse corrections and 75% finished so we can make final corrections. Let them figure out how to do the task. Hold back from checking in at other than the agreed-upon times and percentages.

3. **Too dependent upon yourself.** Look at others' solutions more. Invite discussion and disagreement, welcome bad news, ask that people come up with the second and third solution. A useful trick is to assign issues and questions before you have given them any thought. Two weeks before you are due to decide, ask your people to examine that issue and report to you two days before you have to deal with it. That way, you really don't have any solutions yet. This really motivates people and makes you look less impatient.

4. **Transitions.** Which transitions are the toughest for you? Write down the five toughest for you. What do you have a hard time switching to and from? Use this knowledge to assist you in making a list of discontinuities (tough transitions) you face, such as confronting people vs. being approachable and accepting, leading vs. following, going from firing someone to a business-as-usual staff meeting. Write

down how each of these discontinuities makes you feel and what you may do that gets you in trouble. For example, you may not shift gears well after a confrontation, or you may have trouble taking charge again after passively sitting in a meeting all day. Create a plan to attack each of the tough transitions.

5.   **Control your instant responses to shifts.** Many of us respond to the fragmentation and discontinuities of work as if they were threats instead of the way life is. Sometimes our emotions and fears are triggered by switching from active to passive or soft to tough. This initial anxious response lasts 45–60 seconds, and we need to buy some time before we say or do something inappropriate. Research shows that generally somewhere between the second and third thing you think to say or do is the best option. Practice holding back your first response long enough to think of a second and a third. Manage your shifts, don't be a prisoner of them.

6.   **Use mental rehearsal to think about different ways you could carry out a transaction.** Try to see yourself acting in opposing ways to get the same thing done—when to be tough, when to let them decide, when to deflect the issue because it's not ready to decide. What cues would you look for to select an approach that matches? Practice trying to get the same thing done with two different groups with two different approaches. Did they both work?

D   Being More Strategic

ESFJs value stability and harmony. The disruptive change that strategy brings can be unsettling.

1.   **Not curious?** Many managers are so wrapped up in today's problems that they aren't curious about tomorrow. They really don't care about the long-term future. They may not even be in the organization when the strategic plan is supposed to happen. They believe there won't be much of a future until we perform today. Being a visionary and a good strategist requires curiosity and imagination. It requires playing "what ifs." What are the implications of the growing gap between rich and poor? The collapse of retail pricing? The increasing influence of brand names? What if it turns out there is life on other planets, and we get the first message? What will that change? Will they need our products? What will happen when a larger percentage of the world's population is over the age of 65? The effects of terrorism? What if cancer is cured? Heart disease? AIDS? Obesity? What if the government outlaws or severely regulates some aspect of your

business? True, nobody knows the answers, but good strategists know the questions. Work at developing broader interests outside your business. Subscribe to different magazines. Pick new shows to watch. Meet different people. Join a new organization. Look under some rocks. Think about tomorrow. Talk to others about what they think the future will bring.

2. **Narrow perspective?** Some are sharply focused on what they do and do it very well. They have prepared themselves for a narrow but satisfying career. Then someone tells them their job has changed, and they now have to be strategic. Being strategic requires a broad perspective. In addition to knowing one thing well, it requires that you know about a lot of things somewhat. You need to understand business. You need to understand markets. You need to understand how the world operates. You need to put all that together and figure out what all that means to your organization.

3. **Too busy?** Strategy is always last on the list. Solving today's problems, of which there are many, is job one. You have to make time for strategy. A good strategy releases future time because it makes choices clear and leads to less wasted effort, but it takes time to do. Delegation is usually the main key. Give away as much tactical day-to-day stuff as you can. Ask your people what they think they could do to give you more time for strategic reflection. Another key is better time management. Put an hour a week on your calendar for strategic reading and reflection throughout the year. Don't wait until one week before the strategic plan is due. Keep a log of ideas you get from others, magazines, etc. Focus on how these impact your organization or function.

4. **Can't think strategically?** Strategy is linking several variables together to come up with the most likely scenario. Think of it as the search for and application of relevant parallels. It involves making projections of several variables at once to see how they come together. These projections are in the context of shifting markets, international affairs, monetary movements, and government interventions. It involves a lot of uncertainty, making risk assumptions, and understanding how things work together. How many reasons would account for sales going down? Up? How are advertising and sales linked? If the dollar is cheaper in Asia, what does that mean for our product in Japan? If the world population is aging and they have more money, how will that change buying patterns? Not everyone enjoys this kind of pie-in-the-sky thinking and not everyone is skilled at doing it.

5. **Don't know enough about your business?** Study your annual report and various other financial reports. If you don't know how, the major investment firms have basic documents explaining how to read financial documents. After you've done this, consult a pro and ask him/her what he/she looks at and why. Ask for lunch or just a meeting with the person who is in charge of the strategic planning process in your company. Have him/her explain the strategic plan for the organization. Particularly, have him/her point out the mission-critical functions and capabilities the organization needs to be on the leading edge to win.

6. **Try some broader tasks.** Volunteer for task forces that include people outside your area of expertise. Work on some TQM, ISO or Six Sigma projects that cross functional or business unit boundaries to learn more about the business. Go talk with customers, work actually delivering the product or service, and write down five things you've learned about how the business works. Start up a mock business in something you know intimately. Write a business plan, complete the necessary forms, price equipment, and talk with people in this business about their problems.

7. **Get close to customers.** Customer service is the best place to learn about the business. Arrange a meeting with a counterpart in customer service. Have him or her explain the function to you. If you can, listen in on customer service calls or, even better, handle a couple yourself.

8. **Do you only think about your part of the business?** In order to be a well-running business, all of the pieces and parts need to work together. A business is a closed system. That means doing something in one area affects all of the other areas. Sunbeam decided to have an off-season discount in order to show more booked business in the fourth quarter. That was easy. Customers stocked up on the cheaper goods. Then plant production faltered in the next two quarters as orders decreased. Inventory prices went up for Sunbeam and its customers, which led to dissatisfaction. Margins decreased as Sunbeam tried to fix the problem. What happens in one area always affects everything else. When you make decisions in your area, do you think about possible negative consequences for the other functions? Document your understanding of the drivers that run your business to a few key drivers organized around things like marketing, sales, operations, etc. Share your conclusions with others from other functions or units to see how your key drivers affect them.

E Paying More Attention to Process

ESFJs are very effective at hands-on activities. Setting up a longer-term process is more difficult.

1. **Lay out tasks and work.** Most successful projects begin with a good plan. What do I need to accomplish? What are the goals? What's the time line? What resources will I need? How many of the resources do I control? Who controls the rest of the resources—people, funding, tools, materials, support—I need? Lay out the work from A to Z. Many people are seen as lacking a plan because they don't write down the sequence or parts of the work and leave something out. Ask others to comment on ordering and what's missing.

2. **Set goals.** You should set goals before assigning projects, work, and tasks. Goals help focus people's time and efforts. It allows people to perform more effectively and efficiently. Most people don't want to waste time. Most people want to perform well. Learn about MBO—managing by objectives. Read a book about it. While you may not be interested in a full-blown application, all of the principles of setting goals will be in the book. Go to a course on goal setting.

3. **Vision the plan in process.** What could go wrong? Run scenarios in your head. Think along several paths. Rank the potential problems from highest likelihood to lowest likelihood. Think about what you would do if the highest likelihood things were to occur. Create a contingency plan for each. Pay attention to the weakest links, which are usually groups or elements you have the least interface with or control over (perhaps someone in a remote location, a consultant, or supplier). Stay doubly in touch with the potential weak links.

4. **Visualize.** Set up a process to monitor progress against the goals. People like running measures. They like to gauge their pace. It's like the United Way Thermometer in the lobby.

5. **Feedback.** Give as much in-process feedback as you have time for. Most people are motivated by process feedback against agreed-upon goals for three reasons:

   ■ First, it helps them adjust what they are doing along the way in time to achieve the goal; they can make midcourse corrections.

   ■ Second, it shows them what they are doing is important and that you're eager to help.

■ Third, it's not the "gotcha" game of negative and critical feedback after the fact.

6. **Bargaining for resources.** What do I have to trade? What can I buy? What can I borrow? What do I need to trade for? What do I need that I can't pay or trade for?

7. **Rallying support.** Share your mission and goals with the people you need to support you. Try to get their input. People who are asked tend to cooperate more than people who are not asked. Figure out how the people who support your effort can win along with you.

I tend to make sure my feelings favor a certain solution. I need to slow down and be more open to others' ideas.

– An ESFJ Manager

APPLICATION

Your personal preferences play out in day-to-day problems and situations you face. Below is a case about your type dealing with such a situation. Use this to think through how you will integrate the tips you've considered and coach yourself to be more effective in your type.

ESFJ Application Situation (Part 1)

"Psst. Here comes the new big cheese," Fred says to Larry while they both get coffee in the break room. "Let's give him the business."

"Do you really think that's wise, considering he's only been in the VP role a few weeks? He may be feeling vulnerable," Larry replies.

"Bull," Joy chimes in. "Andy's still one of us, no matter how high he climbs. Why do you think he keeps coming around, even though he's got a bright new office and a sporty car?"

Andrew approaches, and the other three immediately stop talking, deliberately, and put on an act of looking guilty and avoiding Andrew's gaze. Andrew completely ignores their charade, however, and says warmly, "How're the very best salespeople in the Western world?" as he puts his arms around Joy's and Larry's shoulders. "Oh, yeah, and how are you doing, Fred?" he adds slyly, as though he only just noticed Fred standing there.

"Doing fine, pal 'o mine," Fred answers. Larry says, "Aw, shucks." Joy smiles.

"Aah, feels like home," Andrew sighs.

"You oughta stop by more often," Joy answers. "We're not seeing as much of you since you went upstairs," she says, rolling her eyes toward the ceiling, then adding, "Hmm, did any of you notice the ceiling is made of glass?"

"Nope," Andrew says. "Guess you can only see that through a woman's eyes."

"No, but really, how are things going for you? Feeling any more comfortable away from the front line than the last time we talked?"

Andrew thought back to what he was already referring to as "the good old days"—that is, those days before three weeks ago when he was promoted to VP. A guy who prided himself on blending his penchant for managing the details as well as for connecting with people, he now wondered what piece was missing in his job performance since the promotion, feeling for the first time in his career uneasy about success. His boss has only commented that being a VP requires a more strategic skill set, and Andrew isn't even sure what they're talking about half the time when they throw the word "strategy" around as though it had some magical powers.

Thinking It Through: Strategy

- If you were coaching Andrew, what else would you want to know about the situation?

- How do you think it would be best to go about getting that information?

Planning It Out: Tactics

- What tendencies and preferences in Andrew (an ESFJ) would you focus on to help him appreciate how the typical facets of his MBTI type might tend to pose challenges for him in his new role?

- What particular areas would you encourage Andrew to work on? What in his tendencies does he need to alter, do less of, or more of?

- Which of the tactics described in the Being More Effective section are applicable in this situation?

- Which Overused Tendencies are most likely to come into play here?

ESFJ Application Situation (Part 2)

- At his annual performance review, Andrew's boss tells him how pleased he is with the one-on-one coaching Andrew is doing with his salespeople and that he's pleased with the near-term results, but suggests he is worried that Andrew is going to burn out from working too many hours at too many things. He also has concerns about what Andrew's vision is for the sales organization over the longer term.

Reflection

- What is it about Andrew that makes it difficult for him to change? What advice would you give him at this point?

SUGGESTED READINGS

■■■■■■■■ **Being a More Effective ESFJ** ■■■■■■■■

Enhancing Ways to Learn

DeGraff, Jeff and Katherine A. Lawrence. *Creativity at Work: Developing the Right Practices to Make Innovation Happen.* San Francisco: Jossey-Bass, Inc., 2002.

Flynn, Daniel J. *Intellectual Morons: How Ideology Makes Smart People Fall for Stupid Ideas.* New York: Crown Business Publishing, 2004.

Hammond, John S., Ralph L. Keeney and Howard Raiffer. *Smart Choices.* Boston: Harvard University Press, 1999.

Lucas, Robert W. *The Creative Training Idea Book: Inspired Tips and Techniques for Engaging and Effective Learning.* New York: AMACOM, 2003.

Von Oech, Roger. *Expect the Unexpected or You Won't Find It: A Creativity Tool Based on the Ancient Wisdom of Heraclitus.* San Francisco: Berrett-Koehler Publishers, Inc., 2002.

Yates, J. Frank. *Decision Management: How to Assure Better Decisions in Your Company.* San Francisco: Jossey-Bass, Inc., 2003.

Dealing With Ambiguity

Anderson, Dean and Linda S. Ackerman Anderson. *Beyond Change Management: Advanced Strategies for Today's Transformational Leaders.* San Francisco: Jossey-Bass, Inc., 2001.

Bellman, Geoffrey M. *Getting Things Done When You Are Not in Charge.* San Francisco: Berrett-Koehler Publishers, Inc., 2001.

Block, Peter. *The Answer to How Is Yes: Acting On What Matters.* San Francisco: Berrett-Koehler Publishers, Inc., 2001.

Bossidy, Larry, Ram Charan and Charles Burck (Contributor). *Execution: The Discipline of Getting Things Done.* New York: Crown Business Publishing, 2002.

Collins, James C. *Good to Great: Why Some Companies Make the Leap...And Others Don't.* New York: HarperCollins, 2001.

Hammond, John S., Ralph L. Keeney and Howard Raiffer. *Smart Choices.* Boston: Harvard University Press, 1999.

Kotter, John P. *The General Managers.* New York: The Free Press, 1982.

Nutt, Paul C. *Why Decisions Fail: Avoiding the Blunders and Traps That Lead to Decision Debacles.* San Francisco: Berrett-Koehler Publishers, Inc., 2002.

Sofo, Francesco. *Six Myths of Critical Thinking.* Business & Professional Publishing, 2003.

Sternberg, Robert J. *Thinking Styles.* Boston: Cambridge University Press, 1997.

White, R.P., P. Hodgson and S. Crainer. *The Future of Leadership.* London: Pitman, 1996.

Yates, J. Frank. *Decision Management: How to Assure Better Decisions in Your Company.* San Francisco: Jossey-Bass, Inc., 2003.

Being More Innovative

Campbell, David. *Take the Road to Creativity and Get Off Your Dead End.* Greensboro, NC: Center for Creative Leadership, 1985.

Ceserani, Jonne. *Big Ideas: Putting the Zest Into Creativity & Innovation at Work.* London: Kogan Page, 2003.

DeGraff, Jeff and Katherine A. Lawrence. *Creativity at Work: Developing the Right Practices to Make Innovation Happen.* San Francisco: Jossey-Bass, Inc., 2002.

Foster, Jack. *Ideaship: How to Get Ideas Flowing in Your Workplace.* San Francisco: Berrett-Koehler Publishers, Inc., 2001.

Lucas, Robert W. *The Creative Training Idea Book: Inspired Tips and Techniques for Engaging and Effective Learning.* New York: AMACOM, 2003.

Von Oech, Roger. *Expect the Unexpected or You Won't Find It: A Creativity Tool Based on the Ancient Wisdom of Heraclitus.* San Francisco: Berrett-Koehler Publishers, Inc., 2002.

Dealing With Conflict

Cloke, Ken and Joan Goldsmith. *Resolving Conflicts at Work: A Complete Guide for Everyone on the Job.* San Francisco: Jossey-Bass, Inc., 2000.

Dana, Daniel. *Conflict Resolution.* New York: McGraw-Hill Trade, 2000.

Guttman, Howard M. *When Goliaths Clash: Managing Executive Conflict to Build a More Dynamic Organization.* New York: AMACOM, 2003.

Masters, Marick Francis and Robert R. Albright. *The Complete Guide to Conflict Resolution in the Workplace.* New York: AMACOM, 2002.

Taking Charge

Badaracco, Joseph L., Jr. *Defining Moments — When Managers Must Choose Between Right and Right.* Boston: Harvard Business School Press, 1997.

Bennis, Warren G. and Burt Nanus. *Leaders: Strategies for Taking Charge.* New York: HarperBusiness, 2003.

Chaleff, Ira. *The Courageous Follower: Standing Up to and for Our Leaders.* San Francisco: Berrett-Koehler Publishers, Inc., 2003.

Coponigro, Jeffrey R. *The Crisis Counselor: A Step-by-Step Guide to Managing a Business Crisis.* New York: McGraw-Hill/Contemporary Books, 2000.

Cox, Danny and John Hoover. *Leadership When the Heat's On.* New York: McGraw-Hill Trade, 2002.

Levin, Robert A. and Joseph G. Rosse. *Talent Flow: A Strategic Approach to Keeping Good Employees, Helping Them Grow, and Letting Them Go.* New York: John Wiley & Sons, Inc., 2001.

Linsky, Martin and Ronald A. Heifetz. *Leadership on the Line: Staying Alive Through the Dangers of Leading.* Boston: Harvard Business School Press, 2002.

Solomon, Muriel. *Working With Difficult People.* New York: Prentice Hall, 2002.

Delegation and Staffing

Allen, David. *Getting Things Done: The Art of Stress-Free Productivity.* New York: Penguin Books, 2003.

Bolton, Robert and Dorothy Grover Bolton. *People Styles at Work—Making Bad Relationships Good and Good Relationships Better.* New York: AMACOM, 1996.

Bossidy, Larry, Ram Charan and Charles Burck (Contributor). *Execution: The Discipline of Getting Things Done.* New York: Crown Business Publishing, 2002.

Daniels, Aubrey C. *Bringing Out the Best in People.* New York: McGraw-Hill, Inc., 1994.

Genett, Donna M. *If You Want It Done Right, You Don't Have to Do It Yourself! The Power of Effective Delegation.* Sanger, CA: Quill Driver Books, 2004.

Lombardo, Michael M. and Robert W. Eichinger. *FYI For Your Improvement* (4th ed.). Minneapolis, MN: Lominger Limited, Inc., 1996–2004.

Mazzarella, Mark C. and Jo-Ellan Dimitrius. *Reading People: How to Understand People and Predict Their Behavior—Anytime, Anyplace.* New York: Ballantine Books, 1999.

■■■■■■■ Overusing ESFJ Tendencies ■■■■■■■■

Self-Awareness

Bennis, Warren G. *On Becoming a Leader.* Cambridge, MA: Perseus Publishing, 2003.

Lombardo, Michael M. and Robert W. Eichinger. *The Leadership Machine.* Minneapolis, MN: Lominger Limited, Inc., 2004.

Myers, Isabel Briggs with Peter B. Myers. *Gifts Differing: Understanding Personality Type.* Palo Alto, CA: Davies-Black Publishing, 1995.

Stone, Florence M. and Randi T. Sachs. *The High-Value Manager—Developing the Core Competencies Your Organization Needs.* New York: AMACOM, 1995.

Personal Growth

Barner, Robert. *Lifeboat Strategies: How to Keep Your Career Above Water During Tough Times—Or Any Time.* New York: American Management Association, 1994.

Bolles, Richard N. *What Color Is Your Parachute? 2004: A Practical Manual for Job-Hunters & Career-Changers.* Berkeley, CA: Ten Speed Press, 2004.

Dominguez, Linda R. *How to Shine at Work.* New York: McGraw-Hill Trade, 2003.

Glickman, Rosalene. *Optimal Thinking: How to Be Your Best Self.* New York: John Wiley & Sons, Inc., 2002.

Holton, Bill and Cher Holton. *The Manager's Short Course. Thirty-Three Tactics to Upgrade Your Career.* New York: John Wiley & Sons, Inc., 1992.

Lombardo, Michael M. and Robert W. Eichinger. *FYI For Your Improvement* (4th ed.). Minneapolis, MN: Lominger Limited, Inc., 1996–2004.

Lombardo, Michael M. and Robert W. Eichinger. *The Leadership Machine.* Minneapolis, MN: Lominger Limited, Inc., 2004.

McCall, Morgan W., Michael M. Lombardo and Ann M. Morrison. *The Lessons of Experience.* Lexington, MA: Lexington Books, 1988.

Morrison, Ann M., Randall P. White, Ellen Van Velsor and the Center for Creative Leadership. *Breaking the Glass Ceiling: Can Women Reach the Top of America's Largest Corporations?* Reading, MA: Addison-Wesley Publishing Company, 1992.

Niven, David. *The 100 Simple Secrets of Successful People: What Scientists Have Learned and How You Can Use It.* New York: HarperBusiness, 2002.

Being More Flexible/Less Pressuring

Anderson, Dean and Linda S. Ackerman Anderson. *Beyond Change Management: Advanced Strategies for Today's Transformational Leaders.* San Francisco: Jossey-Bass, Inc., 2001.

Barker, Larry, Ph.D. and Kittie Watson, Ph.D. *Listen Up: At Home, at Work, in Relationships: How to Harness the Power of Effective Listening.* Irvine, CA: Griffin Trade Paperback, 2001.

Bellman, Geoffrey M. *Getting Things Done When You Are Not in Charge.* San Francisco: Berrett-Koehler Publishers, Inc., 2001.

Bolton, Robert and Dorothy Grover Bolton. *People Styles at Work—Making Bad Relationships Good and Good Relationships Better.* New York: AMACOM, 1996.

Burke, W. Warner and William Trahant with Richard Koonce. *Business Climate Shifts: Profiles of Change Makers.* Boston: Butterworth-Heinemann, 2000.

Carter, Les. *The Anger Trap: Free Yourself From the Frustrations That Sabotage Your Life.* New York: John Wiley & Sons, Inc., 2003.

Luecke, Richard. *Managing Change and Transition.* Boston: Harvard Business School Publishing, 2003.

Patterson, Kerry, Joseph Grenny, Ron McMillan, Al Switzler and Stephen R. Covey. *Crucial Conversations: Tools for Talking When Stakes Are High.* New York: McGraw-Hill/Contemporary Books, 2002.

Being More Strategic

Bandrowski, James F. *Corporate Imagination Plus—Five Steps to Translating Innovative Strategies Into Action.* New York: The Free Press, 2000.

Birch, Paul and Brian Clegg. *Imagination Engineering—The Toolkit for Business Creativity.* London: Pitman Publishing, 1996.

Chakravorti, Bhaskar. *The Slow Pace of Fast Change: Bringing Innovations to Market in a Connected World.* Boston: Harvard Business School Press, 2003.

Charan, Ram. *What the CEO Wants You to Know: How Your Company Really Works.* New York: Crown Business Publishing, 2001.

Christensen, Clayton M. and Michael E. Raynor. *The Innovator's Solution.* Harvard Business School Press, 2003.

Collins, James C. *Good to Great: Why Some Companies Make the Leap...And Others Don't.* New York: HarperCollins, 2001.

DeGraff, Jeff and Katherine A. Lawrence. *Creativity at Work: Developing the Right Practices to Make Innovation Happen.* San Francisco: Jossey-Bass, Inc., 2002.

Dudik, Evan Matthew. *Strategic Renaissance: New Thinking and Innovative Tools to Create Great Corporate Strategies Using Insights From History and Science.* New York: AMACOM, 2000.

The Futurist Magazine. http://www.wfs.org

Gaynor, Gerard H. *Innovation by Design.* New York: AMACOM, 2002.

Hamel, Gary. *Leading the Revolution.* Boston: Harvard Business School Press, 2002.

Hargadon, Andrew and Kathleen M. Eisenhardt. *How Breakthroughs Happen: The Surprising Truth About How Companies Innovate.* Boston: Harvard Business School Press, 2003.

Harvard Business Review. Phone: 800-988-0886 (US and Canada). Fax: 617-496-1029. Mail: Harvard Business Review. Subscriber Services, P.O. Box 52623. Boulder, CO 80322-2623 USA. http://www.hbsp.harvard.edu/products/hbr

Kaplan, Robert S. and David P. Norton. *The Strategy-Focused Organization: How Balanced Scorecard Companies Thrive in the New Business Environment.* Boston: Harvard Business School Press, 2000.

Porter, Michael E. *Competitive Strategy: Techniques for Analyzing Industries and Competitors.* New York: The Free Press, 1998.

Prahalad, C.K. and Venkat Ramaswamy. *The Future of Competition: Co-Creating Unique Value With Customers.* Boston: Harvard Business School Press, 2004.

Paying More Attention to Process

Allen, David. *Getting Things Done: The Art of Stress-Free Productivity.* New York: Penguin Books, 2003.

Bossidy, Larry, Ram Charan and Charles Burck (Contributor). *Execution: The Discipline of Getting Things Done.* New York: Crown Business Publishing, 2002.

Drucker, Peter F. *The Effective Executive.* New York: HarperBusiness, 2002.

Stone, Florence M. and Randi T. Sachs. *The High-Value Manager— Developing the Core Competencies Your Organization Needs.* New York: AMACOM, 1995.

Ulrich, David, Jack Zenger and Norman Smallwood. *Results-Based Leadership.* Boston: Harvard Business School Press, 1999.

CHAPTER 15

ENFJ
Extraverted Feeling
with
Introverted Intuiting

■■■■■■■■■■■■■■■■■

2.5% of Population
3.4% of Managers

■■■■■■■■■■■■■■■■■

Typical Strengths

Popular
Responsible
Charming
Warm
Good Communicator
Developing Relationships
Initiating
Funny
Coaching and Mentoring

ISTJ	ISFJ	INFJ	INTJ
ISTP	ISFP	INFP	INTP
ESTP	ESFP	ENFP	ENTP
ESTJ	ESFJ	**ENFJ**	ENTJ

Trust is the key to leading others. I've got to work on my circle of trust.

— An ENFJ Manager

Basic Habits of Mind

The lead process for ENFJs is Extraverted Feeling, which often pushes them to seek connections with people in intense ways. They notice subtle differences and cues in the interactions among people and are very engaging and eager to spend time with others. This interest in people is aided by Introverted Intuiting, which helps them immediately see many possibilities for each person with whom they are engaged.

Introverted Sensing and Introverted Thinking also aid ENFJs. Introverted Sensing promotes an awareness of specific changes in their environment. Introverted Thinking pushes them toward precision. Very attentive to their environment, ENFJs notice subtle changes in behavior and spot potential conflicts readily. They then tend to think that if they can get everything into the open, get more precise and hammer things out, that the situation will be worked out.

Unfortunately, this sometimes backfires as people see this behavior as intrusive, overblown, or seeing problems that aren't there. Many ENFJs would be surprised to know that their genuine concern for others can be seen as pushy, overly inclusive, insistent, and adamant.

Typical Communication Patterns

- ENFJs are action-oriented, outgoing individuals who are idealistic about the future.

- They seek out "democratic" roles—sharing responsibilities and seeking cooperation.

- They are gregarious, turning almost any conversation toward a variety of topics through an appreciative and supportive approach.

General Learning Strategy

■ ENFJs usually prefer to learn by creative exploration and like to discover connections among ideas and people. They look for parallel "lessons" from other parts of life.

■ Typical learning strategies are networking with others to explore connections and future uses for what they are learning. They quickly envision how the experience of others is valuable.

■ Their learning is generally enhanced by opportunities to share insights, speculate.

■ They like supportive environments to test out ideas and creative expressions.

Interpersonal Qualities Related to Motivation

■ ENFJs are engaged by working on people (rather than technical) issues.

■ They are resourceful in interactions, which enables them to share the patterns and insights they feel are important.

■ They have an initiating and approachable nature.

Blind Spots

■ ENFJs might be surprised to learn that others see them as needing to be more flexible in dealing with others, demonstrate a quicker understanding of situations, and have fewer disagreements with the direction of upper management.

■ Many feel ENFJs have an overdependence on a select few.

Stress Related Behavior

■ Under stress, they seem to put more energy into being decisive (thus seeming pushy), taking action (seeming impatient), and can spend unusual amounts of time in organizing.

■ As this increases, ENFJs can seem hasty, impulsive, and hardheaded.

■ With sustained stress, they can become reserved and obsessed with internal criticisms of their perceived failures and inadequate accomplishments.

Potential Barriers to Effectiveness

- ENFJs can appear opinionated, manipulating, blunt, and dogmatic, so that all of their relationships are affected.

- At times, their energetic style seems overly pressuring, their methodological approach seems manipulating, and their comments seem overly personal.

- They can lack awareness of their impact on others.

Being a More Effective ENFJ

A **Focusing on Analysis**
B **Selling Ideas**
C **Too Dependent on a Few Relationships**
D **Staffing**
E **Technical Focus**
F **Problems With Higher Management**
G **Dealing With Conflict**

ISTJ	ISFJ	INFJ	INTJ
ISTP	ISFP	INFP	INTP
ESTP	ESFP	ENFP	ENTP
ESTJ	ESFJ	ENFJ	ENTJ

A Focusing on Analysis

As an ENFJ said: "I work on solving the problem before completely analyzing it. I focus too much on other people instead."

1. **Turn off your idea-generation program.** Sometimes you need to just do it as designed. Four ideas to make a procedure better won't help the work get done today. Pick a few causes to change. For the others, just execute them. Don't get into so many permutations of an idea that you don't stop to analyze what is before you.

2. **Check yourself for these common errors in thinking:** Do you state as facts things that are really opinions or assumptions? Are you sure these assertions are facts? State opinions and assumptions as that and don't present them as facts. Do you attribute cause and effect to relationships when you don't know if one causes the other? If sales are down, and we increase advertising and sales go up, this doesn't prove causality. They are simply related. Say we know that the relationship between sales/advertising is about the same as sales/number of employees. If sales go down, we probably wouldn't hire more people, so make sure one thing causes the other before acting on it. Do you

generalize from a single example without knowing if that single example does generalize?

3. **Do a historical analysis.** Do an objective analysis of decisions you have made in the past and what the percentage correct was. Break the decisions into topics or areas of your life. For most of us, we make better decisions in some areas than others. Maybe your decision-making skills need help in one or two limited areas, like decisions about people, decisions about your career, political decisions, technical, etc.

4. **Study decision makers.** Whom do you admire? Bill Gates? Winston Churchill? Read the biographies and autobiographies of a few people you respect, and pay attention to how they made decisions in their lives and careers. Write down five things they did that you can do. For example, Churchill always slept on important decisions, no matter what. He initially only asked questions and tried to understand the problem and argument as given. He kept his views to himself until later. A helpful Web site for finding biographical summaries, books, videos, etc. is www.biography.com. Additionally, they list a monthly schedule for the Biography Channel, a cable channel on the A&E network dedicated to biography shows and specials on significant lives.

5. **Locate the essence of the problem.** What are the key factors or elements in this problem? Experts usually solve problems by figuring out what the deep, underlying principles are and working forward from there; the less adept focus on desired outcomes/solutions and either work backward or concentrate on the surface facts. What are the deep principles of what you're working on? Once you've done this, search the past for parallels—your past, the business past, the historical past. One common mistake here is to search in parallel organizations because "only they would know." Backing up and asking a broader question will aid in the search for solutions. When Motorola wanted to find out how to process orders more quickly, they went not to other electronics firms, but to Domino's Pizza and Federal Express.

6. **Patterns.** Look for patterns in personal, organization, or the world, in general successes and failures. What was common to each success or what was present in each failure but never present in a success? Focus on the successes; failures are easier to analyze but don't in themselves tell you what would work. Comparing successes, while less exciting, yields more information about underlying principles. The bottom line

is to reduce your insights to principles or rules of thumb you think might be repeatable. When faced with the next new problem, those general underlying principles will apply again.

7. **Defining the problem.** Instant and early conclusions, solutions, statements, suggestions, and how we solved it in the past, are the enemies of good problem solving. Studies show that defining the problem and taking action occur almost simultaneously for most people, so the more effort you put on the front end, the easier it is to come up with a good solution. Stop and first define what the problem is and isn't. Since providing solutions is so easy for everyone, it would be nice if they were offering solutions to the right problem. Figure out what causes it. Keep asking why. See how many causes you can come up with and how many organizing buckets you can put them in. This increases the chance of a better solution because you can see more connections. Be a chess master. Chess masters recognize thousands of patterns of chess pieces. Look for patterns in data; don't just collect information. Put it in categories that make sense to you. Ask lots of questions. Allot at least 50% of the time to defining the problem.

B Selling Ideas

Personable as they may be, ENFJs spend more time on relationship building than being persuasive sellers of ideas.

1. **Learn to sell ideas simply as a statement of purpose or mission.** C.K. Prahalad, one of the leading strategic consultants, believes that in order to qualify as a mission statement, it should take less than three minutes to explain it clearly to an audience. Really effective mission statements are simple, compelling, and capable of capturing people's imagination. Mission statements should help everyone allot his/her time. They should signal what's mission-critical and explain what's rewarded in the organization and what's not. Create a simple obvious symbol, visual, or slogan to make the cause come alive. Ford's "Quality is Job One" seems clear enough. Nordstrom's "The Customer is Always Right" tells employees how they should do their jobs. Although the actual mission and vision document would be longer, the message needs to be finely crafted to capture the essence of what's important around here.

2. **Common mind-set.** The power of a mission and vision communication is providing everyone in the organization with a road map on how they are going to be part of something grand and exciting.

Establish common cause. Imagine what the change would look like if fully implemented, then describe the outcome often—how things will look in the future. Help people see how their efforts fit in by creating simple, obvious measures of achievement like bar or thermometer charts. Be succinct. People don't line up behind laundry lists or ambiguous objectives. Missions and visions should be more about where we are going and less about how we are going to get there. Keep your eyes on the prize.

3. **Change management.** Most significant vision and mission statements represent a deviation from the past. They represent a rallying call for a departure from business as usual. They require that people are going to have to think, talk, and act differently. For that reason, underneath the excitement will be apprehension, anxiety, and fear of the unknown. All of the principles of change management apply to communicating a mission. Expect trouble and admit that 20–40% of time will be spent debugging, fixing mistakes, and figuring out what went wrong. Treat each one as a chance to learn—document difficulties and learn from them. Without sounding like you're hedging, present it as a work-in-progress to be improved over time. How changes are made should be as open as possible. Studies show that people work harder and are more effective when they have a sense of choice over how they accomplish stretch goals and objectives. Invite multiple attacks, encourage experimentation, talk with people who have successfully pulled off changes.

4. **Walking your talk.** Many times employees listen more to what you do than to what you say. The largest reason change efforts fail is that the messenger does not act in line with the new vision and mission. Words are wonderful. Actions are stronger. If you want to be credible, make sure you incorporate the new thinking and behavior into your repertoire. Otherwise it will be gone as soon as the echoes of your words are gone.

5. **Inspiring.** Missions and visions are meant to motivate. Don't threaten. Don't say this is our last chance. Don't blame the past. Visions are optimistic, inspirational, about possibilities, about getting to a grand place in the market. Paint a positive "we can do it" picture. You have to blow a little smoke and use fairy dust. It's a performance. You have to get people to see what you see. This is all about how to present well and motivate. Always rehearse. Use a test group before you go public. See it yourself on video. Would you understand and be motivated?

6. **Detractors and resisters.** There will always be those who don't buy it, have seen it all before, haven't yet seen a mission or vision come true. They may be private about it or come at you in public. Before you communicate the mission and vision, think about the 10 critical questions that might come up. "What happened to last year's brand-new mission that we've already abandoned? I don't think that will work. Our customers won't go for it." Be prepared for the most likely criticisms. Mentally rehearse how you might respond to questions. Listen patiently to people's concerns, protecting their feelings, but also reinforcing the perspective of why the change is needed. Attack positions, not the people. Show patience toward the unconverted; maintain a light touch. Remember, there was a time during the crafting of this vision that you were not convinced. Invite alternative suggestions to reach the same outcome. In the end, thank everyone for their time and input and just say the train is leaving. Rarely, you may have to pull a specific person aside and say, "I understand all your worries and have tried to respond to them, but the train is moving on. Are you on or off?"

7. **Managing vision and mission is a lot like selling.** You have a product you think others would buy if they knew about it. Each customer is a little different. What features and benefits would they be looking for? What would they be willing to pay in terms of time and commitment? What are their objections likely to be? How will you answer them? How are you going to ask for the order?

8. **Against the grain tough stands.** Taking a tough stand demands confidence in what you're saying along with the humility that you might be wrong—one of life's paradoxes. To prepare to take the lead on a tough issue, work on your stand through mental interrogation until you can clearly state in a few sentences what your stand is and why you hold it. Build the business case. How do others win? People don't line up behind laundry lists or ambiguous objectives. Ask others for advice—scope the problem, consider options, pick one, develop a rationale, then go with it until proven wrong. Then redo the process. If this doesn't help, find out where the pain is for you. What have you been avoiding? Examine your past and see where taking-charge behavior has gotten you in trouble or you thought it would get you in trouble. Isolate the most troublesome elements, such as forgetting things under pressure, trouble with fierce debate, problems with unpopular stands, and things moving too fast. Devise counter-strategies.

C Too Dependent on a Few Relationships

Although very adept with people, ENFJs usually gravitate to a few close relationships and can be seen as dependent on a small group of insiders. This limits their perspective and their network in an organization.

1. **Spend most of your time with just a few people?** Developed a comfort and liking for the few? Expand your repertoire to get your relationship quota up. Find someone to act as your devil's advocate. Go to the toughest critic first, not those who will basically support you. Be an early adopter of something. Find some new thing, technique, software, tool, system, process, or skill relevant to your activity. Privately become an expert in it. Read the books. Get certified. Visit a location where it's being done. Then surprise everyone and be the first to introduce it into your world. Sell it. Train others. Integrate it into your work.

2. **Pick three tasks you've never done before and go do them.** If you don't know much about customers, work in a store or handle customer complaints; if you don't know what engineering does, go find out; task trade with someone. Meet with your colleagues from other areas and tell each other what and, more importantly, how you do what you do.

3. **Volunteer for task forces.** Task forces/projects are a great opportunity to learn new things in a low-risk environment. Task forces are one of the most common developmental events listed by successful executives. Such projects require learning other functions, businesses, or nationalities well enough that in a tight time frame you can appreciate how they think and why their area/position is important. In so doing, you get out of your own experience and start to see connections to a broader world—how international trade works; or more at home, how the pieces of your organization fit together.

4. **Pick a person in the organization who is different in some aspects from your advocate/mentor.** Observe what he/she does and how he/she does it. He/she is as successful as your advocate/mentor but does it in other ways. If possible, ask for a meeting/lunch to discuss his/her success and the things he/she has learned. See if he/she has any interest in teaching you something and being a temporary coach. Get to know other potential advocates on and off work. Go for maximum variety in the towering strengths they possess.

5. **Are you the same in your personal life?** Do you eat at the same restaurants? Vacation at the same places? Holidays are always done the same as in the past? Buy the same make or type car over and over again? Have the same insurance agent your father had? Expand yourself. Go on adventures with the family. Travel to places you have not been before. Never vacation at the same place again. Eat at different theme restaurants. Go to events and meetings of groups you have never really met. Go to ethnic festivals and sample the cultures. Go to athletic events you've never attended before. Each week, you and your family should go on a personal learning adventure. See how many different perspectives you can add to your knowledge.

D Staffing

ENFJs genuinely like people but may not take the time to look carefully at their assets and liabilities.

1. **When you make a hiring decision or are deciding whom to work with on a problem or project,** do you think you have a tendency to clone yourself too much? Do you have a preference for people who think and act as you do? What characteristics do you value too much? What downsides do you ignore or excuse away? This is a common human tendency. The key is to seek balance, variety, and diversity. Shore up your weaknesses when hiring others. People good at this competency can comfortably surround themselves with people not like them.

2. **Make sure you know what matters most.** Read sources that focus on key competencies at work, such as *The Extraordinary Leader* by Zenger and Folkman or *The Leadership Machine* by Lombardo and Eichinger. Look at the research-based lists of competencies that appear on standardized competency instruments such as VOICES®, PROFILOR®, or BENCHMARKS®.

3. **Become a student of the people around you.** First, try to outline their strengths and weaknesses, their preferences and beliefs. Watch out for traps—it is rarely general intelligence or pure personality that spells the difference in people. Most people are smart enough, and many personality characteristics don't matter that much for performance. Ask a second question. Look below surface descriptions of smart, approachable, technically skilled people to describe specifics. Then try to predict ahead of time what they would do in specific circumstances.

What percent of the time are your predictions correct? Try to increase the percent over time.

4. **What differences make a difference?** For each job, role, task, or assignment, try to create a success profile of what would be required for success. What skills, knowledge, and competencies would be mission-critical to getting the job done? This means that they differentiate superior from average performance. Don't include competencies that, while important, most people on a job would be expected to already have. (For example, integrity is a must, but if people already have it, it can't predict success. Similarly, time management and planning are important, but most people have demonstrated a reasonable proficiency in those in order to be employable. They wouldn't distinguish superior from average performers often.) Go for the critical few, not the important many. Which competencies don't make a difference?

5. **Volunteer to be part of an assessment center team,** or take a course on assessment. You will be trained to observe and assess people as they are going through a number of tasks and assignments. As part of the process, you will compare your notes and assessments with others on the team. That way, you will learn to calibrate your assessments.

E Technical Focus

ENFJs are global thinkers and sometimes lack a detailed, technical focus if the issue is not terribly important to them.

1. **Locate a pro.** Find the seasoned master professional in the technology or function, and ask whether he/she would mind showing you the ropes and tutoring you. Most don't mind having a few "apprentices" around. Help him or her teach you. Ask, "How do you know what's important? What do you look at first? Second? What are the five keys you always look at or for? What do you read? Who do you go to for advice?"

2. **Sign up.** Almost all functions have national and sometimes regional professional associations made up of hundreds of people who do well what you need to learn every day. Sign up as a member. Buy some of the introductory literature. Go to some of their workshops. Go to the annual conference.

3. **Learn to think as an expert in the technology thinks.** Take problems to him/her and ask what are the keys he/she looks for; observe what

he/she considers significant and not significant. Chunk up data into categories so you can remember it. Devise five key areas or questions you can consider each time a technical issue comes up. Don't waste your time learning facts; they won't be useful unless you have conceptual buckets to put them in.

4. **Teach others.** Form a study group and take turns presenting on new, different, or unknown aspects of the technology. Having to teach it will force you to conceptualize and understand it more deeply. The relationships you form in such groups pay off in other ways as well. One company found its technicians learned more from coffee break conversations than from manuals.

F Problems With Higher Management

Since values often come first, ENFJs can be seen as not that supportive of upper management strategy. If anything in the strategy crosses swords with a value of ENFJs, they can dig in their heels.

1. **Consider who bothers you.** If only certain higher-ups bother you and others don't, take a piece of paper and list the styles of the two groups/individuals. What are the similarities? Why does one style bother you and the other doesn't? With the groups/individuals that bother you, how could you respond more comfortably and effectively? Perhaps you could use some of the techniques you use with the more comfortable groups. Probably you should prime yourself to take nothing in personal terms and, no matter what happens, return to a discussion of the problem.

2. **Get to know more top managers.** Try to meet and interact with higher-ups in informal settings like receptions, social or athletic events, charity events, off-sites, etc. You will probably learn that higher-ups are just regular people who are older and therefore higher than you in the hierarchy. You may then feel more comfortable with them when back in the work setting.

3. **Find out how top managers think.** Read the biographies of five "great" people; see what is said about them and their views of people like you. Read five autobiographies and see what they said about themselves and how they viewed people in your position. Write down five things you can do differently or better.

4. **Be ready for Q&A.** Many people get in trouble during questions and answers. Don't fake answers; most high-level managers will tolerate a

"Don't know but I'll get back to you on that." Think of all the questions ahead of time; ask someone else to look at what you are going to say and do and to think of questions they would ask. Rehearse the answers to the questions. Another place people get in trouble when challenged is by retreating to a safe recitation of facts; executives are usually asking for logic and problem analysis, not a repackaging of what you've already said. The worst case, of course, is when an executive rejects your argument. If this happens, draw the person out to see if you've been misunderstood and clarify. If that's not the case, let the disagreement be as it is. Few executives respect someone who drops an argument as soon as challenged. You should listen carefully and respond with logic in 30 seconds or less per point. Don't repeat the entire argument; long answers often backfire since people have already heard it and few may agree with the questioner. In haste to be thorough, you may just look defensive.

5. **Quit arguing.** Most of the time, you may be delivering someone else's view of the future. Top management and a consultant created the mission, vision, and strategy off somewhere in the woods all by themselves. You may or may not have been asked for any input. You may even have some doubts about it yourself. Your role is to manage this vision and mission, not your personal one. Do not offer conditional statements to your audience: "I've got some concerns myself." Don't let it be known to others that you are not fully on board. Your job is to deliver and manage the message. While it's okay to admit your problems in dealing with change, it's not okay to admit them in dealing with this change. If you have better ideas, try to get them to the people who form missions in your organization.

6. **Facing the boss.** Try to have a series of informal, relaxed discussions with your boss about what the problem might be, leading with your contributions—we are seldom completely in the right—to the problem first; then give him/her an opportunity to add to the discussion. Make it easy for him/her by indicating, "You are doing me a favor. I need your help." In return for your boss's help, offer some in return. What are your boss's weakest areas or what can you do to make the job easier? Figure out what those are and pitch in. This is good practice because relationships don't often prosper unless there is some equity built in. Give to get or your boss may soon be uncomfortable with the one-way nature of the help.

7. **Some rules to follow:** Describe. Say "I" not "you." Focus on how to accomplish work better. (If you think the boss is blocking you, instead

of saying this, say, "I need help in getting this done. I've tried the following things, but...")

■ If your boss is reluctant to give criticism, help by making statements rather than asking questions. Saying "I think I focus too much on operations and miss some of the larger strategic connections" is easier for most people to reply to than a question which asks them to tell you this point.

■ If your manager is uninvolved, you will need to provide the structure and aim for a sign-off on your objectives.

■ If you work for a detail-driven micromanager, ask what results you must achieve to be successful (and left alone more).

■ If your manager is well-meaning, but a nuisance, ask if you can check in with him because you are trying to be more autonomous.

■ If you believe the boss is blocking you, access your network for performance help, think of five ways to accomplish anything, and try them all.

8. **Learn to depersonalize and be neutral.** Try to separate the person from the boss role he/she is in; try to objectify the situation. Someone made her/him boss for a reason, and you are never going to please everyone. Deal with him/her as your boss more than as a person. While you don't ever have to invite her/him to your home, you do have to deal with this person as a boss. Ask yourself why you dislike your boss so much or don't like to work with him/her. Write down everything you don't like on the left-hand side of a page. On the right-hand side write a strategy for dealing with it. Consider these strategies: Ask what strengths you can appeal to; ask what you can provide that the boss needs; ask what the boss would like for you to do to be more effective; design a project that you can do together so you can have a success experience; and consult with others for advice. What do people think who have a favorable impression of your boss? Do you share any common interests? Write down everything you've heard him/her say that was favorable. Play to the boss's good points. Whatever you do, don't signal what you think. Put your judgments on hold, nod, ask questions, summarize as you would with anyone else. A fly on the wall should not be able to tell whether you're talking to friend or foe. You can always talk less and ask more questions.

9. **Keep your cool.** Being nervous, anxious, and uncomfortable around one or more higher-ups is fairly normal; the key is not allowing that to prevent you from doing your best. Being uncomfortable can sometimes lead to physical reactions like sweating, hesitating or stuttering speech, mispronounced words, flushing of the face, grumbling in the stomach, running out of breath while talking, etc. When that happens, stop a second or two, take a deep breath, compose yourself, and continue what you were doing; they all have been there before. Remember, all you can do is the best you can do. You probably know more about this topic than they do. You're well prepared—being anxious can prevent you from demonstrating your expertise.

G Dealing With Conflict

ENFJs believe in harmony and typically avoid dealing with conflict situations. When forced to, they tend to personalize the conflict rather than keeping it on the problem.

1. **Clear problem-focused communication.** Follow the rule of equity: Explain your thinking and ask them to explain theirs. Be able to state their position as clearly as they do whether you agree or not—give it legitimacy. Separate facts from opinions and assumptions. Generate a variety of possibilities first rather than stake out positions. Keep your speaking to 30–60 second bursts. Try to get them to do the same. Don't give the other side the impression you're lecturing or criticizing them. Explain objectively why you hold a view; make the other side do the same. Ask lots of questions, make fewer statements. To identify interests behind positions, ask why they hold them or why they wouldn't want to do something. Always restate their position to their satisfaction before offering a response.

2. **Downsizing the conflict.** Almost all conflicts have common points that get lost in the heat of the battle. After a conflict has been presented and understood, start by saying that it might be helpful to see if we agree on anything. Write them on the flip chart. Then write down the areas left open. Focus on common goals, priorities, and problems. Keep the open conflicts as small as possible and concrete. The more abstract it gets, "We don't trust your unit," the more unmanageable it gets. To this respond, "Tell me your specific concern—why exactly don't you trust us; can you give me an example?" Usually after calm discussion, they don't trust your unit on this specific issue under these specific conditions. That's easier to deal

with. Allow others to save face by conceding small points that are not central to the issue—don't try to hit a home run every time. If you can't agree on a solution, agree on a procedure to move forward. Collect more data. Appeal to a higher power. Get a third-party arbitrator. Something. This creates some positive motion and breaks stalemates.

3. **Practice Aikido,** the ancient art of absorbing the energy of your opponent and using it to manage him/her. Let the other side vent frustration or blow off steam, but don't react. Listen. Nod. Ask clarifying questions. Ask open-ended questions like, "What one change could you make so we could achieve our objectives better?" "What could I do that would help the most?" Restate their position periodically to signal you have understood. But don't react. Keep them talking until they run out of venom. Then explore the underlying concern. Separate the people from the problem. When someone attacks you, rephrase it as an attack on the problem. In response to threats, say you'll only negotiate on merit and fairness. If the other side won't play fair, surface their game—"It looks like you're playing good cop, bad cop. Why don't you settle your differences and tell me one thing?" In response to unreasonable proposals, attacks, or a non-answer to a question, you can always say nothing. People will usually respond by saying more, coming off their position a bit, or at least revealing their true interests. Many times, with unlimited venting and your understanding, the actual conflict shrinks.

4. **Questions.** In win-win and something-something negotiations, the more information you have about the other side, the more you will have to work with. What can you learn about what they know before going in? What will they do if they don't reach an agreement with you? In the negotiation, ask more questions, make fewer statements. Ask clarifying questions: "What did you mean by that?" Probes: "Why do you say that?" Motives: "What led you to that position?" When the other side takes a rigid position, don't reject it. Ask why: What are the principles behind the offer? How do we know it's fair? What's the theory of the case? Play out what would happen if their position was accepted. Get everything out that you can. Don't negotiate assumptions, negotiate facts.

5. **Are your problem performers confused?** Do they know what's expected of them? You may not set clear enough performance standards, goals, and objectives. You may be a seat-of-the-pants manager, and some people are struggling because they don't know what is expected or it changes. You may be a cryptic communicator.

You may be too busy to communicate. You may communicate to some and not to others. You may have given up on some and stopped communicating. Or you may think they would know what to do if they're any good, but that's not really true because you have not properly communicated what you want. The first task is to outline the 5 to 10 key results areas and what indicators of success would be. Involve your problem direct reports on both ends—the standards and the indicators. Provide them with a fair way to measure their own progress. Employees with goals and standards are usually harder on themselves than you'll ever be. Often they set higher standards than you would. Sometimes the problem is behavioral, as in someone who can't control outbursts, and only affects performance on the back end in lost cooperation or sabotage. Then the best approach is to note the gap between behavior and expectations, and point out what some of the observed consequences are. If the person agrees, then coaching may suffice. If the person balks, then a 360° feedback process with follow-up may be needed to illuminate the depth of the problem before any help can be given.

6. **Starting the "improve or you're gone" process.** The first meeting. After you have made the assessment that a direct report just isn't making it, document your observations against the standards and arrange the first tough meeting. Experience directs that these first tough meetings should always be in the beginning of the week and in the mornings. They should not occur on Fridays or the day before holidays when most managers deliver them. They should not be at a time when the unit is on a bomb run getting ready for a big presentation. Start the meeting by saying "we" have a performance issue to talk about and fix. Be succinct. You have limited attention span in tough feedback situations. Don't waste time with a long preamble, just get to it. The recipient is likely to know the feedback is negative, so go ahead and say it first. They won't hear or remember anything positive you have to say anyway. Don't overwhelm the person, even if you have a lot to say. Pick the key areas and stick to them. Keep it to the facts and their impact on you, them, and your unit. Talk about specific events and situations. Plan for enough time. This is not a process to rush.

7. **Go in with an improvement plan.** Don't criticize without a solution and a plan. Tell the person what you want—paint a different outcome. Don't expect him/her to guess, and don't spend a lot of time rehashing the past. Suggest steps both of you can take to remedy the problem. Be positive but firm. Be constructive. Be optimistic in the

beginning. Help him/her see the negative consequences and the potential timing—you can ask what he/she thinks and you can tell him/her what the consequences are from your side. Change starts with seeing an unacceptable consequence and a way out. "Improve or else" threats don't work.

Overusing ENFJ Tendencies

If you sometimes overdo your preferred behaviors, you may need to work on:

A **Being Less Pushy and Inclusive**

B **Overmanaging**

C **Being More Personally Flexible**

ISTJ	ISFJ	INFJ	INTJ
ISTP	ISFP	INFP	INTP
ESTP	ESFP	ENFP	ENTP
ESTJ	ESFJ	ENFJ	ENTJ

A Being Less Pushy and Inclusive

Due to their high energy and interest in people, ENFJs can come across as pressuring and opinionated.

1. **To better figure out what drives people, look to:** What do they do first? What do they emphasize in their speech? What do they display emotion around? What values play out for them?

   - First things. Does this person go to others first, hole up and study, complain, discuss feelings, or take action? These are the basic orientations of people that reveal what's important to them. Use these to motivate.

   - Speech content. People might focus on details, concepts, feelings, or other people in their speech. This can tell you again how to appeal to them by mirroring their speech emphasis. Although most of us naturally adjust—we talk details with detail-oriented people—chances are good that in problem relationships you're not finding the common ground. She talks "detail" and you talk "people," for example.

   - Emotion. You need to know what people's hot buttons are because one mistake can get you labeled as insensitive with some people. The only cure here is to see what turns up the volume for them—either literally or what they're concerned about.

■ Values. Apply the same thinking to the values of others. Do they talk about money, recognition, integrity, efficiency in their normal work conversation? Figuring out what their drivers are tells you another easy way to appeal to anyone.

2. **Customer focus.** People who are good at this work from the outside (the customer, the audience, the person, the situation) in, not from the inside out. ("What do I want to do in this situation; what would make me happy and feel good?") Practice not thinking inside/out when you are around others. What are the demand characteristics of this situation? How does this person or audience best learn? Which of my approaches or styles would work best? How can I best accomplish my goals? How can I alter my approach and tactics to be the most effective? The one-trick pony can only perform once per show. If the audience doesn't like that particular trick, no oats for the pony.

3. **Pay particular attention to non-verbal cues.** Common signals of trouble are changes in body posture (especially turning away), crossed arms, staring, or the telltale glancing at one's watch, scribbling on the pad, tapping fingers or the pencil, looking out the window, frowns, and washboard foreheads. When this occurs, pause. Ask a question. Ask how we're doing. Do a live process check. Some people use the same body language to signal that they are done or not interested in what's going on. Get to know their signals. Construct an alternative plan for the five people you work with closely: When Bill begins to stare, I will…. When Sally interrupts for the third time, I will….

4. **Impatience triggers.** Some people probably bring out your impatience more than others. Who are they? What is it about them that makes you more impatient? Pace? Language? Thought process? Accent? These people may include people you don't like, who ramble, who whine and complain, or who are repetitive advocates for things you have already rejected. Mentally rehearse some calming tactics before meeting with people who trigger your impatience. Work on understanding their positions without judging them—you can always judge later. In all cases, focus them on the issues or problems to be discussed, return them to the point, interrupt to summarize, and state your position. Try to gently train them to be more efficient with you next time without damaging them in the process.

5. **Rein in your horse.** Impatient people provide answers, conclusions, and solutions too early in the process. Others haven't even understood the problem yet. Providing solutions too quickly will make your people dependent and irritated. If you don't teach them how you think and how you can come up with solutions so fast, they will never learn. Take the time to really define the problem—not impatiently throw out a solution. Brainstorm what questions need to be answered in order to resolve it. Give your people the task to think about for a day and come back with some solutions. Be a teacher instead of a dictator of solutions. Study yourself. Keep a journal of what triggered your behavior and what the observed consequences were. Learn to detect and control your triggers before they get you in trouble.

6. **Task impatience.** Impatient people check in a lot. How's it coming. Is it done yet? When will it be finished? Let me see what you've done so far. That is disruptive to due process and wastes time. When you give out a task or assign a project, establish agreed-upon time checkpoints. You can also assign percentage checkpoints. Check in with me when you are about 25% finished so we can make midcourse corrections and 75% finished so we can make final corrections. Let them figure out how to do the task. Hold back from checking in at other than the agreed-upon times and percentages.

7. **In conflict situations, what reactions do you have** (such as impatience or non-verbals like flushing or drumming your pen or fingers)? Learn to recognize those as soon as they start and substitute something more neutral. Most emotional responses to conflict come from personalizing the issue. Separate people issues from the problem at hand, and deal with people issues separately and later if they persist. Always return to facts and the problem before the group; stay away from personal clashes. Attack the problem by looking at common interests and underlying concerns, not people and their positions. Try on their views for size—the emotion as well as the content. Ask yourself if you understand their feelings. Ask what they would do if they were in your shoes. See if you can restate each other's position and advocate it for a minute to get inside each other's place. If you get emotional, pause and collect yourself. You are not your best when you get emotional. Then return to the problem.

B Overmanaging

ENFJs lead with enthusiasm. Often, what ENFJs see as checking in, others see as being intrusive. They also can run into problems with workload distribution since they tend to manage with a person-by-person approach.

1. **How to delegate?** Communicate, set time frames and goals, and get out of the way. People need to know what it is you expect. Major chunks of responsibility set? Workload distributed properly? Did you set measures? Find out what your best practices are. Set up a series of delegation practices that can be used as if you're not there. What do you have to be informed of? What feedback loops can people use for midcourse correction? What questions should be answered as the work proceeds? What steps should be followed? What are the criteria to be followed? When will you be available to help?

2. **More what and why, less how.** The best delegators are crystal clear on what and when, and more open on how. People are more motivated when they can determine the how for themselves. Inexperienced delegators include the hows, which turn the people into task automatons instead of an empowered and energized staff. Tell them what and when and for how long, and let them figure out how on their own. Give them leeway. Encourage them to try things. Besides being more motivating, it's also more developmental for them. Add the larger context. Although it is not necessary to get the task done, people are more motivated when they know where this task fits in the bigger picture. Take three extra minutes and tell them why this task needs to be done, where it fits in the grander scheme, and its importance to the goals and objectives of the unit.

3. **If you are impatient and find yourself checking in too frequently,** set up a time table with your people with agreed-upon checkpoints and in-progress checks. Let them initiate this on a schedule you are comfortable with. Ask yourself who your most motivating bosses were. Chances are they gave you a lot of leeway, encouraged you to try things, were good sounding boards, and cheered your successes. Do what they did with you.

4. **Let your team help you.** Periodically, send out a memo asking each person whether there is anything he or she thinks he/she could do that you are now doing or monitoring too closely. Pick one or two things per person and empower them to do it on their own. Make sure the up-front communication is adequate for them to perform well. Explain your standards—what the outcome should be, the key things that need to be taken care of—then ask them to figure out how to do it themselves.

5. **Are you hanging on to too much?** Are you a perfectionist, wanting everything to be just so? Do you have unrealistic expectations of others? Someone made you leader because you are probably better at doing what the team does than some or most of the members. Be careful to set the goals and objectives in a realistic and motivating manner.

6. **Do you delegate but withhold the power and authority to get the job done?** Delegating the work without the authority to make process or how-to decisions is demotivating. People grow if they have a chance to decide and succeed or fail on their own.

7. **What skill do you have that you could pass on to others?** Ask yourself why this is a strength for you. What are the first items you would teach as the keys to help others form umbrellas for understanding? Watch others carefully for their reactions when teaching and coaching. What works and doesn't work for you as a coach? Reveal things that people don't need to know to do their jobs, but which will be interesting to them—and help them feel valued.

8. **Do you help your people learn by looking for repeating patterns?** Help them look for patterns in the situations and problems they deal with. What succeeded and what failed? What was common to each success or what was present in each failure but never present in a success? Focus on the successes; failures are easier to analyze but don't in themselves tell you what would work. Comparing successes, while less exciting, yields more information. The bottom line is help them reduce insights to principles or rules of thumb that might be repeatable. Ask them what they have learned to increase their skills and understanding, making them better managers or professionals. Ask them what they can do now that they couldn't do a year ago. Reinforce this and encourage more of it. Developing is learning in as many ways as possible.

C Being More Personally Flexible

ENFJs can overemphasize relationships and relationship building at the expense of trying different things or thinking things through alone. This singleness of style hampers their problem-solving effectiveness.

1. **Transitions.** Which transitions are the toughest for you? Write down the five toughest for you. What do you have a hard time switching to and from? Use this knowledge to assist you in making a list of discontinuities (tough transitions) you face, such as confronting people vs. being approachable and accepting, leading vs. following, going from firing someone to a business-as-usual staff meeting. Write down how each of these discontinuities makes you feel and what you may do that gets you in trouble. For example, you may not shift gears well after a confrontation, or you may have trouble taking charge again after passively sitting in a meeting all day. Create a plan to attack each of the tough transitions.

2. **Control your instant responses to shifts.** Many of us respond to the fragmentation and discontinuities of work as if they were threats instead of the way life is. Sometimes our emotions and fears are triggered by switching from active to passive or soft to tough. This initial anxious response lasts 45–60 seconds, and we need to buy some time before we say or do something inappropriate. Research shows that generally somewhere between the second and third thing you think to say or do is the best option. Practice holding back your first response long enough to think of a second and a third. Manage your shifts, don't be a prisoner of them.

3. **Use mental rehearsal to think about different ways you could carry out a transaction.** Try to see yourself acting in opposing ways to get the same thing done—when to be tough, when to let them decide, when to deflect the issue because it's not ready to decide. What cues would you look for to select an approach that matches? Practice trying to get the same thing done with two different groups with two different approaches. Did they both work?

I probably consult too much with others, leading to more time in relationship building than in fact assessment or selling my own ideas.

– An ENFJ Manager

■ ■ ■ ■ ■ ■ ■ ■ ■ ■ ■ ■ ■ ■ ■ ■ ■

APPLICATION

Your personal preferences play out in day-to-day problems and situations you face. Below is a case about your type dealing with such a situation. Use this to think through how you will integrate the tips you've considered and coach yourself to be more effective in your type.

ENFJ Application Situation (Part 1)

As National Service Manager for a large specialized medical equipment company, you're seen by both your coworkers and clients as a warm, friendly, open person, and you pride yourself in knowing all about the people you interact with. You think of yourself as a "people person," and pleasing others is rewarding. That personal touch, along with your generally being practical, has contributed to your success in the service organization.

There's a downside, though, to your interest in working with and helping people out: You rarely say "no," and as a result, you often wind up with more on your plate than you can deal with. The problem is, you don't see that as clearly as some of the people do who work with you.

In preparing for your annual performance appraisal, you're tallying up the numbers—among them, percent on-time fulfillment of client requests and orders processed; measures of client satisfaction with quality; peer ratings on teamwork and collaboration; leadership training requirements met—and you're satisfied that the review is going to go well.

Thinking It Through: Strategy

■ If there's something you've overlooked in preparing for your review, what might that be?

■ What kinds of things do you think your boss is likely to focus on as development needs for you?

Planning It Out: Tactics

■ When you've had trouble at work, where has this occurred?

■ What potential barriers to your effectiveness (i.e., actions, behaviors) are inherent in this situation based on your personality type (ENFJ)?

■ What particular areas would present developmental challenges to you, and what competencies would you want to put into play in order not only to accomplish your objectives but to assure that relationships are preserved?

■ Which of the tactics described in the Being More Effective section are applicable in this situation?

■ Which Overused Tendencies are most likely to come into play here?

ENFJ Application Situation (Part 2)

In your performance review, your boss agrees with you that you've met your specific business goals. In fact, she gave you higher ratings on some items than you even gave yourself. She did, however, suggest there are some behaviors that are detrimental to your performance.

■ As an ENFJ, why are you likely to be committing to more than you can handle?

■ What might you focus on to enhance your decision making?

■ What might you need to do less of?

Reflection

- What do you think are the advantages of ENFJs as managers?
- What are the potential liabilities?

SUGGESTED READINGS

■■■■■■■ **Being a More Effective ENFJ** ■■■■■■■

Focusing on Analysis

Flynn, Daniel J. *Intellectual Morons: How Ideology Makes Smart People Fall for Stupid Ideas.* New York: Crown Business Publishing, 2004.

Hammond, John S., Ralph L. Keeney and Howard Raiffer. *Smart Choices.* Boston: Harvard University Press, 1999.

Nutt, Paul C. *Why Decisions Fail: Avoiding the Blunders and Traps That Lead to Decision Debacles.* San Francisco: Berrett-Koehler Publishers, Inc., 2002.

Sofo, Francesco. *Six Myths of Critical Thinking.* Business & Professional Publishing, 2003.

Sternberg, Robert J. *Thinking Styles.* Boston: Cambridge University Press, 1997.

Yates, J. Frank. *Decision Management: How to Assure Better Decisions in Your Company.* San Francisco: Jossey-Bass, Inc., 2003.

Selling Ideas

Arredondo, Lani. *Communicating Effectively.* New York: McGraw-Hill Trade, 2000.

Bennis, Warren G. and Burt Nanus. *Leaders: Strategies for Taking Charge.* New York: HarperBusiness, 2003.

Booher, Dianna. *Speak With Confidence: Powerful Presentations That Inform, Inspire, and Persuade.* New York: McGraw-Hill, Inc., 2002.

Cox, Danny and John Hoover. *Leadership When the Heat's On.* New York: McGraw-Hill Trade, 2002.

Harvard Business School Press (Ed.). *Presentations That Persuade and Motivate (The Results-Driven Manager Series)*. Boston: Harvard Business School Press, 2004.

McCormack, Mark H. *On Communicating*. Los Angeles: Dove Books, 1998.

Zeuschner, Raymond F. *Communicating Today: The Essentials*. Boston: Allyn & Bacon, 2002.

Too Dependent on a Few Relationships

Benton, D.A. *Executive Charisma: Six Steps to Mastering the Art of Leadership*. New York: McGraw-Hill Trade, 2003.

Bolton, Robert and Dorothy Grover Bolton. *People Styles at Work—Making Bad Relationships Good and Good Relationships Better*. New York: AMACOM, 1996.

Brooks, Michael. *Instant Rapport*. New York: Warner Books, 1989.

Maxwell, John C. *Relationships 101*. London: Thomas Nelson, 2004.

Silberman, Melvin L. and Freda Hansburg. *Peoplesmart: Developing Your Interpersonal Intelligence*. San Francisco: Berrett-Koehler Publishers, Inc., 2000.

Niven, David. *The 100 Simple Secrets of Successful People: What Scientists Have Learned and How You Can Use It*. New York: HarperBusiness, 2002.

Staffing

Harvard Business School Press. *Hiring and Keeping the Best People*. Boston: Harvard Business School Press, 2003.

Levin, Robert A. and Joseph G. Rosse. *Talent Flow: A Strategic Approach to Keeping Good Employees, Helping Them Grow, and Letting Them Go*. New York: John Wiley & Sons, Inc., 2001.

Lombardo, Michael M. and Robert W. Eichinger. *The Leadership Machine*. Minneapolis, MN: Lominger Limited, Inc., 2004.

Michaels, Ed, Helen Handfield-Jones and Beth Axelrod. *The War for Talent*. Boston: Harvard Business School Press, 2001.

Myers, Isabel Briggs with Peter B. Myers. *Gifts Differing: Understanding Personality Type*. Palo Alto, CA: Davies-Black Publishing, 1995.

Poundstone, William. *How Would You Move Mount Fiji? Microsoft's Cult of the Puzzle—How the World's Smartest Company Selects the Most Creative Thinkers*. Boston: Little, Brown, 2003.

Smart, Bradford D., Ph.D. *Topgrading—How Leading Companies Win: Hiring, Coaching and Keeping the Best People*. New York: Prentice Hall, 1999.

Zenger, John H. and Joseph Folkman. *The Extraordinary Leader: Turning Good Managers Into Great Leaders*. New York: McGraw-Hill, Inc., 2002.

Technical Focus

DeGraff, Jeff and Katherine A. Lawrence. *Creativity at Work: Developing the Right Practices to Make Innovation Happen*. San Francisco: Jossey-Bass, Inc., 2002.

Drummond, Helga. *The Art of Decision Making*. New York: John Wiley & Sons, Inc., 2001.

Flynn, Daniel J. *Intellectual Morons: How Ideology Makes Smart People Fall for Stupid Ideas*. New York: Crown Business Publishing, 2004.

Hammond, John S., Ralph L. Keeney and Howard Raiffer. *Smart Choices*. Boston: Harvard University Press, 1999.

Lucas, Robert W. *The Creative Training Idea Book: Inspired Tips and Techniques for Engaging and Effective Learning*. New York: AMACOM, 2003.

Yates, J. Frank. *Decision Management: How to Assure Better Decisions in Your Company*. San Francisco: Jossey-Bass, Inc., 2003.

Problems With Higher Management

Charan, Ram. *What the CEO Wants You to Know: How Your Company Really Works*. New York: Crown Business Publishing, 2001.

Dobson, Michael Singer. *Managing Up! 59 Ways to Build a Career-Advancing Relationship With Your Boss*. New York: AMACOM, 2000.

Dominguez, Linda R. *How to Shine at Work*. New York: McGraw-Hill Trade, 2003.

Jay, Ros. *How to Manage Your Boss: Developing the Perfect Working Relationship*. London: Financial Times Management, 2002.

Dealing With Conflict

Cloke, Ken and Joan Goldsmith. *Resolving Conflicts at Work: A Complete Guide for Everyone on the Job.* San Francisco: Jossey-Bass, Inc., 2000.

Dana, Daniel. *Conflict Resolution.* New York: McGraw-Hill Trade, 2000.

Graham, Gini. *A Survival Guide for Working With Humans: Dealing With Whiners, Back-Stabbers, Know-It-Alls, and Other Difficult People.* New York: AMACOM, 2004.

Guttman, Howard M. *When Goliaths Clash: Managing Executive Conflict to Build a More Dynamic Organization.* New York: AMACOM, 2003.

Levin, Robert A. and Joseph G. Rosse. *Talent Flow: A Strategic Approach to Keeping Good Employees, Helping Them Grow, and Letting Them Go.* New York: John Wiley & Sons, Inc., 2001.

Masters, Marick Francis and Robert R. Albright. *The Complete Guide to Conflict Resolution in the Workplace.* New York: AMACOM, 2002.

Solomon, Muriel. *Working With Difficult People.* New York: Prentice Hall, 2002.

■■■■■■■ Overusing ENFJ Tendencies ■■■■■■■■

Being Less Pushy and Inclusive

Badaracco, Joseph L., Jr. *Leading Quietly.* Boston: Harvard Business School Press, 2002.

Barker, Larry, Ph.D. and Kittie Watson, Ph.D. *Listen Up: At Home, at Work, in Relationships: How to Harness the Power of Effective Listening.* Irvine, CA: Griffin Trade Paperback, 2001.

Bellman, Geoffrey M. *Getting Things Done When You Are Not in Charge.* San Francisco: Berrett-Koehler Publishers, Inc., 2001.

Bolton, Robert and Dorothy Grover Bolton. *People Styles at Work—Making Bad Relationships Good and Good Relationships Better.* New York: AMACOM, 1996.

Brooks, Michael. *Instant Rapport.* New York: Warner Books, 1989.

Glickman, Rosalene. *Optimal Thinking: How to Be Your Best Self.* New York: John Wiley & Sons, Inc., 2002.

Mazzarella, Mark C. and Jo-Ellan Dimitrius. *Reading People: How to Understand People and Predict Their Behavior—Anytime, Anyplace.* New York: Ballantine Books, 1999.

Overmanaging

Allen, David. *Getting Things Done: The Art of Stress-Free Productivity.* New York: Penguin Books, 2003.

Bossidy, Larry, Ram Charan and Charles Burck (Contributor). *Execution: The Discipline of Getting Things Done.* New York: Crown Business Publishing, 2002.

Branham, L. *Keeping the People Who Keep You in Business.* New York: AMACOM, 2001.

Genett, Donna M. *If You Want It Done Right, You Don't Have to Do It Yourself! The Power of Effective Delegation.* Sanger, CA: Quill Driver Books, 2004.

Glanz, Barbara A. *Handle With CARE: Motivating and Retaining Employees.* New York: McGraw-Hill Trade, 2002.

Being More Personally Flexible

Anderson, Dean and Linda S. Ackerman Anderson. *Beyond Change Management: Advanced Strategies for Today's Transformational Leaders.* San Francisco: Jossey-Bass, Inc., 2001.

Bellman, Geoffrey M. *Getting Things Done When You Are Not in Charge.* San Francisco: Berrett-Koehler Publishers, Inc., 2001.

Burke, W. Warner and William Trahant with Richard Koonce. *Business Climate Shifts: Profiles of Change Makers.* Boston: Butterworth-Heinemann, 2000.

Fullan, Michael. *Leading in a Culture of Change.* New York: John Wiley & Sons, Inc., 2001.

Gilley, Jerry W. *The Manager As Change Agent.* Cambridge, MA: Perseus Publishing, 2001.

Luecke, Richard. *Managing Change and Transition.* Boston: Harvard Business School Publishing, 2003.

CHAPTER 16

ENTJ
Extraverted Thinking
with
Introverted Intuiting

■■■■■■■■■■■■■■■■■

1.8% of Population
13.1% of Managers

■■■■■■■■■■■■■■■■■

Typical Strengths

Natural Leader
Confident
Well Informed
Future Oriented
Logical/Complex
Commanding
Independent
Avid Learner
Question Everything

ISTJ	ISFJ	INFJ	INTJ
ISTP	ISFP	INFP	INTP
ESTP	ESFP	ENFP	ENTP
ESTJ	ESFJ	ENFJ	ENTJ

I get the big picture and believe we can make it happen now.

– An ENTJ Manager

Basic Habits of Mind

The lead process for ENTJs is Extraverted Thinking. This inclines them to critique information for reasonableness and decide what conclusions the information implies. Aided by Introverted Intuiting, which serves to identify endless connections and interrelationships among facts and ideas, they perpetually build more complex models of whatever their interests may be. This combination leads to a focus on systems and complex problems.

Introverted Sensing and Introverted Feeling also assist ENTJs. Introverted Sensing helps anchor information that is critical for the future. Introverted Feeling promotes within them a sense of mission. Sometimes this is misperceived as being overly certain, picky, and bullying.

Typical Communication Patterns

- Fluent about their ideas and their critique of events or situations, ENTJs like to discuss theory, analysis, and formulas for making things work better.

- They are fast paced in their interactions, which are energetic, action oriented, and communicate high aspirations.

General Learning Strategy

- ENTJs prefer big-picture thinking and challenging assignments to drive their learning.

- Their typical learning strategies are debating ideas and theories and conducting independent research.

- Their learning is generally helped by having complex problems to solve and by environments that reward achievement and analysis.

Interpersonal Qualities Related to Motivation

■ Motivated by systematic and logical action, ENTJs look for ways to improve whatever has gone before.

■ They value intellectual matters and are energized by making things happen; complexity and the strategic elements of problems increase their enthusiasm.

Blind Spots

■ ENTJs might be surprised to learn that their efforts at creating a developmental climate, building relationships, and contributing to teamwork are not received as effectively as they imagine. They often feel that they have fostered good relationships because folks are doing their part. What they may fail to realize is that people often feel they have no other choice, given the vision, passion, and forcefulness of ENTJs. Creating a developmental climate is a bit of a challenge since they often assume that a very challenging, "How high can the bar be?" environment is developmental. They often do not see the relationship between a supportive, coaching-like environment and a developmental climate. Further, teamwork is often seen as everyone doing their part to fulfill the vision, rather than facilitating a common vision toward which everyone can work.

■ They may argue they show caring by building a well-functioning system, but often leave people out of the equation. In 15 years of running an illustration exercise, one of the authors has never seen an ENTJ draw a picture that included another person. Interpersonal savvy tends to be their largest blind spot.

Stress Related Behavior

■ When stressed, ENTJs can become aggressive, demanding, and condescending.

■ They put more energy into getting the job done and getting it done right as stress increases.

■ If stress is persistent enough, they may seem dreamy, reserved, hypersensitive, and somewhat overconcerned about others' views.

Potential Barriers to Effectiveness

■ Because of their quick, verbal, analytical style, observers think that ENTJs could have problems with interpersonal relationships.

■ Further, many feel that their high aspirations and demanding attitudes create problems with personal/work balance.

■ Their generally active and critical nature can be seen as condescending and arrogant.

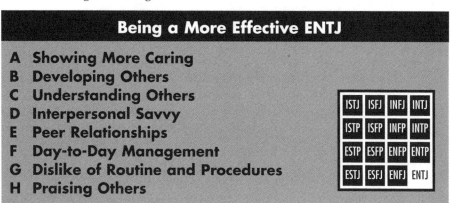

Being a More Effective ENTJ

A **Showing More Caring**
B **Developing Others**
C **Understanding Others**
D **Interpersonal Savvy**
E **Peer Relationships**
F **Day-to-Day Management**
G **Dislike of Routine and Procedures**
H **Praising Others**

ISTJ	ISFJ	INFJ	INTJ
ISTP	ISFP	INFP	INTP
ESTP	ESFP	ENFP	ENTP
ESTJ	ESFJ	ENFJ	ENTJ

A Showing More Caring

ENTJs are very busy people, and they often don't take the time to show much caring for others.

1. **Caring is listening.** Many bosses are marginal listeners. They are action oriented and more apt to cut off people mid-sentence than listen. They also are impatient and finish people's sentences for them when they hesitate. All of these impatient behaviors come across to others as a lack of caring. It's being insensitive to the needs and feelings of others. So, step one in caring is listening longer.

2. **Caring is sharing and disclosing.** Share your thinking on a business issue and invite the advice of direct reports. Pass on tidbits of information you think will help people do their jobs better or broaden their perspectives. Reveal things people don't need to know to do their jobs, but which will be interesting to them—and help them feel valued. Disclose some things about yourself as well. It's hard for people to relate to a stone. Tell them how you arrive at decisions. Explain your intentions, your reasons, and your thinking when announcing decisions. If you offer solutions first, you invite resistance

and feelings of not being cared about—"He/she just dumps things on us."

3. **Caring is knowing.** Know three non-work things about everybody—their interests and hobbies or their children or something you can chat about. Life is a small world. If you ask your people a few personal questions, you'll find you have something in common with virtually anyone. Having something in common will help bond the relationship.

4. **Caring is accepting.** Try to listen without judging initially. Turn off your "I agree; I don't agree" filter. You don't have to agree with it; just listen to understand. Assume when people tell you something they are looking for understanding; indicate that by being able to summarize what they said. Don't offer advice or solutions unless it's obvious the person wants to know what you would do. While offering instant solutions is a good thing to do in many circumstances, it's chilling where the goal is to get people to talk to you more freely.

5. **Caring is understanding.** Study the people you work with. Without judging them, collect evidence on how they think and what they do. What drives them to do what they do? Try to predict what they will do in given situations. Use this to understand how to relate to them. What are their hot buttons? What would they like for you to care about?

6. **Feedback.** People need continuous feedback from you and others to grow. Some tips about feedback:

   ■ Arrange for them to get feedback from multiple people, including yourself, on what matters for success in their future jobs; arrange for your direct reports to get 360° feedback about every two years.

   ■ Give them progressively stretching tasks that are first-time and different for them so that they can give themselves feedback as they go.

   ■ If they have direct reports and peers, another technique to recommend is to ask their associates for comments on what they should stop doing, start doing, and keep doing to be more successful.

   ■ You have to be willing to be straight with your people and give them accurate but balanced feedback. Give as much real-time feedback as you have time for. Most people are motivated by process feedback against agreed-upon goals for three reasons. First, it helps them adjust what they are doing along the way in time to better achieve the goal; they can make midcourse corrections. Second, it shows them what they are doing is important and that you're there to help. Third, it's not the "gotcha" game of negative and critical feedback after the fact. If there are negatives, they need to know as soon as possible.

■ Set up a buddy system so people can get continuing feedback.

■ If your organization has a mentoring program, find out how it works. Best practices begin with those to be mentored writing down goals, objectives, and development needs. They are then carefully matched with mentors and the relationship is outlined. How often will the people meet? On what topics is the mentor to be helpful? What are the responsibilities of the person to be mentored? If your organization doesn't have such a program, look at setting one up within your unit or function.

B Developing Others

Impatient to get on with it, ENTJs also don't naturally spend the time necessary to help others develop. They are more driven by leading others to solve problems and implement fresh ideas.

1. **You have to invest some time.** For most managers, time is what they have the least of to give. For the purposes of developing others beyond today's job, you need to allocate about eight hours per year per direct report. If you have a normal span of seven direct reports, that's 7 of 220 working days or 3% of your annual time. Two of the eight hours are for an annual in-depth appraisal of the person in terms of current strengths and weaknesses and of the competencies he/she needs to develop to move on to the next step. Two of the eight hours are for an in-depth career discussion with each person. What does he/she want? What will he/she sacrifice to get there? What is his/her own appraisal of his/her skills? Two of the eight hours are for creating a three- to five-year development plan and sharing it with the person. The last two hours are to present your findings and recommendations to the organization, usually in a succession planning process, and arranging for developmental events for each person. Start thinking of yourself as a coach or mentor. It's your job to help your people grow.

2. **Help people focus on the right things.** In their study of successful vs. average careers, Citrin and Smith found that the most successful

people force themselves into experiences they need for growth. They do not play it safe. While they demonstrate early competence in a specific area, they also don't overdo working on basic job requirements. They do enough work on the basics while searching for mission-critical job elements and trying to overdeliver on them. They add unexpected value. They call this the 20/80 principle of performance—focusing on the 20% that makes 80% of the difference. In doing so, the successful rack up career freedom points by tackling these tough assignments.

3. **Do you help your people learn by looking for repeating patterns?** Help them look for patterns in the situations and problems they deal with. What succeeded and what failed? What was common to each success or what was present in each failure but never present in a success? Focus on the successes; failures are easier to analyze but don't in themselves tell you what would work. Comparing successes, while less exciting, yields more information. The bottom line is help them reduce insights to principles or rules of thumb that might be repeatable. Ask them what they have learned to increase their skills and understanding, making them better managers or professionals. Ask them what they can do now that they couldn't do a year ago. Reinforce this and encourage more of it. Developing is learning in as many ways as possible.

4. **How to delegate?** Communicate, set time frames and goals, and get out of the way. People need to know what it is you expect. What does the outcome look like? When do you need it by? What's the budget? What resources do they get? What decisions can they make? Do you want checkpoints along the way? How will we both know and measure how well the task is done? One of the most common problems with delegation is incomplete or cryptic up-front communication leading to frustration, a job not well done the first time, rework, and a reluctance to delegate next time. Poor communicators always have to take more time managing because of rework. Analyze recent projects that went well and didn't go well. How did you delegate? Too much? Not enough? Unwanted pieces? Major chunks of responsibility? Workload distributed properly? Did you set measures? Overmanage or abdicate? Find out what your best practices are. Set up a series of delegation practices that can be used as if you're not there. What do you have to be informed of? What feedback loops can people use for midcourse correction? What questions should be answered as the work proceeds? What steps

should be followed? What are the criteria to be followed? When will you be available to help?

5. **More what and why, less how.** The best delegators are crystal clear on what and when, and more open on how. People are more motivated when they can determine the how for themselves. Inexperienced delegators include the hows, which turn the people into task automatons instead of an empowered and energized staff. Tell them what and when and for how long, and let them figure out how on their own. Give them leeway. Encourage them to try things. Besides being more motivating, it's also more developmental for them. Add the larger context. Although it is not necessary to get the task done, people are more motivated when they know where this task fits in the bigger picture. Take three extra minutes and tell them why this task needs to be done, where it fits in the grander scheme, and its importance to the goals and objectives of the unit.

C Understanding Others

ENTJs are visionaries interested in the future and organizational change. They often don't apply that same passion to understanding people.

1. **Learn to be a cultural anthropologist.** In assessing groups, ask yourself: What makes their blood boil? What do they believe? What are they trying to accomplish together? What do they smile at? What norms and customs do they have? What practices and behaviors do they share? Do they not like it if you stand too close? If you get right down to business? Do they like first names or are they more formal? If a Japanese manager presents his card, do you know what to do? Why do they have their cards printed in two languages and executives from the U.S. don't? Do you know what jokes are okay to tell? What do they believe about you and your group or groups? Positive? Neutral? Negative? What's been the history of their group and yours? Is this a first contact or a long history? Don't blunder in; nothing will kill you quicker with a group than showing utter disregard—read disrespect—for it and its norms, or having no idea of how they view your group. Ask people for insights who deal with this group often. If it's an important group to you and your business, read about it.

2. **Be candid with yourself.** Is there a group or groups you don't like or are uncomfortable with? Do you judge individual members of that group without really knowing if your impressions and stereotype is

true? Most of us do. Avoid putting groups in good and bad buckets. Many of us bucket groups as friendly or unfriendly. Once we do, we generally don't talk to the unfriendliest as much and may question their motives. Don't generalize about individuals. A person might belong to a group for many reasons, yet not typify stereotypes of the group. All accountants aren't detail-driven introverts, for example. To deal with this, put yourself in their shoes. Why would you act that way? What do you think they're trying to achieve? Assume that however they act is rational; it must have paid off or they wouldn't be doing it. Describe behavior and motives as neutrally as you can. Listen and observe to understand, not judge. If you are going to interact with a group you have trouble with, be on your guard and best behavior.

3. **Working with groups.** To deal effectively with groups, establish reciprocity. Relationships don't last unless you provide something and so do they. Find out what they want and tell them what you want. Strike a bargain. If one group usually gets the benefit, the other group will eventually become uncooperative and balky. Learn their conceptual categories. People who went on to become successful executives often spoke of their first time dealing with another function. The most common tack for a marketing person dealing with finance for the first time was to show them something he/she was working on and ask them how they would analyze it. What questions would they ask? What were the key numbers and why? What were the four or five key factors they were looking at? Be able to speak their language. Speaking their language shows respect and makes it easier for them to talk with you. Tell them your conceptual categories. To deal with you, they also need to know how you think and why. Tell them your perspective—the questions you ask, the factors you're interested in. If you can't explain your thinking, they won't know how to deal with you effectively.

4. **Getting groups to work together.** The keys are to find the common ground, downsize the differences that will get in the way, and use the differences that add value to form an alliance. Even groups seemingly far apart will have some things in common. Announce that you would first like to see if there are any points on which the two sides could tentatively agree. List those on a board or flip chart. Then list the seemingly far aparts, the real differences. Take each difference and list it as adding value—we can do that and you can't, and you can do something we are not good at—or getting in the way. Use the differences that add value and throw a plan around minimizing the

troublesome differences. Based on the common ground and the value-adding differences, form a common mind-set about how these groups can work together more effectively.

D Interpersonal Savvy

ENTJs can appear cool and impersonal. They are often uncomfortable in the world of people, preferring the world of ideas and learning.

1. **To understand the differences among people, look to the obvious first.** What do they do first? What do they emphasize in their speech? People focus on different things—taking action, details, concepts, feelings, other people. What's their interaction style? People come in different styles—pushy, tough, soft, matter-of-fact, and so on. To figure these out, listen for the values behind their words and note what they have passion and emotion around. One key to getting anything of value done in the work world is the ability to see differences in people and to manage against and use those differences for everyone's benefit. Interpersonal savvy is meeting each person where he/she is to get done what you need to get done. Basically, people respond favorably to ease of transaction. If you make it easy by accepting their normal mode of doing things, not fighting their style, and neither defending your own nor letting style get in the way of performance, things will generally run smoothly.

2. **Does your style chill the transaction?** Arrogant? Insensitive? Distant? Too busy to pay attention? Too quick to get into the agenda? Do you devalue others and dismiss their contributions, resulting in people feeling diminished, rejected, and angry? Do you offer answers, solutions, conclusions, statements, or dictates early in the transaction? That's the staple of people with a non-savvy style. Not listening. Instant output. Sharp reactions. Don't want to be that way? Read your audience. Do you know what people look like when they are uncomfortable with you? Do they back up? Stumble over words? Cringe? Stand at the door hoping not to get invited in? You should work doubly hard at observing others. Always select your interpersonal approach from the other person in, not from you out. Your best choice of approach will always be determined by the other person or group, not you. Think about each transaction as if the other person were a customer you wanted. How would you craft an approach?

3. **The first three minutes.** Managing the first three minutes is essential. The tone is set. First impressions are formed. Work on being open and approachable, and take in information during the beginning of a transaction. This means putting others at ease so that they feel okay about disclosing. It means initiating rapport, listening, sharing, understanding, and comforting. Approachable people get more information, know things earlier, and can get others to do more things. The more you can get them to initiate and say early in the transaction, the more you'll know about where they are coming from, and the better you can tailor your approach.

4. **Manage your non-verbals.** Interpersonally savvy people understand the critical role of non-verbal communications, of appearing and sounding open and relaxed, smiling and calm. They keep consistent eye contact. They nod while the other person is talking. They speak in a paced and pleasant tone. Work to eliminate any disruptive habits, such as speaking too rapidly or forcefully, using strongly worded or loaded language, or going into too much detail. Watch out for signaling disinterest with actions like glancing at your watch, fiddling with paperwork, or giving your impatient "I'm busy" look.

5. **Selective interpersonal skills?** Some people are interpersonally comfortable and effective with some and not others. Some might be interpersonally smooth with direct reports and tense around senior management. What do the people you are comfortable around have in common? What about those you're not comfortable with? Is it level? Style? Gender? Race? Background? The principles of interpersonal savvy are the same regardless of the audience. Do what you do with the comfortable group with the uncomfortable groups. The results will generally be the same.

6. **Being savvy with people you don't like.** What do people see in them who do like them or can at least get along with them? What are their strengths? Do you have any common interests with them? Whatever you do, don't signal to them what you think. Put your judgments on hold, nod, ask questions, summarize as you would with anyone else. A fly on the wall should not be able to tell whether you're talking to friend or foe. You can always talk less and ask more questions; and neither apologize nor criticize. Even if they're contentious, you can respond neutrally by restating the problem you're working on.

E Peer Relationships

ENTJs push visions and ideas that they believe are right. They often don't establish reciprocity and trading with peers.

1. **Influencing.** Peers generally do not have power over each other. That means that influence skills, understanding, and trading are the currencies to use. Don't just ask for things; find some common ground where you can provide help. What do the peers you're contacting need? Do you really know how they see the issue? Is it even important to them? How does what you're working on affect them? If it affects them negatively, can you trade something, appeal to the common good, figure out some way to minimize the work (volunteering staff help, for example)? Go into peer relationships with a trading mentality.

2. **Sometimes the problem is maneuvering through the complex maze called the organization.** How do you get things done sideways? Who are the movers and shakers in the organization? How do they get things done? Who do they rely on for expediting things through the maze? Who are the major gatekeepers who control the flow of resources, information, and decisions? Who are the guides and the helpers? Get to know them better. Who are the major resisters and stoppers? Try to avoid or go around them.

3. **If peers see you as excessively competitive,** they will cut you out of the loop and may sabotage your cross-border attempts. To be seen as more cooperative, always explain your thinking and invite them to explain theirs. Generate a variety of possibilities first rather than stake out positions. Be tentative, allowing them room to customize the situation. Focus on common goals, priorities, and problems. Invite criticism of your ideas.

4. **If peers think you lack respect for them or what they do,** try to keep conflicts as small and concrete as possible. Separate the people from the problem. Don't get personal. Don't give peers the impression you're trying to dominate or push something on them. Without agreeing or disagreeing, try on their views for size. Can you understand their viewpoint? When peers blow off steam, don't react; return to facts and the problem, staying away from personal clashes. Allow others to save face; concede small points; don't try to hit a home run every time. When a peer takes a rigid position, don't reject it. Ask why: What are the principles behind the position? How do we

know it's fair? What's the theory of the case? Play out what would happen if his/her position was accepted.

5. **Separate working smoothly with peers from personal relationships,** contests, competing for incentives, one-upsmanship, not-invented-here, pride, and ego. Working well with peers over the long term helps everyone, makes sense for the organization, and builds a capacity for the organization to do greater things. Usually the least-used resource in an organization is lateral exchanges of information and resources.

6. **If a peer doesn't play fair, avoid telling others all about it.** This often boomerangs. What goes around comes around. Confront the peer directly, politely, and privately. Describe the unfair situation; explain the impact on you. Don't blame. Give the peer the chance to explain, ask questions, let him/her save some face, and see if you can resolve the matter. Even if you don't totally accept what is said, it's better to solve the problem than win the argument.

7. **Monitor yourself in tough situations to get a sense of how you are coming across.** What's the first thing you attend to? How often do you take a stand vs. make an accommodating gesture? What proportion of your comments deals with relationships vs. the issue to be addressed? Mentally rehearse for worst-case scenarios/hard-to-deal-with people. Anticipate what the person might say and have responses prepared so as not to be caught off guard.

F Day-to-Day Management

ENTJs are interested in the next great innovation. They often ignore, even scoff at day-to-day management skills.

1. **Do an upstream and downstream check with the people you work for,** work around, and those who work for you, to create a list of the administrative slip-ups you do that give them the most trouble. Be sure to ask them for help creating the list. That way, you have a focused list of the things you need to fix first. If you fix the top 10, maybe that will do and the rest of your habits can stay the same.

2. **Put the things you have to do in two piles**—things I have to do that are for me, and things I have to do that are for others or that will affect others. Do the second pile first. Further divide the other pile into the mission-critical, important, and things that can wait. Do them in that order.

3. **Manage your time efficiently.** Plan your time and manage against it. Be time sensitive. Value time. Figure out what you are worth per hour and minute by taking your gross salary plus overhead and benefits. Attach a monetary value on your time. Then ask, is this worth $56 of my time? Figure out what your three largest time wasters are, and reduce them 50% by batching activities and using efficient communications like e-mail and voice mail for routine matters.

4. **Lay out tasks and work.** Most successful projects begin with a good plan. What do I need to accomplish? What are the goals? What's the time line? What resources will I need? How many of the resources do I control? Who controls the rest of the resources—people, funding, tools, materials, support—I need? Lay out the work from A to Z. Many people are seen as lacking a plan because they don't write down the sequence or parts of the work and leave something out. Ask others to comment on ordering and what's missing.

5. **Set goals and measures.** Nothing keeps projects on time and on budget like a goal, a plan, and a measure. Set goals for the whole project and the subtasks. Plan for all. Set measures so you and others can track progress against the goals.

6. **Manage efficiently.** Plan the budget and manage against it. Spend carefully. Have a reserve if the unanticipated comes up. Set up a funding time line so you can track ongoing expenditures against plan.

7. **Set up a process to monitor progress against the plan.** How would you know if the plan is on time? Could you estimate time to completion or percent finished at any time? Give progress feedback as you go to people involved in implementing the plan.

G Dislike of Routine and Procedures

The chance that an ENTJ will be interested in routines and procedures is about zero. Easily bored with detail, they need to remind themselves to attend to it.

1. **Try to see the value in routines.** Pick a plan or procedure and do a historical analysis of how it came to be and why it is necessary. Resist the urge to change it or question its usefulness. Understand it first.

2. **Turn off your answer program.** We all have a need to provide answers as soon as possible to questions and problems. We all have preconceived notions, favorite solutions, and prejudices that prevent our intellectual skills from dealing with the real facts of the problem.

For one-half of the time you have to deal with an issue or a problem, shut off your solution machine and just take in the facts.

3. **Compensate for your dislikes.** Find a person you admire and respect to deal with all the procedures you find oppressive. Let this person tell you if anything needs changing. Otherwise, trust his or her judgment.

H Praising Others

Everyone isn't motivated by a grand vision or the work itself, therefore, ENTJs often need to take the time to praise people.

1. **Follow through with positive and negative rewards and consequences.** Celebrate the exceeders, compliment the just-made-its, and sit down and discuss what happened with the missers. Actually deliver the reward or consequence you communicated. If you don't do what you said you were going to do, no one will pay attention to the next goal and consequence you set.

2. **Follow the basic rules of inspiring others** as outlined in classic books like *People Skills* by Robert Bolton or *Thriving on Chaos* by Tom Peters. Communicate to people that what they do is important. Say thanks. Offer help and ask for it. Provide autonomy in how people do their work. Provide a variety of tasks. "Surprise" people with enriching, challenging assignments. Show an interest in their careers. Adopt a learning attitude toward mistakes. Celebrate successes, have visible accepted measures of achievement, and so on. Too often people behave correctly but there are no consequences. Although it's easy to get too busy to acknowledge, celebrate, and occasionally criticize, don't forget to reinforce what you want. As a rule of thumb, 4 to 1 positive to negative is best.

3. **Know and play the motivation odds.** According to research by Rewick and Lawler, the top motivators at work are: (1) Job challenge; (2) Accomplishing something worthwhile; (3) Learning new things; (4) Personal development; and (5) Autonomy. Pay (12th), Friendliness (14th), Praise (15th), or Chance of Promotion (17th) are not insignificant but are superficial compared with the more powerful motivators. Provide challenges, paint pictures of why this is worthwhile, create a common mind-set, set up chances to learn and grow, and provide autonomy, and you'll hit the vast majority of people's hot buttons.

4. **Use goals to motivate.** Most people are turned on by reasonable goals. They like to measure themselves against a standard. They like to see who can run the fastest, score the most, and work the best. They like goals to be realistic but stretching. People try hardest when they have somewhere between one-half and two-thirds chance of success and some control over how they go about it. People are even more motivated when they participate in setting the goals. Set just-out-of-reach challenges and tasks that will be first time for people—their first negotiation, their first solo presentation, etc.

5. **Be able to speak their language at their level.** It shows respect for their way of thinking. Speaking their language makes it easier for them to talk with you and give you the information you need to motivate.

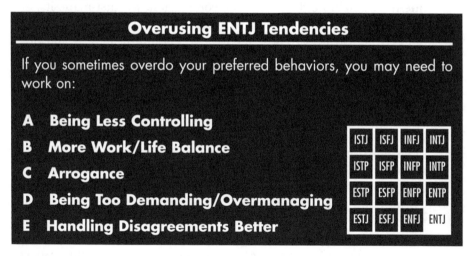

Overusing ENTJ Tendencies

If you sometimes overdo your preferred behaviors, you may need to work on:

A Being Less Controlling

B More Work/Life Balance

C Arrogance

D Being Too Demanding/Overmanaging

E Handling Disagreements Better

ISTJ	ISFJ	INFJ	INTJ
ISTP	ISFP	INFP	INTP
ESTP	ESFP	ENFP	ENTP
ESTJ	ESFJ	ENFJ	ENTJ

A Being Less Controlling

ENTJs often have to gag themselves to keep from pressuring others once they think a situation clearly calls for action.

1. **Rein in your horse.** Impatient people provide answers, conclusions, and solutions too early in the process. Others haven't even understood the problem yet. Providing solutions too quickly will make your people dependent and irritated. If you don't teach them how you think and how you can come up with solutions so fast, they will never learn. Take the time to really define the problem—not impatiently throw out a solution. Brainstorm what questions need to be answered in order to resolve it. Give your people the task to think

about for a day and come back with some solutions. Be a teacher instead of a dictator of solutions. Study yourself. Keep a journal of what triggered your behavior and what the observed consequences were. Learn to detect and control your triggers before they get you in trouble.

2. **Listening chillers?** Don't interrupt before they have finished. Don't suggest words when they hesitate or pause. Don't finish their sentences for them. Don't wave off any further input by saying, "Yes, I know that." "Yes, I know where you're going." "Yes, I have heard that before." If time is really important, you can say, "Let me see if I know where this is going…," or "I wonder if we could summarize to save both of us some time?" Finally, early in a transaction, answers, solutions, conclusions, statements, and dictates shut many people down. You've told them your mind is already made up. Listen first, solve second.

3. **Listening to those who waste a lot of time.** With those you don't have time to listen to, switch to being a teacher. Try to help them craft their communications to you in a more acceptable way. Tell them to be shorter next time. Come with more/less data. Structure the conversation by helping them come up with categories and structures to stop their rambling. Good listeners don't signal to the "bad" people that they are not listening or are not interested. Don't signal to anyone what bucket they're in. Put your mind in neutral, nod, ask questions, be helpful.

4. **Listening to people you don't like.** What do people see in them who do like them or can at least get along with them? What are their strengths? Do you have any common interests? Talk less and ask more questions to give them a second chance. Don't judge their motives and intentions—do that later.

5. **Listening to people you like but…**

   ■ They are disorganized. Interrupt to summarize and keep the discussion focused. While interrupting is generally not a good tactic, it's necessary here.

   ■ They just want to chat. Ask questions to focus them; don't respond to chatty remarks.

   ■ They want to unload a problem. Assume when people tell you something they are looking for understanding; indicate that by being able to summarize what they said. Don't offer any advice.

- They are chronic complainers. Ask them to write down problems and solutions and then let's discuss it. This turns down the volume while, hopefully, moving them off complaining.

- They like to complain about others. Ask if they've talked to the person. Encourage them to do so. If that doesn't work, summarize what they have said without agreeing or disagreeing.

B More Work/Life Balance

ENTJs are often so consumed with their work, their vision, and all the undone tasks of life, that their personal life gets short attention.

1. **All your eggs in one basket?** Add things to your off-work life. This was a major finding of a stress study at AT&T of busy, high-potential women and men. It may seem counterintuitive, but the best-adjusted people forced themselves to structure off-work activities just as much as on-work activities. Otherwise work drives everything else out. Those with dual responsibilities (primary care giver and home manager and a full-time jobholder) need to use their management strengths and skills more at home. What makes your work life successful? Batch tasks, bundle similar activities together, delegate to children, or set up pools with coworkers or neighbors to share tasks, such as car pooling, soccer games, Scouts, etc. Pay to have some things done that are not mission-critical to your home needs. Organize and manage efficiently. Have a schedule. Set up goals and plans. Use some of your work skills more off-work.

2. **There's time and there's focused time.** Busy people with not much time learn to get into the present tense without carrying the rest of their burdens, concerns, and deadlines with them. When you have only one hour to read or play with the kids or play racquetball or sew—be there. Have fun. You won't solve any problems during the 60 minutes anyway. Train your mind to be where you are. Focus on the moment.

3. **Create deadlines, urgencies, and structures off-work.** One tactic that helps is for people to use their strengths from work off-work. If you are organized, organize something. If you are very personable, get together a regular group. If you are competitive, set up a regular match. As commonsensical as this seems, AT&T found that people with poor off-work lives did not use their strengths off-work. They truly left them at the office.

4. **What are your NOs?** If you don't have any, chances are you'll be frustrated on both sides of your life. Part of maturity is letting go of nice, even fun and probably valuable, activities. What are you hanging on to? What can't you say no to at the office that really isn't a priority? Where do you make yourself a patsy? If your saying no irritates people initially, this may be the price. You can usually soften it, however, by explaining what you are trying to do. Most people won't take it personally if you say you're going to pick up your child or maybe coach his/her soccer team or you can't help with this project because of an explicit priority which is critical to your unit. Give reasons that don't downgrade the activity you're giving up. It's not that it's insignificant; it just didn't quite make the cut.

5. **If you can't relax once you leave work,** schedule breakpoints or boundaries. One of the great things about the human brain is that it responds to change; signal it that work is over—play music in your car, immediately play with your children, go for a walk, swim for 20 minutes—give your mind a clear and repetitious breakpoint. Try to focus all your energy where you are. At work, worry about work things and not life things. When you hit the driveway, worry about life things and leave work things at the office. Schedule a time every week for financial management and worries. Try to concentrate your worry time where it will do some good.

6. **If your problem goes beyond that**—you're three days into vacation and still can't relax—write down what you're worried about, which is almost always unresolved problems. Write down everything you can think of. Don't worry about complete sentences—just get it down. You'll usually find it's hard to fill a page, and there will be only three topics—work problems, problems with people, and a to-do list. Note any ideas that come up for dealing with them. This will usually shut off your worry response, which is nothing but a mental reminder of things unresolved. Since we're all creatures of habit, though, the same worries will pop up again. Then you have to say to yourself (as silly as this seems), "I've done everything I can do on that right now," or "That's right, I remember, I'll do it later." Obviously, this tactic works when we're not on vacation as well.

7. **Talk to people who have your best interests at heart,** who accept you for who you are, and with whom you can be candid. What do they want for you? Ask them what they would change.

C Arrogance

If ENTJs have a fatal flaw, arrogance is likely to be it. They push their vision, are impatient with detractors and the unconvinced, and can be quite rough with them. They tend to only respect feedback from fellow experts and visionaries.

1. **Do you value feedback only from those you feel have the experience and expertise to offer it?** If someone points out that you could be somewhat more accommodating, is your reaction to whom, for what purpose, and will that move us toward the goal? Go to the people you respect most and get their feedback on your pluses and minuses. Then think about what modifications in your behavior would help you push your vision through more effectively.

2. **You may view feedback as information,** but this can come across that you just don't care and can increase perceptions of aloofness. Make sure to say thank you for the feedback. Because you may be seen as quite powerful and having high standards, if you don't say thank you or find something to praise or verify in the feedback, you can be seen as indifferent or dismissive.

3. **Although ENTJs are rarely defensive,** they can be if the feedback comes when they are upset about performance or slowness. You will need to work on keeping yourself in a calm state when getting negative feedback. You need to change your thinking. When getting the feedback, your only task is to accurately understand what people are trying to tell you. It is not your task at that point to accept or reject. That comes later. Mentally rehearse how you will calmly react to tough feedback situations before they happen. Develop automatic tactics to shut down or delay your usual emotional response. Some useful tactics are to slow down, take notes, ask clarifying questions, ask them for concrete examples, and thank them for telling you since you know it's not easy for them.

4. **Answers. Solutions. Conclusions. Statements. Dictates.** That's the staple of arrogant people. Instant output. Sharp reactions. This may be getting you in trouble. You jump to conclusions, categorically dismiss what others say, use challenging words in an absolute tone. People then see you as closed to their input or combative. More negatively, they may believe you think they're stupid or ill-informed. Give people a chance to talk without interruption. If you're seen as intolerant or closed, people will often stumble over words in their haste to talk with you or shortcut their argument since they assume you're not listening anyway. Ask a question, invite them to disagree with you, present

their argument back to them softly, let them save face no matter what. Add a 15-second pause into your transactions before you say anything, and add two clarifying questions per transaction to signal you're listening and want to understand.

5. **Arrogant people keep their distance** and don't share much personal data. You may believe you shouldn't mix personal with business. You may believe it's wise to keep distance between you and others you work around and with. Since it's hard for others to relate to an arrogant person in the first place, your reputation may be based on only short, unsatisfactory transactions. The kinds of disclosures people enjoy are: the reasons behind why you do and decide what you do; your self-appraisal; things you know behind what's happening in the business that they don't know—that you are at liberty to disclose; things both good and embarrassing that have happened to you in the past; comments about what's going on around you—without being too negative about others; and things you are interested in and do outside of work. These are areas which you should learn to disclose more than you now do.

6. **Blame and vengeance?** Do you feel a need to punish the people and groups that set you off? Do you become hostile, angry, sarcastic, or vengeful? While all that may be temporarily satisfying to you, they will all backfire and you will lose in the long term. When someone attacks you, rephrase it as an attack on a problem. Reverse the argument—ask what they would do if they were in your shoes. When the other side takes a rigid position, don't reject it. Ask why: What are the principles behind the offer? How do we know it's fair? What's the theory of the case? Play out what would happen if their position was accepted. Let the other side vent frustration or blow off steam, but don't react. When you do reply to an attack, keep it to the facts and their impact on you. It's fine for you to draw conclusions about the impact on yourself—"I felt blindsided." It's not fine for you to tell others their motives—"You blindsided me" means you did it, probably meant to, and I know the meaning of your behavior. So state the meaning for yourself; ask others what their actions meant.

7. **Impatience triggers.** Some people probably bring out your impatience more than others. Who are they? What is it about them that makes you more impatient? Pace? Language? Thought process? Accent? These people may include people you don't like, who ramble, who whine and complain, or who are repetitive advocates for things you have already rejected. Mentally rehearse some calming tactics before meeting with people who trigger your impatience. Work on

understanding their positions without judging them—you can always judge later. In all cases, focus them on the issues or problems to be discussed, return them to the point, interrupt to summarize, and state your position. Try to gently train them to be more efficient with you next time without damaging them in the process.

8. **Task impatience.** Impatient people check in a lot. How's it coming. Is it done yet? When will it be finished? Let me see what you've done so far. That is disruptive to due process and wastes time. When you give out a task or assign a project, establish agreed-upon time checkpoints. You can also assign percentage checkpoints. Check in with me when you are about 25% finished so we can make midcourse corrections and 75% finished so we can make final corrections. Let them figure out how to do the task. Hold back from checking in at other than the agreed-upon times and percentages.

D Being Too Demanding/Overmanaging

ENTJs see clearly how something should be done, and they can be quite pressuring to get it done now. ENTJs often make no secret of what they think of others who are "getting in the way."

1. **Under extended stress, you can become hypercritical of others** and find an endless list of reasons for the unacceptability of some action or fact. You appear skeptical and touchy. Accept this for what it is—you. Think of it as your personal preferences speaking rather than reality. Go to someone you trust and respect and ask this person to assess the issue or people in question. Ask them to tell you the merits of these people or issue. When you get into hypercritical mode, you often don't see them.

2. **In meetings, make sure you include everyone,** and don't direct substantially more remarks toward one person or subgroup to the exclusion of others. Make sure you signal nothing negative to others; a neutral observer should not be able to tell from your demeanor whom you like and don't like. Help the quiet, shy, and reserved have their say. Quiet the loud, assertive, and passionate. Give everyone a fair chance to be heard.

3. **You should work doubly hard at observing others.** Always select your interpersonal approach from the other person in, not from you out. Your best choice of approach will always be determined by the other person or group, not you. Think about each transaction as if the

other person were a customer you wanted. How would you craft an approach?

4. **Equity with information.** Follow the rule of equity of information with everyone. Explain your thinking and ask them to explain theirs. When discussing issues, give reasons first, solutions last. When you give solutions first, people often don't listen to your reasons. Some people get overly directive with some of their reports, and they, in turn, feel that you're not interested in what they think. Invite their thinking and their reasons before settling on solutions. Don't provide information selectively. Don't use information as a reward or a relationship builder with one or just a few and not others.

5. **Pause to:**

   ■ Edit your actions before you act. Before you speak or act in problem situations, ask yourself if you would do the same thing in a parallel situation. Is your value really what should be operating here?

   ■ Pick your battles. Make sure you only pull rank and impose your values on others in really mission-critical situations.

6. **Let your team help you.** Periodically, send out a memo asking each person whether there is anything he or she thinks he/she could do that you are now doing or monitoring too closely. Pick one or two things per person and empower them to do it on their own. Make sure the up-front communication is adequate for them to perform well. Explain your standards—what the outcome should be, the key things that need to be taken care of—then ask them to figure out how to do it themselves.

7. **What skill do you have that you could pass on to others?** Ask yourself why this is a strength for you. What are the first items you would teach as the keys to help others form umbrellas for understanding? Watch others carefully for their reactions when teaching and coaching. What works and doesn't work for you as a coach? Reveal things that people don't need to know to do their jobs, but which will be interesting to them—and help them feel valued.

E Handling Disagreements Better

ENTJs typically dislike emotional situations since they value logic above all else. But they also need to take care of the feelings and viewpoints of others.

1. **Clear problem-focused communication.** Follow the rule of equity: Explain your thinking and ask them to explain theirs. Be able to state their position as clearly as they do whether you agree or not—give it legitimacy. Separate facts from opinions and assumptions. Generate a variety of possibilities first rather than stake out positions. Keep your speaking to 30–60 second bursts. Try to get them to do the same. Don't give the other side the impression you're lecturing or criticizing them. Explain objectively why you hold a view; make the other side do the same. Ask lots of questions, make fewer statements. To identify interests behind positions, ask why they hold them or why they wouldn't want to do something. Always restate their position to their satisfaction before offering a response.

2. **Downsizing the conflict.** Almost all conflicts have common points that get lost in the heat of the battle. After a conflict has been presented and understood, start by saying that it might be helpful to see if we agree on anything. Write them on the flip chart. Then write down the areas left open. Focus on common goals, priorities, and problems. Keep the open conflicts as small as possible and concrete. The more abstract it gets, "We don't trust your unit," the more unmanageable it gets. To this respond, "Tell me your specific concern—why exactly don't you trust us; can you give me an example?" Usually after calm discussion, they don't trust your unit on this specific issue under these specific conditions. That's easier to deal with. Allow others to save face by conceding small points that are not central to the issue—don't try to hit a home run every time. If you can't agree on a solution, agree on a procedure to move forward. Collect more data. Appeal to a higher power. Get a third-party arbitrator. Something. This creates some positive motion and breaks stalemates.

3. **Cooperative relations.** The opposite of conflict is cooperation. Developing cooperative relationships involves demonstrating real and perceived equity, the other side feeling understood and respected, and taking a problem-oriented point of view. To do this more: Increase the realities and perceptions of fairness—don't try to win every battle and take all the spoils; focus on the common-ground issues and interests of both sides—find wins on both sides, give in on little

points; avoid starting with entrenched positions—show respect for them and their positions; and reduce any remaining conflicts to the smallest size possible.

4. **Practice Aikido,** the ancient art of absorbing the energy of your opponent and using it to manage him/her. Let the other side vent frustration or blow off steam, but don't react. Listen. Nod. Ask clarifying questions. Ask open-ended questions like, "What one change could you make so we could achieve our objectives better?" "What could I do that would help the most?" Restate their position periodically to signal you have understood. But don't react. Keep them talking until they run out of venom. Then explore the underlying concern. Separate the people from the problem. When someone attacks you, rephrase it as an attack on the problem. In response to threats, say you'll only negotiate on merit and fairness. If the other side won't play fair, surface their game—"It looks like you're playing good cop, bad cop. Why don't you settle your differences and tell me one thing?" In response to unreasonable proposals, attacks, or a non-answer to a question, you can always say nothing. People will usually respond by saying more, coming off their position a bit, or at least revealing their true interests. Many times, with unlimited venting and your understanding, the actual conflict shrinks.

5. **Bargaining and trading.** Since you can't absolutely win all conflicts unless you keep pulling rank, you have to learn to horse-trade and bargain. What do they need that I have? What could I do for them outside this conflict that could allow them to give up something I need now in return? How can we turn this into a win for both of us?

6. **Questions.** In win-win and something-something negotiations, the more information you have about the other side, the more you will have to work with. What can you learn about what they know before going in? What will they do if they don't reach an agreement with you? In the negotiation, ask more questions, make fewer statements. Ask clarifying questions: "What did you mean by that?" Probes: "Why do you say that?" Motives: "What led you to that position?" Get everything out that you can. Don't negotiate assumptions, negotiate facts.

I am so self-reliant, independent, and demanding that I do not take the time to study, listen, and engage in more personal ways with others.

– An ENTJ Manager

■ ■ ■ ■ ■ ■ ■ ■ ■ ■ ■ ■ ■ ■ ■ ■ ■

APPLICATION

Your personal preferences play out in day-to-day problems and situations you face. Below is a case about your type dealing with such a situation. Use this to think through how you will integrate the tips you've considered and coach yourself to be more effective in your type.

ENTJ Application Situation (Part 1)

"I'm ready for some new challenges," David tells Anne, his wife. "But when I mentioned that to Sheryl, she said that I'm going to have to work on my teaming skills if I expect to go any higher."

"Well, so much for the saying, 'You can't argue with success, huh?'" Anne joked, putting down her fork as she and David finished their late dinner.

"Sheryl thinks the fact that turnover in my group is running at about 25% annually has something to do with my teaming skills."

"You have to admit, you're hard charging and sometimes get pretty headstrong about the things you want to accomplish when the pressure is on."

David reflected, staring out the dining room window, but without really seeing. Under him, in the six years he'd been Director of Operations, the software company had grown 30%. Sure there were other companies that had experienced much faster growth than that, but then some of them had gone down in flames. Sometimes he thought the faster pace at those companies would be attractive, but he had a theory about the value of stability and predictability that counterbalanced the lure of the more glamorous highfliers.

If only Sheryl, the CEO, could see that he was ready for something bigger, maybe that VP job would be his.

"Penny for your thoughts," Anne said, noticing David's dreamlike state.

"Well, it's just that I'm wondering if Sheryl is right when she tells me that I need to change the way I interact with my direct reports. What's wrong with being ambitious and setting stretch goals and then encouraging people to work hard to meet them? If I sit around being patient, the competition gets the jump on us. Why don't people get that?"

Anne doesn't answer his questions. As a practicing therapist, she is more inclined to try to coach him.

Thinking It Through: Strategy

■ How do you think Anne might proceed if she decides to continue to try to coach David?

Planning It Out: Tactics

■ What tendencies and preferences in David (an ENTJ) can Anne focus on to help him appreciate how he's affecting others, both positively and negatively?

■ What particular areas would Anne urge David to work on if he aspires to higher levels of leadership, and how might he be challenged in those areas?

■ Which of the tactics described in the Being More Effective section are applicable in this situation?

■ Which Overused Tendencies are most likely to come into play here?

ENTJ Application Situation (Part 2)

■ Anne thinks David could practice the behaviors and skills at home, with his children and with her, that will serve him better at work. What does she tell him?

Reflection

■ Why do you think the turnover on David's team is high (running well above industry norms for comparable companies and positions)? What characteristics of an ENTJ might present problems in relationships with team members and direct reports, and how might David mitigate those?

SUGGESTED READINGS

■■■■■■■ Being a More Effective ENTJ ■■■■■■■

Showing More Caring

Autry, James A. *The Art of Caring Leadership*. New York: William Morrow and Company, Inc., 1991.

Brantley, Jeffrey and Jon Kabat-Zinn. *Calming Your Anxious Mind: How Mindfulness and Compassion Can Free You From Anxiety, Fear, and Panic.* Oakland, CA: New Harbinger Publications, 2003.

Daniels, Aubrey C. *Bringing Out the Best in People*. New York: McGraw-Hill, Inc., 1994.

Kouzes, James M. and Barry Z. Posner. *Encouraging the Heart: A Leader's Guide to Rewarding and Recognizing Others*. San Francisco: Jossey-Bass, Inc., 2003.

Stone, Douglas. *Difficult Conversations: How to Discuss What Matters Most*. New York: Penguin Books, 2000.

Developing Others

Charan, Ram, James L. Noel and Steve Drotter. *The Leadership Pipeline: How to Build the Leadership Powered Company*. New York: John Wiley & Sons, Inc., 2000.

Daniels, Aubrey C. *Bringing Out the Best in People*. New York: McGraw-Hill, Inc., 1994.

Fulmer, Robert M. and Jay A. Conger. *Growing Your Company's Leaders.* New York: AMACOM, 2004.

Lombardo, Michael M. and Robert W. Eichinger. *The Leadership Machine.* Minneapolis, MN: Lominger Limited, Inc., 2004.

Understanding Others

Ashkenas, Ronald N. (Ed.), Dave Ulrich, Todd Jick, Steve Kerr and Lawrence A. Bossidy. *The Boundaryless Organization: Breaking the Chains of Organization Structure, Revised and Updated.* New York: John Wiley & Sons, Inc., 2002.

Belbin, R. Meredith. *Management Teams.* Boston: Butterworth-Heinemann, 2004.

Bolton, Robert and Dorothy Grover Bolton. *People Styles at Work—Making Bad Relationships Good and Good Relationships Better.* New York: AMACOM, 1996.

Crainer, Stuart. *Motivating the New Generation—Modern Motivation Techniques.* New York: BrownHerron Publishing, 2001.

Deems, Richard S. and Terri A. Deems. *Leading in Tough Times: The Manager's Guide to Responsibility, Trust, and Motivation.* Amherst, MA: HRD Press, 2003.

Glanz, Barbara A. *Handle With CARE: Motivating and Retaining Employees.* New York: McGraw-Hill Trade, 2002.

Interpersonal Savvy

Benton, D.A. *Executive Charisma: Six Steps to Mastering the Art of Leadership.* New York: McGraw-Hill Trade, 2003.

Bolton, Robert and Dorothy Grover Bolton. *People Styles at Work—Making Bad Relationships Good and Good Relationships Better.* New York: AMACOM, 1996.

Brooks, Michael. *Instant Rapport.* New York: Warner Books, 1989.

Maxwell, John C. *Relationships 101.* London: Thomas Nelson, 2004.

Silberman, Melvin L. and Freda Hansburg. *Peoplesmart: Developing Your Interpersonal Intelligence.* San Francisco: Berrett-Koehler Publishers, Inc., 2000.

Peer Relationships

Baker, Wayne E. *Networking Smart*. New York: Backinprint.com, 2000.

Bolton, Robert and Dorothy Grover Bolton. *People Styles at Work—Making Bad Relationships Good and Good Relationships Better*. New York: AMACOM, 1996.

Cartwright, Tatula. *Managing Conflict With Peers*. Greensboro, NC: Center for Creative Leadership, 2003.

Patterson, Kerry, Joseph Grenny, Ron McMillan, Al Switzler and Stephen R. Covey. *Crucial Conversations: Tools for Talking When Stakes Are High*. New York: McGraw-Hill/Contemporary Books, 2002.

Day-to-Day Management

Bandrowski, James F. *Corporate Imagination Plus—Five Steps to Translating Innovative Strategies Into Action*. New York: The Free Press, 2000.

Byfield, Marilyn. *It's Hard to Make a Difference When You Can't Find Your Keys: The Seven-Step Path to Becoming Truly Organized*. New York: Viking Press, 2003.

Champy, James A. *X-Engineering the Corporation: Reinventing Your Business in the Digital Age*. New York: Warner Books, 2002.

Gleeson, Kerry. *The Personal Efficiency Program: How to Get Organized to Do More Work in Less Time*. New York: John Wiley & Sons, Inc., 2000.

Keen, Peter G.W. *The Process Edge—Creating Value Where It Counts*. Boston: Harvard Business School Press, 1998.

MacKenzie, Alec. *The Time Trap: The Classic Book on Time Management*. Fine Communications, 2002.

Dislike of Routine and Procedures

Bossidy, Larry, Ram Charan and Charles Burck (Contributor). *Execution: The Discipline of Getting Things Done*. New York: Crown Business Publishing, 2002.

Keen, Peter G.W. *The Process Edge—Creating Value Where It Counts*. Boston: Harvard Business School Press, 1998.

Lawler, Edward E., III, Susan Albers Mohrman and George Benson. *Organizing for High Performance: Employee Involvement, TQM, Reengineering, and Knowledge Management in the Fortune 1000: The CEO Report.* San Francisco: Jossey-Bass, Inc., 2001.

Niven, P.R. *Balanced Scorecard Step-by-Step: Maximizing Performance and Maintaining Results.* New York: John Wiley & Sons, Inc., 2002.

Praising Others

Bolton, Robert. *People Skills.* New York: Simon & Schuster, 1979.

Crainer, Stuart. *Motivating the New Generation—Modern Motivation Techniques.* New York: BrownHerron Publishing, 2001.

Glanz, Barbara A. *Handle With CARE: Motivating and Retaining Employees.* New York: McGraw-Hill Trade, 2002.

Hiam, Alexander. *Motivational Management: Inspiring Your People for Maximum Performance.* New York: AMACOM, 2003.

Peters, Tom. *Thriving on Chaos: Handbook for a Management Revolution.* New York: HarperCollins, 1987.

■■■■■■■ Overusing ENTJ Tendencies ■■■■■■■

Being Less Controlling

Barker, Larry, Ph.D. and Kittie Watson, Ph.D. *Listen Up: At Home, at Work, in Relationships: How to Harness the Power of Effective Listening.* Irvine, CA: Griffin Trade Paperback, 2001.

Bolton, Robert and Dorothy Grover Bolton. *People Styles at Work—Making Bad Relationships Good and Good Relationships Better.* New York: AMACOM, 1996.

Burley-Allen, Madelyn. *Listening: The Forgotten Skill.* New York: John Wiley & Sons, Inc., 1995.

Gonthier, Giovinella and Kevin Morrissey. *Rude Awakenings: Overcoming the Civility Crisis in the Workplace.* Chicago: Dearborn Trade Publishing, 2002.

Ryan, Mary Jane. *The Power of Patience: How to Slow the Rush and Enjoy More Happiness, Success, and Peace of Mind Everyday.* New York: Broadway Press, 2003.

More Work/Life Balance

Glanz, Barbara. *Balancing Acts.* Chicago, IL: Dearborn Trade Publishing, 2003.

Gordon, Gil E. *Turn It Off: How to Unplug From the Anytime-Anywhere Office Without Disconnecting Your Career.* New York: Three Rivers Press, 2001.

Merrill, A. Roger and Rebecca R. Merrill. *Life Matters: Creating a Dynamic Balance of Work, Family, Time & Money.* New York: McGraw-Hill, Inc., 2003.

St. James, Elaine. *Simplify Your Work Life: Ways to Change the Way You Work So You Have More Time to Live.* New York: Hyperion, 2001.

Arrogance

Bolton, Robert and Dorothy Grover Bolton. *People Styles at Work—Making Bad Relationships Good and Good Relationships Better.* New York: AMACOM, 1996.

Carter, Les. *The Anger Trap: Free Yourself From the Frustrations That Sabotage Your Life.* New York: John Wiley & Sons, Inc., 2003.

Ellis, Albert, Ph.D. *How to Control Your Anxiety Before It Controls You.* New York: Citadel Press, 2000.

Waldroop, James, Ph.D. and Timothy Butler, Ph.D. *Maximum Success: Changing the 12 Behavior Patterns That Keep You From Getting Ahead.* New York: Doubleday, 2000.

Being Too Demanding/Overmanaging

Allen, David. *Getting Things Done: The Art of Stress-Free Productivity.* New York: Penguin Books, 2003.

Bossidy, Larry, Ram Charan and Charles Burck (Contributor). *Execution: The Discipline of Getting Things Done.* New York: Crown Business Publishing, 2002.

Branham, L. *Keeping the People Who Keep You in Business.* New York: AMACOM, 2001.

Genett, Donna M. *If You Want It Done Right, You Don't Have to Do It Yourself! The Power of Effective Delegation.* Sanger, CA: Quill Driver Books, 2004.

Glanz, Barbara A. *Handle With CARE: Motivating and Retaining Employees.*
New York: McGraw-Hill Trade, 2002.

Patterson, Kerry, Joseph Grenny, Ron McMillan, Al Switzler and Stephen
R. Covey. *Crucial Conversations: Tools for Talking When Stakes Are High.*
New York: McGraw-Hill/Contemporary Books, 2002.

Solomon, Muriel. *Working With Difficult People.* New York: Prentice Hall,
2002.

Handling Disagreements Better

Cloke, Ken and Joan Goldsmith. *Resolving Conflicts at Work: A Complete
Guide for Everyone on the Job.* San Francisco: Jossey-Bass, Inc., 2000.

Dana, Daniel. *Conflict Resolution.* New York: McGraw-Hill Trade, 2000.

Guttman, Howard M. *When Goliaths Clash: Managing Executive Conflict to
Build a More Dynamic Organization.* New York: AMACOM, 2003.

Masters, Marick Francis and Robert R. Albright. *The Complete Guide to
Conflict Resolution in the Workplace.* New York: AMACOM, 2002.

SECTION II

Introduction to Facets: A Deeper Look at YOU

A deeper view of the subtleties of type came when Isabel Myers described multiple facets of each dimension of the MBTI tool. Later research confirmed these facets as aspects of each of her dimensions. For example, an individual could be scored for Extraversion but also be described by the facets as being Quiet or Contained, which are associated with Introversion. In other words, having a preference for one type in general does not mean that all aspects of that preference are accurate descriptors. In commonsense terms, this is why all ESTJs are not alike. There are some quiet extraverts.

Another way to think about facets is that there are a minority of pure types. There are few pure INTJs or ESTJs, for example. There are more mixed types. There are INTJs with a little E and a little S, F, and P. Not enough to change their general preference or type but enough to be different from a pure INTJ. This information is contained in Form Q of the MBTI.

Myers found numerous facets under each dimension. The publisher, Consulting Psychologists Press, chose to create a uniform structure such that there are five facets within each dimension. When taking the MBTI Step II tool, an individual gets a four letter type and a score on 20 other dimensions, five within each of the four aspects of the reported type.

As a general rule, these facets are more descriptive of your behaviors than just your type, and from a statistical perspective, have a huge range of variability within the key dimensions. In other words, this means that you can have a clear Thinking preference, and can still exhibit Accommodating (Feeling) behaviors.

The facets are associated with the dimensions of type in the following ways:

Extraverting	↔	Introverting	Thinking	↔	Feeling
Initiating	(1)	Receiving	Logical	(1)	Empathetic
Expressive	(2)	Contained	Reasonable	(2)	Compassionate
Gregarious	(5)	Intimate	Questioning	(5)	Accommodating
Active	(4)	Reflective	Critical	(4)	Accepting
Enthusiastic	(3)	Quiet	Tough	(3)	Tender
Sensing	**↔**	**Intuiting**	**Judging**	**↔**	**Perceiving**
Concrete	(1)	Abstract	Systematic	(3)	Casual
Realistic	(2)	Imaginative	Planful	(1)	Open-Ended
Practical	(5)	Conceptual	Early Starting	(5)	Pressure-Prompted
Experiential	(3)	Theoretical	Scheduled	(2)	Spontaneous
Traditional	(4)	Original	Methodical	(4)	Emergent

In the section that follows, we present each of the 20 facet pairs. To use the first pair (Initiating–Receiving) as an example, there are effectiveness or developmental tips to help you develop more Initiating behaviors (strengthen the Extraverted part of YOU), and tips about what to do if you overdo Initiating (balance the Extraverted part of YOU). With Receiving, you can also scan the tips to strengthen that facet or to compensate for overdoing it.

In the tables, the numbers between each pair (1 through 5) reflect how much the facet reflects preference (1) vs. being more affected by experience (5). Using the Extraverting–Introverting table as an example, Initiating–Receiving (1) is most likely to be a personality preference, and Gregarious–Intimate (5) is more reflective of experience. We are more likely to see people who, while introverted, are gregarious as well. They report that they learned to be more socially engaged in order to enrich their influence.

Extraverting ←→ Introverting Facets

Extraverting	Purpose: Drawing Energy	Introverting
Initiating (Congenial, active) • Easily connect with other people. • Broad base of acquaintances. • Keep continuous lookout for new people.	Strategies for communicating and connecting with others (very broad and general). **1**	**Receiving** (Reserved, low-key) • Engage extensively with those they know. • More likely to be introduced than to introduce themselves. • Prefer to discuss topics they know well. • Often expert at something.
Expressive (Self-revealing) • Emphasis on open and forthright communication of feelings. • Easy to know. • Share feelings without reservation.	Communicating feelings, thoughts, interests. **2**	**Contained** (Controlled, private) • Selective about what and with whom they share. • Personal experience rarely shared. • Process feelings internally at length.
Gregarious (Seek popularity, join groups) • Enjoy associations with a variety of people. • Prefer a wide circle of people. • Sensitive to the "flow" of the group. • Like the give-and-take of relationships.	Breadth and depth of relationships. **5**	**Intimate** (Seek one-to-one conversations) • Maintain a limited range of friendships requiring a significant amount of trust. • Dislike too many activities. • Often provide delayed responses to interactions.
Active (Enjoy contact, listen, speak) • Actively engage with environment. • Learn better by doing, drawn to active rather than intellectual issues.	How we engage with the environment to socialize, learn, and entertain ourselves. **4**	**Reflective** (Prefer space, read, write) • Enjoy stimulation that evokes visual, intellectual, or mental responses. • Learn best from written material.
Enthusiastic (Energetic, lively) • Talkative, hearty, enjoy energetic exchange. • Enjoy being center of attention at times. • Convey humor through stories. • Like being with others.	Level and type of energy in communicating. **3**	**Quiet** (Calm, enjoy solitude) • Interactions with others neither energize nor stimulate them. • They are low-key. • Usually succinct when communicating. • Use understatement.

E↔I

Initiating↔Receiving
Strategies for communicating and connecting with others (very broad and general).

Initiating (Congenial, active)

- Easily connect with other people.

- Broad base of acquaintances.

- Keep continuous lookout for new people.

To develop more of this facet:

1. **For low-risk practice, talk to strangers off-work.** Set a goal of meeting 10 new people at a social gathering; find out what you have in common with them. Initiate contact at your place of worship, at PTA meetings, in the neighborhood, at the supermarket, on the plane, and on the bus. Explore new ground. Learn new things. Practice in your life. Go to theme restaurants you know nothing about. Vacation at places without doing a lot of research. Go to ethnic festivals for groups you have little knowledge about.

2. **You have to put out your hand first.** Make first eye contact. Note the color of the person's eyes to ensure good eye contact. You have to ask the first question or share the first piece of information. You have to make the first three minutes comfortable for the other person. When you see someone you haven't talked with recently, wrap up what you're doing and go talk with him or her.

3. **Confide your thinking on a business issue and invite the response of others.** Pass on tidbits of information you think will help people do their jobs better or broaden their perspectives.

4. **Initiating people work to know and remember important things about the people they work around, for, and with.** Know three things about everybody—their interests or their children or something you can chat about other than the business agenda. Treat life as a small world. Establish things you can talk about with each person you work with that go beyond strictly work transactions. The point is to forge common ground and connections.

5. **Initiating people appear and sound open and relaxed.** They smile. They are calm. They keep eye contact. They nod while the other person is talking. They have an open body posture. They speak in a paced and pleasant tone. Eliminate any disruptive habits, such as speaking too rapidly or forcefully, using strongly worded or loaded

language, or going into too much detail. Watch out for signaling disinterest with actions like glancing at your watch, fiddling with paperwork, or giving your impatient "I'm busy" look.

6. **The magic of questions.** Many people don't ask enough curiosity questions when in their work mode. There are too many informational statements, conclusions, suggestions, and solutions and not enough "what if," "what are you thinking," "how do you see that." In studies, statements outweighed questions 8 to 1. Ask more questions than others. Make fewer solution statements early in a discussion. Keep probing until you understand what they are trying to tell you.

7. **Communicate to people that what they do is important.** Say thanks. Offer help and ask for it. Provide autonomy in how people do their work. Provide a variety of tasks. "Surprise" people with enriching, challenging assignments. Show an interest in their careers. Adopt a learning attitude toward mistakes. Celebrate successes, have visible accepted measures of achievement, and so on.

8. **Disclose more.** The kinds of disclosure that people enjoy reveal the reasons behind why you do what you do, things you know behind what's happening in the business that they don't know, things both good and embarrassing that have happened to you in the past, commentary about what's going on around you, and things you are interested in and do outside of work. Learn to be more comfortable admitting your mistakes. This makes you more human, and it also establishes a routine of learning from inevitable shortcomings. Observe someone who discloses a lot more than you do and does it well. What do they disclose? What type of personal information do they share?

9. **At work, start small so you can recover more quickly.** Go for small wins. Don't blast into a major task to prove your boldness. Break it down into smaller tasks. Take the easiest one for you first. Then build up to the tougher ones.

10. **What's mission-critical?** What are the three to five things that most need to get done to achieve your goals? Effective performers typically spend about half their time on a few mission-critical priorities.

If you sometimes overdo being Initiating:

1. **You may talk too much and turn off others.** They may interpret your behavior as lack of interest in others, egocentrism, or even selfishness. Do a feedback check: Ask for 360° feedback and find out if you are turning people off.

2. **Listen more.** How do people know you are listening? You have eye contact. You take notes. You don't frown or fidget. How do people know you've understood? You paraphrase what they have said to their satisfaction. How do people know if you have accepted or rejected what they said? You tell them. Hopefully in a tactful way if you reject what they had to say. Give your reasons.

3. **Listening chillers?** Don't interrupt before they have finished. Don't suggest words when they hesitate or pause. Don't finish their sentences for them. Don't wave off any further input by saying, "Yes, I know that." "Yes, I know where you're going." "Yes, I have heard that before." If time is really important, you can say, "Let me see if I know where this is going...," or "I wonder if we could summarize to save both of us some time?" Finally, early in a transaction, answers, solutions, conclusions, statements, and dictates shut many people down. You've told them your mind is already made up. Listen first, solve second.

4. **Questions.** Good listeners ask lots of questions to get to a good understanding. Probing questions. Clarifying questions. Confirming—is this what you are saying—questions. Ask one more question than you do now and add to that until people signal you that they think you are truly listening.

5. **Work to get continuous feedback; don't wait for annual feedback events.** There are three ways to get better, continued, high-quality feedback:

   ■ Prepare specific areas you are concerned about, and ask people to respond anonymously in writing. List the areas where you need feedback, and ask them what they would like for you to keep doing, start doing, and stop doing to improve.

   ■ Work with a development partner who knows what you're working on and gives up on-line feedback as you try new things.

   ■ In areas you are working on, ask others who have watched you to debrief events with you shortly after they happen.

Receiving (Reserved, low-key)

- Engage extensively with those they know.
- More likely to be introduced than to introduce themselves.
- Prefer to discuss topics they know well.
- Often expert at something.

To develop more of this facet:

1. **Listen more.** How do people know you are listening? You have eye contact. You take notes. You don't frown or fidget. You paraphrase what they have said to their satisfaction. How do people know if you have accepted or rejected what they said? You tell them. Hopefully in a tactful way if you reject what they had to say. Give your reasons.

2. **Listening chillers?** Don't interrupt before they have finished. Don't suggest words when they hesitate or pause. Don't finish their sentences for them. Don't wave off any further input by saying, "Yes, I know that." If time is really important, you can say, "Let me see if I know where this is going...," or "I wonder if we could summarize to save both of us some time?" Finally, early in a transaction, answers, solutions, conclusions, statements, and dictates shut many people down. You've told them your mind is already made up. Listen first, solve second.

3. **Questions.** Good listeners ask lots of questions to get to a good understanding. Probing questions. Clarifying questions. Confirming—is this what you are saying—questions. Ask one more question than you do now and add to that until people signal you that they think you are truly listening.

4. **Listening to those who waste a lot of time.** With those you don't have time to listen to, switch to being a teacher. Try to help them craft their communications to you in a more acceptable way. Interrupt to summarize. Tell them to be shorter next time. Come with more/less data. Structure the conversation by helping them come up with categories and structures to stop their rambling. Good listeners don't signal to the "bad" people that they are not listening or are not interested. Don't signal to anyone what bucket they're in. Put your mind in neutral, nod, ask questions, be helpful.

5. **Listening to people you don't like.** What do people see in them who do like them or can at least get along with them? What are their strengths? Do you have any common interests? Talk less and ask more questions to give them a second chance. Don't judge their motives and intentions—do that later.

6. **Broaden your perspective.** Pick three unrelated things to study and dabble in that you have not yet paid much attention to—opera, romance novels, technical journals out of your area, MTV, learn a new language, take a magic course, study archeology. Connections can come from anywhere—your brain doesn't care where it gets perspectives. Try to think about how the principles of one tie into the other.

7. **Read international publications** like *The Economist*, the *International Herald Tribune, Commentary*; autobiographies of people like Kissinger; pick a country and study it; read a book on the fall of the Soviet Union; or read "we present all sides" journals like *The Atlantic Monthly* to get the broadest possible view of issues. There are common underlying principles in everything. You need to expose yourself more broadly in order to find and apply those principles to what you're doing today.

8. **Become more of an expert.** Reduce your understanding of how business operates to personal rules of thumb or insights. Write them down in your own words. An example would be, "What are the drivers in marketing anything?" One executive had 25 such drivers that he continually edited, scratched through, and replaced with more up-to-date thinking. Use these rules of thumb to analyze a business that you know something about, possibly one of your hobbies or a sport you are enthusiastic about. Pick what you know. Then pick two businesses that have pulled off clever strategies, one related to yours and one not. Study what they did, talk to people who know what happened, and see what you can learn. Then study two businesses that were not successful and see what they didn't do.

9. **Don't know enough about your business?** Study your annual report and various other financial reports. If you don't know how, the major investment firms have basic documents explaining how to read financial documents. After you've done this, consult a pro and ask him/her what he/she looks at and why. Ask for lunch or just a meeting with the person who is in charge of the strategic planning process in your company. Have him/her explain the strategic plan for the organization. Particularly, have him/her point out the mission-critical functions and capabilities the organization needs to be on the leading edge to win.

10. **Learn to think as an expert in your business does.** Take problems to inside experts or external consultants and ask them what are the keys they look for; observe what they consider significant and not significant. Chunk up data into categories so you can remember it. Devise five key areas or questions you can consider each time a business issue comes up. Don't waste your time just learning facts; they won't be useful unless you have conceptual buckets to put them in. Then present your thinking to experts or write a strategic business plan for your unit and invite their review. There is no need to restrict your choices to just your organization; any astute business person should have some interesting insights.

If you sometimes overdo being Receiving:

1. **Don't like risk?** Sometimes taking action involves pushing the envelope, taking chances, and trying bold new initiatives. Doing those things leads to more misfires and mistakes. Research says that successful executives have made more mistakes in their careers than those who didn't make it. Treat any mistakes or failures as chances to learn. Nothing ventured, nothing gained. Up your risk comfort. Start small so you can recover more quickly. Go for small wins. Don't blast into a major task to prove your boldness.

2. **Show more caring.** Share your thinking on a business issue and invite the advice of others. Pass on tidbits of information you think will help people do their jobs better or broaden their perspectives. Reveal things people don't need to know to do their jobs, but which will be interesting to them—and help them feel valued. Disclose some things about yourself as well. Know three non-work things about everybody—their interests and hobbies or their children or something you can chat about. Life is a small world. If you ask your people a few personal questions, you'll find you have something in common with virtually anyone.

3. **Delegate for development.** Brainstorm with your direct reports all the tasks that aren't being done but are important to do. Ask them for a list of tasks that are no longer challenging for them. (You can also use parts of your own job to develop others. Take three tasks that are no longer developmental for you, but would be for others, and delegate them.) Trade tasks and assignments between two direct reports; have them do each other's work. Assign each of your direct reports an out-of-comfort-zone task that meets the following criteria: The task needs to be done, the person hasn't done it or isn't good at it, and the task calls for a skill the person needs to develop. Remember to focus on varied assignments—more of the same isn't developmental.

4. **Share your thinking.** To help those around you grow and learn from what you know, you have to sometimes think out loud. You have to share your thinking from the initial presentation of the issue through to conclusion. Most of us are on thinking autopilot. We don't think about thinking. When someone else has to or wants to understand how you came up with a decision, it's sometimes difficult to unravel it in your mind. You have to go step-by-step and recreate your thinking. Sometimes it helps if other people ask the questions. They can probably guide you through how you came up with an answer or a decision better than you can. Once in a while, you should document a decision or two. What was the issue? What were the pros and cons you considered? How did you weight things? Then you can use those examples to demonstrate to others how you make decisions.

5. **Inconsistent informing.** Have an information checklist detailing what information should go to whom; pass on summaries or copies of important communications. Determine the information checklist by: keeping tabs on unpleasant surprises people report to you; ask direct reports what they'd like to know to do their jobs better; and check with boss, peers, and customers to see if you pass along too little, enough, or too much of the right kinds of information. It's important to know what to pass, to whom to pass, and when to pass, to become an effective informer.

6. **Set priorities and stick to them.** What's mission-critical? What are the three to five things that most need to get done to achieve your goals? Effective performers typically spend about half their time on a few mission-critical priorities. Don't get diverted by trivia and things you like doing but that aren't tied to the bottom line.

Expressive↔Contained
Communicating feelings, thoughts, interests.

Expressive (Self-revealing)

- Emphasis on open and forthright communication of feelings.

- Easy to know.

- Share feelings without reservation.

To develop more of this facet:

1. **Share your thinking on a business issue and invite advice.** Pass on tidbits of information you think will help people do their jobs better or broaden their perspectives. Reveal things people don't need to know to do their jobs, but which will be interesting to them—and help

them feel valued. Disclose some things about yourself as well. Tell them how you arrive at decisions. Explain your intentions, your reasons, and your thinking when announcing decisions.

2. **Taking a tough stand demands confidence in what you're saying** along with the humility that you might be wrong—one of life's paradoxes. To prepare to take the lead on a tough issue, work on your stand through mental interrogation until you can clearly state in a few sentences what your stand is and why you hold it. Build the business case. How do others win? People don't line up behind laundry lists or ambiguous objectives. Ask others for advice—scope the problem, consider options, pick one, develop a rationale, then go with it until proven wrong.

3. **To sell your leadership, keep your eyes on the prize** but don't specify how to get there. Present the outcomes, targets, and goals without the how to's. Welcome their ideas—good and bad. Any negative response is a positive if you learn from it. Allow them to fill in the blanks, ask questions, and disagree without appearing impatient with them.

4. **Give as much real-time feedback as you have time for.** Most people are motivated by process feedback against agreed-upon goals for three reasons:

   - First, it helps them adjust what they are doing along the way in time to better achieve the goal; they can make midcourse corrections.

   - Second, it shows them what they are doing is important and that you're there to help.

   - Third, it's not the "gotcha" game of negative and critical feedback after the fact.

5. **Help your people learn by looking for repeating patterns?** Help them look for patterns in the situations and problems they deal with. What succeeded and what failed? What was common to each success or what was present in each failure but never present in a success? Focus on the successes; failures are easier to analyze but don't in themselves tell you what would work. Comparing successes, while less exciting, yields more information. The bottom line is help them reduce insights to principles or rules of thumb that might be repeatable. Ask them what they have learned to increase their skills and understanding, making them better managers or professionals. Ask them what they can do now that they couldn't do a year ago. Reinforce this and encourage more of it. Developing is learning in as many ways as possible.

6. **Do an inventory of your personal strengths and weaknesses.** Get some input from others. Ask your people what they appreciate about you as a person and as a manager and what they would prefer you change. What do you do well and what don't you do well personally and as a manager of others?

7. **Seeing more humor in life.** There are topics that can be near universally humorous. There are universal traits such as misers, bad drivers, and absent-minded people. There are things that are funny about your life. Have funny kids, pets, hobbies? What's a ridiculous situation you've been caught in lately? There are funny things in the workplace. The jargon of it, memos, ironic rules. Stories from the picnic or the off-site. There is providing relief from our problems. The weather, taxes, any of life's little indignities and embarrassments. And there is always the news. Most programs have at least one humorous tale, and sometimes the news is funny enough as it is. Humor that unites people rather than puts down people or groups is always safe. Begin to look for and remember the humor around you. Begin to pass on your observation to a few safe people to test your humor judgment.

8. **To help those around you grow and learn from what you know,** you have to sometimes think out loud. You have to share your thinking from the initial presentation of the issue through to conclusion. Most of us are on thinking autopilot. When someone else has to or wants to understand how you came up with a decision, it's sometimes difficult to unravel it in your mind. You have to go step-by-step and recreate your thinking. Sometimes it helps if other people ask the questions. They can probably guide you through how you came up with an answer or a decision better than you can. Once in a while, you should document a decision or two. What was the issue? What were the pros and cons you considered? How did you weight things? Then you can use those examples to demonstrate to others how you make decisions.

9. **Think of yourself as a presenter.** Make a checklist. What's your objective? What's your point? What are five things you want them to remember? What would the ideal audience member say if interviewed 15 minutes after you finish? Who's your audience? How much do they know? What are five techniques you will use to hold their attention? What questions will the audience have? How much time do you have—always take a few minutes less, never more. State your message or purpose in a single sentence. In other words, do the ending first. Then outline the three to five chunks of your argument to support your thesis. Any more and the audience won't follow it.

E↔I

If you sometimes overdo being Expressive:

1. **You may talk too much about your feelings and opinions** and need to gear back somewhat. The kinds of disclosure that people enjoy reveal the reasons behind why you do what you do, your self-appraisal, things you know behind what's happening in the business that they don't know—that you are at liberty to disclose, things both good and embarrassing that have happened to you in the past, commentary about what's going on around you—without being too negative about others, and things you are interested in and do outside of work.

2. **When disclosing beliefs or values stances, always explain why you hold a belief**—give reasons rather than just stating something. Statements cut off discussion and may make you look rigid or simplistic. Bold statements are those that are absolute and because of that, limiting. There is no comeback to "never hire a friend" except to reject your disclosure. Saying "I had to fire someone once; this was the situation, my reasons, what I tried to do to help, and what I learned from it" sets up your belief statements. Making them first comes across as pronouncements ("Never hire a friend").

3. **Sometimes sharing your feelings too willingly can turn off or upset others.** Do they get a chance to share their feelings? Are they comfortable with talking about feelings? Observe people carefully, especially their non-verbal communication to see how they are reacting. Make it a practice to talk no more than others get to talk. Make it your goal to get others to initiate topics. You don't have to dominate topic selection.

4. **If you share your feelings too often,** people may come to think that you run hot and lack perspective on situations. Balance this tendency with keeping it to the facts so that you balance your communications with others.

Contained (Controlled, private)

- Selective about what and with whom they share.
- Personal experience rarely shared.
- Process feelings internally at length.

To develop more of this facet:

1. **Once the emotional response is triggered, it has to run its course.** If no threat follows the initial trigger, it lasts from 45–60 seconds in most people. That's why your grandmother told you to count to 10.

Emotions can shut you down and leave you speechless, neither choosing to fight (argue, respond) or flee (calmly shut down the transaction and exit). You'll have to fight these reactions to learn to be cool under pressure.

2. **Decreasing triggers.** Write down the last 25 times you lost your composure. Most people who have composure problems have three to five repeating triggers. Criticism. Loss of control. A certain kind of person. An enemy. Being surprised. Spouse. Children. Money. Authority. Angry at yourself because you can't say no? Try to group 90% of the events into three to five categories. Once you have the groupings, ask yourself why these are a problem. Is it ego? Losing face? Being caught short? Being found out? Causing you more work? In each grouping, what would be a more mature response? Mentally and physically rehearse a better response. Try to decrease by 10% a month the number of times you lose your composure.

3. **Increasing impulse control.** People say and do inappropriate things when they lose their composure. The problem is that they say or do the first thing that occurs to them. Research shows that generally somewhere between the second and third thing you think of to say or do is the best option. Practice holding back your first response long enough to think of a second. When you can do that, wait long enough to think of a third before you choose. By that time, 50% of your composure problems should go away.

4. **Count to 10.** Our thinking and judgment are not at their best during the emotional response. Create and practice delaying tactics. Go get a pencil out of your briefcase. Go get a cup of coffee. Ask a question and listen. Go up to the flip chart and write something. Take notes. See yourself in a setting you find calming. Go to the bathroom. You need about a minute to regain your composure after the emotional response is triggered. Don't do or say anything until the minute has passed.

5. **When you do reply to an attack, keep it to the facts and their impact on you.** It's fine for you to draw conclusions about the impact on yourself—"I felt blindsided." It's not fine for you to tell others their motives—"You blindsided me" means you did it, probably meant to, and I know the meaning of your behavior. So state the meaning for yourself; ask others what their actions meant.

6. **Too much invested at work?** Find a release for your pent-up emotions. Get a physical hobby. Start an exercise routine. Jog. Walk. Chop wood. Sometimes people who have flair tempers hold it in too much, the pressure builds, and the teakettle blows. The body stores

energy. It has to go somewhere. Work on releasing your work frustration off-work.

7. **The simple courtesies.** Impatient people interrupt, finish other people's sentences when they hesitate, ask people to hurry, ask people to skip the next few transparencies and get to the last slide, urge people to finish and get to the point. All these behaviors of the impatient person intimidate, irritate, demotivate, and frustrate others and lead to incomplete communications, damaged relationships, a feeling of injustice, and leave others demeaned in the process. Add five seconds to your average response/interrupt tolerance time until you stop doing these things most of the time. Learn to pause to give people a second chance. People often stumble on words with impatient people, hurrying to get through before their first or next interruption.

8. **Impatient people provide answers, conclusions, and solutions too early in the process.** Others haven't even understood the problem yet. Providing solutions too quickly will make your people dependent and irritated. If you don't teach them how you think and how you can come up with solutions so fast, they will never learn. Take the time to really define the problem—not impatiently throw out a solution. Brainstorm what questions need to be answered in order to resolve it. Give your people the task to think about for a day and come back with some solutions. Be a teacher instead of a dictator of solutions.

9. **Impatient people check in a lot.** How's it coming? Is it done yet? That is disruptive to due process and wastes time. When you give out a task or assign a project, establish agreed-upon time checkpoints. You can also assign percentage checkpoints. Check in with me when you are about 25% finished so we can make midcourse corrections and 75% finished so we can make final corrections. Let them figure out how to do the task. Hold back from checking in at other than the agreed-upon times and percentages.

If you sometimes overdo being Contained:

1. **Practice being more expressive.** Write down in advance three things you're willing to say. Force yourself to stop processing and make it a goal to make more feeling statements and share more of your personal experiences. If you are too contained, people won't know how to relate to you and may start guessing about what you think. It's better for them to hear it from you.

2. **Act faster.** Always do 10% of each task immediately after it is assigned so you can better gauge what it is going to take to finish the rest. Break

the task down into smaller pieces. Commit to doing a piece a day. Don't even think of the larger goal. Just do something on it each day.

3. **For low-risk practice, talk to strangers off-work.** Set a goal of meeting 10 new people at a social gathering; find out what you have in common with them. Initiate contact at your place of worship, at PTA meetings, in the neighborhood, at the supermarket, on the plane, and on the bus. Explore new ground. Learn new things. Practice in your life. Go to theme restaurants you know nothing about. Vacation at places without doing a lot of research. Go to ethnic festivals for groups you have little knowledge about.

4. **Do an inventory of the common management techniques and practices** you do well and those that you do not do so well or often enough. Think about the practices below in particular:

   ■ Do a communication check on yourself. How well do you inform? Explain? Get back to people? Give feedback?

   ■ Do you delegate enough? Do you give the people under you the authority to do their work? Do you over- or undermanage? Periodically, ask your people to give you a list of the things they think you are doing yourself that they believe they could do a good job on; delegate some of the things on everybody's list.

   ■ Are you organized and planful? Can people follow what you want? Do you lay out work and tasks to be done clearly? Do you set clear goals and objectives that can guide their work?

   ■ Do you confront problems directly and quickly or do you let things fester?

5. **Rather go it alone?** Are you interested in getting work done through others or would you rather do it all yourself? Maybe management isn't for you. Maybe you would be better off being a senior personal contributor. Maybe you don't really care to relate to people very deeply.

6. **Become a better reader of people.** People focus on different things— taking action, details, concepts, feelings, other people. What's their interaction style? People come in different styles—pushy, tough, soft, matter-of-fact, and so on. To figure these out, listen for the values behind their words and note what they have passion and emotion around. One key to getting anything of value done in the work world is the ability to see differences in people and to manage against and use those differences for everyone's benefit. Interpersonal savvy is meeting each person where he/she is to get done what you need to get done. Basically, people respond favorably to ease of transaction. If

you make it easy by accepting their normal mode of doing things, not fighting their style, and neither defending your own nor letting style get in the way of performance, things will generally run smoothly.

7. **Tend to shy away from managerial courage situations?** Why? What's getting in your way? Are you prone to give up in tough situations, fear exposing yourself, don't like conflict, what? Ask yourself—what's the downside of delivering a message you think is right and will eventually help the organization but may cause someone short-term pain. What if it turns out you were wrong? Treat any misinterpretations as chances to learn. What if you were the target person or group? Even though it might hurt, would you appreciate it if someone brought the data to your attention in time for you to fix it with minimal damage? What would you think of a person whom you later found out knew about it and didn't come forward, and you had to spend inordinate amounts of time and political currency to fix it? Follow your convictions. Follow due process. Step up to the plate and be responsible, win or lose. People will think better of you in the long term.

Gregarious↔Intimate
Breadth and depth of relationships.

Gregarious (Seek popularity, join groups)

■ Enjoy associations with a variety of people.

■ Prefer a wide circle of people.

■ Sensitive to the "flow" of the group.

■ Like the give-and-take of relationships.

To develop more of this facet:

1. **Join one group.** List all the positive benefits group members get out of group memberships. List no negatives. Turn off your judgment program because, after all, you're not terribly interested in joining groups. After three months, write down all the benefits you've gotten from group membership—what you've learned about, whom you have met, what you have in common, how this has broadened your thinking.

2. **You should work doubly hard at observing others.** Always select your interpersonal approach from the other person in, not from you out. Your best choice of approach will always be determined by the other person or group, not you. Think about each transaction as if the

other person were a customer you wanted. How would you craft an approach?

3. **Select three people to observe who are good in interpersonal transactions.** Write down what they say or do when problems arise. What kinds of words do they use? How do they monitor what's happening? Do they ask questions or make statements? Do they state things in hard, moderate, or soft ways? How much time do they talk vs. others? Compare this with what you do in these same situations. What differences do you see? Interview these people to see if they can take you inside their minds and explain why they did what they did and especially why they changed tactics midstream.

4. **Gregarious people get more information,** know things earlier, and can get others to do more things. The more you can get people to initiate and say early in the transaction, the more you'll know, and the better you can connect with them. Make it your goal to get the latest "news."

5. **Being savvy with people you don't like.** What do people see in them who do like them or can at least get along with them? What are their strengths? Do you have any common interests with them? Whatever you do, don't signal to them what you think. Put your judgments on hold, nod, ask questions, summarize as you would with anyone else. A fly on the wall should not be able to tell whether you're talking to friend or foe. You can always talk less and ask more questions; and neither apologize nor criticize. Even if they're contentious, you can respond neutrally by restating the problem you're working on.

6. **For low-risk practice, talk to strangers off-work.** Set a goal of meeting 10 new people at a social gathering; find out what you have in common with them. Initiate contact at your place of worship, at PTA meetings, in the neighborhood, at the supermarket, on the plane, and on the bus. Explore new ground. Learn new things. Practice in your life. Go to theme restaurants you know nothing about. Vacation at places without doing a lot of research. Go to ethnic festivals for groups you have little knowledge about.

7. **You have to put out your hand first.** Make first eye contact. Note the color of the person's eyes to ensure good eye contact. You have to ask the first question or share the first piece of information. You have to make the first three minutes comfortable for the other person. When you see someone you haven't talked with recently, wrap up what you're doing and go talk with him or her.

8. **Confide your thinking on a business issue and invite the response of others.** Pass on tidbits of information you think will help people do their jobs better or broaden their perspectives.

9. **Initiating people work to know and remember important things about the people they work around, for, and with.** Know three things about everybody—their interests or their children or something you can chat about other than the business agenda. Treat life as a small world. Establish things you can talk about with each person you work with that go beyond strictly work transactions. The point is to forge common ground and connections.

10. **Gregarious people appear and sound open and relaxed.** They smile. They are calm. They keep eye contact. They nod while the other person is talking. They have an open body posture. They speak in a paced and pleasant tone. Eliminate any disruptive habits, such as speaking too rapidly or forcefully, using strongly worded or loaded language, or going into too much detail. Watch out for signaling disinterest with actions like glancing at your watch, fiddling with paperwork, or giving your impatient "I'm busy" look.

11. **Interpersonal savvy is meeting each person where he/she is** to get done what you need to get done. Basically, people respond favorably to ease of transaction. If you make it easy by accepting their normal mode of doing things, not fighting their style, and neither defending your own nor letting style get in the way of performance, things will generally run smoothly.

If you sometimes overdo being Gregarious:

1. **You may be busy talking but not listening or engaging with others.** Remember the basics. You have eye contact. You take notes. You don't frown or fidget. How do people know you've understood? You paraphrase what they have said to their satisfaction. How do people know if you have accepted or rejected what they said? You tell them. Hopefully in a tactful way if you reject what they had to say. Give your reasons.

2. **Listening chillers?** Don't interrupt before they have finished. Don't suggest words when they hesitate or pause. Don't finish their sentences for them. Don't wave off any further input by saying, "Yes, I know that." "Yes, I know where you're going." "Yes, I have heard that before." If time is really important, you can say, "Let me see if I know where this is going…," or "I wonder if we could summarize to save both of us some time?" Finally, early in a transaction, answers, solutions, conclusions, statements, and dictates shut many people

down. You've told them your mind is already made up. Listen first, solve second.

3. **Questions.** Good listeners ask lots of questions to get to a good understanding. Probing questions. Clarifying questions. Confirming— is this what you are saying—questions. Ask one more question than you do now and add to that until people signal you that they think you are truly listening.

4. **You may value the one-on-one relationships but not take the time to understand group dynamics.** If it is a voluntary/interest group, people usually belong for three reasons: The group fulfills social needs; it provides a sense of belonging and gives emotional support and identification; and it helps people achieve their goals by sharing information and helping each other. Find out all you can about what groups the people you need to deal with and manage belong to. It can help you deal with them and help them perform better.

5. **Learn to be a cultural anthropologist.** In assessing groups, ask yourself: What makes their blood boil? What do they believe? What are they trying to accomplish together? What do they smile at? What norms and customs do they have? What practices and behaviors do they share? Do they not like it if you stand too close? If you get right down to business? Do they like first names or are they more formal? If a Japanese manager presents his card, do you know what to do? Why do they have their cards printed in two languages and executives from the U.S. don't? Do you know what jokes are okay to tell? What do they believe about you and your group or groups? Positive? Neutral? Negative? What's been the history of their group and yours? Is this a first contact or a long history? Don't blunder in; nothing will kill you quicker with a group than showing utter disregard—read disrespect—for it and its norms, or having no idea of how they view your group. Ask people for insights who deal with this group often. If it's an important group to you and your business, read about it.

Intimate (Seek one-to-one conversations)

■ Maintain a limited range of friendships requiring a significant amount of trust.

■ Dislike too many activities.

■ Often provide delayed responses to interactions.

To develop more of this facet:

1. **Intimate people are very good at listening.** They listen without interrupting. They ask clarifying questions. They don't instantly judge. They listen to understand. Judgment may come later. They restate what the other person has said to signal understanding. They nod. They may jot down notes. Listeners don't always offer advice or solutions unless it's obvious the person wants to know what they would do.

2. **Intimate people work to know and remember important things about the people they work around, for, and with.** Know three things about everybody—their interests or their children or something you can chat about other than the business agenda. Treat life as a small world. If you ask a few questions, you'll find you have something in common with virtually anyone. Establish things you can talk about with each person you work with that go beyond strictly work transactions. The point is to forge common ground and connections.

3. **The magic of questions.** Many people don't ask enough curiosity questions when in their work mode. There are too many informational statements, conclusions, suggestions, and solutions and not enough "what if," "what are you thinking," "how do you see that." In studies, statements outweighed questions 8 to 1. Ask more questions than others. Make fewer solution statements early in a discussion. Keep probing until you understand what they are trying to tell you.

4. **Caring is sharing and disclosing.** Share your thinking on a business issue and invite the advice of direct reports. Pass on tidbits of information you think will help people do their jobs better or broaden their perspectives. Reveal things people don't need to know to do their jobs, but which will be interesting to them—and help them feel valued. Disclose some things about yourself as well. Tell them how you arrive at decisions. Explain your intentions, your reasons, and your thinking when announcing decisions.

5. **Caring is accepting.** Try to listen without judging initially. Turn off your "I agree; I don't agree" filter. You don't have to agree with it; just listen to understand. Assume when people tell you something they are looking for understanding; indicate that by being able to summarize what they said. Don't offer advice or solutions unless it's obvious the person wants to know what you would do. While offering instant solutions is a good thing to do in many circumstances, it's chilling where the goal is to get people to talk to you more freely.

6. **Caring is understanding.** Study the people you work with. Without judging them, collect evidence on how they think and what they do. What drives them to do what they do? Try to predict what they will do in given situations. Use this to understand how to relate to them. What are their hot buttons? What would they like for you to care about?

7. **When someone is troubled, simply imagine how you would feel in this situation and respond with that.** Tell the person how sorry you are this has happened or has to be dealt with. Offer whatever help is reasonable. Offer hope of a better day. This is what the person can use most.

8. **Compassion is not always advice.** Don't offer advice unless asked. Indicate support through listening and a helpful gesture. There will be time for advice when the situation isn't so emotionally charged. Many times we are too quick with advice before we really understand the problem.

9. **Be candid with yourself.** Is there a group or groups you don't like or are uncomfortable with? Do you judge individual members of that group without really knowing if your stereotype is true? Most of us do. Do you show compassion for one group's problems but not another's? To deal with this:

    ▪ Put yourself in their case. Why would you act that way? What do you think they're trying to achieve? Assume that however they act is rational to them; it must have paid off or they wouldn't be doing it. Don't use your internal standards.

    ▪ Avoid putting groups in buckets. Many of us bucket groups as friendly or unfriendly, good or bad, like me or not like me. Once we do, we generally don't show as much compassion toward them and may question their motives. Apply the logic of why people belong to the group in the first place. See if you can predict accurately what the group will say or do across situations to test your understanding of the group. Don't use your agreement program.

    ▪ Listen. Even though this tip may seem obvious, many of us tune out when dealing with difficult or not-well-understood groups, or reject what they're saying before they say it. Just listen. Mentally summarize their views, and see if you can figure out what they want from what they say and mean. The true test is whether you can clearly figure it out, even though you don't think that way.

If you sometimes overdo being Intimate:

1. **You may be slow to step up in conflict situations.** Taking a tough stand demands confidence in what you're saying along with the humility that you might be wrong—one of life's paradoxes. To prepare to take the lead on a tough issue, work on your stand through mental interrogation until you can clearly state in a few sentences what your stand is and why you hold it. Build the business case. How do others win? Ask others for advice. Scope the problem, consider options, pick one, develop a rationale, then go with it until proven wrong. Consider the opposing view. Develop a strong case against your stand. Prepare responses to it. Expect pushback.

2. **Standing alone usually involves dealing with pure hand-to-hand confrontations.** You believe one thing, they want something else. When that happens, keep it to any facts that are available. You won't always win. Stay objective. Make the business case. Listen as long as they will talk. Ask a lot of clarifying questions. Sometimes they talk themselves to your point of view if you let them talk long enough. Always listen to understand first, not judge. Restate their points until they say that's right. Find something to agree with, however small that may be. Then refute their points starting with the one you have the most objective information for first. Move down the line. You will always have points left that didn't get resolved. Acknowledge those. The objective is to get the list as small as possible.

3. **Clear problem-focused communication.** Follow the rule of equity: Explain your thinking and ask them to explain theirs. Be able to state their position as clearly as they do whether you agree or not—give it legitimacy. Separate facts from opinions and assumptions. Generate a variety of possibilities first rather than stake out positions. Keep your speaking to 30–60 second bursts. Try to get them to do the same. Don't give the other side the impression you're lecturing or criticizing them. Explain objectively why you hold a view; make the other side do the same. Ask lots of questions, make fewer statements. To identify interests behind positions, ask why they hold them or why they wouldn't want to do something. Always restate their position to their satisfaction before offering a response.

Active↔Reflective
How we engage with the environment to socialize, learn, and entertain ourselves.

Active (Enjoy contact, listen, speak)

■ Actively engage with environment.

■ Learn better by doing, drawn to active rather than intellectual issues.

To develop more of this facet:

1. **You may be late taking action.** Start earlier. Always do 10% of each task immediately after it is assigned so you can better gauge what it is going to take to finish the rest. Break the task down into smaller pieces. Commit to doing a piece a day.

2. **Take a course or work with a tutor to bolster your confidence in one skill or area at a time.** Focus on the strengths you do have; think of ways you can use these strengths when making nerve-wracking actions. If you are interpersonally skilled, for example, see yourself smoothly dealing with questions and objections to your actions. The only way you will ever know what you can do is to act and find out.

3. **Research says that successful executives have made more mistakes in their careers than those who didn't make it.** Treat any mistakes or failures as chances to learn. Nothing ventured, nothing gained. Up your risk comfort. Start small so you can recover more quickly. Go for small wins. Don't blast into a major task to prove your boldness. Break it down into smaller tasks. Take the easiest one for you first. Then build up to the tougher ones. Review each one to see what you did well and not well, and set goals so you'll do something differently and better each time.

4. **Make a list of what you like and don't like to do.** Concentrate on doing at least a couple of liked activities each day. Work to delegate or task trade the things that are no longer motivating to you. Do your least preferred activities first; focus not on the activity, but your sense of accomplishment. Change your work activity to mirror your interests as much as you can. Volunteer for task forces and projects that would be motivating for you.

5. **Taking action requires that you get others on board.** Work on your influence and selling skills. Lay out the business reason for the action. Think about how you can help everybody win with the action. Get others involved before you have to take action. Involved people are

easier to influence. Learn better negotiation skills. Learn to bargain and trade.

6. **Don't inform enough.** Are you a minimalist? Do you tell people only what they need to know to do their little piece of the puzzle? People are motivated by being aware of the bigger picture. They want to know what to do in order to do their jobs and more. How does what they are doing fit into the larger picture? What are the other people working on and why? Many people think that's unnecessary information and that it would take too much time to do. They're wrong. The sense of doing something worthwhile is the number two motivator at work! It results in a high return on motivation and productivity. (Try to increase the amount of more-than-your-job information you share.) Focus on the impact on others by figuring out who information affects. Put five minutes on your meeting agenda. Ask people what they want to know and, assuming it's not confidential information, tell them. Pick a topic each month to tell your people about.

7. **According to behavioral research studies, the most effective communicators:** speak often, but briefly (15–30 seconds); ask more questions than others; make fewer solution statements early in a discussion; headline their points in a sentence or two; summarize frequently, and make more frequent "here's where we are" statements; invite everyone to share their views; and typically interject their views after others have had a chance to speak, unless they are passing on decisions.

8. **Think of yourself as a presenter.** Make a checklist. What's your objective? What's your point? What are five things you want them to remember? What would the ideal audience member say if interviewed 15 minutes after you finish? Who's your audience? How much do they know? What are five techniques you will use to hold their attention? What questions will the audience have? How much time do you have—always take a few minutes less, never more. State your message or purpose in a single sentence. In other words, do the ending first. Then outline the three to five chunks of your argument to support your thesis. Any more and the audience won't follow it.

If you sometimes overdo being Active:

1. **Control your instant responses to shifts.** Many of us respond to the fragmentation and discontinuities of work as if they were threats instead of the way life is. Sometimes our emotions and fears are triggered by switching from active to passive or soft to tough. This initial anxious response lasts 45–60 seconds, and we need to buy some

time before we say or do something inappropriate. Research shows that generally somewhere between the second and third thing you think to say or do is the best option. Practice holding back your first response long enough to think of a second and a third. Manage your shifts, don't be a prisoner of them.

2. **Use mental rehearsal to think about different ways you could carry out a transaction.** Try to see yourself acting in opposing ways to get the same thing done—when to be tough, when to let them decide, when to deflect the issue because it's not ready to decide. What cues would you look for to select an approach that matches? Practice trying to get the same thing done with two different groups with two different approaches. Did they both work?

3. **You may be quite impatient,** and some people probably bring out your impatience more than others. Who are they? What is it about them that makes you more impatient? Pace? Language? Thought process? Accent? These people may include people you don't like, who ramble, who whine and complain, or who are repetitive advocates for things you have already rejected. Mentally rehearse some calming tactics before meeting with people who trigger your impatience. Work on understanding their positions without judging them—you can always judge later. In all cases, focus them on the issues or problems to be discussed, return them to the point, interrupt to summarize, and state your position. Try to gently train them to be more efficient with you next time without damaging them in the process.

4. **Rein in your horse.** Don't provide answers, conclusions, and solutions too early in the process. Others haven't even understood the problem yet. Providing solutions too quickly will make your people dependent and irritated. If you don't teach them how you think and how you can come up with solutions so fast, they will never learn. Take the time to really define the problem—not impatiently throw out a solution. Brainstorm what questions need to be answered in order to resolve it. Give your people the task to think about for a day and come back with some solutions. Be a teacher instead of a dictator of solutions. Study yourself. Keep a journal of what triggered your behavior and what the observed consequences were. Learn to detect and control your triggers before they get you in trouble.

5. **Do you check in a lot?** How's it coming. Is it done yet? When will it be finished? Let me see what you've done so far. That is disruptive to due process and wastes time. When you give out a task or assign a project, establish agreed-upon time checkpoints. You can also assign percentage checkpoints. Check in with me when you are about 25%

finished so we can make midcourse corrections and 75% finished so we can make final corrections. Let them figure out how to do the task. Hold back from checking in at other than the agreed-upon times and percentages.

Reflective (Prefer space, read, write)

■ Enjoy stimulation that evokes visual, intellectual, or mental responses.

■ Learn best from written material.

To develop more of this facet:

1. **Complex problems are hard to visualize.** They tend to be either oversimplified or too complex to solve unless they are put in a visual format. Cut it up into its component pieces. Examine the pieces to see if a different order would help, or how you could combine three pieces into one. Chart them with mind mapping, an easy to learn technique. Another technique is a pictorial chart called a storyboard, where a problem is illustrated by its components being depicted as pictures. A variation of this is to tell stories that illustrate the +'s and –'s of a problem, then flowchart those according to what's working and not working. Another is a fishbone diagram used in Total Work Systems.

2. **Sometimes going to extremes helps.** Adding every condition, every worst case you can think of sometimes will suggest a different solution. Taking the present state of affairs and projecting into the future may indicate how and where the system will break down.

3. **Sleep on it.** Take periodic breaks, whether stuck or not. This allows the brain to continue to work on the issue. Most breakthroughs come when we're "not thinking about it." Put it away; give it to someone else; sleep on it. Once you've come up with every idea you can think of, throw them all out and wait for more to occur to you. Force yourself to forget about the issue.

4. **Analogies.** Lots of creative solutions come from analogies to nature or other fields. Come up with a list (electrical engineering, cats, trees, the sea, biology, shipbuilding), any list will do, and insert it after you describe the problem to the group in the first or second option. Many times this will trigger novel ideas that no other process will.

5. **Look for distant parallels.** Don't fall into the mental trap of searching only in parallel organizations because "only they would know." Back up and ask a broader question to aid in the search for solutions. When Motorola wanted to find out how to process orders more quickly, they

went not to other electronics firms, but to Domino's Pizza and Federal Express. For more ideas, an interesting—and fun—book on the topic is *Take the Road to Creativity and Get Off Your Dead End* by David Campbell.

6. **Patterns.** Look for patterns in personal, organization, or the world, in general successes and failures. What was common to each success or what was present in each failure but never present in a success? Focus on the successes; failures are easier to analyze but don't in themselves tell you what would work.

7. **Use experts.** Find an expert or experts in your functional/ technical/business area and go find out how they think and solve new problems. Ask them what are the critical principles/ drivers/things they look for.

8. **How do people know you are listening?** You have eye contact. You take notes. You don't frown or fidget. How do people know you've understood? You paraphrase what they have said to their satisfaction. How do people know if you have accepted or rejected what they said? You tell them. Hopefully in a tactful way if you reject what they had to say. Give your reasons.

9. **Listening chillers?** Don't interrupt before they have finished. Don't suggest words when they hesitate or pause. Don't finish their sentences for them. Don't wave off any further input. Don't mentally prepare your remarks while they are talking.

10. **Select three people to observe who are thoughtful and reflective.** Write down what they say or do when problems arise. What kinds of words do they use? How do they monitor what's happening? Do they ask questions or make statements? Do they state things in hard, moderate, or soft ways? How much time do they talk vs. others? Compare this with what you do in these same situations. What differences do you see? Interview these people to see if they can take you inside their minds and explain why they did what they did and especially why they changed tactics midstream.

11. **Read international publications** like *The Economist*, the *International Herald Tribune, Commentary*; autobiographies of people like Kissinger; pick a country and study it; read a book on the fall of the Soviet Union; or read "we present all sides" journals like *The Atlantic Monthly* to get the broadest possible view of issues. There are common underlying principles in everything. You need to expose yourself more broadly in order to find and apply those principles to what you're doing today.

12. **Figure out the rules of the game.** Reduce your understanding of how your business operates to personal rules of thumb or insights. Write them down in your own words. Use these rules of thumb to analyze a business that you know something about, possibly one of your hobbies or a sport you are enthusiastic about. Pick what you know. Then pick two businesses that have pulled off clever strategies, one related to yours and one not. Study what they did, talk to people who know what happened, and see what you can learn. Then study two businesses that were not successful and see what they didn't do.

If you sometimes overdo being Reflective:

1. **Practice being more expressive.** Write down in advance three things you're willing to say. Force yourself to stop processing and make it a goal to make more statements, opinions, and share more of your personal experiences. If you are too reflective, people won't know how to relate to you and may start guessing about what you think. It's better for them to hear it from you.

2. **Share your thinking.** To help those around you grow and learn from what you know, you have to sometimes think out loud. You have to share your thinking from the initial presentation of the issue through to conclusion. When someone else has to or wants to understand how you came up with a decision, it's sometimes difficult to unravel it in your mind. You have to go step-by-step and recreate your thinking. Sometimes it helps if other people ask the questions. They can probably guide you through how you came up with an answer or a decision better than you can. Once in a while, you should document a decision or two. What was the issue? What were the pros and cons you considered? How did you weight things? Then you can use those examples to demonstrate to others how you make decisions.

3. **Don't inform enough.** Are you a minimalist? Do you tell people only what they need to know to do their little piece of the puzzle? People are motivated by being aware of the bigger picture. They want to know what to do in order to do their jobs and more. How does what they are doing fit into the larger picture? What are the other people working on and why? Many people think that's unnecessary information and that it would take too much time to do. They're wrong. The sense of doing something worthwhile is the number two motivator at work! It results in a high return on motivation and productivity. (Try to increase the amount of more-than-your-job information you share.) Focus on the impact on others by figuring out who information affects. Put five minutes on your meeting agenda. Ask people what they want to know and, assuming it's not

confidential information, tell them. Pick a topic each month to tell your people about.

4. **A loner.** Do people around you know what you're doing and why? Are you aware of things others would benefit from, but you don't take the time to communicate? In most organizations, these things and things like it will get you in trouble. Organizations function on the flow of information. Being on your own and preferring peace and privacy are okay as long as you communicate things to bosses, peers, and teammates that they need to know and would feel better if they knew. Don't be the source of surprises.

5. **Cryptic informer.** Some people just aren't good at informing. Their communication styles are not effective. According to behavioral research studies, the most effective communicators: speak often, but briefly (15–30 seconds); ask more questions than others; make fewer solution statements early in a discussion; headline their points in a sentence or two; summarize frequently, and make more frequent "here's where we are" statements; invite everyone to share their views; and typically interject their views after others have had a chance to speak, unless they are passing on decisions. Compare these practices to yours. Work on those that are not up to standard.

Enthusiastic↔Quiet
Level and type of energy in communicating.

Enthusiastic (Energetic, lively)

- Talkative, hearty, enjoy energetic exchange.

- Enjoy being center of attention at times.

- Convey humor through stories.

- Like being with others.

To develop more of this facet:

1. **Turn up the volume more.** Everyone has passions. Pick one or two brief but engaging stories and "act" them out for others in a way that people will enjoy. Think of yourself as a presenter. Make a mental checklist. What's your objective? What's your point? What are three things you want them to remember? Who's your audience? How much do they know? What are some techniques you will use to hold their attention? What questions will the audience have?

2. **Build a sense of fun for those around you.** Parties, roasts, gag awards, and outings build cohesion. Start celebrating wins, honor those who have gone the extra mile, but don't honor anyone twice before everyone has been honored once. Working with the whole person tends to build teams.

3. **See more humor in life.** There are topics that can be near universally humorous. There are universal traits such as misers, bad drivers, and absent-minded people. There are things that are funny about your life. Have funny kids, pets, hobbies? What's a ridiculous situation you've been caught in lately? There are funny things in the workplace. The jargon of it, memos, ironic rules. Stories from the picnic or the off-site. There is providing relief from our problems. The weather, taxes, any of life's little indignities and embarrassments. And there is always the news. Most programs have at least one humorous tale, and sometimes the news is funny enough as it is. Humor that unites people rather than puts down people or groups is always safe. Begin to look for and remember the humor around you. Begin to pass on your observation to a few safe people to test your humor judgment.

4. **Follow the basic rules of inspiring others** as outlined in classic books like *People Skills* by Robert Bolton or *Thriving on Chaos* by Tom Peters. Communicate to people that what they do is important. Say thanks. Offer help and ask for it. Provide autonomy in how people do their work. Provide a variety of tasks. "Surprise" people with enriching, challenging assignments. Show an interest in their careers. Adopt a learning attitude toward mistakes. Celebrate successes, have visible accepted measures of achievement, and so on. Too often people behave correctly but there are no consequences. Although it's easy to get too busy to acknowledge, celebrate, and occasionally criticize, don't forget to reinforce what you want. As a rule of thumb, 4 to 1 positive to negative is best.

5. **To better figure out what drives people, look to:** What do they do first? What do they emphasize in their speech? What do they display emotion around? What values play out for them?

- First things. Does this person go to others first, hole up and study, complain, discuss feelings, or take action? These are the basic orientations of people that reveal what's important to them. Use these to motivate.

- Speech content. People might focus on details, concepts, feelings, or other people in their speech. This can tell you again how to appeal to them by mirroring their speech emphasis. Although most of us naturally adjust—we talk details with detail-oriented people—chances are good that in problem relationships you're not finding the common ground. She talks "detail" and you talk "people," for example.

- Emotion. You need to know what people's hot buttons are because one mistake can get you labeled as insensitive with some people. The only cure here is to see what turns up the volume for them—either literally or what they're concerned about.

- Values. Apply the same thinking to the values of others. Do they talk about money, recognition, integrity, efficiency in their normal work conversation? Figuring out what their drivers are tells you another easy way to appeal to anyone.

6. **You have to put out your hand first.** Make first eye contact. Note the color of the person's eyes to ensure good eye contact. You have to ask the first question or share the first piece of information. You have to make the first three minutes comfortable for the other person. When you see someone you haven't talked with recently, wrap up what you're doing and go talk with him or her.

7. **Know three things about everybody**—their interests or their children or something you can chat about other than the business agenda. Treat life as a small world.

If you sometimes overdo being Enthusiastic:

1. **You may have problems with composure and need to decrease the triggers that set you off.** Write down the last 25 times you lost your composure. Most people who have composure problems have three to five repeating triggers. Criticism. Loss of control. A certain kind of person. An enemy. Being surprised. Spouse. Children. Money. Authority. Angry at yourself because you can't say no? Try to group 90% of the events into three to five categories. Once you have the groupings, ask yourself why these are a problem. Is it ego? Losing face? Being caught short? Being found out? Causing you more work? In each grouping, what would be a more mature response? Mentally and physically rehearse a better response. Try to decrease by 10% a month the number of times you lose your composure.

2. **Increasing impulse control.** People say and do inappropriate things when they lose their composure. The problem is that they say or do the first thing that occurs to them. Research shows that generally somewhere between the second and third thing you think of to say or do is the best option. Practice holding back your first response long enough to think of a second. When you can do that, wait long enough

EXTRAVERTING–INTROVERTING FACETS

to think of a third before you choose. By that time, 50% of your composure problems should go away.

3. **Count to 10.** Our thinking and judgment are not at their best during the emotional response. Create and practice delaying tactics. Go get a pencil out of your briefcase. Go get a cup of coffee. Ask a question and listen. Go up to the flip chart and write something. Take notes. See yourself in a setting you find calming. Go to the bathroom. You need about a minute to regain your composure after the emotional response is triggered. Don't do or say anything until the minute has passed.

4. **Get anxious and jump to conclusions?** Take quick action? Don't like ambiguity and uncertainty and act to wipe it out? Solutions first, understanding second? Take the time to really define the problem. Let people finish. Try not to interrupt. Don't finish others' sentences. Ask clarifying questions. Restate the problem in your own words to everyone's satisfaction. Ask them what they think. Throw out trial solutions for debate. Then decide.

Quiet (Calm, enjoy solitude)

■ Interactions with others neither energize nor stimulate them.

■ They are low-key.

■ Usually succinct when communicating.

■ Use understatement.

To develop more of this facet:

1. **Decreasing triggers.** Write down the last 25 times you lost your composure. Most people who have composure problems have three to five repeating triggers. Criticism. Loss of control. A certain kind of person. An enemy. Being surprised. Spouse. Children. Money. Authority. Angry at yourself because you can't say no? Try to group 90% of the events into three to five categories. Once you have the groupings, ask yourself why these are a problem. Is it ego? Losing face? Being caught short? Being found out? Causing you more work? In each grouping, what would be a more mature response? Mentally and physically rehearse a better response. Try to decrease by 10% a month the number of times you lose your composure.

2. **Increasing impulse control.** People say and do inappropriate things when they lose their composure. The problem is that they say or do the first thing that occurs to them. Research shows that generally somewhere between the second and third thing you think of to say or do is the best option. Practice holding back your first response long

enough to think of a second. When you can do that, wait long enough to think of a third before you choose. By that time, 50% of your composure problems should go away.

3. **Count to 10.** Our thinking and judgment are not at their best during the emotional response. Create and practice delaying tactics. Go get a pencil out of your briefcase. Go get a cup of coffee. Ask a question and listen. Go up to the flip chart and write something. Take notes. See yourself in a setting you find calming. Go to the bathroom. You need about a minute to regain your composure after the emotional response is triggered. Don't do or say anything until the minute has passed.

4. **Blame and vengeance?** Do you feel a need to punish the people and groups that set you off? Do you become hostile, angry, sarcastic, or vengeful? While all that may be temporarily satisfying to you, they will all backfire and you will lose in the long term. When someone attacks you, rephrase it as an attack on a problem. Reverse the argument—ask what they would do if they were in your shoes. When the other side takes a rigid position, don't reject it. Ask why: What are the principles behind the offer? How do we know it's fair? What's the theory of the case? Play out what would happen if their position was accepted. Let the other side vent frustration or blow off steam, but don't react.

5. **When you do reply to an attack, keep it to the facts and their impact on you.** It's fine for you to draw conclusions about the impact on yourself—"I felt blindsided." It's not fine for you to tell others their motives—"You blindsided me" means you did it, probably meant to, and I know the meaning of your behavior. So state the meaning for yourself; ask others what their actions meant.

6. **How do people know you are listening?** You have eye contact. You take notes. You don't frown or fidget. How do people know you've understood? You paraphrase what they have said to their satisfaction. How do people know if you have accepted or rejected what they said? You tell them. Hopefully in a tactful way if you reject what they had to say. Give your reasons.

7. **Listening chillers?** Don't interrupt before they have finished. Don't suggest words when they hesitate or pause. Don't finish their sentences for them. Don't wave off any further input. Don't mentally prepare your remarks while they are talking.

8. **Avoid know-it-all terms and use understatement.** "I think that, but what do you think?" "It may be," "A factor here is." Don't make all or nothing statements including words like always and never or demeaning statements like "What you need to realize is...."

If you sometimes overdo being Quiet:

1. **You may run into problems with your boss.** Focus on the three key problems you need to work on with him/her and do them. Focus on expectations, ask what results indicate success. Find out about your boss's job and what sorts of pressures he/she is under. Consider these strategies: Ask what strengths you can appeal to; ask what you can provide that the boss needs; ask what the boss would like for you to do to be more effective; design a project that you can do together so you can have a success experience; and consult with others for advice.

2. **You start.** Being approachable means you have to initiate the transaction. You have to put out your hand first. Make first eye contact. Note the color of the person's eyes to ensure good eye contact. You have to ask the first question or share the first piece of information. You have to make the first three minutes comfortable for the other person or group so they can accomplish what they came to you to do.

3. **Work to know and remember important things about the people you work around, for, and with.** Know three things about everybody—their interests or their children or something you can chat about other than the business agenda. Treat life as a small world. If you ask a few questions, you'll find you have something in common with virtually anyone. Establish things you can talk about with each person you work with that go beyond strictly work transactions. These need not be social—they could be issues of strategy, global events, market shifts. The point is to forge common ground and connections.

4. **Watch your non-verbals.** Approachable people appear and sound open and relaxed. They smile. They are calm. They keep eye contact. They nod while the other person is talking. They have an open body posture. They speak in a paced and pleasant tone. Eliminate any disruptive habits, such as speaking too rapidly or forcefully, using strongly worded or loaded language, or going into too much detail. Watch out for signaling disinterest with actions like glancing at your watch, fiddling with paperwork, or giving your impatient "I'm busy" look.

5. **The magic of questions.** Many people don't ask enough curiosity questions when in their work mode. There are too many informational statements, conclusions, suggestions, and solutions and not enough "what if," "what are you thinking," "how do you see that." In studies, statements outweighed questions 8 to 1. Ask more questions than others. Make fewer solution statements early in a discussion. Keep probing until you understand what they are trying to tell you.

6. **For low-risk practice, talk to strangers off-work.** Set a goal of meeting 10 new people at a social gathering; find out what you have in common with them. Initiate contact at your place of worship, at PTA meetings, in the neighborhood, at the supermarket, on the plane, and on the bus. See if any of the bad and scary things you think might happen to you if you initiate people contact actually happen.

7. **Follow the basic rules of inspiring others** as outlined in classic books like *People Skills* by Robert Bolton or *Thriving on Chaos* by Tom Peters. Communicate to people that what they do is important. Say thanks. Offer help and ask for it. Provide autonomy in how people do their work. Provide a variety of tasks. "Surprise" people with enriching, challenging assignments. Show an interest in their careers. Adopt a learning attitude toward mistakes. Celebrate successes, have visible accepted measures of achievement, and so on.

8. **Bring people into your world.** Tell them your conceptual categories. To deal with you, they need to know how you think and why. Tell them your perspective—the questions you ask, the factors you're interested in. If you can't explain your thinking, they won't know how to deal with you effectively. It's easier to follow someone and something you understand.

9. **The easiest way to motivate someone is to get him/her involved deeply in the work he/she is doing.** Delegate and empower as much as you can. Get him/her involved in setting goals and determining the work process to get there. Ask his/her opinion about decisions that have to be made. Have him/her help appraise the work of the unit. Share the successes. Debrief the failures together. Use his/her full tool set.

Sensing ←→ Intuiting Facets

Sensing	Purpose: Perceiving Information	Intuiting
Concrete (Exact facts, literal) • Verify information experientially. • Enjoy specific instructions, emphasis on tangible. • Preference for sensory data that are verifiable.	General focus of perception and attention. **1**	**Abstract** (Figurative, symbolic) • Meaning resides in ideas and abstractions. • Follow patterns of associations. • Language does not describe but connotes what is real.
Realistic (Matter-of-fact, seek efficiency) • Emphasis on doing things. • Developing routines. • Being more efficient with time and energy, a hands-on person.	Meaning given to information especially as related to tasks/problem solving. **2**	**Imaginative** (Inventive, seek novelty) • Facts only stimulate important associations. • Like to mentally play with ideas. • Enjoy the opportunity to envision new markets, ingenious.
Practical (Results-oriented, applied) • Attend to physical characteristics. • Pull together known, verifiable, tested, facts. • See change as a step-by-step evolution.	What is made or created out of what we know. **5**	**Conceptual** (Idea-oriented, intellectual) • Reality beyond the senses. • Make connections among ideas, enjoy exchange of ideas. • Enjoy looking at a collage rather than specifics.
Experiential (Hands-on, empirical) • Prefer validation by repeated experience. • Enjoy active participation. • Adept at trial-and-error, and like established procedures.	How we make meanings, patterns of perceptions. **3**	**Theoretical** (Conceptual, hypothetical) • Explore by looking for interconnections. • Learn best by theory. • Adept at discovering new ideas. • Generally uninterested in routine matters.
Traditional (Conventional, customary) • Do things in established ways because it is safe and secure to do so. • Like to do things according to customs and norms. • Social environment confirms their way of doing things.	Role of social context and traditions in life. **4**	**Original** (Unconventional, unusual) • Seek innovation. • Change established ways as a method of self-expression. • Enjoy finding unique ways of doing routine things.

S↔N

Concrete←→Abstract
General focus of perception and attention.

Concrete (Exact facts, literal)

■ Verify information experientially.

■ Enjoy specific instructions, emphasis on tangible.

■ Preference for sensory data that are verifiable.

To develop more of this facet:

1. **Locate a pro.** Find the seasoned master professional in the technology or function, and ask whether he/she would mind showing you the ropes and tutoring you. Most don't mind having a few "apprentices" around. Help him or her teach you. Ask, "How do you know what's important? What do you look at first? Second? What are the five keys you always look at or for? What do you read? Who do you go to for advice?"

2. **Teach others.** Form a study group and take turns presenting on new, different, or unknown aspects of the technology. Having to teach it will force you to conceptualize and understand it more deeply. The relationships you form in such groups pay off in other ways as well. One company found its technicians learned more from coffee break conversations than from manuals.

3. **Be an early tester of new and emerging technology.** Don't wait until you have to hurry and catch up. Whenever a new technology surfaces, volunteer to learn and try it first. That gives you a head start and allows you to stumble a bit because you are the first.

4. **Practice by picking some technology somewhat related to your work and quietly become an expert at it.** Introduce it at work. Demonstrate it to your workmates. Market for others to learn it and adopt it for the business. Form a study group and take turns presenting on new, different, or emerging technologies. Having to teach it will force you to conceptualize and understand it more deeply.

5. **If you have trouble going back the second or third time to get something done, then switch approaches.** Sometimes people get stuck in a repeating groove that's not working. Do something different next time. If you visited the office of someone you have

difficulties with, invite him/her to your office next time. Think about multiple ways to get the same outcome. For example, to push a decision through, you could meet with stakeholders first, go to a single key stakeholder, study and present the problem to a group, call a problem-solving session, or call in an outside expert. Be prepared to do them all when obstacles arise.

6. **Start earlier.** Reduce the time between attempts. Always start 10% of each attempt immediately after it is apparent it will be needed so you can better gauge what it is going to take to finish it. Always assume it will take more time than you think it's going to take.

7. **Finishing.** While it's true that sometimes you get 80% of what you are pushing for with the first 20% of the effort, it unfortunately then takes another 80% of the time to finish the last 20%. When you get caught in this situation, create a checklist with the 20% that remains to be done. Plan to do a little on it each day. Cross things off and celebrate each time you get to take something off the list. Remember, it's going to challenge your motivation and attention. Try to delegate finishing to someone who would see the 20% as a fresh challenge. Get a consultant to finish it. Task trade with someone else's 20% so you both would have something fresh to do.

8. **Manage your time efficiently.** Figure out what you are worth per hour and minute by taking your gross salary plus overhead and benefits. Attach a monetary value on your time. Then ask, is this worth $56 of my time? Review your calendar over the past 90 days to figure out what your three largest time wasters are, and reduce them 50% by batching activities and using efficient communications like e-mail and voice mail for routine matters. Make a list of points to be covered in phone calls; set deadlines for yourself; use your best time of day for the toughest projects—if you're best in the morning, don't waste it on B and C level tasks.

9. **Set goals.** Nothing manages time better than a goal, a plan, and a measure. Set goals for yourself. These goals are essential for setting priorities. If you do not have goals, you can't set time priorities. Using the goals, separate what you need to do into mission-critical, important to get done, nice if there is time left over, and not central to what you are trying to achieve. When faced with choices or multiple things to do, apply the scale.

10. **Focus on measures.** How would you tell if the goal was accomplished? If the things I asked others to do were done right, what

outcomes could we all agree on as measures of success? Most groups can easily come up with success measures that are different from, and more important to them, than formal measures. Ask them to do so.

If you sometimes overdo being Concrete:

1. **You may have trouble dealing with situations that are ambiguous and everything seems up in the air.** People who deal well with ambiguity make a series of smaller decisions, get instant feedback, correct the course, get a little more data, move forward a little more, until the bigger problem is under control. They don't try to get it right the first time. Many problem-solving studies show that the second or third try is when we really understand the underlying dynamics of problems. They also know that the more uncertain the situation is, the more likely it is they will make mistakes in the beginning. So, you need to work on two practices: Start small so you can recover more quickly. Do little somethings as soon as you can and get used to trial-and-error learning.

2. **Perfectionist?** Need or prefer or want to be 100% sure? Recognize your perfectionism for what it might be—collecting more information than others to improve your confidence in making a fault-free decision and thereby avoiding risk and criticism. Try to decrease your need for data and your need to be right all the time slightly every week until you reach a more reasonable balance between thinking it through and taking action. Try making some small decisions on little or no data. Anyone with a brain and 100% of the data can make good decisions. The real test is who can act the soonest with a reasonable amount, but not all, of the data. Some studies suggest successful general managers are about 65% correct. Trust your intuition. Let your brain do the calculations.

3. **Develop creative thinking skills.** Creative thought processes do not follow the formal rules of logic, where one uses cause and effect to prove or solve something. Some rules of creative thought are:

   - Not using concepts but changing them; imagining this were something else.

   - Move from one concept or way of looking at things to another, such as from economic to political.

   - Generate ideas without judging them initially.

   - Use information to restructure and come up with new patterns.

- Jump from one idea to another without justifying the jump.

- Look for the least likely and odd.

- Look for parallels far from the problem, such as how is an organization like a big oak tree?

- Ask what's missing or what's not here.

- Fascination with mistakes and failure as learning devices.

4. **Brainstorming with a group.** Outline the problem for the group; tell them what you've tried and learned from the tries. Include things that may have happened only once. Invite the group to free-form respond. Any idea is okay—no criticism allowed. Record all ideas on a flip chart. When the group has exhausted the possibilities, take the most interesting ones and ask the group to first name positive features of the ideas, then negative features, and finally what's interesting about the ideas. Follow this process until you've covered all the ideas that interest you. Then ask the group what else they would select as interesting ideas to do a plus, minus, interesting analysis. This process can usually be done in an hour or two.

5. **Delegate for development.** Brainstorm with your direct reports all the tasks that aren't being done but are important to do. Ask them for a list of tasks that are no longer challenging for them. (You can also use parts of your own job to develop others. Take three tasks that are no longer developmental for you, but would be for others, and delegate them.) Trade tasks and assignments between two direct reports; have them do each other's work. Assign each of your direct reports an out-of-comfort-zone task that meets the following criteria: The task needs to be done, the person hasn't done it or isn't good at it, and the task calls for a skill the person needs to develop. Remember to focus on varied assignments—more of the same isn't developmental.

6. **Don't know how to be strategic?** The simplest problem is someone who wants to be strategic and wants to learn. Strategy is a reasonably well-known field. Read the gurus (Michael Porter, Ram Charan, C.K. Prahalad, Gary Hamel, Fred Wiersema, and Vijay Govindarajan). Scan the *Harvard Business Review* and *Sloan Review* regularly. Read the three to five strategic case studies in *BusinessWeek* every issue. Go to a three-day strategy course taught by one of the gurus. Get someone from the organization's strategic group to tutor you in strategy. Watch CEOs

talk about their businesses on cable. Volunteer to serve on a task force on a strategic issue. Join the Strategic Leadership Forum for a year, read their publication, *Strategy and Leadership,* and attend one national convention. Attend The Conference Board's Annual Conference on Strategy, where CEOs talk about their companies. Read 10 annual reports a year outside your industry and study their strategies.

7. **Inspiring.** Missions and visions are meant to motivate. Don't threaten. Don't say this is our last chance. Don't blame the past. Visions are optimistic, inspirational, about possibilities, about getting to a grand place in the market. Paint a positive "we can do it" picture. You have to blow a little smoke and use fairy dust. It's a performance. You have to get people to see what you see. This is all about how to present well and motivate. Always rehearse. Use a test group before you go public. See it yourself on video. Would you understand and be motivated?

Abstract (Figurative, symbolic)

- Meaning resides in ideas and abstractions.

- Follow patterns of associations.

- Language does not describe but connotes what is real.

To develop more of this facet:

1. **Problem definition.** Under uncertainty, it really helps to get as firm a handle as possible on the problem. Figure out what causes it. Keep asking why. See how many causes you can come up with and how many organizing buckets you can put them in. This increases the chance of a better solution because you can see more connections. The evidence from decision-making research makes it clear that thorough problem definition with appropriate questions to answer leads to better decisions.

2. **Practice picking out anomalies**—unusual facts that don't quite fit, like sales going down when they should have gone up. What do these odd things imply for strategy? Naturally creative people are much more likely to think in opposite cases when confronted with a problem. Turn the problem upside down: Ask what is the least likely thing it could be, what the problem is not, what's missing from the problem, or what the mirror image of the problem is.

3.   **Look for distant parallels.** Don't fall into the mental trap of searching only in parallel organizations because "only they would know." Back up and ask a broader question to aid in the search for solutions. When Motorola wanted to find out how to process orders more quickly, they went not to other electronics firms, but to Domino's Pizza and Federal Express.

4.   **Experts usually solve problems** by figuring out what the deep, underlying principles are and working forward from there; the less adept focus on desired outcomes/solutions and either work backward or concentrate on the surface facts. What are the deep principles of what you're working on?

5.   **Patterns.** Look for patterns in personal, organization, or the world, in general successes and failures. What was common to each success or what was present in each failure but never present in a success? Focus on the successes; failures are easier to analyze but don't in themselves tell you what would work. Comparing successes, while less exciting, yields more information about underlying principles.

6.   **Jump start your mind.** There are all kinds of mental exercises to increase your problem-solving repertoire. You can create checklists so you don't forget anything. You can run scenarios. You can ask what's missing. You can do pros and cons. You can visualize. You can diagram a problem. You can practice seeing how many patterns you can see in something or how many ways you can mentally organize it.

7.   **Try to add one minute to your thinking time.** Go through a mental checklist to see if you have thought about all of the ramifications of the problem or challenge. Go into any learning event with a goal. Ask questions about what you read. Chunk up what you learn. Put it in categories that make sense to you.

8.   **Pick three unrelated things to study and dabble in that you have not yet paid much attention to**—opera, romance novels, technical journals out of your area, MTV, learn a new language, take a magic course, study archeology. Connections can come from anywhere— your brain doesn't care where it gets perspectives. Try to think about how the principles of one tie into the other.

9.   **Task forces/projects are a great opportunity.** If the project is important, is multi-functional, and has a real outcome which will be taken seriously (not a study group), it is one of the most common developmental events listed by successful executives. You get out of

your own experience and start to see connections to a broader world—how international trade works; or more at home, how the pieces of your organization fit together. You can build perspective.

10. **Each situation we deal with is different.** In order to be truly effective across situations and people, we are called upon to shift behavior with the demands of each situation. Work on first reading the situation and the people. Monitor your gear-shifting behavior for a week at work and at home. What switches give you the most trouble? The least? Why? Off-work, practice gear-shifting transitions. Go from a civic meeting to a water fight with your kids, for example. On the way between activities, if only for a few seconds, think about the transition you're making and the frame of mind needed to make it work well.

If you sometimes overdo being Abstract:

1. **Getting the idea right may become more important than delivery.** Do you miss deadlines because you like to tinker with the idea or project until it's perfect? Unless you're lucky and work in a very stable niche, this behavior will get you left behind. You won't respond quickly enough to change; you won't learn new things; people will be increasingly frustrated as you hold them up. The rewards are to the swift. David Ulrich, a top strategic business consultant, says that in the past there was a premium on being right. That is shifting to being first. You may associate timely decisions with sloppy decisions, but this is not the case. Timely means sooner, as soon as possible or by a time-certain date, but not sloppy. Timely, thoughtful decisions can be of high quality. It's quality incrementalism.

2. **People who are good at making the abstract more concrete are incrementalists.** They make a series of smaller decisions, get instant feedback, correct the course, get a little more data, move forward a little more, until the bigger problem is under control. They don't try to get it right the first time. Many problem-solving studies show that the second or third try is when we really understand the underlying dynamics of problems. They also know that the more uncertain the situation is, the more likely it is they will make mistakes in the beginning. So, you need to work on two practices: Start small so you can recover more quickly. Do little somethings as soon as you can and get used to heat.

3. **If you think something is an elegant idea, you may jump on it before others are ready.** Here, you need to rein back your enthusiasm

and follow due process. Others may not be ready and are still processing it through. Don't let your natural inclination rule. Give others a chance.

4. **Do an inventory of the common management techniques and practices** you do well and those that you do not do so well or often enough. Think about the practices below in particular:

    ■   Do a communication check on yourself. How well do you inform? Explain? Get back to people? Give feedback?

    ■   Do you delegate enough? Do you give the people under you the authority to do their work? Do you over- or undermanage? Periodically, ask your people to give you a list of the things they think you are doing yourself that they believe they could do a good job on; delegate some of the things on everybody's list.

    ■   Are you organized and planful? Can people follow what you want? Do you lay out work and tasks to be done clearly? Do you set clear goals and objectives that can guide their work?

    ■   Do you confront problems directly and quickly or do you let things fester?

5. **Cryptic informer.** Some people just aren't good at informing. Their communication styles are not effective. According to behavioral research studies, the most effective communicators: speak often, but briefly (15–30 seconds); ask more questions than others; make fewer solution statements early in a discussion; headline their points in a sentence or two; summarize frequently, and make more frequent "here's where we are" statements; invite everyone to share their views; and typically interject their views after others have had a chance to speak, unless they are passing on decisions. Compare these practices to yours. Work on those that are not up to standard.

6. **Figure out the rules of the game.** Reduce your understanding of how business operates to personal rules of thumb or insights. Write them down in your own words. An example would be, "What are the drivers in marketing anything?" One executive had 25 such drivers that he continually edited, scratched through, and replaced with more up-to-date thinking. Use these rules of thumb to analyze a business that you know something about, possibly one of your hobbies or a sport you are enthusiastic about. Pick what you know. Then pick two businesses that have pulled off clever strategies, one related to yours

and one not. Study what they did, talk to people who know what happened, and see what you can learn. Then study two businesses that were not successful and see what they didn't do.

7. **Locate a pro.** Find the seasoned master professional in the technology or function, and ask whether he/she would mind showing you the ropes and tutoring you. Most don't mind having a few "apprentices" around. Help him or her teach you. Ask, "How do you know what's important? What do you look at first? Second? What are the five keys you always look at or for? What do you read? Who do you go to for advice?"

8. **Think of speaking with others as you would in a presentation.** What are five things you want them to remember? What would the ideal audience member say if interviewed 15 minutes after you finish? Who's your audience? How much do they know? What are five techniques you will use to hold their attention? What presentation technology would work best? What questions will the audience have? What's the setting? How much time do you have—always take a few minutes less, never more. State your message or purpose in a single sentence. In other words, do the ending first. Then outline the three to five chunks of your argument to support your thesis. Any more and the audience won't follow it.

Realistic↔Imaginative
Meaning given to information especially as related to tasks/problem solving.

Realistic (Matter-of-fact, seek efficiency)

- Emphasis on doing things.

- Developing routines.

- Being more efficient with time and energy, a hands-on person.

To develop more of this facet:

1. **Focus more on the mission-critical few decisions.** Don't get diverted by trivial work and other decisions. Get better organized and disciplined. Keep a decision log. When a decision opportunity surfaces, immediately log it along with the ideal date it needs to be made. Plan backwards to the work necessary to make the decision on time.

2. **Create two columns.** Left side are the areas where you seem to make timely and speedy decisions. What's common about those areas? Right side are the areas where you hold back, hesitate, and wait too long to decide. What's common to that list? Money involved? People? Risk? Higher management's involved? Are you avoiding detail or strategy or a technical area you dislike or know little about? Since you already make timely decisions in at least one area, transfer your decision behaviors and practices to the other areas. You already have the skills.

3. **Write down the decisions you would make right now,** then compare them with the decisions you actually make and announce later. Are the decisions more the same than different? If they are more the same, you are too slow to act. Since the noise and the heat are the same, the simple solution is to declare as soon as you have made the decision. Better to be done with it. If there is any useful data in the noise and heat, you can adjust your decision sooner.

4. **Think of a big decision as a series of smaller ones.** The essence of timely decision making is the tolerance of increased errors and mistakes, and absorbing the possible heat and criticism that follow. Acting on an ill-defined problem with no precedents to follow in a hurry means shooting in the dark with as informed a decision as you can make at the time. Incrementalists make a series of smaller decisions, get instant feedback, correct the course, get a little more data, move forward a little more, until the bigger decision gets made. They don't try to get it right the first time. They try their best educated guess now, and then correct as feedback comes in. Many problem-solving studies show that the second or third try is when we really understand the underlying dynamics of problems.

5. **Do an inventory of your personal strengths and weaknesses.** Get some input from others. Ask your people what they appreciate about you as a person and as a manager and what they would prefer you change. What do you do well and what don't you do well personally and as a manager of others?

6. **Set goals.** Nothing manages time better than a goal, a plan, and a measure. Set goals for yourself. These goals are essential for setting priorities. If you do not have goals, you can't set time priorities. Using the goals, separate what you need to do into mission-critical, important to get done, nice if there is time left over, and not central to

S↔N

what you are trying to achieve. When faced with choices or multiple things to do, apply the scale.

7. **Focus on measures.** How would you tell if the goal was accomplished? If the things I asked others to do were done right, what outcomes could we all agree on as measures of success? Most groups can easily come up with success measures that are different from, and more important to them, than formal measures. Ask them to do so.

8. **Lay out the process.** Most well-running processes start out with a plan. What do I need to accomplish? What's the time line? What resources will I need? Who controls the resources—people, funding, tools, materials, support—I need? What's my currency? How can I pay for or repay the resources I need? Who wins if I win? Who might lose? Buy a flowcharting software program. Lay out the work from A to Z. Many people are seen as lacking because they don't write down the sequence or parts of the work and leave something out. Ask others to comment on ordering and what's missing.

9. **Manage your time efficiently.** Figure out what you are worth per hour and minute by taking your gross salary plus overhead and benefits. Attach a monetary value on your time. Then ask, is this worth $56 of my time? Review your calendar over the past 90 days to figure out what your three largest time wasters are, and reduce them 50% by batching activities and using efficient communications like e-mail and voice mail for routine matters. Make a list of points to be covered in phone calls; set deadlines for yourself; use your best time of day for the toughest projects—if you're best in the morning, don't waste it on B and C level tasks.

10. **Do an upstream and downstream check with the people you work for,** work around, and those who work for you, to create a list of the administrative slip-ups you do that give them the most trouble. Be sure to ask them for help creating the list. That way, you have a focused list of the things you need to fix first. If you fix the top 10, maybe that will do and the rest of your habits can stay the same.

If you sometimes overdo being Realistic:

1. **Transitions.** Which transitions are the toughest for you? Write down the five toughest for you. What do you have a hard time switching to and from? Use this knowledge to assist you in making a list of discontinuities (tough transitions) you face, such as confronting people vs. being approachable and accepting, leading vs. following,

going from firing someone to a business-as-usual staff meeting. Write down how each of these discontinuities makes you feel and what you may do that gets you in trouble. For example, you may not shift gears well after a confrontation, or you may have trouble taking charge again after passively sitting in a meeting all day. Create a plan to attack each of the tough transitions.

2. **Go for more variety at work.** Take a risk, then play it safe. Set tasks for yourself that force you to shift gears, such as being a spokesperson for your organization when tough questions are expected, making peace with an enemy, or managing people who are novices at a task. If you already have these tasks as part of your job, use them to observe yourself and try new behaviors.

3. **Use mental rehearsal to think about different ways you could carry out a transaction.** Try to see yourself acting in opposing ways to get the same thing done—when to be tough, when to let them decide, when to deflect the issue because it's not ready to decide. What cues would you look for to select an approach that matches? Practice trying to get the same thing done with two different groups with two different approaches. Did they both work?

4. **You may deny the complexity of getting things done in an organization and see issues as simpler than others do.** You may have trouble getting things done through others. Get an assessment. Try to do the most honest self-assessment you can on why you aren't skilled at getting things done smoothly and effectively in the organization. Ask at least one person from each group you work with for feedback.

5. **Find out who the movers and shakers in the organization are.** How do they get things done? Who do they rely on for expediting things through the maze? How do you compare to them? Who are the major gatekeepers who control the flow of resources, information, and decisions? Who are the guides and the helpers? Get to know them better. Who are the major resisters and stoppers? Try to avoid or go around them.

6. **Shake things up.** What you are doing now apparently isn't working. Do something different. Try things you generally don't do. Look to what others do who are more effective than you. Keep a log on what worked and what didn't.

7. **Think equity.** Relationships that work are built on equity and considering the impact on others. Don't just ask for things; find some

common ground where you can provide help, not just ask for it. What does the unit you're contacting need in the way of problem solving or information? Do you really know how they see the issue? Is it even important to them? How does what you're working on affect them? If it affects them negatively and they are balky, can you trade something, appeal to the common good, figure out some way to minimize the work or other impact (volunteering staff help, for example)?

Imaginative (Inventive, seek novelty)

■ Facts only stimulate important associations.

■ Like to mentally play with ideas.

■ Enjoy the opportunity to envision new markets, ingenious.

To develop more of this facet:

1. **Remove the restraints.** What's preventing you from being more creative? Perfectionist? Being creative operates at well below having everything right. Cautious and reluctant to speculate? Being creative is the opposite. Worried about what people may think? Afraid you won't be able to defend your idea? By its very nature, being creative means throwing uncertain things up for review and critique. Narrow perspective, most comfortable with your technology and profession? Being creative is looking everywhere. More comfortable with what is very practical? Being creative begins as being impractical. Too busy to reflect and ruminate? Being creative takes time. Get out of your comfort zone. Many busy people rely too much on solutions from their own history. They rely on what has happened to them in the past. They see sameness in problems that isn't there. Beware of "I have always…" or "Usually, I…." Always pause and look under rocks and ask yourself is this really like the problems you have solved in the past? You don't have to change who you are and what you're comfortable with other than when you need to be more creative.

2. **Unearthing creative ideas.** Creative thought processes do not follow the formal rules of logic, where one uses cause and effect to prove or solve something. Some rules of creative thought are:

   ■ Not using concepts but changing them; imagining this were something else.

   ■ Move from one concept or way of looking at things to another, such as from economic to political.

■ Generate ideas without judging them initially.

■ Use information to restructure and come up with new patterns.

■ Jump from one idea to another without justifying the jump.

■ Look for the least likely and odd.

■ Look for parallels far from the problem, such as how is an organization like a big oak tree?

■ Ask what's missing or what's not here.

■ Fascination with mistakes and failure as learning devices.

■ Sleep on it. Take periodic breaks, whether stuck or not. This allows the brain to continue to work on the issue. Most breakthroughs come when we're "not thinking about it." Put it away; give it to someone else; sleep on it. Once you've come up with every idea you can think of, throw them all out and wait for more to occur to you. Force yourself to forget about the issue.

3. **When attacking a tough problem** which has eluded attempts to solve it, get the broadest group you can. Involve different functions, levels, and disciplines. Pull in customers and colleagues from other organizations. Remember that you're looking for fresh approaches; you're not convening a work task force expected to implement or judge the practicality of the notions. Believe it or not, it doesn't matter if they know anything about the problem or the technology required to deal with it. That's your job.

4. **Strategy is linking several variables together to come up with the most likely scenario.** Think of it as the search for and application of relevant parallels. It involves making projections of several variables at once to see how they come together. These projections are in the context of shifting markets, international affairs, monetary movements, and government interventions. It involves a lot of uncertainty, making risk assumptions, and understanding how things work together. How many reasons would account for sales going down? Up? How are advertising and sales linked? If the dollar is cheaper in Asia, what does that mean for our product in Japan? If the world population is aging and they have more money, how will that change buying patterns?

5. **Become a strategic activist.** Pick one distinctive competence or driving force. That's what the mediocre companies who became

successful over time did in James Collins' latest research. Create a strategic plan for your unit around one distinctive competence—include breakthrough process and product improvements, justify your conclusions by pointing to hard data that points toward your conclusions. Have the plan reviewed by people you trust. Form a consortium with three other individuals or companies; each of you will present a strategic issue and a plan backed up with data and rationale. Agree to review your thinking every three months with this group and write down lessons learned. Analyze three business/organizational success stories in your area and the same number of failures. What did each have in common? How would these principles apply in your situation? What was common to the failures that was never present in the successes?

If you sometimes overdo being Imaginative:

1. **Set goals.** You should set goals before assigning projects, work, and tasks. Goals help focus people's time and efforts. It allows people to perform more effectively and efficiently. Most people don't want to waste time. Most people want to perform well. Learn about MBO—managing by objectives. Read a book about it. While you may not be interested in a full-blown application, all of the principles of setting goals will be in the book. Go to a course on goal setting.

2. **Focus on measures.** How would you tell if the goal was accomplished? If the things I asked others to do were done right, what outcomes could we all agree on as measures of success? Most groups can easily come up with success measures that are different from, and more important to them, than formal measures. Ask them to do so.

3. **Clarity.** You need to be clear about goals, how they are going to be measured, and what the rewards and consequences will be for those who exceed, just make, or miss their goals. Communicate both verbally and in writing if you can.

4. **Visualize.** Set up a process to monitor progress against the goals. People like running measures. They like to gauge their pace. It's like the United Way Thermometer in the lobby.

5. **Feedback.** Give as much in-process feedback as you have time for. Most people are motivated by process feedback against agreed-upon goals for three reasons:

- First, it helps them adjust what they are doing along the way in time to achieve the goal; they can make midcourse corrections.

- Second, it shows them what they are doing is important and that you're eager to help.

- Third, it's not the "gotcha" game of negative and critical feedback after the fact.

6. **Laying out the work.** Most resourcefulness starts out with a plan. What do I need to accomplish? What's the time line? What resources will I need? Who controls the resources—people, funding, tools, materials, support—I need? What's my currency? How can I pay for or repay the resources I need? Who wins if I win? Who might lose? Lay out the work from A to Z. Many people are seen as disorganized because they don't write down the sequence or parts of the work and leave something out. Ask others to comment on ordering and what's missing.

7. **Vision the plan in process.** What could go wrong? Run scenarios in your head. Think along several paths. Rank the potential problems from highest likelihood to lowest likelihood. Think about what you would do if the highest likelihood things were to occur. Create a contingency plan for each. Pay attention to the weakest links, which are usually groups or elements you have the least interface with or control over (perhaps someone in a remote location, a consultant, or supplier). Stay doubly in touch with the potential weak links.

Practical←→Conceptual
What is made or created out of what we know.

Practical (Results-oriented, applied)

- Attend to physical characteristics.

- Pull together known, verifiable, tested facts.

- See change as a step-by-step evolution.

To develop more of this facet:

1. **Locate a pro.** Find the seasoned master professional in the technology or function, and ask whether he/she would mind showing you the ropes and tutoring you. Most don't mind having a few "apprentices"

around. Help him or her teach you. Ask, "How do you know what's important? What do you look at first? Second? What are the five keys you always look at or for? What do you read? Who do you go to for advice?"

2. **Find the bible on your function/technology.** Almost every function and technology has a book people might call the "bible" in the area. It is the standard reference everyone looks to for knowledge. There is probably a journal in your technology or function. Subscribe for a year or more. See if they have back issues available.

3. **Set goals.** You should set goals before assigning projects, work, and tasks. Goals help focus people's time and efforts. It allows people to perform more effectively and efficiently. Most people don't want to waste time. Most people want to perform well. Learn about MBO— managing by objectives. Read a book about it. While you may not be interested in a full-blown application, all of the principles of setting goals will be in the book. Go to a course on goal setting.

4. **Focus on measures.** How would you tell if the goal was accomplished? If the things I asked others to do were done right, what outcomes could we all agree on as measures of success? Most groups can easily come up with success measures that are different from, and more important to them, than formal measures. Ask them to do so.

5. **Clarity.** You need to be clear about goals, how they are going to be measured, and what the rewards and consequences will be for those who exceed, just make, or miss their goals. Communicate both verbally and in writing if you can.

6. **Visualize.** Set up a process to monitor progress against the goals. People like running measures. They like to gauge their pace. It's like the United Way Thermometer in the lobby.

7. **Measure activity** (in addition to measuring outcomes and results). Say you bought some equipment. How many people are needed to run it? How much time will this take? Repairs? How much time? Activity-based accounting measures the cost of doing or not doing a task. By looking at work carefully in terms of time, core and non-core tasks (those less important because the time spent isn't worth it) can be determined. Using this method, a group of nurses doubled their productivity.

8. **Setting priorities?** What's mission-critical? What are the three to five things that most need to get done to achieve your goals? Effective

performers typically spend about half their time on a few mission-critical priorities. Don't get diverted by trivia and things you like doing but that aren't tied to the bottom line.

9. **When faced with a new issue, challenge, or problem,** figure out what causes it. Keep asking why. See how many causes you can come up with and how many organizing buckets you can put them in. This increases the chance of a better solution because you can see more connections. Chess masters recognize thousands of possible patterns of chess pieces. Look for patterns in data; don't just collect information. Put it in categories that make sense.

10. **Patterns.** Look for patterns in personal, organization, or the world, in general successes and failures. What was common to each success or what was present in each failure but never present in a success? Focus on the successes; failures are easier to analyze but don't in themselves tell you what would work. Comparing successes, while less exciting, yields more information about underlying principles.

11. **Increasing impulse control.** People say and do inappropriate things when they lose their composure. The problem is that they say or do the first thing that occurs to them. Research shows that generally somewhere between the second and third thing you think of to say or do is the best option. Practice holding back your first response long enough to think of a second. When you can do that, wait long enough to think of a third before you choose.

If you sometimes overdo being Practical:

1. **Reject strategy?** There are people who reject strategic formulation as so much folly. They have never seen a five-year strategic plan actually happen as projected. They think the time they use to create and present strategic plans is wasted. They think it's where the rubber meets the sky. While it's true that most strategic plans never work out as planned, that doesn't mean that it was a wasted effort. Strategic plans lead to choices about resources and deployment. They lead to different staffing actions and different financial plans. Without some strategic plans, it would be a total shot in the dark. Most failed companies got buried strategically, not tactically. They were still making high-quality buggy whips when they went under. They picked the wrong direction or too many directions. Not being able to produce a quality product or service today is generally not the problem.

2. **Can't think strategically?** Strategy is linking several variables together to come up with the most likely scenario. Think of it as the search for and application of relevant parallels. It involves making projections of several variables at once to see how they come together. These projections are in the context of shifting markets, international affairs, monetary movements, and government interventions. It involves a lot of uncertainty, making risk assumptions, and understanding how things work together. How many reasons would account for sales going down? Up? How are advertising and sales linked? If the dollar is cheaper in Asia, what does that mean for our product in Japan? If the world population is aging and they have more money, how will that change buying patterns? Not everyone enjoys this kind of pie-in-the-sky thinking and not everyone is skilled at doing it.

3. **Subscribe to** *The Systems Thinker*®, Pegasus Communications, Inc., Cambridge, MA, 781-398-9700. This is a group dedicated to finding out how things work and why they work that way. They have a monthly publication as well as workshops, seminars, and other materials available to help you see the world as a series of recurring systems or archetypes. They analyze everyday events and processes and try to see why they work the way they do. The material will help you view things in terms of whole systems.

4. **Try to picture things in the form of flows.** Buy a flowcharting software program that does PERT and GANTT charts. Become an expert in its use. Use the output of the software to communicate the systems you manage to others. Use the flowcharts in your presentations.

5. **Managing remotely is the true test of delegation and empowerment.** It's impossible for you to do it all. Successful managers report high involvement in setting parameters, exceptions they want to be notified of, and expected outcomes. They detail what requires their involvement and what doesn't. When people call them for a decision, they always ask, "What do you think? What impact will it have on you—customers, etc.—if we do this?" rather than just render a judgment. If you don't, people will begin to delegate upward, and you'll be a close-in manager from a remote location. Help people think things through, and trust them to follow the plan. Delegation requires this clear communication about expectations and releasing the authority to decide and act.

6. **Managing vision and mission is a lot like selling.** You have a product you think others would buy if they knew about it. Each customer is a little different. What features and benefits would they be looking for? What would they be willing to pay in terms of time and commitment? What are their objections likely to be? How will you answer them? How are you going to ask for the order?

7. **C.K. Prahalad, one of the leading strategic consultants, believes that in order to qualify as a mission statement,** it should take less than three minutes to explain it clearly to an audience. Really effective mission statements are simple, compelling, and capable of capturing people's imagination. Mission statements should help everyone allot his/her time. They should signal what's mission-critical and explain what's rewarded in the organization and what's not. Create a simple obvious symbol, visual, or slogan to make the cause come alive.

Conceptual (Idea-oriented, intellectual)

■ Reality beyond the senses.

■ Make connections among ideas, enjoy exchange of ideas.

■ Enjoy looking at a collage rather than specifics.

To develop more of this facet:

1. **Under uncertainty, it really helps to get as firm a handle as possible on the problem.** Figure out what causes it. Keep asking why. See how many causes you can come up with and how many organizing buckets you can put them in. This increases the chance of a better solution because you can see more connections. The evidence from decision-making research makes it clear that thorough problem definition with appropriate questions to answer leads to better decisions. Focusing on solutions or information first often slows things down since we have no conceptual buckets in which to organize our thinking.

2. **Visualize the problem.** Complex processes or problems with a lot of uncertainty are hard to understand. They tend to be a hopeless maze unless they are put in a visual format. One technique is a pictorial chart called a storyboard, where a process or vision or strategy is illustrated by its components being depicted as pictures. A variation of this is to do the old pro and con, +'s and −'s of a problem and process, then flowchart those according to what's working and not

working. Another is the fishbone diagram used in Total Work Systems. It is a method of breaking down the causes of a problem into categories. Buy a flowcharting software program to help you visualize problems quickly.

3. **Check yourself for these common errors in thinking:** Do you state as facts things that are really opinions or assumptions? Are you sure these assertions are facts? State opinions and assumptions as that and don't present them as facts. Do you attribute cause and effect to relationships when you don't know if one causes the other? If sales are down, and we increase advertising and sales go up, this doesn't prove causality. They are simply related. Say we know that the relationship between sales/advertising is about the same as sales/number of employees. If sales go down, we probably wouldn't hire more people, so make sure one thing causes the other before acting on it. Do you generalize from a single example without knowing if that single example does generalize?

4. **Access great minds.** Study a few great thinkers and philosophers like John Stuart Mill who outlined the basic logic of problem solving. Read their biographies or autobiographies for clues into how they used their intellectual skills.

5. **Turn off your answer program.** We all have a need to provide answers as soon as possible to questions and problems. We all have preconceived notions, favorite solutions, and prejudices that prevent our intellectual skills from dealing with the real facts of the problem. For one-half of the time you have to deal with an issue or a problem, shut off your solution machine and just take in the facts.

6. **Think systems.** Subscribe to *The Systems Thinker®*, Pegasus Communications, Inc., Waltham, MA, 781-398-9700. This is a group dedicated to finding out how things work and why they work that way. They have a monthly publication as well as workshops, seminars, and other materials available to help you see the world as a series of recurring systems or archetypes. They analyze everyday events and processes and try to see why they work the way they do. They take complex problems and try to show how almost all problems are some form of seven classic models.

7. **Locate the essence of the problem.** What are the key factors or elements in this problem? Experts usually solve problems by figuring out what the deep, underlying principles are and working forward from there; the less adept focus on desired outcomes/solutions and

either work backward or concentrate on the surface facts. What are the deep principles of what you're working on? Once you've done this, search the past for parallels—your past, the business past, the historical past.

8. **Use others.** Teams of people with the widest diversity of backgrounds produce the most innovative solutions to problems. Get others with different backgrounds to analyze and make sense with you. When working together, come up with as many questions about the problem as you can. Set up a competition with another group or individual, asking them to work on exactly what you are working on. Set a certain time frame and have a postmortem to try to deduce some of the practices and procedures that work best. Find a team or individual that faces problems quite similar to what you face and set up dialogues on a number of specific topics.

9. **Envision the process unfolding.** What could go wrong? Run scenarios in your head. Think along several paths. Rank the potential problems from highest likelihood to lowest likelihood. Think about what you would do if the highest likelihood things were to occur. Create a contingency plan for each. Pay attention to the weakest links, which are usually groups or elements you have the least interface with or control over (perhaps someone in a remote location, a consultant, or supplier). Stay doubly in touch with the potential weak links.

If you sometimes overdo being Conceptual:

1. **You may overly complicate issues.** Analysis paralysis? Break out of your examine-it-to-death mode and just do it. Sometimes you hold back acting because you don't have all the information. Some like to be close to 100% sure before they act. Anyone with a brain and 100% of the data can make good decisions. The real test is who can act the soonest with a reasonable amount, but not all, of the data. Some studies suggest successful general managers are about 65% correct. If you learn to make smaller decisions more quickly, you can change course along the way to the correct decision.

2. **Go back to your basic problem-solving skills.** First define what the problem is and isn't. Figure out what causes it. Keep asking why. See how many causes you can come up with and how many organizing buckets you can put them in. This increases the chance of a better solution because you can see more connections. Look for patterns in

data; don't just collect information. Put it in categories that make sense to you. Ask lots of questions. Allot at least 50% of the time to defining the problem. Then select an alternative or two to test, get feedback, and modify. This tip should be easy for you because you already know all this, you've just gotten sidetracked by overanalysis.

3. **Set goals.** You should set goals before assigning projects, work, and tasks. Goals help focus people's time and efforts. It allows people to perform more effectively and efficiently. Most people don't want to waste time. Most people want to perform well. Learn about MBO—managing by objectives. Read a book about it. While you may not be interested in a full-blown application, all of the principles of setting goals will be in the book. Go to a course on goal setting.

4. **Focus on measures.** How would you tell if the goal was accomplished? If the things I asked others to do were done right, what outcomes could we all agree on as measures of success? Most groups can easily come up with success measures that are different from, and more important to them, than formal measures. Ask them to do so.

5. **Clarity.** You need to be clear about goals, how they are going to be measured, and what the rewards and consequences will be for those who exceed, just make, or miss their goals. Communicate both verbally and in writing if you can.

6. **Laying out the work.** Most resourcefulness starts out with a plan. What do I need to accomplish? What's the time line? What resources will I need? Who controls the resources—people, funding, tools, materials, support—I need? What's my currency? How can I pay for or repay the resources I need? Who wins if I win? Who might lose? Lay out the work from A to Z. Many people are seen as disorganized because they don't write down the sequence or parts of the work and leave something out. Ask others to comment on ordering and what's missing.

7. **Vision the plan in process.** What could go wrong? Run scenarios in your head. Think along several paths. Rank the potential problems from highest likelihood to lowest likelihood. Think about what you would do if the highest likelihood things were to occur. Create a contingency plan for each. Pay attention to the weakest links, which are usually groups or elements you have the least interface with or control over (perhaps someone in a remote location, a consultant, or supplier). Stay doubly in touch with the potential weak links.

8. **You may also not be clear with problem performers.** Do they know what's expected of them? You may not set clear enough performance standards, goals, and objectives. You may be a cryptic communicator. You may communicate to some and not to others. You may have given up on some and stopped communicating. Or you may think they would know what to do if they're any good, but that's not really true because you have not properly communicated what you want. The first task is to outline the 5 to 10 key results areas and what indicators of success would be. Involve your problem direct reports on both ends—the standards and the indicators. Provide them with a fair way to measure their own progress.

9. **Realism.** They are not performing up to standard? It's common to see 90-day improve-or-else plans that no one can accomplish: be more strategic, improve your interpersonal skills, learn about the business, be less arrogant. Ask yourself how long did it take you to become proficient at what you are criticizing this person for. Because managers hesitate delivering negative messages, we get to people late.

Experiential←→Theoretical
How we make meanings, patterns of perceptions.

Experiential (Hands-on, empirical)

■ Prefer validation by repeated experience.

■ Enjoy active participation.

■ Adept at trial-and-error, and like established procedures.

To develop more of this facet:

1. **Start earlier.** Always do 10% of each task immediately after it is assigned so you can better gauge what it is going to take to finish the rest. Break the task down into smaller pieces. Commit to doing a piece a day. Don't even think of the larger goal. Just do something on it each day.

2. **Perfectionist?** Need to be 100% sure? Perfectionism is tough to let go of because it's a positive trait for most. Recognize your perfectionism for what it might be—collecting information to improve your confidence and avoid criticism, examining opportunities so long you miss them, or waiting for the perfect solution. Try to decrease your need for all of the data and your need to be right all the time slightly

every week, until you reach a more reasonable balance between thinking it through and taking action. Some studies suggest successful general managers are about 65% correct. If you learn to make smaller decisions more quickly, you can change course along the way to the correct decision.

3. **Maybe you're slow to act because you don't think you're up to the task.** If you boldly act, others will shoot you down and find you out. Take a course or work with a tutor to bolster your confidence in one skill or area at a time. Focus on the strengths you do have; think of ways you can use these strengths when making nerve-wracking actions. If you are interpersonally skilled, for example, see yourself smoothly dealing with questions and objections to your actions. The only way you will ever know what you can do is to act and find out.

4. **Treat any mistakes or failures as chances to learn.** Nothing ventured, nothing gained. Up your risk comfort. Start small so you can recover more quickly. Go for small wins. Don't blast into a major task to prove your boldness. Break it down into smaller tasks. Take the easiest one for you first. Then build up to the tougher ones. Review each one to see what you did well and not well, and set goals so you'll do something differently and better each time. End up accomplishing the big goal and taking the bold action.

5. **The essence of dealing comfortably with uncertainty is the tolerance of errors and mistakes, and absorbing the possible heat and criticism that follow.** People who are good at this are incrementalists. They make a series of smaller decisions, get instant feedback, correct the course, get a little more data, move forward a little more, until the bigger problem is under control. They don't try to get it right the first time. Many problem-solving studies show that the second or third try is when we really understand the underlying dynamics of problems.

6. **To increase learning from your mistakes,** design feedback loops to be as immediate as possible. The faster and the more frequent the cycles, the more opportunities to learn—if we do one smaller thing a day for three days instead of one bigger thing in three, we triple our learning opportunities. There will be many mistakes and failures; after all, since you're not sure, it's very likely no one else knows what to do either. They just have a right to comment on your errors. The best tack when confronted with a mistake is to say, "What can we learn from this?"

7. **Locate a pro.** Find the seasoned master professional in the technology or function, and ask whether he/she would mind showing you the ropes and tutoring you. Most don't mind having a few "apprentices" around. Help him or her teach you. Ask, "How do you know what's important? What do you look at first? Second? What are the five keys you always look at or for? What do you read? Who do you go to for advice?"

8. **Sign up.** Almost all functions have national and sometimes regional professional associations made up of hundreds of people who do well what you need to learn every day. Sign up as a member. Buy some of the introductory literature. Go to some of their workshops. Go to the annual conference.

9. **Find the bible on your function/technology.** Almost every function and technology has a book people might call the "bible" in the area. It is the standard reference everyone looks to for knowledge. There is probably a journal in your technology or function. Subscribe for a year or more. See if they have back issues available.

10. **Meet the notables.** Identify some national leaders in your function/technology and buy their books, read their articles, and attend their lectures and workshops.

11. **Learn from those around you.** Ask others in your function/technology which skills and what knowledge is mission-critical and ask them how they learned it. Follow the same or a similar path.

12. **Take a course.** Your local college or university might have some nighttime or weekend courses you could take in your technology. Your organization may have training classes in your technology.

13. **Enjoy the moment more.** Be on the lookout for the ridiculous around you. Jot down funny things that happen around you so you can remember them. Self-humor is usually safe, seen as positive by others, and most of the time leads to increased respect. Funny and embarrassing things that happened to you (when the airline lost your luggage and you had to wash your underwear in an airport restroom and dry it under the hand dryer). Your flaws and foibles (when you were so stressed over your taxes that you locked the keys in your car with the motor running). Mistakes you've made. Blunders you've committed. Besides adding humor to the situation, it humanizes you and endears people to you.

S↔N

If you sometimes overdo being Experiential:

1. **You may not understand fully how careers are built in the long term.** It's easy to get cynical and believe that successful people are political or sell out, suck up, knife people in the back, it's who you know, and so on. The facts are dramatically different from this. Those behaviors get people in trouble eventually. What has staying power is performing and problem solving on the current job, having a few notable strengths, and seeking new tasks you don't know how to do. It's solving every problem with tenacity, while looking for what you haven't yet done and getting yourself in a position to do it. Read *The Lessons of Experience* by McCall, Lombardo and Morrison for the careers of men and *Breaking the Glass Ceiling* by Morrison, White and Van Velsor for the careers of women to see how successful careers really happen.

2. **Focus on the right things.** In their study of successful vs. average careers, Citrin and Smith found that the most successful people force themselves into experiences they need for growth. They do not play it safe. While they demonstrate early competence in a specific area, they also don't overdo working on basic job requirements. They do enough work on the basics while searching for mission-critical job elements and trying to overdeliver on them. They add unexpected value. They call this the 20/80 principle of performance—focusing on the 20% that makes 80% of the difference. In doing so, the successful rack up career freedom points by tackling these tough assignments.

3. **Break out of your career comfort zone.** Maybe you haven't seen enough. Pick some activities you haven't done before but might find exciting. Take a course in a new area. Task trade—switch tasks with a peer. Volunteer for task forces and projects that are multi-functional or multi-business in nature. Read more broadly.

4. **Not comfortable marketing yourself?** You don't know how to get promoted. You dislike people who blow their own horns. Here's how to do it. Build a performance track record of variety—start up things, fix things, innovate, make plans, come under budget. This is what will get you promoted. All organizations are looking for broad thinkers to give fresh opportunities to. Start by thinking more broadly.

5. **You may enjoy doing and not delegate.** How to delegate? Communicate, set time frames and goals, and get out of the way. People need to know what it is you expect. What does the outcome look like? When do you need it by? What's the budget? What

resources do they get? What decisions can they make? Do you want checkpoints along the way? How will we both know and measure how well the task is done? One of the most common problems with delegation is incomplete or cryptic up-front communication leading to frustration, a job not well done the first time, rework, and a reluctance to delegate next time. Poor communicators always have to take more time managing because of rework. Analyze recent projects that went well and didn't go well. How did you delegate? Too much? Not enough? Unwanted pieces? Major chunks of responsibility? Workload distributed properly? Did you set measures? Overmanage or abdicate? Find out what your best practices are. Set up a series of delegation practices that can be used as if you're not there. What do you have to be informed of? What feedback loops can people use for midcourse correction? What questions should be answered as the work proceeds? What steps should be followed? What are the criteria to be followed? When will you be available to help?

6. **You may keep your focus fairly narrow.** At work, pick three tasks you've never done and go do them. If you don't know much about customers, work in a store or handle customer complaints; if you don't know what engineering does, go find out; task trade with someone. Seek the broadest possible exposure inside the organization. Do lunch with counterparts of the organization and tell each other what you do. Task forces/projects are a great opportunity. If the project is important, is multi-functional, and has a real outcome which will be taken seriously (not a study group), it is one of the most common developmental events listed by successful executives.

7. **Read international publications** like *The Economist*, the *International Herald Tribune, Commentary;* autobiographies of people like Kissinger; pick a country and study it; read a book on the fall of the Soviet Union; or read "we present all sides" journals like *The Atlantic Monthly* to get the broadest possible view of issues. There are common underlying principles in everything. You need to expose yourself more broadly in order to find and apply those principles to what you're doing today.

S↔N

Theoretical (Conceptual, hypothetical)

- Explore by looking for interconnections.

- Learn best by theory.

- Adept at discovering new ideas.

- Generally uninterested in routine matters.

To develop more of this facet:

1. **Become a better student of people.** Observe more than you do now. See if you can predict what people are going to say and do before they do it. See if their behavior shows a pattern. What do they do over and over again? By scoping out people better, you can better adjust to their responses.

2. **Customer focus.** People who are good at this work from the outside (the customer, the audience, the person, the situation) in, not from the inside out. ("What do I want to do in this situation; what would make me happy and feel good?") Practice not thinking inside/out when you are around others. What are the demand characteristics of this situation? How does this person or audience best learn? Which of my approaches or styles would work best? How can I best accomplish my goals? How can I alter my approach and tactics to be the most effective?

3. **Think systems.** Subscribe to *The Systems Thinker®*, Pegasus Communications, Inc., Waltham, MA, 781-398-9700. This is a group dedicated to finding out how things work and why they work that way. They have a monthly publication as well as workshops, seminars, and other materials available to help you see the world as a series of recurring systems or archetypes. They analyze everyday events and processes and try to see why they work the way they do. They take complex problems and try to show how almost all problems are some form of seven classic models.

4. **Access great minds.** Study a few great thinkers and philosophers like John Stuart Mill who outlined the basic logic of problem solving. Read their biographies or autobiographies for clues into how they used their intellectual skills.

5. **People focus on different things**—taking action, details, concepts, feelings, other people. What's their interaction style? People come in

different styles—pushy, tough, soft, matter-of-fact, and so on. To figure these out, listen for the values behind their words and note what they have passion and emotion around. One key to getting anything of value done in the work world is the ability to see differences in people and to manage against and use those differences for everyone's benefit.

6. **To better figure out what drives people, look to:** What do they do first? What do they emphasize in their speech? What do they display emotion around? What values play out for them?

   ■ First things. Does this person go to others first, hole up and study, complain, discuss feelings, or take action? These are the basic orientations of people that reveal what's important to them. Use these to motivate.

   ■ Speech content. People might focus on details, concepts, feelings, or other people in their speech. This can tell you again how to appeal to them by mirroring their speech emphasis. Although most of us naturally adjust—we talk details with detail-oriented people—chances are good that in problem relationships you're not finding the common ground. She talks "detail" and you talk "people," for example.

   ■ Emotion. You need to know what people's hot buttons are because one mistake can get you labeled as insensitive with some people. The only cure here is to see what turns up the volume for them—either literally or what they're concerned about.

   ■ Values. Apply the same thinking to the values of others. Do they talk about money, recognition, integrity, efficiency in their normal work conversation? Figuring out what their drivers are tells you another easy way to appeal to anyone.

7. **Learn to think as experts in technology do.** Take problems to them and ask what are the keys they look for; observe what they consider significant and not significant. Chunk data into categories so you can remember it better. Devise five key areas or questions you can consider each time a technical issue comes up. Don't waste your time learning facts; they won't be useful unless you have conceptual buckets to put them in.

8. **Locate the essence of the problem.** What are the key factors or elements in this problem? Experts usually solve problems by figuring out what the deep, underlying principles are and working forward from there; the less adept focus on desired outcomes/solutions and either work backward or concentrate on the surface facts. What are the deep principles of what you're working on? Once you've done this, search the past for parallels—your past, the business past, the historical past.

9. **Patterns.** Look for patterns in personal, organization, or the world, in general successes and failures. What was common to each success or what was present in each failure but never present in a success? Focus on the successes; failures are easier to analyze but don't in themselves tell you what would work. Comparing successes, while less exciting, yields more information about underlying principles. The bottom line is to reduce your insights to principles or rules of thumb you think might be repeatable. When faced with the next new problem, those general underlying principles will apply again.

10. **Become a strategic activist.** Pick one distinctive competence or driving force. That's what the mediocre companies who became successful over time did in James Collins' latest research. Create a strategic plan for your unit around one distinctive competence— include breakthrough process and product improvements, justify your conclusions by pointing to hard data that points toward your conclusions. Have the plan reviewed by people you trust. Form a consortium with three other individuals or companies; each of you will present a strategic issue and a plan backed up with data and rationale. Agree to review your thinking every three months with this group and write down lessons learned. Analyze three business/ organizational success stories in your area and the same number of failures. What did each have in common? How would these principles apply in your situation? What was common to the failures that was never present in the successes?

11. **Learn to be a cultural anthropologist.** In assessing groups, ask yourself: What makes their blood boil? What do they believe? What are they trying to accomplish together? What do they smile at? What norms and customs do they have? What practices and behaviors do they share? Do they not like it if you stand too close? If you get right down to business? Do they like first names or are they more formal? If a Japanese manager presents his card, do you know what to do? Why do they have their cards printed in two languages and

executives from the U.S. don't? Do you know what jokes are okay to tell? What do they believe about you and your group or groups? Positive? Neutral? Negative? What's been the history of their group and yours? Is this a first contact or a long history? Don't blunder in; nothing will kill you quicker with a group than showing utter disregard—read disrespect—for it and its norms, or having no idea of how they view your group. Ask people for insights who deal with this group often. If it's an important group to you and your business, read about it.

12. **Share the future with others.** The power of a mission and vision communication is providing everyone in the organization with a road map on how they are going to be part of something grand and exciting. Establish common cause. Imagine what the change would look like if fully implemented, then describe the outcome often—how things will look in the future. Help people see how their efforts fit in by creating simple, obvious measures of achievement like bar or thermometer charts. Be succinct. People don't line up behind laundry lists or ambiguous objectives. Missions and visions should be more about where we are going and less about how we are going to get there. Keep your eyes on the prize.

If you sometimes overdo being Theoretical:

1. **You may value the scientific method over other ways of thinking.** To break out of a thinking box, try some creative problem solving techniques that do not follow the formal rules of logic, where one uses cause and effect to prove or solve something. Some rules of creative thought are:

- Not using concepts but changing them; imagining this were something else.

- Move from one concept or way of looking at things to another, such as from economic to political.

- Generate ideas without judging them initially.

- Use information to restructure and come up with new patterns.

- Jump from one idea to another without justifying the jump.

- Look for the least likely and odd.

623

S↔N

- Look for parallels far from the problem, such as how is an organization like a big oak tree?

- Ask what's missing or what's not here.

- Fascination with mistakes and failure as learning devices.

2. **You may not pay much attention to building a team.** Establish a common cause and a shared mind-set. A common thrust is what energizes dream teams. As in light lasers, alignment adds focus, power, and efficiency. It's best to get each team member involved in setting the common vision. Establish goals and measures. Most people like to be measured. People like to have checkpoints along the way to chart their progress. Most people perform better with goals that are stretching. Again, letting the team participate in setting the goals is a plus.

3. **Follow the basic rules of inspiring team members** as outlined in classic books like *People Skills* by Robert Bolton or *Thriving on Chaos* by Tom Peters. Tell people what they do is important. Say thanks. Offer help and ask for it. Provide autonomy in how people do their work. Provide a variety of tasks. "Surprise" people with enriching, challenging assignments. Show an interest in their careers. Adopt a learning attitude toward mistakes. Celebrate successes, have visible accepted measures of achievement, and so on.

4. **You may need to write more succinctly.** Prepare an outline before you write. Too many people write without a plan. Go through a checklist. What's your objective? What are your main points? Outline your main points in logical support of the objective. What are five things you want them to know and remember about each point? When you write, any sentence that does not relate to the objective and the points shouldn't be there. What would the ideal reader say if interviewed 15 minutes after he/she finishes reading your piece? Who's your audience? How much do they know that you don't have to repeat? How much background should you include? What questions will the audience have when they read your piece? Are they covered? What's the setting for readers? How much time will they spend? How long can it be? Pick up something you've written lately and take a test. Does it have a thesis? Does each paragraph have a topic sentence—a subject? If you state one sentence per paragraph, do the statements follow logically?

5. **Don't drown the reader in detail he/she doesn't need or can't use.** Use detail only when it's essential to understanding your argument/thesis. What are five facts that show your point? Even if writing a lengthy report, those five facts should be highlighted in a paragraph or two, not revealed slowly. Readers will forget why they are reading about each problem since problems usually have more than one cause, and they will become distracted thinking about other matters. Few people read an almanac. If your argument is data driven, use the few; put the many in appendices.

Traditional←→Original
Role of social context and traditions in life.

Traditional (Conventional, customary)

■ Do things in established ways because it is safe and secure to do so.

■ Like to do things according to customs and norms.

■ Social environment confirms their way of doing things.

To develop more of this facet:

1. **Equity with information.** Follow the rule of equity of information with everyone. Explain your thinking and ask them to explain theirs. When discussing issues, give reasons first, solutions last. When you give solutions first, people often don't listen to your reasons. Some people get overly directive with some of their reports, and they, in turn, feel that you're not interested in what they think. Invite their thinking and their reasons before settling on solutions. Don't provide information selectively. Don't use information as a reward or a relationship builder with one or just a few and not others.

2. **In meetings, make sure you include everyone,** and don't direct substantially more remarks toward one person or subgroup to the exclusion of others. Make sure you signal nothing negative to others; a neutral observer should not be able to tell from your demeanor whom you like and don't like. Help the quiet, shy, and reserved have their say. Quiet the loud, assertive, and passionate. Give everyone a fair chance to be heard.

3. **Locate a pro.** Find the seasoned master professional in the technology or function, and ask whether he/she would mind showing you the ropes and tutoring you. Most don't mind having a few "apprentices"

around. Help him or her teach you. Ask, "How do you know what's important? What do you look at first? Second? What are the five keys you always look at or for? What do you read? Who do you go to for advice?"

4. **Find the bible on your function/technology.** Almost every function and technology has a book people might call the "bible" in the area. It is the standard reference everyone looks to for knowledge. There is probably a journal in your technology or function. Subscribe for a year or more. See if they have back issues available.

5. **Are you a hedger?** Do you hold back and qualify everything? Don't speak up when you should? Do you not know how to say what needs to be said, so you go bland and qualify everything to death? Do you hesitate or slow down when you are sharing something that is difficult for you? Does your voice go up in volume? Freudian slips? Stumble over words? Even though it's not your intention, do people think you are not disclosing what you really know? Practice coming up with two or three clear statements you are prepared to defend. Test them with people you trust. Keep them on the facts and on the problems. Be specific and don't blame. Don't qualify or make your statements conditional. Just say it.

6. **Don't promise something unless you can deliver.** If you don't know for sure, say, "I'll let you know when I do." Either promise or don't—don't say "I'll try." If you don't know, just say so and follow up when you do know. Try to reduce your sales pitches to the actual merits of the case.

7. **Think about multiple ways to get the same outcome.** For example, to push a decision through, you could meet with stakeholders first, go to a single key stakeholder, study and present the problem to a group, call a problem-solving session, or call in an outside expert. Be prepared to do them all when obstacles arise.

8. **When your initiative hits resistance, keep it on the problem and the objectives.** Depersonalize. If attacked, return to what you're trying to accomplish and invite people's criticisms and ideas. Listen. Correct if justified. Stick to your point. Push ahead again. Resistance is natural.

9. **All your eggs in one basket?** Add things to your off-work life. This was a major finding of a stress study at AT&T of busy, high-potential women and men. It may seem counterintuitive, but the best-adjusted people forced themselves to structure off-work activities just as much

as on-work activities. Otherwise work drives everything else out. Those with dual responsibilities (primary care giver and home manager and a full-time jobholder) need to use their management strengths and skills more at home. What makes your work life successful? Batch tasks, bundle similar activities together, delegate to children, or set up pools with coworkers or neighbors to share tasks, such as car pooling, soccer games, Scouts, etc. Pay to have some things done that are not mission-critical to your home needs. Organize and manage efficiently. Have a schedule. Set up goals and plans. Use some of your work skills more off-work.

If you sometimes overdo being Traditional:

1. **You may be stuck.** Break out of your career comfort zone. Maybe you haven't seen enough. Pick some activities you haven't done before but might find exciting. Take a course in a new area. Task trade—switch tasks with a peer. Volunteer for task forces and projects that are multi-functional or multi-business in nature. Read more broadly.

2. **Focus on the right things.** In their study of successful vs. average careers, Citrin and Smith found that the most successful people force themselves into experiences they need for growth. They do not play it safe. While they demonstrate early competence in a specific area, they also don't overdo working on basic job requirements. They do enough work on the basics while searching for mission-critical job elements and trying to overdeliver on them. They add unexpected value. They call this the 20/80 principle of performance—focusing on the 20% that makes 80% of the difference. In doing so, the successful rack up career freedom points by tackling these tough assignments.

3. **You may get caught up in your own views and not readily see those of others.** Stereotypes? You have to understand your own subtle stereotyping. Helen Astin's research showed that both men and women rated women managers at the extremes (very high or very low) while they rated men on a normal curve. Do you think redheads have tempers? Blondes have more fun? Overweight people are lazy? Women are more emotional at work? Men can't show emotion? Find out your own pattern. Attend a course which delves into perception of others. Most stereotyping is false. Even if there are surface differences, they don't make a difference in performance.

4. **When you make a hiring decision** or are deciding whom to work with on a problem or project, do you think you have a tendency to clone yourself too much? Do you have a preference for people who

think and act as you do? What characteristics do you value too much? What downsides do you ignore or excuse away? This is a common human tendency. The key is to seek balance, variety, and diversity.

5. **You may not understand diversity issues as well as you might.** Try to see people more as individuals than members of a group. Avoid putting people in grouped buckets. Many of us bucket people as can or can't do this. We have good buckets and bad buckets. Buckets I like/am comfortable with and buckets that bother me. Once we bucket, we generally don't relate as well to the off bucket people. Much of the time bucketing is based on like me—the good bucket; not like me—the bad bucket. Across time, the can do/like me bucket gets the majority of your attention, more feedback, stretching tasks, develops the most and performs the best, unfortunately proving your stereotyping again and again. To break this cycle, understand without judging. Be candid with yourself. Is there a group or groups you don't like or are uncomfortable with? Do you judge individual members of that group without really knowing if your stereotype is true? Most of us do. Try to see people as people.

6. **You may not champion innovation.** You need raw creative ideas to be able to manage innovation. While you may not be and don't need to be the source for the creative ideas, you need to understand the process. Creative thought processes do not follow the formal rules of logic where one uses cause and effect to prove or solve something. The rules of creative thought lie not in using existing concepts but in changing them—moving from one concept or way of looking at things to another. It involves challenging the status quo and generating ideas without judging them initially. Jumping from one idea to another without justifying the jump. Looking for the least likely and the odd. The creative process requires freedom and openness and a non-judgmental environment. The creative process can't be timed. Setting a goal and a time schedule to be creative will most likely chill creativity.

7. **Getting creativity out of a group.** Many times the creative idea comes from a group, not single individuals. When working on a new idea for a product or service, have them come up with as many questions about it as you can. Often we think too quickly of solutions. In studies of problem-solving sessions, solutions outweigh questions 8 to 1. Asking more questions helps people rethink the problem and come to more and different solutions. Have the group take a current product you are dissatisfied with and represent it visually—a flowchart or a

series of pictures. Cut it up into its component pieces and shuffle them. Examine the pieces to see if a different order would help, or how you could combine three pieces into one. Try many experiments or trials to find something that will work. Have the group think beyond current boundaries. What are some of the most sacred rules or practices in your organization? Unit? Think about smashing them— what would your unit be doing if you broke the rules? Talk to the most irreverent person you know about this. Buffer the group. It's difficult to work on something new if they are besieged with all the distractions you have to deal with, particularly if people are looking over your shoulder asking why isn't anything happening.

8. **Selecting the idea.** Creativity relies on freedom early, but structure later. Once the unit comes up with its best notion of what to do, subject it to all the logical tests and criticism any other alternative is treated to. Testing out creative ideas is no different than any other problem-solving/evaluation process. The difference is in how the ideas originate.

Original (Unconventional, unusual)

■ Seek innovation.

■ Change established ways as a method of self-expression.

■ Enjoy finding unique ways of doing routine things.

To develop more of this facet:

1. **Innovation through diversity.** Studies show that heterogeneous or diverse groups are more innovative than homogeneous groups. They view opportunities from different perspectives. The majority of the U.S. labor market will shortly be former minorities. Females and minorities collectively will be in the majority. Companies known in the marketplace for managing diversity well will get their pick of the best and the brightest. A broader talent pool means more to choose from; more effective managers tend to have a more diverse array of people around them. The rest will get the leftovers. Are you known for managing diversity well? Want increased motivation and productivity? There is a positive relationship between perceived equity/feeling valued and the performance of organizations. The business case boils down to more perspectives, more chances to learn, more ways to appeal to different market segments, and a more productive workforce where all employees think merit is what counts

in an organization. Read "Making Differences Matter: A New Paradigm for Managing Diversity" by Thomas and Ely in the *Harvard Business Review,* (HBR OnPoint Enhanced Edition) November 1, 2002.

2. **The first step to managing innovation is to understand your markets**—historically, today, and most importantly tomorrow. What have your customers done in the past? Which new products succeeded and which failed? What do they buy today? Among your current customers, what more do they want and are willing to pay for? For those who did not buy your product or service, what was missing? What do your competitors have that you don't? Talk to the strategic planners in your organization for their long-term forecasts. Talk to your key customers. What do they think their needs will be?

3. **Unearthing creative ideas.** Creative thought processes do not follow the formal rules of logic, where one uses cause and effect to prove or solve something. Some rules of creative thought are:

- Not using concepts but changing them; imagining this were something else.

- Move from one concept or way of looking at things to another, such as from economic to political.

- Generate ideas without judging them initially.

- Use information to restructure and come up with new patterns.

- Jump from one idea to another without justifying the jump.

- Look for the least likely and odd.

- Look for parallels far from the problem, such as how is an organization like a big oak tree?

- Ask what's missing or what's not here.

- Fascination with mistakes and failure as learning devices.

4. **Most innovations fail,** most proposals fail, most change efforts fail, anything worth doing takes repeated effort. To increase learning from your mistakes, design feedback loops to be as immediate as possible. The faster and the more frequent the cycles, the more opportunities to learn—if we do one smaller thing a day for three days instead of one bigger thing in three, we triple our learning opportunities.

5. **Change management.** Most significant vision and mission statements represent a deviation from the past. They represent a rallying call for a departure from business as usual. They require that people are going to have to think, talk, and act differently. For that reason, underneath the excitement will be apprehension, anxiety, and fear of the unknown. All of the principles of change management apply to communicating a mission. Expect trouble and admit that 20–40% of time will be spent debugging, fixing mistakes, and figuring out what went wrong. Treat each one as a chance to learn—document difficulties and learn from them. Without sounding like you're hedging, present it as a work-in-progress to be improved over time. How changes are made should be as open as possible. Studies show that people work harder and are more effective when they have a sense of choice over how they accomplish stretch goals and objectives. Invite multiple attacks, encourage experimentation, talk with people who have successfully pulled off changes.

If you sometimes overdo being Original:

1. **You may have significant trouble with time management.** Manage your time efficiently. Plan your time and manage against it. Be time sensitive. Value time. Figure out what you are worth per hour and minute by taking your gross salary plus overhead and benefits. Attach a monetary value on your time. Then ask, is this worth $56 of my time? Review your calendar over the past 90 days to figure out what your three largest time wasters are, and reduce them 50% by batching activities and using efficient communications like e-mail and voice mail for routine matters. Make a list of points to be covered in phone calls; set deadlines for yourself; use your best time of day for the toughest projects—if you're best in the morning, don't waste it on B and C level tasks.

2. **Set goals.** Nothing manages time better than a goal, a plan, and a measure. Set goals for yourself. These goals are essential for setting priorities. If you do not have goals, you can't set time priorities. Using the goals, separate what you need to do into mission-critical, important to get done, nice if there is time left over, and not central to what you are trying to achieve. When faced with choices or multiple things to do, apply the scale.

3. **Laying out tasks and work on a time line.** Most successful time managers begin with a good plan for time. What do I need to accomplish? What are the goals? What's mission-critical and what's

trivial? What's the time line? How will I track it? Buy a flowcharting software program that does PERT and GANTT charts. Become an expert in its use. Use the output of the software to plan your time. Alternatively, write down your work plan. Many people are seen as lacking time management skills because they don't write down the sequence or parts of the work and leave something out. Ask others to comment on ordering and what's missing.

4. **Be careful not to be guided by just what you like and what you don't like to do.** That way of using your time will probably not be successful over time. Use data, intuition, and even feelings to apportion your time, but not feelings alone.

5. **Another common time waster is inadequate disengagement skills.** Some poor time managers can't shut down transactions. Either they continue to talk beyond what would be necessary or, more commonly, they can't get the other party to quit talking. When it's time to move on, just say, "I have to get on to the next thing I have to do; we can pick this up some other time."

Thinking←→Feeling Facets

Thinking	Purpose: Making Decisions	Feeling
Logical (Impersonal, objective analysis) • Comprehension based on logical sense. • Seek internally consistent logical principles. • Point out implicit premises of situations. • Logical discrepancies weaken others' credibility.	Ideal decision-making strategy and decision-related criteria. **1**	**Empathetic** (Personal, feeling) • Prefer frameworks of relationships among people. • Identify motivations. • See logic as unique view of others. • Value different abilities, enjoy complexity.
Reasonable (Justice, cause and effect) • Seek to be consistently fair. • Want equitable solutions to problems. • Task-focused attention. • No favorites as they rely on principles of fairness and acceptable standards.	Standards for implementing decisions and maintaining relationships with others. **2**	**Compassionate** (Sympathy, tactful) • See the world as personalized and interconnected. • Enjoy unique needs of different people. • Care about the hopes, dreams, hurts, and discouragements of those around them.
Questioning (Precise, enjoy debate) • Ask questions to gain clarity and to solve problems. • Challenge established practices, designs, facts. • Find a common understanding.	How you handle differences of opinion. **5**	**Accommodating** (Approving, seek harmony) • Concerned with how "truth" is understood and valued. • Value harmony, seek consensus, keep peace. • May work to avoid confrontations.
Critical (Skeptical, want proof) • Critique to improve situations and to get at "the truth." • Honesty is more valuable than tact. • Sometimes hold suspect those who moderate viewpoints. • Judgment errors are more damning than a person's hurt feelings.	General action after an initial decision. **4**	**Accepting** (Tolerant, trusting) • Seek to affirm contributions and would rather act to develop relationships than to be critical and lose them. • Often overlook lapses in others. • Active in encouraging others to achieve and fulfill goals.
Tough (Firm, ends-oriented) • Stand firm in decisions made, feel secure that their judgment is good given the data. • Believe in the soundness of their decision-making processes. • Highly value detached judgment.	The way we stand by the impact of decisions. **3**	**Tender** (Gentle, means-oriented) • Effect of decisions on others is more important than the processes used in deciding. • Focus on how to give attention to each person. • There is no "absolute truth," so human interdependence is primary.

T↔F

Logical ◄─►Empathetic
Ideal decision-making strategy and decision-related criteria.

Logical (Impersonal, objective analysis)

■ Comprehension based on logical sense.

■ Seek internally consistent logical principles.

■ Point out implicit premises of situations.

■ Logical discrepancies weaken others' credibility.

To develop more of this facet:

1. **Don't know enough about your business?** Study your annual report and various other financial reports. If you don't know how, the major investment firms have basic documents explaining how to read financial documents. After you've done this, consult a pro and ask him/her what he/she looks at and why. Ask for lunch or just a meeting with the person who is in charge of the strategic planning process in your company. Have him/her explain the strategic plan for the organization. Particularly, have him/her point out the mission-critical functions and capabilities the organization needs to be on the leading edge to win.

2. **Are your problem performers confused?** Do they know what's expected of them? The first task is to outline the 5 to 10 key results areas and what indicators of success would be. Involve your problem direct reports on both ends—the standards and the indicators. Provide them with a fair way to measure their own progress. Employees with goals and standards are usually harder on themselves than you'll ever be. Often they set higher standards than you would.

3. **One of the most common problems with delegation** is incomplete or cryptic up-front communication leading to frustration, a job not well done the first time, rework, and a reluctance to delegate next time. Poor communicators always have to take more time managing because of rework. Analyze recent projects that went well and didn't go well. How did you delegate? Too much? Not enough? Unwanted pieces? Major chunks of responsibility? Workload distributed properly? Did you set measures? Overmanage or abdicate? Find out what your best practices are. Set up a series of delegation practices

that can be used as if you're not there. What do you have to be informed of? What feedback loops can people use for midcourse correction? What questions should be answered as the work proceeds? What steps should be followed? What are the criteria to be followed? When will you be available to help?

4. **Do an inventory of your personal strengths and weaknesses.** Get some input from others. Ask your people what they appreciate about you as a person and as a manager and what they would prefer you change. What do you do well and what don't you do well personally and as a manager of others?

5. **Do an inventory of the common management techniques and practices you do well** and those that you do not do so well or often enough. You can get a list of those techniques from any introductory text on management, from a course for first-time managers, or from the Human Resource function. Ask your people for input on those you do well and those you need to work on. Create a management practices skill-building plan for yourself.

6   **Fairness standards.** Install objective standards to determine the fairness of a treatment (pay, office choice, day off)—criteria, statistical models, professional standards, market value, cost models. Set standards anyone could independently measure and come up with the same conclusion.

7. **In meetings, make sure you include everyone,** and don't direct substantially more remarks toward one person or subgroup to the exclusion of others. Make sure you signal nothing negative to others; a neutral observer should not be able to tell from your demeanor whom you like and don't like. Help the quiet, shy, and reserved have their say. Quiet the loud, assertive, and passionate. Give everyone a fair chance to be heard.

8. **Think systems.** Subscribe to *The Systems Thinker®*, Pegasus Communications, Inc., Waltham, MA, 781-398-9700. This is a group dedicated to finding out how things work and why they work that way. They have a monthly publication as well as workshops, seminars, and other materials available to help you see the world as a series of recurring systems or archetypes. They analyze everyday events and processes and try to see why they work the way they do. They take complex problems and try to show how almost all problems are some form of seven classic models.

T↔F

9. **Lay out tasks and work.** Most successful projects begin with a good plan. What do I need to accomplish? What are the goals? What's the time line? What resources will I need? How many of the resources do I control? Who controls the rest of the resources—people, funding, tools, materials, support—I need? Lay out the work from A to Z.

10. **Watch your biases.** Some people have solutions in search of problems. They have favorite solutions. They have biases. They have universal solutions to most situations. They pre-judge what the problem is without stopping to consider the nuances of this specific problem. Do honest and open analysis first. Did you state as facts things that are really assumptions or opinions? Are you sure these assertions are facts? Did you generalize from a single example.

11. **Stop and first define what the problem is and isn't.** Since providing solutions is so easy for everyone, it would be nice if they were offering solutions to the right problem. Figure out what causes it. Keep asking why. See how many causes you can come up with and how many organizing buckets you can put them in. This increases the chance of a better solution because you can see more connections. Look for patterns in data; don't just collect information. Put it in categories that make sense to you. Ask lots of questions. Allot at least 50% of the time to defining the problem.

If you sometimes overdo being Logical:

1. **You may have problems with approachability.** Approachable people share more information and get more in return. Confide your thinking on a business issue and invite the response of others. Pass on tidbits of information you think will help people do their jobs better or broaden their perspectives. Disclose some things about yourself. It's hard for people to relate to an enigma. Reveal things that people don't need to know to do their jobs, but which will be interesting to them—and help them feel valued.

2. **Personalizing.** Approachable people work to know and remember important things about the people they work around, for, and with. Know three things about everybody—their interests or their children or something you can chat about other than the business agenda. Treat life as a small world. If you ask a few questions, you'll find you have something in common with virtually anyone. Establish things you can talk about with each person you work with that go beyond strictly work transactions. These need not be social—they could be

issues of strategy, global events, market shifts. The point is to forge common ground and connections.

3. **Watch your non-verbals.** Approachable people appear and sound open and relaxed. They smile. They are calm. They keep eye contact. They nod while the other person is talking. They have an open body posture. They speak in a paced and pleasant tone. Eliminate any disruptive habits, such as speaking too rapidly or forcefully, using strongly worded or loaded language, or going into too much detail. Watch out for signaling disinterest with actions like glancing at your watch, fiddling with paperwork, or giving your impatient "I'm busy" look.

4. **You may need to appear more accepting.** Try to listen without judging initially. Turn off your "I agree; I don't agree" filter. You don't have to agree with it; just listen to understand. Assume when people tell you something they are looking for understanding; indicate that by being able to summarize what they said. Don't offer advice or solutions unless it's obvious the person wants to know what you would do. While offering instant solutions is a good thing to do in many circumstances, it's chilling where the goal is to get people to talk to you more freely.

5. **You may need to show more compassion.** A primary reason for problems with compassion is that you don't know how to deal with strong feelings and appear distant or uninterested. You're uncomfortable with strong displays of emotion and calls for personal help. Simply imagine how you would feel in this situation and respond with that. Tell the person how sorry you are this has happened or has to be dealt with. Offer whatever help is reasonable. A day off. A loan. A resource. If you can, offer hope of a better day. This is what the person can use most.

6. **You may need to read people better.** To understand people, look to the obvious. What do they do first? What do they emphasize in their speech? People focus on different things—taking action, details, concepts, feelings, other people. What's their interaction style? People come in different styles—pushy, tough, soft, matter-of-fact, and so on. To figure these out, listen for the values behind their words and note what they have passion and emotion around. One key to getting anything of value done in the work world is the ability to see differences in people and to manage against and use those differences for everyone's benefit. Interpersonal savvy is meeting each person

where he/she is to get done what you need to get done. Basically, people respond favorably to ease of transaction. If you make it easy by accepting their normal mode of doing things, not fighting their style, and neither defending your own nor letting style get in the way of performance, things will generally run smoothly.

7. **You may need to read the politics of situations better.** For close-in political savvy (live in a meeting) you need to learn how to read non-verbals. Common signals of trouble are changes in body posture (especially turning away), crossed arms, staring, or the telltale glancing at one's watch, scribbling on the note pad, tapping one's fingers or a pencil, looking out the window, frowns, and washboard foreheads. When this occurs, pause. Ask a question. Ask how we're doing. Do a live process check.

Empathetic (Personal, feeling)

- Prefer frameworks of relationships among people.

- Identify motivations.

- See logic as unique view of others.

- Value different abilities, enjoy complexity.

To develop more of this facet:

1. **Try to see people more as individuals than members of a group.** Avoid putting people in grouped buckets. Many of us bucket people as can or can't do this. We have good buckets and bad buckets. Buckets I like/am comfortable with and buckets that bother me. Once we bucket, we generally don't relate as well to the off bucket people. Much of the time bucketing is based on like me—the good bucket; not like me—the bad bucket. Across time, the can do/like me bucket gets the majority of your attention, more feedback, stretching tasks, develops the most and performs the best, unfortunately proving your stereotyping again and again. To break this cycle, understand without judging. Be candid with yourself. Is there a group or groups you don't like or are uncomfortable with? Do you judge individual members of that group without really knowing if your stereotype is true? Most of us do. Try to see people as people.

2. **People focus on different things**—taking action, details, concepts, feelings, other people. What's their interaction style? People come in different styles—pushy, tough, soft, matter-of-fact, and so on. To

figure these out, listen for the values behind their words and note what they have passion and emotion around. One key to getting anything of value done in the work world is the ability to see differences in people and to manage against and use those differences for everyone's benefit. Always select your interpersonal approach from the other person in, not from you out. Your best choice of approach will always be determined by the other person or group, not you.

3. **To better figure out what drives people, look to:** What do they do first? What do they emphasize in their speech? What do they display emotion around? What values play out for them?

- First things. Does this person go to others first, hole up and study, complain, discuss feelings, or take action? These are the basic orientations of people that reveal what's important to them. Use these to motivate.

- Speech content. People might focus on details, concepts, feelings, or other people in their speech. This can tell you again how to appeal to them by mirroring their speech emphasis. Although most of us naturally adjust—we talk details with detail-oriented people—chances are good that in problem relationships you're not finding the common ground. She talks "detail" and you talk "people," for example.

- Emotion. You need to know what people's hot buttons are because one mistake can get you labeled as insensitive with some people. The only cure here is to see what turns up the volume for them—either literally or what they're concerned about.

- Values. Apply the same thinking to the values of others. Do they talk about money, recognition, integrity, efficiency in their normal work conversation? Figuring out what their drivers are tells you another easy way to appeal to anyone.

4. **Be able to speak their language at their level.** It shows respect for their way of thinking. Speaking their language makes it easier for them to talk with you and give you the information you need to motivate.

5. **How to start.** Start with three things you can talk about with almost anyone without risking uncomfortable personal disclosure. Vacations, hobbies, business interests, your thinking on business issues, children,

etc. Decide what they are and make a conscious effort to sprinkle them into some of your interactions with others you have generally had only a business relationship with before. Notice the reaction. Did they also share for the first time? Usually yes. And that's the point. Within limits, the more you know about each other, the better the working relationship will be.

6. **How do people know you are listening?** You have eye contact. You take notes. You don't frown or fidget. How do people know you've understood? You paraphrase what they have said to their satisfaction. How do people know if you have accepted or rejected what they said? You tell them. Hopefully in a tactful way if you reject what they had to say. Give your reasons.

7. **Challenge yourself to practice listening to those you don't usually listen to.** Listen for content. Separate the content from the person. Try to ferret out some value from everyone.

8. **Listening chillers?** Don't interrupt before they have finished. Don't suggest words when they hesitate or pause. Don't finish their sentences for them. Don't wave off any further input by saying, "Yes, I know that." "Yes, I know where you're going." "Yes, I have heard that before." If time is really important, you can say, "Let me see if I know where this is going…," or "I wonder if we could summarize to save both of us some time?" Finally, early in a transaction, answers, solutions, conclusions, statements, and dictates shut many people down. You've told them your mind is already made up. Listen first, solve second.

9. **Get feedback from a wide group**—boss, peers, higher management, direct reports, even friends and colleagues from off-work. Find out how you impact each group and individual. To increase empathy, you need a start point of how you come across now. A good, safe mechanism to get you started is 360° feedback.

If you sometimes overdo being Empathetic:

1. **You may get caught in the various emotions flying about and fail to take action.** Don't like risk? Sometimes taking action involves pushing the envelope, taking chances, and trying bold new initiatives. Doing those things leads to more misfires and mistakes. Research says that successful executives have made more mistakes in their careers than those who didn't make it. Treat any mistakes or failures as chances to learn. Nothing ventured, nothing gained. Up your risk

comfort. Start small so you can recover more quickly. Go for small wins. Don't blast into a major task to prove your boldness. Break it down into smaller tasks. Take the easiest one for you first. Then build up to the tougher ones. Review each one to see what you did well and not well, and set goals so you'll do something differently and better each time.

2. **Leading is riskier than following.** While there are a lot of personal rewards for leading, leading puts you in the limelight. Think about what happens to political leaders and the scrutiny they face. Leaders have to be internally secure. Do you feel good about yourself? They have to please themselves first that they are on the right track. Can you defend to a critical and impartial audience the wisdom of what you're doing? They have to accept lightning bolts from detractors. Can you take the heat? People will always say it should have been done differently. Listen to them, but be skeptical. Even great leaders are wrong sometimes. They accept personal responsibility for errors and move on to lead some more. Don't let criticism prevent you from taking the lead. Build up your heat shield. Conduct a postmortem immediately after finishing milestone efforts. This will indicate to all that you're open to continuous improvement whether the result was stellar or not.

3. **You may be nervous around higher management.** Worst case it. List all of your worst fears; what bad things do you think might happen; envision yourself in each of those situations; mentally practice how you would recover. Can't think of the right words? Pause, don't fill the void with "uhs." Refer to your notes. Feeling defensive? Ask a question. Running overtime? Go straight to the conclusion. Practice the more realistic recoveries live in front of a mirror or with a colleague playing the audience.

4. **You may have problems with conflict.** Most emotional responses to conflict come from personalizing the issue. Separate people issues from the problem at hand, and deal with people issues separately and later if they persist. Always return to facts and the problem before the group; stay away from personal clashes. Attack the problem by looking at common interests and underlying concerns, not people and their positions. Try on their views for size—the emotion as well as the content. Ask yourself if you understand their feelings. Ask what they would do if they were in your shoes. See if you can restate each other's position and advocate it for a minute to get inside each other's

place. If you get emotional, pause and collect yourself. You are not your best when you get emotional. Then return to the problem.

5. **You may need to broaden your perspective.** At work, pick three tasks you've never done and go do them. If you don't know much about customers, work in a store or handle customer complaints; if you don't know what engineering does, go find out; task trade with someone. Seek the broadest possible exposure inside the organization. Do lunch with counterparts of the organization and tell each other what you do. Task forces/projects are a great opportunity. If the project is important, is multi-functional, and has a real outcome which will be taken seriously (not a study group), it is one of the most common developmental events listed by successful executives.

6. **During World War II, the military discovered the most creative groups were those where the members had little or nothing in common and knew little about the issue.** Their freewheeling approach yielded fresher solutions. They were not trapped by the past. Take a current challenge to the most disparate group you can find (a historian, a college student, a theologian, a salesperson, a plumber, etc.) and see what insights they have into it. Find some problems outside of your area and see what you can add.

Reasonable←→Compassionate
Standards for implementing decisions and maintaining relationships with others.

Reasonable (Justice, cause and effect)

- Seek to be consistently fair.

- Want equitable solutions to problems.

- Task-focused attention.

- No favorites as they rely on principles of fairness and acceptable standards.

To develop more of this facet:

1. **Fairness seems simple; treat all people the same.** Lack of fairness plays out in many ways: Do you treat high performers differently than everyone else? Do you have favorite and less favorite groups? Do you develop some but not others? Do your ethics seem variable to

direct reports? Does your candor vary? It's usually best to think of fairness as equity toward others and not signaling to others what your assessment is of them in your day-to-day behavior. A more subtle way to think of fairness is to treat each person equitably, that is according to his or her needs. The treatment would actually differ somewhat from person to person but the outcome or effect would be the same; each person would feel fairly treated. A large part of each person's motivation will be determined by his/her feelings about fair treatment. Unfair treatment causes all kinds of noise in the relationship between a boss and a direct report and causes noise in the group. Unfair treatment leads to less productivity, less efficiency, and wasted time seeking justice.

2. **Equity with information.** Follow the rule of equity of information with everyone. Explain your thinking and ask them to explain theirs. When discussing issues, give reasons first, solutions last. When you give solutions first, people often don't listen to your reasons. Some people get overly directive with some of their reports, and they, in turn, feel that you're not interested in what they think. Invite their thinking and their reasons before settling on solutions. Don't provide information selectively. Don't use information as a reward or a relationship builder with one or just a few and not others.

3. **Equity with groups.** Monitor yourself carefully to see if you treat different groups or people differently. Common patterns are to treat low performers, people with less status, and people from outside your unit with less respect. Be candid with yourself. Is there a group or individuals you don't like or are uncomfortable with? Have you put them in your not very respected bucket? Many of us do. To break out of this, ask yourself why they behave the way they do and how you would like to be treated if you were in their position. Turn off your judgment program.

4. **Equity with standards.** Check to make sure you are not excusing a behavior in a high performer that you wouldn't tolerate in someone else. Does everyone have the same rules and get held to the same standard? Install objective standards to determine the fairness of a treatment (pay, office choice, day off)—criteria, statistical models, professional standards, market value, cost models. Set standards anyone could independently measure and come up with the same conclusion.

T↔F

5. **Do you help your people learn by looking for repeating patterns?** Help them look for patterns in the situations and problems they deal with. What succeeded and what failed? What was common to each success or what was present in each failure but never present in a success? Focus on the successes; failures are easier to analyze but don't in themselves tell you what would work. Comparing successes, while less exciting, yields more information. The bottom line is help them reduce insights to principles or rules of thumb that might be repeatable. Ask them what they have learned to increase their skills and understanding, making them better managers or professionals. Ask them what they can do now that they couldn't do a year ago. Reinforce this and encourage more of it. Developing is learning in as many ways as possible.

6. **Clear problem-focused communication.** Follow the rule of equity: Explain your thinking and ask them to explain theirs. Be able to state their position as clearly as they do whether you agree or not—give it legitimacy. Separate facts from opinions and assumptions. Generate a variety of possibilities first rather than stake out positions. Keep your speaking to 30–60 second bursts. Try to get them to do the same. Don't give the other side the impression you're lecturing or criticizing them. Explain objectively why you hold a view; make the other side do the same. Ask lots of questions, make fewer statements. To identify interests behind positions, ask why they hold them or why they wouldn't want to do something. Always restate their position to their satisfaction before offering a response.

7. **Delivering tough messages.** Don't overwhelm the person/group, even if you have a lot to say. Go from specific to general points. Keep it to the facts. Don't embellish to make your point. No passion or inflammatory language. Don't do it to harm or out of vengeance. Don't do it in anger. If feelings are involved for you, wait until you can describe them, not show them.

If you sometimes overdo being Reasonable:

1. **You may delegate, but then become hands-on and overmanage.** How to delegate? Communicate, set time frames and goals, and get out of the way. People need to know what it is you expect. What does the outcome look like? When do you need it by? What's the budget? What resources do they get? What decisions can they make? Do you want checkpoints along the way? How will we both know and measure how well the task is done?

2. **Analyze recent projects that went well and didn't go well.** How did you delegate? Too much? Not enough? Unwanted pieces? Major chunks of responsibility? Workload distributed properly? Did you set measures? Overmanage or abdicate? Find out what your best practices are. Set up a series of delegation practices that can be used as if you're not there. What do you have to be informed of? What feedback loops can people use for midcourse correction? What questions should be answered as the work proceeds? What steps should be followed? What are the criteria to be followed? When will you be available to help?

3. **More what and why, less how.** The best delegators are crystal clear on what and when, and more open on how. People are more motivated when they can determine the how for themselves. Inexperienced delegators include the hows, which turn the people into task automatons instead of an empowered and energized staff. Tell them what and when and for how long, and let them figure out how on their own. Give them leeway. Encourage them to try things. Besides being more motivating, it's also more developmental for them. Add the larger context. Although it is not necessary to get the task done, people are more motivated when they know where this task fits in the bigger picture. Take three extra minutes and tell them why this task needs to be done, where it fits in the grander scheme, and its importance to the goals and objectives of the unit.

4. **Monitoring delegated tasks.** Do you micromanage? If you're constantly looking over shoulders, you're not delegating. A properly communicated and delegated task doesn't need to be monitored. If you must monitor, set time-definite checkpoints: by the calendar, every Monday, by percentage, after each 10% is complete, or by outcome—such as when you have the first draft. Be approachable for help, but not intrusive. Intervene only when agreed-upon criteria are not being followed or expectations are not being met. This focuses on the task, not the person. Let people finish their work.

5. **You may talk more about tactics than strategy. Become a strategic activist.** Pick one distinctive competence or driving force. That's what the mediocre companies who became successful over time did in James Collins' latest research. Create a strategic plan for your unit around one distinctive competence—include breakthrough process and product improvements, justify your conclusions by pointing to hard data that points toward your conclusions. Have the plan reviewed by people you trust. Form a consortium with three other

individuals or companies; each of you will present a strategic issue and a plan backed up with data and rationale. Agree to review your thinking every three months with this group and write down lessons learned. Analyze three business/organizational success stories in your area and the same number of failures. What did each have in common? How would these principles apply in your situation? What was common to the failures that was never present in the successes?

Compassionate (Sympathy, tactful)

■ See the world as personalized and interconnected.

■ Enjoy unique needs of different people.

■ Care about the hopes, dreams, hurts, and discouragements of those around them.

To develop more of this facet:

1. **Caring is treating people differently.** Caring is not treating people equally, it's treating people equitably. People are different. They have different needs. They respond differently to you. They have different dreams and concerns. Each person is unique and feels best when treated uniquely.

2. **Know three things about everybody**—their interests or their children or something you can chat about other than the business agenda. Treat life as a small world. If you ask a few questions, you'll find you have something in common with virtually anyone. Establish things you can talk about with each person you work with that go beyond strictly work transactions.

3. **Try to listen without judging initially.** Turn off your "I agree; I don't agree" filter. You don't have to agree with it; just listen to understand. Assume when people tell you something they are looking for understanding; indicate that by being able to summarize what they said. Don't offer advice or solutions unless it's obvious the person wants to know what you would do. While offering instant solutions is a good thing to do in many circumstances, it's chilling where the goal is to get people to talk to you more freely.

4. **Study the people you work with.** Without judging them, collect evidence on how they think and what they do. What drives them to do what they do? Try to predict what they will do in given situations.

Use this to understand how to relate to them. What are their hot buttons? What would they like for you to care about?

5. **Imagine how you would feel in this situation and respond with that.** Tell the person how sorry you are this has happened or has to be dealt with. Offer whatever help is reasonable. A day off. A loan. A resource. If you can, offer hope of a better day. This is what the person can use most.

6. **Compassion is not always advice.** Don't offer advice unless asked. Indicate support through listening and a helpful gesture. There will be time for advice when the situation isn't so emotionally charged. Many times managers are too quick with advice before they really understand the problem.

7. **Do you show compassion for one group's problems but not another's?** To deal with this:

   ■ Put yourself in their case. Why would you act that way? What do you think they're trying to achieve? Assume that however they act is rational to them; it must have paid off or they wouldn't be doing it. Don't use your internal standards.

   ■ Avoid putting groups in buckets. Many of us bucket groups as friendly or unfriendly, good or bad, like me or not like me. Once we do, we generally don't show as much compassion toward them and may question their motives. Apply the logic of why people belong to the group in the first place. See if you can predict accurately what the group will say or do across situations to test your understanding of the group. Don't use your agreement program.

8. **Being sensitive.** You need to know what people's compassion hot buttons are because one mistake can get you labeled as insensitive with some people. The only cure here is to see what turns up the volume for them—either literally or what they're concerned about. Be careful of downplaying or demeaning someone else's cause (like the Native American community trying to remove Indian nicknames from athletic teams).

9. **Caring is signaling that you care.** Watch out for unintentionally signaling to people that you don't care. A—"I leave the details to others"; B—"I'm not very organized"; C—"I've always believed in taking action then sorting it out later"; might mean A—"What I do isn't important"; B—"I'm left to pick up the pieces"; and C—"I have

to deal with the havoc," to your direct reports. Think about impact on them when you speak.

If you sometimes overdo being Compassionate:

1. **You may focus on individuals more than the vision or goal of the project or group.** First, get clear on your purpose, then work on common mind-set. The power of a mission and vision communication is providing everyone in the organization with a road map on how they are going to be part of something grand and exciting. Establish common cause. Imagine what the change would look like if fully implemented, then describe the outcome often—how things will look in the future. Help people see how their efforts fit in by creating simple, obvious measures of achievement like bar or thermometer charts. Be succinct. People don't line up behind laundry lists or ambiguous objectives. Missions and visions should be more about where we are going and less about how we are going to get there. Keep your eyes on the prize.

2. **Results may come second.** Hard as that may be to consider, if you are overdoing being compassionate, results may be suffering. Go back to your priorities. What's mission-critical? What are the three to five things that most need to get done to achieve your goals? Effective performers typically spend about half their time on a few mission-critical priorities. Don't get diverted by trivia and things you like doing but that aren't tied to the bottom line.

3. **You may attend too much to people at the expense of your work.** Do an inventory of the common management techniques and practices you do well and those that you do not do so well or often enough. Think about the practices below in particular:

   ■ Do a communication check on yourself. How well do you inform? Explain? Get back to people? Give feedback?

   ■ Do you delegate enough? Do you give the people under you the authority to do their work? Do you over- or undermanage? Periodically, ask your people to give you a list of the things they think you are doing yourself that they believe they could do a good job on; delegate some of the things on everybody's list.

   ■ Are you organized and planful? Can people follow what you want? Do you lay out work and tasks to be done clearly? Do you set clear goals and objectives that can guide their work?

■ Do you confront problems directly and quickly or do you let things fester?

4. **You may need to improve in sizing up people.** Become a student of the people around you. First, try to outline their strengths and weaknesses, their preferences and beliefs. Watch out for traps—it is rarely general intelligence or pure personality that spells the difference in people. Most people are smart enough, and many personality characteristics don't matter that much for performance. Ask a second question. Look below surface descriptions of smart, approachable, technically skilled people to describe specifics. Then try to predict ahead of time what they would do in specific circumstances. What percent of the time are your predictions correct? Try to increase the percent over time.

5. **You need to match people differences and differences in task requirements.** People are different; tasks are different. People have different strengths and have different levels of knowledge and experience. Instead of thinking of everyone as equal, think of them as different. Equal treatment is really giving each person tasks to do that match their capacities. Look at the success profile of each assignment and line it up with the capabilities of each person. Assign things based upon that match.

Questioning↔Accommodating
How you handle differences of opinion.

Questioning (Precise, enjoy debate)

■ Ask questions to gain clarity and to solve problems.

■ Challenge established practices, designs, facts.

■ Find a common understanding.

To develop more of this facet:

1. **Try to add one minute to your thinking time.** Go through a mental checklist to see if you have thought about all of the ramifications of the problem or challenge. Go into any learning event with a goal. Ask questions about what you read. Chunk up what you learn. Put it in categories that make sense to you. Other research has shown that the first thing or solution you think of is seldom the best choice. Usually

somewhere between the second and third choice turns out to be the most effective.

2. **When faced with a new issue, challenge, or problem, figure out what causes it.** Keep asking why. See how many causes you can come up with and how many organizing buckets you can put them in. This increases the chance of a better solution because you can see more connections. Chess masters recognize thousands of possible patterns of chess pieces. Look for patterns in data; don't just collect information. Put it in categories that make sense to you.

3. **Locate the essence of the problem.** What are the key factors or elements in this problem? Experts usually solve problems by figuring out what the deep, underlying principles are and working forward from there; the less adept focus on desired outcomes/solutions and either work backward or concentrate on the surface facts. What are the deep principles of what you're working on? Once you've done this, search the past for parallels—your past, the business past, the historical past.

4. **Patterns. Look for patterns in personal, organization, or the world, in general successes and failures.** What was common to each success or what was present in each failure but never present in a success? Focus on the successes; failures are easier to analyze but don't in themselves tell you what would work. Comparing successes, while less exciting, yields more information about underlying principles. The bottom line is to reduce your insights to principles or rules of thumb you think might be repeatable. When faced with the next new problem, those general underlying principles will apply again.

5. **Use experts.** Find an expert or experts in your functional/ technical/business area and go find out how they think and solve new problems. Ask them what are the critical principles/ drivers/things they look for. Have them tell you how they thought through a new problem in this area, the major skills they look for in sizing up people's proficiency in this area, key questions they ask about a problem, how they would suggest you go about learning quickly in this area.

6. **Too often we think first and only of solutions.** In studies of problem-solving sessions, solutions outweigh questions 8 to 1. Most meetings on a problem start with people offering solutions. Early solutions are not likely to be the best. Set aside 50% of the time for questions and problem definition, and the last 50% for solutions. Asking more

questions early helps you rethink the problem and come to more and different solutions.

7. **Studies show that defining the problem and taking action occur almost simultaneously for most people,** so the more effort you put on the front end, the easier it is to come up with a good solution. Stop and first define what the problem is and isn't. Since providing solutions is so easy for everyone, it would be nice if they were offering solutions to the right problem.

8. **Try many experiments or trials to find something that will work.** Have the group think beyond current boundaries. What are some of the most sacred rules or practices in your organization? Unit? Think about smashing them—what would your unit be doing if you broke the rules? Talk to the most irreverent person you know about this. Buffer the group. It's difficult to work on something new if they are besieged with all the distractions you have to deal with, particularly if people are looking over your shoulder asking why isn't anything happening.

If you sometimes overdo being Questioning:

1. **You may come across as critical and invasive.** Pause, and explain why you are asking what you are asking. People are put off by question after question. They almost immediately ask why am I being asked all these questions? What is behind this?

2. **Share your thinking.** To help those around you grow and learn from what you know, you have to sometimes think out loud. You have to share your thinking from the initial presentation of the issue through to conclusion. Most of us are on thinking autopilot. We don't think about thinking. When someone else has to or wants to understand how you came up with a decision, it's sometimes difficult to unravel it in your mind. You have to go step-by-step and recreate your thinking. Sometimes it helps if other people ask the questions. They can probably guide you through how you came up with an answer or a decision better than you can. Once in a while, you should document a decision or two. What was the issue? What were the pros and cons you considered? How did you weight things? Then you can use those examples to demonstrate to others how you make decisions.

3. **Cryptic informer.** Some people just aren't good at informing. Their communication styles are not effective. According to behavioral research studies, the most effective communicators: speak often, but

briefly (15–30 seconds); ask more questions than others; make fewer solution statements early in a discussion; headline their points in a sentence or two; summarize frequently, and make more frequent "here's where we are" statements; invite everyone to share their views; and typically interject their views after others have had a chance to speak, unless they are passing on decisions. Compare these practices to yours. Work on those that are not up to standard.

4. **You may run into problems with peers who may view this as competitiveness.** If peers see you as excessively competitive, they will cut you out of the loop and may sabotage your cross-border attempts. To be seen as more cooperative, always explain your thinking and invite them to explain theirs. Generate a variety of possibilities first rather than stake out positions. Be tentative, allowing them room to customize the situation. Focus on common goals, priorities, and problems. Invite criticism of your ideas.

5. **Influencing.** Peers generally do not have power over each other. That means that influence skills, understanding, and trading are the currencies to use. Don't just ask for things; find some common ground where you can provide help. What do the peers you're contacting need? Do you really know how they see the issue? Is it even important to them? How does what you're working on affect them? If it affects them negatively, can you trade something, appeal to the common good, figure out some way to minimize the work (volunteering staff help, for example)? Go into peer relationships with a trading mentality.

6. **Your boss may see you as difficult to deal with.** Do you question almost everything as a matter of course or to learn, but receive stares or exasperation in return? Then focus on the three key problems you need to work on with him/her and do them. Keep your conversations with the boss directed at these core agenda. Focus on expectations, ask what results indicate success. Find out about your boss's job and what sorts of pressures he/she is under. Explain more and make more statements. Consider these strategies: Ask what strengths you can appeal to; ask what you can provide that the boss needs; ask what the boss would like for you to do to be more effective; design a project that you can do together so you can have a success experience; and consult with others for advice.

7. **Your questioning nature may get you in trouble** with people who don't think that way and see your questioning as doubting the

competence of other ethnic groups or disapproval of difference. Stereotypes? You have to understand your own subtle stereotyping. Helen Astin's research showed that both men and women rated women managers at the extremes (very high or very low) while they rated men on a normal curve. Do you think redheads have tempers? Blondes have more fun? Overweight people are lazy? Women are more emotional at work? Men can't show emotion? Find out your own pattern. Attend a course which delves into perception of others. Most stereotyping is false. Even if there are surface differences, they don't make a difference in performance.

8. **You may not understand diversity issues as well as you might.** Try to see people more as individuals than members of a group. Avoid putting people in grouped buckets. Many of us bucket people as can or can't do this. We have good buckets and bad buckets. Buckets I like/am comfortable with and buckets that bother me. Once we bucket, we generally don't relate as well to the off bucket people. Much of the time bucketing is based on like me—the good bucket; not like me—the bad bucket. Across time, the can do/like me bucket gets the majority of your attention, more feedback, stretching tasks, develops the most and performs the best, unfortunately proving your stereotyping again and again. To break this cycle, understand without judging. Be candid with yourself. Is there a group or groups you don't like or are uncomfortable with? Do you judge individual members of that group without really knowing if your stereotype is true? Most of us do. Try to see people as people.

9. **Learn to be a cultural anthropologist.** In assessing groups, ask yourself: What makes their blood boil? What do they believe? What are they trying to accomplish together? What do they smile at? What norms and customs do they have? What practices and behaviors do they share? Do they not like it if you stand too close? If you get right down to business? Do they like first names or are they more formal? If a Japanese manager presents his card, do you know what to do? Why do they have their cards printed in two languages and executives from the U.S. don't? Do you know what jokes are okay to tell? What do they believe about you and your group or groups? Positive? Neutral? Negative? What's been the history of their group and yours? Is this a first contact or a long history? Don't blunder in; nothing will kill you quicker with a group than showing utter disregard—read disrespect—for it and its norms, or having no idea of how they view your group. Ask people for insights who deal with this

group often. If it's an important group to you and your business, read about it.

Accommodating (Approving, seek harmony)

- Concerned with how "truth" is understood and valued.

- Value harmony, seek consensus, keep peace.

- May work to avoid confrontations.

To develop more of this facet:

1. **Equity with groups.** Monitor yourself carefully to see if you treat different groups or people differently. Common patterns are to treat low performers, people with less status, and people from outside your unit with less respect. Be candid with yourself. Is there a group or individuals you don't like or are uncomfortable with? Have you put them in your not very respected bucket? Many of us do. To break out of this, ask yourself why they behave the way they do and how you would like to be treated if you were in their position. Turn off your judgment program.

2. **Do you show compassion for one group's problems but not another's?** To deal with this:

   - Put yourself in their case. Why would you act that way? What do you think they're trying to achieve? Assume that however they act is rational to them; it must have paid off or they wouldn't be doing it. Don't use your internal standards.

   - Avoid putting groups in buckets. Many of us bucket groups as friendly or unfriendly, good or bad, like me or not like me. Once we do, we generally don't show as much compassion toward them and may question their motives. Apply the logic of why people belong to the group in the first place. See if you can predict accurately what the group will say or do across situations to test your understanding of the group. Don't use your agreement program.

   - Listen. Even though this tip may seem obvious, many of us tune out when dealing with difficult or not-well-understood groups, or reject what they're saying before they say it. Just listen. Mentally summarize their views, and see if you can figure out what they want from what they say and mean. The true test is whether you can clearly figure it out, even though you don't think that way.

3. **Caring is accepting.** Try to listen without judging initially. Turn off your "I agree; I don't agree" filter. You don't have to agree with it; just listen to understand. Assume when people tell you something they are looking for understanding; indicate that by being able to summarize what they said. Don't offer advice or solutions unless it's obvious the person wants to know what you would do. While offering instant solutions is a good thing to do in many circumstances, it's chilling where the goal is to get people to talk to you more freely.

4. **Caring is understanding.** Study the people you work with. Without judging them, collect evidence on how they think and what they do. What drives them to do what they do? Try to predict what they will do in given situations. Use this to understand how to relate to them. What are their hot buttons? What would they like for you to care about?

5. **Establish a common cause and a shared mind-set.** A common thrust is what energizes dream teams. As in light lasers, alignment adds focus, power, and efficiency. It's best to get each team member involved in setting the common vision. Establish goals and measures. Most people like to be measured. People like to have checkpoints along the way to chart their progress. Most people perform better with goals that are stretching. Again, letting the team participate in setting the goals is a plus.

6. **There are as many interpretations of what's fair as there are people in your world.** Try to get the whole group involved in questions of fairness. Get everyone's opinion about how fair a particular program or treatment is. Let them tell you what's fair before you make that judgment for them without input. Everyone will feel better treated when they have had a hand in determining the rules.

7. **In negotiations, set rapport and boundaries.** Start slow until you know where the other party is coming from. Pay attention to positioning. You and your team on one side and them on the other sets up a contest. Try to mix team members together on both sides. If you're the host, start with small talk unrelated to the subject of the negotiation. Give everyone time to settle in and get comfortable. When it's time, ask whether it would be useful for each side to lay out its goals, starting positions, and any boundaries, such as we aren't here to negotiate costs at this time. Volunteer to go first. Give reasons

first, positions last. When you offer goals and positions, people often don't listen to your reasons.

8. **In win-win and something-something negotiations,** the more information you have about the other side, the more you will have to work with. What can you learn about what they know before going in? What will they do if they don't reach an agreement with you? In the negotiation, ask more questions, make fewer statements. Ask clarifying questions: "What did you mean by that?" Probes: "Why do you say that?" Motives: "What led you to that position?" When the other side takes a rigid position, don't reject it. Ask why: What are the principles behind the offer? How do we know it's fair? What's the theory of the case? Play out what would happen if their position was accepted. Get everything out that you can. Don't negotiate assumptions, negotiate facts.

If you sometimes overdo being Accommodating:

1. **You may have problems with conflict.** Most emotional responses to conflict come from personalizing the issue. Separate people issues from the problem at hand, and deal with people issues separately and later if they persist. Always return to facts and the problem before the group; stay away from personal clashes. Attack the problem by looking at common interests and underlying concerns, not people and their positions. Try on their views for size—the emotion as well as the content. Ask yourself if you understand their feelings. Ask what they would do if they were in your shoes. See if you can restate each other's position and advocate it for a minute to get inside each other's place. If you get emotional, pause and collect yourself. You are not your best when you get emotional. Then return to the problem.

2. **Clear problem-focused communication.** Follow the rule of equity: Explain your thinking and ask them to explain theirs. Be able to state their position as clearly as they do whether you agree or not—give it legitimacy. Separate facts from opinions and assumptions. Generate a variety of possibilities first rather than stake out positions. Keep your speaking to 30–60 second bursts. Try to get them to do the same. Don't give the other side the impression you're lecturing or criticizing them. Explain objectively why you hold a view; make the other side do the same. Ask lots of questions, make fewer statements. To identify interests behind positions, ask why they hold them or why they wouldn't want to do something. Always restate their position to their satisfaction before offering a response.

3. **Tend to shy away from managerial courage situations?** Why? What's getting in your way? Are you prone to give up in tough situations, fear exposing yourself, don't like conflict, what? Ask yourself—what's the downside of delivering a message you think is right and will eventually help the organization but may cause someone short-term pain. What if it turns out you were wrong? Treat any misinterpretations as chances to learn. What if you were the target person or group? Even though it might hurt, would you appreciate it if someone brought the data to your attention in time for you to fix it with minimal damage? What would you think of a person whom you later found out knew about it and didn't come forward, and you had to spend inordinate amounts of time and political currency to fix it? Follow your convictions. Follow due process. Step up to the plate and be responsible, win or lose. People will think better of you in the long term.

4. **You may also not be clear with problem performers.** Do they know what's expected of them? You may not set clear enough performance standards, goals, and objectives. You may be a cryptic communicator. You may communicate to some and not to others. You may have given up on some and stopped communicating. Or you may think they would know what to do if they're any good, but that's not really true because you have not properly communicated what you want. The first task is to outline the 5 to 10 key results areas and what indicators of success would be. Involve your problem direct reports on both ends—the standards and the indicators. Provide them with a fair way to measure their own progress.

5. **Realism.** They are not performing up to standard? It's common to see 90-day improve-or-else plans that no one can accomplish: be more strategic, improve your interpersonal skills, learn about the business, be less arrogant. Ask yourself how long did it take you to become proficient at what you are criticizing this person for. Because managers hesitate delivering negative messages, we get to people late.

THINKING–FEELING FACETS

T↔F

Critical↔Accepting
General action after an initial decision.

Critical (Skeptical, want proof)

- Critique to improve situations and to get at "the truth."

- Honesty is more valuable than tact.

- Sometimes hold suspect those who moderate viewpoints.

- Judgment errors are more damning than a person's hurt feelings.

To develop more of this facet:

1. **Clear problem-focused communication.** Follow the rule of equity: Explain your thinking and ask them to explain theirs. Be able to state their position as clearly as they do whether you agree or not—give it legitimacy. Separate facts from opinions and assumptions. Generate a variety of possibilities first rather than stake out positions. Keep your speaking to 30–60 second bursts. Try to get them to do the same. Don't give the other side the impression you're lecturing or criticizing them. Explain objectively why you hold a view; make the other side do the same. Ask lots of questions, make fewer statements. To identify interests behind positions, ask why they hold them or why they wouldn't want to do something. Always restate their position to their satisfaction before offering a response.

2. **Give reasons first, solutions last.** When you give solutions first, people often directly challenge the solutions instead of defining the problem. Pick words that are other-person neutral. Pick words that don't challenge or sound one-sided. Pick tentative and probabilistic words that give others a chance to maneuver and save face. Pick words that are about the problem and not the person. Avoid direct blaming remarks; describe the problem and its impact.

3. **Developing cooperative relationships** involves demonstrating real and perceived equity, the other side feeling understood and respected, and taking a problem-oriented point of view. To do this more: Increase the realities and perceptions of fairness—don't try to win every battle and take all the spoils; focus on the common-ground issues and interests of both sides—find wins on both sides, give in on little points; avoid starting with entrenched positions—show respect for

658

them and their positions; and reduce any remaining conflicts to the smallest size possible.

4. **Let the other side vent frustration or blow off steam, but don't react.** Listen. Nod. Ask clarifying questions. Ask open-ended questions like, "What one change could you make so we could achieve our objectives better?" "What could I do that would help the most?" Restate their position periodically to signal you have understood. But don't react. Keep them talking until they run out of venom. When the other side takes a rigid position, don't reject it. Ask why: What are the principles behind the position? How do we know it's fair? What's the theory of the case? Play out what would happen if their position was accepted. Then explore the underlying concern. Separate the people from the problem.

5. **Be succinct.** You have limited attention span in tough feedback situations. Don't waste time with a long preamble, particularly if the feedback is negative. If the feedback is negative and the recipient is likely to know it, go ahead and say it directly. They won't hear anything positive you have to say anyway. Don't overwhelm the person/group, even if you have a lot to say. Go from specific to general points. Keep it to the facts. Don't embellish to make your point. No passion or inflammatory language. Don't do it to harm or out of vengeance. Don't do it in anger. If feelings are involved for you, wait until you can describe them, not show them. Managerial courage comes in search of a better outcome, not destroying others. Stay calm and cool. If others are not composed, don't respond. Just return to the message.

6. **Tough concern.** Don't forget the pathos of the situation—even if you're totally right, feelings may run high. If you have to be critical, you can still empathize with how he/she feels, and you can help with encouragement when the discussion turns more positive. Mentally rehearse for worst-case scenarios. Anticipate what the person might say and have responses prepared so as not to be caught off guard.

7. **Keeping your cool.** Sometimes our emotional reactions lead others to think we are weak and have problems with tough situations. How do you show emotions? In negotiations, what emotional reactions do you have, such as impatience, interrupting, denials, or non-verbals like fidgeting or drumming your fingers? Learn to recognize those as soon as they start and ask a question instead to bide time, or ask the person to tell you more about his/her point of view. Let the other side vent

T↔F

frustration or blow off steam, but don't react. Return to facts and the problem before the group, staying away from personal clashes.

8. **Put balance in your messages.** Don't get the reputation of being the executioner or the official organization critic. Try to deliver as much positive information as negative over time. Keep track of the losers— if you have to work with these people again, do something later to show goodwill. Compliment them on a success, share something, help them achieve something. You have to balance the scales.

9. **In the case of dealing with upper management, being more critical means explaining your thinking in a way that solves/informs major problems they face.** Learn their language and how they think, then tailor your communications to focus on critical problems and critical solutions. Simply being critical won't work. It may get you the reputation of being negative and offering little that is constructive.

If you sometimes overdo being Critical:

1. **Turn off your judgment program.** In trying to reach someone, work on not judging him/her. You don't have to agree, you just have to understand in order to motivate. The fact that you wouldn't be motivated that way isn't relevant.

2. **Be able to speak their language at their level.** It shows respect for their way of thinking. Speaking their language makes it easier for them to talk with you and give you the information you need to motivate.

3. **If peers see you as excessively competitive, they will cut you out of the loop and may sabotage your cross-border attempts.** To be seen as more cooperative, always explain your thinking and invite them to explain theirs. Generate a variety of possibilities first rather than stake out positions. Be tentative, allowing them room to customize the situation. Focus on common goals, priorities, and problems. Invite criticism of your ideas.

4. **If peers think you lack respect for them or what they do, try to keep conflicts as small and concrete as possible.** Separate the people from the problem. Don't get personal. Don't give peers the impression you're trying to dominate or push something on them. Without agreeing or disagreeing, try on their views for size. Can you understand their viewpoint? When peers blow off steam, don't react; return to facts and the problem, staying away from personal clashes.

Allow others to save face; concede small points; don't try to hit a home run every time. When a peer takes a rigid position, don't reject it. Ask why: What are the principles behind the position? How do we know it's fair? What's the theory of the case? Play out what would happen if his/her position was accepted.

5. **People who are politically savvy work from the outside (audience, person, group) in.** They determine the demand characteristics or requirements of each situation and each person they face and select from among their various skills, tone, and styles to find the best approach to make things work. Practice not thinking inside/out when you are around others.

6. **Strong advocates for narrow views don't usually fare well politically in organizations.** Initially be tentative. Give others some room to maneuver. Make the business or organizational case first. Be prepared to counter arguments that your objective is less important than theirs. A lot of political noise is caused by making extreme statements right out of the box.

7. **Follow the basic rules of inspiring team members** as outlined in classic books like *People Skills* by Robert Bolton or *Thriving on Chaos* by Tom Peters. Tell people what they do is important. Say thanks. Offer help and ask for it. Provide autonomy in how people do their work. Provide a variety of tasks. "Surprise" people with enriching, challenging assignments. Show an interest in their work. Adopt a learning attitude toward mistakes. Celebrate successes, have visible accepted measures of achievement, and so on. Each team member is different, so good team managers deal with each person uniquely while being fair to all.

8. **The first three minutes.** Managing the first three minutes is essential. The tone is set. First impressions are formed. Work on being open and approachable, and take in information during the beginning of a transaction. This means putting others at ease so that they feel okay about disclosing. It means initiating rapport, listening, sharing, understanding, and comforting. Approachable people get more information, know things earlier, and can get others to do more things. The more you can get them to initiate and say early in the transaction, the more you'll know about where they are coming from, and the better you can tailor your approach.

T↔F

Accepting (Tolerant, trusting)

- Seek to affirm contributions and would rather act to develop relationships than to be critical and lose them.

- Often overlook lapses in others.

- Active in encouraging others to achieve and fulfill goals.

To develop more of this facet:

1. **People focus on different things**—taking action, details, concepts, feelings, other people. What's their interaction style? People come in different styles—pushy, tough, soft, matter-of-fact, and so on. To figure these out, listen for the values behind their words and note what they have passion and emotion around. One key to getting anything of value done in the work world is the ability to see differences in people and to manage against and use those differences for everyone's benefit. Interpersonal savvy is meeting each person where he/she is to get done what you need to get done. Basically, people respond favorably to ease of transaction. If you make it easy by accepting their normal mode of doing things, not fighting their style, and neither defending your own nor letting style get in the way of performance, things will generally run smoothly.

2. **You should work doubly hard at observing others.** Always select your interpersonal approach from the other person in, not from you out. Your best choice of approach will always be determined by the other person or group, not you. Think about each transaction as if the other person were a customer you wanted. How would you craft an approach?

3. **The first three minutes.** Managing the first three minutes is essential. The tone is set. First impressions are formed. Work on being open and approachable, and take in information during the beginning of a transaction. This means putting others at ease so that they feel okay about disclosing. It means initiating rapport, listening, sharing, understanding, and comforting. Accepting people get more information, know things earlier, and can get others to do more things.

4. **Manage your non-verbals.** Accepting people appear and sound open and relaxed, smiling and calm. They keep consistent eye contact. They nod while the other person is talking. They speak in a paced and pleasant tone. Work to eliminate any disruptive habits, such as

speaking too rapidly or forcefully, using strongly worded or loaded language, or going into too much detail. Watch out for signaling disinterest with actions like glancing at your watch, fiddling with paperwork, or giving your impatient "I'm busy" look.

5. **Too dependent upon yourself.** Look at others' solutions more. Invite discussion and disagreement, welcome bad news, ask that people come up with the second and third solution. A useful trick is to assign issues and questions before you have given them any thought. Two weeks before you are due to decide, ask your people to examine that issue and report to you two days before you have to deal with it. That way, you really don't have any solutions yet. This really motivates people and makes you look less impatient.

6. **Rein in your horse.** Impatient people provide answers, conclusions, and solutions too early in the process. Others haven't even understood the problem yet. Providing solutions too quickly will make your people dependent and irritated. If you don't teach them how you think and how you can come up with solutions so fast, they will never learn. Take the time to really define the problem—not impatiently throw out a solution. Brainstorm what questions need to be answered in order to resolve it. Give your people the task to think about for a day and come back with some solutions. Be a teacher instead of a dictator of solutions. Study yourself. Keep a journal of what triggered your behavior and what the observed consequences were. Learn to detect and control your triggers before they get you in trouble.

7. **Follow the basic rules of inspiring others** as outlined in classic books like *People Skills* by Robert Bolton or *Thriving on Chaos* by Tom Peters. Communicate to people that what they do is important. Say thanks. Offer help and ask for it. Provide autonomy in how people do their work. Provide a variety of tasks. "Surprise" people with enriching, challenging assignments. Show an interest in their careers. Do you know what their hopes and dreams are? Find out and encourage them. Adopt a learning attitude toward mistakes. Celebrate successes, have visible accepted measures of achievement, and so on.

8. **Caring is accepting.** Try to listen without judging initially. Turn off your "I agree; I don't agree" filter. You don't have to agree with it; just listen to understand. Assume when people tell you something they are looking for understanding; indicate that by being able to summarize what they said. Don't offer advice or solutions unless it's

obvious the person wants to know what you would do. While offering instant solutions is a good thing to do in many circumstances, it's chilling where the goal is to get people to talk to you more freely.

If you sometimes overdo being Accepting:

1. **You may be a casual delegator.** Analyze recent projects that went well and didn't go well. How did you delegate? Too much? Not enough? Unwanted pieces? Major chunks of responsibility? Workload distributed properly? Did you set measures? Overmanage or abdicate? Find out what your best practices are. Set up a series of delegation practices that can be used as if you're not there. What do you have to be informed of? What feedback loops can people use for midcourse correction? What questions should be answered as the work proceeds? What steps should be followed? What are the criteria to be followed? When will you be available to help?

2. **Are your standards for staffing too low?** Do you hire the first close candidate that comes along? Always try to wait long enough to have choices but not long enough to lose a very good candidate while you wait for the perfect one to come along. Learn how to set reasonable standards by looking at a competency model and selecting key skills. Make sure you know what matters most. Read sources that focus on key competencies at work, such as *The Extraordinary Leader* by Zenger and Folkman or *The Leadership Machine* by Lombardo and Eichinger. Look at the research-based lists of competencies that appear on standardized competency instruments such as VOICES®, PROFILOR®, or BENCHMARKS®.

3. **You may have only a vague idea of the skill sets of others.** Become a student of the people around you. First, try to outline their strengths and weaknesses, their preferences and beliefs. Watch out for traps—it is rarely general intelligence or pure personality that spells the difference in people. Most people are smart enough, and many personality characteristics don't matter that much for performance. Ask a second question. Look below surface descriptions of smart, approachable, technically skilled people to describe specifics. Then try to predict ahead of time what they would do in specific circumstances. What percent of the time are your predictions correct? Try to increase the percent over time.

4. **Volunteer to be part of an assessment center team or take a course in assessing competencies.** You will be trained to observe and assess people as they are going through a number of tasks and assignments. As part of the process, you will compare your notes and assessments with others on the team. That way, you will learn to calibrate your assessments.

5. **You may not take a stand.** Taking a tough stand demands confidence in what you're saying along with the humility that you might be wrong—one of life's paradoxes. To prepare to take the lead on a tough issue, work on your stand through mental interrogation until you can clearly state in a few sentences what your stand is and why you hold it. Build the business case. How do others win? Ask others for advice. Scope the problem, consider options, pick one, develop a rationale, then go with it until proven wrong. Consider the opposing view. Develop a strong case against your stand. Prepare responses to it. Expect pushback.

6. **People may get away with poor performance because you won't confront them.** Are your problem performers confused? Do they know what's expected of them? You may not set clear enough performance standards, goals, and objectives. You may be a seat-of-the-pants manager, and some people are struggling because they don't know what is expected or it changes. The first task is to outline the 5 to 10 key results areas and what indicators of success would be. Involve your problem direct reports on both ends—the standards and the indicators. Provide them with a fair way to measure their own progress.

7. **Learn to deal with conflict better.** Separate people from the problem and don't personalize conflict. Simply explain your thinking and ask them to explain theirs. Be able to state their position as clearly as they do whether you agree or not—give it legitimacy. Separate facts from opinions and assumptions. Generate a variety of possibilities first rather than stake out positions. Keep your speaking to 30–60 second bursts. Try to get them to do the same. Don't give the other side the impression you're lecturing or criticizing them. Explain objectively why you hold a view; make the other side do the same. Ask lots of questions, make fewer statements. To identify interests behind positions, ask why they hold them or why they wouldn't want to do something.

T↔F

Tough←→Tender
The way we stand by the impact of decisions.

Tough (Firm, ends-oriented)

- Stand firm in decisions made, feel secure that their judgment is good given the data.

- Believe in the soundness of their decision-making processes.

- Highly value detached judgment.

To develop more of this facet:

1. **Leading is riskier than following.** While there are a lot of personal rewards for leading, leading puts you in the limelight. People will always say it should have been done differently. Listen to them, but be skeptical. Even great leaders are wrong sometimes. They accept personal responsibility for errors and move on to lead some more. Don't let criticism prevent you from taking the lead. Build up your heat shield. Conduct a postmortem immediately after finishing milestone efforts. This will indicate to all that you're open to continuous improvement whether the result was stellar or not.

2. **Against the grain tough stands.** Taking a tough stand demands confidence in what you're saying along with the humility that you might be wrong—one of life's paradoxes. To prepare to take the lead on a tough issue, work on your stand through mental interrogation until you can clearly state in a few sentences what your stand is and why you hold it. Build the business case. How do others win? People don't line up behind laundry lists or ambiguous objectives. Ask others for advice—scope the problem, consider options, pick one, develop a rationale, then go with it until proven wrong. Then redo the process. If this doesn't help, find out where the pain is for you. What have you been avoiding? Examine your past and see where taking-charge behavior has gotten you in trouble or you thought it would get you in trouble. Isolate the most troublesome elements, such as forgetting things under pressure, trouble with fierce debate, problems with unpopular stands, and things moving too fast. Devise counter-strategies.

3. **Selling your leadership.** To sell your leadership, keep your eyes on the prize but don't specify how to get there. Present the outcomes,

targets, and goals without the how to's. Welcome their ideas—good and bad. Any negative response is a positive if you learn from it. Allow them to fill in the blanks, ask questions, and disagree without appearing impatient with them. Allow others to save face; concede small points, invite criticism of your own. Help them figure out how to win. Keep to the facts and the problem before the group; stay away from personal clashes.

4. **Keep your cool.** Manage your emotional reactions. Sometimes your emotional reactions lead others to think you have problems with tough leadership situations. In the situations where this happens, what emotional reactions do you have? Do you show impatience or non-verbals like increasing voice volume or drumming your fingers? Learn to recognize those as soon as they start. Substitute something more neutral. If you tend to blurt out disagreement when uncomfortable or surprised by a point of view, ask a question instead to buy time. Or, ask the person to tell you more about his/her point of view. Don't go for the quick, obvious response. That's stress getting the better of you. Or, ask yourself questions.

5. **One-on-one combat.** Leading always involves dealing with pure one-on-one confrontation. You want one thing, he/she wants something else. When that happens, keep it to the facts. You won't always win. Stay objective. Listen as long as he/she will talk. Ask a lot of questions. Sometimes he/she will talk himself/herself into your point of view if you let him/her talk long enough. Always listen to understand first, not judge. Then restate his/her points until he/she says that's right. Then find something to agree with, however small that may be. Refute his/her points starting with the one you have the most objective information on. Then move down the line. You will always have points left that didn't get resolved. Document those and give a copy to your opponent. The objective is to get the list as small as possible. Then decide whether you are going to pull rank and go ahead. Delay and get more data. Go to a higher source for arbitration.

6. **Leadership presence.** Leading takes presence. You have to look and sound like a leader. Voice is strong. Eye contact. Intensity. Confidence. A lot of leadership presence has to do with forceful presentation skills. Giving good presentations is a known technology. There are several books and workshops you can take. Look to workshops that use videotaping. Join your local Toastmasters Club for some low-risk training and practice. Look to small things such as do you look like a leader? What colors do you wear? Do you dress the part? Are your

glasses right? Is your office configured right? Do you sound confident? Do you whine and complain or do you solve problems? If I met you for the first time in a group of 10, would I pick you as the leader?

7. **Recognize perfectionism for what it might be**—collecting more information than others do to improve confidence in making a fault-free decision and thereby avoiding the risk and criticism that would come from making decisions faster. Some studies suggest even successful general managers are about 65% correct. If you need to be more timely, you need to reduce your own internal need for data and the need to be perfect. Try to decrease your need for data and your need to be right all the time slightly every week until you reach a more reasonable balance between thinking it through and taking action.

8. **Most problems are ill-defined and ambiguous.** When facing this, don't try to get it right the first time. Try your best educated guess now, and then correct as feedback comes in. Many problem-solving studies show that the second or third try is when we really understand the underlying dynamics of problems. So, you need to work on two practices: Start smaller so you can recover more quickly. Do something as soon as you can and get used to heat.

9. **Delivering tough messages.** Don't overwhelm the person/group, even if you have a lot to say. Go from specific to general points. Keep it to the facts. Don't embellish to make your point. No passion or inflammatory language. Don't do it to harm or out of vengeance. Don't do it in anger. If feelings are involved for you, wait until you can describe them, not show them. Managerial courage comes in search of a better outcome, not destroying others. Stay calm and cool. If others are not composed, don't respond. Just return to the message.

10. **Hesitate in the face of resistance and adverse reaction?** Conflict slows you down? Shakes your confidence in your decision? Do you backpedal? Give in too soon? Try to make everyone happy? Do your homework first. Scope the problem, consider options, pick one, develop a rationale, then go to others. Be prepared to defend your selection; know what they will ask, what they will object to, how this decision will affect them. Listen carefully, invite criticism of your idea and revise accordingly in the face of real data. Otherwise, hold your ground.

If you sometimes overdo being Tough:

1. **You may run into problems with customers.** Customers complain; it's their job. Be ready for the good news and the bad news; don't be defensive; just listen and respond to legitimate criticisms and note the rest. Vocal customers will usually complain more than compliment; you need to not get overwhelmed by the negative comments; people who have positive opinions speak up less often.

2. **Put yourself in your customer's shoes.** If you were a customer of yours, what would you expect; what kind of turnaround time would you tolerate; what price would you be willing to pay for the quality of product or service you provide; what would be the top three things you would complain about? Answer all calls from customers in a timely way; if you promise a response, do it; if the time frame stretches, inform them immediately; after you have responded, ask them if the problem is fixed.

3. **You may be so sure you're right you don't listen.** How do people know you're listening? You have eye contact. You take notes. You don't frown or fidget. How do people know you've understood? You paraphrase what they have said to their satisfaction. How do people know if you have accepted or rejected what they said? You tell them. Hopefully in a tactful way if you reject what they had to say. Give your reasons.

4. **Listening chillers?** Don't interrupt before they have finished. Don't suggest words when they hesitate or pause. Don't finish their sentences for them. Don't wave off any further input by saying, "Yes, I know that." "Yes, I know where you're going." "Yes, I have heard that before." If time is really important, you can say, "Let me see if I know where this is going…," or "I wonder if we could summarize to save both of us some time?" Finally, early in a transaction, answers, solutions, conclusions, statements, and dictates shut many people down. You've told them your mind is already made up. Listen first, solve second.

5. **Questions.** Good listeners ask lots of questions to get to a good understanding. Probing questions. Clarifying questions. Confirming— is this what you are saying—questions. Ask one more question than you do now and add to that until people signal you that they think you are truly listening.

T↔F

6. **You may get into political trouble.** Being politically sensitive includes being people sensitive. You have to be able to read people. You have to be able to predict how they are going to react to you and to what you are trying to get done. The magic and the complexity of life is that people are different. Each requires special consideration and treatment. If you are able to predict what individuals or groups will do, you will be able to select from among your various tactics, skills, and styles to get done what you need.

7. **For close-in political savvy (live in a meeting) you need to learn how to read non-verbals.** Common signals of trouble are changes in body posture (especially turning away), crossed arms, staring, or the telltale glancing at one's watch, scribbling on the note pad, tapping one's fingers or a pencil, looking out the window, frowns, and washboard foreheads. When this occurs, pause. Ask a question. Ask how we're doing. Do a live process check.

8. **Because you take strong stands, you may come across as a know-it-all.** Too quick to get into the agenda? Do you devalue others and dismiss their contributions, resulting in people feeling diminished, rejected, and angry? Do you offer answers, solutions, conclusions, statements, or dictates early in the transaction because you've already decided? Take the time to really define the problem—not impatiently throw out a solution. Brainstorm what questions need to be answered in order to resolve it. Give your people the task to think about for a day and come back with some solutions. Be a teacher instead of a dictator of solutions. Study yourself. Keep a journal of what triggered your behavior and what the observed consequences were. Learn to detect and control your triggers before they get you in trouble.

Tender (Gentle, means-oriented)

- Effect of decisions on others is more important than the processes used in deciding.

- Focus on how to give attention to each person.

- There is no "absolute truth," so human interdependence is primary.

To develop more of this facet:

1. **How to start.** Start with three things you can talk about with almost anyone without risking uncomfortable personal disclosure. Vacations, hobbies, business interests, your thinking on business issues, children,

etc. Decide what they are and make a conscious effort to sprinkle them into some of your interactions with others you have generally had only a business relationship with before. Notice the reaction. Did they also share for the first time? Usually yes. And that's the point. Within limits, the more you know about each other, the better the working relationship will be. Try to get to know three non-work things about everybody—their interests or their children or something you can chat about with them other than the weather or the weekend sports results.

2. **Deeper disclosure.** More serious personal disclosure involves talking about your self-appraisal. This involves talking about your personal strengths, weaknesses, limitations, and beliefs. Most others are more comfortable with people who do reasonable disclosure. The funny thing about self-assessment disclosure is that most of the people around you already know what you're going to disclose! If you say, "I'm not the most organized person in the world," most around you will do a smiling nod because they suffer the consequences of your disorganization. But, that brief mention of a problem you have or a belief you hold will help the person feel more comfortable. This tells them they are not alone, that you have some of the same problems and worries they do.

3. **Being approachable means you have to initiate the transaction.** You have to put out your hand first. Make first eye contact. Note the color of the person's eyes to ensure good eye contact. You have to ask the first question or share the first piece of information. You have to make the first three minutes comfortable for the other person or group so they can accomplish what they came to you to do.

4. **Approachable people are very good at listening.** They listen without interrupting. They ask clarifying questions. They don't instantly judge. They listen to understand. Judgment may come later. They restate what the other person has said to signal understanding. They nod. They may jot down notes. Listeners don't always offer advice or solutions unless it's obvious the person wants to know what they would do.

5. **Watch your non-verbals.** Approachable people appear and sound open and relaxed. They smile. They are calm. They keep eye contact. They nod while the other person is talking. They have an open body posture. They speak in a paced and pleasant tone. Eliminate any disruptive habits, such as speaking too rapidly or forcefully, using

strongly worded or loaded language, or going into too much detail. Watch out for signaling disinterest with actions like glancing at your watch, fiddling with paperwork, or giving your impatient "I'm busy" look.

6. **The magic of questions.** Many people don't ask enough curiosity questions when in their work mode. There are too many informational statements, conclusions, suggestions, and solutions and not enough "what if," "what are you thinking," "how do you see that." In studies, statements outweighed questions 8 to 1. Ask more questions than others. Make fewer solution statements early in a discussion. Keep probing until you understand what they are trying to tell you.

7. **Caring is accepting.** Try to listen without judging initially. Turn off your "I agree; I don't agree" filter. You don't have to agree with it; just listen to understand. Assume when people tell you something they are looking for understanding; indicate that by being able to summarize what they said. Don't offer advice or solutions unless it's obvious the person wants to know what you would do. While offering instant solutions is a good thing to do in many circumstances, it's chilling where the goal is to get people to talk to you more freely.

8. **Caring is understanding.** Study the people you work with. Without judging them, collect evidence on how they think and what they do. What drives them to do what they do? Try to predict what they will do in given situations. Use this to understand how to relate to them. What are their hot buttons? What would they like for you to care about?

If you sometimes overdo being Tender:

1. **You may focus too little on decision quality and too much on the effects of a decision on people.** Know your biases. Be clear and honest with yourself about your attitudes, beliefs, biases, opinions and prejudices, and your favorite solutions. We all have them. The key is not to let them affect your objective and cold decision making. Before making any sizable decision, ask yourself, are any of my biases affecting this decision? Do you play favorites, deciding quickly in one area, but holding off in another? Do you avoid certain topics, people, groups, functional areas because you're not comfortable or don't know? Do you drag out your favorite solutions often?

2. **Do you do enough analysis?** Thoroughly define the problem. Figure out what causes it. Keep asking why. See how many causes you can come up with and how many organizing buckets you can put them in. This increases the chance of a better solution because you can see more connections. Look for patterns in data, don't just collect information. Put it in categories that make sense to you. A good rule of thumb is to analyze patterns and causes to come up with alternatives. Many of us just collect data, which numerous studies show increases our confidence but doesn't increase decision accuracy. Think out loud with others; see how they view the problem. Studies show that defining the problem and taking action usually occur simultaneously, so to break out of analysis paralysis, figure out what the problem is first. Then when a good alternative appears, you're likely to recognize it immediately.

3. **People concerns affect your priority setting.** In your case, you probably get distracted by people concerns and this can lead to an activity trap. John Kotter, in *The General Managers*, found that effective managers spent about half their time working on one or two key priorities—priorities they described in their own terms, not in terms of what the business/organizational plan said. Further, they made no attempt to work as much on small but related issues that tend to add up to lots of activity. So, rather than consuming themselves and others on 97 seemingly urgent and related smaller activities, they always returned to the few issues that would gain the most mileage long term.

4. **Set goals for yourself and others.** Most people work better if they have a set of goals and objectives to achieve and a standard everyone agrees to measure accomplishments against. Most people like stretch goals. They like them even better if they have had a hand in setting them. Set checkpoints along the way to be able to measure progress. Give yourself and others as much feedback as you can.

5. **People may get away with poor performance because you won't confront them.** Are your problem performers confused? Do they know what's expected of them? You may not set clear enough performance standards, goals, and objectives. You may be a seat-of-the-pants manager, and some people are struggling because they don't know what is expected or it changes. The first task is to outline the 5 to 10 key results areas and what indicators of success would be. Involve your problem direct reports on both ends—the standards and

the indicators. Provide them with a fair way to measure their own progress.

6. **You have trouble delivering tough messages.** Be succinct. You have limited attention span in tough feedback situations. Don't waste time with a long preamble, particularly if the feedback is negative. If the feedback is negative and the recipient is likely to know it, go ahead and say it directly. They won't hear anything positive you have to say anyway. Don't overwhelm the person/group, even if you have a lot to say. Go from specific to general points. Keep it to the facts. Don't embellish to make your point. No passion or inflammatory language. Don't do it to harm or out of vengeance. Don't do it in anger. If feelings are involved for you, wait until you can describe them, not show them. Managerial courage comes in search of a better outcome, not destroying others. Stay calm and cool. If others are not composed, don't respond. Just return to the message.

7. **Bring a solution if you can.** Everybody appreciates a problem solver. Give people ways to improve; don't just dump and leave. Tell others what you think would be better—paint a different outcome. Help others see the consequences—you can ask them what they think, and you can tell them what the consequences are from your side if you are personally involved ("I'd be reluctant to work with you on X again").

8. **Take a stand.** This demands confidence in what you're saying along with the humility that you might be wrong—one of life's paradoxes. To take the lead on a tough issue, work on your stand through mental interrogation until you can clearly state in a few sentences what your stand is and why you hold it. Build the business case. How do others win? Ask others for advice. Scope the problem, consider options, pick one, develop a rationale, then go with it until proven wrong. Consider the opposing view. Develop a strong case against your stand. Prepare responses to it. Expect pushback. Stick to your guns. Once a decision is reached, don't dilute it by asking questions like "Is everyone okay with this?"

Judging ←→Perceiving Facets

Judging	Purpose: Dealing with the World	Perceiving
Systematic (Orderly, structured) • Methodical and structured even in small tasks. • Feel they make the most of jobs and pleasures by being deliberately systematic, dislike inefficiency and waste. • Desire for order reflects a need for control, insist on closure.	Flow of events, tasks, and the general organization of life. 3	**Casual** (Relaxed, easygoing) • Approach work with spontaneity and openness to seeing things in new ways. • Actively seek variety. • Interruptions are expected to keep work from being boring, will wait to make decisions until they feel all appropriate data are explored.
Planful (Future-focused, advance planner) • Prefer a definite schedule. • Tend to structure time in orderly ways and to know advance dates for social events, otherwise they are unlikely to be available. • Feel that planning means doing what you want to do.	Arranging leisure activities, in the daily plan and future plan. 1	**Open-Ended** (Present-focused, flexible) • Prefer unscheduled leisure time so they can take advantage of unexpected opportunities. • Place self in a flow of events that match inclinations. • Variety and improvisational opportunities are desired.
Early Starting (Steady progress, self-discipline) • Work best when they start their own work way ahead of deadlines. • Like to complete their work in time to review it. • Like extra time to check for errors and make last-minute refinements.	Managing deadlines, time pressures. 5	**Pressure-Prompted** (Bursts, spurts, pressure) • Work well with a deadline and under time pressure. • Often enjoy meeting a tight schedule. • Require a time period to think through projects before starting on them.
Scheduled (Routine, structure) • Routine is appealing because it is a way of getting things done correctly and with efficiency. • Gain energy from a predictable flow of tasks. • Structure provides an anchor for maintaining relationships.	Degree of scheduling in daily life. 2	**Spontaneous** (Variety, unexpected) • Work best when they have constant variety. • Find different ways of doing regular events. • Break monotony by exploring new activities. • Feel a need to introduce variation into events.
Methodical (Plan specific tasks, organized) • Organize materials and arrange in order needed, note what needs to be done in specific order to get the job done. • Take pleasure in organizing work and materials, make complete plans with specific time allotments for each task.	Sequencing or ordering of smaller to larger tasks without concern for time or schedule. 4	**Emergent** (Plan loosely, adaptable) • Treat projects as explorations and discoveries, take delight in finding out what to do as they go along. • Do minimal preparation, often discover how to complete things by trial-and-error, follow trail of associations when involved in new projects.

Systematic ↔ Casual
Flow of events, tasks, and the general organization of life.

Systematic (Orderly, structured)

- Methodical and structured even in small tasks.

- Feel they make the most of jobs and pleasures by being deliberately systematic, dislike inefficiency and waste.

- Desire for order reflects a need for control, insist on closure.

To develop more of this facet:

1. **Do you do enough analysis?** Thoroughly define the problem. Figure out what causes it. Keep asking why. See how many causes you can come up with and how many organizing buckets you can put them in. This increases the chance of a better solution because you can see more connections. Look for patterns in data, don't just collect information. Put it in categories that make sense to you. A good rule of thumb is to analyze patterns and causes to come up with alternatives. Many of us just collect data, which numerous studies show increases our confidence but doesn't increase decision accuracy. Think out loud with others; see how they view the problem. Studies show that defining the problem and taking action usually occur simultaneously, so to break out of analysis paralysis, figure out what the problem is first. Then when a good alternative appears, you're likely to recognize it immediately.

2. **Set goals.** Nothing manages time better than a goal, a plan, and a measure. Set goals for yourself. These goals are essential for setting priorities. If you do not have goals, you can't set time priorities. Using the goals, separate what you need to do into mission-critical, important to get done, nice if there is time left over, and not central to what you are trying to achieve. When faced with choices or multiple things to do, apply the scale.

3. **Laying out the work.** Most resourcefulness starts out with a plan. What do I need to accomplish? What's the time line? What resources will I need? Who controls the resources—people, funding, tools, materials, support—I need? What's my currency? How can I pay for or repay the resources I need? Who wins if I win? Who might lose? Lay out the work from A to Z. Many people are seen as disorganized

because they don't write down the sequence or parts of the work and leave something out. Ask others to comment on ordering and what's missing.

4. **Watch out for the activity trap.** John Kotter, in *The General Managers,* found that effective managers spent about half their time working on one or two key priorities—priorities they described in their own terms, not in terms of what the business/organizational plan said. Further, they made no attempt to work as much on small but related issues that tend to add up to lots of activity. So, rather than consuming themselves and others on 97 seemingly urgent and related smaller activities, they always returned to the few issues that would gain the most mileage long term.

5. **When you are stuck, write down the pros and cons for each option.** Check what effect each would have both on the short and long term. Are there cost differences? Is one resource more efficient than the other? Is one apt to be more successful than the other? Think about the interaction of both short- and long-term goals. Sometimes what you decide to do today will hurt you or the organization downstream. When making either a short-term or long-term choice, stop for a second and ask what effect this might have on the other. Adjust as necessary.

6. **Manage your time efficiently.** Plan your time and manage against it. Be time sensitive. Value time. Figure out what you are worth per hour and minute by taking your gross salary plus overhead and benefits. Attach a monetary value on your time. Then ask, is this worth $56 of my time? Review your calendar over the past 90 days to figure out what your three largest time wasters are, and reduce them 50% by batching activities and using efficient communications like e-mail and voice mail for routine matters. Make a list of points to be covered in phone calls; set deadlines for yourself; use your best time of day for the toughest projects—if you're best in the morning, don't waste it on B and C level tasks.

7. **Another common time waster is inadequate disengagement skills.** Some poor time managers can't shut down transactions. Either they continue to talk beyond what would be necessary or, more commonly, they can't get the other party to quit talking. When it's time to move on, just say, "I have to get on to the next thing I have to do; we can pick this up some other time."

8. **Don't get diverted by trivial work and other decisions.** Get better organized and disciplined. Keep a decision log. When a decision opportunity surfaces, immediately log it along with the ideal date it needs to be made. Plan backwards to the work necessary to make the decision on time. If you are not disciplined in how you work and are sometimes late making decisions and taking action because of it, buy books on TQM, ISO and Six Sigma. Go to one workshop on efficient and effective work design.

If you sometimes overdo being Systematic:

1. **You may be quite uncomfortable with change, uncertainty, and loose ends.** According to studies, 90% of the problems of middle managers and above are ambiguous—it's neither clear what the problem is nor what the solution is. Most people with a brain, given unlimited time, and 100% of the information, could make accurate and good decisions. The real rewards go to those who can comfortably make more good decisions than bad with less than all of the information, in less time, with few or no precedents on how it was solved before.

2. **The essence of dealing comfortably with uncertainty is the tolerance of errors and mistakes, and absorbing the possible heat and criticism that follow.** Acting on an ill-defined problem with no precedents to follow means shooting in the dark with as informed a decision as you can make at the time. People who are good at this are incrementalists. They make a series of smaller decisions, get instant feedback, correct the course, get a little more data, move forward a little more, until the bigger problem is under control. They don't try to get it right the first time. Many problem-solving studies show that the second or third try is when we really understand the underlying dynamics of problems. They also know that the more uncertain the situation is, the more likely it is they will make mistakes in the beginning. So, you need to work on two practices: Start small so you can recover more quickly. Do little somethings as soon as you can and get used to heat.

3. **Perfectionist?** Need or prefer or want to be 100% sure? Lots might prefer that. Perfectionism is tough to let go of because most people see it as a positive trait for themselves. Recognize your perfectionism for what it might be—collecting more information than others to improve your confidence in making a fault-free decision and thereby avoiding risk and criticism. Try to decrease your need for data and your need

to be right all the time slightly every week until you reach a more reasonable balance between thinking it through and taking action. Try making some small decisions on little or no data. Anyone with a brain and 100% of the data can make good decisions. The real test is who can act the soonest with a reasonable amount, but not all, of the data. Some studies suggest successful general managers are about 65% correct. Trust your intuition. Let your brain do the calculations.

4. **Stuck with what you know?** Do you feel best when you know everything that's going on around you, and you are in control? Most do. Few are motivated by uncertainty and chaos. But many are challenged by it. They enjoy solving problems no one has solved before. They enjoy cutting paths where no one has been before. You need to become more comfortable being a pioneer. Explore new ground. Learn new things. Practice in your life. Go to theme restaurants you know nothing about. Vacation at places without doing a lot of research. Go to ethnic festivals for groups you have little knowledge about.

5. **Develop a philosophical stance toward failure/criticism.** After all, most innovations fail, most proposals fail, most change efforts fail, anything worth doing takes repeated effort. To increase learning from your mistakes, design feedback loops to be as immediate as possible. The faster and the more frequent the cycles, the more opportunities to learn—if we do one smaller thing a day for three days instead of one bigger thing in three, we triple our learning opportunities. There will be many mistakes and failures; after all, since you're not sure, it's very likely no one else knows what to do either. They just have a right to comment on your errors. The best tack when confronted with a mistake is to say, "What can we learn from this?"

6. **You may get pushy because of your need for closure.** You may fixate on details and drive for an answer when none is readily apparent. You're not at your best when anxious, frustrated, upset, or when you lose your cool. What brings out your emotional response? Write down why you get anxious: when you don't know what to do; don't want to make a mistake; afraid of the unknown consequences; don't have the confidence to act. When you get emotional, drop the problem for awhile. Count to 10. Ask more questions and make fewer statements. Go do something else. Come back to it when you are under better control. Let your brain work on it while you do something safer.

7. **You may drive too hard for the win in negotiations.** Losers are not happy people. Good win-win negotiators focus on the target, the issues, and the underlying interests of both sides. They generally use commonly accepted ethical principles and fairness. They deal with personal issues separately if at all, deflect personal assaults, and stay away from early rigid positions.

8. **Start slow until you know where the other party is coming from.** Pay attention to positioning. You and your team on one side and them on the other sets up a contest. Try to mix team members together on both sides. If you're the host, start with small talk unrelated to the subject of the negotiation. Give everyone time to settle in and get comfortable. When it's time, ask whether it would be useful for each side to lay out its goals, starting positions, and any boundaries, such as we aren't here to negotiate costs at this time. Volunteer to go first. Give reasons first, positions last. When you offer goals and positions, people often don't listen to your reasons.

Casual (Relaxed, easygoing)

■ Approach work with spontaneity and openness to seeing things in new ways.

■ Actively seek variety.

■ Interruptions are expected to keep work from being boring, will wait to make decisions until they feel all appropriate data are explored.

To develop more of this facet:

1. **According to studies, 90% of the problems of middle managers and above are ambiguous**—it's neither clear what the problem is nor what the solution is. The essence of dealing comfortably with uncertainty is the tolerance of errors and mistakes, and absorbing the possible heat and criticism that follow. People who are good at this are incrementalists. They make a series of smaller decisions, get instant feedback, correct the course, get a little more data, move forward a little more, until the bigger problem is under control. They don't try to get it right the first time. Many problem-solving studies show that the second or third try is when we really understand the underlying dynamics of problems. They also know that the more uncertain the situation is, the more likely it is they will make mistakes in the beginning.

2. **When facing where it's not clear what to do, try many experiments or trials to find something that will work.** Think beyond current boundaries. What are some of the most sacred rules or practices in your organization? Unit? Think about smashing them—what would your unit be doing if you broke the rules? Talk to the most irreverent person you know about this.

3. **Impatience triggers.** Some people probably bring out your impatience more than others. Who are they? What is it about them that makes you more impatient? Pace? Language? Thought process? Accent? These people may include people you don't like, who ramble, who whine and complain, or who are repetitive advocates for things you have already rejected. Mentally rehearse some calming tactics before meeting with people who trigger your impatience. Work on understanding their positions without judging them—you can always judge later. In all cases, focus them on the issues or problems to be discussed, return them to the point, interrupt to summarize, and state your position. Try to gently train them to be more efficient with you next time without damaging them in the process.

4. **Turn off your judgment program.** In trying to reach someone, work on not judging him/her. You don't have to agree, you just have to understand in order to motivate. The fact that you wouldn't be motivated that way isn't relevant.

5. **Rein in your horse.** Impatient people provide answers, conclusions, and solutions too early in the process. Others haven't even understood the problem yet. Providing solutions too quickly will make your people dependent and irritated. If you don't teach them how you think and how you can come up with solutions so fast, they will never learn. Take the time to really define the problem—not impatiently throw out a solution. Brainstorm what questions need to be answered in order to resolve it. Give your people the task to think about for a day and come back with some solutions. Be a teacher instead of a dictator of solutions. Study yourself. Keep a journal of what triggered your behavior and what the observed consequences were. Learn to detect and control your triggers before they get you in trouble.

6. **You start.** Being approachable means you have to initiate the transaction. You have to put out your hand first. Make first eye contact. Note the color of the person's eyes to ensure good eye contact. You have to ask the first question or share the first piece of

information. You have to make the first three minutes comfortable for the other person or group so they can accomplish what they came to you to do.

7. **Know three things about everybody**—their interests or their children or something you can chat about other than the business agenda. Treat life as a small world. If you ask a few questions, you'll find you have something in common with virtually anyone. Establish things you can talk about with each person you work with that go beyond strictly work transactions.

8. **Watch your non-verbals.** Approachable people appear and sound open and relaxed. They smile. They are calm. They keep eye contact. They nod while the other person is talking. They have an open body posture. They speak in a paced and pleasant tone. Eliminate any disruptive habits, such as speaking too rapidly or forcefully, using strongly worded or loaded language, or going into too much detail. Watch out for signaling disinterest with actions like glancing at your watch, fiddling with paperwork, or giving your impatient "I'm busy" look.

9. **Pick something you've never done but which would broaden your perspective off-work.** Serve with a community group, volunteer to be a Big Sister/Brother, travel to an unvisited country, follow a group of ten-year-olds around for a few days.

10. **At work, pick three tasks you've never done and go do them.** If you don't know much about customers, work in a store or handle customer complaints; if you don't know what engineering does, go find out; task trade with someone. Seek the broadest possible exposure inside the organization. Do lunch with counterparts of the organization and tell each other what you do.

If you sometimes overdo being Casual:

1. **Manage your time efficiently.** Plan your time and manage against it. Be time sensitive. Value time. Figure out what you are worth per hour and minute by taking your gross salary plus overhead and benefits. Attach a monetary value on your time. Then ask, is this worth $56 of my time? Review your calendar over the past 90 days to figure out what your three largest time wasters are, and reduce them 50% by batching activities and using efficient communications like e-mail and voice mail for routine matters. Make a list of points to be covered in phone calls; set deadlines for yourself; use your best time of day for

the toughest projects—if you're best in the morning, don't waste it on B and C level tasks.

2. **Another common time waster is inadequate disengagement skills.** Some poor time managers can't shut down transactions. Either they continue to talk beyond what would be necessary or, more commonly, they can't get the other party to quit talking. When it's time to move on, just say, "I have to get on to the next thing I have to do; we can pick this up some other time."

3. **You love variety and get caught up in activity rather than priorities.** John Kotter, in *The General Managers*, found that effective managers spent about half their time working on one or two key priorities— priorities they described in their own terms, not in terms of what the business/organizational plan said. Further, they made no attempt to work as much on small but related issues that tend to add up to lots of activity. So, rather than consuming themselves and others on 97 seemingly urgent and related smaller activities, they always returned to the few issues that would gain the most mileage long term.

4. **You may be disorganized and not very timely.** Keep a decision log. When a decision opportunity surfaces, immediately log it along with the ideal date it needs to be made. Plan backwards to the work necessary to make the decision on time. If you are not disciplined in how you work and are sometimes late making decisions and taking action because of it, buy books on TQM, ISO and Six Sigma. Go to one workshop on efficient and effective work design.

5. **You take in too much input.** Collecting more data may be more interesting and may increase your confidence, but it is also a way of making a fault-free decision and avoiding risk and criticism. Try to decrease your need for data and your need to be right all the time slightly every week until you reach a more reasonable balance between thinking it through and taking action. Try making some small decisions on little or no data. Anyone with a brain and 100% of the data can make good decisions. The real test is who can act the soonest with a reasonable amount, but not all, of the data. Some studies suggest successful general managers are about 65% correct. Trust your intuition. Let your brain do the calculations.

6. **You may not make timely decisions.** To check this out, write down the decisions you would make right now, then compare them with the decisions you actually make and announce later. Are the decisions more the same than different? If they are more the same, you may

have this problem. Since the noise and the heat are the same, the simple solution is to declare as soon as you have made the decision. Better to be done with it. If there is any useful data in the noise and heat, you can adjust your decision sooner.

7. **You won't cut off debate and take a stand.** Taking a tough stand demands confidence in what you're saying along with the humility that you might be wrong—one of life's paradoxes. To prepare to take the lead on a tough issue, work on your stand through mental interrogation until you can clearly state in a few sentences what your stand is and why you hold it. Build the business case. How do others win? People don't line up behind laundry lists or ambiguous objectives. Ask others for advice—scope the problem, consider options, pick one, develop a rationale, then go with it until proven wrong. Then redo the process. If this doesn't help, find out where the pain is for you. What have you been avoiding? Examine your past and see where taking-charge behavior has gotten you in trouble or you thought it would get you in trouble. Isolate the most troublesome elements, such as forgetting things under pressure, trouble with fierce debate, problems with unpopular stands, and things moving too fast. Devise counterstrategies.

8. **You confuse others by not setting direction.** Do an inventory of the common management techniques and practices you do well and those that you do not do so well or often enough. Think about the practices below in particular:

   ■ Do a communication check on yourself. How well do you inform? Explain? Get back to people? Give feedback?

   ■ Do you delegate enough? Do you give the people under you the authority to do their work? Do you over- or undermanage? Periodically, ask your people to give you a list of the things they think you are doing yourself that they believe they could do a good job on; delegate some of the things on everybody's list.

   ■ Are you organized and planful? Can people follow what you want? Do you lay out work and tasks to be done clearly? Do you set clear goals and objectives that can guide their work?

   ■ Do you confront problems directly and quickly or do you let things fester?

9. **You have one style, which is casual, and sometimes this comes across as lacking seriousness of purpose.** You may not be picked for choice assignments you want, use an unvarying off-the-cuff presentation style, or be seen as not driving hard enough for results. Think about your career prospects. Is this how you want to be seen? If not, it's time to do these things differently.

Planful↔Open-Ended
Arranging leisure activities, in the daily plan and future plan.

Planful (Future-focused, advance planner)

■ Prefer a definite schedule.

■ Tend to structure time in orderly ways and to know advance dates for social events, otherwise they are unlikely to be available.

■ Feel that planning means doing what you want to do.

To develop more of this facet:

1. **Add things to your off-work life.** This was a major finding of a stress study at AT&T of busy, high-potential women and men. It may seem counterintuitive, but the best-adjusted people forced themselves to structure off-work activities just as much as on-work activities. Otherwise work drives everything else out. Those with dual responsibilities (primary care giver and home manager and a full-time jobholder) need to use their management strengths and skills more at home. What makes your work life successful? Batch tasks, bundle similar activities together, delegate to children, or set up pools with coworkers or neighbors to share tasks, such as car pooling, soccer games, Scouts, etc. Pay to have some things done that are not mission-critical to your home needs. Organize and manage efficiently. Have a schedule. Set up goals and plans. Use some of your work skills more off-work.

2. **Create deadlines, urgencies, and structures off-work.** One tactic that helps is for people to use their strengths from work off-work. If you are organized, organize something. If you are very personable, get together a regular group. If you are competitive, set up a regular match. As commonsensical as this seems, AT&T found that people with poor off-work lives did not use their strengths off-work. They truly left them at the office.

3. **Lay out tasks and work.** Most successful projects begin with a good plan. What do I need to accomplish? What are the goals? What's the time line? What resources will I need? How many of the resources do I control? Who controls the rest of the resources—people, funding, tools, materials, support—I need? Lay out the work from A to Z. Many people are seen as lacking a plan because they don't write down the sequence or parts of the work and leave something out. Ask others to comment on ordering and what's missing.

4. **Set the plan.** Buy a flowcharting software program that does PERT and GANTT charts. Become an expert in its use. Use the output of the software to communicate your plans to others. Use the flowcharts in your presentations.

5. **Set goals and measures.** Nothing keeps projects on time and on budget like a goal, a plan, and a measure. Set goals for the whole project and the subtasks. Plan for all. Set measures so you and others can track progress against the goals.

6. **Manage multiple plans or aspects of big plans.** Many attempts to accomplish complex plans involve managing parallel tracks or multiple tasks at the same time. It helps if you have a master plan. Good planning decreases the chances you will lose control by spreading yourself too thin.

7. **Manage efficiently.** Plan the budget and manage against it. Spend carefully. Have a reserve if the unanticipated comes up. Set up a funding time line so you can track ongoing expenditures against plan.

8. **You need to match people and tasks.** People are different. They have different strengths and have differing levels of knowledge and experience. Instead of thinking of everyone as equal, think of them as different. Really equal treatment is giving people tasks to do that match their capacities.

9. **Vision the plan in process.** What could go wrong? Run scenarios in your head. Think along several paths. Rank the potential problems from highest likelihood to lowest likelihood. Think about what you would do if the highest likelihood things were to occur. Create a contingency plan for each. Pay attention to the weakest links, which are usually groups or elements you have the least interface with or control over (perhaps someone in a remote location, a consultant, or supplier). Stay doubly in touch with the potential weak links.

10. **Set up a process to monitor progress against the plan.** How would you know if the plan is on time? Could you estimate time to completion or percent finished at any time? Give people involved in implementing the plan progress feedback as you go.

11. **Find someone in your environment who is better at planning than you are to see how it's done.** How does that compare against what you typically do? Try to increase doing the things he/she does. Ask for feedback from some people who have had to follow your plans. What did they like? What did they find difficult?

12. **Get others to help.** Share your ideas about the project with others, possibly the people you need to support you later. Get their input on the plan. Delegate creating the plan to people who are better at it than you are. You provide the goals and what needs to be done, and let others create the detailed plan.

If you sometimes overdo being Planful:

1. **You miss learning opportunities because you structure too much.** When faced with a new issue, challenge, or problem, figure out what causes it. Keep asking why. See how many causes you can come up with and how many organizing buckets you can put them in. This increases the chance of a better solution because you can see more connections. Chess masters recognize thousands of possible patterns of chess pieces. Look for patterns in data; don't just collect information. Put it in categories that make sense to you. To better understand new and difficult learning, read *The Future of Leadership* by White, Hodgson and Crainer.

2. **Locate the essence of the problem.** What are the key factors or elements in this problem? Experts usually solve problems by figuring out what the deep, underlying principles are and working forward from there; the less adept focus on desired outcomes/solutions and either work backward or concentrate on the surface facts. What are the deep principles of what you're working on? Once you've done this, search the past for parallels—your past, the business past, the historical past. One common mistake here is to search in parallel organizations because "only they would know." Backing up and asking a broader question will aid in the search for solutions. When Motorola wanted to find out how to process orders more quickly, they went not to other electronics firms, but to Domino's Pizza and Federal Express.

J↔P

3. **You gravitate to safe solutions.** Don't expect to get it right the first time. This leads to safe and stale solutions. Many studies show that the second or third try is when we really understand the underlying dynamics of problems. To increase learning, shorten your act and get feedback loops aiming to make them as immediate as possible. The more frequent the cycles, the more opportunities to learn; if we do something in each of three days instead of one thing every three days, we triple our learning opportunities and increase our chances of finding the right answer. Be more willing to experiment.

4. **Use others more.** Teams of people with the widest diversity of backgrounds produce the most innovative solutions to problems. Get others with different backgrounds to analyze and make sense with you. When working together, come up with as many questions about it as you can. Set up a competition with another group or individual, asking them to work on exactly what you are working on. Set a certain time frame and have a postmortem to try to deduce some of the practices and procedures that work best. Find a team or individual that faces problems quite similar to what you face and set up dialogues on a number of specific topics.

5. **You overmanage.** Let your team help you. Periodically, send out a memo asking each person whether there is anything he or she thinks he/she could do that you are now doing or monitoring too closely. Pick one or two things per person and empower them to do it on their own. Make sure the up-front communication is adequate for them to perform well. Explain your standards—what the outcome should be, the key things that need to be taken care of—then ask them to figure out how to do it themselves.

6. **If you are impatient and find yourself checking in too frequently,** set up a timetable with your people with agreed-upon checkpoints and in-progress checks. Let them initiate this on a schedule you are comfortable with. Ask yourself who your most motivating bosses were. Chances are they gave you a lot of leeway, encouraged you to try things, were good sounding boards, and cheered your successes. Do what they did with you.

7. **You get too much into how people should do their work.** The best delegators are crystal clear on what and when, and more open on how. People are more motivated when they can determine the how for themselves. Inexperienced delegators include the hows, which turn the people into task automatons instead of an empowered and

energized staff. Tell them what and when and for how long, and let them figure out how on their own. Give them leeway. Encourage them to try things. Besides being more motivating, it's also more developmental for them. Add the larger context. Although it is not necessary to get the task done, people are more motivated when they know where this task fits in the bigger picture. Take three extra minutes and tell them why this task needs to be done, where it fits in the grander scheme, and its importance to the goals and objectives of the unit.

Open-Ended (Present-focused, flexible)

■ Prefer unscheduled leisure time so they can take advantage of unexpected opportunities.

■ Place self in a flow of events that match inclinations.

■ Variety and improvisational opportunities are desired.

To develop more of this facet:

1. **Do you feel best when you know everything that's going on around you, and you are in control?** Most do. Few are motivated by uncertainty and chaos. But many are challenged by it. They enjoy solving problems no one has solved before. They enjoy cutting paths where no one has been before. You need to become more comfortable being a pioneer. Explore new ground. Learn new things. Practice in your life. Go to theme restaurants you know nothing about. Vacation at places without doing a lot of research. Go to ethnic festivals for groups you have little knowledge about.

2. **Make your off-work life more exciting.** Many of us want as little stress as we can get off-work and seeking this comfort ends up as boredom. What are three really exciting things you and/or your family could do? Work will always be exciting or at least full of activity. Combating this stimulus overload means finding something you can be passionate about off the job.

3. **If you can't relax once you leave work, schedule breakpoints or boundaries.** One of the great things about the human brain is that it responds to change; signal it that work is over—play music in your car, immediately play with your children, go for a walk, swim for 20 minutes—give your mind a clear and repetitious breakpoint. Try to focus all your energy where you are. At work, worry about work

things and not life things. When you hit the driveway, worry about life things and leave work things at the office. Schedule a time every week for financial management and worries. Try to concentrate your worry time where it will do some good.

4. **Perfectionist?** Need or prefer or want to be 100% sure? Lots might prefer that. Perfectionism is tough to let go of because most people see it as a positive trait for themselves. Recognize your perfectionism for what it might be—collecting more information than others to improve your confidence in making a fault-free decision and thereby avoiding risk and criticism. Try to decrease your need for data and your need to be right all the time slightly every week until you reach a more reasonable balance between thinking it through and taking action. Try making some small decisions on little or no data. Anyone with a brain and 100% of the data can make good decisions. The real test is who can act the soonest with a reasonable amount, but not all, of the data. Some studies suggest successful general managers are about 65% correct. Trust your intuition. Let your brain do the calculations.

5. **Some get stressed with increased ambiguity and uncertainty.** We lose our anchor. We are not at our best when we are anxious, frustrated, upset, or when we lose our cool. What brings out your emotional response? Write down why you get anxious: when you don't know what to do; don't want to make a mistake; afraid of the unknown consequences; don't have the confidence to act. When you get emotional, drop the problem for awhile. Go do something else. Come back to it when you are under better control. Let your brain work on it while you do something safer.

If you sometimes overdo being Open-Ended:

1. **Manage your time efficiently.** Plan your time and manage against it. Be time sensitive. Value time. Figure out what you are worth per hour and minute by taking your gross salary plus overhead and benefits. Attach a monetary value on your time. Then ask, is this worth $56 of my time? Review your calendar over the past 90 days to figure out what your three largest time wasters are, and reduce them 50% by batching activities and using efficient communications like e-mail and voice mail for routine matters. Make a list of points to be covered in phone calls; set deadlines for yourself; use your best time of day for the toughest projects—if you're best in the morning, don't waste it on B and C level tasks.

2. **You may be disorganized and not very timely.** Keep a decision log. When a decision opportunity surfaces, immediately log it along with the ideal date it needs to be made. Plan backwards to the work necessary to make the decision on time. If you are not disciplined in how you work and are sometimes late making decisions and taking action because of it, buy books on TQM, ISO and Six Sigma. Go to one workshop on efficient and effective work design.

3. **You may not make timely decisions.** To check this out, write down the decisions you would make right now, then compare them with the decisions you actually make and announce later. Are the decisions more the same than different? If they are more the same, you may have this problem. Since the noise and the heat are the same, the simple solution is to declare as soon as you have made the decision. Better to be done with it. If there is any useful data in the noise and heat, you can adjust your decision sooner.

4. **You love variety and get caught up in activity rather than priorities.** John Kotter, in *The General Managers,* found that effective managers spent about half their time working on one or two key priorities—priorities they described in their own terms, not in terms of what the business/organizational plan said. Further, they made no attempt to work as much on small but related issues that tend to add up to lots of activity. So, rather than consuming themselves and others on 97 seemingly urgent and related smaller activities, they always returned to the few issues that would gain the most mileage long term.

5. **Set goals and measures.** Nothing keeps projects on time and on budget like a goal and a measure. Set goals for the whole project and the subtasks. Set measures so you and others can track progress against the goals.

6. **Laying out the work.** Most resourcefulness starts out with a plan. What do I need to accomplish? What's the time line? What resources will I need? Who controls the resources—people, funding, tools, materials, support—I need? What's my currency? How can I pay for or repay the resources I need? Who wins if I win? Who might lose? Lay out the work from A to Z. Many people are seen as disorganized because they don't write down the sequence or parts of the work and leave something out. Ask others to comment on ordering and what's missing.

Early Starting↔Pressure-Prompted
Managing deadlines, time pressures.

Early Starting (Steady progress, self-discipline)

■ Work best when they start their own work way ahead of deadlines.

■ Like to complete their work in time to review it.

■ Like extra time to check for errors and make last-minute refinements.

To develop more of this facet:

1. **Procrastinator?** Are you a procrastinator? Get caught short on deadlines? Do it all at the last minute? Not only will you not be timely, your decision quality and accuracy will be poor. Procrastinators miss deadlines and performance targets. If you procrastinate, you might not produce consistent decisions. Start earlier. Always do 10% of thinking about the decision immediately after it is assigned so you can better gauge what it is going to take to finish the rest. Divide decisions into thirds or fourths, and schedule time to work on them spaced over the delivery period. Remember one of Murphy's Laws: It takes 90% of the time to do 90% of the project, and another 90% of the time to finish the remaining 10%. Always leave more time than you think it's going to take. Set up checkpoints for yourself along the way. Schedule early data collection and analysis. Don't wait until the last moment. Set an internal deadline one week before the real one.

2. **Disorganized?** Don't always get to everything on time? Forget deadlines? Lose requests for decisions? Under time pressure and increased uncertainty, you have to put the keel in the water yourself. You can't operate helter-skelter and make quality timely decisions. You need to set tighter priorities. Focus more on the mission-critical few decisions. Don't get diverted by trivial work and other decisions. Get better organized and disciplined. Keep a decision log. When a decision opportunity surfaces, immediately log it along with the ideal date it needs to be made. Plan backwards to the work necessary to make the decision on time. If you are not disciplined in how you work and are sometimes late making decisions and taking action because of it, buy books on TQM, ISO and Six Sigma. Go to one workshop on efficient and effective work design.

3. **Selective timeliness.** It's very common for people to be timely in some areas (budget decisions) and untimely in others (give an employee negative feedback). Sometimes we avoid certain areas. Create two columns. Left side are the areas where you seem to make timely and speedy decisions. What's common about those areas? Right side are the areas where you hold back, hesitate, and wait too long to decide. What's common to that list? Money involved? People? Risk? Higher management's involved? Are you avoiding detail or strategy or a technical area you dislike or know little about? Since you already make timely decisions in at least one area, transfer your decision behaviors and practices to the other areas. You already have the skills. You just need to get over the barriers (most likely attitude barriers) in the more difficult areas. If you lack expertise, access your network. Go to the two wisest people you know on the decision, hire a consultant, convene a one-time problem-solving group. You don't have to be an expert in the area, but you do need to know how to access expertise to make timely decisions.

4. **Sometimes we avoid hard-to-deal-with people,** leaving them to the last minute because we want to be right and not get punished or demeaned. Mentally rehearse for worst-case scenarios/hard-to-deal-with people. Anticipate what the person might say and have responses prepared so as not to be caught off guard. Focus on two or three key points in conflict situations and stick to those clearly and politely. Try not to bring up everything you can think of, but instead focus on essence. Try trial balloons with difficult people. Sometime before a decision is due, float up a small trial balloon on a direction you are thinking of.

5. **Give up after one or two tries?** If you have trouble going back the second or third time to get something done, then switch approaches. Sometimes people get stuck in a repeating groove that's not working. Do something different next time. If you visited the office of someone you have difficulties with, invite him/her to your office next time. Think about multiple ways to get the same outcome. For example, to push a decision through, you could meet with stakeholders first, go to a single key stakeholder, study and present the problem to a group, call a problem-solving session, or call in an outside expert. Be prepared to do them all when obstacles arise.

6. **The final 20%.** When you get caught in this situation, create a checklist with the 20% that remains to be done. Plan to do a little on it each day. Cross things off and celebrate each time you get to take

something off the list. Remember, it's going to challenge your motivation and attention. Try to delegate finishing to someone who would see the 20% as a fresh challenge. Get a consultant to finish it. Task trade with someone else's 20% so you both would have something fresh to do.

7. **Stress and conflict under time pressure.** Some are energized by time pressure. Some are stressed with time pressure. It actually slows us down. We lose our anchor. We are not at our best when we are pushed. We get more anxious, frustrated, upset. What brings out your emotional response? Write down why you get anxious under time pressure. What fears does it surface? Don't want to make a mistake? Afraid of the unknown consequences? Don't have the confidence to decide? When you get stressed, drop the problem for a moment. Go do something else. Come back to it when you are under better control. Let your brain work on it while you do something safer.

If you sometimes overdo being Early Starting:

1. **You may miss opportunities to learn differently because you are so organized and step-by-step.** When faced with a new issue, challenge, or problem, figure out what causes it. Keep asking why. See how many causes you can come up with and how many organizing buckets you can put them in. This increases the chance of a better solution because you can see more connections. Chess masters recognize thousands of possible patterns of chess pieces. Look for patterns in data; don't just collect information. Put it in categories that make sense to you. To better understand new and difficult learning, read *The Future of Leadership* by White, Hodgson and Crainer.

2. **Locate the essence of the problem.** What are the key factors or elements in this problem? Experts usually solve problems by figuring out what the deep, underlying principles are and working forward from there; the less adept focus on desired outcomes/solutions and either work backward or concentrate on the surface facts. What are the deep principles of what you're working on? Once you've done this, search the past for parallels—your past, the business past, the historical past. One common mistake here is to search in parallel organizations because "only they would know." Backing up and asking a broader question will aid in the search for solutions. When Motorola wanted to find out how to process orders more quickly, they went not to other electronics firms, but to Domino's Pizza and Federal Express.

3. **You gravitate to safe solutions.** Don't expect to get it right the first time. This leads to safe and stale solutions. Many studies show that the second or third try is when we really understand the underlying dynamics of problems. To increase learning, shorten your act and get feedback loops aiming to make them as immediate as possible. The more frequent the cycles, the more opportunities to learn; if we do something in each of three days instead of one thing every three days, we triple our learning opportunities and increase our chances of finding the right answer. Be more willing to experiment.

4. **Use others more.** Teams of people with the widest diversity of backgrounds produce the most innovative solutions to problems. Get others with different backgrounds to analyze and make sense with you. When working together, come up with as many questions about it as you can. Set up a competition with another group or individual, asking them to work on exactly what you are working on. Set a certain time frame and have a postmortem to try to deduce some of the practices and procedures that work best. Find a team or individual that faces problems quite similar to what you face and set up dialogues on a number of specific topics.

5. **Use oddball tactics.** What is a direct analogy between something you are working on and a natural occurrence? Ask what in nature parallels your problem. When the terrible surfs and motion of the tide threatened to defeat their massive dam project, the Delta Works, the Dutch used the violence of the North Sea to drive in the pilings, ending the danger of the south of the Netherlands flooding. Practice picking out anomalies—unusual facts that don't quite fit, like sales going down when they should have gone up. What do these odd things imply for strategy?

6. **Encourage yourself to do quick experiments and trials.** Studies show that 80% of innovations occur in the wrong place, are created by the wrong people (dye makers developed detergent; Post-it® Notes was an error in a glue formula), and 30–50% of technical innovations fail in tests within the company. Even among those that make it to the marketplace, 70–90% fail. The bottom line on change is a 95% failure rate, and the most successful innovators try lots of quick, inexpensive experiments to increase the chances of success.

J↔P

Pressure-Prompted (Bursts, spurts, pressure)

■ Work well with a deadline and under time pressure.

■ Often enjoy meeting a tight schedule.

■ Require a time period to think through projects before starting on them.

To develop more of this facet:

1. **Spend more time thinking through projects in advance.** Delay doing anything while you mull it over. Wait even a bit too long to act, and let the pressure build. Then, seemingly at the last minute, go at the project full bore. Notice how quickly your mind works, how exhilarating working under time pressure can be.

2. **For some safe practice, pick a few off-work activities where time pressure is everything.** Try timed chess or bridge matches, or numerous board games where your turn lasts until the sand goes through the hourglass. Practice timing yourself to do simple tasks, then try to beat your best time until you reach the limit of how quickly you can do it. Up your tolerance for last-minute activities.

3. **Perfectionist?** Need to be 100% sure? Perfectionism is tough to let go of because it's a positive trait for most. Worried about what people will say when you mess up? When every "t" isn't crossed? Recognize your perfectionism for what it might be—collecting information to improve your confidence and avoid criticism, examining opportunities so long you miss them, or waiting for the perfect solution. Try to decrease your need for all of the data and your need to be right all the time slightly every week, until you reach a more reasonable balance between thinking it through and taking action. Also, you may hold on to too much of the work, fail to delegate, and are becoming a bottleneck preventing action around you. One way to overcome this is to begin to believe in others and let them do some of the work for you.

4. **Analysis paralysis?** Break out of your examine-it-to-death mode and just do it. Sometimes you hold back acting because you don't have all the information. Some like to be close to 100% sure before they act. Anyone with a brain and 100% of the data can make good decisions. The real test is who can act the soonest with a reasonable amount, but not all, of the data. Some studies suggest successful general managers are about 65% correct. If you learn to make smaller decisions more

quickly, you can change course along the way to the correct decision. You may examine things to death because you are a chronic worrier who focuses on the downsides of action. Write down your worries, and for each one, write down the upside (a pro for each con). Once you consider both sides of the issue, you should be more willing to take action. Virtually any conceivable action has a downside, but it has an upside as well. Act, get feedback on the results, refine, and act again.

5. **Build up your confidence.** Maybe you're slow to act because you don't think you're up to the task. If you boldly act, others will shoot you down and find you out. Take a course or work with a tutor to bolster your confidence in one skill or area at a time. Focus on the strengths you do have; think of ways you can use these strengths when making nerve-wracking actions. If you are interpersonally skilled, for example, see yourself smoothly dealing with questions and objections to your actions. The only way you will ever know what you can do is to act and find out.

6. **Don't like risk?** Sometimes taking action involves pushing the envelope, taking chances, and trying bold new initiatives. Doing those things leads to more misfires and mistakes. Research says that successful executives have made more mistakes in their careers than those who didn't make it. Treat any mistakes or failures as chances to learn. Nothing ventured, nothing gained. Up your risk comfort. Start small so you can recover more quickly. Go for small wins. Don't blast into a major task to prove your boldness. Break it down into smaller tasks. Take the easiest one for you first. Then build up to the tougher ones. Review each one to see what you did well and not well, and set goals so you'll do something differently and better each time. End up accomplishing the big goal and taking the bold action. Challenge yourself. See how creative you can be in taking action a number of different ways.

If you sometimes overdo being Pressure-Prompted:

1. **You wait way too long to start.** Many, many tasks can't be done at the last minute. You may get it done, but your decision quality and accuracy will be poor. Procrastinators miss deadlines and performance targets. If you procrastinate, you might not produce consistent decisions. Start earlier. Always do 10% of thinking about the decision immediately after it is assigned so you can better gauge what it is going to take to finish the rest. Divide decisions into thirds

or fourths, and schedule time to work on them spaced over the delivery period. Remember one of Murphy's Laws: It takes 90% of the time to do 90% of the project, and another 90% of the time to finish the remaining 10%. Always leave more time than you think it's going to take. Set up checkpoints for yourself along the way. Schedule early data collection and analysis. Don't wait until the last moment. Set an internal deadline one week before the real one.

2. **Think of a big decision as a series of smaller ones.** The essence of timely decision making is the tolerance of increased errors and mistakes, and absorbing the possible heat and criticism that follow. Acting on an ill-defined problem with no precedents to follow in a hurry means shooting in the dark with as informed a decision as you can make at the time. Incrementalists make a series of smaller decisions, get instant feedback, correct the course, get a little more data, move forward a little more, until the bigger decision gets made. They don't try to get it right the first time. They try their best educated guess now, and then correct as feedback comes in. Many problem-solving studies show that the second or third try is when we really understand the underlying dynamics of problems.

3. **You don't persevere on tasks because you get bored.** Then go for variety. If you visited the office of someone you have difficulties with, invite him/her to your office next time. Think about multiple ways to get the same outcome. For example, to push a decision through, you could meet with stakeholders first, go to a single key stakeholder, study and present the problem to a group, call a problem-solving session, or call in an outside expert. Be prepared to do them all to keep yourself motivated.

4. **You get in trouble with your boss.** Last-minute performers often don't fare well in organizations. Strike a deal with your boss and stick to it. Focus on expectations, ask what results indicate success. Find out about your boss's job and what sorts of pressures he/she is under.

5. **You dump work on your direct reports at the last minute and overwhelm them.** Communicate earlier, set time frames and goals, and get out of the way. People need to know what it is you expect. What does the outcome look like? When do you need it by? What's the budget? What resources do they get? What decisions can they make? Do you want checkpoints along the way? How will we both know and measure how well the task is done? One of the most common problems with delegation is incomplete or cryptic up-front

communication leading to frustration, a job not well done the first time, rework, and a reluctance to delegate next time. Poor communicators always have to take more time managing because of rework. Analyze recent projects that went well and didn't go well. How did you delegate? Too much? Not enough? Unwanted pieces? Major chunks of responsibility? Workload distributed properly? Did you set measures? Set up a series of delegation practices that can be used as if you're not there. What do you have to be informed of? What feedback loops can people use for midcourse correction? What questions should be answered as the work proceeds? What steps should be followed? What are the criteria to be followed? When will you be available to help?

6. **You don't manage your time well.** Plan your time and manage against it. Be time sensitive. Value time. Figure out what you are worth per hour and minute by taking your gross salary plus overhead and benefits. Attach a monetary value on your time. Then ask, is this worth $56 of my time? Review your calendar over the past 90 days to figure out what your three largest time wasters are, and reduce them 50% by batching activities and using efficient communications like e-mail and voice mail for routine matters. Make a list of points to be covered in phone calls; set deadlines for yourself; use your best time of day for the toughest projects—if you're best in the morning, don't waste it on B and C level tasks.

7. **You don't work on priorities, you work on what creates the most pressure and excitement.** Be careful not to be guided by just what you like and what you don't like to do. That way of using your time will probably not be successful over time. Use data, intuition, and even feelings to apportion your time, but not feelings alone. John Kotter, in *The General Managers*, found that effective managers spent about half their time working on one or two key priorities—priorities they described in their own terms. They didn't respond much to the tactical pressures of the moment.

J↔P

Scheduled↔Spontaneous
Degree of scheduling in daily life.

Scheduled (Routine, structure)

■ Routine is appealing because it is a way of getting things done correctly and with efficiency.

■ Gain energy from a predictable flow of tasks.

■ Structure provides an anchor for maintaining relationships.

To develop more of this facet:

1. **Try to see the value in routines.** Pick a plan or procedure and do a historical analysis of how it came to be and why it is necessary. Resist the urge to change it or question its usefulness. Understand it first.

2. **Compensate for your dislikes.** Find a person you admire and respect to deal with all the procedures you find oppressive. Let this person tell you if anything needs changing. Otherwise, trust his or her judgment.

3. **Using your work goals, separate what you need to do into mission-critical,** important to get done, nice if there is time left over, and not central to what we are trying to achieve. When faced with choices or multiple things to do, apply the scale and always choose the highest level. Be time sensitive. Taking time to plan and set priorities actually frees up more time later than just diving into things hoping that you can get it done on time. Most people out of time claim they didn't have the time to plan their time.

4. **Laying out tasks and work on a time line.** Most successful time managers begin with a good plan for time. What do I need to accomplish? What are the goals? What's mission-critical and what's trivial? What's the time line? How will I track it? Buy a flowcharting software program that does PERT and GANTT charts. Become an expert in its use. Use the output of the software to plan your time. Alternatively, write down your work plan. Many people are seen as lacking time management skills because they don't write down the sequence or parts of the work and leave something out. Ask others to comment on ordering and what's missing.

5. **Manage your time efficiently.** Plan your time and manage against it. Be time sensitive. Value time. Figure out what you are worth per hour and minute by taking your gross salary plus overhead and benefits. Attach a monetary value on your time. Then ask, is this worth $56 of my time? Review your calendar over the past 90 days to figure out what your three largest time wasters are, and reduce them 50% by batching activities and using efficient communications like e-mail and voice mail for routine matters. Make a list of points to be covered in phone calls; set deadlines for yourself; use your best time of day for the toughest projects—if you're best in the morning, don't waste it on B and C level tasks.

6. **Find someone in your environment who is better at time management than you are.** Watch what he/she does and compare against what you typically do. Try to increase doing the things he or she does and doesn't do. Ask for feedback from some people who have commented on your poor time management. What did they find difficult?

7. **Be careful not to be guided by just what you like and what you don't like to do.** That way of using your time will probably not be successful over time. Use data, intuition, and even feelings to apportion your time, but not feelings alone.

8. **Others will always ask you to do more than you can do.** An important time saver is the ability to constructively say no. One technique people use is to ask the requester which of the other things they have asked you to do would they like to cancel or delay in order to do the most recent request. That way, you say both yes and no and let the requester choose.

9. **Another common time waster is inadequate disengagement skills.** Some poor time managers can't shut down transactions. Either they continue to talk beyond what would be necessary or, more commonly, they can't get the other party to quit talking. When it's time to move on, just say, "I have to get on to the next thing I have to do; we can pick this up some other time."

If you sometimes overdo being Scheduled:

1. **Routine isn't always the best way to get things done efficiently.** According to studies, 90% of the problems of middle managers and above are ambiguous—it's neither clear what the problem is nor what the solution is. Most people with a brain, given unlimited time, and

100% of the information, could make accurate and good decisions. The real rewards go to those who can comfortably make more good decisions than bad with less than all of the information, in less time, with few or no precedents on how it was solved before.

2. **The essence of dealing comfortably with uncertainty is the tolerance of errors and mistakes, and absorbing the possible heat and criticism that follow.** Acting on an ill-defined problem with no precedents to follow means shooting in the dark with as informed a decision as you can make at the time. People who are good at this are incrementalists. They make a series of smaller decisions, get instant feedback, correct the course, get a little more data, move forward a little more, until the bigger problem is under control. They don't try to get it right the first time. Many problem-solving studies show that the second or third try is when we really understand the underlying dynamics of problems. They also know that the more uncertain the situation is, the more likely it is they will make mistakes in the beginning. So, you need to work on two practices: Start small so you can recover more quickly. Do little somethings as soon as you can and get used to heat.

3. **Perfectionist?** Need or prefer or want to be 100% sure? Lots might prefer that. Perfectionism is tough to let go of because most people see it as a positive trait for themselves. Recognize your perfectionism for what it might be—collecting more information than others to improve your confidence in making a fault-free decision and thereby avoiding risk and criticism. Try to decrease your need for data and your need to be right all the time slightly every week until you reach a more reasonable balance between thinking it through and taking action. Try making some small decisions on little or no data. Anyone with a brain and 100% of the data can make good decisions. The real test is who can act the soonest with a reasonable amount, but not all, of the data. Some studies suggest successful general managers are about 65% correct. Trust your intuition. Let your brain do the calculations.

4. **Do you feel best when you know everything that's going on around you, and you are in control?** Most do. Few are motivated by uncertainty and chaos. But many are challenged by it. They enjoy solving problems no one has solved before. They enjoy cutting paths where no one has been before. You need to become more comfortable being a pioneer. Explore new ground. Learn new things. Practice in your life. Go to theme restaurants you know nothing about. Vacation

at places without doing a lot of research. Go to ethnic festivals for groups you have little knowledge about.

5. **You may be avoiding risk.** Sometimes taking action involves pushing the envelope, taking chances, and trying bold new initiatives. Doing those things leads to more misfires and mistakes. Research says that successful executives have made more mistakes in their careers than those who didn't make it. Treat any mistakes or failures as chances to learn. Nothing ventured, nothing gained. Up your risk comfort. Start small so you can recover more quickly. Go for small wins. Don't blast into a major task to prove your boldness. Break it down into smaller tasks. Take the easiest one for you first. Then build up to the tougher ones. Review each one to see what you did well and not well, and set goals so you'll do something differently and better each time.

6. **You may struggle when a straight-ahead style runs up against organizational realities.** Get lost in the maze? Some people know the steps necessary to get things done but are too impatient to follow the process. Maneuvering through the maze includes stopping once in awhile to let things run their course. It may mean waiting until a major gatekeeper has the time to pay attention to your needs. One additional problem might be in diagnosing the paths, turns, dead ends, and zags.

7. **Get rattled when what you try doesn't work or gets rejected?** If you tend to lose your cool and get frustrated, practice responses before the fact. What's the worst that could happen and what will you do? You can pause, count to 10, or ask why it can't be done. You can take in information and develop counter moves. So don't react, learn.

8. **Who are the movers and shakers in the organization?** How do they get things done? Who do they rely on for expediting things through the maze? How do you compare to them? Who are the major gatekeepers who control the flow of resources, information, and decisions? Who are the guides and the helpers? Get to know them better. Who are the major resisters and stoppers? Try to avoid or go around them.

J↔P

Spontaneous (Variety, unexpected)

- Work best when they have constant variety.

- Find different ways of doing regular events.

- Break monotony by exploring new activities.

- Feel a need to introduce variation into events.

To develop more of this facet:

1. **Make a list of what you like and don't like to do.** Concentrate on doing at least a couple of liked activities each day. Work to delegate or task trade the things that are no longer motivating to you. Do your least preferred activities first; focus not on the activity, but your sense of accomplishment. Change your work activity to mirror your interests as much as you can. Volunteer for task forces and projects that would be motivating for you.

2. **Do you feel best when you know everything that's going on around you, and you are in control?** Most do. Few are motivated by uncertainty and chaos. But many are challenged by it. They enjoy solving problems no one has solved before. They enjoy cutting paths where no one has been before. You need to become more comfortable being a pioneer. Explore new ground. Learn new things. Practice in your life. Go to theme restaurants you know nothing about. Vacation at places without doing a lot of research. Go to ethnic festivals for groups you have little knowledge about.

3. **Make your off-work life more exciting.** Many of us want as little stress as we can get off-work and seeking this comfort ends up as boredom. What are three really exciting things you and/or your family could do? Work will always be exciting or at least full of activity. Combating this stimulus overload means finding something you can be passionate about off the job. Volunteer, take a course, join a service club, be a coach or a referee.

4. **Pick three unrelated things to study and dabble in that you have not yet paid much attention to**—opera, romance novels, technical journals out of your area, MTV, learn a new language, take a magic course, study archeology. Connections can come from anywhere—your brain doesn't care where it gets perspectives. Try to think about how the principles of one tie into the other.

5. **Pick something you've never done but which would broaden your perspective off-work.** Serve with a community group, volunteer to be a Big Sister/Brother, travel to an unvisited country, follow a group of ten-year-olds around for a few days.

6. **At work, pick three tasks you've never done and go do them.** If you don't know much about customers, work in a store or handle customer complaints; if you don't know what engineering does, go find out; task trade with someone. Seek the broadest possible exposure inside the organization. Do lunch with counterparts of the organization and tell each other what you do.

7. **Task forces.** Task forces/projects are a great opportunity. If the project is important, is multi-functional, and has a real outcome which will be taken seriously (not a study group), it is one of the most common developmental events listed by successful executives. Such projects require learning other functions, businesses, or nationalities well enough that in a tight time frame you can appreciate how they think and why their area/position is important. In so doing, you get out of your own experience and start to see connections to a broader world—how international trade works; or more at home, how the pieces of your organization fit together.

8. **When faced with a new issue, challenge, or problem, figure out what causes it.** Keep asking why. See how many causes you can come up with and how many organizing buckets you can put them in. This increases the chance of a better solution because you can see more connections. Chess masters recognize thousands of possible patterns of chess pieces. Look for patterns in data; don't just collect information. Put it in categories that make sense to you.

9. **Don't expect to get it right the first time.** This leads to safe and stale solutions. Many studies show that the second or third try is when we really understand the underlying dynamics of problems. To increase learning, shorten your act and get feedback loops aiming to make them as immediate as possible. The more frequent the cycles, the more opportunities to learn; if we do something in each of three days instead of one thing every three days, we triple our learning opportunities and increase our chances of finding the right answer. Be more willing to experiment.

10. **Encourage yourself to do quick experiments and trials.** Studies show that 80% of innovations occur in the wrong place, are created by the wrong people (dye makers developed detergent; Post-it® Notes was

an error in a glue formula), and 30–50% of technical innovations fail in tests within the company. Even among those that make it to the marketplace, 70–90% fail. The bottom line on change is a 95% failure rate, and the most successful innovators try lots of quick, inexpensive experiments to increase the chances of success.

If you sometimes overdo being Spontaneous:

1. **You love variety and get caught up in activity rather than priorities.** John Kotter, in *The General Managers*, found that effective managers spent about half their time working on one or two key priorities— priorities they described in their own terms, not in terms of what the business/organizational plan said. Further, they made no attempt to work as much on small but related issues that tend to add up to lots of activity. So, rather than consuming themselves and others on 97 seemingly urgent and related smaller activities, they always returned to the few issues that would gain the most mileage long term.

2. **You don't manage your time well.** Plan your time and manage against it. Be time sensitive. Value time. Figure out what you are worth per hour and minute by taking your gross salary plus overhead and benefits. Attach a monetary value on your time. Then ask, is this worth $56 of my time? Review your calendar over the past 90 days to figure out what your three largest time wasters are, and reduce them 50% by batching activities and using efficient communications like e-mail and voice mail for routine matters. Make a list of points to be covered in phone calls; set deadlines for yourself; use your best time of day for the toughest projects—if you're best in the morning, don't waste it on B and C level tasks.

3. **Many tasks are straight-ahead A,B,C, finish.** Set goals and measures. Nothing keeps projects on time and on budget like a goal and a measure. Set goals for the whole project and the subtasks. Set measures so you and others can track progress against the goals.

4. **Laying out the work.** Most resourcefulness starts out with a plan. What do I need to accomplish? What's the time line? What resources will I need? Who controls the resources—people, funding, tools, materials, support—I need? What's my currency? How can I pay for or repay the resources I need? Who wins if I win? Who might lose? Lay out the work from A to Z. Many people are seen as disorganized because they don't write down the sequence or parts of the work and

leave something out. Ask others to comment on ordering and what's missing.

5. **Vision the plan in process.** What could go wrong? Run scenarios in your head. Think along several paths. Rank the potential problems from highest likelihood to lowest likelihood. Think about what you would do if the highest likelihood things were to occur. Create a contingency plan for each. Pay attention to the weakest links, which are usually groups or elements you have the least interface with or control over (perhaps someone in a remote location, a consultant, or supplier). Stay doubly in touch with the potential weak links.

6. **Set up a process to monitor progress against the plan.** How would you know if the plan is on time? Could you estimate time to completion or percent finished at any time? Give people involved in implementing the plan progress feedback as you go.

7. **You may not have developed your technical skills sufficiently.** Locate a pro. Find the seasoned master professional in the technology or function, and ask whether he/she would mind showing you the ropes and tutoring you. Most don't mind having a few "apprentices" around. Help him or her teach you. Ask, "How do you know what's important? What do you look at first? Second? What are the five keys you always look at or for? What do you read? Who do you go to for advice?"

8. **Find the bible on your function/technology.** Almost every function and technology has a book people might call the "bible" in the area. It is the standard reference everyone looks to for knowledge. There is probably a journal in your technology or function. Subscribe for a year or more. See if they have back issues available.

Methodical↔Emergent
Sequencing or ordering of smaller to larger tasks without concern for time or schedule.

Methodical (Plan specific tasks, organized)

■ Organize materials and arrange in order needed, note what needs to be done in specific order to get the job done.

■ Take pleasure in organizing work and materials, make complete plans with specific time allotments for each task.

To develop more of this facet:

1. Subscribe to *The Systems Thinker®*, Pegasus Communications, Inc., Cambridge, MA, 781-398-9700. This is a group dedicated to finding out how things work and why they work that way. They have a monthly publication as well as workshops, seminars, and other materials available to help you see the world as a series of recurring systems or archetypes. They analyze everyday events and processes and try to see why they work the way they do.

2. **Lay out the process.** Most well-running processes start out with a plan. What do I need to accomplish? What's the time line? What resources will I need? Who controls the resources—people, funding, tools, materials, support—I need? What's my currency? How can I pay for or repay the resources I need? Who wins if I win? Who might lose? Buy a flowcharting software program that does PERT and GANTT charts. Become an expert in its use. Use the output of the software to communicate your plans to others. Use the flowcharts in your presentations. Nothing helps move a process along better than a good plan. It helps the people who have to work under the plan. It leads to better use of resources. It gets things done faster. It helps anticipate problems before they occur. Lay out the work from A to Z. Many people are seen as lacking because they don't write down the sequence or parts of the work and leave something out. Ask others to comment on ordering and what's missing.

3. **Have an information checklist detailing what information should go to whom;** pass on summaries or copies of important communications. Determine the information checklist by: keeping tabs on unpleasant surprises people report to you; ask direct reports what they'd like to know to do their jobs better; and check with boss, peers,

and customers to see if you pass along too little, enough, or too much of the right kinds of information. It's important to know what to pass, to whom to pass, and when to pass, to become an effective informer.

4. **Do you tell people only what they need to know to do their little piece of the puzzle?** Being aware of the bigger picture motivates people. They want to know what to do in order to do their jobs and more. How does what they are doing fit into the larger picture? What are the other people working on and why? Many people think that's unnecessary information and that it would take too much time to do. They're wrong. The sense of doing something worthwhile is the number two motivator at work! It results in a high return on motivation and productivity. (Try to increase the amount of more-than-your-job information you share.) Focus on the impact on others by figuring out who information affects. Put five minutes on your meeting agenda. Ask people what they want to know and, assuming it's not confidential information, tell them. Pick a topic each month to tell your people about.

5. **Set goals and measures.** Nothing keeps projects on time and on budget like a goal and a measure. Set goals for the whole project and the subtasks. Set measures so you and others can track progress against the goals.

6. **Some people know the steps and the process necessary to get things done but they are too impatient to follow the process.** Following a process to get things done includes stopping once in awhile to let things run their course. It may mean waiting until a major gatekeeper has the time to pay attention to your needs. Due process takes time.

7. **Envision the process unfolding.** What could go wrong? Run scenarios in your head. Think along several paths. Rank the potential problems from highest likelihood to lowest likelihood. Think about what you would do if the highest likelihood things were to occur. Create a contingency plan for each. Pay attention to the weakest links, which are usually groups or elements you have the least interface with or control over—perhaps someone in a remote location, a consultant, or supplier. Stay doubly in touch with the potential weak links.

8. **Bargaining for resources.** What do I have to trade? What can I buy? What can I borrow? What do I need to trade for? What do I need that I can't pay or trade for?

9. **Manage your time efficiently.** Plan your time and manage against it. Be time sensitive. Value time. Figure out what you are worth per hour and minute by taking your gross salary plus overhead and benefits. Attach a monetary value on your time. Then ask, is this worth $56 of my time? Review your calendar over the past 90 days to figure out what your three largest time wasters are, and reduce them 50% by batching activities and using efficient communications like e-mail and voice mail for routine matters. Make a list of points to be covered in phone calls; set deadlines for yourself; use your best time of day for the toughest projects—if you're best in the morning, don't waste it on B and C level tasks.

If you sometimes overdo being Methodical:

1. **You may be blocking your creative instincts.** Remove the restraints. What's preventing you from being more creative? Perfectionist? Being creative operates at well below having everything right. Cautious and reluctant to speculate? Being creative is the opposite. Worried about what people may think? Afraid you won't be able to defend your idea? By its very nature, being creative means throwing uncertain things up for review and critique. Narrow perspective, most comfortable with your technology and profession? Being creative is looking everywhere. More comfortable with what is very practical? Being creative begins as being impractical. Too busy to reflect and ruminate? Being creative takes time. Get out of your comfort zone. Many busy people rely too much on solutions from their own history. They rely on what has happened to them in the past. They see sameness in problems that isn't there. Beware of "I have always..." or "Usually, I...." Always pause and look under rocks and ask yourself is this really like the problems you have solved in the past? You don't have to change who you are and what you're comfortable with other than when you need to be more creative. Then think and act differently; try new things; break free of your restraints.

2. **Value-added approaches.** To be more personally creative, immerse yourself in the problem. Getting fresh ideas is not a speedboating process; it requires looking deeply.

   ■ Carve out dedicated time—study the problem deeply, talk with others, look for parallels in other organizations and in remote areas totally outside your field. If your response to this is that you don't have the time, that also usually explains why you're not having any fresh ideas.

■ Think out loud. Many people don't know what they know until they talk it out. Find a good sounding board and talk to him/her to increase your understanding of a problem or a technical area. Talk to an expert in an unrelated field. Talk to the most irreverent person you know. Your goal is not to get his/her input, but rather his/her help in figuring out what you know—what your principles and rules of thumb are.

■ Practice picking out anomalies—unusual facts that don't quite fit, like sales going down when they should have gone up. What do these odd things imply for strategy? Naturally creative people are much more likely to think in opposite cases when confronted with a problem. Turn the problem upside down: Ask what is the least likely thing it could be, what the problem is not, what's missing from the problem, or what the mirror image of the problem is.

■ Look for distant parallels. Don't fall into the mental trap of searching only in parallel organizations because "only they would know." Back up and ask a broader question to aid in the search for solutions. When Motorola wanted to find out how to process orders more quickly, they went not to other electronics firms, but to Domino's Pizza and Federal Express. For more ideas, an interesting—and fun—book on the topic is *Take the Road to Creativity and Get Off Your Dead End* by David Campbell.

3. **Use others to help.** Try brainstorming. Outline the problem for the group; tell them what you've tried and learned from the tries. Include things that may have happened only once. Invite the group to free-form respond. Any idea is okay—no criticism allowed. Record all ideas on a flip chart. When the group has exhausted the possibilities, take the most interesting ones and ask the group to first name positive features of the ideas, then negative features, and finally what's interesting about the ideas. Follow this process until you've covered all the ideas that interest you. Then ask the group what else they would select as interesting ideas to do a plus, minus, interesting analysis. This process can usually be done in an hour or two.

4. **Your perspective may need to be broadened.** Read international publications like *The Economist,* the *International Herald Tribune, Commentary;* autobiographies of people like Kissinger; pick a country and study it; read a book on the fall of the Soviet Union; or read "we present all sides" journals like *The Atlantic Monthly* to get the broadest

possible view of issues. There are common underlying principles in everything. You need to expose yourself more broadly in order to find and apply those principles to what you're doing today.

5.   **At work, pick three tasks you've never done and go do them.** If you don't know much about customers, work in a store or handle customer complaints; if you don't know what engineering does, go find out; task trade with someone. Seek the broadest possible exposure inside the organization. Do lunch with counterparts of the organization and tell each other what you do.

6.   **Task forces/projects are a great opportunity.** If the project is important, is multi-functional, and has a real outcome which will be taken seriously (not a study group), it is one of the most common developmental events listed by successful executives. Such projects require learning other functions, businesses, or nationalities well enough that in a tight time frame you can appreciate how they think and why their area/position is important. In so doing, you get out of your own experience and start to see connections to a broader world—how international trade works; or more at home, how the pieces of your organization fit together. You can build perspective.

Emergent (Plan loosely, adaptable)

■   Treat projects as explorations and discoveries, take delight in finding out what to do as they go along.

■   Do minimal preparation, often discover how to complete things by trial-and-error, follow trail of associations when involved in new projects.

To develop more of this facet:

1.   **Remove the restraints.** What's preventing you from being more creative? Perfectionist? Being creative operates at well below having everything right. Cautious and reluctant to speculate? Being creative is the opposite. Worried about what people may think? Afraid you won't be able to defend your idea? By its very nature, being creative means throwing uncertain things up for review and critique. Narrow perspective, most comfortable with your technology and profession? Being creative is looking everywhere. More comfortable with what is very practical? Being creative begins as being impractical. Too busy to reflect and ruminate? Being creative takes time. Get out of your comfort zone. Many busy people rely too much on solutions from

their own history. They rely on what has happened to them in the past. They see sameness in problems that isn't there. Beware of "I have always..." or "Usually, I...." Always pause and look under rocks and ask yourself is this really like the problems you have solved in the past? You don't have to change who you are and what you're comfortable with other than when you need to be more creative. Then think and act differently; try new things; break free of your restraints.

2. **Unearthing creative ideas.** Creative thought processes do not follow the formal rules of logic, where one uses cause and effect to prove or solve something. Some rules of creative thought are:

- Not using concepts but changing them; imagining this were something else.

- Move from one concept or way of looking at things to another, such as from economic to political.

- Generate ideas without judging them initially.

- Use information to restructure and come up with new patterns.

- Jump from one idea to another without justifying the jump.

- Look for the least likely and odd.

- Look for parallels far from the problem, such as how is an organization like a big oak tree?

- Ask what's missing or what's not here.

- Fascination with mistakes and failure as learning devices.

3. **During World War II, it was discovered that teams of people with the widest diversity of backgrounds produced the most creative solutions to problems.** The teams included people who knew absolutely nothing about the area (i.e., an English major working on a costing problem). When attacking a tough problem which has eluded attempts to solve it, get the broadest group you can. Involve different functions, levels, and disciplines. Pull in customers and colleagues from other organizations. Remember that you're looking for fresh approaches; you're not convening a work task force expected to implement or judge the practicality of the notions. Believe it or not, it doesn't matter if they know anything about the problem or the technology required to deal with it. That's your job.

4. **Experiment and learn.** Whether the ideas come from you or a brainstorming session, encourage yourself to do quick experiments and trials. Studies show that 80% of innovations occur in the wrong place, are created by the wrong people (dye makers developed detergent, Post-it® Notes was a failed glue experiment), and 30–50% of technical innovations fail in tests within the company. Even among those that make it to the marketplace, 70–90% fail. The bottom line on change is a 95% failure rate, and the most successful innovators try lots of quick, inexpensive experiments to increase the chances of success.

5. **Getting creativity out of a group.** Many times the creative idea comes from a group, not single individuals. When working on a new idea for a product or service, have them come up with as many questions about it as you can. Often we think too quickly of solutions. In studies of problem-solving sessions, solutions outweigh questions 8 to 1. Asking more questions helps people rethink the problem and come to more and different solutions. Have the group take a current product you are dissatisfied with and represent it visually—a flowchart or a series of pictures. Cut it up into its component pieces and shuffle them. Examine the pieces to see if a different order would help, or how you could combine three pieces into one. Try many experiments or trials to find something that will work. Have the group think beyond current boundaries. What are some of the most sacred rules or practices in your organization? Unit? Think about smashing them— what would your unit be doing if you broke the rules? Talk to the most irreverent person you know about this. Buffer the group. It's difficult to work on something new if they are besieged with all the distractions you have to deal with, particularly if people are looking over your shoulder asking why isn't anything happening.

6. **Patterns.** Look for patterns in personal, organization, or the world, in general successes and failures. What was common to each success or what was present in each failure but never present in a success? Focus on the successes; failures are easier to analyze but don't in themselves tell you what would work. Comparing successes, while less exciting, yields more information about underlying principles. The bottom line is to reduce your insights to principles or rules of thumb you think might be repeatable. When faced with the next new problem, those general underlying principles will apply again.

7. **Share the future with others.** The power of a mission and vision communication is providing everyone in the organization with a road

map on how they are going to be part of something grand and exciting. Establish common cause. Imagine what the change would look like if fully implemented, then describe the outcome often—how things will look in the future. Help people see how their efforts fit in by creating simple, obvious measures of achievement like bar or thermometer charts. Be succinct. People don't line up behind laundry lists or ambiguous objectives. Missions and visions should be more about where we are going and less about how we are going to get there. Keep your eyes on the prize.

If you sometimes overdo being Emergent:

1. **You may get blindsided because you haven't set up proper measures.** How would you tell if the goal was accomplished? If the things I asked others to do were done right, what outcomes could we all agree on as measures of success? Most groups can easily come up with success measures that are different from, and more important to them, than formal measures. Ask them to do so. Set up a process to monitor progress against the goals. People like running measures. They like to gauge their pace. It's like the United Way Thermometer in the lobby.

2. **Give as much in-process feedback as you have time for.** Most people are motivated by process feedback against agreed-upon goals for three reasons:

   ■ First, it helps them adjust what they are doing along the way in time to achieve the goal; they can make midcourse corrections.

   ■ Second, it shows them what they are doing is important and that you're eager to help.

   ■ Third, it's not the "gotcha" game of negative and critical feedback after the fact.

3. **Measure activity** (in addition to measuring outcomes and results). Say you bought some equipment. How many people are needed to run it? How much time will this take? Repairs? How much time? Activity-based accounting measures the cost of doing or not doing a task. By looking at work carefully in terms of time, core and non-core tasks (those less important because the time spent isn't worth it) can be determined. Using this method, a group of nurses doubled their productivity.

J↔P

4. **You don't plan ahead and have the wrong people on board.** Do you have a long-term view of the talent it's going to take to produce both current and long-term results? Do you have a replacement plan for yourself? Do you use a success profile with the competencies you know you are going to need? Have you hired someone who now has, or will have in a short period of time, the ability to take your job? Have you selected someone you would sponsor for promotion to another job at your level, possibly passing you up in time? The best managers surround themselves with talent, and eventually some of the talent turns out to be better than the person who hired and trained them. That's a good thing and reason for a celebration.

5. **Make sure you know what matters most.** Read sources that focus on key competencies at work, such as *The Extraordinary Leader* by Zenger and Folkman or *The Leadership Machine* by Lombardo and Eichinger. Look at the research-based lists of competencies that appear on standardized competency instruments such as VOICES®, PROFILOR®, or BENCHMARKS®.

6. **You let events emerge and get caught up in activity rather than priorities.** John Kotter, in *The General Managers,* found that effective managers spent about half their time working on one or two key priorities—priorities they described in their own terms, not in terms of what the business/organizational plan said. Further, they made no attempt to work as much on small but related issues that tend to add up to lots of activity. So, rather than consuming themselves and others on 97 seemingly urgent and related smaller activities, they always returned to the few issues that would gain the most mileage long term.

7. **You need to think more in systems terms than you do.** Subscribe to *The Systems Thinker®*, Pegasus Communications, Inc., Cambridge, MA, 781-398-9700. This is a group dedicated to finding out how things work and why they work that way. They have a monthly publication as well as workshops, seminars, and other materials available to help you see the world as a series of recurring systems or archetypes. They analyze everyday events and processes and try to see why they work the way they do. The material will help you view things in terms of whole systems.

8. **You lose effectiveness when you are not hands-on.** Managing remotely is the true test of delegation and empowerment. It's impossible for you to do it all. Successful managers report high involvement in setting parameters, exceptions they want to be notified of, and expected outcomes. They detail what requires their involvement and what doesn't. When people call them for a decision, they always ask, "What do you think? What impact will it have on you—customers, etc.—if we do this?" rather than just render a judgment. If you don't, people will begin to delegate upward, and you'll be a close-in manager from a remote location. Help people think things through, and trust them to follow the plan. Delegation requires this clear communication about expectations and releasing the authority to decide and act.

SECTION III

Effectiveness and Development Planning

Remember, it's all about being a more effective YOU. Most people are capable, at least for short bursts, of rendering all of the behaviors of all the types, albeit not as well or against a high standard of effectiveness. An introvert can smile and shake hands and have an animated dialogue. An intuitive thinker can collect data from others. A highly logical and conceptual person can have a burst of compassion. A highly structured and planful person can do something spontaneous. The question is what is your preferred mode of operation and how pure of a type are you? At what frequency do you stick with your type and your facets?

In an ideal world of maximum effectiveness, you would have a preferred type and style that you use most of the time, and then for short periods you could credibly behave against your type and your facets. The fast could slow down. The futurist could attend to practical details today. The private loner could contribute value to a team effort. The rigid could adapt to something.

Developing an "unnatural to YOU" behavior has two component parts. First, you have to want to and be willing to take a risk and, second, you have to have the skill.

The motive for wanting to develop a behavior is to achieve a goal or get something done that is important to you and others. The motive includes knowing what kind of adaptation you have to make. This requires being type wise or type smart. Who are YOU? Who are THEY? What works and what doesn't? What does the situation call for? What would you need to be able to do differently to make it all happen?

The skill is fairly simple if the motivation is there. You need to do something different than you normally do.

The Five Strategies

There are five strategies you can use when faced with the need to do something different to bring about a more favorable outcome.

1. You can build the skill(s) for temporary or permanent use.

2. You can substitute something else for the lack of skill. You can use another skill to cover for, substitute for, or neutralize the negative effects of the lack of skill.

3. You can use a workaround strategy to neutralize the lack of the skill. You can use any of 10 workaround strategies to cover for your lack of skill.

4. You can compensate for overused skills (usually strengths).

5. Finally, although not a very attractive strategy, you can also just live with it. At least you know what it is because you are type wise and are willing to admit that you have a lack of skill in this area. In this case, you should use your strengths more often. Know the collage of your strongest competencies and leverage them more often. If you excel at problem solving and strategy, get into more situations that allow you to use and hone your strengths. Get into roles, jobs, organizations, and career paths that use your specific strengths. Stay away from situations that call on your weak areas.

Building the Skill

If you choose to work directly on your lack of skills in one or more areas:

1. Look at the specific tips and pick the ones that apply. Each tip is written against a specific issue with being unskilled. It is highly unlikely that all of the tips will apply to any one person. Think back to your feedback and the description of typical patterns for your type.

2. Lay out a plan and a schedule. Your plan should include at least three tips you will work on immediately. You should measure the number of times you did this or didn't do that and record these efforts so you can track your improvement. Set a specific time frame of no more than a month to try these items repeatedly; if your time frame is longer or indefinite, you'll be less likely to do anything. Start today.

3.   Other things you can do are:

■   Neutralize your weaker areas. If you're not terribly personable, or hate to deal with conflict, your first goal should be to turn this from a negative to a neutral. Start small, using the tips in this book.

■   Seek further feedback. Little happens without feedback. Get a developmental partner, get formal 360° feedback, poll people you work with about what you should keep doing, keep doing with slight modifications, stop doing, and start doing.

■   Test the unknown. Some competencies or performance dimensions you might be low on reflect lack of experience that we call an untested area. Maybe you don't build teams well, but have never really built or led a team. Pick something small that needs doing, and give it a try using the tips.

■   Go against your natural grain. If you're ambitious or if you seek a different kind of job, you'll have to work on your downsides more vigorously than the suggestions above. Few succeed in a different job by simply repeating past successful behavior. This is a strong lesson from career research. You'll have to stretch in uncomfortable areas. For example, whether you gravitate toward team building or not, you can learn the behaviors of excellent team builders. You might even come to enjoy it. It's important not to confuse what you like to do with what's necessary to do.

■   Use jobs for development.

(a)   The number one developer of competence by far is stretching, challenging jobs—not feedback, not courses, not role models, but jobs where you develop and exercise significant and varied competencies. If you really want to grow, these are the best places to do it.

(b)   If you are ambitious, handling a variety of jobs is what matters most for long-term success. In the Center for Creative Leadership studies, executives who remained successful had been tested in start-ups and fix its and by transitioning to different businesses/organizations. You have a rich opportunity to use your job to learn better from experience. What specifically about the job demands that you work on this need? Write down these challenges; focus your development on them.

(c) Part-time assignments. Unless you have challenging job tasks where you either perform against the need or fail, not much development will occur. This is the essence of action learning or learning from experience—not practice, not trying things out, but getting better in order to perform. Take the example of listening skills, a common need. Everyone's had a million chances (practices) to listen better but they don't, usually because there are some people or some situations where they don't want to listen and have gotten away with it. To listen better, then, how about if they were in a tough negotiation or running a task force of experts when they're not an expert. Get the idea? It's listen or else you can't do the job. Any plan you write must have "perform this or else" tasks in it to work. Otherwise you'll revert to your old ways. To use these tasks, shape them to your job and organization. What tasks like these are available? If you have a significant need (you are really weak in this area), start with smaller challenges and build up to the tougher ones.

(d) You don't have to be good at everything. Most successful leaders have four to six major strengths, but tend to lack glaring weaknesses. Developing in all areas is unlikely. Use the strategies above to select wisely. If directly working on improvement seems unlikely, use the indirect strategies below.

Substitute

If you don't care to work on your need directly, you can use another strength to neutralize a weakness. Here are a few examples of how you could substitute a strength to attack a weakness in presentation skills.

1. You are not good at formal presentation but are humorous and have the potential of being funny. Upgrade the use of humor (already a high skill) in your presentations. Using cartoons and humorous dialog would increase audience acceptance and lead to a higher evaluation of the success of the presentation even though basic presentation skills would not have been improved.

2. Facilitate (already a high skill) instead of present. Minimize presentation time and increase discussion and audience participation.

3. Tape portions of the presentation where you could rehearse, do multiple takes and insert taped portions into the live presentation.

4. Write (already a high skill) out your points and distribute them ahead of the meeting and then have a discussion instead of making a speech.

Again, the outcome is to reduce the impact of being a marginal presenter by substituting things you are already good at to get the same thing done. This approach is relatively easy to do if you have the skills necessary to counter your need.

Work Around the Weakness

Use other resources to get the same thing done. The goal of a workaround is to reduce the noise caused by the need. While there may or may not be any learning attached to the workaround, this gets done what has to be done without directly addressing the personal need.

Essential to this approach is self-knowledge. You have to know you have the need and acknowledge its importance. There are 10 workaround strategies:

■ **Using Other People Workarounds**

1. Find an internal person to stand in for you when the weakness is in play. A peer. An internal consultant. A friend. A person from your staff. So if you are a marginal presenter, get someone who is a good presenter to present your material.

2. Find an external person to stand in for you when the weakness is in play. This is usually a consultant who specializes in doing what you are not good at. If you are marginal on strategic thinking, hire a consultant or a firm who creates strategic plans you can choose from.

3. Hire people for your team who are good in the areas you are not. Delegate the tasks that bring the weakness into play.

■ **Task Workarounds**

4. Trade tasks with a peer. Trade for something you are good at and trade away the one you are struggling with. You help a peer with his or her strategic planning and he or she helps you with your presentations to senior management.

5. Share tasks. Partner with someone to combine tasks and share so that each of you does the tasks you are best at.

6. Structure the weakness out. Redesign your job (with your boss) so that you are not responsible for the task(s) that brings your weakness into play. Change your job so that you no longer have to give lots of speeches to strangers. Assign that task to another unit.

■ **Change Workarounds**

7. Change jobs (companies, units, divisions). If you decide that you don't want to work on your needs, do an honest assessment of your strengths and find an organization, a job, or another unit that fits those strengths. You are in sales and you are good at everything except cold calling and lead generation. Find a sales job where leads are provided or customers come to you.

8. Change careers. If you decide that you don't want to address this need, do an honest assessment of your strengths and find a different career that does not call upon your areas of weakness and requires the portfolio of strengths you do have. If you are in sales promotion and are not a comfortable presenter or cold caller, then consider marketing analysis where those two requirements are greatly decreased.

■ **Self Workarounds**

9. Pre-declare your weakness. Research shows that admitting weaknesses (within limits) will actually increase people's evaluations of you. So if you start by saying, "As most of you know, speaking is not one of my strengths," people will not be as critical.

10. Redefine yourself. Live with it. If you decide not to address the need, concentrate harder on the things you do well.

Addressing an Overused Tendency

Many people get to very responsible positions with a handful of remarkable strengths. Much of the time it's competencies like intelligence, a drive for results, problem solving, action orientation, project management skills, taking chances, presentation and political skills. This kind of person is a self-starter, self-reliant, and often a loner who gets things done. They are better managers of projects and ideas than people. They are stress carriers who drive other people to keep up with them. They get repeated promotions until they get to a job that calls for more than what they used to get there.

Others get little feedback coupled with good performance evaluations. Whether promoted or not, they are encouraged to do more of the same, use the strengths that got them where they are. This is fine, of course, until something changes—a new strategy, a change in job responsibilities, a new leadership direction in the organization. Then, new skills are called for and the current skill portfolio needs an overhaul.

In either case, they come to a fork in the road. Which path they take makes a big difference.

The left fork is taken by the open, learning agile, curious, continuous improvers. They detect that the assignment is going to require something different. A break from the past. A new direction. A transition. They figure out what the new ways of thinking or new skills need to be and address them with a number of strategies. They develop them or use workarounds. They might also look to compensators that get the same thing done without developing new skills.

The right fork is taken by the larger group. When their aims get frustrated, when things are not going the way they are used to, when they are stretched to their limit, they turn up the volume on the handful of strengths that they already have. The operating theory is that if a lot is good, more must be even better, or if someone can't understand what you are saying, increase the volume.

If some in this group have the strengths listed above, they become relentless drivers, driving everyone else into burnout. Trusting few, they do too much themselves. They are frustrated when pure intellectual horsepower can't solve all problems. They begin to believe that it's the people who are causing the problems.

Others may simply have no idea what to do differently. Lacking feedback and a target, they don't know what success looks like and repeat what has worked for them in the past.

If either case is you, if you have gotten feedback that you do too much of a good thing, here are some general strategies to address this problem.

1. Isn't it obvious? Stop overdoing it. Do it less. Decrease the volume. As straightforward as that sounds, few can do it. Why? Because this is what it sounds like. The mentor says:

    ■ Be less smart.

    ■ Be less results oriented.

    ■ Be less self-sufficient, start delegating more.

    ■ Slow down; listen; reflect.

    ■ Be less hard-charging.

    ■ Do less yourself.

    ■ Take fewer risks.

    Most have trouble with that advice. Why? Because those are the things that account for their success to date. These are the things you have been rewarded for. It's pretty scary thinking about DOING LESS of what you are good at. So even though this sounds like a no-brainer, it's really hard in real life to crank back on your strengths. It can, however, work.

2. Another strategy is to put a coating on the aspirin to prevent damage to the stomach. Use some other skills you have to lessen the noise and the damage you are causing by the overuse. Keep driving for results, but do so in a softer way by adding more listening skills and humor. Keep charging hard but increase communication and feedback. Keep taking risks but keep people better informed. Each of the tips is intended to help you decrease the noise and make your strengths more comfortable to others. How many should you use? As many as it takes to get the noise down to a reasonable level.

3. You can use a workaround or substitution strategy as mentioned previously.

If you are having trouble putting together a satisfactory plan from the rest of the book or just need some additional ideas, what follows is a generalized plan for any need.

General Development Plan

Universal Development Plan For Any Need

1. **Get specific.** Get more detailed and behavioral feedback on the need. Most of the time, people are weak in some aspect of a competency. It's almost never all interpersonal skills. It's usually something specific—for example, interpersonal skills with upper management under the pressure of tough questions from two of the seven on the management committee on topics you care deeply about. To find out more about what your need is specifically, go to a few people who know and who will tell you if you ask. Accept that you have a need. Don't be defensive or try to rationalize away the need. Say you are concerned about the need and request more detailed information so you can focus on an efficient plan for growth and development. Ask them for specific examples. When? Where? With whom? In what settings? Under what conditions? How many times? Might anyone they know be of help? Get as specific as you can. Listen, don't rebut. Take notes. Thank them for the input.

2. **Creating the plan.** If you have accepted the need as true and you are ready to do something about it, you need three kinds of action plans. You need to know what to stop doing, start doing, and keep doing. Since you have a need in this area (you don't do this well), you need to stop some things you are doing that aren't working. In their place, you need to start doing some things you either don't like doing, haven't ever done, or don't even know about. Even if you are bad at something, there are things you do in this area that you are probably good at. Send a form or e-mail to a number of people who would be willing to help you work on this skill. Tell them you have discovered and taken ownership of this need, want to do something about it, list the specific need you discovered in step one, and ask them for the things you should stop doing, start doing, and keep doing.

3. **Learning from others.** Research shows that we learn best from others when we: (a) Pick multiple models, each of whom excels at one thing rather than looking for the whole package in one person. Think more broadly than your current job for models; add some off-work models. (b) Take both the student and the teacher role. As a student, study other people—don't just admire or dislike what they do. One key to learning from others is to reduce what they do or don't do to a set of principles or rules of thumb to integrate into your behavior. As a teacher, it's one of the best ways to learn something as it forces you to

think it through and be concise in your explanation. (c) Rely on multiple methods of learning—interview people, observe them without speaking with them, study remote models by reading books or watching films, get someone to tutor you, or use a contrast strategy. Sometimes it's hard to see the effects of your behavior because you are too close to the problem. Pick two people, one who is much better than you are at your need and one who is much worse. Copy what the good model does that leads to good outcomes. Get rid of the behaviors that match what the bad model does.

4. **Read the "bible" on this need.** Every skill or competency has had one or more books written about it. How to negotiate to win. How to get along with bad bosses. How to win friends. How to be more creative. Go to a large business bookstore and buy at least two books covering your need. Take one hour and scan each book. Just read the first sentence of every paragraph. Don't read to learn. Just read to see the structure of the book. Pick the one that seems to be right for you and read it thoroughly. That book may reference or lead you to other books or articles on the skill. Use your reading to answer the following questions: What's the research on the skill? What are the 10 how to's all the experts would agree to? How is this skill best learned?

5. **Learn from autobiographies and biographies.** Try to find books by or on two famous people who have the skill you are trying to build. Mother Teresa on compassion. Harry Truman on standing alone. Norman Schwarzkopf on leadership. Helen Keller on persistence. Try to see how they wove the skill you are working on into their fabric of skills. Was there a point in their lives when they weren't good at this skill? What was the turning point?

6. **Learn from a course.** Find the best course you have access to. It might be offered in your organization or more likely it will be a public program. Find one that is taught by the author of a book or a series of articles on this need. Be sure to give it enough time. It usually takes three to five days to learn about any skill or competency. One- to two-day courses are usually not long enough. Find one where you learn the theory and have a lot of practice with the skill. Find one that videotapes if the skill lends itself to the lens. Take your detailed plan with you and take notes against your need. Don't just take notes following the course outline. For example, if you're attending a listening course and one of your need statements is how to listen when people ramble, take notes against that specific statement; or if your need involves a task or project, write down action steps you can take immediately. Throw yourself into the course. No phone calls.

Don't take any work with you. No sightseeing. Just do the course. Be the best student in the course and learn the most. Seldom will a course alone be sufficient to address a need. A course always has to be combined with the other remedies in this Universal Development Plan, especially stretching tasks so you can perform against your need under pressure.

7. **Get a partner.** Sometimes it's easier to build a skill if you have someone to work with. If you can find someone working on the same need, you can share learnings and support each other. Take turns teaching each other some to do's—one of the best ways to cement your learning. Share books you've found. Courses you've attended. Models you've observed. You can give each other progress feedback. Or get a learning buddy, someone who will help you grow. Have him/her agree to observe and give you feedback against your learning objectives.

8. **Try some stretching tasks, but start small.** Seventy percent of skills development happens on the job. As you talk with others while building this skill, get them to brainstorm tasks and activities you can try. Write down five tasks you will commit to doing, tasks like: initiate three conversations, make peace with someone you've had problems with, write a business plan for your unit, negotiate a purchase, make a speech, find something to fix. You can try tasks off the job as well: teach someone to read, be a volunteer, join a study group, take up a new hobby—whatever will help you practice your need in a fairly low-risk way. After each task, write down the +'s and –'s of your performance and note things you will try to do better or differently next time.

9. **Track your own progress.** You are going to need some extra motivation to get through this. You need to be able to reward yourself for progress you've made. Others may not notice the subtle changes for awhile. Set progress goals and benchmarks for yourself. If you were working on approachability for instance, have a goal of initiating conversations with five new people a week. Keep a log. Make a chart. Celebrate incremental progress. Noting times you didn't interrupt others or made two strategy suggestions that people grabbed and discussed will reinforce your continued efforts.

10. **Get periodic feedback.** Get a group of people who haven't known you very long. They don't have a history of seeing you not do well in this skill over a long period of time. Get feedback from them a third of the way into your skill-building plan. Also, go back to the original

group who helped you see and accept this need. Their ratings will lag behind the first group because they know your history in this skill. Use both groups to monitor your progress.

Parting Note

A plan can also be all of the things we talked about above. After you know exactly what need you have, you could start with a substitute plan that has an immediate effect. Then, midterm, you could use one or more workaround strategies to continue to cover for your lack of skill. While all of this is going on, you can use the development tips in this book to actually build the skill as well as watch the people you use in your workaround plan to learn from what they do. Then, if even further development is needed, use tasks, special projects, part-time assignments, and even different jobs to finish your development. You can string different strategies together for a more powerful and permanent result.

The goal of YOU *is action. So, above all, do something.*

Lominger Limited, Inc.
offers these additional publications:

The Leadership Machine

Architecture to develop leaders for any future
by
Michael M. Lombardo
Robert W. Eichinger

FYI For Your Improvement™
4th Edition

Includes 7 International Focus Areas
by
Michael M. Lombardo
Robert W. Eichinger

100 Things You Need to Know: Best People Practices for Managers and HR

THE resource book every HR practitioner MUST HAVE
by
Robert W. Eichinger
Michael M. Lombardo
Dave Ulrich